SHADOWS

Airlift and Airwar in Biafra and Nigeria
1967-1970

Michael I. Draper

HIKOKI
PUBLICATIONS

First published in Great Britain in 1999 by
Hikoki Publications Ltd
16 Newport Road, Aldershot, Hants, GU12 4PB
Tel: 01252 319935 Fax: 01252 655593
email: hikoki@dircon.co.uk
Website: http//www.hikoki.dircon.co.uk/
© 1999 Hikoki Publications

All rights reserved. Apart from any fair dealing for the purpose of private study, research, criticism or review, as permitted under the Copyright, Design and Patents Act 1988, no part of this publication may be reproduced, stored in a retrieval system, or transmitted in any form or by any means, electronic, electrical, chemical, mechanical, optical, photocopying, recording or otherwise, without prior written permission. All enquiries should be directed to the publisher.

ISBN 1 902109 63 5

Edited by Barry Ketley
Artwork by David Howley
Design by Hikoki Publications
Printed in England by Ian Allan Printing

Distribution & Marketing
in UK and Europe
by
Midland Counties Publications
24 The Hollow, Earl Shilton, Leicester LE9 7NA
Tel: 01455 233 747 Fax: 01455 233 737

Distribution & Marketing
in North America
by
Howell Press Inc
1713-2D Allied Lane, Charlottesville, Virginia
22903-5336, USA
Tel: 001 804 977 4006 Fax: 001 804 971 7204
email: HowellPres@aol.com

Caption to rear cover: *One of the lasting images of the Nigerian Civil War was of the starving and dying children in Biafra. For a while the world stood helplessly by. Then the relief airlift started. For eighteen months religious groups of different faiths worked together to feed a nation. Father Joe Prendergast was one of a number of Catholic priests of the Irish Holy Ghost Order who worked in appalling conditions to help save lives of the most vulnerable. Here he offers comfort to one of his "little fella's" who is suffering from kwashiorkor, an often fatal condition caused by extreme protein deficiency. This was the main inspiration behind the massive airlift. Joe Prendergast now lives quietly in California; hopefully the "little fella", now 30 years on, also enjoys a peaceful life.*

Caption to title page: *2 hours 46 minutes into its flight from Abidjan to Sao Tome on 16 August 1968 and Anson G-AWMG's instruments indicate a satisfactory cruising speed and dead on course. The co-pilot's face, however, expresses concern over the rate of fuel flow from an untested and unorthodox auxiliary fuel system. In reality the main cabin floor was awash in aviation fuel. The flight-deck windows had already been opened to reduce the fumes inside the aircraft as well as trying to reduce the effect of an overhead tropical sun. Biafra proved to be a place unfit for the faint-hearted (Ray Roberts)*

ALSO AVAILABLE

Eyes for the Phoenix
Allied Aerial Photo-Reconnaissance Operations in
South-East Asia 1941-1945
by
Geoffrey Thomas
ISBN 0 9519899 4 4

Courage Alone
The Italian Air Force 1940-1943
by
Chris Dunning
ISBN 1 902109 02 3

The Secret Years
Flight Testing at Boscombe Down 1939-1945
by
Tim Mason
ISBN 0 9519899 9 5

Emblems of the Rising Sun
Imperial Japanese Army Air Force Unit Markings
by
Peter Scott
ISBN 1 902109 55 4

Luftwaffe Emblems 1939-1945
by
Barry Ketley & Mark Rolfe
ISBN 0 9519899 7 9

FORTHCOMING

Stormbird
Flying through fire as a Luftwaffe ground-attack
pilot and Me 262 ace
by
Oberst (i.R.) Hermann Buchner
ISBN 0 902109 00 7

White Eagles
The Aircraft, Men and Operations
of the Polish Air Force 1918-1939
by
Bartlomiej Belcarz & Robert Peczkowski
ISBN 0 902109 73 2

Condor
The Luftwaffe in Spain 1936-1939
by
Patrick Laureau
ISBN 0 902109 10 4

CONTENTS

ACKNOWLEDGMENTS   4

FOREWORD
By Frederick Forsyth   8

INTRODUCTION
And a crash in the Cameroons   9

CHAPTER 1
Crisis and Action   15
The Declaration of Secession

CHAPTER 2
Establishing Biafra's 'first' Air Force   23

CHAPTER 3
The arms airlift to Biafra   51

CHAPTER 4
Federal Nigerian Air Force   71
Formation, delivery and recruitment

CHAPTER 5
Biafran relief aid starts   96
Politics of relief; the war grinds on

COLOUR SECTION 1   97

CHAPTER 6
Uli and Uga   134
The lifeline airstrips

CHAPTER 7
Nordchurchaid airlift begins   142
Joint Church Aid emerges; International Red Cross Operation 'Inalwa' started

CHAPTER 8
"Fly now—pray later"   157
The Church airlift is consolidated; Joint Church Aid is launched; the IRC opens a new base at Cotonou

CHAPTER 9
Biafra   185
Old faces; old aircraft; new faces; new aircraft

COLOUR SECTION 2   193

CHAPTER 10
Biafran Air Force Operations   217
Establishing Biafra's 'second' Air Force

CHAPTER 11
The Meteor Job   231

CHAPTER 12
The Nigerians close in   239
Biafra's final hour

CHAPTER 13
Postscript   259

APPENDIXES   263

PREFACE & ACKNOWLEDGMENTS

Africa, throughout the 1960s, was a continent in turmoil. The former Belgian Congo had witnessed civil war since the state of Katanga had been declared in June 1960; unrest in Angola had escalated into a war against the Portuguese colonialist regime as was the case in another Portuguese colony, Mozambique. Rhodesia had made a unilateral declaration of independence in November 1965 and other conflicts involved Ethiopia, Eritrea and Sudan. The Nigerian Civil War (in which the Eastern State of Nigeria declared itself as the independent sovereign state of Biafra) was a particularly vicious African war. That it lasted from July 1967 until January 1970 was, for the most part, the result of considerable external assistance for both sides. Landlocked from early-1968 the Biafrans fought for their very existence–a fight against starvation and a well-armed enemy. A hugely successful publicity campaign launched by the Biafrans during 1968 brought the conflict to the forefront of world conscience. As a result the Churches, the International Red Cross and other agencies raised sufficient funds to launch a relief airlift into Biafra, an airlift which, in tonnage proportions, was second only to the 1948-49 Berlin Air Lift. But unlike the Berlin affair the airlift to Biafra was almost entirely a civil airlift and operated only at night into an airstrip converted from a bush road. It was, and still remains, the largest civilian airlift since the Second World War.

The author has been concerned to present the happenings of a 30-month conflict in an objective and as systematic a manner as possible. Some of it was seen first hand when, in July 1968, he was asked to join the crew of an ex-R.A.F. Avro Anson. It was at a time when no food was being flown in and the Anson had been designated to ferry relief supplies from the island of Fernando Póo to Biafra.* But it was during a stopover on São Tomé that he witnessed a small fleet of recently-gathered DC-7C aircraft that took his interest. They all had clearly false identities. On several return visits to São Tomé he met a number of crews in the bar of the Pousada São Geronimo, and gained a fascinating and first-hand insight into Biafra's support operations from that island.

Subsequently the author became embroiled in a naive attempt to export a number of ex-R.A.F. Provosts to Biafra. This, as well as having spent some considerable time at Blackbushe in the company of pilots specifically hired to fly a batch of proposed Biafran Air Force Hunter jets, convinced him that one day a story would unfold.

It was during the earliest period of researching the Biafran operation that the author met with Peter J. Marson‡. Renowned for his extensive knowledge of the Lockheed Constellation series Peter had, and with the help of Luis Tavares in Lisbon, closely monitored the operation

2 Above: *Jakob Ringler arrived at São Tomé in June 1969 to assist Father Tony Byrne, the Irish Priest and instigator of the CARITAS relief airlift to Biafra. Through his camera lens Jakob subsequently captured every significant event on the island. In this simplistic view an International Red Cross Boeing C-97G brings in a cargo of urgent relief aid after the Red Cross airlift from Cotonou had been suspended on 6 June 1969. The twin-fish insignia of JOINT CHURCH AID became an instantly-recogniseable symbol of the massive Church effort from Sao Tome as did the rather drab-looking C-97G in the far background*

of Biafra's principle gun-runner, Hank Warton. It was Luis' first-hand notes and his outstanding sketches that form the basis for colour schemes contained within this book.

In 1970, after the Nigerian Civil War had ended, Peter Marson and the author embarked upon a gradual process of piecing the story together. The publisher has put my name on the cover but Peter's should be up there as well. Although virtually complete by 1982, the work came to a halt when both began separately developing other non-related projects, the author collaborating on a book covering the Falklands Air War. Pressure of other work then kept Biafra on the back-burner until the end of 1996 when an article by João Vidal on Biafran T-6G Texan operations appeared in the journal *Air Enthusiast*. This article provided many answers to the only remaining 'grey area' and it is to the credit of João and the journal's editor, Ken Ellis, that this book was then dragged screaming onto a word-processor and finally completed.

But a word of warning. This is not the tale of air combat. Apart from the shoot-down of a Red Cross DC-7B, to the best of the author's knowledge there were no incidents of air-to-air combat. There were some incidents that came close to that description and on several occasions Nigerian MiG-17s attempted to intercept Biafran T-6Gs and MFI-9Bs. Virtually all operational sorties by both sides were ground-attack missions in support of army commanders. Some of the target locations were therefore quite obscure and the measurement of success difficult to define. Some details of specific air sorties are included but this is primarily the story of the individual aircraft involved; where they originated, where they were based and where they ended their days. It is a story driven by colour schemes, markings, destinations and cargoes. Inevitably, in a work such as this, the story will be incomplete and despite exhaustive research details of some events are lacking. If it inspires other researchers to delve new sources then its objective has been achieved.

A word on the inclusion of Chapter Notes. An eminent scholar once rightly claimed that there is no such thing as 'oral history'; there is only 'oral evidence', 'history' being what historians make of all their evidence. Again and again during work on this book the author has been struck by the fallibility and the treachery of human memory, especially when the teller is looking back 30-plus years. Given the nature of the subject primary reference sources in the form of official documentation are not generally available. Because of this, and the need to rely upon 'oral evidence' which normally would only help in leavening the narrative with anecdotal recollections, the author has quoted the verbal source wherever possible.

Many of these verbal sources, for quite understandable reasons, demand no mention, nor seek any credit. Some have related unbelievably colourful details of various incidents–which are probably true–but the author has tried to be careful in only repeating those which can be substantiated by some degree of factual evidence. It has not been easy to exclude some stories but without any corroborative evidence, excluded they have been. One international arms dealer spent many hours answering the most searching of questions on the strict understanding that his identity would not be revealed. It hasn't, but his assistance was crucial, as was also the un-named source who acquired, on the author's behalf, various extracts from confidential French Police records on Baron Oppenheim's activities.

If the book had a start-point then it probably occurred in the Queen Elizabeth Hospital at Umuahia, Biafra, during September 1968, with several all-too-brief conversations with Count Gustav von Rosen, and with Godwin Ezeilo, a Biafran Air Force officer. Von Rosen had recently broken an air blockade into Biafra and was visiting relief administrators. On each occasion the author was there to visit an injured crew member from the Anson G-AWMG but would occasionally join impromptu meetings and it was from those discussions that the germ of an idea for this book began to grow.

Being on the spot at the right time helped enormously. On São Tomé, Axel Duch, having left Air America and Vietnam to take up a position with Nordchurchaid, offered a much-valued insight into the early attempts to launch a relief airlift. On Fernando Póo island the employees of Bristow Helicopters Ltd freely opened up old Situation Reports and other records which helped to describe the final days at Port Harcourt. One of the engineers, Ian McLeod, had also kept a diary of daily events. In spite of the language barrier, the Santa Isabel Air Traffic Control staff also allowed access to tower logs etc, as well as proving to be a font of much knowledge.

Biafra was something of a dichotomy; on occasions missionaries mixed freely with international arms dealers; many missionaries, especially those Catholic priests from Ireland, put up with the most appalling hardships to help feed the civilian population. They loaded aircraft on the islands; they offloaded them at Uli, often under a very real threat of bombing. They knew most of the aircrews; they even buried some of them after the inevitable accidents and crashes. (The author highly recommends Fr Tony Byrne's book, *Airlift To Biafra* for a modest, yet honest, recollection of the airlift. Also Fr Billy Butler's autobiography *To Places Far Away - A Wanderer For Christ* which successfully portrays Father Butler's unique humour, often in the face of human misery).

The late Reverend William Aitken proved an enormous help during the early days of research. At Port Harcourt and then at Uli for much of the war, Bill had the foresight to keep a diary to which he allowed full access. Fr Anthony Byrne (who featured so prominently in setting up the São Tomé airlift) offered considerable support and acted as a much-valued conduit for contacting aircrew. So did Fr Billy Butler, Fr Tom Cunningham and Fr Joe Prendergast, all of whom did much of the unglamorous work on the relief airlift. Fr Leo Laden provided vital material from church archives in Dublin.

Accident investigators and assessors Peter J. Cooper, and Fred Kirby helped enormously as did John Humphreys, of Amnesty International, to whom the author is grateful for details of the L-749A '5N85H' accident. Sister Ann Bent, former Matron at Umuahia's Queen Elizabeth Hospital and a passenger on the last flight of Warton's ill-fated L-1049D '5T-TAC', offered a unique insight into the Bissau incident. Alex Rumley (late of Templewood Aviation Ltd) made available his own personal files, without which some of the grey areas of the arms-supply chain would have remained distinctly dark grey!

Bruce Ronaldson (late of OXFAM) allowed access to his records; Pastor Mollerup allowed extracts from the Nordchurchaid Operations Report and Chamrong Lo (Comité International de la Croix-Rouge) undertook searches of ICRC records.

Aircrew and groundcrew on both sides provided invaluable detail of operations and incidents. Jimmy Webb, Ares Klootwyk, Paul Jenner, David Priest, Rod Price and Keith Sissons all offered important mission details from their Flying Log-Books, as did Paul Martin who spent many hours recounting his time on Nigerian Jet Provosts and MiG-17s–and who maintained an amazingly detailed Flying Log Book. Alan Beardmore, Peter Carter, Jim Whelan, Jim Leahy, Ted Chatsfield and Roy Pawson also provided background information to the Federal side. The late Marian Kozubski always insisted that he "did nuzzing extr-r-r-aordinary" but fellow Pole Roman Hrycak, apart from recounting his own exploits, talked so much and so highly of his extraordinary friend Marian! So did Marian's widow, Sheila Kozubski, who kindly made various papers available. Mike Downing and Mick Peckham were especially helpful with details of early movements at Kano.

On the Biafran side acknowledgment is due to Marcel Tschudin (of Balair) and also to many Nordchurchaid aircrew. They include Verdun Polley, Eddie Roocroft, Phil Phillp, Amund Klepp, Harold Snelholm, Einer Gudlaugsson, Runolfur Sigurdsson and also Bernie Murphy who somehow managed to operate on both sides of the conflict–food to one side; arms to the other! David Nicoll kindly lent the Flying Log-Books and personal papers of his late father, Alex Nicoll. Ground crews Phil Townsend, Ron Blake and Frank Strainge provided a different but much-valued perspective on the support aspect and the author gratefully acknowledges Malcolm Finnis who made some of the initial introductions.

A number of pilots operating on the French relief airlift from Libreville were also helpful, especially Jean-Renaud Guillemot and Emmanuel d'Herbes. Two other pilots gave valuable time and information; they were Biafran Air Force pilots Willy Murray-Bruce and Larry Obechie.

In the USA, Stefan Bailis and Bob Cobaugh helped clarify the situation regarding the Biafran B-25s; Scott Thompson (author of *The B-25 in Civil Service*) added further details. Jack Malloch and Hank Warton both personally provided a unique insight into their respective flying experiences, especially Hank who allowed access to his personal papers. Hank's Operations Manager, Bertram Peterson, through his brother Frank, also made available his collection of documents and photographs. Other former employees of Hank Warton who helped enormously include John Trent, Larry Raab, Jack Crosson, Clyde Arnspeiger and Derick 'Red' Mettrick. Flight crews from Jack Malloch's operation, including Malcolm Porter, Ian Rodwell, Colin Miller, Cliff Hawthorne, Dave Goldsmith, Brian Ditcham, Jack Wight and Henry Kinnear all generously offered time, assistance and details from personal Flying Log-Books. The author is also grateful to Christopher Halse for allowing access to the log-books of his late Father, Clive Halse.

Roy Chuck, Harold Peall and the late Harold Bunday, all formerly of Hawker Siddeley Aviation, helped to fit pieces of the jigsaw together, as did John F Coggins, Simon Hare, Guy Kremer, Richard Humberstone, Stuart Marshall, Anton le Nobel, Stenn Addler, Solveig Aasbrenn (of Fred Olsen), Dr David Nicolle and especially Paul Baxter who helped start the engines of the errant Meteor NF.14 G-AXNE at Blackbushe and then unwittingly took a genuine holiday in Faro–much to the concern of HM Customs & Excise who promptly arrested him on his return! The author is also indebted to the late John Squire, former Managing-Director of Aer Turas, whose amusing–yet true–stories have provided colour to some incidents. Other former associates of Aer Turas, notably Capt W.H. 'Bluey' Gardiner, Malcolm Nason, Eamon Power and Frank Smith added vital bits of the story. Nic Taaffe offered valuable assistance at difficult times as did Bryan Mather, 'Sandy' Burns, Tony Merton-Jones, Paul Howard, Paul Wigley, Alan Brough, Dave Cotterell and members of the Keegan dynasty, especially Kevin Keegan. Jim Wilde and Tony Mabelis of Bristow Helicopters added important information on that company's activities as did 'Jock' MacCaskel who, within days of the Biafran collapse, travelled to the former enclave to inspect various wrecks and damaged aircraft.

The author has also made use of specialists within the aviation historical association, Air-Britain. My good friend of many years, Bob Ruffle, dug deep into his files on Soviet-built aircraft to unravel some of the details relating to the Federal Nigerian side. Jeremy Parkin, Ken Measures, Terry Sykes, Peter-Michael Gerhardt, Jennifer Gradidge and especially Geoff Russell all provided valuable details on their chosen subjects. For details of French aircraft involved the author is indebted to Jacques Chillon and Jean-Pierre Dubois. From Canada, Brian Harris made available original documentation on Canairelief's operation; Larry Milberry also assisted in no small way.

The author thanks Sue Bellamy of the Bermuda Civil Aviation Authority, Tony Beales and Jerry Boyd (of British Airways) and Nicky Pearce who provided a valuable link with former aircrew on Jack Malloch's arms flights.

Two aviation historians have been kind enough to allow their respective published works to be used as a primary source and parts quoted within these pages. Leif Hellström, joint-author of *Foreign Invaders*, extensively researched the Biafran B-26 operation and was particularly helpful, as was João Vidal who unearthed the complex story of Biafra's T-6G operations. Without their respective input these subjects would have been considerably shorter on detail. Lennart Burns also helped enormously by liaising with the publisher of the late Gunnar Haglund's book *Guerillapilot* in which the Biafran MFI-9B saga is related. Stefan Sjödin very kindly undertook all of the translating process.

Unearthing photographs of aircraft and events covered in this book has been an utter joy. It should not be under-emphasised that taking photographs in Nigeria was strictly forbidden. Many shots were taken secretly from doorways and cockpit windows. Needless to say being caught with a camera at Uli was an offence likely to attract instant arrest. Such is the rarity of some views. Of the many shots taken at São Tomé most originate from Jakob Ringler's prized slide collection. Jakob spent a year on the island working as Fr Byrne's assistant–and if it moved, he photographed it! So did Keith Sissons (on the Federal side) and whose collection of Nigerian Air Force MiG-17s and Ilyushin 28s is equally unrivalled. In South Africa, Dave Becker has kindly allowed access to his collection. The author has tried in every instance to locate and identify the rightful copyright owner of each picture and to acknowledge accordingly. Inevitably, in an age of scanning and copying, there will unknowingly be some errors and omissions–for that both the author and publisher apologise. Some illustrations show a 'Confidential Source'. In such cases the photographer has specifically requested anonymity. All may rest in the knowledge that many of their photographs have provided the basis for David Howley's colour drawings.

Finally, the author wishes to acknowledge a dear old friend, John Mitchell-Smith, without whose telephone call just over thirty years ago, Biafra–to the author–would still have been just another small and long-forgotten African war.

Michael I. Draper,
Hampshire, UK, September 1999

AUTHOR'S NOTE:

All place-names are shown as they were known at the time of the 1967-70 conflict. Since then some countries have changed name as have capital cities, airports and state boundaries etc.

The island of Fernando Póo, together with Rio Muni on the mainland, constituted Spanish Equatorial Guinea. On the island the main town (which gave its name to the airport) was Santa Isabel.

During October 1968 Spanish Equatorial Guinea gained independence from Spain to become The Republic of Equatorial Guinea. Fernando Póo was renamed Bioko and Santa Isabel became Malabo. The first President of independent Equatorial Guinea, Francisco Macias Ngueme, ran the State in a harsh dictatorial manner until overthrown in a coup on 3 August 1979. However the island remains one of the few places in the world where outside visitors are distinctly unwelcome. Throughout the text the pre-October 1968 names have been used.

The islands of São Tomé and the smaller Principé formed part of the Portuguese Overseas Provinces until gaining independence in 1974. By 1975 a classic Marxist single-party regime had become established on São Tomé and the islands became increasingly isolated. However eventually, in 1990, a referendum sought a democracy within the islands and closer ties with Portugal.

Of the main protagonists General Gowon remained in power in post-war Nigeria but was finally overthrown on 29 September 1975. He later settled in the UK. On the other hand Ojukwu, the former Biafran leader, remained in exile in the Ivory Coast until mid-1982 when he was quietly allowed back to Nigeria where he entered normal business life.

* Bruce Hilton tells the story of the Ansons' involvement in Biafra in the book *Highly Irregular* (published by The Macmillan Company 1969). The Ansons also provide the backdrop and inspiration for the novel, *The Blind Side* by Francis Clifford (published by Hodder & Stoughton 1971)

‡ Peter J Marson is the author of *The Lockheed Constellation Series*, published by Air Britain (Historians) Ltd 1982.

Note that times shown within the text are given either in Greenwich Mean Time (or Zulu), or Local time (Local).

FOREWORD
by
Frederick Forsyth

Memory fades with the passing years, yet most of us have some recollections and images so firmly blazed into our minds that we can never forget them.

So it certainly is for those who, thirty years ago, witnessed the agony of a small self-styled West African state called Biafra. Before that thirty-month conflict with Nigeria was over and Biafra had been conquered and reabsorbed into the Nigerian federation, something close to a million people had died of starvation–a hunger that stemmed directly from the food blockade imposed as a concomitant of the war.

But there would have been another million children starved into oblivion save for one thing: so horrifying were the pictures emerging from this African war that the consciences of the West were touched. from the USA and from Europe, from the Catholic and Protestant relief agencies, from the Red Cross and from private donors, the funds were supplied to send emergency relief food to the dying children.

But there was a major problem: Biafra was blockaded by land, sea and air. The only feasible way to get sacks of the relief food into the enclave that Biafra had become was to set up an air-bridge from two offshore islands, Fernando Póo (Spanish) and São Tomé (Portuguese).

And so it was. The Joint Church Aid air operation remains to this day unique in the annals of air operations. It was non-governmental. The pilots were mercenaries or volunteers. The aircraft were a ramshackle collection of time-expired or phased-out workhorses of the skies, culled from boneyards all over the world.

The 'airport' inside Biafra was no airport at all, but a single strip converted from a section of motorway. Being under constant threat of nocturnal bombing by the Nigerians, it had lead-in lights that flashed on for a few seconds each time a relief plane approached and gave the pilot a tiny 'window' of illuminated runway on which to touch down or die.

As they approached the darkened concrete strip in a totally black African night, they could hear the mercenary pilots flying the Nigerian bombers on the same wavelength, jeering at them, daring them to land when the lights flashed on for a few elusive seconds.

It was crazy, it was hairy, it was impossibly dangerous; it should never have worked. But somehow it did–night after night after night. When the planes landed and taxied into the welcome darkness by the side of the motorway-turned-landing-strip, willing hands hauled the sacks of milk powder and bundles of stockfish out of the fuselages and away into the feeding centres. That done, the pilots taxied back to the take-off point, the lights flickered on for a few seconds, and they were gone; back to the islands to sleep through the day and do it again the following night.

There have been books about the Nigeria-Biafra war before; about the fighting, about the priests and missionaries who helped on the ground, about the labyrinthine political and diplomatic intrigues that went on through the chancelleries of Europe. But Mike Draper has here concentrated mostly on the air-bridge itself; on the creaking, patched-up planes that flew, and on the often oddball risk-takers prepared to drive them. This is the story of how the strangest air-bridge the world has ever seen (or, in fact, not seen for it flew only by night) was put together and operated.

Frederick Forsyth, Hertford, UK, 1999

3 Above: "...the airplanes were a ramshackle collection of time-expired or phased-out workhorses of the skies, culled from boneyards all over the world." No description could better describe this line-up of Flughjalp's DC-6s and DC-6Bs at the end of the world's largest civilian airlift (Phil Phillp)

INTRODUCTION
And a crash in the Cameroons

"The East", claimed Lieutenant-Colonel Odumegwu Ojukwu, the Military Governor of Nigeria's Eastern Region, after attending the Aburi Peace Conference in January 1967 "can take care of itself and should the Government in Lagos, or the Government in the North—in their lunatic frenzy—think of attacking the East we would not only repulse them but we will certainly be sure that they would never again want to attack the East. As early as July (1966) I was in a position; I had all the paraphanalia with which to set up an alternative government but then, as now, I have been very much concerned with the amount of lives lost."[1] The threat, as well as the concerns, was real enough but by the time they were uttered Nigeria was deep in crisis and moving headlong towards military conflict.

Civil wars are particularly distasteful and it is often difficult to benchmark a singular event which leads directly to full-scale war. In the case of the Nigerian Civil War it could, to coin an over-used contemporary expression, have been a war just waiting to happen. Until 1 October 1960, when Nigeria gained Independence from the British

4 Above: *Nigeria Airways' fleet was headquartered at Lagos-Ikeja where the company maintained an Engineering Base. This typical pre-war view shows C-47A/DC-3s 5N-AAN and 5N-AAP, both of which were impressed into Nigerian Air Force service in August 1967. Inside the hangar can be seen the fin of F-27 Friendship 5N-AAV which was later hijacked by Eastern Nigerian soldiers in April 1967 in an incident which fuelled the political turmoil that ultimately led to civil war (Dave Becker Collection)*

Commonwealth, the country had been administered along traditional Crown Colony lines. But independent Nigeria had been established with almost no obvious consideration for tribal distribution or language groupings. At one stage Nigeria could boast at least 250 different languages.

Independent Nigeria was divided into three distinct Regions with the North considerably larger than the other two. These Regions largely corresponded with the three main tribes, each of which was fundamentally different from either of the other two. The Northern Region consisted of predominantly the *Hausa* tribe, traditionally of Muslim faith and very much feudal in outlook. The Western Region, primarily the Catholic *Yoruba* tribe, tended to be the nation's traders whilst the Christian *Ibo* tribe—dominant in the Eastern Region—held most of Nigeria's civil service and public life positions. Independence allowed the differences in Nigeria's peoples to come out into the open and it was this, above all else, which laid the foundation for the civil war which broke out seven years later.

By sheer force of numbers the North had captured overall control of the newly-independent Central Government in Lagos and despite their greater sophistication members of the Western and Eastern Regions were never likely to get any control for a long time, at least not through a democratic election process. This realisation led to widespread discontent which, on 15 January 1966, resulted in a number of young Army officers from the East launching a coup against the Lagos administration. The timing of the coup was perfect; it took place on the day after the first Commonwealth Conference to be held outside the United Kingdom ended. Amongst those killed were the Nigerian Prime Minister and most of his Ministers, including the Premiers of the Northern and Western Regions. Not surprisingly the new leader to emerge from the coup, Major-General Aguiyi-Ironsi, and despite being an *Ibo*, made all the right promises for a future and stable peace. "Tribal loyalties", claimed Ironsi, "would give way to national reconstruction."

In trying to defuse the volatile situation in Nigeria Ironsi dispensed with the traditional offices of President, Prime Minister, as well as the role of Premier. Instead he appointed five military Commanders to govern the four Regions and the Federal territory of Lagos. Among those appointments was the naming of a young Nigerian Army battalion commander, Lieutenant-Colonel Odumegwu Ojukwu as the new Military Governor of the Eastern Region. But after only seven months, on 28 July 1966 — and again by the bullet — Ironsi was removed from power during a Northern-led counter coup.

Only in the East did the second coup fail and where Ojukwu remained firmly in control. But many *Ibo* easterners were killed in the counter coup, especially those *Ibos* who had long settled in the Northern Region. Ojukwu pleaded for calm but many elected to return to their eastern homeland. At the same time Ojukwu reaffirmed his refusal to accept the military authority of Lagos, led by Lt Colonel Yakubu Gowon since the July 1966 coup. For several months the tension worsened throughout Nigeria[2].

In the autumn of 1966 the situation changed dramatically and the fragile peace finally snapped in the North. *Hausas* struck against those *Ibos* still living outside their homeland; thousands were killed and most of those who survived fled southwards. Many of the more fortunate ones managed to take flights from Kano to Makurdi just to get out; onlookers at Kano airport witnessed up to 80 *Ibos* at a time, all without any luggage, clambering aboard 45-seater Nigeria Airways' F-27 Friendships ahead of Northern police armed with horse-whips. Pan African Airline's DC-6A 5N-AFT was also used for evacuating *Ibos* out of the North by flying large numbers from Kano to Lagos and then on to Port Harcourt.

Once again, Nigeria faced almost certain political disintegration and the threat of further assassinations did little to instil any confidence in a lasting peace. Rather surprisingly the *Hausas* and the *Ibos* did appear to display some outward patience towards the close of 1966 by placing some reliance upon the Central Government to sort out the chaos and to hold together what was by then an extremely fragile Federation. But in reality the lull simply offered an opportunity for both sides to build up their stocks of arms for what was being seen by many Nigerians as an inevitable civil war.

Many attempts were made to reconcile the differences between Ojukwu and Gowon but all failed — until January 1967, when a meeting was arranged in Aburi, Ghana and to which all of the military governors had agreed to attend. Aburi undoubtedly offered a turning point in Nigerian politics and Ojukwu secured a number of political successes at the meeting but as soon as he was back in Lagos, Gowon seemed unwilling to implement most of the decisions taken. Ojukwu did not disguise his irritation and even began to talk of civil war.

The secret build-up of arms

When Ojukwu announced that the East could take care of itself he did so with the clear knowledge that the Federal Military Government in Lagos had began building stocks of arms. What had become known as the 'Apollo arms deal' *(sic)* had involved a team of individuals led by a Northern Army Officer, a Major Sule Apolo, being despatched by Lagos to Europe in order to negotiate arms purchases. One of the largest deals allegedly struck by Apolo was for a huge quantity of Italian weapons and ammunition which was delivered almost immediately and stored in a military warehouse at Kaduna, northern Nigeria. Gowon did admit that such a transaction had taken place but stated that the weapons were for the entire Nigerian Army including, under normal circumstances, those units based in the East. But Ojukwu argued that the situation was far from being normal and it was therefore highly unlikely that any of the Italian arms would be issued to the East. As a counter-point Gowon accused Ojukwu of secretly building up his own arms stocks in the East. And so it went on. Gowon was, of course, quite correct in his assertions and the evidence later emerged when a Canadair DC-4M2, piloted by two well-known American adventurers, crashed whilst en route to Eastern Nigeria. The two pilots on board had a known track record of running illegal guns around Africa. Ojukwu's secret arms deals in Europe no longer remained a secret.

The aircraft in question had had a chequered life before the arms flight to Eastern Nigeria. Built originally under licence by Canadair in 1948 for Trans Canada Airlines, as CF-TFM, it had been sold to a British charter company in 1961 and later stored at Baginton/Coventry for a couple of years. Despite its registration marks having been cancelled, it was later flown north to Newcastle but remained on the ground and was later impounded by the airport authority there and sold by auction. Its next flight, again without any legal documentation, but with a false Panamanian registration 'HP-925', was to Limburg, Holland on 9 February 1965. In Holland the aircraft received some rudimentary maintenance before being once again impounded, this time by the Dutch at Rotterdam airport. The Dutch authorities had learnt that an American adventurer-pilot, Lucien H Pickett, was about to use it to run guns illegally into Algeria.

By October 1965 a Swiss-American entrepreneur, Heinrich Heuer, claimed to the Dutch that he had purchased the aircraft as part of a deal to establish a new airline in the African State of Burundi. Unfortunately for Heuer the West German police, who wanted him to answer charges relating to fraud, embezzlement, arson and "recruiting for a foreign army" heard of his arrival and managed to have him extradited to Germany before the aircraft could be flown out. With Heuer in custody yet another German-American pilot, Henry 'Hank' Warton, appeared at Rotterdam shortly afterwards and with some helpful persuasion from the Burundian Embassy in Paris, managed to convince the Dutch to let him fly the DC-4M out, ostensibly on a test-flight to Frankfurt. The Dutch were probably pleased to see the aircraft depart and allowed Warton to fly it out of Rotterdam, on 19 December 1965. But Warton did not fly to Frankfurt; instead he flew the DC-4M to the small airfield at Albenga, in northern Italy.[3]

During the summer of 1966 Warton announced that he had secured a contract to start a regular run of flowers from Italy to Germany. Warton later claimed to have visited Heuer, who was by then serving a jail sentence in West Germany, and paid over cash for the aircraft, receiving in return all of the aircraft's documentation. (Warton did subsequently learn that there was some doubt as to whether Heuer himself had actually paid for the aircraft; the previous owner in Britain later claimed that he had not.)

Before he had a chance to start the flower charter flights Warton claims to have been approached by a German gentleman who—although he did not announce the fact at the time—he later discovered was acting as a middle-man between the French arms-dealer Paul Favier and an emissary from the Eastern Nigeria Government, Christopher Okigbo. The un-named German made an offer that involved Warton flying just over 1,000 guns from Rotterdam to Port Harcourt, Eastern Nigeria.

The deal involved a mixed shipment of British and American weapons that had originally been supplied to Holland at the end of the Second World War and which Favier had purchased from an Israeli entrepreneur (named Arazi) during early 1964. Shortly afterwards part of the haul, including 500 US Browning machine-guns had been shipped to Intor Ltd, one of the UK's largest independent arms dealers, run by an ex-British Army Major, Robert Turp. The machine-guns were reconditioned at Turp's outer London factory at Bexleyheath and, with full government approval, were resold; the profit was reportedly divided equally between Favier and Intor Ltd. By 1966 Favier had become anxious over the balance of unsold stock, said to consist of 3,600 US Thompson machine-guns and an equal quantity of old British Lanchester rifles, all of which were still stored in Favier's Dutch naval warehouse.

Robert Turp had, it seems, refused offers to purchase Favier's stock on a number of occasions but eventually did agree to store the weapons after Favier had complained about the high storage costs in Holland. The agreement was, however, dependent on Favier securing a Board of Trade import licence. In fact a licence had previously been issued but Favier had allowed it to lapse. It was therefore simply a straightforward renewal and without any real difficulty the transfer of Favier's weapons was legalised by the issue of a UK Import Licence and the essential UK Import Certificate. Although they were becoming increasingly suspicious the Dutch authorities appear to have been finally satisfied.

Several months later, and before any of the weapons had been shipped, Favier returned to London in an attempt to purchase a quantity of recently-reconditioned German MG42 machine-guns from Intor. He also requested that Robert Turp arrange for a British-registered aircraft to deliver them to Favier's Nigerian client (the Eastern Region) at Port Harcourt. Turp claims to have rejected both requests and Favier returned to Paris to arrange for delivery of his own stocks—ostensibly from Holland to London for temporary storage.

Several weeks after refusing Favier's request the infamous DC-4M, and still carrying the false Italian marks 'I-ACOA', landed at Rotterdam's Zestienhoven airport, inbound from Italy, during the evening of 8 October 1966. The appearance of the DC-4M immediately aroused the suspicions of the Dutch airport authorities especially as Warton made no secret that he had been instructed to uplift the guns. Only after a Piper Aztec landed from Geneva just after midnight on the morning of 9 October, with four people aboard—almost certainly including Favier—was the correct flight documentation able to be produced. The Dutch had little alternative but to allow the aircraft to be loaded. There was a moment of concern during the loading when one crate fell off a fork-lift truck, hit the ground and scattered guns over the tarmac. From the airport bar Warton's co-pilot, 'Chuck' Pollock, watched the loaders gather up the spilled machine-guns; he was also watching the Dutch customs men watching the loaders and immediately grabbed his coat, declared himself "counted out of the deal", and walked out.

Despite remaining wary of Warton's intentions the Dutch had no sound reason to stop the depleted crew from climbing aboard and taking off. (Had the Rotterdam authorities been aware that the Italian police had earlier impounded the aircraft owing to some doubt over the aircraft's ownership then the Dutch may have intervened. Had they also known that Warton had just spirited the aircraft out of Albenga on the pretence of making a local flight to test the state of the aircraft's engines, they undoubtedly would have intervened. Presumably the

Rotterdam authorities were also unaware that the Italian registration marks were false!)

Apart from Warton, the DC-4M crew included an American Flight Engineer, Elliot Vought and an Italian Loadmaster, Pasquale Laveni, who also doubled as a navigator. Warton's co-pilot was Orvis M. Nelson—one of the most colourful men in the history of American aviation. (A former US Air Force and United Air Lines pilot, Orvis Nelson had formed Transocean Air Lines in 1946, building it up into the world's largest contract air carrier. When government regulations and financial problems caused Transocean's collapse in the early 1960s, Nelson somehow arranged financing for another venture, Aeronaves de Panama, and began building another empire. Success, however, denied Nelson second-time around.[4]

Christopher Okigbo, the Nigerian poet, had planned to take the opportunity of hitching a ride back to Eastern Nigeria aboard the DC-4M but Warton and Nelson jointly persuaded him to take a scheduled flight. Neither American wanted to have to explain to any suspicious airport authority why a Nigerian government official was aboard an aircraft carrying 1,000 machine-guns.

At Zestienhoven airport, Rotterdam, Warton lodged a flight-plan showing Birmingham as the destination. As all other papers appeared to be in order the aircraft was allowed to depart exactly on schedule, during the mid-afternoon of 9 October. At 15.56Z Warton reported the aircraft position as abeam Clacton and heading west on Red One airway. Shortly afterwards 'I-ACOA' entered the Birmingham air traffic control zone but instead of requesting clearance to land, Warton reported that the aircraft's charterer—shown on the flight-plan as 'Silver Line Airways'— had instructed him by radio to divert to Palma airport, in Majorca. Without landing in the UK Warton turned the aircraft around and flew south. Immediately after landing at Palma the aircraft was quickly refuelled before taking-off to head further southwards and out across the Sahara to Hassi Messaoud, an Algerian oil base on the edge of the desert. Again the aircraft took on more fuel before being parked for a day and night stopover.

The original plan had been for Warton and Nelson to share the flying. In that way whilst one was flying the aircraft the other would rest in the makeshift sleeping area in the cabin galley area. Warton had flown almost continuously throughout the first day having flown both sectors. For the next sector it was to be Nelson's turn at the controls but when 'I-ACOA' took-off from Hassi Messaoud, at 07:44 on 11 October 1966 it did so with Warton again in the captain's seat. Then, and shortly after take-off, Warton handed over control to Nelson and climbed back to the sleeping area.

Warton and Nelson had advised the Algerian authorities of their next, and final, destination to be Fort Lamy, in Chad but the aircraft inadvertently overflew Chad. Orvis Nelson had, whilst Warton was asleep in the main cabin, maintained a southerly heading but as their ETA for Fort Lamy approached nobody on the flight-deck caught sight of Lake Chad. Eventually Warton returned to the flight-deck and when he enquired as to the aircraft's position Nelson admitted that they were lost. With fuel running low and light fading Warton took over control of the aircraft and elected to continue flying southwards until the fuel position became critical. Inevitably one engine cut. When a second engine failed shortly afterwards Warton decided to make an emergency forced-landing and chose what appeared to be flat area beside a river.[5]

First reports from the crash site indicated that the aircraft had "sustained irreparable damage" and that the crew, consisting of "three Americans and one Italian" were critically injured. There was little doubt that the aircraft was beyond repair; it broke into four sections immediately upon impact and its seven-tonne cargo (of 960 Lanchester sub-machine guns, 2060 magazines for the guns, and 600 chargettes) was scattered along the marshy riverbank. But, considering the extent of the damage to the aircraft, the injuries were minimal—Warton escaped with mild concussion and the worst injury sustained by the crew affected Orvis Nelson who suffered a broken leg.

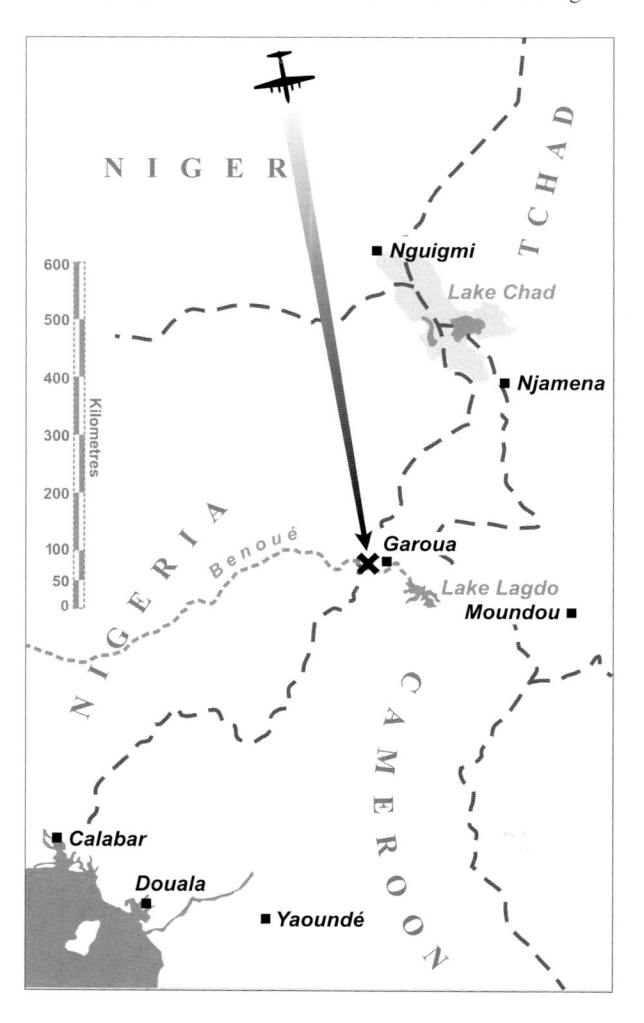

5: The crash of Hank Warton's DC-4M 'I-ACOA' (on 11 October 1966) could have caused much embarrassment to the British Government had anybody believed rumours at the time (allegedly originating in the US Embassy in the Cameroons) that the flight had started in Birmingham, UK. The British Ambassador in Yaoundé, Cameroon, kept his London masters up to date with developments through a series of confidential despatches. This letter, one of the series, outlines the precise breakdown of the DC-4M's cargo when it crashed in northern Cameroon and also adds a fascinating postscript (Reproduced by kind permission of the Public Record Office)

```
(1382/66)                                   BRITISH EMBASSY
                                                YAOUNDE
                                            4 November, 1966.
                        CONFIDENTIAL

Dear Renwick,
        Would you please refer to your telegram No. 252 of
27 October about the arms smugglers' forced landing near
Garoua.

2.      We now have a copy of the "Sunday Times" of 23 October.
Luckily, the news of the Board of Trade's Import Licence has
not, so far as we know, got through to the Cameroonians and
we are not yet subject to any criticism or even suggestions
of British involvement in the affair.  Indeed, the Cameroonians
seem to be keeping everything very much to themselves.  This
may change when the trial comes up, of course.

3.      Our informant has taken another look at the official
report and you may be interested to know what the Cameroonians
say about the European end of the deal.  They think, apparently,
that a Mr. Rasmussen from Enelslagen Airport, Frankfurt, acted
as intermediary between Silverline and Inter, run by a
former French Commissioner of Police.  They go on to say that
Inter sold the arms to the Nigerian Government (sic) through
a Dutchman named Muller.  The arms are listed as 24 cases
of Lanchester sub-machine guns, each case containing 40
weapons;  13 cases, each containing 144 magazines for the
above.  A further 188 magazines were found loose and 4 cases
each containing 150 chargettes.  The report also claims that
a fifth European passenger or crew should or could have been
aboard the aircraft.  Papers were found for a man named
Pollock, whose name appeared on the flight list.

                                   Yours ever,
                                   (R.N. Dales)

R.W. Renwick, Esq.,
  West & Central Africa Department,
    Foreign Office,
      London, S.W.1.

                         CONFIDENTIAL
```

6: When the illegally-registered DC-4M, 'I-ACOA', crashed in the Cameroons on 11 October 1966 it brought the illegal arms build-up by Eastern Nigeria into the open. Hank Warton and Orvis Nelson had taken off from Rotterdam two days previously and in a circuitous route flew south to Palma and on to Hassi Messaoud in Algeria. The crew missed their intended stop at Fort Lamy, Chad and consequently ran out of fuel. All on board survived the crash and later, when Biafra declared itself as an independent state, Warton emerged as one of Biafra's principal suppliers of arms (Karl Kramer)

The aircraft had crash-landed some 400kms south of Fort Lamy, beside the Benoué River in the French Cameroons. All four crew were taken to a hospital at Garoua, the relatively obscure capital of northern Cameroons, and about 30kms to the east of the point on the Benoué River where the crash had occurred. In the meantime the Cameroonian authorities began to investigate the crash.

As one would expect in an incident such as this, there was much speculation and rumour. One story, which seems to have originated from the US Embassy in Yaoundé, identified the crew as American but that they were "renegades and that the whole operation was mounted by the British". It also emerged that just before the aircraft abandoned its attempt to land at Birmingham, Warton had asked Birmingham Air Traffic to request new freight instructions from 'Instone Air Transport Ltd of London EC.3'. It also emerged that Birmingham Air Traffic had been unable to contact 'Instone'. The Board of Trade subsequently investigated the company but could find no connection between Instone and Intor. Therefore, according to the B.O.T, the decision to divert to Majorca must have been Warton's.

As a result of their attempted flight over the Cameroons without having lodged a flight-plan, Warton and his crew were charged with "illegally flying over Cameroons airspace and of flying an aircraft without the proper documentation." They were also charged with "transporting arms without authority". A court in Garoua later, on 6 January 1967, sentenced all four to a month in jail but in view of the period held awaiting trial all four men were released immediately. Warton was also fined 200,000francs CFA (£300) while Nelson was fined just 100,000francs CFA (£150).

Repercussions of the Cameroons incident were widespread. The fraudulent use of an import licence innocently granted by the Board of Trade caused embarrassment in London; Paul Favier's involvement focused attention upon his activities and, despite Congo-Brazzaville's President Massamba Débat claiming (in a radio broadcast on 24 December 1966) that the arms had been destined for the Congo, Eastern Nigeria's secret build-up of illicit arms suddenly became very public knowledge. When the crew were brought to trial in Garoua it was alleged that papers relating to the *Ibo* poet, Christopher Okigbo, were discovered amongst the wreckage of the DC-4M. This had even led to some reports that Okigbo was on board the aircraft when it crashed but that he had managed to escape on foot into the Cameroons bush. This was, of course, pure speculation; Okigbo had not been aboard at Warton's insistence. Ultimately Okigbo was killed in the fighting in Biafra.

The *Sunday Times* 'Insight' article, on 23 October 1966, had not only proved to have been extremely accurate but did much to highlight the arms build-up in Eastern Nigeria. One British charter airline even contacted the Ministry of Aviation on 24 October to announce that they had been asked to tender for arms flights between Prague and Enugu. Two days later, the M.O.A. was aware of other British operators being asked to make arrangements for flying consignments of Czech arms, ostensibly for Dahomey, but known to be destined for Enugu. [6]

In view of the time awaiting trial, Warton was released from jail shortly after the court passed judgement. But it was not a simple matter of just catching the next flight out of the country. It was to be some while yet before Henry Arthur Warton could resume his gun-running activities but when he did manage to re-organise his operation he did, for a short while, become Biafra's most important benefactor of clandestine arms and ammunition.

Notes

Note 1   Lt-Col Ojukwu, speaking after the Aburi Peace Conference, January 1967.

Note 2   Although both men were born into different tribes their upbringing and military training followed similar traditional patterns. Lieutenant-Colonel Yakubu 'Jack' Gowon was born in 1935 in the Middle Belt of Nigeria. The son of an evangelist, Gowon was a Northerner, from the Angas minority tribe, yet was a devout Christian. After secondary education in the northern Muslim town of Zaria, he joined the Nigerian Army and undertook officer training, firstly in Ghana, and later in the UK at the Royal Military Academy, Sandhurst. Gowon saw service with the Nigerian contingent in support of UN Forces in the Congo, before returning to the UK for a second spell at the Army Staff College. He had been, in the mind of General Aguiyi-Ironsi, the natural choice for the appointment of Army Chief of Staff.

Ironsi's appointment of Lieutenant-Colonel Chukwuemeka Odumegwu Ojukwu as Military Governor of the Eastern Region had brought to prominence another Nigerian Army man with officer training in the UK. Ojukwu was born in a small Northern Nigeria town during November 1933. He was an Ibo and the second son of transport millionaire Sir Louis Odumegwu Ojukwu. His education in Nigeria and England was followed, in 1956, by acceptance to the military officer academy at Eaton Hall, Chester. During 1961, and by then a Major in the Nigerian Army, Ojukwu spent –as did Gowon– a spell with the Nigerian detachment in the Congo. Subsequently he rose to the rank of Lieutenant-General, taking on the role of Military Commandant of Kano after the 1966 coup which brought General Ironsi to power; later taking up the position of Military Governor of the Eastern Region. Ojukwu was also a wealthy man, having inherited the rewards of his father's successful business.

Note 3   The spelling of Hank Warton's name has often been quoted as Wharton. On seeing a biography of his experiences in Propliner magazine his one comment to the author was a dislike of his name spelt with an 'h'–despite the fact that most published references do include it. Much of the detail relating to the flight of 'I-ACOA' was originally published by the Sunday Times Insight Team on 23 October 1966. Comments later by the Foreign & Commonwealth Office judged the Insight report to be factually correct.

Note 4   American Aviation Historical Journal, Summer 1980

Note 5   A full verbal description of the events leading up to the accident was given to the author by Hank Warton.

Note 6   Foreign & Commonwealth Office Papers, Public Record Office FO371/187848

CRISIS AND ACTION
The Declaration of Secession

Hijacks and seizures

General Gowon's apparent reluctance to implement a number of principles agreed at the January 1967 Aburi talks did little to boost confidence in the Eastern Region. Increasingly, Nigeria's easterners became hostages to the inability of Lagos to stabilise tension throughout the country. The situation was further fuelled when, during a dawn broadcast from the Eastern capital, Enugu on 25 February, Ojuwku warned that if the Aburi agreements were not fully implemented by the end of the Nigerian financial year—31 March 1967—he would take unilateral action and force them into effect.

As the deadline approached so an air of expectancy began to emerge; there was also a widespread expectation that the Eastern Region would break from the Federation. When the day came Ojukwu called a press conference in Enugu; a special announcement had been anticipated, but instead of the expected break, Ojukwu simply announced the first part of a survival plan in the shape of the Revenue Edict. The new ruling demanded that all monies collected in Eastern Nigeria on behalf of the Federal Government should be paid to the Government Treasury in the Eastern Region.

Lagos described the Revenue Edict as a means of funding Ojukwu's rehabilitation programme and for securing financial support for the increasing number of refugees still arriving in the East, mostly from the North. It was not, however, seen as affecting the huge oil revenue which was collected in Lagos.

On 1 April 1967, the day following Ojukwu's Revenue Edict, the Lagos Government declared the Edict to be "illegal and unconstitutional" and immediately retaliated by imposing a complete diplomatic, economic and military blockade against the East. The ban also included a suspension of all scheduled Nigeria Airways flights into the Region, the ban becoming effective from Tuesday, 4 April. Ironically, all scheduled services into, and out of, the Eastern Region were operated by Nigeria Airways and, apart from a twice-weekly through service to Tiko in the Cameroons, all were part of the airline's domestic network. These schedules, were flown by the airline's six DC-3s (5N-AAK/AAL/AAM/AAN/AAP/AAQ) and five F-27 Friendship 200s (5N-AAV/AAW/AAX/AAY & AAZ).

At the time of the government ban on flights into the Eastern Region, Nigeria Airways still had an obligation to fly a group of passengers who had pre-booked seats for the scheduled Enugu to Lagos (Flight WT141) service on

8 Above: The Government of Eastern Nigeria purchased the Hawker Siddeley 125 Srs 1B 5N-AER during the autumn of 1966 and on 23 December 1966 it began its delivery flight from Luton. In fact the jet progressed no further than Lagos before returning to the UK for storage. It is seen here, at Luton, immediately after its return. The crest on the fuselage cheat-line contains what was later to become Biafra's coat of arms and the 'rising-sun' national insignia. (via Brian Gates)

Wednesday, 5 April—in spite of the fact that money collected from the sale of these tickets (as well for other services in the Eastern Region) had not yet been paid over to the airline's Lagos headquarters.[7] Nevertheless the suspension of flights was lifted for just one day only to allow Nigeria Airways' DC-3 5N-AAK to be positioned from Lagos-Ikeja to Enugu, probably not routeing on that occasion via Port Harcourt. However, and immediately after 5N-AAK had landed at Enugu the airport authorities there impounded the aircraft and arranged instead for a number of vehicles to convey the passengers as well as the DC-3's crew back to Lagos.[8]

Ojukwu's Revenue Edict was followed, on 17 April, by the Legal Education Edict and by the Statutory Bodies Edict. The latter was designed to establish a Statutory Bodies Council in Eastern Nigeria and as a consequence ten central Government-owned agencies were transferred to the Council's control, amongst which was Nigeria Airways (WAAC) Ltd.

One effect of the Statutory Bodies Edict was to enable Corporation services to be continued throughout Eastern Nigeria as well as offering a means of paying those *Ibo* refugees who were employed by the Corporations, including the national airline. The other effect of Ojukwu's new Edict was simply to 'legalise' the Eastern Region government's impounding of the DC-3 5N-AAK which, since its enforced grounding on 5 April, had been kept under a heavily-armed guard at Enugu.

As if to underline newly-declared statutory powers the Eastern Region made a second assault against Nigeria Airways when, within only a week of announcing the Statutory Bodies Edict, two armed *Ibo* men hijacked an F-27 Friendship, 5N-AAV, on Sunday 23 April. The incident occurred just three minutes into the scheduled afternoon Benin-Lagos (WT123) service when the Pakistani captain (reported to have been named Cooper) had his headphones forcibly removed at gunpoint. The aircraft was flown to the Eastern Capital of Enugu where the sixteen passengers—who included Nigerians, Americans, British, Irish and Italians—were searched before taken to a luxury Enugu hotel where they spent the night.[9]

During the course of the following morning all of the passengers were returned to Benin by road; the hijacker, thought by the Benin airport authorities to have been an Eastern Nigeria soldier, remained in Enugu.[10] There was, considerably later, a suggestion that the hijacker had not been a soldier but, in fact, the F-27's co-pilot. Other reports identified the hijacker as a Nigerian *Ibo*, and which later identified him as Ibikare 'Ibi' Allwell Brown, an *Ibo* pilot who was eventually to fly MFI-9Bs with the Biafran Air Force.[11] Whatever the true facts surrounding the hijack were, 5N-AAV remained at Enugu and under the terms of Ojukwu's Statutory Bodies Edict became the property of the Eastern State Government. (As an aside, all available official documentation relating to 5N-AAV shows that the Nigerian Certificate of Airworthiness expired on 12 April 1967. The author could find no evidence that the C. of A had been renewed, suggesting that the aircraft may have been operating, perhaps rather surprisingly, without a valid certificate.)

Shortly after the hijacking of 5N-AAV, an attempt to seize a second F-27 Friendship almost succeeded in Ghana. A group of *Ibo*s had planned to board the aircraft for the return sector of a scheduled Lagos to Accra service but on that occasion details had been apparently leaked and security officials at Accra airport foiled the attempt.[12]

Equally foiled, but for very different reasons, was an attempt by Ojukwu to acquire a Hawker Siddeley 125 executive jet. The aircraft, a Series 1B/522, had been purchased by the Eastern Nigerian government, through the Swiss agent Transair Suisse SA, back in the autumn of 1966. Registered in Switzerland as HB-VAU, the 125 had made its first flight at Chester on 19 September 1966 before being handed over to the Swiss agency on 26 October 1966. It was re-sold almost immediately to the Eastern Region government. At the same time its paint scheme

9: When Eastern Nigeria issued its Revenue Edict all scheduled Nigeria Airways flights to the Region were suspended, on 4 April 1967. However the ban was lifted for one day to allow DC-3 5N-AAK to fly to Enugu to collect a group of stranded passengers. When the aircraft landed at Enugu on 5 April 1967 the Eastern Region simply impounded it and it was later impressed into the Biafran Air Force. (Roger Caratini, via Jennifer M. Gradidge)

was marginally altered, and it was re-registered as 5N-AER. But its delivery flight to Enugu, Eastern Nigeria, which began from Luton on 23 December 1966, ended prematurely after an unscheduled en route landing at Lagos.[13]

It was during a refuelling stop at Accra, in Ghana, when the pilot, Trevor Copplestone, was notified that flight clearance to Enugu had been cancelled (possibly due to the fact that Enugu was not officially a 'customs' airfield). The instruction added that the aircraft was to be flown instead to Lagos where further orders would be issued. 5N-AER plied on to Lagos but after landing it seems that the airport authorities there simply refused to allow the crew to fly further east. In fact the jet was surrounded by half-a-dozen Land Rovers of the Nigerian Army and the crew placed under house arrest.

Whether or not Lagos refused to allow Ojukwu to receive his 125 or whether Ojukwu simply declined to accept it is still very much open for conjecture. One popular theory to emerge at the time suspected the Federal Government of employing a local witchdoctor to place a *ju-ju* curse upon the aircraft, and thus making it virtually impossible for Ojukwu to accept! A more plausible explanation is put forward by Ntieyong Akpan, later Ojukwu's Chief Secretary and Head of the Civil Service.[14] In reflecting upon Ojukwu's state of mind during this period, Akpan believes that Ojukwu was being intimidated by close relatives who professed to be more interested in his personal safety than anything else. Akpan described the 125 incident as probably "the most ridiculous and embarrassing act of intimidation" and went on to explain that "on its way to the East the pilot, owing to some misunderstanding, landed in Lagos. For this the Governor was advised to reject the plane which would have been 'bugged' in Lagos. The assurances of both the dealer and the pilot that nobody in Lagos had got even near the plane, which had been kept locked by the pilot all the time it was at the airport, did not make any impression." In the event, the 125 was flown back to the UK, arriving at Luton on 12 January 1967 and where it was placed into storage.[15] Just after its return to Luton Mike Keegan, owner of Keegan Aviation, spoke publicly, on 28 April 1967, of the situation regarding the 125. "There has been some talk that when the plane was delivered a witch doctor put a magic spell on it. I do not know whether this is true–all I am interested in at present is selling it!"[16]

Oil: Aerial support operations and Biafran secesssion

Lying surreptitiously behind the political bickering and the general deterioration of the delicate alliance between East and the remainder of Nigeria, laid the nation's greatest prize–rich and sulphur-free oil deposits.

The extent of Nigeria's oil resources was still largely unknown in 1967. The flow of crude from fields in the East and Mid-West had already begun and virtually all of the Mid-West oil was shipped out via the Trans-Niger pipeline to the Bonny Terminal in the East. Other fields were being drilled from offshore rigs and these, together with the Mid-West fields, suggested that the extent of underground reserves were potentially immense. But all of these fields were in the Eastern Region, as was Nigeria's only oil refinery near Port Harcourt. As Governor of the Eastern Region, Ojukwu effectively controlled the physical flow of oil from source to coastal terminals.[17]

However hard Ojukwu tried not to involve any direct conflict with the oil companies or to involve the oil companies in his dispute with Lagos, there is no doubt that those companies were becoming increasingly caught within a situation that was almost as volatile as the very product itself.[18]

It was not just the oil companies who were now embroiled in the worsening political situation; a host of support operators were also involved, including a fairly widespread helicopter support network. In spite of Enugu being the Eastern Regional capital, it was the oil companies' support activity in supplying the rigs and fields, who were responsible for making Port Harcourt the busiest airport in Eastern Nigeria.

There were essentially two helicopter operators based at Port Harcourt in support of the Nigerian oil industry. Aero Contractors Co of Nigeria operated throughout the south and east of Nigeria, principally in support of the French oil company, SAFRAEP. Aero Contractors, which operated mainly Alouette helicopters, was almost wholly owned (97%) by the Dutch company, Schreiner Air Transport NV.

By far the larger of the two operators offering local support to the oil industry was Bristow Helicopters (Nigeria) Ltd, a locally-registered offshoot of the British company. Although Bristow's operations were spread across the south of Nigeria the company's main base for both administrative and front-line servicing work was Port Harcourt.

It came as no real surprise when Ojukwu finally announced, in the early hours of Tuesday, May 30 1967 that the Eastern state of Nigeria was to become the Independent State of Biafra with immediate effect. Enugu celebrated, Ojukwu was sworn in as Biafra's first Head of State and took a triumphant ride around Enugu township. Some senior Ibos believed that secession was one step too far and sought to escape to the West. For others life and work continued almost normally.

At the time of secession Bristows had eleven helicopters committed to oil-support work, all technically based at Port Harcourt. These involved two Westland Whirlwind Srs.3, four Hiller 360 UH-12Es and five Westland Widgeon (licence-built Sikorsky S-51) helicopters, all of which were semi-permanently allocated to the three oil companies Shell-BP, AMOSEAS and Mobil:[19]

Allocation of helicopters to Oil Companies As at 30 May 1967

	Shell-BP	Amoseas	Mobil
Whirlwind 3	–	5N-AGI	5N-AGK
Hiller 360 UH-12E	5N-ABY 5N-AGE	5N-ABZ	5N-AGB
Widgeon	5N-ABV 5N-ABW	5N-AGL	5N-AGA G-APTE*

Operated on lease from Westland Aircraft Ltd; allocated marks 5N-AGM but not taken up due to the domestic political situation.

In fact, Shell had ceased its operations from Port Harcourt during late-April 1967 and had moved to Ughelli in the Mid-West. Accordingly, Bristows had also deployed the two Hiller UH-12Es, 5N-ABY and 5N-AGE (the former with standard skid undercarriage; the latter on floats) to Ughelli, although both were technically based at Port Harcourt for routine maintenance etc. The two Widgeons, 5N-ABV and 5N-ABW, both of which were also allocated to Shell-BP were being held in reserve and were therefore kept, out of use, at Port Harcourt.

In many respects the declaration of secession did little, at first, to hamper Bristows' operation. The company continued to ferry supplies to and from the offshore rigs albeit these flights were now being made under the watchful eyes of the Federal Nigerian Navy as it began to police a blockade of Eastern ports. But on no occasion did the Nigerian Navy attempt to interfere with Bristow's activities in supporting the oil rigs. In fact the only restriction placed upon Bristow Helicopters came from the Biafrans. That involved a ban on flying across the border into the neighbouring Mid-West Region. The reason for this ban was more from a fear of helicopters being able to fly Nigerian 'spies' back into Biafra unnoticed, than for any other reason.

Bristows, however, did take some precautionary measures. Within a week of secession the company decided to evacuate employees' wives and families, together with some of the oil companys' families. The Biafran Army did allow these flights to take place but still insisted that none should cross the border into Federal Nigeria. But Bristows argued their case and questioned the ban while at the same time helicopters had been allowed to cross the border in order to support oil operations at Ughelli. These flights certainly meant crossing the state border. The Biafrans relented and allowed evacuation flights to head for Ughelli. Because of their larger capacity Bristows used their two Whirlwinds (5N-AGI and 5N-AGK) for these evacuation flights, the first of which was made by 5N-AGK, on 8 June 1967. Then, and amidst a growing nervousness within the Biafran Army, clearance for cross-border flights was refused and all further flights flew only to the eastern bank of the river Niger. From there evacuees were taken across to Federal territory by boat and completed their journeys to Lagos aboard helicopters based on the Federal side. In consideration of the shorter flight-time to the border, and the fact that the mood-swing of the local Biafran Army commander was becoming increasingly erratic, Bristows supplemented the Whirlwinds with two of the Widgeons.

Equally concerned for the safety of their employees' families had been the oil companies themselves and they too had set about arranging a series of evacuation flights. Eager not to display any obvious aggression towards the oil companies, the Biafrans did agree to requests for several aircraft to land at Port Harcourt and make such flights. The first of these evacuation flights took place early on 4 June when one of Shell's DH Herons (undoubtedly 5N-AGM) landed at Port Harcourt. Shortly afterwards on the same day the Pan African Airways DC-6A 5N-AFT landed, the latter having been specially chartered for evacuating families of Mobil and AMOSEAS employees.

Shell's Heron made just the one evacuation flight to Lagos on 4 June; the DC-6A managed to complete three round Lagos-Port Harcourt-Lagos trips. On the following day the Heron undertook a second, and its final, evacuation flight.[20]

Other evacuation flights proved to be not quite so straightforward. Fears for the safety of a number of British schoolchildren in the former Eastern State led the British High Commission in Accra to organise their immediate evacuation. Anxious not to risk losing another Nigeria Airways aircraft to the Biafrans, the Commission arranged for the charter of a DC-3 from Ghana Airways.

10: The Port Harcourt ramp, 19 May 1966 when Air Ferry DC-4 G-ASFY arrived to uplift four Hiller UH-12Es (5N-ABX, 5N-AGC, 5N-AGG & 5N-AGH) to the UK. Helicopters supporting oil companies drilling from offshore rigs, eg the Hiller 360 and the Whirlwind here, were fitted with flotation gear as standard, unlike Widgeon 5N-ABW (background) which operated on wheels for inland tasks. (Unknown)

11: The Ghana Airways DC-3 9G-AAD was chartered by the British High Commission in Accra for a series of evacuation flights from Biafra. On 7 June 1967 it was flown to Port Harcourt to bring out a group of British school-children but developed an apparent engine fault on the ground. Suspicious that it was part of an invasion plot, the Biafran Army ordered the crew to abandon the aircraft and leave by road. 9G-AAD was immediately handed over to the Biafran Air Force although it was soon written-off after the fighting started. (Roger Caratini, via Jennifer M Gradidge)

The aircraft, 9G-AAD, flew from Accra to Port Harcourt during the morning of 7 June. It had been anticipated that the DC-3 would complete the evacuation of all of the children in just two flights but difficulties arose before the first had been completed. Immediately after taking-off for the first trip to Lagos the captain advised Port Harcourt Air Traffic Control that his aircraft was suffering an engine malfunction and that an emergency landing was necessary. Back on the ground at Port Harcourt several local engineers assisted the crew in removing the troubled engine's cowling and to help locate the source of the problem. No obvious fault could be found and Biafran soldiers, who were nervously overseeing every movement, began to get wary that something untoward was happening. They reacted by ordering all of the crew and engineers to move away from the aircraft. The DC-3 captain, a short, dark-haired South African and known to his crew as David, did manage to convince the Biafrans to allow him to make a telephone call to Ghana in order to explain the predicament and at the same time request that a new engine be ferried in the next day.[21]

Ghana Airways did arrange for a replacement engine and assembled a team of engineers and equipment within the required deadline, but when the Biafran Army Commander realised that the airline was planning to fly the engine into Port Harcourt aboard a DHC-4 Caribou of the Ghana Air Force he suspected the flight to be part of an elaborate airborne assault. He promptly refused the Caribou permission to land. Ghana Airways then tried to send the engine into Port Harcourt by ship but this was also denied, this time by the Federal Nigerian Government which refused to lift its blockade of Eastern ports just to allow one aircraft engine to be delivered.

The stranded schoolchildren were eventually evacuated aboard the Pan African DC-6A 5N-AFT but not before a further drama took place. Both the Lagos authorities, as well as the Biafrans, agreed to allow the DC-6A to make one final flight to Port Harcourt on 9 June but as 'AFT was on final approach to the airport it too suffered an engine malfunction. The aircraft was grounded at Port Harcourt for several days until the fault was rectified. By now the Biafrans were almost beside themselves with invasion-fever but eventually the DC-6A fault was rectified and the remaining evacuees finally ferried back to Lagos–all, that is, except the crew of the Ghana Airways DC-3. They were held in Biafra until 15 June when the Biafran Army formally ordered their expulsion although they insisted that they abandon the DC-3.

When, afterwards, Biafran engineers inspected the Ghana Airways DC-3 they discovered that the cockpit fuel levers had been set to select an empty fuel tank; the engine failure, it seemed, had been caused simply through fuel starvation. There was a growing feeling among the Bristows' mechanics at Port Harcourt that the DC-3's South African pilot had possibly engineered his enforced landing there. Whatever the true facts of the situation were, and those were very strange times, the embryonic Biafran Air Force had just gained its second DC-3.

In spite of their suspicions surrounding the Ghana Airways aircraft, the Biafrans did allow evacuation flights by Bristow Helicopters from Port Harcourt to the Federal border to continue. Within several days Bristows had evacuated all of the families without any difficulty or harrassment. The other oil-support helicopter operator in the area, Aero Contractors Co of Nigeria, also began to evacuate its employees' families but it seems that, unlike Bristows, the company had elected not to seek official clearance to do so from the Biafran Army.

Aero Contractors had at least two Alouette II helicopters (5N-AIA & 5N-AIB)–and possibly a third (5N-ACR)–at Port Harcourt and it is likely that all were used for evacuation flights during this period. When, on 12 June, Biafran soldiers made one of their routine inspections of the company's base it has been alleged that they discovered documents which related to the recent evacuation of personnel. As these flights had never been officially sanctioned it had to be assumed by the ever-suspicious Biafrans that Aero Contractors' helicopters had, unlike Bristows', crossed the border and into Federal territory. A report on this assumption was signalled back to Army HQ at Enugu whose response was to order the immediate expulsion of all Aero Contractors' personnel. The order to leave Biafra was announced early the next morning, 13 June, by a group of soldiers who simply marched into the company's Port Harcourt office and demanded that all personnel leave Biafra before sunset on that day and that all of the equipment, including the helicopters, be abandoned. Together with a number of assorted cars and caravans, and a supply of vital Jet-A1 fuel the Biafran Air Force had acquired two (or possibly three) more Alouette II helicopters. Aero Contractors also operated a Dornier Do 28A-1 at Port Harcourt during this period and although no positive identity is known, it is believed to have been 5N-ACQ (c/n 3006). Even so it is thought that it did manage to escape from Port Harcourt before the Biafrans issued their dismissal notice.[22]

In spite of the increasingly delicate political and military situation existing during this period, Shell still found time to recognise the effort put in by Bristow Helicopters in evacuating non-essential personnel to the border by hosting a small dinner during the evening of 14 June. All air and ground crews attended. Even better news followed the next morning when one of Bristow's pilots, flying a Whirlwind to the border, succeeded in quietly collecting the first mail to reach Port Harcourt since the country declared independence. Under considerable secrecy groundcrews delivered the mail around the base throughout the day.

The main discussion topic at the Shell-Bristow dinner had been to question how long the helicopters could continue to be operated with any degree of normality before they, and the pilots, would have to be evacuated. Having just witnessed the expulsion of Aero Contractors, Bristows took a decision, by the end of the evening, to fly out at the earliest opportunity all those personnel not directly involved in flying operations. There were obvious difficulties, especially as the Biafran Army had become increasingly nervous over any movements at the airport, but some personnel were successfully flown out under cover of normal flights. The most obvious sign of Biafran nerves becoming dangerously stretched had occurred earlier in the day and had involved the Bristow Helicopters' Riley Dove (5N-AGF), which normally operated on behalf of Shell, out of Port Harcourt.[23]

For some time rumours had persisted that a seaborne assault by Federal troops against the island of Bonny was imminent. Indeed, some local reports even talked of a build-up of Nigerian ships just outside the proposed landing-area. Of course, the Biafrans had no real way of confirming such reports until the morning of 14 June 1967 when the first act of aggressive interference took place.

The Biafran Army ordered Bristows' pilot to take a group of officers aboard the Riley Dove and undertake a coastal reconnaissance sortie.

The flight headed east to Calabar and then turned back to cover the entire coastal area, over Bonny oil terminal and further west over Brass and the Niger delta. Bristows' pilot was then ordered to fly northwards along the river Niger to a point beyond Onitsha. The pilot had had little alternative but to make the flight as had the group of very nervous soldiers on board, some of whom were clearly making their first flights in an aeroplane. None of those aboard saw any sign of a pending invasion although, back at Port Harcourt, the pilot did comment quietly to colleagues that the oil terminal at Bonny was unusually congested with ships awaiting clearance.

The Lagos government, although still blockading ports in the East, did continue to allow ships into the Bonny terminal, even after Ojukwu announced on 25 June that oil royalties of £7m, due to be paid on 1 July, were to be paid instead to the Government of Biafra. The possible imposition of fines against those oil companies not making payments was clearly an indication that oil was shortly to become a military issue. But the 1 July deadline passed with no payments being made to either government; in fact little happened for several days until 4 July when General Gowon quietly announced that the naval blockade would be extended to include a ban on all shipping from and to the Bonny terminal. Shell announced shortly afterwards that oil production in East Nigeria would be cut back. This tempted Lagos to qualify its shipping ban as only applying to any oil company that paid over any royalties to the Biafran government. Radio Biafra simply announced that "the oil companies were co-operating" but other reports that royalties of £250,000 had been paid over were strenuously denied by Shell.

On 2 July the Nigerian Navy opened fire on a Panamanian-registered steamer, *Rigel*, which it suspected of running the blockade in spite of assurances from the captain that his ship–now with a three-foot hole in its side just above the waterline–was on a course from Douala to Lomé. The effect of this incident was to confirm the Federal Government's threat against the oil companies and which led to a stoppage in oil production and the temporary closure of the Bonny oil terminal.

In the light of these events there remained a real sense of a pending Federal military assault and with its domination of coastal approaches a seaborne attack was still considered to be more likely.

The fighting starts: Bristow Helicopters evacuate

The first shots of the Nigerian Civil War were fired just after 05:00 hours on 6 July 1967; they were not, as the

Biafrans had expected, fired from the sea but in the rugged and hilly terrain of the north, at a point near Okoja. When the Federal Nigerian Army later reported its action on Biafra's northern border to the international press it was described as merely a "police action to quash a minor rebellion". In fact the Nigerian forces consisted of two Infantry Brigades (1 & 2 Brigade), each with three Battalions.

Despite the outbreak of fighting along Biafra's northern border, and the likelihood that it could eventually develop into a full-scale civil war, Bristow Helicopters continued to fly in support of Mobil from Port Harcourt (and to a lesser degree in support of Shell), albeit flying was now on a much-reduced scale. The Biafrans continued to believe that an assault would be launched from the south and saw the Nigerian 'police action' in the north as simply a diversionary measure. On 8 July, and as if to underline this fear, the Biafran Army marched into Bristow's offices and produced a government order declaring that all normal flying duties were to cease. Furthermore, and from immediate effect according to the same declaration, all helicopters and crews were to be placed at the Army's disposal for the purpose of reconnaissance flights. The crews did attempt to put up some resistance and argued that Ojukwu had insisted that British subjects working within Biafra were not to be molested or hindered in carrying out their normal duties. But the nerve of the Army Commander for the Port Harcourt area had finally cracked to such a degree that he had now begun to turn a deaf ear to instructions from Enugu. The situation facing Bristow Helicopters did not recommend a prolonged political dialogue and so, and in fear for their own safety, Bristow's personnel began immediate preparations for their own evacuation.

Even at this late stage, Bristows still had some six helicopters at Port Harcourt, plus two Hiller 360s (5N-ABY and 5N-AGE) that had been detached to the Shell-BP field at Ughelli, in the Mid-West State, although these were considered to be well out of the danger area. Since the stoppage in oil production the need for this number of helicopters had reduced and several of those based at Port Harcourt (including Widgeon 5N-ABW and Whirlwind 5N-AGI) had already been flown out to the offshore rigs for safety–and before the Biafran Army could ground them. The Hiller 360 5N-ABZ (which had sustained damage at a storage tanker offshore from Escravos on 26 May, but had been speedily repaired at Port Harcourt during the early days of Biafran independence) had also been flown out of Biafra, to the offshore Rig 52. In the meantime Bristows curtly refused to undertake any more support flights on behalf of the Biafran Army and for ten days the Biafrans stopped the company making any further flights.

Eventually, on 18 July, Bristows received the final order to move all remaining personnel out to four offshore rigs: Rig 52 (AMOSEAS), Rig 59 (Mobil), the Sedco Rig (Shell), and the large Oceanmaster Rig (Mobil), for safety. Three helicopters were allowed, by the Biafran Army, to shuttle the last seventy oilmen out of Port Harcourt; among the last flights involved Hiller 5N-AGB to the Mobil Rig 59, while Widgeon G-APTE made for the nearer Oceanmaster Rig. The final departure from Biafra was made by the Whirlwind 5N-AGK, flown by Mike Ratcliffe, and which also made for the Oceanmaster rig.

12: Biafra's 'rising sun' insignia did not just appear on the day of secession. It was taken from the crest of Nigeria's Eastern Region. The crest was applied to the 125 jet 5N-AER when it was purchased in 1966 by the Eastern Government. Either side of the crest can be seen part of the 125's fuselage cheat-line, as well as the panel riveting. Prophetically the links in the chain signifying 'PEACE, UNITY, FREEDOM' appear to have already broken reflecting Nigerian life over the next three years (Peter Obe)

Unfortunately three of the Widgeons (5N-ABV, 5N-AGA and 5N-AGL, all of which were fitted with standard undercarriage, ie non-flotation gear) had to be left behind at Port Harcourt, together with the Riley Dove 5N-AGF. Although a handful of Bristows' personnel did remain at Port Harcourt for several more weeks until they too were evacuated, by road to the Nigerian border, there really was no scope for retrieving the abandoned equipment. The Biafran Air Force had become considerably larger as a result.[24]

Notes

Note 7 *London Times* 5 April 1967

Note 8 The point of seizure has also been identified as Port Harcourt and quoted as such within The Struggle for One Nigeria, published by the Federal Ministry of Information, Lagos 1967. However, most contemporary reports locate the incident at Enugu.

Note 9 *London Times* 25 April 1967

Note 10 As also reported to the author by Captain Roman Hrycak, London, 18 January 1982.

Note 11 Interview with Willy Murray-Bruce, London, 6 February 1974. Willy and Ibi Brown both later flew MFI-9Bs with the Biafran Air Force; both were also firm friends.

Note 12 *The Struggle for One Nigeria*, published by Federal Ministry of Information, Lagos 1967.

Note 13 *RAF Flying Review*, March 1968 issue

Note 14 *The Struggle For Secession 1966-1970*, by N.U. Akpan (published by Frank Cass & Co, 1971)

Note 15 *RAF Flying Review*, March 1968 issue

Note 16 *London Times*, 29 April 1967

Note 17 With hindsight it may seem strange that Ojukwu did not simply "hijack" the oil-fields; but the underlying problem within Nigeria was not the result of a dispute over oil, nor was the Biafran war an oil war in the truest sense and Ojukwu appears to have gone to some lengths to avoid a direct conflict with the oil companies. In any case had a stoppage occurred then the companies involved would undoubtedly have stopped paying royalty payments to the Central Treasury and more than anything else Ojukwu desperately needed a cash allocation from Lagos to finance his programme of rehabilitating thousands of refugees that had fled back to the East.

Note 18 During early 1967 three companies were extracting crude oil from the Nigerian fields: the American Gulf Corporation from offshore drilling platforms along the Mid-West coastline; the French SAFRAP company from on-shore fields inside the Eastern State, and Shell-BP which, by far the largest of the local producers, was shipping out crude oil from a number of ports in both States. The flow of oil had already been affected to a certain extent by the Federal blockade of shipping to ports in the East and with little evidence of Lagos being prepared to release financial aid to Ojukwu, Shell began to voice its concern over a possible shutdown of its Nigerian operation.

Note 19 Extracted from Situation Reports compiled by Bristow Helicopters Ltd.

Note 20 Ian McLeod (of Bristow Helicopters Ltd) recorded in his diary the arrival of the Heron but on this occasion made no record of the identity. It was probably 5N-AGM (c/n 14050) which was owned by Executive Air Engineering but leased to Bristow Helicopters Ltd between 24 April 1967 and 25 September 1967.

Note 21 As recorded by Ian McLeod at the time.

Note 22 Dornier Do28A-1 5N-ACQ was cancelled from the Nigerian register (date unknown) as withdrawn from use and later returned to the Netherlands where it was preserved.

Note 23 As recorded by Ian McLeod of Bristow Helicopters.

Note 24 After Bristow Helicopters had evacuated the Port Harcourt area, the company set about re-establishing its Nigerian oil-support work. AMOSEAS, which had been one of five companies exploring in the Eastern Region, stopped all operations during July 1967. This allowed the Bristow Whirlwind 5N-AGI, which had been ferried to one of the offshore rigs and later flown to Lagos with a number of evacuees, to be flown on to Cotonou to await a decision on its future. (In fact it was flown back to the UK, arriving at Gatwick 17.10.67 before completing the journey to Redhill.)

The ex-AMOSEAS Hiller UH-12E 5N-ABZ, together with the Mobil Hiller 5N-AGB, was flown from the temporary base aboard Rig 52 to Santa Isabel Airport on Fernando Póo where a new maintenance base was set up by Bristows and for continued support operations for those rigs offshore between the island and the Nigerian coast. Shortly afterwards it was decided to replace the Hillers with Whirlwinds and so the two redundant Hillers were flown back to Rig 52 for a "lazy" ferry back to Lagos, the rig being towed back to the capital for maintenance. The Hillers were then prepared for air-freighting back to Redhill, UK.

13: After the recapture of Port Harcourt by the Nigerian Army, Bristow Helicopters resumed limited operations in support of onshore oil fields in the south-east. Whirlwind Srs 3 5N-ABP was written-off on 27 November 1968 after suffering engine overspeed and failure on a flight from Bonny to Warri. The crash occurred near the village of Iba, approximately 15 miles north-west of Port Harcourt, when the pilot attempted to force-land in the bush. 5N-ABP was declared a total loss with the fuselage and rotor blades sustaining most of the damage as clearly evident in this view. Bristow's Technical Director Bill Petrie and fitter Tony Mabelis survey the wreck (via Peter J Cooper)

ESTABLISHING BIAFRA'S 'FIRST' AIR FORCE
1967-1968

More than anything else the Declaration of Biafran Independence, on 30 May 1967, fuelled an immediate build-up of arms by both sides. Unfortunately, most of the traditional sources were being put into a position that they would have preferred to avoid. Timing was the most unfortunate; the outbreak of fighting in Nigeria, on 6 July 1967, came just one month after the Six-Day War between Israel and the surrounding Arab countries. The USA was still very much entrenched in a hopeless war in Vietnam and across south-east Asia; the United Kingdom, although not directly involved in any foreign war, had just completed a strategic withdrawal of its military forces from Aden and was continuing to face up to the secessionist Smith regime in Rhodesia. Other civil wars were being waged in the Sudan, Yemen, and Angola while the former Belgian Congo was in a constant state of unrest. All of these conflicts offered sound reasoning for avoiding any involvement in another African conflict, especially an internal one.

Britain, while not ignoring the issue, tried to take a stance of neutrality towards Nigeria, a stance which involved the continued supply of 'traditional' weapons (small-arms, armoured cars etc), but which flatly denied the delivery of aircraft and heavy armaments. Notwithstanding that the Wilson government unsuccessfully tried to persuade the Nigerian Air Force to purchase a squadron of Hawker-Siddeley Andover transport aircraft –but it fell to the Soviet Union to fill the void in Nigeria's fighter and bomber roles.

Several potential arms suppliers simply refused to become involved in either side of the Nigerian civil war at any time; these countries included Switzerland, Germany, Italy, the Scandinavian countries and the United States. Hitherto Germany had demonstrated the greatest willingness to offer material support by helping to establish an embryonic Nigerian Air Force during the early '60s but withdrew its training personnel from the country as soon as the fighting started. In the period leading up to secession the Swiss government had also, albeit probably unwittingly, supplied a sizeable quantity of anti-aircraft guns to Federal Nigeria but then took a decisive stand as the country began to exhibit an unavoidable path to civil war.

On the other hand, the role of Portugal in providing help for Biafra was invaluable and included the provision of staging and refuelling facilities for both Biafran arms and relief aid at Lisbon airport (later, at Faro), the west African port and airport of Bissau and, of even greater value, the island of São Tomé, in the Gulf of Guinea–situated just some 200 miles south of Port Harcourt. Inevitably, without that support Biafra would have collapsed long before it did.

In terms of 'below-the-line' support there is little doubt that France became Biafra's major benefactor, although

14 Above: Biafra's Air Force was effectively established on 29 June 1967 with the arrival at Enugu of former French Air Force B-26R N12756. The aircraft was later camouflaged and with shark's teeth insignia for added effect. (Jean Zumbach)

the degree to which the French Government, under President de Gaulle, took a knowing part has never been–and no doubt never will be–formally admitted. De Gaulle's right-hand man in the 'cloak and dagger upper reaches'of French politics was Jacques Foccart, whose official title was 'Secretaire-General aux Affaires Africaines et Malgaches aupres de la Presidence'. Many contemporary reports openly pinpoint Foccart as the primary architect of French support for Biafra, but the *Quai d'Orsay*–the French Foreign Office–possessed greater sympathy, in the early period of the conflict, for the Federal Nigerian side. However, the *Quai d'Orsay* was relatively powerless to exert any influence and as black Africa was not considered to be the most important focus of foreign interest, it tended to accept Foccart's supremacy in such matters. The nature of French support was therefore strictly unofficial and necessitated the Biafran government relying on several groups of adventurers and mercenaries. This attitude could well explain the manner in which Biafra received its squadron of French Alouette helicopters.

Biafran helicopter operations

Even thirty years after the conflict, the extent to which the Biafrans made use of its helicopter element still remains largely vague. Few were ever flown, if ever, outside Biafra and those pilots who flew them kept no written record of operations. At least two Biafran Air Force pilots, Augustus Okpe and Willy Murray-Bruce, were seconded to the helicopter unit and both were trained inside Biafra by a French instructor.

Not only are precise details vague but even the precise number of helicopters used in Biafra has never been accurately established although one of the few published references to offer a figure quotes "six French-built Alouette helicopters".[25] Another reference suggests a different quantity but agrees with the source, claiming that "before the war the French Sud-Aviation factory had delivered three Alouette helicopters to Nigeria, together with a pilot-instructor. The Biafran trainee pilots spirited them away just before the outbreak of hostilities......."[26] A further reference to a clandestine purchase of helicopters by the Eastern Region Government has been made by Ntieyong U. Akpan, later the Chief Secretary to the Biafran Military Government. He claimed that two ship-loads of arms had been smuggled into Port Harcourt towards the end of January 1967 and also that "a number of helicopters had been acquired". "From Port Harcourt", Akpan goes on to claim, the arms and ammunition were unloaded and taken ".......not to Enugu, but somewhere in Nnewi."[27]

There is therefore little doubt that the former Eastern Region Government did acquire a number of Alouettes in a covert deal with the French manufacturer. This is again supported by a former Biafran Air Force pilot, Augustus Okpe, who subsequently claimed that the deal, which had been negotiated by a former Sud Aviation instructor named André Cessou, had consisted of at least one Alouette II and one Alouette III.[28] Okpe also maintains that they were delivered to Eastern Nigeria, not during late-January (as Akpan suggests) but much closer to secession, ie during April 1967. A further source (and the only known official documentation to be publicly released) is the Foreign & Commonwealth Office Annual Review of the Cameroons 1967. This does not offer precise dates, nor further details, but does support the theory that they arrived very close to secession. The Review reports that "the Cameroonian Federal authorities were probably more unable than unwilling to stop the smuggling of small arms into the Eastern Region from West Cameroon and they failed to prevent some French helicopters from getting through via a French firm in Douala."

Willy Murray-Bruce, one of the other Biafran pilots recruited for helicopter training, believes the quantity to have been greater than that suggested by Okpe but does agree that the Alouettes did consist of Mark IIs and IIIs. There is, of course, no official record as to any identities for these helicopters but two new-build Alouette IIs were registered in France as F-OCJS (c/n 1980) and F-OCJT (c/n 1982), both to Sud Aviation on 24 February 1967 as Sud SA.3180 'Astazou Alouettes', a variant that was subsequently re-styled as SA.318C Alouette II. On precisely the same date two Sud SE.3160 Alouette IIIs were also registered, again in the name of the manufacturer, as F-OCJP (c/n 1389) and F-OCJQ (c/n 1394).

Certificates of Airworthiness were officially issued after inspections at the Marignanne factory, for the two Alouette IIIs, on 15 February 1967 (F-OCJQ) and 17 February 1967 (F-OCJP); certificates for the two Alouette IIs were issued on 20 February 1967. All of the certificates were issued for a six-month period but none of the Alouettes ever had their C of As renewed, suggesting that either all four had become permanently non-airworthy or that they had been exported. The latter does tend to be more likely and especially by the manner in which the registrations were cancelled–in an administrative 'tidy-up' by the French authorities during 1969. If French government records are rather vague, then the manufacturer's records are even more so. No details of their fates have been recorded and the only recorded information is identical for all four. The declared customer is shown as "Loc vente Petroliers" which literally translates as "Local Sale Oil Tankers".[29] The implication that all were sold under a local arrangement with an oil company and which was obviously sufficient to satisfy the French authorities. But in view of none ever being re-registered after their cancellation in France, or indeed reported since their initial factory inspections, is strong evidence that all four were part of a clandestine sale overseas. Also speculative, but supported by one former Biafran Air Force pilot, is the fact that the deal had been negotiated by a former Sud Aviation instructor, André Cessou, who had also travelled to Eastern Nigeria to assist with pilot-instruction.

15: Widgeon 5N-AGA was abandoned at Port Harcourt on 18 July 1967. It was later used by the Biafran Air Force without any attempt to remove either company titling, or the registration letters. It survived a number of attacks by the Nigerian Air Force and was finally captured at Udi in February 1968. Several days later it was flown to Lagos by South African mercenary Ares Klootwyk (Lagos Daily Times)

16: Also captured at Udi was the remains of the Biafran Air Force Alouette III BAF-040. This was one of the original Alouettes acquired in a clandestine deal just prior to secession and is either the former F-OCJP or F-OCJQ. The remains were conveyed back to Lagos and later dumped at Oji Camp, where this view was taken just after the end of the civil war (Confidential Source)

17 Below: Operating out of Makurdi, Jet Provost NAF 702 seriously interrupted helicopter sorties when Britons Paul Martin and Mike Thompsett attacked the Biafran base. Details of the 9 October raid are contained within the logbook of Paul Martin

Unfortunately it is difficult to confirm this report as Cessou was later killed aboard the Biafran Air Force F-27 Friendship.

On the evidence of the Bristow Helicopters' personnel it seems certain that Aero Contractors were forced to abandon at least two Alouette II helicopters at Port Harcourt and which undoubtedly involved 5N-AIA and 5N-AIB. However the former Managing Director of Schreiner Airways (which owned Aero Contractors) is said to have later admitted privately that the company had sold "several" Alouettes to the Biafran government just prior to stopping their operations at Port Harcourt.[30] At least one of the former Aero Contractors' Alouettes (5N-AIA) did remain with the Biafrans and was, much later, observed at Cascais, Portugal during March 1970, ie just after the fighting had stopped. Another Alouette II, in a typically Biafran camouflage scheme, was seen to be aboard an L-1049H Super Constellation (N563E) at São Tomé during the war's final phase. It was reportedly being positioned inside Biafra for use by Ojukwu should he need to make a hurried escape.[31] Schreiner Airways has always officially denied that any of its helicopters were involved in the civil war yet did admit, again privately, that at least one of their Alouette IIs was lost in a crash at Owerri while being flown by a Biafran Air Force pilot. But this had occurred after the fighting had begun.[32] Another Schreiner Alouette II, 5N-ACR, is known to have been returned to the Netherlands when it was reported at Rotterdam in April 1970.

The Biafran Air Force formed a Helicopter Training Unit at Udi, just south of the capital Enugu. It was also from Udi that the Air Force conducted most of its helicopter operations which were primarily restricted to reconnaissance sorties along Biafra's northern border, ie where the fighting started during July 1967. Some bombing missions were also conducted by Biafra's helicopter unit and which were carried out, again along the northern border, from rough strips close to the line of fighting. These sorties were flown with a minimum fuel load in order to maximise lift with a full weapons load on board.[33] These raids were of sufficient nuisance value for front-line Nigerian officers to call upon the Air Force for support on at least one occasion. On 9 October 1967 the Nigerian Air Force Jet Provost NAF702, flown by British pilots Paul Martin and Mike Thompsett, flew a reconnaissance mission from Makurdi to Udi to search for the Biafran helicopter base. They eventually found it but had to return to Makurdi immediately as fuel had begun to run low. Later on the same date the same crew returned to the area and strafed Udi. The crew claimed the destruction of several helicopters in the process.[34]

One of the Biafran Air Force Alouettes is thought to have crash-landed near Uzuakoli during the early Summer 1968 period. An Air Force pilot later reported that villagers in Uzuakoli believed the helicopter to have been part of a Federal landing force and promptly lynched the crew.[35] Another is thought to have crashed during the early phase of the war when it was flying from Enugu to Calabar with the head of the Biafran Navy, Lieutenant-Commander Anuku, aboard. Anuku, it was reported during September 1967, was "still nursing injuries which he sustained in the crash".[36] At least one other Alouette was damaged beyond repair at Udi; this was an Alouette III sporting a unique camouflage scheme of maroon, blue and dull green as well as the Biafran serial, BAF040. The damaged Alouette was captured by Federal forces when they overran Udi in January 1968. It was later conveyed to Lagos where the rear section was still in existence at the end of the war.

Of the three former Bristow Helicopters' Widgeons, two were most definitely flown by the Biafran Air Force, the exception being 5N-ABV which is known to have suffered 'on ground' damage at Port Harcourt, the incident occurring shortly after its acquisition when a Biafran Air Force pilot tried to get the helicopter airborne.[37] A second Widgeon, 5N-AGL, was used by Biafran forces for a while and flown to the Udi helicopter base but was later wrecked during a heavy landing near Uli airstrip during early-1968. A post-war examination of the wreckage suggested that the pilot had clearly lost control, probably as a result of inexperience with the sophisticated nature of the helicopter's gear interchange between the main and the tail rotors. This explanation was supported by the fact that when Bristows' personnel later inspected the damaged main rotor blades they still retained earth deposits on the leading edge of the blade tips.

Widgeon 5N-AGA had a more dramatic end after it was captured intact when the Federal Nigerian Army 1st Division overran Biafra's base at Udi during January 1968. The Widgeon had been abandoned by fleeing Biafrans but surprisingly it was still in flying condition. It had clearly been used by the Biafran Air Force although no attempt had been made to remove the standard Bristows colour scheme or the registration marks. After a brief hover-test flight it was ferried, by the South African mercenary Ares Klootwyk, from Udi to Enugu on 2 February and then from Enugu to Makurdi, via Oturkpo on the following day. Four days later, on 7 February 1968, the same pilot ferried 5N-AGA from Makurdi to Benin and on to Lagos/Ikeja. At that stage, and firmly denying that it had any connections with a former Bristow Helicopters' Widgeon, the Nigerian Air Force impressed the helicopter into service with a fresh repaint.

By 14 February 5N-AGA had been transposed into NAF510 and operated for a while with the Nigerian Air Force.[38]

Apart from the helicopters impounded at Port Harcourt the Biafrans did gain access to two Hiller 360s, both of which were operated by Bristow Helicopters on behalf of Shell-BP from Ughelli in the Mid-West Region - in an area initially thought to have been quite safe. During the early hours of 9 August 1967 the Biafran Army had launched a dramatic attack across the river Niger and into the Mid-West Region. The assault, in brigade strength, made astonishing progress in its advance, so much so that by dusk on the same day almost the entire Region had been captured, including the southern parts of Sapele and Warri and the oil complex at Ughelli.

Such was the speed of the Biafran attack that workers at Ughelli simply fled in sheer panic. Bristow's two Hiller 360s (5N-ABY and 5N-AGE) were on the Ughelli helipad at the time of the attack; there was simply not the time available to fly them out to safety. An attempt to disable them was made, even as Biafran soldiers began to enter the outer part of the complex, when a local mechanic, Lambert Abali, ran out to the helipad and "with the aid of a spanner, put 5N-AGE out of action". Within two hours of Abali's action both Hillers were in the hands of advancing Biafran soldiers.[39]

Curiously neither of the two Ughelli-based helicopters were ever used by the Biafran Air Force and when the Biafrans were later forced out of the Region, both Hillers remained exactly as they had been abandoned.[40]

For the remainder of the war Bristows continued to provide the oil companies with helicopter support from bases outside the area of conflict. A new base was established, during July 1967, at Santa Isabel airport, on the island of Fernando Póo, for operations in support of Mobil while logistical support for Shell was later re-established from Ughelli.[41]

The full story of Biafra's use of helicopters may never be unravelled and one mystery which does remain unanswered is a reference made by former Biafran Air Force helicopter pilot, Willy Murray-Bruce. During his tour of duty with the Helicopter Unit at Udi, and where much of his flying was aboard the Alouette IIs, he did claim to have undertaken several flights aboard "a camouflaged Bell 47". While this cannot be totally discounted there have been no other confirmed reports of a Bell 47 operating inside Biafra.

Biafra arms; other sources

Support for Biafra was not wholly French; it has been said that a Madrid-based group of businessmen (which apparently included Otto Skorzeny, the former SS officer renowned for having rescued Mussolini from his Italian captors at a mountain hotel in Campo Imperatore in September 1943) wielded considerable power in support of Biafra. It is probable that another member of this Madrid-based group, albeit maybe a distant member, was one Baron Christian von Oppenheim. Various reports have connected Skorzeny, Oppenheim–as well as the German-American gunrunner Hank Warton–to the small state of Burundi.

Oppenheim, according to one published source, was "one of Ojukwu's oldest friends in Europe. They had met sometime before the Biafran secession. He was chairman of a company in Madrid, and it was through him that Ojukwu made his first European arms contracts when he decided to break with Nigeria". The writer met Oppenheim on a number of occasions in Paris, Lisbon and Enugu, enough times "to realize his power behind the scenes".[42]

At best von Oppenheim can be described as having been an import and export agent. He operated from a private address at Cinca 23, Madrid 2; his company was Camer International. Subsequent investigations after von Oppenheim's death revealed that Camer International had obtained an export licence from the Spanish Government for the export of arms and ammunition to Port Harcourt to the value of £541,477, of which Camer's commission amounted to £108,295. The licence had been issued on 7 March 1967, the application apparently being supported by a document allegedly from the Defence Department of the Federal Government of Nigeria and dated 16 December 1966. In other words, two months after Hank Warton's highly-publicised crash had brought Eastern Nigeria's secret stockpiling of arms to public notice, von Oppenheim's company appears to have secured an order to supply the Eastern Nigerian government with more arms. The document which purported to confirm the order, against which the Spanish government granted the export licence, contained three signatures, two of which were by the Officer Controlling Vote, and the Permanent Secretary, Ministry of Finance; all three signatures were identical. The destination of this consignment, as apparently instructed by the Federal Government of Nigeria, was stated to be the Ministry of Works, Enugu.[43]

Even after Eastern Nigeria declared independence von Oppenheim appears to have spent much of the period between May and July 1967 either in Biafra, or commuting between Biafra and Europe on a number of special missions. At the beginning of June 1967 a Swiss-based company, named as INCOS and operating from 92 Rue de Thone, Geneva, signed an open charter agreement with Geneva-based Executive Jet Aviation SA for the use of one or more Lear Jets. Under the agreement three Lear Jet 23s were used on numerous occasions between 3 June 1967 until early-October 1967: HB-VBA (c/n 026), HB-VBB (c/n 045A) and an American-registered example N428EJ (c/n 022).[44]

Evidence of von Oppenheim's close association with the Biafran high command is revealed within documentation raised by Executive Jet Aviation and which included a bill addressed to "Mr Christian von Oppenheim" requesting confirmation of an outstanding balance of a debt of US$19,010. An accompanying statement of the account was detailed as follows:

1. Daily Charges June thru July 1, 1967	
27 days at $1,500 per day	US$ 40,500.00
2. Flight Hours June 4 thru July 1 1967	
84h. 25 at $250 per hour	US$ 21,103.00
3. Crew Expenses June 4 thru July 2, 1967	
29 days at $35 per day	US$ 1,015.00
4. Landing and Handling Fees June 4 thru July 2, 1967	
29 days at $25 per day	US$ 725.00
	US$ 63,343.00
Less: your check of June 3, 1967	US$ 13,000.00
Received from Banque Romande:	
on June 15, 1967	US$ 10,500.00
on June 25, 1967	US$ 20,833.00
Balance in our favour as at July 25, 1967	US$ 19,010.00

Most of the chartered flights described within Executive Jet Aviation's statement had been made between Enugu and various other points in Africa, especially to the island of São Tomé. Other flights had involved trips between Enugu and Lisbon, between Geneva and Zurich and from Geneva to various European cities, eg Nice and Paris.

The same Lear Jets were also used by senior Biafran Government officials, including Louis Mbanefo, the Biafran Secretary of State, as well as Ojukwu himself on visits to various African capitals. The primary purpose of these flights was undoubtedly in connection with the Biafran leadership's desperate efforts to obtain diplomatic recognition by other governments. It is also reported that the Lear Jets were used on several occasions for transferring large amounts of Nigerian currency from Enugu to Geneva and Zurich, via Lisbon. The one person said to have been the organiser of these flights was Baron Christian von Oppenheim, again underlining the suggestion that a close relationship existed between Oppenheim and Ojukwu. The last of the Executive Jet Aviation charter flights, on behalf of the Biafran government, took place on 17 October 1967, ie shortly after the death of von Oppenheim. But by that time Biafra's own executive jet, the Hawker Siddeley 125, 5N-AER, had been delivered to Port Harcourt.

If Oppenheim was indeed Ojukwu's most influential business contact, then undoubtedly his primary source of arms, during this early period, was via the French dealer Pierre Laureys. Based in Paris, Laureys had a long history of clandestine arms deals with African governments, notably with Moise Tshombé's rebel Katanga Air Force to whom he had supplied a number of ex-French Air Force T-6G Texans.[45] Certainly by January 1968 Laureys has even been described as one of Biafra's principle agents and was reported to have been negotiating, in Lisbon, with the French mercenery leader Bob Denard over recruits for Biafra.[46] Laureys also operated–at least on paper–a small 'charter' airline, registered in Panama, under the rather simplistic title, *Compagnie Aeromaritime des Transportes*. The airline was run from an address in Paris although during the initial period of Biafra's secession Laureys was also known to have operated from Casa Ravina, Avenida de Venezuela, Monte-Estoril Portugal–the same address as Baron Christian von Oppenheim. This was the address for Laureys as recorded by Executive Jet Aviation with whom a credit account for Lear Jet charter flights had also been opened, and which like Oppenheim's flights, were mostly sectored between Enugu and Europe. (Laureys is also thought to have been the owner or operator of a Grumman Mallard, G-ASCS, formerly operated by Ferranti Ltd. On 1 November 1967 the Civil Aviation Authority recorded a change in registered ownership from Ferranti to a Mr F.M. Lawreys (sic) of 28a Vereker Road, London W.14)

The Biafran B-26 Invaders arrive

Having appropriated two civil DC-3s (5N-AAK & 9G-AAD), and one F-27 Friendship (5N-AAV), the Biafrans had the basis for a small national airline; the small number of helicopters located at Udi formed the basis for a military wing. But the Biafran Air Force needed an attack/bomber element to help establish national security. It is likely that it was at this early stage in Biafra's existence that the arms dealer Pierre Laureys first emerged and most likely on the recommendation of Ojuwku's closest adviser, Baron von Christian Oppenheim.

Not surprisingly, therefore, the initial acquisitions for the erstwhile Biafran Air Force came from French sources. Two ex-French Air Force Douglas B-26 Invaders were acquired. Both had been demobbed some time previously; both were secured through the services of Pierre Laureys.

The first of the two Invaders to be delivered was a B-26R variant which had operated with the Armée de l'Air as 4139531. Until its retirement from military service, it had been on the strength of the French research establishment, Centre d'Essais en Vol, at Brétigny. Then, disposed of through the Administration des Domaines (possibly by auction) on 11 July 1966, it had been bought by a Luxembourg-based dealer, Pan Eurasian Trading Company, on 2 August 1966. The price paid was reported to have been 9720 Francs. Two weeks later, on 22 September 1966, the B-26R was officially recorded as sold to a Mr Ernest A Koenig and who, during the course of the following month, had the aircraft civilian-registered in the USA, as N12756. Several weeks later found the aircraft in Belgium and effectively in storage at Courtrai-Wevelghem.[47]

Ernest Koenig became involved in several deals involving arms and aircraft which ended up in Biafra. He was one of several dealers with dual nationality that enabled him to move fairly freely throughout Europe and Africa. He was born in New York, sometime in 1930, to German parents who had earlier emigrated to the USA in the late-

18: Attention is focused upon a damaged nose-wheel of the the newly-camouflaged Biafran B-26R at Enugu after it suffered a tyre burst. Ground crews are preparing to tow the aircraft clear of the runway (Jean Zumbach)

19: In this view the exposed nose-wheel rim is clearly visible as is the sharks' teeth insignia. In his autobiography Jean Zumbach described the incident as interrupting sorties for a week. Eventually the French dealer Pierre Laureys brought a replacement down from France (Jean Zumbach)

20: Biafra's second B-26 Invader was an RB-26P variant and also a former French Air Force example. It was, however, acquired from the French aerial survey company, Société Carta to whom it had been registered F-BMJR. During mid-August 1967 one of Jack Malloch's pilots, the American Derick 'Red' Mettrick was offered the job of delivering F-BMJR from Creil to Port Harcourt. The generally poor condition of this RB-26P dogged progress and even after delivery it frequently suffered engine snags (Unknown)

1920s. After the death of his father the young Koenig returned, with his mother, to Europe and to a Germany then rallying under the influence of Adolf Hitler. When the Second World War broke out the Koenigs were forced to stay within Germany although both mother and son managed to survive the obvious hardships and any possible persecution of having such a close association with the USA. At the end of the war, and in taking advantage of his American citizenship and therefore being technically a 'displaced person', Ernest Koenig opted to take up residency in America where, in 1950, he enlisted into the United States Air Force. He rose to the rank of Major and was later transferred to the embryonic German Luftwaffe - with full pension rights. When his tour of duty with the German forces came to an end Koenig stayed in Germany where he re-entered civilian life as an aircraft dealer, living in Mannheim but operating, at the time of the Biafran period from a PO Box address in Luxembourg City.[48] It is highly probable that Koenig and Pan Eurasian Trading Company were, in fact, one and the same.

It is, of course, also possible that, in his purchase of the French B-26R, Koenig was simply acting as an agent on behalf of Eastern Nigeria. At least one contemporary source believed that the real buyer at the initial sale was a "French company, which paid good money for the aircraft". It has also been suggested that eventually the Biafrans paid up to $320,000 for it. Equally likely is that the French company involved at the outset was closely associated with Pierre Laureys although, apart from several rather vague references within Jean Zumbach's autobiography, no documented evidence is to hand to support this fact.

Zumbach, a former Congo mercenary flier, became Biafra's first white mercenary pilot, and described a certain *"Pierre Follorey"* as the prime mover in securing the B-26R and crew but he does admit to having changed the names of some of those characters involved. Zumbach writes:

"Walking down the Champs-Elysees in the Spring of 1967, I ran across an old acquaintance whom I shall refer to in these pages as Pierre Follorey. We had met in England during the war, and after the liberation of France he had gone into journalism, as an air-correspondent, before taking up "business"; mainly arms-dealing. I had seen very little of him since the end of our Katangan adventure."[49]

Zumbach's contract was apparently twofold; firstly to deliver the B-26R from Lisbon to Biafra and then to fly it operationally inside Biafra. He first travelled to Lisbon to wait for the arrival of N12756 down from Belgium. Zumbach describes his wait in a Lisbon hotel with another likely reference to Laureys:

"Three weeks later, Follorey joined me in Lisbon at the Ritz Hotel ... I was just starting to get bored when we were informed that the B-26 had landed. Follorey was now joined by a distinguished-looking gentleman, anxious to preserve his anonymity, but loaded with dollars. I had already guessed the broad outline of my mission, but Follorey filled in the details" ... *"(the B-26)* has been bought by this gentleman here. He represents Colonel Ojukwu, the leader of Biafra."[50]

These are virtually the only published references to those who were personally involved in the Biafran B-26 purchase, and it is pertinent to repeat that it is only assumed that the name of *Pierre Follorey* is, in reality, a pseudonym for Pierre Laureys. On the other hand one is left only to imagine the true identity of *Follorey's* companion but–and with all deference to those involved– apart from Baron Christian von Oppenheim there were few other wealthy and distinguished-looking gentlemen sufficiently close enough to Ojukwu's secret activities who would have warranted such a fine description.

Before its departure from Belgium, the B-26R had been taken out of storage at Courtrai-Wevelghem and prepared for its delivery flight to Africa; preparations involved a thorough inspection and the fitment of additional avionics. The problem of finding a suitably-licenced pilot was solved by contracting a former Congo flyer, one Jan van Rissegheim, to ferry N12756 from Wavelgheim to Lisbon. In an attempt to guarantee getting paid for the flight, the Belgian ferry pilot unscrewed and removed the aircraft manufacturer's plate during the delivery flight! Then, and immediately after its arrival at Lisbon, the B-26R was fitted with additional internal fuel tanks to ensure its delivery flight involved the minimum of refuelling stops.[51]

In the meantime those responsible for ensuring the Invader's safe delivery had contracted one of the few civilian-rated pilots in Europe in order to take the aircraft on from Lisbon for a quite astonishing fee of 10,000 Francs. He was reported to have been one Jacques Lestrade who, for several years, had been with the Centre d'Essais en Vol (CEV) and also as a fighter pilot with 4ème Escadre de Chasse (EC.4) of the French Air Force. Accompanying Lestrade was the 52-year old Jean Zumbach, also known as 'Johnny 'Kamikaze' Brown' or simply 'Mr Brown'.[52]

Without doubt a highly-experienced pilot, Zumbach was one of Biafra's more colourful characters. He was born in Poland, near Warsaw in April 1915, and while he later admitted to being a Pole at heart, an admission which reflected his upbringing, his birth had in fact been registered with the Swiss consular authorities in Warsaw, and therefore was accorded Swiss citizenship. At the age of 21, Zumbach enlisted into the Polish Air Force and later gained his flying wings in November 1938. When Hitler's forces invaded Poland Zumbach elected to flee the country and successfully escaped, via Hungary, Rumania and Bulgaria to Beirut from where, as a fighter pilot, he was later absorbed into the French Air Force. When the German forces successfully invaded France Zumbach had again been forced to escape, this time to England where he joined the newly-formed 303 (Polish) Squadron, RAF, flying Hurricanes and later Spitfires. By the end of the war Jean Zumbach had achieved a distinguished war record, having risen to the rank of Wing Commander. After being demobbed in 1946 he–by his own admission–had been involved in various flying ventures, many of which can at best be described as semi-legal; he had also served with the Katangese Air Force for a year, from January 1962.[53]

Biafra's first B-26 took off from Lisbon on 26 June 1967 with Lestrade at the controls, Zumbach taking the right-hand seat and a third (and unidentified) person also aboard, reportedly present to ensure that the aircraft arrived at its destination safely.[54] After pre-planned refuelling and overnight stops were made at Dakar, in Senegal and at Abidjan, Ivory Coast, B-26R N12756 landed at Port Harcourt on 29 June, watched by, among others, the resident Bristow Helicopters' crews. Later on the same day the aircraft flew the short distance north to Enugu.[55]

Immediately after the B-26R arrived at Enugu, Jacques Lestrade returned to France and Zumbach was formally contracted to fly the aircraft operationally, and for which he was reportedly paid two months salary of $8,000.[56] Several weeks later the whole operation was completed when Ernest Koenig lodged a Bill of Sale with the American FAA to indicate that N12756 had (ostensibly) been sold to a 'Mr Moises Broder' of Port Gentil, Gabon, allegedly for aerial survey work. Yet the aircraft remained registered to Ernest Koenig throughout 1969.

Almost three weeks after Zumbach's arrival in Biafra a second French pilot arrived at Enugu, around 17 July. He was known to be a former French Air Force pilot, he came from Avignon, and used the name 'Mr Black'. Others have described him as a gold-toothed Frenchman and named M. Durang–which may well have been his true identity. The arrival of Durang, if indeed that was his correct name, was not coincidental; nor was the appointment of two Biafran Air Force pilots, Godwin Ezeilo and Jimmy Yates to the B-26 unit.[57]

Biafra's second Invader should have arrived later in July 1967 but suffered from snags before delivery. Like the first Invader, the second example also originated from French sources. It differed, however, from the earlier aircraft in that it was a glazed-nose RB-26P variant and almost certainly the former F-BMJR, one of five RB-26P examples that had been sold by the French Air Force to the aerial survey company Societe Carta during 1966.

The RB-26P was ferried to Enugu by a 44-year old American pilot, Derick 'Red' Mettrick. An experienced pilot who had flown with 408 (Canadian) Squadron, RAF during the Second World War, Mettrick had just spent a little over a year flying for Jack Malloch in Rhodesia. He had first met Malloch in Miami, in April 1966, when the Rhodesian was buying the DC-7C N7326A/VP-WAJ. Malloch had asked Mettrick to test-fly the DC-7C and then offered him the job of delivering it to Salisbury. Mettrick accepted and in fact stayed with Malloch for some eighteen months. For a while he had been flying on Jack Malloch's L-1049G Super Constellation (VP-WAW) and made several flights into Biafra aboard this aircraft. When his contract with Malloch ended Mettrick had planned to return to Miami but during a stopover in Lisbon he met up with Hank Warton who, at the time, was trying to establish a gun-running airlift from Lisbon to Biafra. Mettrick was staying at Lisbon's Phoenix Hotel when a call came in from the nearby Ambassador Hotel. The caller was the French arms dealer Pierre Laureys who asked Mettrick if for a fee, thought to be considerably more than that paid to Lestrade, he would fly the RB-26P south to Port Harcourt.

Mettrick agreed to ferry F-BMJR to Biafra for $3,000. He collected the aircraft at Creil and intended to fly direct from there to Lisbon, but discovered en route that a number of instruments were not functioning properly. The ADF was unserviceable, the HF Radio was also out of action and only one of the two VHF Radios was working. As darkness approached and the weather worsened Mettrick abandoned the attempt to make Lisbon and instead diverted to Oporto. After an overnight stay, the RB-26P was flown from Oporto to Lisbon on the following morning.

The response by Pierre Laureys to Mettrick's report of the aircraft's serviceability state was to ask for a complete list of faults and then have T.A.P. work on the aircraft at Lisbon–at any cost. It is believed that the RB-26P underwent remedial work at Lisbon for almost two weeks.

Mettrick had flown F-BMJR from Creil to Lisbon on his own. For the onward journey the aircraft was fitted with additional fuel tanks (actually three 55-gallon drums) but Mettrick needed somebody to operate a 'waddle-pump' and thereby pump the fuel into the main fuel tanks. Laureys introduced a locally-based Portuguese mechanic, Luis Texeria, who was immediately recruited as Flight Engineer.

The flight from Lisbon to Port Harcourt was made with the minimum of stops. Only for refuelling purposes did Mettrick and Texeira land at Dakar and Bissau. The visit to Dakar was extremely brief but long enough to alarm the airport authorities there. Fully refuelled, the RB-26P was sitting at the Runway Holding Point when the ATC controller requested the crew to taxi back to the ramp area. Mettrick was sure that the French would try and stop the flight proceeding and so immediately lined-up and took off. At Bissau the aircraft landed for an overnight stay, but, like the visit to Dakar, the stop-over was not straightforward. During the evening a high-ranking Portuguese Air Force official tried to persuade Mettrick to return to Lisbon but Mettrick argued that the Officer had no jurisdiction over an American pilot flying a demilitarised French-registered aircraft–even if the Officer did suspect the ultimate destination to be Biafra. Texeria, on the other hand, was more than a little worried but spoke sufficiently good English to convince the Officer that he was not a Portuguese national. The RB-26P successfully took-off just after dawn on the following morning and was in Port Harcourt by the late afternoon. By dusk, French and Biafran technicians had begun fitting armaments.[58]

The 'Pink Lady' and the 'Grey Ghost'

Biafra's 'Grey Ghost' was simply the former Air France L-1049G F-BGNE. Inactive at Orly, Paris since its certificate of airworthiness expired on 4 October 1963, the Super Constellation was earmarked for quite an astonishing end to its career. In preparation for a sale to the French dealer *Établissements Jean Godet*, F-BGNE was taken out of storage on 27 July 1967; the sale was officially recorded on 9 August 1967. Repainted in an overall drab grey-green colour scheme, F-BGNE was officially restored to the French register on 16 August for ferrying purposes. On the following day, and via Lisbon, the L-1049G was flown to the Biafran capital, Enugu. On its arrival it carried the overtly-spurious marks '5N-07G'.[60]

Établissements Godet can be best described as no more than a second-hand dealer. Documentation lodged with the French authorities by Godet reveal that the aircraft was resold immediately, officially to a Portuguese company, but in such a manner that suggested two separate sales were made, firstly to Rhodesian Airlines *(sic)* who, in turn, resold the aircraft to an equally tenuous company, Transportader do Ar, the latter being simply Portuguese for 'Air Transport'. Both companies appear to have been part of a 'paper cover' for the sale to the Biafran government who reportedly paid some US$350,000 for the aircraft–a sizeable mark-up when considering that Air France was paid approximately US$84,000 for it.[60]

Whilst Jean Godet is reported to have sold the aircraft to the Biafrans it does appear, from later events, that he may have retained a degree of responsibility for '5N-07G's operation and also for the hiring of a crew. From the start Frenchman Jacques Languillaume made most–if not all–of the flights, including the initial delivery flight from Paris-Orly.

Languillaume was undoubtedly quite familiar with the aircraft as he had previously flown it during his time with Air France. He was also known to the French legal authorities as, at the time of the Biafran operation, Languillaume was the subject of a French police investigation into the financial collapse of SOGESTA, the pension fund for Air France pilots. Languillaume had been formally arrested back in 1966 but released from custody in November of that year pending a court trial. As of August 1967 the trial had yet to commence.

But Languillaume's involvement may have been more than just 'doing a job'. There have been suggestions (from contemporaries of Languillaume) that he was given an option by the French government; the option being to either fly on behalf of the Biafrans or face his immediate trial. There is, of course, no official evidence to support this fact. Nor is there much supportive documentation to prove the Rhodesian connection apart from the fact that Jack Malloch offered one of his own employees, Henry Kinnear, the Flight Engineer's position on the 'Grey Ghost' alongside Languillaume. That Malloch was offering his own staff positions on the 'Grey Ghost' Super Constellation does suggest more than a passing interest. In the event Kinnear declined the offer and Languillaume's regular crew consisted of two other Frenchmen, co-pilot Roger Fontenau and Flight Engineer Gilbert Kermerec.[61]

21: The one aircraft which operated the Biafra run longer than any others was Biafra's own 'Grey Ghost' Super Constellation which operated the Biafra run for almost two years. During that time it carried the curious identity 5N07G. In all that time it was rarely photographed and this poor shot of the L-1049G shows it landing at Lisbon on 3 September 1968 with what appears to be an open crew door (Luis A. Tavares)

The 'Grey Ghost' Super Constellation began operating regular flights on behalf of the Biafran government immediately after its arrival. Most of its destinations involved Portuguese (or Portuguese colonial) airports, eg Bissau (Guinea), Luanda (Angola) as well as São Tomé and, of course, Lisbon. But to ensure an uninterrupted operation it was vital to secure another aircraft as a back-up.

It was not long after secession was declared (on 30 May 1967) that Biafra's London-based agent, Austin Okwesa, began discussing acquisitions with an aircraft broker at Windsor. for a suitable transport aircraft. The two men travelled to Cambridge to inspect a DC-7CF, G-ATOB, which had just been retired by Trans Meridian Airways, and was being offered for sale or lease by sister company Trans World Leasing. A cash deal was agreed upon and the aircraft was flown, shortly afterwards, from Cambridge to Lisbon.[62] One condition of the purchase, it seems, was that the seller did not "rush" to advise details of the transaction to the UK Civil Aviation Authority. In fact the deal was not officially announced for some four (or even five) months. G-ATOB was ferried to Lisbon towards the end of June 1967 but the British registration marks were not cancelled until 2 November 1967. Interestingly, the marks were cancelled as "sold to Switzerland", the location for Biafra's principle banker.[63]

From the outset DC-7CF G-ATOB was plagued with various snags; even after landing at Lisbon, at the end of its initial delivery flight, some fairly basic maintenance had to be carried out by T.A.P. engineers. Nevertheless the problems were never cured and G-ATOB continued to suffer engine problems throughout its life on the Biafran arms airlift. On at least one occasion, when returning to Lisbon, the aircraft was nearly lost when the crew failed to realise that the auto-pilot stabilizer trim was malfunctioning badly.

G-ATOB was known by the Biafrans as the 'Pink Lady' (due to the name *'Lady Thelma'* having been painted on the nose by the previous owner); other pilots referred to 'TOB as *'The Old Bitch'*. Initially, it was flown on behalf of the Biafrans by a Dutch ex-Schreiner Airways pilot, Peter Woolf, but his association with the aircraft lasted only a very short period after the aircraft purportedly sustained several direct hits during an approach to Port Harcourt airfield. He was later replaced by a Swedish crew although by that time the Biafrans were starting to train local pilots for both the DC-7CF and the 'Grey Ghost' L-1049G. The object of training their own crews was, in time, to reduce the dependence on French and other foreign crews.

It is ironic that the DC-7CF was purchased by the Biafrans specifically to act as a 'back-up' for the 'Grey Ghost' Super Constellation. The L-1049G provided excellent service given the difficult operational circumstances but the DC-7CF was grounded for much of its time on the Biafran run. Details of its movements have passed largely unnoticed. The few recorded sightings include one known visit to Lisbon on 6 March 1968 (and another on 10 March) before being abandoned at Madrid-Barajas during early-April 1968. In fact it remained inactive at Madrid for the next three months.[64]

Another Riley Dove

Without doubt aircraft movements at Enugu and Port Harcourt increased significantly during the early days of secession as a variety of adventurers flew in. One arrival at Port Harcourt, on 6 July 1967 involved an American-registered Riley Dove, N477PM.[65] The Swiss pilot, André Juillard, is thought to have arrived with a cargo of Czech machine-guns which he reportedly offered to sell to the Biafrans. He also appears to have offered the aircraft as well and as part of the offer performed several coastal reconnaissance sorties, on 7 July and 8 July. The flights were made by the two Europeans and a single Biafran

22: Early in 1967 the Stuckeys Inc Riley Dove N477PM was flown to Europe and was briefly involved in the Nigerian Civil War. It arrived at Port Harcourt on 6 July 1967 with a cargo of guns and remained within Biafra for approximately a week before flying back to Europe. It was later impounded by the Algerian authorities and its crew arrested on espionage charges. Nothing further was heard of the aircraft until 15 October 1973 when the US FAA cancelled the marks as 'reported stolen and held in a foreign country'. An accompanying note reported 'State Department says it can be released via the Swiss authorities' (Terry Sykes Collection)

Army major aboard, but after landing on the second day the Biafrans immediately placed a 24-hour guard around the aircraft, denying Juillard the chance of making any further flights. Zumbach refers to the incident:

"....a Swiss called André Girard *(sic)* had brought 2,000 Hungarian sporting guns. The man in charge of the Enugu 'arsenal' had made a practice of consulting with me before ordering any of these job lots. Too often they had the disadvantage of coming in miscellaneous shapes and sizes, which complicated the problem of ammunition supply. I recommended buying the Hungarian guns because they were so easy to handle that even a raw recruit stood a fair chance of hitting the target."[66]

After a week the Biafran Army guard was stood down and Juillard was allowed to fly the Riley Dove out of Port Harcourt. It is assumed that, together with his two passengers–at least one of whom was another Swiss national –Juillard then flew the Riley Dove directly back north to Europe, this assumption being made after reports emerged that the crew had been arrested at Algiers on 13 July while making a transitionary refuelling stop. The aircraft was also impounded by the Algerian authorities,[67] and reportedly handed over to the Algerian Air Force.

The air war starts

By mid-July 1967 the Biafran Air Force B-26R had finally been made ready for service. Since arriving at Enugu on 29 June the US registration marks N12756 had been removed and the aircraft was repainted. A light shade of blue, perhaps even azure, was applied to the under-surfaces while upper-surfaces were finished in a gloss khaki green and dark brown camouflage. No external serial or identity was applied although the Biafran 'national' flag was hand-painted on both sides of the upper part of the rudder. The yellow rising sun superimposed on the red, black and green bars looked quite striking but these markings were later removed. The initial repainting was completed by the addition of red and white shark's mouth and teeth insignia on the nose, together with the obligatory, yet menacing, black and white eye.

At the same time as the repaint, the Biafrans began to instal a rather crude weapons-fit. At one stage of the aircraft's career, and while allocated to the French CEV for radar and radio trials the Invader had been fitted with a distinctively-shaped modified nose cone. The Biafran mechanics made use of this cone by boring a hole through the front of it and fitting a single tripod-mounted machine gun inside. The gun, which is said to have been of Czech origin, was never linked to any electrical firing system and is said to have been operated blindly by a rather crude communications system between pilot and gunner. According to Zumbach this system involved a piece of cord tied to the gunner's arm; one tug from the pilot signalled 'open fire' and two tugs told him to stop firing. A second gun was reportedly fitted to the rear end of the bomb bay and which fired downwards through open bomb-bay doors.

The Biafran B-26R was also used in a bombing role using what became known as 'Willy bombs' (after the name of the local Biafran designer/manufacturer). Again, a lack of a suitable internal electrical system meant that the bombs were released, by hand, by bombardiers strapped into the fuselage.[68]

Some reports claim that an air-raid against Lagos took place on 10 July 1967 but it is more likely that the first Biafran raid came later, on 26 July 1967. Certainly at some time in mid-July 1967 the aircraft's nosewheel burst while landing at Enugu. This did put the aircraft out of action for about a week while a spare wheel was flown in from France aboard a chartered Mystère jet. (See later) The raid on 26 July 1967 was against the three battalions of the Lagos Garrison Organisation which, late on the previous day, had carried out a successful sea-landing at Bonny.

Although a relatively small force, Nigeria's navy had effected a blockade of Biafra's ports since secession. The military advantages of capturing Bonny were not great but the action did have a further and neutralising effect on Biafra's key town of Port Harcourt, some 40 miles up the Bonny river. The wharves at Port Harcourt, essential for its sea trade, were now completely cut off from the sea.

The Biafran Air Force attack against the landing forces at Bonny involved the B-26R and possibly one of the Biafran DC-3s, probably the former Nigeria Airways 5N-AAK. The B-26R attacked the Nigerian frigate, *Nigeria,* with home-produced Willy bombs. The Nigerians described the bombs as closely resembling oil drums and which did little damage; even the Biafrans were disappointed with the results but the frigate continued to be attacked by the B-26R over the next few days. In the end the frigate did sustain sufficient damage to cause its temporary withdrawal.

Zumbach claims to have flown most, if not all, of the early sorties. He did, however, have several Biafran crew members to draw from. His usual navigator and bombardier was a Canadian-trained Biafran officer, Captain (later Major) Godwin Ezeilo. On some occasions another Biafran, Jimmy Yates, took on the role. The navigator's position was inevitably filled by a Lieutenant Oraeki while Corporal Peter Akachukwu and Sergeant Anthony Alaribe fulfilled the combined gunner/bombardier function. Two other Biafran Air Force officers flew occasional missions on the B-26R, namely Lieutenant Felix Ayinotu and Lieutenant Akitu.[69]

A surprisingly daring land assault across the Niger river was launched by the Biafran Army just before dawn on 9 August 1967. The assault, which took Biafran soldiers into the Mid-West region, came as a complete shock to the

Nigerian Army and, as a result, by dusk Benin and the southern river ports of Sapele and Warri, the oil centre at Ughelli and virtually the whole of the Mid-West had been overrun.

Several sorties were carried out by the B-26R (together with the ex-Bristow Helicopters' Riley Dove) in support of the Biafran surprise offensive. The Biafrans succeeded in capturing much of the Mid-West State and there were genuine fears within Lagos that the Biafran Army had become unstoppable. But just as the Biafran B-26R had begun to instill fear into the Nigerian Army, the Biafrans–having already learnt of the arms agreement between Lagos and Moscow–began to receive reports of an airlift consisting of Soviet Air Force freighters into Kano, northern Nigeria.

On Friday 18 August 1967 some fifteen Antonov An-12s landed at Kano in 10-minute intervals. Within a very short time these aircraft began to disgorge a number of MiG-17F jets. Jean Zumbach did not fly on the Kano raid; instead it was Durang who took the B-26R on what was undoubtedly the longest raid carried out by the Biafran Air Force. Durang took-off from Enugu late on the morning of 19 August and attacked the airfield around lunchtime. Little damage was caused.[70]

The ability to strike out at Nigerian targets could have given the Biafran Air Force a major military advantage. The bombs, however, were crude and ineffective. The ability of those pilots recruited to carry out the sorties has also to be questioned. One sortie involved one of the B-26s attacking Kaduna airfield, the main Nigerian Air Force training base. Again the attacking aircraft inflicted little damage and managed to kill just one person. He was a Chief Engineer named Mumu, and who had been responsible for the fleet of Chipmunks at Lagos-Ikeja before the war had started.

The Nigerians did go as far as publicly admitting that attacks by the "rebel B-26" were *regular and persistent*.[71] But to refute allegations by Lagos that the Americans were aiding the rebels, Washington issued a statement which underlined the illegality of the B-26:

"The B-26 aircraft said to be operating in the former Eastern Region of Nigeria formerly belonged to the French Air Force which sold it as surplus. Although the aircraft bears an American registration number, it was never issued a Certificate of Airworthiness from any U.S. source, hence such registration is not valid. The history of the aircraft indicates that in June it was flown from Ostend, Belgium by a Belgian pilot to Lisbon, Portugal where it was reputedly sold to a French citizen. With an illegal registration number and without air worthiness certificate, the aircraft subsequently was flown by a French crew from Lisbon to Dakar to Abidjan, and then to Enugu."[72]

The first operational mission involving Biafra's second Invader, the RB-26P (ex F-BMJR) is thought to have been launched against Nigerian soldiers (of 1 Brigade) near the town of Nsukka, the aircraft being flown by 'Captain Mike', one of the two American pilots who had delivered the aircraft into Biafra. The area of Nsukka and Opi provided targets for further air-raids by the Biafran RB-26P as two Federal battalions (21 and 22 Battalions) consolidated their position just short of Obukpa. Meanwhile, on Biafra's southern front Biafran Army defences near Bonny were regularly being shelled by the Federal Nigerian Navy gunboat. Towards the end of August 1967 the Biafran Air Force turned its attention towards trying to remove the naval threat. Yet again the effect was fairly minimal.

From August 1967 Zumbach appears to have gradually reduced his involvement with the B-26R. The gold-toothed Frenchman, Durang, flew a number of missions until permanently taking over the aircraft when Jean Zumbach left Biafra on 10 September 1967 for a spell of leave in France. In fact he did not return.

Retaliatory action against the Biafran Air Force began on 6 September 1967, not by the MiG-17s being assembled at Kano, but by a Nigerian Air Force Jet Provost T.51, NAF701. The Jet Provost, one of two operated by the Nigerians, carried out a dawn raid against Enugu airfield. Flown by two ex-R.A.F. pilots, Paul Martin and Ralph Swift, NAF701 was operating out of Makurdi from where it had taken off a little after 06:00. As they approached Enugu airfield the two-man crew could see a B-26 being 'bombed-up' in, somewhat surprisingly, an open part of the airfield. It was very obvious to the attackers that the Biafrans had not anticipated an air raid. Martin and Swift made three very low strafing runs across the airfield and although the Jet Provost was only fitted with .303 Brownings it is thought that the B-26R did sustain some damage. A second Biafran Invader, the RB-26P, was also on the airfield and was similarly attacked, as was a single DC-3. Both crew were unsure how much damage they had inflicted although they were certain that the DC-3 (which was undoubtedly the former 5N-AAK) was beyond repair.

A second attack against Enugu airfield by the Nigerian Air Force took place four days later, on 10 September. Both Jet Provosts, NAF701 & 702, were used in the attack. On that occasion the DC-3 was observed to be in the same position and "down on its undercarriage"; one B-26 was seen and attacked. It is likely that this B-26 was the B-26R. The second Invader, the RB-26P, is known to have been re-positioned to Port Harcourt around this time and thereby escaped the second raid on Enugu.[73]

Biafra's first Invader, the shark-toothed B-26R never, in fact, flew again. The Biafrans did attempt some repairs to the fin and rudder and it was probably during this remedial work that the Biafran fin insignia was removed. The aircraft was then towed into the airfield's only hangar where mechanics began to strip it of essential parts as part of an effort to keep the RB-26P airworthy.

More than anything else Biafra's B-26 operations were hindered by the lack of spare parts and while Biafran ingenuity could produce relatively-effective weapons, there were limits in operational support capability. There was a period, after the RB-26P had been transferred to Port Harcourt when the starboard engine was malfunctioning almost constantly. When the Rhodesian DC-4, VP-YTY, landed at Port Harcourt on one occasion the Biafrans sought assistance from the aircraft's Flight Engineer, Henry Kinnear. Kinnear supervised the changing of the engine's plugs before giving it an engine run at full throttle. He recalls that the brakes were totally ineffective and the RB-26P had spun round almost three times. Fortunately nothing was hit–but he managed to cure the engine

Among modifications reportedly incorporated into the RB-26P were home-made rocket launchers, with a total of forty-eight light and six heavy rockets installed beneath the wings. The aircraft, which had undergone this weapons fit (partially at Port Harcourt and completed at Enugu) before entering service, is also reported to have had guns installed in the wings. But this remains unconfirmed. However, what is known is that the overall black scheme in which it was delivered to Biafra, was later overpainted–towards the end of August 1967–in a similar scheme to its sister B-26R. The colours were almost identical but the RB-26P did not receive the shark's teeth so prominent on the first aircraft.

The Rhodesian Heron; the fall of Enugu

There had been occasions during the early days of secession when Biafran Army personnel had been flown along coastal and border areas as part of a reconnaissance operation. There were other occasions when even Ojukwu himself had wanted to view the front-line areas but suitable aircraft were not readily available to him. Undoubtedly the most unsuitable aircraft was his own Hawker Siddeley 125 (which at the time was lying damaged at Port Harcourt–see later). Ojuwku therefore turned to Jack Malloch for a solution.

Malloch operated a DH.114 Heron 1B which, along with the DC-4 VP-YTY, had been a gift to him from President Moise Tshombé. It was, according to its new owner, the most delightful aircraft to fly and one in which he had shared many close shaves in the Congo conflict. Jack Malloch agreed terms for the charter of the Heron, VP-WAM, just as the battle for Enugu began.

VP-WAM was flown up from Luanda to São Tomé by Bill Conduit with two engineers, Geoff Mason and Tom Ryder, on board. After taking-off from São Tomé the Heron then flew north to the Biafran coast but the crew got lost and are reputed to have descended to almost ground level in order to try and read roadside directional signs for a route north from Port Harcourt. Eventually, and after several hours of anxious searching the Heron found Enugu and was cleared for landing. After parking beside the airfield's single hangar the Heron's crew settled into an Enugu hotel to await their next flight detail. But several days after its arrival it sustained slight damage during a raid by Nigerian Air Force Jet Provosts. It was then pushed into the hangar but could not be fully repaired before the town, and airport, was overrun.

At least one observer reflected upon the loss of Biafra's capital, Enugu, as a "blow to Biafran prestige, but not as psychologically damaging as might have been expected." The writer continued to describe Enugu as a "British administrative creation but never regarded as a truly *Ibo* town. Umuahia, Aba and Owerri were the real heartland towns while Onitsha and Port Harcourt outstripped Enugu commercially."[74]

But those directly involved in the fighting believed that the fall of Enugu would lead to the automatic collapse of Biafra. It was a view held by the Nigerian Army's 1st Division which rested after capturing the capital and then took some six months to move its Divisional Headquarters in from Makurdi.[75]

Enugu airfield, on the north-eastern outskirts of the town, had simply been abandoned by the Biafrans just several days before the town fell. Several aircraft were left on Enugu airfield, including a DC-3–undoubtedly the former Nigeria Airways 5N-AAK–which was lying damaged at one side of the airfield. Also abandoned was the Biafran Air Force B-26R which had been left half inside the hangar and beneath a cover of crude foliage camouflage, as well as the Heron VP-WAM. The loss of the DC-3 was particularly ironic as it had been kept airworthy for a while by cannibalising the ex-Ghana Airways DC-3 9G-AAD after the latter had been damaged during a strafing attack by Nigerian L-29 Delfins at Port Harcourt two months beforehand.[76]

The RB-26P had been transferred to Port Harcourt before the Federal Army re-captured Enugu and thus escaped. So did the F-27 Friendship 5N-AAV, which was also at Port Harcourt.

By most accounts the F-27 Friendship had always been kept at Port Harcourt and often plied between there and São Tomé. It is also thought that the original 'NIGERIA AIRWAYS' titling may well have been replaced by 'BIAFRA AIRWAYS'. For a while the F-27's paint scheme remained untouched but during the autumn of 1967 a rather crude attempt to camouflage it was made. The white fuselage top was overpainted grey with irregular green 'squiggles' applied on top in a similar fashion to that applied to the Biafran Air Force T-6Gs much later on in the war.[77]

23: *Air Trans Africa's DH.114 Heron 1b VP-WAM was literally caught at Enugu when the airport was overrun by Federal Nigerian soldiers in October 1967. Jack Malloch had personally lent the aircraft to Ojukwu after the Biafran leader's Hawker Siddeley 125 had been damaged at Port Harcourt. The Heron was also seen as enabling Ojukwu to observe battle areas from the air and help raise the morale of his army. VP-WAM is seen here in an almost undamaged state shortly after its capture at Enugu (Oseni Oladigbol)*

24: *Also falling into Nigerian Army hands was the Biafran Air Force B-26R. Despite Enugu having been attacked on several occasions by Jet Provosts and L-29s the only apparent problem seems associated with the engines. The final flight of the aircraft is thought to have been on 21 August, possibly just after the Kano raid (Oseni Oladigbol)*

The 'camouflage' pattern applied to the F-27 was part of a scheme to render the aircraft less visible from the air but also to turn the aircraft into a makeshift bomber. Such was the state of the Biafran Air Force at the end of September 1967. Two B-25 Mitchells were expected, one even thought to be sitting on São Tomé island, but neither had arrived in Biafra.

It has been said that the same Biafran technicians who fitted armaments to the two B-26s also converted the F-27 to a bomber role. Evidence of a crude bomber conversion emerged much later from an inspection of several pieces of wreckage. Some details, albeit rather sketchy, were later related by a former Biafran based at Port Harcourt, where the work was carried out. It seemed that a round hole was simply cut through the rear fuselage where the outer skin sweeps up to the cabin floor. The hole was just large enough for a home-made cylindrical bomb to be dropped through. Inside the aircraft there was little evidence of any conversion work other than a cover which resembled an old-fashioned dustbin lid. The conversion was completed during the first week of October 1967.

Biafra: The 'Oppenheim Affair'

Just days after the loss of Enugu, the Biafran F-27 'bomber' was launched and lost on its first mission. It was quite the most bizarre of incidents, hastily-planned and ill-conceived from the outset. The target was Lagos but it brought very tragic results.

Events began to unfold at Port Harcourt with the arrival, at 04:00 on 3 October, of the Biafran 'Grey Ghost' Super Constellation '5N-07G'. The crew of three: Captain Jacques Languillaume, Flight Engineer Gilbert Kermarec and a Biafran co-pilot, were tired. They had originally left Lisbon with a cargo of Czech arms on 1 October and routed via Bissau to Luanda before flying north to São Tomé and then into Biafra. On the final approach to Port Harcourt the Biafran defences opened fire on the aircraft and literally "peppered it with bullet holes".[78]

The aircraft did manage to land safely and the arms unloaded. Because of the damage sustained Languillaume decided to fly immediately back to São Tomé and arrange for the repairs to be carried out locally. In fact it was Kermarec who stayed to organise the repairs; Languillaume elected to return to Port Harcourt on the following day (4 October) aboard the 'Biafran Airways' F-27 bomber which had flown in to São Tomé en route to Enugu (sic). The F-27 was being flown by its regular crew, Andre Cessou in command and co-pilot Alfred Anoway. Also on board the F-27 was Bernard Bret, a mechanic, and Cessou's girlfriend.

Languillaume collected his wages and decided to wait at Port Harcourt until word came out from São Tomé island that the repairs to '5N-07G' had been completed. It is even likely that, considering the grounding of the L-1049G as well as the situation in Enugu, a degree of frustration or boredom set in amongst the group of European pilots gathered in Port Harcourt. It is further likely that some members of the group had consumed a fair amount of alcohol before the plan to bomb Lagos was hatched.

The bombing mission took place during the night of 6/7 October 1967. The aircraft was loaded with approximately fifty locally-made bombs, reportedly contained within oil drums and, with a full fuel load, took-off from Port Harcourt late in the evening of 6 October. André Cessou, the F-27's regular pilot, was in charge of the flight, together with another Frenchman, Bernard Bret.

25: The Biafran Air Force F-27 Friendship, the former Nigeria Airways 5N-AAV, was used for a misguided bombing sortie against Lagos late on 5 October 1967. Despite claims by Federal Nigerian authorities that anti-aircraft defences had shot it down, it is widely assumed that the aircraft exploded in flight, possibly due to one of the bombs exploding prematurely. "Other causes" have never been totally ruled out especially as in these two views, taken on the following morning, no scorch or burn marks are evident. The upper view shows the rear fuselage underside section lying on its starboard side. The tail skid is visible to the extreme left. Through the square hatch and inside the fuselage can be seen the heat exchangers for the tropical air conditioning system - a feature standard to the Nigeria Airways' fleet

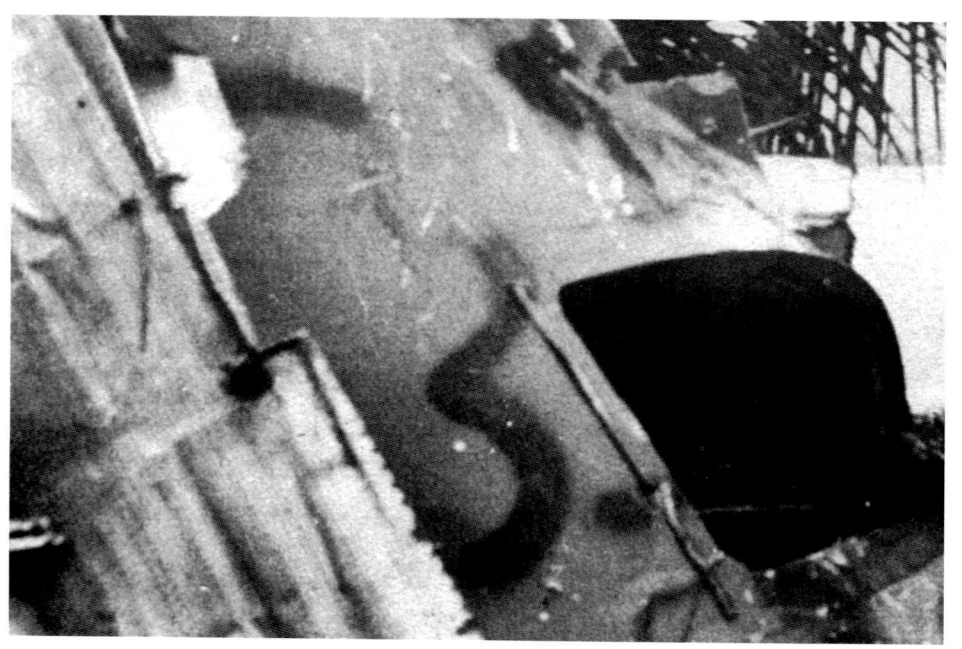

26: The lower view shows the rear fuselage section from the other side with the main passenger entrance door clearly visible. The door appears to have been removed rather than blown out which would point away from an explosion. If Cessou had made a slow run over Lagos with just 40° of flap then any movement of "bombs" towards the doorway would have increased the aft C of G. That would caused the nose to rise, created a stall, and led to the F-27 falling out of the sky. The picture lends credence to reports by one of Biafra's other mercenary pilots that the aircraft's upper surfaces wre crudely camouflaged in a matt green with added "squiggle" areas in darker green. (pictures by Peter Obe; assessed by Tim Gibbs)

Cessou's regular co-pilot, Alfred Anoway, had refused to join the flight in the belief that the aircraft was already heavily overloaded and as it is known that Languillaume was aboard, it is likely that he took Anoway's place in the co-pilot's seat.

Several passengers were also on board the F-27, presumably for the ride. These included Baron Christian von Oppenheim (known locally as Christian Schmidt), André Cessou's girlfriend (thought to be a Tunisian woman, aged about 20), and three Biafran Air Force officers, two of whom were later identified as Oyii Emmanuel and Charles Nweke.[79] The identity of the third officer has never been fully established. One other Biafran Air Force officer, Johnny Obianior, should have been aboard but was otherwise engaged when the aircraft took-off and therefore missed the flight.[80] (The Tunisian woman is thought to have been the same girl who worked as a cabin attendant aboard the Biafran Government Hawker Siddeley 125, and who was known as Simone.)

Curiously, the Nigerian Government did not immediately release all of the details of the F-27 incident; in fact the initial release talked of an American-built aircraft crashing with the loss of eight men, described as four whites and four Africans. The release issued by Lagos also went on to question the aircraft's point of departure in the mistaken belief that all of the airfields in Biafra had been put out of action.[81]

The Nigerians officially claimed to have shot down the F-27 as it was attempting to carry out the raid over Lagos; others suspected that one of the home-made bombs simply exploded while still on board. Whatever did cause the F-27 to explode it had quite tragic results, all eight people being killed, and the Biafran Government losing half of its regular pilots and one of its key advisers.

It was Jean Zumbach, in his autobiography, who introduced evidence that the bombing raid over Lagos had been something of a hotch-potch of a scheme, created almost out of boredom. Zumbach describes an air of deep despondency amongst the pilots following the loss of Enugu. There was also some despair over the state of Languillame's 'Grey Ghost' L-1049G, grounded at São Tomé and awaiting repair from small-arms damage. It seemed that the Biafrans asked Languillame to use the F-27 for the raid but that the Frenchman initially refused. Oppenheim allegedly responded by asking if he "was chicken", whereupon Languillame agreed to undertake the mission.[82]

Zumbach attributes the source of his F-27 story to 'Jean Bonnel', a Frenchman who had been hired by the Biafran Government as a 'supply agent' but whom Zumbach had earmarked for flying the second Biafran B-26. 'Bonnel', according to Zumbach, had previously worked with Fouga as a flying instructor on the company's Magister jets. In Biafra, 'Bonnel' had flown one of the Biafran Air Force DC-3s (presumably the ex-Nigeria Airways, 5N-AAK), and even accompanied the B-26 on several bombing-raids. On 10 September 1967 Zumbach left Biafra and returned to Paris; he quotes 'Bonnel' as then taking over as Head of the Biafran Air Force *(sic)* , but 'Bonnel' too returned to Paris after the F-27 incident, reportedly sick with malaria and in need of hospital treatment. *(Strangely, Zumbach makes no mention of two other French pilots known to be in Biafra at this time; the co-pilot, Alfred Anoway, who became disillusioned after the F-27 incident and the mysterious "gold-toothed Frenchman", Durang. It is just possible that Durang may ha e been appointed a senior post in the Biafran Air Force, and it is therefore equally possible that Durang and Zumbach's 'Jean Bonnel' are in fact the same person. Anoway is known to ha e returned to France not long after the F-27 incident and quietly disappeared into normal life.)*[83]

Neither the Nigerians, nor the Biafrans, released any elaborate details of the F-27 incident and none of those aboard were positively identified at the time. The Nigerian police did retrieve certain items from the wreckage but kept them under lock and key and did not make them publicly known. Among those items was a number of traveller's cheques, issued by the African Continental Bank in Port Harcourt, and in the name of the French pilot, Jacques Languillame. A week afterwards the Nigerian police added a cable to their secret file on the crash. It had been received from Arthur Forbes Granard (the Earl of Granard) and read *(literally)* as follows:

"HE SIR DAVID HUNT AMBASSADRE DE GRANDE BRETAGNE LAGOSNIGERIA

SHOULD BE MOST GRATEFUL TO YOU IF YOU COULD ASCERTAIN WHEREABOUTS CHRISTIAN OPPENHEIMER GERMAN JOURNALIST WAS ON BOARD THE BIAFRA PLANE WHICH CRASHED SATURDAY NIGHT LAGOS OPPENHEIMER'S WIFE IS NIECE OF MINE PLEASE CABLE ME CARE BRITISH EMBASSY PARIS AT MY EXPENSE BEST WISHES
ARTHUR FORBES GRANARD"

The cable is undated but reference to 'Saturday night' suggests that it was sent within a week of the crash; Saturday was, in fact, 7 October 1967.[84] Interestingly Oppenheim's name is given as Oppenheimer while the reference to him being a German journalist is also of note. Similarly of interest is the date of the crash–referred to here as Saturday night, ie night of 7/8 October. Contemporary press reports tell of the crash occurring in the early hours of Saturday morning, ie night of 6/7 October.

Shortly after the crash Oppenheim's body was released by the Nigerians for return to Spain and on 17 October 1967 the following memorium notice (interestingly giving another variation of the date for the crash) was placed in a local Madrid newspaper:

"Baron Christian von Oppenheim, who died as a victim of an aviation accident on the 8th October 1967. His wife Ione Stuart Walker, sons Corina, Eduardo, Flora and Maria Gabriela; his parents, the marquesses of Casteja; his parents-in-law, Mr Alan and Lady Mary Walker; his brothers, brothers-in-law, uncles, nephews, cousins and the rest of his family and his faithful servants Miguelina Marga and Ines Sierra... The funeral services will be celebrated tomorrow, the 18th at one o'clock in the afternoon in the church of San Fermin de los Navarros, Eduardo Dato 10, for his eternal rest."

Some of the evidence collected by the Nigerian police was later passed over to the French police. They were more interested in confirming that Languillaume was aboard the Biafran F-27. Under French judicial procedure, any criminal proceedings can only be officially and legally terminated in the event of the death of the accused. French police files in Versailles contain a reference that outstanding charges against Languillaume, relating to the Air France Pension Fund, were dropped due to his death –on 5 October 1967. (This is a fourth variation of the crash date!)

The same French police files include details of a fairly substantial investigation into the activities in Biafra of French personnel, most of whom were out of favour with the French authorities due to their involvement in Algeria. There are references to the L-1049G 'Grey Ghost' ('5N-07G') being operated into Biafra under the orders of a Mr Godet and that it was being flown regularly by Languillaume. The same files reveal that Godet visited Madame Languillaume at her home in Paris, on 12 October 1967, to break the news of her husband's death. A statement by the Super Constellation's regular Flight Engineer, Gilbert Kermerec (and who had remained with the damaged aircraft at São Tomé) alleges that he learnt of Languillaume's death several days afterwards. The news had come from the crew of an Air Trans Africa DC-4 which landed at São Tomé for refuelling, on 10 October, while returning from a supply run into Port Harcourt. On the following day Alfred Anoway (the Biafran F-27's regular co-pilot) flew from Port Harcourt to São Tomé (possibly aboard the former Bristow Riley Dove, 5N-AGF) where he met up with Kermerec and explained the full circumstances leading up to the F-27 crash. Although Kermerec lived in Douala he returned to Europe immediately afterwards and visited Languillaume's widow in Paris. At the same time he handed over her late husband's personal belongings and papers.

So what did cause the F-27 to crash? Anti-aircraft fire by Lagos defences, even if a lucky shot in the dead of night at a blacked-out target, can almost certainly be ruled out. No official investigation ever took place but when it was realised that the aircraft had been the former Nigeria Airways' F-27 (5N-AAV) several accident investigators inspected the wreckage. The engines were later retrieved by Fokker, and inspected by Rolls-Royce. No major defects were found. An inspection of the wreckage, however, did not reveal any obvious sign of an explosion on board nor did it point to any other immediate cause. The outflow valves had reportedly blown out but this was not proven. It just seemed to have fallen out of the sky, so Lagos claimed a shoot-down.

Under normal circumstances that would have been the end of the F-27 affair, but something else emerged much later–after the war–and which put another, and perhaps a rather more colourful, theory to the background of the F-27 crash. It was put forward by Ralph Huwonchey, an ex-Eton diplomat who, at the outbreak of hostilities, had elected to join the Biafran side. When Huwonchey was interviewed by the French Police it was he who suggested that Oppenheim was a double-agent acting for both the Nigerians and the Biafrans. It was not so much of a "may have been" but more of a "definitely was" suggestion.

Huwonchey then went on to make a further suggestion –that Oppenheim had intended to hijack the F-27 to Lagos and for this he had taken on board two large pistols. The former Biafran strongly doubted that the Nigerian Army had managed to shoot the F-27 down, in spite of the fact that Lagos had paraded one Corporal James Ewa as the soldier responsible for firing the fatal shell; even claiming that he had been promoted only the day beforehand and supplied with fresh ammunition at the same time. In Huwonchey's opinion the aircraft had crashed rather than having been shot down but when pursued on this point he could offer no real evidence to support this theory. On the other hand not all of Biafra's mercenary pilots had boarded the F-27. It had become something of a custom to throw a party after each mission; on this occasion it was the turn of a Portuguese pilot, Gil Pinto de Sousa, to act as host and he therefore remained at Port Harcourt to prepare for the party. De Sousa did later recall that just as the F-27 was getting ready for taxying out from Port Harcourt, Oppenheim had asked him for the loan of his 9mm pistol. De Sousa handed his gun over, despite believing that Oppenheim already had a pistol in his possession.[85] The fact that at least one of the F-27 occupants had a hand-gun, or even two hand-guns, does not in itself offer proof-positive that the operation was an attempted hijack; but it does add a rather colourful twist to one of Biafra's most intriguing episodes.

Biafra: the B-25 Mitchells

The Portuguese pilot who had watched the F-27 leave Port Harcourt on its fateful raid was one of two new arrivals in Biafra just before the fall of Enugu. Gil Pinto de Sousa was a former Portuguese Air Force NCO pilot and had just completed a tour of duty with AB4 at Henrique de Carvalho, in Angola. De Sousa had been looking for a new assignment when, on 1 September 1967, an Air Trans Africa DC-4 (VP-YTY) landed at Henrique de Carvalho. De Sousa learnt from the aircraft's Portuguese

27: *The Biafran Air Force operations involving the two B-25 Mitchells are the least written about This is undoubtedly due to their extremely brief operational life. They arrived in Biafra during October 1967 and both were effectively lost during one night sortie some six weeks later. Both aircraft were acquired from a Miami-based dealer who was later issued with a subpoena instructing the owner to explain what was reported as an unauthorised export of B-25J N8013 and TB-25N N9868C. The latter is seen here at Miami just prior to being flown out across the Atlantic to São Tomé island (Harold J. Martin)*

28: *What purports to be one of the Biafran Air Force B-25s at rest at Port Harcourt. Although a poor photocopy the palm trees surrounding the PSP hardstanding supports the assumption. The armaments fitted to the nose of the B-25 appear more potent than that fitted to the B-26s. A camouflage pattern is just discernable aft of the cockpit glazing and which clearly extends down to the bottom of the fuselage. It is just possible that the solid nose configuration of this machine matches that of the civilianised former RCAF aircraft, N8013 (via Leif Hellström)*

29: *Marian Kozuba-Kozubski, amongst a group of Nigerian Army officers at Port Harcourt shortly after the airport's capture, looks every part the Polish pilot-adventurer that he was. Sadly, this photograph is of very poor quality but the background is believed to show the wreckage of one of the former Biafran Air Force B-25 Mitchells–possibly the one-time N9868C (via Sheila Kozubski)*

41

U.S. DEPARTMENT OF COMMERCE
BUREAU OF INTERNATIONAL COMMERCE
WASHINGTON, D.C. 20230

SUBPOENA TO APPEAR AND TESTIFY AND TO PRODUCE BOOKS, RECORDS, AND OTHER WRITINGS, AS SET FORTH HEREIN.

TO: Tripoint Aviations Associates
3901 N.W. 37th Court
Miami, Florida 33142

At the instance of Mr. Charles B. Clements, Director, Investigations Division, Office of Export Control, Bureau of International Commerce, you are hereby required to appear before _____ of the Bureau of International Commerce at Customs Agency Service, 621 N.E. 1st Ave, Miami, Florida, in the city of XXXXXXXXXXXXXXXXXXXXX, on the 6 day of October, 19 67, at 3 o'clock, P. M. of that day to testify in the matter of an investigation necessary and incidental to the enforcement of the Export Control Act of 1949, as amended.

And you are hereby required to bring with you and produce at said time and place the following books, records, and other writings:

all records pertaining to B-25 aircraft N-8013 and N-9868C.

Failure to comply with this subpoena will render you liable to proceedings in a DISTRICT COURT of the UNITED STATES to compel you to appear and testify and produce books, records, and other writings, as

30 Above: After the two B-25 Mitchells had been exported from the USA, their owner–Tripoint Associates –was issued with a subpoena to appear before the US Department of Commerce offices in Miami. The aircraft, it was alleged, had been exported to Biafra without a valid export licence. This document appears to be one of the very few official references to the fact that the two aircraft were indeed exported. The outcome of any investigation by the US Customs, or any other Agency, remains unknown. (Robert Cobaugh, via Peter J. Marson)

navigator that they were about to make an air-drop of ammunition to a group of mercenaries stranded at Bukavu. He also learnt that the DC-4 was then due to fly on to Luanda and ultimately to Biafra. The aircraft's captain, Jack Malloch, agreed to take de Sousa to Biafra, or at least as far as São Tomé island. (In fact, VP-YTY did not fly into Biafra on this occasion.) From São Tomé, de Sousa managed to secure another lift, on 3 September, aboard an Air Trans Africa L-1049G Super Constellation (VP-WAW) to Enugu where he was introduced to the Biafran Air Force Commander, Lt-Col Chude Sokei and to whom he offered his services as a pilot. A formal contract was agreed and signed by both parties on the following day, 4 September 1967.[86]

The other pilot who arrived in Biafra just before Enugu fell was something of an enigma. He was a 40-year old West German and a former Luftwaffe pilot-instructor. Friedrich 'Freddy' Herz had even, before the conflict, spent some time instructing trainee Nigerian pilots. In fact he is thought to have become friendly with a number of *Ibo* pilots when they had been training with the Nigerian Air Force detachment at the Luftwaffe Training Unit *Flugzeugfuhrerschule (FFS-C)* at Uetersen in Germany. But Herz's arrival in Biafra had not been quite straightforward; he had arrived in Biafra from the Cameroons, during September 1967 and for a short time the Biafrans suspected him of being a Nigerian spy. Word has it that the Biafrans even considered arresting him at one stage but in the end they changed their minds and the former Luftwaffe pilot remained loyal to the Biafrans until the final collapse.[87]

Both Friedrich Herz and Gil Pinto de Sousa had been hired specifically to fly the two North American B-25 Mitchells which the Biafrans were expecting to take delivery of very shortly. Herz has often been credited with flying for the Biafran Air Force out of conviction and that being paid to do was immaterial. One cannot imagine that everything he did in Biafra was out of idealistic conviction. De Sousa's terms included US$600 for a month's retainer (half of which was paid in Biafran currency) together with free accommodation and food at Enugu's Progress Hotel.[88] Their stay in Enugu was extremely short-lived before the Nigerians began attacking the town and when the time to evacuate came neither had time to make it to the airport. Together, Herz and de Sousa drove south to Port Harcourt.

Although both pilots were waiting for the delivery of the two B-25s, one may even have arrived on São Tomé island some time previously–perhaps even as early as July 1967. The first of the two aircraft had been flown from Opa Locka airport, Florida to São Tomé by an American pilot who had previously flown with Trans World Airlines. According to one source on São Tomé island the American pilot requested, immediately after landing there, that the B-25 be loaded with salt before he left the aircraft parked at São Tomé and then returned to the USA, presumably to collect the second aircraft. The same source declared that the aircraft had remained at São Tomé "for almost six months". (Six months may have been an overestimation, but clearly one of the two aircraft was at São Tomé for some while.)[89] The identity of the American ferry pilot has never been firmly established but he is thought to have been one George 'Robbie' Robertson, who was known to have flown with T.W.A. Robertson did become one of Hank Warton's most loyal of mercenary pilots and remained in Biafra after Warton was fired.[90]

The identities of the two aircraft are rather easier to establish as they were both entered, as N8013 and N9868C, on a subpoena issued by the US Department of Commerce. The subpoena ordered Tripoint Aviation Associates, of 3901 NW 37th Court, Miami, to appear before the Director, Investigations Division Office of Export Control, Bureau of International Commerce, on 26 October 1967. The allegations clearly suggested that the two B-25s had been flown out of the USA prior to this date and in doing so had possibly broken export customs controls.[91]

One of the partners, if not the sole proprietor, of Tripoint Associates was Robert 'Bob' Cobaugh and who is known to have kept a number of B-25s at Florida's Opa Locka airport during 1967. At least three aircraft, N8011, N8013 and N9868C had stood in open storage for at least a year, although one of the trio (N9868C) had been used for Civil Air Patrol duties off the Florida coastline. Cobaugh was a member of the Miami C.A.P. and regularly flew a number of operations on their behalf, ostensibly watching out for illegal smuggling flights *(sic)*. (Cobaugh was, much later, associated with the Biafran arms airlift out of Faro, throughout 1969).[92]

Both of the two Mitchells exported to Biafra had originally been built as B-25J-NC variants during 1944 for the USAAF; N8013 was built as a 'Block 30', 44-31491, and after USAAF service had been transferred, in December 1951, to the Royal Canadian Air Force as 5245. Immediately after its transfer it had been re-designated as a TB-25J variant and remained in service until November 1961. After disposal locally, it was later registered in the USA and at the time of its sale to Biafra was registered to the Intercontinental Trading Corporation (of 1515 North West 12th Street, Fort Lauderdale, Florida).

N9868C was built as B-25J-25-NC 44-29919 but re-designated as a TB-25J almost immediately. '919 was later converted, by the Hughes Tool Company, to TB-25N standard in 1954 but disposed of by the USAF in autumn 1958. For a while it had been operated by a Florida-based company, Caribbean Air Transport but by 1967 was registered to Aerographic Inc (of 846 North Krome Avenue, Homestead, Florida).[93]

It is believed that the two B-25s exported to Biafra had one fundamental difference which distinguished them from each other. Contemporary photographs of N9868C at Miami show it to have a glazed upper nose panel, while N8013 is believed to have had a solid nose cone section. Otherwise the two aircraft were broadly identical.

Surviving documentation shows that Bob Cobaugh of Tripoint Aviation Associates instructed another local company, Aviation Machinists Company, to provide "new and modified fuel tank fittings" to the B-25s under the verbal instructions of one Mike Bailee. The modification work was carried out at Miami during July 1967 and clearly implies that long-range fuel tanks were fitted to the aircraft, possibly for the trans-atlantic ferry flight to São Tomé. It also implies that the two aircraft were still in the USA at that time.

The first of the two B-25s was flown on the final leg from São Tomé to Port Harcourt some time during October 1967, ie just after the fall of Enugu. For a brief period it was said to have been flown operationally by a Cuban pilot who called himself 'Captain Yas', together with an American pilot, both of whom had apparently negotiated the sale to Biafra. As well as these two men, an American mechanic was also flown in to Port Harcourt to install the armaments. *(The American mechanic is almost certainly Ed Short who is said to have later married a Biafran girl, left Port Harcourt and worked for a while at the Biafran European base at Faro, Portugal.)*

Operational readiness of the B-25s was not declared until almost two weeks after their arrival at Port Harcourt by which time the sole surviving RB-26P was also at Port Harcourt and being flown regularly by the Frenchman Durang. The Biafran Air Force could therefore effectively boast three operational aircraft–or theoretically, at least. In fact one of the B-25s was continually dogged with engine trouble and for almost the whole of November 1967 it was permanently grounded. The Portuguese pilot, Gil Pinto de Sousa, did make several training flights aboard one of the B-25s from Port Harcourt under the guidance of the Cuban delivery pilot. He also flew as an observer on several operational sorties aboard the serviceable B-25 and in company with the RB-26P, including a number of attacks against Nigerian forces advancing northwards from Calabar.

The very fact that the Nigerian Army was advancing northwards signalled a turnaround in the fortunes of both armies. By the end of September 1967 a substantial part of the Mid-West state had been recaptured by the Nigerian Army which had then turned its attention towards the southern half of Biafra, initially involving a seaborne assault landing. The campaign had opened with the Nigerian Navy heavily bombarding the beaches early on 18 October 1967. NSS *Lokoja* sailed into Calabar River later in the day with men of 3 Commando Division's 8 Battalion. Other Battalions landed at pre-designated points elsewhere in the Calabar area with surprisingly little opposition.

Although the circumstances are still unclear, it was during this autumn period that the Commander of the Biafran Air Force, Lieutenant-Colonel Chude Sokei was mortally injured during fierce fighting within the Abagana sector. With immediate effect Major Godwin Ezeilo was appointed Acting Commander and under his directive the Port Harcourt-based B-25s and RB-26P were tasked with an increased number of sorties. Often these involved up to three operations per day, most of which were concentrated against the build-up of Nigerian artillery units in the Calabar area.

At the end of November 1967 the Biafran High Command learnt of a deployment of Nigerian Air Force jets to the airfield at Calabar. It could only have involved a number of L-29 Delfins or possibly several MiG-17Fs. The threat was taken seriously and detailed planning began immediately for a bombing raid against Calabar airfield. The timing of the attack was planned for midnight on 2 December 1967.[94]

Only two of Biafra's three bombers were involved in the Calabar raid, the exception being one of the B-25s, still grounded with severe engine snags. Of the two aircraft that did make the raid, the B-25 was crewed by Freidrich Herz (pilot), Major Godwin Ezeilo (co-pilot), Captain Sam Ezunor (navigator) and Peter Akachukwu as gunner/bombardier while aboard the RB-26P was Mnsr Durang (pilot), Captain Onuorah (co-pilot), Captain Ochulor (navigator) and Anthony Alaribe (gunner/bombardier).

In view of its inferior speed, the B-25 took off some fifteen minutes before the Invader. After making a wide sweep around the target area both aircraft made their run across the airfield almost simultaneously, the B-25 bombing from a relatively high altitude, while the RB-26P attacked at low-level.

Precisely how many of the Nigerian jets were damaged or even destroyed has never been claimed or admitted by either side, but the raid proved far more costly for the Biafrans. As the RB-26P began its return approach to Port Harcourt, Durang reported difficulty in lowering the aircraft's main undercarriage at which point Herz agreed to circle away from the airfield to allow the stricken aircraft to land first. Durang elected to make an enforced belly-landing on Port Harcourt's grass runway but although he managed to land with no serious injuries to the crew the aircraft sustained serious and irrepairable damage.

When Freidrich Herz brought his B-25 in for landing he made a long approach but which proved to be at too low an altitude, possibly in an affort to land short of the damaged RB-26P. In the event the aircraft clipped the tops of palm-trees and touched-down short of the runway. As the B-25 hit the ground both of the wings were torn off and it too was written off as a result. Somewhat surprisingly only the navigator, Sam Ezunor, was killed in the crash. Herz suffered a broken leg and lost a finger; the other crew members sustained minor injuries. After spending a short period in a Port Harcourt hospital Herz was then invalided back to Europe for recuperation over the Christmas holiday. He later returned to Biafra during January 1968 but by then there was little, if any, of the Biafran Air Force in flyable condition.

Daylight on 3 December had brought the full realisation that virtually the entire Biafran Air Force had been written-off. Herz's B-25 was lying wrecked to one end of the runway, the only surviving RB-26P was also lying wrecked on the runway and de Sousa's B-25 was grounded with severe engine trouble. In fact the second B-25 was never again brought to a serviceable state and it continued to stand at Port Harcourt for six months before being finally destroyed during the Nigerian assault of the airfield in May 1968.

Only the former Bristow Helicopters' Riley Dove (5N-AGF) was in a marginal flying condition but that too was effectively written-off when it struck a truck and ground-looped at Uli during early 1968, reportedly being taxied by Major Godwin Ezeilo. Although the extent of damage to the Riley Dove was relatively minor, repairs were aggravated by a lack of available spare engines or propellers.[95]

The Presidential 125

Port Harcourt airfield, at the end of 1967, presented a sad reflection of Biafra's independence. Apart from Herz' wrecked B-25, the damaged RB-26P was undergoing repairs and the second B-25 was almost permanently unserviceable. The former Ghana Airways DC-3 (9G-AAD) lay written-off after a Nigerian Air Force attack and in another compound one of the former Bristow Helicopters' Westland Widgeons (5N-ABV) sat damaged beyond repair. One other aircraft was lying in a damaged condition at the side of Port Harcourt airfield. This was Colonel Ojukwu's personal Hawker Siddeley 125, 5N-AER.

Since returning to Luton on 12 January 1967 after its frustrated delivery flight had ended at Lagos, 5N-AER had been kept under the care of McAlpine Aviation. Some reports suggest that it was placed into long-term storage at Luton, others that Mike Keegan was looking for a buyer for the aircraft. 5N-AER certainly did remain inactive for a six-month period, during which time the Eastern Region had become the independent state of Biafra. On 24 June 1967 it was flown from Luton to Le Bourget by two British pilots for what was clearly a positioning flight. For almost a month the same two pilots flew European-based Biafran emissaries around Europe and West Africa under what was most likely a 'private operator's category'. The arrangement was not quite straightforward as the pilots were employed by McAlpine Aviation but Gregory Air Taxis Ltd was picking up the tab for landing fees, fuel and such like.[96] It was almost as if the Biafrans were dry-leasing their own aircraft to themselves!

The two pilots received their flight instructions almost on a daily basis–not directly from the Biafrans, but from a Frenchman named Monsieur Houchard.[97] The aircraft was by all accounts based at Le Bourget and was certainly operating on behalf of the Biafrans but, rather surprisingly, it did not, during the period in question, land on Biafran soil. In fact, the furthest south that 5N-AER ventured was Casablanca, in Morocco. A summary of flights made between 24 June and 18 July 1967, taken from one of the British pilots' Flying Log Book, shows that the 125 amassed almost 60 flying hours, as follows:

Government of Biafra, Hawker Siddeley 125 5N-AER Flight Log, June-July 1967

Date	Flight Routeing	Times (GMT)	Time
24.6.67	Luton-Le Bourget	1000-1105	1.05
25.6.67	Le Bourget-Nice	0730-0905	1.35
25.6.67	Nice-Le Bourget	1230-1350	1.20
	Le Bourget-Luton	1435-1530	0.55
	Luton-Nice	1640-1845	2.05
	Nice-Le Bourget	2025-2200	1.35
27.6.67	Le Bourget-Southampton	0805-0900	0.55
	Southampton-Amsterdam	1300-1410	1.10
	Amsterdam-Le Bourget	1905-2000	0.55
29.6.67	Le Bourget-Lisbon	0740-1015	2.35
	Lisbon Casablanca	1120-1300	1.40
	Casablanca-Rabat	1840-1905	0.25
	Rabat Casablanca	1920-1945	0.25
30.6.67	Casablanca-Rabat	1115-1140	0.20
	Rabat Biarritz	1155-1350	1.55
	Biarritz-Heathrow	1510-1645	1.35
1.7.67	Heathrow-Orly	0600-0700	1.00
2.7.67	Orly-Deauville	1010-1100	0.50
	Deauville-Orly	1810-1855	0.45
3.7.67	Orly-Nice	1225-1405	1.40
4.7.67	Nice-Le Bourget	1750-1920	1.30
5.7.67	Le Bourget-Deauville	1205-1240	0.35
	Deauville-Le Bourget	1735-1810	0.35
	Le Bourget-Nice	1900-2030	1.30
6.7.67	Nice-Rome	1105-1200	0.55
	Rome-Nice	2005-2110	1.05
7.7.67	Nice-Le Bourget	0740-0900	1.20
	Le Bourget-Nice	1315-1440	1.25
	Nice-Luton	1540-1745	2.05
11.7.67	Luton-Le Bourget	0540-0635	0.55
	Le Bourget-Biarritz	0710-0825	1.15
	Biarritz-Rabat	0910-1115	2.05
12.7.67	Rabat-Lisbon	1115-1230	1.15
	Lisbon-Le Bourget	1410-1625	2.15
	Le Bourget-Heathrow	1735-1830	0.55
	Heathrow-Le Bourget	1840-1940	1.00
13.7.67	Le Bourget-Deauville	1130-1200	0.30
	Deauville-Le Bourget	1810-1850	0.40

Date	Flight Routeing	Times (GMT)	Time
14.7.67	Le Bourget-Lisbon	1155-1420	2.25
	Lisbon-Rabat	1520-1625	1.05
16.7.67	Rabat-Casablanca	1145-1215	0.30
	Casablanca-Rabat	2145-2220	0.35
17.7.67	Rabat-Nice	1210-1500	2.50
	Nice-Le Bourget	1545-1715	1.30
18.7.67	Le Bourget-Dublin	0740-0920	1.40
	Dublin-Luton	1030-1125	0.55

After positioning from Dublin to Luton on 18 July, the British crew involved in the above flights did not fly 5N-AER again and the jet remained at Luton for a short while; certainly, on 21 July 1967 it underwent a routine Check 1 inspection.[98]

Subsequently, and flown by a French crew contracted by Transair SA, (and who may well have involved the Frenchmen, René Leclerc and André Cessou), the aircraft was delivered to Biafra. The date of its arrival in Biafra remains in some doubt. One source suggests that "it had not been seen at Luton since the end of July"[99] but another records the aircraft being based at Le Bourget during July and August 1967 before finally being flown to Port Harcourt on 13 September 1967.[100]

The extent to which the Biafran leadership utilised the 125 5N-AER during July and August 1967 is unknown but there are approximately 150 flying hours unaccounted for. What turned out to be its penultimate flight, and last for the Biafran leadership, took place about two weeks after being based in Biafra when, on 26 September 1967, Leclerc and Cessou flew the jet into Port Harcourt, inbound from São Tomé. As part of a routine precautionary measure against air attack it was immediately pushed into its hangar.

Very shortly afterwards the Federal Nigerian Air Force launched a sortie against Port Harcourt. It is still unclear whether the sortie was flown by a MiG-17F or an L-29 Delfin (but more likely the latter). What *is* clear is that rockets fired by the attacking aircraft hit the hangar containing Ojukwu's 125. One rocket penetrated the side of the hangar and exploded inside, close to the 125. The main damage sustained by 5N-AER in the explosion was around the rear equipment bay door–the 'hell-hole'– while shrapnel severed the electrical wiring loom, and caused several skin tears along the underside of the port wing and along the port upper rear fuselage. Ironically the attacker probably never realised the extent of the damage caused in the raid.

A little while after the raid a Rhodesian pilot, 'Bunny' Warren signed a contract with the Biafrans, on 26 October, to arrange for the aircraft to be repaired. Warren was also hired as the 125's new captain, the usual crew having been killed in the crash of the Biafran F-27. Warren did have some type-experience, it was said that he had previously flown a 125 owned by Mines Air Services Ltd in Zambia until the authorities there became convinced that he was a Rhodesian spy and apparently arrested him. Put on a BOAC flight out of Zambia, Warren later got off at the first opportunity and made his way back to Rhodesia where, in August 1967, he signed up with Air Trans Africa as a co-pilot on Jack Malloch's DC-4, VP-YTY but later transferred to the L-1049G, VP-WAW. This had brought him into contact with the Biafrans.[101]

Bunny Warren's first action in Biafra was to arrange for a clearing to be made in the jungle surrounding Port Harcourt airfield and then move the damaged 125 into it. The next concern was to complete all the repairs before the natural camouflage of surrounding trees shed their leaves and expose it to another raid by the Nigerian Air Force.[102]

During early December 1967 the Hawker Siddeley factory at Hatfield received an unexpected visit from Warren. The reason for his visit was to try to persuade the manufacturer in sending a team of engineers to Port Harcourt and repair the damaged 125 on site; also to arrange for the shipment of the necessary spare parts. Not unnaturally, the offer was politely declined on the basis that a previous application for UK Board of Trade approval to export a standard free-issue modification kit for this particular aircraft had been refused. Apart from the mod kit Hawker Siddeley had even faced difficulty in persuading the Board of Trade to allow the despatch of a 125 Mandatory Safety Modification (Mod 25/1894), associated with the introduction of a redesigned flap centre hinge bolt.[103]

There was never any likelihood that anybody from Hawker Siddeley would be allowed to travel into a warzone to repair the 125. Warren knew it too and on his return he convinced the Biafrans into allowing him and a team of local workers to make sufficient repairs for a single flight to São Tomé. At least hangarage facilities on the island were better than at Port Harcourt, and the aircraft would also be considered as out of the war zone. The patching-up process included the plugging of the smaller holes with a locally-made filler while larger tears were covered with crude patches, all pop-riveted with metal plates. At least one of the patches was made from a flattened Nestlé Milk tin.

The flight from Port Harcourt to São Tomé was made on (or about) 15 February 1968 and by any account it was an ususual flight. Apart from the various holes and tears in the fuselage skin and wings, 5N-AER's hydraulic system had also been seriously damaged in the raid. Only temporary repairs had been effected and the flight to São Tomé was made without the use of air-brakes or flaps. Even the undercarriage jack piston had been crudely sleeved, so that the main undercarriage was 'fixed and welded' in the down position.[104]

Shortly after its arrival on the Portuguese island, the Biafrans again attempted to get Hawker Siddeley to

31: The Government of Biafra's executive Hawker Siddeley 125, 5N-AER, suffered serious damage during a rocket attack against its hangar at Port Harcourt during October 1967. After the attack it was pushed into a jungle clearing at the side of the airfield where most of the damage was sufficiently, albeit very crudely, patched-up for a single flight to São Tomé island. The upper view shows a fuselage skin tear measuring approximately 6in x 3in just forward of the inverted cooling outlet. Also damaged was the production joint frame together with the electric cable loom which was completely severed

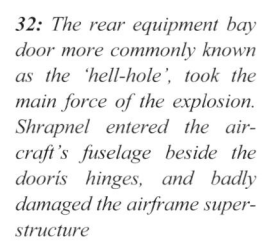

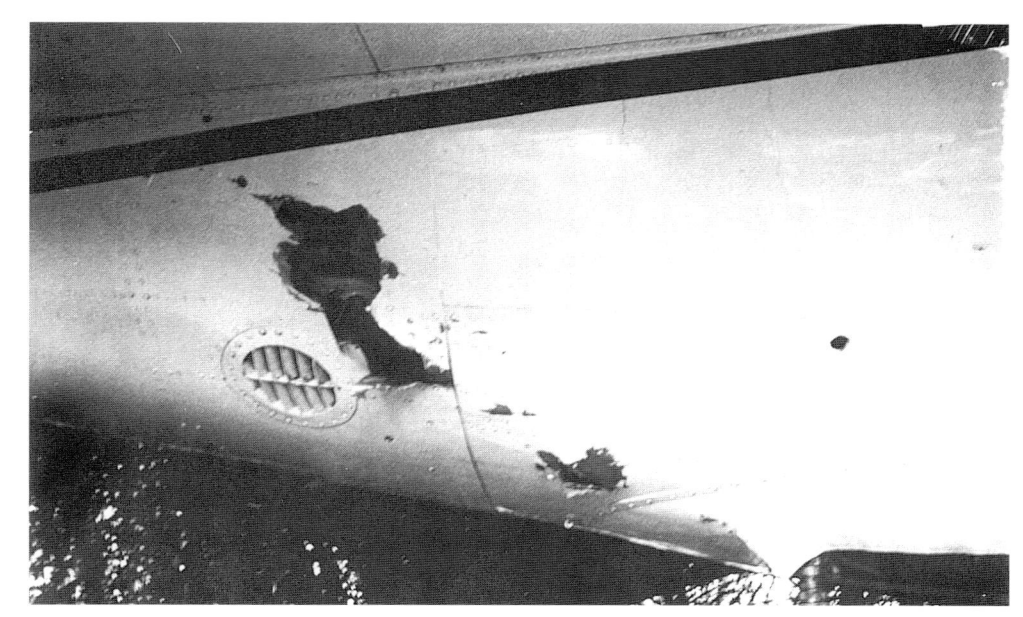

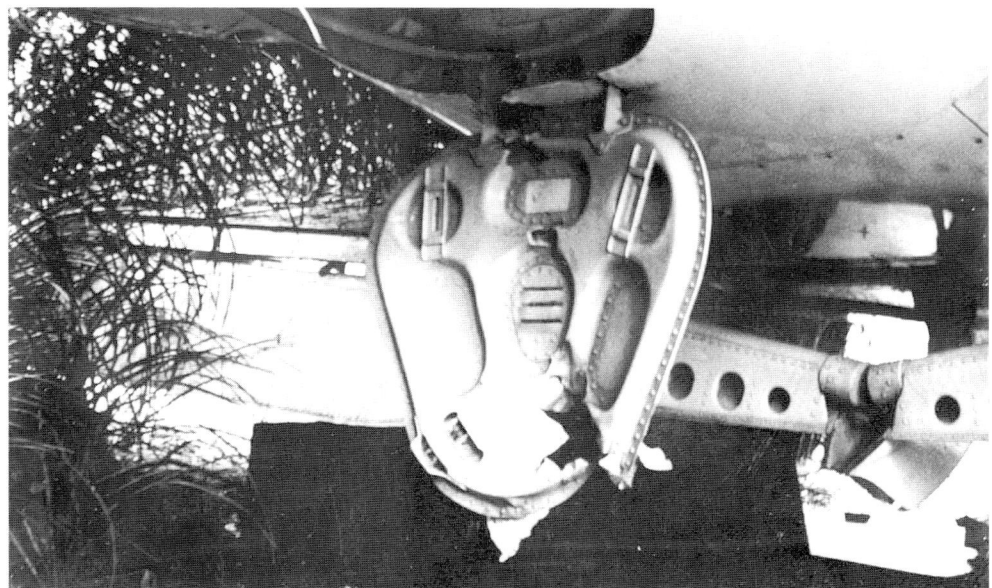

32: The rear equipment bay door more commonly known as the 'hell-hole', took the main force of the explosion. Shrapnel entered the aircraft's fuselage beside the door's hinges, and badly damaged the airframe superstructure

33: The port wing of Ojukwu's 125 5N-AER sustained a skin tear directly in line where the flap and aileron meet. The tear was subsequently patched by whatever metal was available locally, including a flattened Nestlé milk tin which was then pop-riveted. Metal fragments that were rightly suspected to have entered the wing itself were simply left in position (All by 'Bunny' Warren)

repair the aircraft. On this occasion, however, the approach was made through the agent Transair SA in an effort to by-pass the complex Board of Trade export ruling. But even though the aircraft was technically out of the war zone, nobody in the UK would touch it and the flight from Port Harcourt to São Tomé proved to be 5N-AER's final flight; it had amassed a total airframe time of just 238.25 hours and approximately 150 landings. 5N-AER was pushed into a corner of São Tomé's hangar and remained there for the next six-and-a-half years. (During its long sojurn at São Tomé a number of individuals laid claim to 5N-AER; gun-runners, Swiss banks and various dealers attempted to recover it as either war-booty or as compensation for debts not paid. The Federal Nigerian government also claimed ownership as the victor of the civil war. There is even some cause to suspect the manufacturer might have had a rightful claim as there seems to be some doubt as to whether anybody had actually paid for the aircraft in the first instance. Eventually, in 1974, it *was* examined, on behalf of one of the claimants, by a team of mechanics from Hawker Siddeley. The aircraft, by then home for countless tropical insects, was assessed to be a 'technical write-off' and the team therefore ensured–in a manner that only mechanics know–that 5N-AER would never fly again. Only then was it released to the Nigerian government and airlifted, by a N.A.F. C-130H, from São Tomé to Nigeria where it took up a permanent ground instructional role at the Air Force's Zaria Technical School.)[105]

Notes

Note 25   *Towards One Nigeria* No:3 (page 67), published by the Federal Ministry of Information, Lagos September 1967.

Note 26   *On Wings Of War* by Jean Zumbach; published by André Deutsch 1975

Note 27   Ibid, N.U. Akpan.

Note 28   As related by Biafran Air Force pilot Augustus Okpe to João M. Vidal. André Cessou remained in Biafra and later became the regular

34: Together with the Air Trans Africa Heron, Biafra's first B-26R also fell into Nigerian hands when the latter recaptured Enugu airfield. Despite Enugu having been attacked on numerous occasions by Jet Provosts and L-29s very little external damage appears evident in this view, taken just after its capture. The Biafran 'national' markings, evident in a view on page 97 taken in an earlier period, appear to have been removed from the aircraft's rudder before its capture. This picture is taken from the same sequence as the nose view on page 37 (Oseni Oladigbol)

35: After delivery Biafra's second Invader was repainted in a camouflage scheme similar to the first. A landing accident at Port Harcourt in December 1967 is thought to hav caused some damage to this RB-26P. The aircraft was never fully serviceable afterwards and in late May 1968 the former F-BMJR fell into the hands of the advancing Nigerian Army. In this view soldiers of Nigeria's 3rd Marine Brigade stand in front of the palm-covered aircraft. There appears to be lettering on the nose below the navigator's canopy (Peter Obe)

pilot of the Biafran Air Force F-27 Friendship 5N-AAV.

Note 29   These details are taken directly from the sales records of Sud Aviation. No other records are held.

Note 30   As related by former Managing Director Capt Cornelius Reichgeld to João Vidal 1995.

Note 31   See final chapter for further details of these events.

Note 32   Reported by Schreiner to João M. Vidal. This crash might relate to the same incident that injured Lt-Cdr Anuku.

Note 33   Interview between Willy Murray-Bruce and the author, London 6 February 1974.

Note 34   As reported by Paul Martin and supported by entries in his Flying Log Book.

Note 35   As related to the author by a Biafran Air Force pilot in Umuahia, September 1968.

Note 36   *Towards One Nigeria* No:3 (page 11), published by the Federal Ministry of Information, Lagos September 1967.

Note 37   Details of Biafran useage have been supplied by Mr 'Jock' Macaskill of Bristow Helicopters.

Note 38   As recorded by Ares Klootwyk, a South African pilot hired by Federal Nigeria.

Note 39   Interview with Jim Wilde of Bristow Helicopters, who was at Ughelli at the time of the Biafran advance.

Note 40   After Biafran forces had been pushed out of the Mid-West Region, Shell was able to re-start its operations there and a new support contract was signed with Bristow Helicopters on 15 December 1967. With renewed access to the area Bristows were able to inspect the two Hillers (5N-ABY and 5N-AGE) that had been abandoned some four months earlier. Their serviceability state was obviously suspect especially as neither had been inhibited, such was the speed of the Biafran advance. In fact 5N-AGE was found to be still in flyable condition but the other Hiller was in clear need of repair and maintenance. In order to resume operations with a minimum of delay the ex-AMOSEAS Hiller (5N-ABZ), which was still at Lagos awaiting shipment to the UK (but not yet crated), was flown to Ughelli during December 1967 to replace the damaged 5N-ABY.
Shortly afterwards the other Hiller at Lagos (5N-AGB), and which had been crated, was unpacked and flown to Ughelli to supplement the other two helicopters. All three Hillers operated from Ughelli until February 1968 when the first Jet Ranger (G-AVSW/5N-AHM) arrived in Nigeria to replace Hiller 5N-ABZ. A second Jet Ranger (G-AWFV/5N-AHN) arrived at Ughelli shortly afterwards to replace Hiller 5N-AGE. Apart from a very brief period during the summer of 1968, when the Jet Rangers were temporarily grounded with engine suppressor problems, the Hillers were crated and finally returned to the UK.

Note 41   When Bristow Helicopters established its new base at Santa Isabel there was no need for those helicopters transferred there to be registered in Nigeria. The Whirlwind 3 5N-AGK was therefore restored to British registry, as G-ASOU. The use of British registrations, rather than Nigerian, was also seen as avoiding any diplomatic disadvantage with the rather unpredictable Spanish Equatorial Guinea authorities. Subsequently, during August 1967, a second Whirlwind 3, G-AOCZ, was sent out from the UK. Both Whirlwinds operated from Santa Isabel in float-undercarriage configuration.

Note 42   *Ibid.*, Jean Zumbach

Note 43   Much of the detail relating to Oppenheim's activity in Nigeria and Biafra have been taken from two confidential reports, one investigating a claim against Oppenheim's life (on behalf of Orion Insurance Co) and another into activities by French personnel in Biafra during 1967. A copy of these reports was made available to the author.

Note 44   Extracted from the original account statement by Executive Jet Aviation, Switzerland.

Note 45   One published reference to Pierre Laureys exists within *Mercenary Commander* by Brian Pottinger and featuring the story of Col Jerry Puren in the Congo/Katanga war. The book includes the following extract, "On his last trip to Europe, Tshombé had contacted an international arms dealer in Paris, Pierre Laureys by name, and bought a consignment of ten T-6's and two Vampire jets for an undisclosed sum. Part of the package deal involved the hire of the necessary pilots. Lorez (sic.) had contacted swashbuckling adventurer-cum-smuggler, Jean Zumbach, then running a restaurant in Paris, and asked him to take care of the details."

Note 46   As reported in the *London Times* 9 January 1968. The French dealer's name was spelt Pierre Lorez.

Note 47   *Foreign Invaders*, Dan Hagedorn and Leif Hellström (MPL 1994)

Note 48   As related by Nic Taaffe.

Note 49   *Ibid.*, Jean Zumbach

Note 50   *Ibid.*, Jean Zumbach

Note 51   As related to the author by João Vidal.

Note 52   *Ibid.*, Dan Hagedorn and Leif Hellström

Note 53   *Ibid.*, Jean Zumbach

Note 54   *Ibid.*, Dan Hagedorn and Leif Hellström

Note 55   Ian McLeod, an Engineer with Bristow Helicopters at Port Harcourt, noted the B-26 landing there on 29 June and that it "was in dark olive grey overall scheme with American registration marks". He also believed that the crew consisted of a French pilot and at least one member of the crew was a Cuban.

Note 56   *Ibid.*, Jean Zumbach

Note 57   As related by João M. Vidal and also by Henry Kinnear, a Flight Engineer with Air Trans Africa and who was in Biafra at the time.

Note 58   As related to the author by Derick 'Red' Mettrick.

Note 59   Peter J. Marson, *The Lockheed Constellation Series*; published by Air-Britain 1982

Note 60   *Ibid.*, Peter J. Marson

Note 61   Confidential French sources; augmented by Flight Engineer Henry Kinnear

Note 62   The precise date of departure from the UK has eluded the author. However a search through the Airport Movement Log Books for various UK airports of the period has revealed that G-ATOB appears to have made very few flights within the UK during 1966/67. Its final recorded movement was an evening "training flight" from Cambridge to Heathrow, via Stansted on 20 June 1967.

Note 63   As related to the author by Tony Griffin, 1981

Note 64   *Aviation Letter* 1968

Note 65   N477PM was originally converted by Riley Aeronautics Inc and operated under a lease arrangement by a Mr Stuckey, known to be the proprietor of a chain of highway snack-shops, and whose company, Stuckeys Inc of Eastman, Georgia was a subsidiary of the Pet Milk Corporation; hence the 'PM' suffix letters to the registration. Prior to its arrival at Port Harcourt, N477PM staged through Geneva on 29 May 1967.

Note 66   *Ibid.*, Jean Zumbach

Note 67   *Interavia*, August 1968 issue. At the time Juillard and his passengers were still being held in an Algerian jail.

Note 68   *Ibid.*, Jean Zumbach

Note 69   *Ibid.*, Dan Hagedorn and Leif Hellström

Note 70   *Ibid.*, Dan Hagedorn and Leif Hellström

Note 71   *My Command: An Account of the Nigerian Civil War 1967-70*, by General Olusegun Obasanjo.

Note 72   *Ibid.,* Olusegun Obasanjo. The American statement was factually accurate except that the B-26 was flown to Port Harcourt initially.

Note 73   Details (and dates) are confirmed by Paul Martin's flying logbook. It is interesting to note that *The Struggle For One Nigeria*, published by the Federal Ministry of Information in October 1967 gives the date for the Enugu raid as 5 September 1967.

Note 74   *Ibid.,* Olusegun Obasanjo.

Note 75   *Ibid.,* Olusegun Obasanjo.

Note 76   Details of the loss of 9G-AAD were reported by Ghana Airways to British Aviation Insurance Company who fully investigated and honoured the claim.

Note 77   *New Nigerian*, 9 October 1967

Note 78   Quite why '5N-07G' routed via Luanda on this occasion is not known. Visits to Luanda were made to uplift arms from part of a 50 ton consignment of arms and ammunition delivered there during 1967. According to a report in the *London Times* (12.3.1968) the arms originated from South Africa and later left Luanda abord Biafra-bound aircraft.

Note 79   Fr Billy Butler was based at Port Harcourt at the time and knew those Biafrans on board. Earlier he had taught them at the local school.

Note 80   According to Rod Price, a British pilot with Nigeria Airways, who flew with Johnny Obianior after the war.

Note 81   *London Times*, 9 October 1967

Note 82   Correspondence between Gil Pinto de Sousa and J.M. Vidal.

Note 83   *Ibid.,* Jean Zumbach

Note 84   Copies of this cable were privately released by the Lagos authorities.

Note 85   Correspondence between Gil Pinto de Sousa and João M. Vidal. Huwonchey was also interviewed by Insurance Investigators to whom he raised the suggestion of an intended hijack.

Note 86   Correspondence between Gil Pinto de Sousa and João M. Vidal; also conversation between de Sousa and the author 20 November 1997.

Note 87   Correspondence between Gil Pinto de Sousa and João M. Vidal.

Note 88   João M Vidal, *Air Enthusiast Quarterly* 65, September/October 1994.

Note 89   The source was Captain José Matos who flew for São Tomé Airways

Note 90   As related to the author by Derick 'Red' Metrick

Note 91   Private papers of Bob Cobaugh, via Stef Baylis and Peter J. Marson

Note 92   The other B-25s in the area included N8011 at Opa Locka and N3451G at Miami. N8011 was reported to have been sold in Bolivia while it is possible that N3451G provided a source of spares to enable N8013 and N9868C to be declared fully airworthy.

Note 93   Federal Aviaion Administration Civil Aircraft Register, January 1970 issue.

Note 94   Much of the detail for this raid appeared in *Guerillapilot* by Gunnar Haglund and in *Foreign Invaders*, Dan Hagedorn and Leif Hellström (MPL 1994)

Note 95   Interview between a Biafran Air Force officer and the author in Umuahia, Biafra September 1968. The officer did not identify himself but could well have been Major Godwin Ezeilo himself.

Note 96   As recorded in Southampton Airport Customs Log and also the Aircraft Movements Log.

Note 97   The name may be mis-spelt but is a phonetic spelling as recalled by one of the pilots.

Note 98   The airframe log-books show that this was the final recorded servicing.

Note 99   Recorded within *Air Britain Digest*, November 1967 issue (Page 298)

Note 100   Hawker Siddeley Aviation aircraft incident file; Item 30240048.

Note 101   Details as related to the author by former Jack Malloch pilots in Harare, Zimbabwe.

Note 102   Hawker Siddeley Aviation internal memo by C. Humphreys, dated 14 December 1967.

Note 103   Hawker Siddeley Aviation internal memo by C. Humphreys, dated 14 December 1967.

Note 104   The aircraft was hangared at São Tomé for a number of years since early-1968. A number of attempts were made to retrieve it (both during and after the civil war), firstly by Hank Warton who tried to claim it in lieu of monies owed to him by the Biafran Government. The marks 5N-AER were officially cancelled on 8 July 1968 as "sold to the USA"and on the same date Warton's company, North American Aircraft Trading Corporation, laid claim to being its owner. On 10 August 1968 registered-ownership passed to the Swiss banker Seligman-Schurch & Co of Basle, until 10 September 1969 when it reverted to North American Aircraft Trading Corp and registered in the USA as N2246. On 10 February 1972 it was cancelled by the FAA as "improperly registered" but it re-appeared on 24 August 1973 when it was allocated the marks N121AC to Ronald L Hauck, of Fort Lauderdale, Florida. Shortly afterwards, on 31 October 1973 its registered owner reverted to North American Aircraft Trading Corp and noted as sold (on the same date) to Miami Aircraft Ventures Inc.
During 1974 Hawker Siddeley Aviation sent an Inspector, Harold Bunday and an Engineer, Harold Peall, to São Tomé to assess the state of the HS-125, still carrying the Nigerian marks 5N-AER. In a telephone conversation with the author on 20 January 1982 Bunday quoted from his report and revealed that the damage was the same as observed by the author in 1968. Bunday was also under the impression that a local São Tomé-based company was (in 1974) buying the aircraft (the cost of which equalled six years of hangarage fees) and that some consideration was given to airlifting the jet back to Chester aboard a Boeing 377 Guppy. However the political situation at São Tomé became increasingly desperate and HSA abandoned the idea of repairing the jet. Bunday and Peall, on realising the danger,contacted their Hatfield base and were advised to leave São Tomé "by any means available"and render the aircraft "unflyable". Bunday and Peall then contacted the British Consulate in Luanda, Angola for assistance and who managed to secure two seats aboard an F-27 Friendship "prison flight"from São Tomé to Luanda. They were the only two passengers aboard the flight who were not shackled to the aircraft's seats!
In further conversations with Harold Peall, it emerged that the purpose of the 1974 visit to São Tomé by the two men was to "covertly sabotage the 125 to ensure that it never flew again". It seemed that Hawker-Siddeley had never been fully paid for the aircraft. Shortly afterwards another Hawker-Siddeley employee, "Jock" McColm, went to Lagos and was flown from Lagos to São Tomé by the Nigerian Air Force in order to airfreight the "unflyable" HS-125 back to Lagos in 1975, as the Federal Nigerian Government had claimed ownership of the jet. The aircraft never did fly again and was issued to the Aircraft Trades School at Zaria.
The history of 5N-AER did not stop with its return to Nigeria. On 5.4.78 c/n 25099 was again registered as N121AC to Orbis Travel Agency Inc as probably a final attempt to lay claim to ownership. By this time the aircraft was firmly grounded in Nigeria where it presumably still remains.

Note 105   As related to the author by Harold Peale 28 May 1997.

THE ARMS AIRLIFT TO BIAFRA

When the fighting started, on 6 July 1967, at two points along Biafra's northern border it brought–for the Biafrans–the stark reality of importing arms or facing surrender. But in importing munitions there were some difficult hurdles to overcome. Many western countries initially viewed Biafra as a breakaway rebel state that only Nigeria itself could resolve; the dispute was seen simply as an internal problem. In any case, any supplier of military aid to Biafra had firstly to break the Federal Nigerian naval blockade of Biafra's ports. Arms and ammunition therefore had to be flown in to either of Biafra's two major airfields, Enugu or Port Harcourt.

Denied legitimate government suppliers, Ojukwu was forced to deal with an intricate web of arms dealers. The financial margins did attract a number of willing sellers,

36 Above: The arms airlift to Biafra involved a wide variety of weapons and ammunition. Some was legally-purchased, much was illegally smuggled via an internecine web of dealers. Other military supplies were captured from the retreating Federal Nigerian Army. In this view Biafran soldiers guard British 76mm and Spanish 7.62mm ammunition (via Hank Warton)

especially in southern Africa and eastern Europe. There were also a number of individuals willing to run the munitions into Biafra by air. Getting these arms to Biafra became one of the most intriguing and clandestine airlifts of the decade.

For the first six months of the Nigerian Civil War there were, apart from the Biafran government's own operation, two major operators contracted to run arms into Biafra. They were the Rhodesian entrepreneur, Jack Malloch, and the German-American adventurer Hank Warton. Both ran arms into Biafra although they operated independently of each other.

Enter Jack Malloch

It was Pierre Laureys, the French arms dealer known to have close connections with Rhodesia and having worked with Jack Malloch in the Congo, who convinced Ojukwu that Malloch be enlisted to help establish a clandestine arms airlift. But Jack Malloch did not need to rely on recommendations from Laureys; he was already well known for various exploits throughout black Africa. He is known, for example, to have had a very good relationship with Houphouet Boigny, President of the Ivory Coast. He was also accepted and trusted by both the Portuguese and South African governments, both of whom were offering covert military support for Biafra. Even in his native Rhodesia, Jack Malloch could count himself as a close and long-time friend of Governer Ian Smith; both had flown Spitfires with the RAF's 237 Squadron during World War II.[106]

Jack Malloch had formed Rhodesian Air Services Ltd in 1960 to operate Inclusive Tour services and charter flights within East Africa. But other work undertaken offered a much better financial return such as performing air-drops of arms and ammunition to the Imam's army during the Yemen crisis from August 1963. The civil war in the Congo, which lingered on for much of that decade, also provided a number of opportunities for clandestine arms flights. Malloch forged a close friendship with Moise Tshombé (leader of the breakaway Katanga regime) and undertook a reliable gun-running operation in support of Tshombé's attempt to establish an independent state. But Tshombe was eventually overthrown on 5 November 1965 and left the Congo for a life in exile. General Mobutu seized power on 25 November and retained some of the mercenary forces for security purposes. Then, in 1966, a pro-Tshombe group based in Belgium plotted Mobutu's downfall and the reinstatment of Tshombe. It failed but a second attempt, with stronger support, began in June 1967. But that too was thrown into confusion when Tshombe's Hawker Siddeley 125 was hijacked on a flight out of Spain on 30 June 1967. The jet was forced to fly to Algeria where Tshombe was thrown into jail.

When Ian Smith declared Unilateral Declaration of Independence for Rhodesia in 1965 Jack Malloch's Air Trans Africa became the nominated company to 'officially' (and successfully) break the UN sanctions imposed against the breakaway Rhodesian regime. Malloch's aircraft operated a number of fuel flights between Zambia and Rhodesia. It almost went without saying that Malloch should add gun-running to Biafra to an already-established set-up in and out of Salisbury as well as maintaining vital arms-supply flights to those remaining parts of the Congo still under mercenary control.

During 1967, Air Trans Africa operated one Rhodesian-registered DC-4, VP-YTY, and a single L-1049G Super Constellation, VP-WAW; it was with these two aircraft that Malloch began his Biafran operation. The very first arms flight into Biafra, after the fighting had started, was quite a marathon affair.[107]

The saga began after Pierre Laureys had contracted Malloch to fly approximately 50 tonnes of guns and ammunition into Biafra in what was seen to involve an initial series of six flights. At the time Malloch's DC-4, VP-YTY, had just suffered an engine failure, on 15 June 1967, mid-way through a sanctions-breaking fuel flight to Livingstone. Apart from causing a delay by needing to replace an engine, the position worsened because of Malloch's difficulty in being able to pay for the replacement. In the end Malloch was forced to take out a loan against his house bond to settle the account for the engine–then Shell refused to supply fuel 'on carnet'. To overcome that problem Malloch's co-pilot, Paul Rex, personally paid over cash for sufficient fuel to enable the DC-4 to fly from Salisbury to Luanda, and on to São Tomé. (At São Tomé, Pierre Laureys advanced sufficient cash funds to meet other costs en route.)

Under the command of Jack Malloch and Clive Halse the DC-4 VP-YTY eventually left Salisbury at 11:00 on 9 July 1967 for the first leg to Luanda and where it landed at 17:15 hrs. Apart from Malloch and Halse, the crew consisted of two Flight Engineers, Henry Kinnear and Thomas 'Bull' Brown and spare pilot, Paul Rex. From Luanda VP-YTY took-off at 19:55 and staged overnight to Bissau where the aircraft was again refuelled before leaving immediately for Lisbon and where it finally landed at 18:05 on 10 July.

With a full cargo of arms and ammunition the DC-4 left Lisbon late on 11 July with Malloch and Halse at the controls with Flight Engineers Kinnear and Brown also sharing the flightdeck. VP-YTY routed to Bissau and on to São Tomé where it night-stopped before flying north to Enugu on 13 July. Biafra's first delivery of clandestine arms had arrived without too many hitches.

There was a sequel to Biafra's first arms delivery. Immediately behind the Rhodesian DC-4 into Enugu was a Swiss-registered Mystère carrying the arms-dealer Pierre Laureys. In spite of a general call out to the Biafran anti-aircraft units not to fire at any aircraft seen landing at Enugu, the Mystère came under intense, albeit inaccurate, flak fire. After landing safely, the pilot of the chartered Mystère voiced his displeasure at having been made to fly into a war zone. As soon as the passengers and sundry items of baggage (including a spare nosewheel for Biafra's B-26R) had been unloaded the Mystère hurriedly departed. Minutes later Laureys discovered that he had left some important papers etc aboard the Mystère and from the airport tower called the pilot to return. The Mystère pilot was, understandably, reluctant to do so and only agreed to return after Laureys had threatened to alert a squadron of Biafran Air Force jet fighters. There were, of course, no Biafran fighters but the Mystère did return to Enugu. It cost the chartered jet dearly. By making the unscheduled extra flight meant that the crew had to dip into the aircraft's reserve fuel tanks and by all accounts only just managed to reach the island of São Tomé safely.

The Rhodesian DC-4 had stayed at Enugu airport overnight before departing to São Tomé and then back to Lisbon, via Bissau. The crew waited at Lisbon for a week to allow off-duty Portuguese Air Force personnel carry out some essential maintenance on the aircraft. Then, on 25 July 1967, and with another full cargo of arms, Clive Halse took VP-YTY out of Lisbon at 01:40 for the long haul to São Tomé. Including a 1-hour refuelling stop at Bissau the flight took almost 20½ hours. VP-YTY landed at the island at 23:00. After a short rest, the same crew took-off at 06:25 the next morning for the short hop to Enugu. The aircraft remained on the ground at Enugu for the next day-and-a-half before leaving to return to São Tomé at 14:55 on 27 July. This was the early period of the war–the 'phoney' period–when a white-topped gun-running aircraft could sit out in the open at Enugu airport for 30 hours and then fly out during the mid-afternoon.

VP-YTY left São Tomé later on 27 July and, with a brief refuelling stop at Luanda, flew back to Salisbury. The DC-4's next flight into Biafra began early on 8 August when it was flown, by Malloch, Rex and Kinnear, from Salisbury to Luanda and on to São Tomé and in to Enugu.

The crew of VP-YTY stayed at Enugu's Presidential Hotel. Coincidentally, Hank Warton was also staying at the same hotel that night although Biafran military personnel (acting as security officials) refused to allow any of the DC-4 crew, even including Malloch, to liaise with Warton.

Warton had arrived in Biafra aboard one of Biafra's own aircraft and his presence in Enugu was in connection with setting up a second arms airlift from Lisbon. Ironically he needed to return to Lisbon and the only flight out was the Air Trans Africa DC-4. The next day, 9 August, VP-YTY departed Enugu for the long haul north to Bissau and Lisbon. At the controls were Jack Malloch, Bunny Warren and Henry Kinnear as Flight Engineer. Hank Warton was also aboard but in a passenger seat.

Not only did Malloch have commitments in Biafra he still had some priority commitment in the Congo, despite the fact that Tshombé had been kidnapped and thrown into an Algerian jail. (The Congo crisis was about to reach a dramatic conclusion since a group of mercenaries led by the Frenchman, Jean 'Black Jack' Schramme, had taken Bukavu but had become surrounded by Congolese forces. They were also short of medical aid and ammunition. Some of Schramme's men had seized a DC-3 at Kamambi from where they had flown across to Luanda to uplift some arms. The DC-3, flown by a Belgian mercenary pilot, Leon Libert, flew to Bukavu but promptly overran a hastily-prepared landing strip and was written-off. It was for this reason that Malloch was then asked to make an air-drop of ammunition to Schramme, an operation which bore all the hallmarks of collusion by the South African and Portuguese governments. On 1 September 1967, Malloch flew VP-YTY from Salisbury south to Swartkops AFB, South Africa to uplift a sizeable cargo of ammunition. Accompanied on the flight-deck by Paul Rex and Henry Kinnear, together with a Portuguese navigator Castelo Branco, the DC-4 was then positioned to Henrique de Carvalho, Angola from where the air-drop would be made. (It was from here that the former Portuguese Air Force pilot, Gil Pinto de Sousa, hitched a ride aboard the DC-4 to São Tomé island enabling him to get into Biafra.)

From Henrique de Carvalho the cargo of ammunition uplifted from Swartkops by VP-YTY was flown over the mountainous Bukavu area early on 2 September 1967. But as the DC-4 approached the dropping-zone it came under attack from two Congolese Air Force T-28 fighters. Malloch immediately reduced altitude and began to fly the DC-4 at a dramatically very low-level through the valleys. The T-28s broke off their chase and Malloch made his way back to Henrique de Carvalho where he landed safely. According to his crew, not for the first time VP-YTY returned with green propellers and the oil coolers full of leaves.

37: While Jack Malloch languished in a Togo jail his two surviving aircraft were overhauled by Aviolanda at Woensdrecht, Holland. By July 1968 the DC-4 had been re-painted into a scheme not dissimilar to Malloch's former Südflug DC-7C VP-WBO. An all-blue fin, two-tone blue fuselage cheat-line and a complete lack of any titling provided the new scheme. VP-YTY was eventually ferried from Woensdrecht to Libreville, via Las Palmas and Abidjan on 16-18 September 1968 (via Peter J. Marson)

The arms were offloaded and Malloch then flew the DC-4 up to Luanda and on to São Tomé before positioning to Lisbon to uplift a cargo of arms bound for Biafra–the seventh arms flight into Enugu. Then, late on 9 September, Jack Malloch, Paul Rex and and Henry Kinnear flew VP-YTY across to Bukavu and on to Henrique de Carvalho to attempt another air-drop of arms to 'Black Jack' Schramme. Again the drop was frustrated, this time by heavy thunderstorms over the target forcing the crew to return, once again, to Henrique de Carvalho. Eventually the air-drop was carried out just after midday on 10 September and after several runs across the target the crew had manhandled 7½ tonnes of mortars and ammunition out of the rear door. The drop took just 30 minutes but the *Armie Nationale de Congolais* (ANC) had been alerted and began shooting at the DC-4. The aircraft was hit by small-arms fire in the under-fuselage and once again Malloch was forced to take evasive action. Back at Henrique de Carvalho the navigator, Castelo Branco, found a 7.62mm bullet lodged in the underfloor area. He claimed it and thereafter wore it on a chain around his neck.

In the meantime, the arms drop had enabled Schramme's men to fight their way out of trouble. All were later evacuated by the International Red Cross and repatriated safely out of Africa. That effectively signalled the end of the Congo crisis and certainly ended Jack Malloch's affair in the Congo.

Malloch flew the DC-4 back to Salisbury on 11 September. Not only did the aircraft need repairing but Jack Malloch had contracted malaria and also needed urgent treatment. For a short period the Biafran arms runs were carried out by the L-1049G Super Constellation, VP-WAW. A summary of all flights made by the DC-4 VP-YTY for the period which included the initial series of Biafran arms flights is as follows:

Flight Movements by DC-4 VP-YTY July-Sept 1967
(Arms Flights to Biafra highlighted in parenthesis)

Date	Routeing	Hours
9.7.67	Salisbury-Luanda	6.15
9/10.7.67	Luanda-Bissau-Lisbon	21.00
11.7.67	Lisbon-Bissau	10.15
12.7.67	Bissau-São Tomé	9.40
13.7.67	São Tomé-Enugu (1)	2.35
14.7.67	Enugu-São Tomé	2.30
16.7.67	São Tomé-Bissau	8.50
17.7.67	Bissau-Lisbon	10.25
25.7.67	Lisbon-Bissau-São Tomé	20.20
26.7.67	São Tomé-Enugu (2)	2.25
27.7.67	Enugu-São Tomé-Luanda	6.10
28.7.67	Luanda-Salisbury	7.05
4.8.67	Salisbury-Salisbury	2.55
8.8.67	Salisbury-Luanda-São Tomé-Enugu (3)	12.00
9.8.67	Enugu-São Tomé-Bissau	11.30
10.8.67	Bissau-Lisbon	9.15
12.8.67	Lisbon-Bissau-Enugu (4)	20.25
15.8.67	Enugu-São Tomé-Enugu (5)	5.15
16.8.67	Enugu-São Tomé-Bissau	12.00
17.8.67	Bissau-Lisbon	9.20
23.8.67	Lisbon-Bissau-São Tomé	19.50
24.8.67	São Tomé-Enugu (6)	2.20
26.8.67	Enugu-São Tomé-Luanda	6.35
27.8.67	Luanda-Salisbury	6.35
31.8.67	Salisbury-Swartkops	3.00
1.9.67	Swartkops-Henrique de Carvalho	5.40
2.9.67	Henrique de Carvalho-Bukavu-Henrique de Carvalho	9.25
	Henrique de Carvalho-Luanda	2.25
3.9.67	Luanda-São Tomé-Bissau	12.05
4.9.67	Bissau-Lisbon	10.00
6.9.67	Lisbon-Bissau	9.40
7.9.67	Bissau-São Tomé-Enugu (7)	12.15
8.9.67	Enugu-São Tomé-Luanda	6.15
9.9.67	Luanda-Henrique de Carvalho-Bukavu-Henrique de Carvalho	11.05
10.9.67	Henrique de Carvalho-Bukavu- Henrique de Carvalho	8.30
11.9.67	Henrique de Carvalho-Salisbury	3.30

38: At first glance there was little to distinguish Jack Malloch's DC-7CF and those aircraft operating from São Tomé by Hank Warton on behalf of the German Churches. In this view VP-WBO is parked at Basle during January 1968 having just arrived with a cargo of Nigerian banknotes taken out of Biafra's bank vaults. Very shortly after this picture was taken the aircraft staged to Lisbon and on to Lomé where it was impounded with several million pounds worth of banknotes still aboard (Guido E. Buehlmann)

Despite the end of the Congo crisis the demand for Malloch's services continued to increase. His primary objective was to provide Biafra with a steady supply of arms flights. Two aircraft, however, were proving to be insufficient and so, in November 1967, Malloch purchased a former Südflug DC-7C, D-ABAN. It was immediately re-registered in Rhodesia as VP-WBO and joined the small fleet of aircraft now making regular arms flights into Port Harcourt.

One major source of arms was a stockpile at Luanda. Some fifty tonnes of arms had been landed during the course of the year. Under a secret tripartite alliance (referred to as the Council of Three) between Portugal, Rhodesia and South Africa the arms were reloaded aboard Biafra-bound aircraft.[108]

Re-enter Hank Warton

Hank Warton was, of course, already known to the Biafrans. His first arms flight had ended in the disastrous crash in the Cameroons (during November 1966) long before the Eastern region had broken away. But Warton had spent the intervening months extricating himself from a succession of difficult situations.[109]

Immediately after the court in Garoua had fined Warton and his crew, Orvis Nelson began to believe that his boss still had a considerable amount of money available. They also began to lose patience with each other. So much so that Nelson had gone to the Court of Labour in Garoua and elected to sue Warton for 'several thousand dollars in lost earnings as a result of being incarcerated in a Cameroon jail.' The case had little chance of succeeding but it had the effect of delaying Warton's departure from the country. Not only that but by the time the case was ready to be heard the Garoua court had closed for its late-Spring recess. In the meantime the Garoua Chief of Police did allow Warton to travel to the town's airport each day to have lunch with the local Air Cameroun pilots, some of whom were Columbian exiles and whom Warton had first met in the Congo some years earlier. Eventually they hatched a plan to get Warton out of the country.

Air Cameroun operated a daily service through Garoua which made several stops at various bush strips en route to Douala. Warton's girlfriend, Ziggy Harder, who had flown down from Europe to help resolve the situation, agreed to go on to Douala and spend several days making arrangements for Warton to stay with a friendly and sympathetic French family.

On a signal from Ziggy, Hank Warton was driven by jeep through the Cameroonian bush to the next airstrip on the Air Cameroun service. It was known that, unlike Garoua, there were no barriers at the airstrip and therefore no difficulty on getting aboard. But by sheer coincidence when the flight landed the Chief of Garoua Police stepped down and walked to the small makeshift terminal.

On seeing Warton in the terminal, the American had to 'explain' that he had just got a job with Air Cameroun and that it was his first day in the job. The Police Chief simply wished him success and allowed Warton to step aboard the aircraft which took-off for Douala. At Douala airport Hank Warton walked, with the crew, through the Operations Department office and out into the street to meet a waiting Ziggy.

Warton remained in hiding for almost two weeks until his French friends arranged for him to receive a visitor's pass onto a passing cruise ship. At the same time they had raised just sufficient money for a one-way ticket (from Douala to Marseilles) for Ziggy. Warton walked aboard as a visitor and then hid in Ziggy's berth. After the ship had sailed from Douala and around the African coast Warton made his presence known to the captain who agreed to firstly telex the US Consulate at Dakar for a passport and then telex Warton's Swiss Bank to arrange for money to be wired to the ship. But it was not quite straightforward. Knowing that Hank Warton was on the run from the Cameroons the US Consulate would only issue travel documents for a one-way trip to Washington. Warton therefore stayed on board until the ship reached Palma where he and Ziggy calmly walked ashore, then crossed to Tenerife for a brief holiday. The holiday allowed just sufficient time for a friend in Germany to arrange a passport for him. Dual nationality had benefits. Warton and Ziggy then flew back to Lisbon. Hank Warton was back in business.

Henry 'Hank' Warton was born Heinrich Warski on 22 December 1916 in the German town of Gratz (later renamed Godzisk when the region became part of Poland). Warton had emigrated to the USA at the age of twenty-one, where he later became an American citizen and volunteered for US Army service in 1941. During the Second World War he is reported to have seen action at Guadalcanal and also to have worked with US military intelligence–he spoke fluent Spanish as well as his native German. In 1947, and out of the US Armed Forces, Warton gained an FAA Commercial flying-licence and immediately embarked upon quite an illustrious flying career, reportedly starting with supply-flying into the newly-established state of Israel. He later flew freight services with Air India and, in 1961, flew with the United Nations in the Congo.[110]

Much of Warton's activities during the 'sixties involved a series of non-scheduled airlines, many of which just bordered on the right side of aviation law. He became 'credited' with just about any semi-legal operation in Europe, including the unauthorised night departure of a Trans Atlantic Airlines DC-4 from Basle while it was still impounded for non-payment of airport fees. (The DC-4 later landed at Brussels without lights, unannounced, and with a false registration, N2894C).

Towards the end of 1963 Henry 'Hank' Warton, by then

39: Hank Warton (centre) speaks with two of his mechanics at Lisbon during the summer of 1968. Servicing of Warton's L-1049 Super Constellations was fairly basic and often snags delayed flights to Biafra, sometimes causing dire shortages of ammunition at crucial periods. American John Fluney (far left) worked for Warton from the earliest days of the Biafra run and later worked for the Biafran Government's 'Phoenix' operation at Faro (Ghislaine Morel)

40: The French arms dealer, Pierre Laureys, played a significant role in aiding the Biafran Government during the early days of Secession. He was certainly involved during the later stages when French Government involvement increased significantly in mid-1968. Laureys (right) is seen here at an Abidjan restaurant (on 6 June 1968) during a stopover on a flight from France to Libreville aboard his Grumman G.73 Mallard G-ASCS. In the centre is a Greek gentlemen thought to have been involved in financing one of the Frenchman's deals. For personal reasons the British pilot's identity is hidden (Confidential Source)

41: Jack Malloch was rarely photographed during the Biafran war period. After the Biafran war and a lengthy period managing a complex sanctions-busting operation in and out of Rhodesia, he effectively retired in the late-1970s. On 26 March 1982 he was killed while flying his personal Spitfire F22 (PK 350) north of Harare. This view was taken shortly before his tragic death and shows 'Uncle Jack' i typical hands on hips stance. To the left is Chris Dixon, one of his many loyal Rhodesian pilots (John Fairey) believed to be operating under the aegis of Atlanta Airways, secured a short-term contract with Lufthansa for freight services within Europe for which he used two C-46 Commandos (N2074A and N355W) and a DC-4 (N6404). The Lufthansa work ended in February 1964 and little was heard of Warton until 17 February 1965 when a PASCO Aviation DC-4 (N11712) landed at Amsterdam while en route to Prague to uplift a cargo of arms that were ultimately destined for the Sudan. Warton was allegedly flying that aircraft.[111] However that operation was frustrated when the aircraft's owner, Heinrich J. Heuer was arrested and extradited to Germany to face various charges. Warton later acquired Heuer's other aircraft, the infamous Canadair DC-4M2 that, at the time, was standing idle at Schiphol airport, Amsterdam since the authorities there had impounded it. It was aboard the DC-4M2 that Warton subsequently escaped serious injury in the forced landing in the Cameroons some months prior to Biafran independence (See Introduction).

After the court case in Garoua, which followed the crash of 'I-ACOA', Warton returned to Europe to re-organise his activities. In doing so he used his Florida-based company, North American Aircraft Trading Corporation, registered at 221, Security Trust Building, Miami. This proved useful in acquiring new aircraft under American registry, of which there was no shortage during mid-1967.

International Aerodyne Inc, a long-established dealer also based in Miami, purchased the entire Iberia fleet of six redundant L-1049G Super Constellations, all of which had been converted to freight configuration and fitted with large rear cargo doors. All six aircraft had been issued with a ferry permit by the US Civil Aviation Bureau (CAB) to allow each to make a one-way flight from Madrid to Miami in order for them to be issued with an American Certificate of Airworthiness. For ferrying purposes, the six had been consecutively registered as N8021 through N8026. All were indeed flown across the Atlantic to Florida with the exception of one, N8025 (c/n 4645), the former Iberia EC-AQN. This exception had been re-sold to Warton who, with his long-time associate, Larry Raab, promptly flouted the American Civil Aviation Bureau ruling by flying the aircraft from Madrid to Lisbon, on 29 June 1967.[112]

In the meantime Hank Warton, now based at the Hotel Tivoli in Lisbon, began to plan a series of arms flights from Lisbon to Biafra, using the military side of Lisbon's international airport. Warton's single L-1049G Super Constellation, N8025, spent a short period at Lisbon undergoing preparations. Part of this involved the removal of the Iberia insignia and the traditional red fuselage cheat-line. The cheat-line was replaced by a solid blue line running the entire length of the fuselage. Finally, the American registration was removed and in its place Warton painted the Mauritanian marks '5T-TAC'. This change took place at Lisbon on 12 August 1967.[113]

It is just a possibility that Warton did try to place his aircraft onto the Mauritanian civil register, maybe even with unofficial assistance from the French. Either that or Warton simply obtained a contemporary copy of the Bureau Veritas and took a personal decision to allocate the vacant identities to his own aircraft. Either way, none of Warton's aircraft were legally registered. The official, and legal, allocations within the '5T-TAx' series at that time were as follows:[114]

Official Civil Aircraft Register (Extract) of Mauritania (5T-TAx series) 1967

Reg	Type	C/n	Remarks
5T-TAA	Jodel D.117A	1159/09	Registered March 1963; current 1967
5T-TAB	CP.301C-2 Emeraude	570	Registered 1963; current 1967
5T-TAC	Not officially allocated until July 1968 when issued to a PA-24 Comanche 260		
5T-TAD	CP.301C-2 Emeraude	586	Registered July 1964; current 1967
5T-TAE	MS.881 Rallye	401	Registered 1964; cancelled Dec 1967
5T-TAF	Cessna 206	0253	Registered Dec 1964; current 1967
5T-TAG	CP.1315-C3 Emeraude	901	Registered Feb 1965; canx April 1967
5T-TAH	Aero Commander 500B	1229-104	Registered July 1964; canx Dec 1967
5T-TAI	MS.892A Commodore	10472	Registered May 1965; current 1967
5T-TAJ	PA-28 Cherokee 140	28-22046	Registered Dec 1966; current 1967

Two months later, during October 1967, Warton purchased a second L-1049G Super Constellation, again through the Miami dealer, International Aerodyne Inc. This second aircraft had formerly operated, as CS-TLC, with Portugal's national airline, Transportes Aereos Portugueses (T.A.P.). In fact it had flown T.A.P.'s last piston-engined flight when it flew from Rio de Janeiro to Lisbon on 13 September 1967. Official records show that Warton purchased CS-TLC on 8 November, after which the Portuguese marks were cancelled on 23 November. But by that time Warton had already applied it with another Mauritanian registration, '5T-TAF'; these marks, like those applied to his first aircraft, were again spurious. However, on this occasion the marks *had* already been legally issued to a Cessna 206. That was a mistake that would later lead to his arrest in Malta.

Warton is known to have spent 48 hours under house arrest in Liberia at some time around this period and it is likely that he had visited the country in an attempt to register three aircraft with the Liberian authorities, one of which was undoubtedly the ex-Iberia L-1049G. Reports suggest that having been arrested (the charge being unrecorded) Warton succeeded in convincing a US official to exert pressure upon the Liberians not to jail him but to allow him to return to his hotel but under house-arrest, whereupon, and by his own account, he escaped through Robertsfield airport under the disguise of an airline pilot.[115]

Warton's two Super Constellations, '5T-TAC' and '5T-TAF', began operating an irregular arms shuttle from Lisbon with an average frequency of two/three times per week. Operations were effectively based at Lisbon-

Portela (the military side of the main Lisbon airport), and flights were almost always timed to depart early in the morning, at approximately 05:00 hours. Routeing around the west African coastline flights normally staged to Bissau, in Portuguese Guinea (a sector of 2,200 miles) after a flight time of some nine hours. After refuelling and a short crew-rest, the aircraft was then flown the eight-hour leg from Bissau to Port Harcourt. The final part of the flight involved a wide arc to the south in order to keep at least 150 miles south of the Nigerian coastline and to avoid possible interception by the Nigerian Air Force.[116]

Total radio silence was maintained during the second sector from Bissau, except for one final pre-arranged call to Port Harcourt in order to alert the Biafrans of an imminent arrival. Apart from maintaining radio silence, the crew also blacked-out the aircraft about an hour before landing, the period of greatest risk.

Warton reportedly charged the Biafran Government $22,000 for each round Lisbon to Port Harcourt flight, the crew receiving approximately $1,000 each for the flight, payable almost always in cash, on their return to Lisbon. It was a high payment for what was viewed as a high-risk business, but if there was any risk to the crew it was more likely to be associated with engine failures, hydraulic trouble and burst tyres. These were the greatest hazards which resulted from the minimum of maintenance.

Biafra: The arms support chain

Considerably less of a risk but nevertheless equally clandestine was the supply of weaponry from a variety of sources to Lisbon. Typical of these nocturnal movements of clandestine arms for Biafra was a series of flights operated by one company, Belgian International Air Services. The flights involved shipments of Czech and Spanish weapons into Lisbon during the autumn of 1967.

The flights began during the night of 25/26 October 1967. B.I.A.S. DC-6A OO-ABE flew from Brussels to Prague to collect a 10-tonne load of Czech arms. Despite landing at Prague in total darkness, at 04:25 hours, the aircraft was parked well away from the main terminal area. The crew was instructed to wait inside the aircraft. Then, a convoy of lorries drove up to the aircraft at which point the crew noticed that all were typical Czech Army vehicles but with their registration plates covered over with a khaki cloth. As soon as loading had been completed, the DC-6A departed Prague at 07:20 and flew direct to Lisbon where it landed at 13:40 hours and taxied to the military side of the airport where the cargo was unloaded.

OO-ABE remained at Lisbon for the rest of that day and much of the night. At 06:30 hrs on 28 October it took-off for the relatively short flight to Bilbao, in northern Spain, where it took on board a quantity of Spanish arms and ammunition. By 12:55 hours the DC-6A had returned to Lisbon where again the cargo was unloaded in the same manner as two days earlier. Curiously the B.I.A.S. DC-6A then remained at Lisbon for a week until, and once again under cover of darkness, it took-off at 02:05 hours on 3 November 1967. On this occasion it headed back to Prague, where it landed at 07:25 hours. Unlike the previous visit just over a week beforehand the crew, this time, were not allowed to stay with their aircraft during the loading process.

Immediately after shutting down their aircraft the crew of three were taken, under a fairly heavily armed guard, to a small side room in the main Terminal building where, and still under the eyes of their Czech guards, they were offered a meal and drink. When the aircraft was fully loaded the crew were driven out to it - in three separate cars. Two of the cars then remained with the aircraft during the start-up procedure and in fact followed the aircraft, one car on each side, all the way to the runway threshold. At 13:55 hours OO-ABE, fully loaded with its second Czech arms shipment, took-off for its return flight to Lisbon where the cargo was offloaded for transfer to Hank Warton's L-1049G Super Constellations.[117]

The 'money' flights

It was not just for the running of guns and ammunition that Hank Warton's or Jack Malloch's aircraft were used for. Occasionally there were other priorities, none more so than the so-called 'money' flights of January 1968. The need arose after the Federal Government announced, without warning, what was obviously a well-planned and highly-secretive decision to change the nation's currency notes. A mere nineteen days notice was given for the change, after which the 'old' notes would be deemed worthless. There is no doubt that the Biafran government, whose reserves still included a vast sum in Nigerian currency, had been taken by complete surprise. Within days of the announcement the Biafrans began offloading literally planeloads of Nigerian currency notes onto the European money-markets, often at rock-bottom prices. It has been reckoned that the Biafrans lost an estimated £30million in the trading of heavily discounted Nigerian banknotes on the world's currency centres, not just in trading at unbelievable discounts, but also from those couriers who, it was alleged, simply disappeared with the occasional suitcase full of cash.[118]

At least two of Hank Warton's L-1049G Super Constellations were used for flying huge consignments of cash from Port Harcourt to Switzerland: '5T-TAC' arrived at Basle early on 6 January and '5T-TAF' which made two visits to Basle for the same purpose, on 10 and 13 January 1968. It is just possible that the visit of Jack Malloch's DC-7CF VP-WBO to Basle, on 11 January, was also involved in the transfer of tonnes of Nigerian banknotes to Europe. Whether or not the DC-7CF *was* involved in flying cash to

Switzerland remains unconfirmed; it certainly was involved in cash transfers a week later.

The attempt to transfer some of Biafra's Nigerian banknotes (probably as part of a money-laundering operation) aboard the Rhodesian-registered DC-7CF proved disastrously unsuccessful. The aircraft was impounded after landing at Lomé, Togo, with Nigerian banknotes to the face value of £7million aboard. In all, there were eight people aboard the DC-7CF, including the captain, Jack Malloch himself. Malloch's co-pilot was a Briton, John Aldridge while the remaining crew consisted of a 'Brazilian' navigator, Vaso Luis de Abren, and a South African Flight Engineer, Alexander Forsyth. Others on board the flight were William Terence Keating, a British engineer from Yorkshire and two other Britons, John Deegan and Major Alastair Wicks, the latter being on board in a purely supernumerary role.[119] The only other person on board was passenger William Kurt Samuel Wallersteiner, a German-born financier, and widely known as Dr. Kurt Wallersteiner. Wallersteiner had allegedly bought the banknotes in Switzerland for a tenth of their face value and was attempting to take advantage of the change in Nigerian currency.[120]

All of those involved in the Lomé incident were immediately arrested and held in custody. The aircraft was impounded, together with its nine tonne cargo of banknotes, the latter being handed over to the Nigerian government. (Two days later the old-style Nigerian banknotes were declared worthless.) Malloch was arrested for having twenty automatic pistols on board the aircraft; two of the crew had 9mm pistols and ammunition.[121] Among other charges facing Malloch was one of flying an aircraft with an illegal registration–the aircraft letters had been altered to read 'ZP-WBO' prior to its flight to Togo.

Shortly after his release from Togo Malloch made a statement describing the loss of the aircraft and the circumstances surrounding his arrest. It could, of course, be argued that any statement of this kind, and offered some months following the main event, might present some of the facts in a slightly different colour (and this statement does tend to suggest a degree of naivity and innocence for such an experienced gun-runner) but nevertheless the general tone does tend to describe the complex nature of clandestine flights involved in Biafra-style operations:

"Late in the afternoon of 18 January 1968, Mr Woodnutt, Mr *(Alastair)* Wicks and I *(Jack Malloch)*, while visiting the Tivoli Hotel, Lisbon saw Dr Kurt Wallersteiner who was staying there and who I already knew from previous occasions as being an influential German businessman with some Swiss banking connections. The gist of our conversation was that he had a charter flight on behalf of his banking concern in Switzerland that he wanted us to perform for him between Lisbon and a point in Africa, which was the only destination revealed at that stage. Mr Woodnutt and I then discussed the charter proposition with him more thoroughly, at which time he advised us that the load would be Nigerian currency that he wanted flown to Togoland for his bank and that he had permission of the Togolese Government and had made arrangements with a banking representative, which we assumed to be a banker in Togo, as his contact there for offloading...

...(During the late afternoon of 19 June) we prepared to exit Lisbon airport. Unfortunately on the take-off run, we had a fire warning in Number 3 engine and abandoned take-off. The fault was with the P.R.T. on this engine and therefore a replacement had to be fitted. *(The Power Recoery Turbines proed extremely troublesome on this DC-7CF, as well as on other DC-7C/Fs operated by Malloch.)* I then rang Mr Woodnutt from the airport to advise him of this fault, which would take four to five hours to remedy, but that there was no need for him to come out and that I would wait at the airport until the job had been done. However the repair work took longer than anticipated and during this time I had further discussion with Dr Wallersteiner, with Mr Wicks present, and this time he showed me a copy of the contract... and also the approval of the Togolese Government. This document put my mind completely to rest as far as operating a Rhodesian-registered aircraft into Togoland was concerned. At the same time a request was made by the Togolese authorities–in order to avoid them any embarrassment with the Press etc –could we make the registration marks on the side of the fuselage illegible. This caused me a little concern but I did understand the embarrassment that it would cause this African country if it were publicised in the local Press that a Rhodesian plane had landed in Lomé. (The fuselage registration marks VP-WBO were altered to read 'ZP-WBO', although letters beneath the wings were not altered.)...

...We eventually took off at about 04:00 on the morning of 20 January, intending to fly direct to Lomé but as the estimated flight time could be affected by winds the flight-plan was shown as Lisbon to Bissau; if flight conditions were satisfactory we intended to call overhead Bissau and file a further flight-plan to Lomé. However, even before reaching Bissau one of our crew, First Officer Rex, got severe stomach pains and in spite of weather conditions allowing a direct flight to Lomé, we decided to land at Bissau to seek medical attention.

"We continued our flight to Lomé on a Visual Flight Rules (VFR) Flight Plan as a security move. It was by then broad daylight, weather conditions were good... and at no time crossed any African country's borders. As this was a Rhodesian aircraft, avoidance of any publicity of its movements has, in any event, always been one of our company's objectives, provided that all flight regulations and safety factors are met.

"70 miles south of Lomé, I called Lomé tower and asked if they had any knowledge of our anticipated arrival. The tower replied that he had not been notified... but that I could continue and land in Lomé and should there be any reason why we could not offload our cargo, we would have to take-off again for either Libreville or Abidjan, due to a customs arrangement between ex-French territories.

"We were marshalled in and Dr Wallersteiner then left the aircraft to make the necessary declarations and arrangements for the offloading. After about 20 minutes it appeared to me that something was not in order. Wallersteiner had no explanation in detail but told me we should arrange to take-off again immediately with the load. The Air Traffic Controller refused to accept a new Flight Plan.

"I was then instructed to get the crew off the aircraft and we were ushered through the customs barrier at gunpoint and taken to the local prison. The next morning Dr Wallersteiner and I were collected by the Chief de Sûreté and the Minister of the Interior and taken to the airport where the money was offloaded, weighed and registered. A search of the aircraft hold found two pistols, belonging to the Flight Engineers. We were then taken back to the jail but were not interviewed for several weeks.

"On 3 February we were interrogated and formally charged with the illegal importation of merchandise. As Captain I was charged with illegally importing firearms"

In spite of presenting facts that might have cleared Malloch and his crew the charges were retained and eventually all appeared in a Lomé court on Wednesday, 5 June 1968. Only the charges against Malloch were proven; those related to changing the aircraft's registration marks, of carrying arms and not having a cargo manifest. All of the others on board were acquitted. The court sentenced Malloch to three month's imprisonment but in view of the time already spent behind bars he, and his crew, were immediately released and allowed to board a scheduled Air Afrique flight back to Europe. The DC-7CF was technically returned to Malloch but he was advised to leave the country quickly and as the aircraft had not been tended to for nearly six months it was abandoned at Lomé. Over a period of time it gradually rotted away.[122]

The six months spent inside a Togo jail cost Jack Malloch dearly. His L-1049G VP-WAW had made just two round Lisbon-Port Harcourt arms flights (on 7/8 January and 11/12 January) before being ferried (on 17 January 1968) to Woensdrecht, Netherlands for an overhaul by the Dutch company, Aviolanda. The DC-4, VP-YTY, was also flown to Woensdrecht for the same reason. With both aircraft in Holland and Jack languishing in jail it was a difficult period for the company. With no money coming in outstanding bills could not be paid, including the charges for overhauling the two aircraft in Holland. Both aircraft were impounded by Aviolanda. Aircrew were stood down or released; some, including Flight Engineers 'Bull' Brown and Jim Townsend, moved across to Hank Warton's operation which now had a virtual monopoly on arms supply flights to Biafra. For 'Bull' Brown the move had a tragic outcome.[123]

Hank Warton; new aircraft

With Jack Malloch in a Togo jail, Hank Warton consolidated his position on the airlift although events were not always to be in his favour. Warton's brush with the Federal Aviation Agency over the earlier misuse of the ferry registration N8025 (in connection with the former Iberia aircraft) proved to be an obstacle on each occasion that he tried to purchase additional aircraft from the USA. Instead he turned to friends in Germany and successfully purchased three L-1049G Super Constellations from the German carrier, Lufthansa. The first of the trio, D-ALOF, was delivered from Hamburg to Lisbon on 13 December 1967 where the illegal marks '5T-TAG' were applied.[124]

Warton entered 1968 with three L-1049Gs but at the beginning of February he suffered his first loss when '5T-TAC' crashed on landing at Port Harcourt. Ironically the aircraft, which was being flown by an American pilot, George 'Robbie' Robertson, was carrying a full load of medical supplies donated to the Biafrans by the Vatican. According to witnesses on the airfield the aircraft landed a little too short and swerved violently. It continued its run for several hundred yards but a wing brushed the ground and was torn off. Then it made another sudden swerve and turned over, fire breaking out as it did so. '5T-TAC' was quickly and completely burnt out. Amazingly the crew, as well as passengers Father Fintan Kilbride, four Sisters, two young African Novices from France and five Biafran officers, all escaped with only very minor injuries.[125]

About a week after the Port Harcourt crash a second incident involved another of Warton's aircraft at Malta. Warton's former Portuguese-registered L-1049G, '5T-TAF', was impounded by the Luqa Airport authorities on 16 February 1968 when they realised that the registration marks were false. (The marks were legally issued to a Cessna 206.) '5T-TAF' had flown into Malta from Lisbon as part of a ruse to avoid paying high export taxes on 113 tyres which Warton had bought from the Portuguese airline, T.A.P. When the L-1049G took-off from Lisbon, Warton had managed to convince the customs authority that he was *not* exporting the tyres but that he would be returning after a short test flight. Customs had agreed to let the flight depart but Warton's plan had been to fly to Malta, land and immediately take-off again for a return flight to Lisbon where, by then, the cargo would technically be 'in transit' from Malta to Bissau.

Although Warton was aboard '5T-TAF' when it landed at Luqa he was not, in fact, flying the aircraft. In the captain's seat was a 49-year old American, Bob Major; Wolfgang Boden was acting as First Officer/Co-pilot and a British Flight Engineer, Rex Holding, completed the crew. The German Embassy immediately arranged for Boden's flight to Germany and the British Embassy organised a fast departure for Holding but Warton and Major were both arrested. Both were granted bail pending a court case but successfully managed, according to

42: In an effort to avoid paying Portuguese authorities a tax on exporting a cargo of Super Constellation tyres, Hank Warton flew the cargo aboard L-1049G '5T-TAF' from Lisbon to Malta on 16 February 1968. The intention was then to fly back to Lisbon where he could argue that the cargo was now 'in transit' from Malta to his base at Bissau. The Air Traffic Controller at Luqa Airport, however, realised '5T-TAF' were marks that legally belonged to a Cessna 206. The aircraft was impounded and the crew of four were arrested. Within hours Warton and the aircraft's captain, Robert Major, were spirited to Catania aboard a fishing boat–courtesy of 'a friendly organisation based in Sicily' (Unknown)

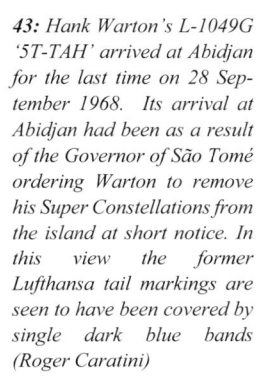

43: Hank Warton's L-1049G '5T-TAH' arrived at Abidjan for the last time on 28 September 1968. Its arrival at Abidjan had been as a result of the Governor of São Tomé ordering Warton to remove his Super Constellations from the island at short notice. In this view the former Lufthansa tail markings are seen to have been covered by single dark blue bands (Roger Caratini)

local reports, to charter a small boat and escape back to Portugal. Ironically, the engine on the fishing-boat failed shortly after leaving Malta leaving all temporarily marooned in mid-Mediterranean.[126] For very obvious reasons Warton himself has never chosen to say too much about his activities in Biafra but when Fr Anthony Byrne, the CARITAS co-ordinator on São Tomé, met Warton at Lisbon he expressed his surprise at seeing Warton free. The newspapers had just broken the story of his arrest in Malta. Byrne mentioned the news item to Warton and wondered how, given the circumstances, he had managed to avoid being kept in a Maltese jail. Warton simply replied that his "good friends in Italy had arranged for his escape". (Many years later Warton did admit that the Italian Mafia had helped organise his escape from Malta.)[127]

Whatever the circumstances of Warton's escape from Malta were, he was forced to abandon '5T-TAF' at Luqa airport, together with its cargo of valuable spare tyres.

The two losses left Warton with just one aircraft, the ex-Lufthansa '5T-TAG', and in order to maintain his commitment to Biafra's demand for military supplies he made up the losses by quickly completing cash deals on the two remaining Lufthansa L-1049G Super Constellations. Export permits were issued in Germany for single flights only, from Hamburg to Lisbon, D-ALID on 23 February 1968 and D-ALEC on 9 March 1968. Like all of Warton's previous aircraft they immediately had their markings removed and replaced with false Mauritanian registrations. In the case of the latest arrivals they were re-registered as '5T-TAH' and '5T-TAK'.[128] Warton's fleet now consisted of the following three aircraft:

Warton Identity	Type	C/n	Lufthansa Identity
5T-TAG	L-1049G	4642	D-ALOF
5T-TAH	L-1049G	4647	D-ALID
5T-TAK	L-1049G	4640	D-ALEC

The 'Schreiner' DC-7C

Even before the Biafran DC-7CF, G-ATOB, was reported at Madrid during the spring of 1968, its condition, especially its engines, had frequently given cause for concern. Among other recurring technical snags on the aircraft was a "runaway stabilizer" which badly affected the autopilot system and on at least one occasion an unintended ditching was narrowly avoided by the crew. In view of this the Biafrans sought a replacement for G-ATOB and which again came from Trans World Leasing's store at Cambridge.

As a result of mounting financial losses, the Dutch charter company, Schreiner Airways had restructured its operations on 1 October 1967 and which effectively involved disposing of its three DC-7C aircraft. Two, PH-SAE and PH-SAO, were sold to Trans World Leasing on 16 November 1967 and flown from Schiphol to Cambridge, the first of which (PH-SAE) arrived on 15 December.[129]

Both aircraft remained in open storage at Cambridge for almost three months. As was normal procedure, the Dutch registration marks were officially cancelled on 1 March 1968. It had been expected that the two aircraft might join Trans World Leasing's sister company, Trans Meridian, but neither did. Instead, one of the two aircraft (PH-SAE) was leased to a Panamian-registered company, simplistically known as Compagnie Aeromaritime des Transportes. The apparent owner of the company was the French arms dealer Pierre Laureys. It was then flown out of Cambridge without, it seems, any attempt to acquire a new Certificate of Registration. Still carrying the marks PH-SAE, the DC-7C took off from Cambridge at 11:46 on 6 March 1968 and was flown direct to Lisbon by a Trans Meridian Airlines captain named Webb. Under the terms of the lease agreement with the French dealer, the crew had been supplied by Trans World Leasing.[130]

Details of subsequent flights by PH-SAE remain fairly sketchy but it is believed to have operated on behalf of the Biafran Government for a while although whether or not it was purchased outright by the Biafrans is still unclear. The aircraft certainly made a number of flights outside the traditional Biafra 'loop', causing Dutch officials to make several demands upon Trans World Leasing to have the aircraft re-registered.

For a while the former Schreiner DC-7C was flown by a Rhodesian captain and a Portuguese (ex T.A.P.) co-pilot, José Rafael Pereira Rebordao. Both crew members had regularly been flying the Air Trans Africa L-1049G Super Constellation until Malloch's arrest in Togo brought the Rhodesian operation to a halt. The Rhodesian captain was subsequently replaced by a Portuguese pilot, Manuel Reis, another former T.A.P. captain but who was also rated on a Super Constellation and not a DC-7C–not that it mattered much to the Biafrans. One report relates how, on his first flight into Biafra, Reis was forced to feather one of the DC-7Cs engines and during the landing that followed, three of the mainwheel tyres burst. The Portuguese crew were forced to abandon PH-SAE in Biafra at which point Rebordao decided to return to Portugal leaving Manuel Reis on São Tomé island in the hope of finding another aircraft to fly.[131]

At some stage, and probably during early May 1968, PH-SAE was flown out of Biafra and positioned to the island of São Tomé where its state of airworthiness was declared as 'marginal'. For several weeks it was grounded. In fact few believed that it would ever fly again but Trans World Leasing sent an engineer, Tom Beavers, down to São Tomé to assess the true state of the DC-7C. This does suggest that Trans World Leasing still retained an interest in the aircraft (which in turn suggests that it *was* being operated under a leasing arrangement). Beavers spent some time at São Tomé working on the DC-7C's engines and it was during this time that he was approached by two American pilots, Derek 'Red' Mettrick and Clyde Arnspiger. According to Mike Keegan, PH-SAE's reputed owner, both Americans expressed a serious interest in purchasing the aircraft. Negotiations, which involved a number of telex calls back to the UK, - again suggesting that Trans World Leasing technically still owned the aircraft - followed and according to the UK owner a price was agreed upon. Furthermore, as the potential new owners were type-rated for the DC-7C there seemed to be no need to send a new crew down to São Tomé. It was therefore agreed that Mettrick and Arnspeiger readily agreed to fly the aircraft back to the UK for "essential maintenance".

Essential maintenance was most certainly required; in fact there is little evidence to hand that any attention had been given to the aircraft since its sale by Schreiner Airways. Documentation that accompanied the sale showed that its Certificate of Airworthiness had expired on 21 October 1967. It had not been renewed. The total flying hours recorded by Schreiner, since its last overhaul, was 4,068 hours. According to accepted maintenance schedules the permitted time between airframe overhauls was 4,000 hours. There are no indications that any work was carried out at Cambridge after its arrival in the UK. It was only the engines, or at least three of them, which had any measurable life-until-next-overhaul.[132] When it had made the flight from Cambridge to Lisbon, the aircraft still carried the officially-cancelled marks PH-SAE, and was therefore being flown without a certificate of registration and, of course, a valid certificate of airworthiness. Furthermore it had operated a number of flights into Biafra; little wonder that its crew was considerably worried over the general state of the aircraft.

When PH-SAE took-off from São Tomé at 06:40 hours on 7 June 1968, it was ostensibly being flown back to the U.K. for maintenance, but it never arrived; instead it landed in Federal Nigeria in quite strange circumstances. Offi-

44: At the end of the Nigeria-Biafra war almost every major airfield in West Africa had an abandoned DC-7C rotting away. In spite of its generally poor condition, the former Schreiner Airways DC-7C PH-SAE operated several flights into Biafra. Abandoned at São Tomé, it was later flown to Lagos and handed over to the Federal Nigerian Government who claimed to have 'hijacked' the aircraft. Two Polish pilots, Roman Hrycak and Marian Kozubski then made a number of ammunition supply flights between Lagos and Port Harcourt during September 1968 but the state of the aircraft eventually overtook even the strongest of Polish nerves and it was dumped at the edge of Lagos airport (Stephen Piercey Collection)

45: By November 1971 PH-SAE had weathered considerably, having stood in the open for just over three years (Confidential Source)

cial reports, released some ten days later, indicated that the aircraft had been intercepted by Nigerian Air Force MiG-17s and, rightly suspecting the DC-7C to be part of the Biafran gun-running fleet, forced it to land at Lagos. The Nigerian official announcement further claimed that the aircraft had immediately been flown to Kaduna, northern Nigeria and that the two American pilots were under arrest after documentation aboard the DC-7C showed that it had in fact been used in arms supply flights to Biafra.[133]

Quite how long the two Americans were held in Lagos is unclear, if indeed they were held at all. Both were reported to have travelled on to Geneva immediately afterwards and another report suggested that they had jointly received an agreed $30,000 from the Nigerian Government for "delivering the aircraft to Lagos". Mettrick later confirmed that he and Arnspiger had flown the aircraft to Lagos and then up-country to Kaduna but insisted that they had been asked to do this by Beavers who, in turn, was apparently acting on instructions from George Batchelor, who, of course, was associated with Trans Meridian and Trans World Leasing. Mettrick has always denied that he was paid any additional sum of money for doing so, claiming that such reports were simply the whim of an imaginative Nigerian press agency.[134]

Equally unclear is whether or not the Frenchman Pierre Laureys still had any involvement with the DC-7C. At the time of its 'defection' to Lagos, Laureys was being flown from Cotonou to Libreville with the French Ambassador to the Ivory Coast and a Greek financier aboard a Grumman G.73 Mallard, G-ASCS. The Mallard's flight had originated from Cambridge and was being flown by a British commercial pilot.[135] Its route was as follows:

Grumman G.73 Mallard G-ASCS - Flight Log 1-24 June 1968

Date	Route	ATD (Z)	ATA (Z)	Remarks
1.6.68	Cambridge-Luton	1805	1830	Outbound UK customs clearance
2.6.68	Luton-Brussels	0655	0845	One Portuguese passenger
	Brussels-Geneva	1245	1525	Pierre Laureys embarks at Brussels
	Geneva-Geneva	1830	2015	Planned destination was Madrid; returned to Geneva due to heavy icing conditions over Lyon.
3.6.68	Geneva-Barcelona	1155	1550	
	Barcelona-Madrid	1705	1935	
	Madrid-Lisbon	2315	0130	
4.6.68	Lisbon-Agadir	1245	1625	
	Agadir-Las Palmas	1745	2005	
5.6.68	Las Palmas-Dakar	1030	1630	
6.6.68	Dakar-Freetown	0450	0815	
	Freetown-Abidjan	0925	1400	
	Abidjan-Cotonou	1620	1915	French Ambassador embarks at Abidjan
7.6.68	Cotonou-Libreville	0925	1325	
9.6.68	Libreville-Lomé	0745	1145	French Ambassador to Lomé
9.6.68	Lomé-Libreville	1345	1810	
11.6.68	Libreville-Abidjan	0515	1105	
	Abidjan-Freetown	1325	1725	
	Freetown-Dakar	1825	2120	
12.6.68	Dakar-El Aauin	0840	1400	
	El Aauin-Casablanca	1535	1900	Fuel pump failure
13.6.68	Casablanca-Biarritz	1015	1510	
	Biarritz-Le Bourget	1715	2025	Hydraulic failure & tyre badly scuffed on landing. Greek financier deplaned
21.6.68	Le Bourget-Lympne	1720	1825	Inbound UK Customs clearance
24.6.68	Lympne-Cambridge	0950	1040	

Registered ownership of the Mallard had just been transferred from a Mr 'F.M. Lawreys' to J.A. Goldschmidt Ltd (of Dunster House, Mincing Lane, London EC3). Goldschmidt also traded from an address in Biarritz, where Lawreys also had one of his bases.[136]

The fact that the aircraft's flight originated at Cambridge, the same original start-point as the Trans World Leasing DC-7C, may be no more than pure coincidence. So might the fact that Pierre Laureys was known to be involved in deals at Libreville - where the Mallard ended its flight. Whatever the connection is, if indeed there is one, there is no evidence to suggest that the Mallard was ever flown in to Biafra.

The war drags on; Biafra seeks a new Air Force

At the end of January 1968 the Federal Nigerian Army Command had issued orders to the 3rd Marine Commando Division to spearhead a northward advance into Biafran territory. The assignment was to cross into Uyo Province, liberate Obubra, and then advance westwards towards Ikot Ekpene and Port Harcourt.

Two Nigerian Brigades (12 & 13 Brigades) converged on Obubra in March 1968 after a six-week battle; Port Harcourt became the next target, a drive for which began in the third week of April. The Nigerian Air Force, using Calabar as a base, provided air support, from unchallenged skies. The plan had been to advance on three fronts and after some initial indecisive fighting by both sides, Nigerian soldiers entered Port Harcourt on 19 May 1968. The Biafran exodus was dispirited and disorganised.

It was not long after the threat of Federal Nigerian MiG-17Fs and L-29s had become a very real one before the Biafran Government set about the acquisition of a jet fighter element of its air force. Ojukwu had briefed his principal emissary in Europe, Christopher C. Mojekwu, to conclude deals that would secure aircraft to counter the Soviet-supplied jets. One broker that had established a trusting relationship with the various Biafran emissaries was the Windsor-based Templewood Aviation Ltd and its Swiss-based associate company, Texsel Sales & Services.[137]

Templewood Aviation Ltd had been formed on 1 November 1967 by two aviation consultants, Anthony 'Tony' Griffin and John Snedden. Snedden was based in Geneva and it was from there that various financial deals were set up. Templewood had already been involved with Biafra's UK emissary, Austin Okwesa, when the latter contracted to purchase twelve ex-French Air Force T-6G Texans.

At the beginning of 1968 Mojekwu instructed Okwesa to raise the question of jet fighter aircraft with Templewood Aviation. Initial discussions centred around a small number of F-86 Sabres but these were dropped in favour of Hawker Hunters which had a proven record as a fighter and a ground-attack aircraft. Okwesa's brief to acquire jet aircraft was not only to enable the Biafran Air Force to match the MiG-17s and L-29s of the Federal Air Force but also to help create a ground-attack squadron with an offensive capability. The primary target in mind was the Federal Nigerian Navy frigate *Nigeria* which, since it had started patrolling the mouth of the river Cross, had become a major threat to Biafra's export shipments of rubber resin.

The proposed Biafran Hunter contract was a straightforward sale & purchase deal and involved four Mk.4 (Mk F.50) variants from Swedish Air Force stocks. Templewood Aviation acted as broker and agreed to supply the four aircraft at a unit price of US$230,000; the price including delivery to São Tomé and on to Biafra. A full ground servicing and maintenance equipment facility, together with a 15% spares holding, was also agreed upon at an additional cost of US$250,000. Templewood also arranged for the aircraft to be fully crewed. (The contract also included the projected sale of a de Havilland DH.114 Heron 2E. This was added to Ojukwu's shopping-list simply to enable him to repay Jack Malloch. It was Malloch's much-valued Heron which had been stranded at Enugu and captured by Federal Nigerian forces.)

The first step in operating the Biafran Hunters was through an advertisement in *Flight International* magazine which sought pilots with Hunter experience, preferably with the R.A.F. From the applicants four pilots, Charles Marsh, Rod Freeman, Alexander 'Sandy' Rumley and Peiter Dezeeuw, were hired expressly for the operation, although Marsh was later replaced by an ex-Fleet Air Arm pilot, John Duncan. One other person was recruited. He was an ex-RAF Corporal Armourer who had recently left No.2 School of Technical Training at RAF St Athan and whose function was to help with assembling the Hunters at São Tomé and then preparing them for action once they were positioned inside Biafra. He was flown immediately to São Tomé to await delivery of the Hunters.

The Biafran Hunter deal was financed by a private Swiss banker who put up $200,000 in promissory notes and which were lodged with the African Continental Bank. The financial arrangements had been completed on 11 April 1968 and were dependent on one primary factor –if the aircraft failed to leave Sweden the monies advanced would be returned in full. In fact the aircraft did fail to leave Sweden but not directly due to any financial irregularity. It was simply that the Swiss financier died unexpectedly and as a result the affair became public. The deal collapsed.

Having waited on São Tomé island for several weeks for the Magisters to arrive, the only person to really gain from the frustrated Hunter deal was the former RAF Corporal. One evening the Biafran 'Grey Ghost' L-1049G ('5N-07G') landed at São Tomé with an engine out. The captain displayed a high degree of irritation and complained–to almost anybody within earshot–about the general state of the aircraft's engines and threatened to simply abandon the aircraft at São Tomé. The former Royal Air Force man offered to look at the engine and later discovered two blown cylinders. By working throughout the night the young Corporal had all four engines running smoothly just after dawn. Immediately after cutting the engines he was offered a job as Flight Engineer aboard Biafra's nocturnal freighter. (In fact, he retained this position until the very end of the war, transferring to the L-749As towards the end of the conflict. After the Nigerian Civil War, he then secured a Flight Engineer's role with one of Europe's leading airlines).

Denied the Swedish Hunters, Templewood sought to procure very quickly, on behalf of their Biafran client, an alternative aircraft and discovered that the Austrian Air Force had begun to retire its fleet of French-built Fouga Magisters. The Magister was considered an inferior substitute for the Hunter but nevertheless several were available. Up to five aircraft (in two shipments) were involved in the Austrian affair with two examples making up the first shipment. By now Templewood was dealing directly with Christopher Mojekwu who had by then become the most important Biafran outside Biafra; he had fired Okwesa and adopted the role of the main negotiator himself. This should have made things a lot easier but the contract involving the Magisters became quite a complex one and the deal subsequently became quite the most bizarre episode of the entire Biafran war.

The contract agreed between Templewood and Mojekwu was two-fold. Biafra paid US$156,000 for two Magisters and a deposit on two others. Included in that sum was the cost of armaments for the two aircraft as well as delivery from Graz to São Tomé. The contract also stipulated that two fully-crewed and armed aircraft should be positioned inside Biafra by Saturday, 29 June 1968. The second part of the contract involved a payment of $102,800 for the remaining Magisters (and spares) to be delivered to Biafra by Friday 5 July 1968. All of the Magisters were to be re-assembled at São Tomé from where Templewood had secured clearance from the island's governor for just one single outbound flight by each aircraft. In other words they could take-off from São Tomé but not return. The "single flight" was therefore regarded as a delivery flight into Biafra but in reality the plan was to take-off from São Tomé and then carry out a low-level strike against the Federal Navy's frigate, *Nigeria*. After the attack the two Magisters were then expected to land at Uli.

The first two aircraft (4D-YF/199 and 4D-YI/212) were air-freighted from Graz to Lisbon on 22 May 1968 aboard a CL-44D, N604SA (owned by Airlift International but one of several wet-leased to Trans Mediterranean Airways). The plan had been to air-freight the dismantled jets on from Lisbon (aboard the CL-44D) but the Airlift crew feared that a suitable starter-trolley might not be available on São Tomé island. As it turned out the fears were fully justified and the crew flatly refused therefore to fly beyond Lisbon. The dismantled aircraft, still clearly showing signs of their previous Austrian insignia and serials, were therefore unloaded at Lisbon airport to await an alternative means of getting them to São Tomé.

One company specialising in freight charter work but flying much less sophisticated aircraft was the Irish company, Aer Turas. Templewood called Aer Turas with an offer to convey the Magisters to São Tomé. The Biafrans were more cautious. They agreed to Aer Turas taking the fuselages but insisted on Warton's aircraft handling the wings.

Aer Turas operated a Bristol 170 Freighter Mk.31E, EI-APC, primarily for race-horse charter work around Europe and on 27 May 1968 the aircraft undertook such a flight from Dublin to Cork and on to Gatwick, where it landed at 15:38hrs (GMT). Then, after an overnight stay, Captain Tommy Thompson and co-pilot John Squire (the company's Managing Director) flew the empty aircraft from Gatwick (departing at 08:10hrs GMT) on a positioning flight to Lisbon. It did not take too long to load just one of the Fouga Magister fuselages into the Bristol 170; however much of the day was spent in rigging up a most unorthodox auxilliary fuel system.[138]

Unlike the DC-7Cs and L-1049 Super Constellations which regularly plied the Biafra run, the Aer Turas Bristol 170 lacked the range to make the journey in one hop, or even at best with one stopover at Bissau. In fact, its maximum range was just over 800 miles and so in order to fly longer sectors (and only land in countries unlikely to be concerned at the cargo and destination) Squire rigged up a number of 45-gallon oil drums, all inter-linked by hosepipe and which fed directly into the fuel crossfeed system; he also took on board a stirrup-pump.

Although it worked well the fuel modification system was unorthodox to the extreme. Two of the engineers involved in the temporary conversion later referred to the 170 as the Bristol 'Frightener' but it did enable the crew to route via Portuguese territories or through countries sympathetic to the Biafran cause.

EI-APC departed Lisbon for the first flight to São Tomé early on 29 May 1968. Flown by Thompson and Squire the aircraft made Sal by the end of the day for an overnight stop. On the following day the 170 was flown on to Bissau for another overnight stop before making the final stages to Abidjan and on to São Tomé late on 31 May. No details of its cargo were ever recorded, apart from a manifest which stated "1,683kgs of freight" but at São Tomé the first of the two Magister fuselages (4D-YI/212) was manhandled out of the Freighter. The crew of the Airlift International CL-44D had been right to have suspected the quality of facilities at São Tomé; in fact the facilities were still very basic. So much so that it took a dozen local porters almost an entire day to manhandle the Magister fuselage safely out of the Bristol 170.

The Aer Turas Freighter was flown back to Lisbon on 2/3 June 1968 to collect the second Magister fuselage. Then, early on 5 June, and with Squire in the left-hand seat EI-APC repeated the journey south to São Tomé in virtually the same manner.

The 'fuel modification' worked well and considerably extended the range of the 170.[139] The standard 'book' range of a Mk.31E Freighter was 820 miles but several of the sectors flown by EI-APC during these two trips significantly exceeded this figure–almost doubling it on one occasion–as the following table illustrates:

46: Biafra's senior representative in Lisbon was H.N. Onobogu and it was he who signed Templewood Aviation Ltd's receipt for the first of two Fouga Magisters (c/n 212) on 30 May 1968. In fact, contrary to the wording, it had been dispatched to São Tomé aboard Bristol 170 EI-APC on the previous day (A. Rumley Personal Papers)

```
TEMPLEWOOD AVIATION Ltd.,
3, High St., Windsor

                                    Tel.: Windsor 66811
30th May 1968


        Received from the above named company the under-
mentioned goods:

        (a) - 1 Fouga Magister jet aircraft, airframe No.
FM 212.

        (b) - Complete installations of aircraft and ground-
-air radio equipment.

        Goods received at Lisbon airport in good condition
and dispatched by Aer Turas to São Tomé on Bristol Freighter
No. EI-APC on the above Date


                                Signed

                                ..................
                                (H. N. Onubogu)
```

47: *The Magister fuselages were air-freighted from Lisbon to São Tomé aboard the Aer Turas Bristol 170 EI-APC, seen here at Southampton in July 1968. The 170 made two flights, each with one fuselage and a number of oil drums containing sufficient fuel to make the journey in as few stages as possible. Fuel was pumped into the cross-feed by a single stirrup pump, a system later explained by its pilot, John Squire, to the British crew of Mercy Missions Anson G-AWMG (Peter J Marson)*

Aer Turas Bristol 170 EI-APC Flight Log 29 May 1968 10 June 1968

Date	Routeing	Miles
29.5.68	Lisbon-Porto Santo	625
	Porto Santo-Sal	1250
30.5.68	Sal-Bissau	450
31.5.68	Bissau-Abidjan	1025
	Abidjan-São Tomé	800
2.6.68	São Tomé-Abidjan	800
	Abidjan-Bissau	1025
3.6.68	Bissau-Port Etienne	625
	Port Etienne-Lisbon	1380
5.6.68	Lisbon-Port Santo	625
	Porto Santo-Bissau	1450
6.6.68	Bissau-Abidjan	1025
	Abidjan-São Tomé	800
7.6.68	São Tomé-Abidjan	800
8.6.68	Abidjan-Dakar	1575
9.6.68	Dakar-Las Palmas	950
	Las Palmas-Lisbon	920
10.6.68	Lisbon-Dublin	1050

In the meantime attempts to get the Magister wings down to São Tomé were progressing slowly. About a week before the Fouga Magister deal, Hank Warton had acquired a freighter variant Super Constellation, the L-1049D, LV-ILW. The aircraft had previously been brought up to L-1049H standard (to become an L-1049D/01) and had operated for a South American company, L.A.P.A.[140] Immediately after its sale to Warton (by dealer International Aerodyne Inc) the aircraft was flown from Miami to Lisbon where the false marks '5T-TAC' were painted on. It was the second of Warton's aircraft to carry these marks, the first having crashed at Port Harcourt almost four months beforehand. But, despite the new L-1049D having a larger freight door than any of Warton's other aircraft, ground-crews at Lisbon still had some difficulty in loading the Magister wings aboard.

There was, as usual, a small gathering of passengers at Lisbon and whose only method of travelling from Europe to Biafra was to be allocated one of 12 or 16 seats fitted towards the front of each of Warton's Super Constellations.[141] Waiting at Lisbon on 28 May were nine passengers: Father Doran (the CARITAS representative in Lisbon), Alan Hart (ITV Journalist/Reporter) together with two ITV cameramen, Sister Ann Bent (Matron, Queen Elizabeth Hospital, Umuahia), one *Ibo* Envoy from Biafra State House and three pilot-cum-engineers (travelling to São Tomé to assemble and fly the Magisters, one of whom was Templewood Aviation's David Webster; the other two were also Templewood employees). All of the passengers were given seats at the front except for the Envoy who took one of two seats beside the rear freight-doors.

David Webster's role was an interesting one. The second part of the Magister deal involved a special project at the personal request of Ojukwu himself. It involved the setting up of a mobile HF transceiver system for communications between Biafra and Europe; more precisely to enable Ojukwu to discuss urgent matters with Mojekwu in Europe. Webster had just returned to the UK from Aden, having completed a British Government contract in Aden as a Communications Officer with Airwork Ltd. He was immediately seconded by Templewood's Alex Rumley to work on Ojukwu's HF link. By the time the Magisters were ready for delivery to São Tomé most of the HF equipment had been acquired and assembled.

The departure of '5T-TAC' from Lisbon was originally scheduled for 28 May but successive delays were announced owing to snags with the aircraft as well as the difficulty in getting the Magister wings aboard the aircraft; in fact departure was delayed for a full five days. The Super Constellation finally took-off from Lisbon at 06:30 hours on Sunday 2 June. The only scheduled stop was at Bissau where it landed at 12:30 hours. It was not long after

48: For much of the duration of the Nigerian civil war Ojuwku's personal 125 remained in the corner of São Tomé's single hangar in company with the two Biafran Fouga Magister fuselages. The Magister's wings had been destroyed aboard one of Warton's Super Constellations in an act of sabotage. Attempts to purchase replacement wings was eventually successful but they arrived at Lisbon just too late (Jakob Ringler)

landing at Bissau that word from the South African pilot, warned of recurring trouble with one of the engines and that the aircraft's hydraulic braking system had sustained some damage in the landing at Bissau. An enforced delay of, initially, several hours was therefore deemed necessary. But shortly afterwards another announcement from the captain claimed that spare parts would have to be flown down from Lisbon which could take up to 48 hours. Passengers and crew took to a nearby hotel and waited.

L-1049D '5T-TAC' was declared serviceable on Tuesday 4 June, just after a second of Warton's aircraft ('5T-TAH') had delivered the necessary spares from Lisbon. Nevertheless five of the passengers were ordered to change aircraft and immediately left Bissau aboard the replacement aircraft. '5T-TAH' was flown direct to Biafra but low mist over Uli made a night landing too hazardous and so the crew, having circled for almost an hour, abandoned the approach and diverted to São Tomé. When they arrived at São Tomé, the passengers aboard '5T-TAH' had fully expected to see their original aircraft, '5T-TAC', already there, together with the Biafran Envoy and the Magister crews but there was no sign of it.

In fact '5T-TAC' never left Bissau. Not long after the replacement aircraft had taken off (or early the next morning, 5 June) an explosion ripped through the forward section of the aircraft and the ensuing fire destroyed not only the L-1049D but also its valuable cargo of Fouga Magister wings. The cause of the explosion has never been fully explained but sabotage by one of the crew was strongly suspected. It was alleged that the person responsible had disappeared immediately afterwards with a bounty of US$146,000.

An attempt to get the three other Fouga Magisters (4D-YD/192, 4D-YE/193, and 4D-YG/200) out of Graz was made during February 1969. On that occasion the two key characters involved an arms dealer, Harry Briggs, and an Irishman, Steve Cooney, of Cooney Contractors Ltd. An End User Certificate was issued by the Irish Department of Industry & Commerce on 5 February 1969 citing Cooney Contractors Ltd (of 163, West End Lane, London NW6) as having undertaken to import three CM.170 Magister jets from the Austrian Air Ministry. Shannon Aircraft Holdings Ltd was shown as the ultimate recipient. Two days later, the same document was presented to the Austrian authorities who granted an export licence to a Mr S. Cooney for the sale of the three aircraft subject to the conditions of the End User Certificate.

Aer Turas' Bristol 170 EI-APC was and DC-4 EI-APK (or AOR) were both flown from Dublin to Graz on 11 February 1969 to collect the Fouga Magisters. But none of the aircraft were released by the Austrians. The 170 then returned to Dublin two days later, via London-Heathrow, while the DC-4 flew on to Prague on the same day to uplift a cargo of arms.[142] Administratively the sale was finalised on 23 February 1969 and the Magisters struck off Austrian Air Force charge but the Biafrans never received the aircraft.[143]

The loss of the Fouga Magisters was a serious blow and denied the Biafran Air Force an ability to re-establish an offensive air element although several months later a small force of MFI-9Bs was successfully delivered to Biafra. But for the rest of the war (and some time beyond) the two original Magister fuselages laid dormant to one side of the hangar at São Tomé. A replacement set of wings was eventually obtained by a German dealer Herbert Berg from surplus Luftwaffe sources at Karlsruhe and even delivered to Faro, Portugal during early January 1970 but just too late; the war was over three days afterwards.

For Hank Warton the Bissau incident had been equally disastrous. He had lost his latest acquisition, the L-1049D '5T-TAC', and was being suspected of organising what was clearly an act of sabotage. Warton flew down to Bissau shortly afterwards and discovered that there was little left of his aircraft. One of Warton's mechanics reported that he had been tensioning a Power Recovery Turbine (P.R.T.) on one of '5T-TAC's engines while the crew and passengers were taking a meal in the Terminal building. Minutes after completing work on the engine the mechanic had joined the others, immediately after which the explosion occurred. The manner in which the aircraft burned suggested that the explosion had occurred in the rear fuselage area and Warton later claimed that a number of 5-gallon acid bottles stowed by the rear freight-doors had leaked and under the hot Bissau sun caught alight. The fire soon spread to cases of ammunition. Warton, quite naturally, never attributed the cause of the fire to sabotage.[144]

On the other hand nobody could explain to David Webster why he had been quietly warned by the Super Connie's crew that "for the benefit of your health it is strongly adviseable not to venture outside the airport Terminal building for the time being".[145]

Notes

Note 106 Various sources describe Malloch's adventures before the Biafran episode. Many emerged in the press just after Jack Malloch was killed in Rhodesia in 1982. Other background details are related from an unpublished biography of Jack Malloch, courtesy of Alan Brough.

Note 107 Details of the early arms flights to Bukavu and to Biafra are taken from Flying Log-Books of aircrew who performed these flights. Further descriptions were provided by Flight Engineer Henry Kinnear who was aboard most of the flights.

Note 108 The *London Times* 12 March 1968. The quoted phrase and other details of the Luanda arms stockpile are taken from a feature article on The Council of Three.

Note 109 Much of the aforegoing detail was provided by Hank Warton personally during the course of many conversations with the author.

Note 110 *Der Spiegel* magazine.

Note 111 As reported by Fred Kirby, a former London insurance assesor who investigated many claims of stolen aircraft and illegal flights etc.

Note 112 *Ibid.*, Peter J. Marson

Note 113 Correspondence between Luis A Tavares and Peter J Marson.

Note 114 *Air Britain Civil Aircraft Registers of Africa,* Air Britain 1981.

Note 115 As related to the author by Peter J. Marson.

Note 116 As related to the author by Peter J. Marson.

Note 117 Details taken from the Flying Log-Books of Bernie Murphy and subsequent correspondence with the author.

Note 118 A number of third-hand reports related to the author by former Warton crews at São Tomé 1968. Dates of aircraft visits to Switzerland are taken from contemporary issues of *Aviation Letter*.

Note 119 *London Times* 20 June 1968. The presence of a Brazilian navigator is interesting. Jack Malloch is not known to have employed a Brazilian navigator but there were occasions when Portuguese personnel described themselves as Brazilian when caught in embarrassing situations in Africa. Another report (by Malloch himself) shows the navigator on this flight as V. Branco. A Portuguese navigator, Castelo Branco, (full name João Manuel Arrobas Castelo Branco) is known to have flown with Malloch during this period but his movements are (coincidentally) unknown for the January-June 1968 period. It is likely therefore that the Brazilian navigator described in the Times report and the Portuguese navigator, Branco, are one and the same person.

Note 120 The satirical magazine *Private Eye* ran a series of articles (Issues 314, 316, 318 & 343) concerning the banking activities of Dr Kurt Wallersteiner under the heading "Fatswallersteiner's Greatest Hits". There were also references in a 1969 issue of *Der Spiegel* which "associated Wallersteiner with Otto Skorzeny in supplying arms to needy Africans."

Note 121 *London Times*, 26 January 1968.

Note 122 The statement was made by Jack Malloch to British Aviation Insurance Co as part of a claim against the hull value of the DC-7CF. A full copy of the report was passed on to the author.

Note 123 Later killed in the tragic accident involving Warton L-1049G '5T-TAG'.

Note 124 D-ALOF was sold to Warton's company, North American Aircraft Trading Corporation on 8.12.67 and ferried to Lisbon on 13.12.67.

Note 125 *To Places Far Away – A Wanderer For Christ* by Father Billy Butler. Details reproduced by kind permission of Fr Butler who was in Port Harcourt at the time of the crash.

Note 126 *Sunday Times*, 5 January 1969

Note 127 Conversation between Larry Raab and the author 12 October 1997.

Note 128 The identity tie-ups are unconfirmed but a close study of colour schemes and timings of sightings at Lisbon and São Tomé offer sufficient evidence for believing these to be confirmed.

Note 129 Contemporary issues of *Anglia Aeronews* which identified movements at Cambridge Airport. The original Log-Books have unfortunately been destroyed.

Note 130 Trans World Leasing subsequently lodged an insurance claim for the hull-value of PH-SAE after its arrival in Lagos. The insurance company investigated the claim and the movement details for this aircraft are taken from that report.

Note 131 Correspondence between João M. Vidal and the author

Note 132 Documentation raised by Schreiner Airways at the time of sale showed that the number 1 engine (serial 707748) had flown 1216 hrs since last overhaul; number 2 (707714) flown 1317 hours and number 4 engine (707815) just 323 hours. The number 3 engine (707802) had recorded 2084 hours. The scheduled time between overhauls was 2000 hours but it is not known if the engine was overhauled after delivery to Trans World Leasing.

Note 133 Documentation released by investigators following an insurance claim for the loss of the aircraft.

Note 134 As related to the author by Derick 'Red' Mettrick

Note 135 The details of this flight were taken from the Flying Log-Book and a conversation between the pilot and the author. The pilot seeks anonymity.

Note 136 As recorded by Civil Avition Authority library files at Gatwick. Later, on 5 March 1969 G-ASCS was re-registered to Terravia Trading Services Ltd but cancelled on 14 March 1969 on being sold to Canada.

Note 137 Much of the aforegoing details relating to Texsel Sales & Services and other related activity are contained within the private papers of

Alex Rumley, extracted and reproduced by kind permission.

Note 138   Details of flight-times etc have been extracted from the Aircraft Journey Log-Book, courtesy of anonymous sources in Ireland.

Note 139   Six weeks after the delivery of the Magister wings, the author met John Squire during a brief stop-over in Jersey. John Squire explained to the author precisely how the system was rigged up and recommended a similar principle for enabling the Mercy Missions' Anson G-AWMG to fly direct from Abidjan to São Tomé.

Note 140   *Ibid.*, Peter J. Marson.

Note 141   A description of the flight from Lisbon to Bissau, together with subsequent events, was given by Sister Ann Bent at Umuahia (in September 1968) and later confirmed by correspondence between the author and Sister Ann Bent during October 1970.

Note 142   Details of flight-times etc have been extracted from the Aircraft Journey Log-Books of those aircraft involved.

Note 143   Of the initial batch of six 1959-build CM170 Magisters, 211/4D-YH was written-off in service on 18.1.61. Five others (192/4D-YD, 193/4D-YE, 199/4D-YF, 200/4D-YG and 212/4D-YI) were all struck off charge on 23 February 1968, reportedly as sold to Biafra. The three Magisters 192, 193 and 200 were eventually acquired by the Bangladesh Air Force with whom they were first noted in 1989.

Note 144   Interview between Hank Warton and the author 7 December 1997. It should be stated that on this occasion Hank Warton was trying to recall a "relatively insignificant (sic) incident from 30 years ago".

Note 145   As related by Alex Rumley to the author. Alex was waiting at São Tomé for the arrival of the Bristol 170 and later spoke with David Webster to determine precisely what had happened at Bissau. On this occasion the author declares an open verdict.

```
THIS IS A REPEAT OF EARLIER TELEX
PLEASE DISREGARD EALIER TELEX

TWO BICYCLES LEAVING TONIGHT

WILL CALL CHRISTOPHER BEFORE DEPARTURE WITH EXACT TIME SO HE
CAN ARRANGE CLEARENCE .

THIS THE ONLY WAY TO TRANSPORT- REPEAT ONLY WAY  MAXIMUM RANGE
800 MILES .

YOUR FULLEST CO-OPERATION ESSENTIAL.
CHRISTOPHER MUST WAIT IN LISBON ==

TONY +

OWAV




OKAY THANKS X PLEASE WHEN CALLING FOR CONFIRMATION OF TIME OF
DEPARTURE CALL LISBON PHONE 612789 IF IT WILL BE BY PHONE
X AS SOMEONE ELSE MIGHT HAVE TO ANSWER FOR CHRISTOPHER - MR IKPA.
```

49: The telex operator at London's Hilton Hotel must have wondered what on earth the well-dressed gentlemen guests were up to if she ever read the stream of coded messages sent from there to Graz, Lisbon and São Tomé. The "bicycles" referred to are in fact the two dismantled Magisters. "Christopher" is Biafra's Christopher Mojekwu, the most senior Biafran envoy in Europe, who personally handled the clearance procedures at Lisbon. The "maximum range 800 miles" relates to the Aer Turas Bristol 170 EI-APC which was used for ferrying the fuselages onward from Lisbon (Alex Rumley Personal Papers)

50: The DC-7C PH-SAE was flown from São Tomé to Kaduna on 4 June 1968 by two Americans who, it was alleged, stood to gain handsome personal rewards for 'hijacking' an aircraft from the arms airlift to Biafra. The aircraft remained grounded at Kaduna until September 1968 when two Polish pilots, Marian Kozubski and Roman Hrycak, were offered the task of flying the DC-7C on the Lagos to Port Harcourt arms run. Curiously no identity for this aircraft was ever revealed officially but this extract from Marian Kozubski's Flying Log-Book shows an identity of '5N-AOW' for flights on 14 and 19 September. The aircraft's final flight was made on 23 September 1968 when it turned back to Lagos on three engines. It never flew again. Much later, after the war was over, Hrycak and Kozubski both remarked upon the terrifyingly poor condition of the DC-7C (Reproduced by kind permission from Mrs Sheila Kozubski)

FEDERAL NIGERIAN AIR FORCE
Formation, deliveries and recruitment

Nigerian Air Force: formation

Despite gaining independence on 1 October 1960, it was not until January 1964 that Nigeria formally constituted a national Air Force. Organisational aid came initially, not from Britain, but from India, and later from West Germany. Flying and technical training for pilots and engineers was also provided by West Germany as well as by Canada. At the same time the embryonic Nigerian Air Force began to receive its first aircraft; ten former Luftwaffe Dornier Do27A-4s for communications duties (NAF101-NAF110) and fourteen Piaggio P.149D (NAF201-NAF214) ab initio trainers, all of which were delivered to Kaduna, northern Nigeria during 1964/65. A fleet of West German-built N.2501D Noratlas aircraft was also planned but, of the ten aircraft which should have reached the Nigerian Air Force, no more than two (NAF301-NAF302) are thought to have arrived in Nigeria and there remains some doubt whether or not these ever flew in Nigerian markings. Both aircraft were returned to West Germany when the political situation in Nigeria worsened. So did Colonel Wolfgang Thiming, the head of the 75-man West German advisory group.[146]

51: Mechanics at Enugu gather around MiG-17F NAF616 to carry out routine after-flight checks at the end of a sortie over Biafra. MiG-17F NAF612 sits to the left and displays the 'hand-painted' style of serial presentation applied to a small batch of aircraft. MiG-17Fs became the standard fighter-bomber element of the Nigerian Air Force throughout the war (Keith E. Sissons)

By the turn of 1967 the Nigerian Air Force strength had increased with further deliveries from West Germany, involving ten additional Do27A-4s (NAF151-NAF160), and five Dornier Do28-B1s (NAF170-NAF174) to fulfill a light transport role. Some reports talk of a projected supply of front-line jet fighters being met by a number of surplus Luftwaffe Fiat G.91s but nothing further developed. In fact the whole question of German involvement in Nigeria had been an unhappy one. Language difficulties had hindered field training and even a British Foreign Office assessment in 1967 described the embryonic Nigerian Air Force as a "rather difficult-sounding baby".

The Italians were thought to have made a reasonably firm offer to cover training and equipment in late-1965 and a batch of Aermacchi MB326 ground attack trainers was later negotiated. This sale, however, was prohibited by the Italian Foreign Ministry when Nigeria's domestic situation began to deteriorate rapidly.[147]

As western governments sought to impose an embargo on arms and military aircraft, Nigeria's search within the West for an effective fighter element fell largely on unsympathetic ears. Long before fighting broke out many traditional suppliers had already become increasingly wary of fuelling Nigeria's internal troubles, a wariness that undoubtedly prompted a number of quasi-clandestine deals. When, for example, a visiting Nigerian Government team approached Switzerland for arms the Swiss Defence Ministry was forbidden by the Foreign Ministry to conclude any sale, yet by August 1967 the Swiss Embassy in Lagos reported that two Oerlikon-Buhrle employees were instructing Nigerians in the use of Oerlikon 20mm anti-aircraft guns.[148] The guns, which were presumably the same guns that Lagos later (and erroneously) claimed were used to shoot down the Biafran F-27 5N-AAV, had clearly been exported illegally.

Nigeria and the arms embargo

The arms embargo imposed by most western governments, including the British, was enforced in a curious manner. So much so, that it was an open secret that a clandestine supply of arms to Nigeria had began to be flown in from Europe and the Middle East. One such series of flights was flown during the autumn of 1967 by the Belgian International Air Services DC-6A, OO-ABE. The roundabout route flown by the crew displayed all the hallmarks of a clandestine arms run. Flown by a Belgian captain, Harry Chang, an unknown co-pilot and a British Flight Engineer, Bernie Murphy, the DC-6A first made a positioning flight from Brussels to Bilbao, in northern Spain, during the early hours of 26 September 1967. The aircraft then spent much of the day at Bilbao being loaded with arms before taking off at 16:15 hours, routeing back to Brussels. The sole reason for returning to Brussels was to allow administrative changes to the cargo manifest so as to show the country of origin as Belgium. After a two-hour stopover OO-ABE departed Brussels and flew south to Lagos, via a brief refuelling stop at Tripoli during the early hours of 27 September.[149]

Immediately after unloading, the B.I.A.S. DC-6A took-off from Lagos and headed north to Bilbao, via a refuelling stop at Palma. Re-loaded with a second cargo of Spanish armaments, OO-ABE took-off at 08:15 hours on 29 September for another positioning flight to Brussels, again for the same administrative reasons that were carried out on the first flight. From Brussels, the aircraft took-off at 17:00 hours and once again flew, via Tripoli, to Lagos where it landed early on 30 September.

Having completed two arms flights from Bilbao the crew received instructions to fly to Jedda to undertake a second series of arms flights to Nigeria, this time from Saudi Arabia. Routeing via Tripoli OO-ABE landed at Jeddah at 16:15 hours on 1 October where, to their horror, the crew discovered their cargo of rockets waiting on the main apron, unprotected from the Middle East sun. The rockets, destined for arming Nigerian Air Force L-29 Delfins, were loaded throughout the day and after an overnight crew rest the aircraft departed at 08:00 hours the following morning for a direct flight to Kano, in northern Nigeria. OO-ABE made three further flights between Jeddah and Kano during which it airlifted some 40 tonnes of ammunition to Nigeria's main Air Force base. Details of individual flights made by DC-6A OO-ABE from Jeddah are as follows:

BIAS DC-6A OO-ABE - Flight Details for Jeddah-Nigeria arms flights, Sept/Oct 1967

Date	Route	Times (Z)	Flight time
30.9.67	Lagos-Tripoli	1145-2005	8.20
1.10.67	Tripoli-Jedda	0955-1615	6.20
2.10.67	Jedda-Kano	0800-1630	8.30
2.10.67	Kano-Jedda	1900-0300	8.00
4.10.67	Jedda-Kano	0400-1250	8.50
4.10.67	Kano-Jedda	1500-2250	7.50
6.10.67	Jedda-Kano	0305-1150	8.45
6.10.67	Kano-Jedda	1430-2220	7.50
7.10.67	Jedda-Kano	2005-0455	8.55
8.10.67	Kano-Brussels	0725-1750	10.25

Arms shipments to Nigeria continued throughout 1967 and 1968. Seldom did any of these flights attract any publicity until 13 July 1968 when a SABENA Boeing 707-329C (OO-SJK, c/n 19211) was reported missing while approaching Lagos Airport. The Nigerian Air Force launched several Whirlwind helicopters to help search for the 707 until the wreckage was found just 8kms from the airport. The jet had been carrying a large consignment of 10,000 G-3 rifles manufactured in Belgium under sub-contract to a German producer. Their discovery aboard the aircraft was not only an embarrassment to SABENA but also to the Belgian Government who had issued an export licence for the sale of these rifles to Federal Nigeria. Belgium's policy towards Nigeria had suddenly become very public. An outcry quickly closed a loophole through which the guns had been exported; it also brought forth a new law by the Belgians which prohibited all export and transit licences for arms and munitions destined for Nigeria. At the same time similar bans were also announced by Holland, Italy and France—not, however, by the UK.[150]

Britain supplied Lagos with military aid throughout the Civil War. In fact the British policy, which had been outlined at a Downing Street Cabinet Meeting on 7 September 1967, was "to supply the Federal Government with reasonable quantities of arms similar to those supplied in the past (eg rifles) but to refuse sophisticated weapons (eg aircraft, rockets etc). It had been decided not to stop arms supplies to the Federal Government since they were the legitimate government and there were some 17,000 British lives at stake in Federal-controlled territory." There was, some observers believed, another reason for Britain's stand. The Nigerian Civil War had begun just one month after the Six-Day War (which cut off the Suez Canal); Britain could become dependent on Nigeria for up to a quarter of its imported oil.[151]

The situation was re-assessed several months afterwards when at another Downing Street meeting, on 23 November 1967, the Cabinet was told that "the Federal Military Government was winning the war and that, negotiations having so far failed to lead to a settlement, British interests would best be served by a quick Nigerian victory." The assessment continued with a decision taken by the Defence & Overseas Policy Committee which "agreed that British policy on arms should be relaxed so that we could now supply such items as mortars and Stirling sub-machine guns, although there would be no question of allowing the export of aircraft or weapons of mass destruction." The Cabinet learnt also that supplies of British ammunition to Nigeria would increase.[152]

By mid-December 1967 the Ministry of Defence had agreed to release from British Army stocks some 5million rounds of 7.62mm ammunition and 2million rounds each of 0.30 Browning and .303 ammunition. 76mm, 81mm and 105mm ammunition was also released at the same time and all supplied to Nigeria on a "strictly cash" basis.[153] Much of this was flown to Lagos and Kano by a number of charter flights out of the UK by several British independent operators. Exactly how many arms flights were made from Britain is difficult to determine but as somebody suggested, "one doesn't go to Lagos for the benefit of one's health!". Conversely, not all of these flights may have carried arms, some definitely did. Flights were primarily routed out of Gatwick and Stansted and it is interesting to note that most of the outbound flights needed to refuel at Idris/Tripoli but on the return flights, when presumably flying empty, the trip was made non-stop. Examples of such flights made during 1967/68 are as follows:

Date	Aircraft	Operator	Flight details (times shown in Z)
4.9.67	Britannia 102 G-ANBN	Laker	Departed Gatwick 2315 to Idris/Tripoli. Arrived Gatwick 1840 (6.9.67) from Lagos as GK1020
5.9.67	Britannia 312 G-AOVH	Caledonian	Departed Gatwick 2026 to Lagos as CA465. Arrived Gatwick 1644 (7.9.67) from Lagos as CA466
6.9.67	Britannia 102 G-ANBN	Laker	Departed Gatwick 2258 to Idris/Tripoli. Arrived Gatwick 1859 (on 8.9.67) from Lagos
17.9.67	Britannia 312 G-AOVI	Caledonian	Departed Gatwick 2303 to Lagos as CA467
20.9.67	Britannia 102 G-ANBM	Transglobe	Arrived Gatwick 1928 from Lagos as IK1038
22.9.67	Britannia 102 G-ANBN	Laker	Arrived Gatwick 1933 from Lagos
14.11.67	Britannia 314 G-ATGD	Transglobe	Departed Gatwick 1828 to Idris/Tripoli as IK1131. Arrived Gatwick 1504 (on 16.11.67) from Lagos
26.11.67	Britannia 312 G-AOVI	Caledonian	Arrived Gatwick 1612 from Lagos as CA498
19.12.67	DC-7CF G-ATMF	TMAC	Departed Gatwick 1950 to Idris/Tripoli. Arrived Gatwick 2156 (on 21.12.67) from Kano
16.2.68	Britannia 102 G-ANBN	Laker	Departed Gatwick 2119 to Idris/Tripoli as GK057. Arrived Gatwick 1813 (18.2.68) from Lagos as GK058
18.2.68	Britannia 102 G-ANBM	Laker	Arrived Gatwick 1906 from Lagos as GK060
5.3.68	Britannia 102 G-ANBM	Laker	Departed Gatwick 1947 to Idris/Tripoli. Arrived Gatwick 1959 (on 7.3.68) from Lagos
10.4.68	Britannia 102 G-ANBM	Laker	Departed Gatwick 1905 to Idris/Tripoli. Arrived Gatwick 1826 (on 12.4.68) from Lagos
18.4.68	Britannia 314 G-ATLE	Transglobe	Departed Gatwick 0032 to Idris/Tripoli as IK290. Arrived Gatwick 0450 (on 19.4.68) from Lagos
18.4.68	Britannia 314 G-ATGD	Transglobe	Departed Gatwick 1911 to Idris/Tripoli. Arrived Gatwick 2331 (on 19.4.68) from Lagos
21.4.68	Britannia 314 G-ATLE	Transglobe	Departed Gatwick 2132 to Idris/Tripoli as IK298. Arrived Gatwick 2150 (on 30.4.68) from Lagos
21.4.68	DC-7CF G-AVXH	TMAC	Departed Stansted 1139 to Gatwick; departed Gatwick 1307 to Idris/Tripoli. Returned to Stansted 1517 (on 25.4.68) from Dublin
21.4.68	DC-7CF G-AWBI	TMAC	Departed Stansted 1146 to Gatwick. Arrived Stansted 1926 (on 29.4.68) from Lagos
25.4.68	Britannia 314 G-ATGD	Transglobe	Departed Gatwick 1818 to Idris/Tripoli. Arrived Gatwick 2017 (on 26.4.68) from Lagos
20.5.68	CL-44D-4 G-AWDK	Transglobe	Departed Gatwick 2050 to Lagos. Arrived Gatwick 2135 (on 21.5.68) from Lagos
23.5.68	CL-44D-4 G-AWDK	Transglobe	Departed Gatwick 2114 to Lagos. Arrived Gatwick 2022 (on 24.5.68) from Lagos
7.6.68	CL-44D-4 G-AWGT	Transglobe	Arrived Gatwick 1910 from Lagos
21.6.68	CL-44D-4 G-AWDK	Transglobe	Departed Gatwick 1731 to Manston. Arrived Gatwick 0307 (on 23.6.68) from Lagos

Several flights also originated from Manston. On 7 June 1968, Trans Meridian Air Cargo DC-7CF G-AVXH visited Manston, followed by two British Eagle Airways Britannia 312s, G-AOVC and G-AOVN, on 11 June. All three aircraft are known to have cleared outbound customs to Lagos with full loads of British arms.[154]

Nigerian DC-3s and Whirlwinds

The question of logistical support to airfields closer to the war zone clearly necessitated a squadron of transport aircraft. In what was seen initially as a temporary measure was the transfer of Nigeria Airways' remaining five Douglas DC-3s (5N-AAL, 5N-AAM, 5N-AAN, 5N-AAP & 5N-AAQ) to the Nigerian Air Force. Although only a temporary measure the Nigerian authorities still displayed administrative disciplines by officially cancelling the civilian marks as each aircraft was formally accepted. Thus 5N-AAN, 5N-AAP and 5N-AAQ were cancelled on 4 August 1967, followed by 5N-AAL on 16 August and 5N-AAM on 28 August. Curiously none of these aircraft were allocated Nigerian Air Force serials in the standard fashion underlining the perceived temporary nature of their transfer. Instead the national 5N- prefix was deleted and the aircraft operated simply as 'AAN', 'AAP' etc throughout the entire war period. Towards the end of the civil war, during the autumn of 1969, five additional DC-3s were purchased directly from SABENA and which became NAF303-NAF307, these serials presumably following on from the two N.2501D Noratlas transports.[155]

The manner in which the Federal authorities allocated serial blocks in an almost strict numerical sequence suggests that delivery of a batch of eight Westland Whirlwind Srs.2 helicopters took place during late-July or early-August 1967. All were purchased from the Austrian Air Force after they had been withdrawn from use in 1964, apparently due to their poor performance at high altitude. All arrived at Lagos by ship and conveyed to Lagos-Ikeja for rudimentary servicing and test-flights.

Operationally, the Whirlwinds were not used to any great degree in the war effort. Each of the airfields where L-29s or MiG-17s were operational (ie Benin, Calabar,

52: A March 1968 view of Lagos/Ikeja airport shows three Nigerian Air Force Whirlwind Mk.2s. An unmarked example (thought to be NAF506) takes to the air and clearly displays a darkened patch on the doors where the former Austrian Air Force serial and insignia have been crudely erased. The other Whirlwinds in this view are NAF503 (left) and NAF505 (right); in the centre background is L-29 Delfin NAF401 (Ares Klootwyk)

53: The Nigerian Air Force Whirlwinds were dispersed to front-line airfields where they acted in a search-and-rescue role as well as being used for communications. NAF504 was ferried from Lagos to Port Harcourt, via Benin, on 8 November 1969 (possibly to augment or replace NAF508). NAF504 is seen at Port Harcourt in standard scheme (Ares Klootwyk)

54: The Nigerian Air Force acquired the C-54B G-ARWI from Lloyd International on 14 December 1968 and immediately re-serialled it as NAF311. Marian Kozubski undertook an acceptance test-flight at Lagos on 17 December 1968 but it is doubtful that many subsequent flights were made. Reports suggest that the aircraft suffered from continuous engine problems and eventually it was discarded at the side of Lagos airport. In this view NAF311 is accompanied by one of the former Austrian Air Force Westland Whirlwind Mk.2 helicopters (Confidential Source)

Enugu, and Port Harcourt) had a locally-based Whirlwind for search-and-rescue duty.

The Whirlwind 2s were augmented, in September 1967, by a single Gnome-powered Srs 3 example (G-APDY) which the Nigerian Air Force purchased from Bristow Helicopters Ltd, with the blessing of the Ministry of Defence. This had become NAF502 and by March 1968 was based at Calabar for local communications duties as well as performing a search and rescue in that area.[156]

With the exception of NAF508 (which is known to have been the former Austrian Air Force 4D-XS) it has not been possible to confirm precise links between Nigerian and the original Austrian Air Force serials. Nor has much been recorded about their fates within Nigeria. It is, of course, just possible that it was aboard one of the ex-Austrian Whirlwinds that the Nigerian Chief of Staff, Colonel Joe Akahan was killed when it crashed near Makurdi on 9 August 1967. Contemporary reports state only that he was killed aboard a Nigerian Air Force helicopter.[157]

Moscow and the L-29

Ultimately, it was the embargo imposed by the west that led Nigeria towards Moscow. Exploratory talks between Nigeria and the Soviet Union had started during the spring of 1967 but only after Ojukwu had declared his independent state of Biafra did any sense of real urgency emerge. Then, towards the end of June 1967, a delegation from Lagos arrived in Moscow ostensibly to make an official inspection of the Nigerian embassy there; in reality the delegation talked further to the Russians about arms. To the Soviets, Nigeria was seen as a strategically-important new customer for jet aircraft.

At the end of July 1967 a second delegation travelled to Moscow where a cultural agreement, initialled in Lagos four months previously, was signed on 2 August 1967 by Anthony Enahoro, the Nigerian Commissioner of Information. Less than two weeks later, two Czech-built LET L-29 Delfin jets were ferried by air to Nigeria. When the aircraft made a refuelling stop at Accra, Ghana, both were seen to be in full Nigerian Air Force insignia and markings.[158] At the same time a number of new-build examples were shipped to Lagos where they were assembled and test-flown by Czech technicians and pilots. The L-29s, which were serialled in the NAF401-408 range and allegedly cost the Nigerians a unit price of US$238,000, were equipped to carry both rockets and small bombs. All were initially based at Lagos-Ikeja airport but later operated a Detachment at Benin. For a while they were Federal Nigeria's primary ground-attack aircraft.[159]

The L-29s were the first of Nigeria's jets to enter operational service towards the end of August 1967, one of the earliest sorties being against Port Harcourt when the Ghana Airways DC-3, 9G-AAD, was hit by rockets.[160]

Precisely how many L-29s were supplied at the start of the Nigerian Civil War is still unclear. So is the source of this initial batch. At least eight aircraft were in Nigeria by September 1967 but according to LET production records only seven were supplied ex-factory. This could indicate that several were second-hand aircraft; considering the speed by which the first two were flown to Nigeria, it is just possible that the first two L-29s (NAF401/402) were, in fact, former Soviet Air Force examples.[161]

The first MiGs arrive and the Biafrans attack

In mid-August 1967, Kano airport was closed to international air traffic and remained so for three weeks afterwards. Only a handful of domestic flights by Nigeria Airways' F-27 Friendships were allowed to land there amidst very strict security measures. Apart from those issued with special passes, all members of the public were prohibited from entering the airport area. Then, on 18 August and with the mid-point of Nigeria's rainy season providing a murky backdrop for their arrival, fifteen overall drab-grey Soviet Air Force Antonov An-12s landed at Kano. The first arrival was met by numerous senior-ranking Nigerian government officials as well as the Emir of Kano and staff from the Soviet embassy. For just over two hours An-12s landed at approximately 10-minute intervals. (Although there can be little doubt that these aircraft were being operated by the Soviet Air Force, each did carry small Aeroflot titles and civil registrations to facilitate easier overflying of countries en route. In landing sequence the An-12s were CCCP-11217, CCCP-11416, CCCP-11397, CCCP-11113, CCCP-11659, CCCP-11109, CCCP-11433, CCCP-11655, CCCP-11115, CCCP-11401, CCCP-11105, CCCP-11102, CCCP-11420, CCCP-11431 and CCCP-11432.) But it was not simply the arrival of Soviet Air Force An-12s which had warranted the closure of Kano; it was their cargo. The An-12s had brought in Nigeria's first delivery of MiG-17F fighters as well as a pair of MiG-15UTI trainers. Accompanying the MiGs was a task force of some thirty Soviet technicians all of whom remained at Kano, setting up base in the old and disused terminal building, to assemble the fighters–all of the MiGs had been airfreighted in minus their wings and top tail sections–and help with flight-instruction.[162]

The Antonov An-12s began leaving Kano early on Saturday morning, 19 August 1967, all flying back to the Soviet Union via Annaba (in Algeria) and Sarajevo (Jugoslavia), reportedly the same route back as the one they took on the way down. But it had not taken long for news of events at Kano to leak through to Biafran High Command; in fact so good was Biafran intelligence that on Saturday 19 August, the day after the MiGs had arrived, the Biafran Air Force launched a sortie by its B-26R Invader against Kano airport. Not only was the intelligence good but it seemed as though the B-26R crew knew precisely when the An-12s were departing; the B-26R

55: L-29 Delfin NAF407 is positioned at Benin sometime in mid-1968. Notable in this view are the underwing rails for unguided rockets. Like the MiG-17F it was aircraft in this role that the Biafrans feared most. (The author recalls being subjected to an air-to-ground rocket attack by a single Nigerian Air Force L-29 when it targeted the wreckage of the Anson G-AWMG at Uzuakoli on 4 Sept 1968) (Nigerian Air Force)

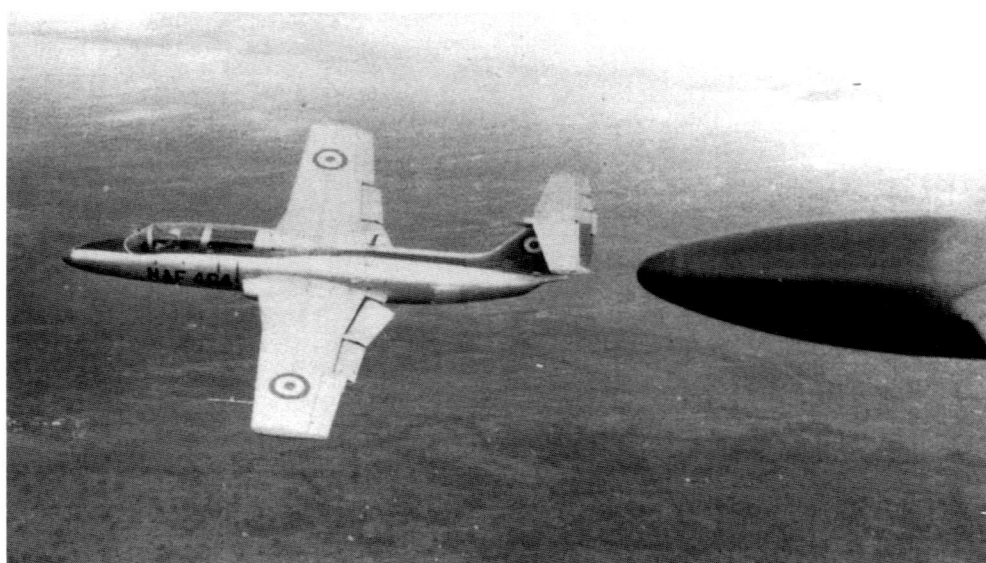

56: A fine air-to-air view of L-29 NAF404, taken from the Nigerian Air Force Jet Provost NAF701. The simplistic scheme applied to the L-29s was considerably enhanced by the green trim, especially along the dorsal spine (Ares Klootwyk)

57: Benin City, November 1968. Ares Klootwyk, Jimmy Webb and Derek Calderhead pose in front of a Nigerian Air Force L-29 Delfin. Calderhead (right) later gained an infamous reputation as 'Genocide' after he began transmitting threatening broadcasts from the Nigerian DC-3 bomber to relief pilots approaching the Biafran strip at Uli (Ares Klootwyk Collection)

arrived over Kano just after the final Soviet aircraft had departed. Piloted by the French mercenary, Durang, and with Ezeilo as co-pilot, it was the Biafran gunner, Anthony Alaribe, who later described the sortie.[163]

"The weather was fine at first, but between Makurdi and Lafia dark clouds closed in and the pilot gained altitude to avoid them. We got to Kano after almost two hours' flight, keeping a vigilant look-out for interceptors from any direction. We now sighted Kano's old terminal building, with the jets already parked in front of it.

"We went into a dive, levelled off and on our first pass strafed the aircraft, hitting their engines and landing gears, before they passed out of sight. On the second pass we nearly ran into an anti-aircraft gun, but the pilot outsmarted the gunner. We came in again, this time from the rear, and I blasted that gun position with bullets, leaving nobody to man it.

"We then climbed and dropped our bombs, aiming at the aircraft. One bomb hit a wing of the terminal building. The bomb blasts left many of the aircraft completely destroyed. On that pass when we pulled away again we narrowly escaped colliding with the side of a building, as we were still trying to avoid the many anti-aircraft guns, Russian Oerlikons that fired bursts like machine-guns. We did not want to run short on ammunition as there might be jet fighters waiting for us on our way home.

"Now we headed for home; we immediately turned away towards Cameroon and spent about thirty minutes waiting and observing. We then headed for Enugu and home, and finally landed safely with the aircraft."

Although Alaribe claimed to have destroyed a number of MiG-17s during the Kano raid there is no evidence from those on the ground at Kano to support that claim. Some workers at Kano had seen the Biafran aircraft rather haphazardly drop what closely resembled oil-drums filled with explosive. Even so there was an official admission after the raid that some crates containing spares had been damaged and that the old airport terminal building had sustained some damage. But that was all. What tends to suggest that some of the MiGs may have been damaged beyond repair is the fact that each of the Soviet An-12s had reportedly brought in one MiG. Therefore it can be assumed that fifteen MiGs were unloaded from fifteen An-12s on 18 August, yet the first block of Nigerian Air Force MiG serial numbers consisted of only ten aircraft, the first two of which were MiG-15UTI trainers and serialled NAF601-602, the remainder (NAF603-610) being MiG-17F variants. This would suggest that five aircraft may have been badly damaged or written-off during the Biafran Air Force attack. Alternatively, five of the An-12s may have been carrying only spares and that Nigeria in fact received just ten MiGs on the August 1967 airlift. But whatever the true extent of damage was at Kano the Nigerians could count themselves extremely fortunate. Had the Biafran attack been a little more professional and with bombs other than a homemade variety, Nigeria's entire front-line strike force of MiG-17Fs, all of which were being assembled in the open air almost at the point of unloading, could have been wiped out. Instead, work continued and the first re-assembled example took to the air at Kano on Monday, 21 August. Piloted by a Soviet officer, the MiG made two low-level runs across Kano and promptly put the fear of the devil into an already frightened local population.

The source of Nigeria's MiG-17Fs has been one of constant debate. The popular belief is that they originated from Egypt. All arrived in Nigeria in a clean finish, ie devoid of any national insignia or markings–with the possible exception of (at least) one MiG-17F. This exception (which became NAF605) carried a rear fuselage band in a manner exclusive to the Egyptian Air Force. It is this example which supports the theory that all of the MiGs were indeed acquired from Egypt and which may well have been the case. (Standard Kremlin procedure would have been to supply equipment from the United Arab Republic against subsequent replacement by the Soviets.) However, it is the source of the An-12s used to ferry the MiGs to Nigeria which serve to inject some doubt. It would have made sense, even by Soviet standards, to position fifteen An-12s based in Eastern Europe or in the Moscow area to Eqypt–there certainly was no shortage. Instead, all of the An-12s used for ferrying the MiGs to Nigeria appear to have originated from fairly obscure transport units in Siberia where, coincidentally, the MiG-17 Overhaul & former Production facility existed, at Novosibirsk. It is just possible therefore that these MiGs simply originated from Siberia, ie Soviet stocks, but included several Egyptian examples that had been returned to Siberia for extensive overhauls. Whatever the source of the MiGs was they had, together with the L-29 Delfins, considerably raised the stakes in the shooting war.[164]

The first MiG-17F sortie took place on 30 August 1967 when a single aircraft carried out a strafing attack along Biafra's northern border. The results were hard to define, a factor that became a major problem within the Nigerian Air Force. But a greater problem facing the Nigerians was the question of who would fly the MiGs. Some Nigerians had previously received jet training in Canada and West Germany before the civil war none had any combat experience. A small group of Czech pilots were based at Lagos and from whom Nigerian Air Force pilots underwent conversion training. There was also a handful of Soviet pilots at Kano but their responsibility was solely to test-fly the MiGs and to train Nigerian pilots; Moscow had specifically refused to allow its pilots to fly combat missions. But Nigeria did not have to look far afield, the Soviet Union had arranged for a group of Egyptians (certainly no more than 25 or 30) to fly and maintain the MiG-17Fs until a sufficient number of Nigerians had been fully trained. But the reliance upon Egyptian pilots had, for the Nigerians, never been a satisfactory arrangement.

The MiG-15UTI trainers were permanently stationed at Kano where all of the initial jet training and conversion flying was carried out. Some Nigerian pilots did successfully convert to the MiG-17 but few achieved operational combat experience. Without doubt Egyptian pilots carried out all of the operations throughout 1967 and until mid-1968. Two young Nigerians, Major Usman Jibrin and a Major Gammal, did later achieve a standard sufficient to act as Instructor on the MiG-15UTI and went on to convert most of the mercenary pilots at Kano.[165]

Nigerian Jet Provosts

Not all of Nigeria's front-line jet force originated from the Soviet bloc; six weeks after the fighting had started two Jet Provost T.51s (export versions of the standard R.A.F. Mk. T.3) were acquired, ostensibly as a gift from the Sudanese government.[166] Both aircraft had been declared surplus to Sudan's requirements and flown from the Sudan to Kano by two British ex-R.A.F. pilots, Ralph Swift and Mike Thompsett.

It would be unfair to suggest that the British government was instrumental in the transfer from Sudan to Nigeria, or that the two pilots were 'seconded' to Nigeria. Certainly the British were aware that the pilots, one of whom had been allowed to resign his commission in the RAF (at extremely short notice), had been hired by the Nigerian Air Force. The British government also knew that the aircraft were in Nigeria; so much so that among military supplies flown from Britain to Nigeria in September 1967 were "three wheel covers for Jet Provosts and a quantity of ejector seat cartridges".[167]

From Kano the Jet Provosts were flown on to the Nigerian Air Force base at Kaduna where, towards the end of August 1967, a third pilot, Paul Martin, (who had also recently resigned a commission with the RAF) joined the Nigerian Air Force Training & Tactical Wing's newly-formed Jet Provost Flight. The aircraft, armed with two .303 Browning machine-guns and underwing rocket launchers, were re-serialled NAF701 and NAF702 and briefly air-tested. Very little attention appears to have been given to their serviceability status although the only recorded snag was a tendency for the guns on NAF702 to frequently jam. Nevertheless both Jet Provosts were quickly pressed into service and ferried to their operational base at Makurdi; NAF701 on 2 September, followed by '702 six days later. Interestingly, Makurdi was the base of No.1 Fighter/Bomber Squadron, NAF but there was no official change of unit allocation for the Jet Provosts and both continued to operate under of the aegis of the Training & Tactical Wing.

The first operational raid by a Nigerian Jet Provost took place on 4 September when Ralph Swift and Paul Martin carried out an attack over Ogugru. Two days later, and using NAF701 again, the same crew made a dawn raid against Enugu airfield where the crew reported success at hitting one of the Biafran B-26s and also seriously damaged a Biafran Air Force DC-3, presumably the former Nigeria Airways' 5N-AAK. Biafran anti-aircraft defences had proved to be fairly intense and accurate. The Jet Provost suffered six direct hits by small-arms fire and was immediately flown back to Kaduna for repairs.

There can be few doubts that the two Jet Provosts performed admirably, both in a training and ground-attack role. It was also easier to fly than the Soviet MiG-17F and thereby allowed a greater opportunity for Nigerian pilots to undertake offensive missions over Biafra. During a regular meeting between Enahoro and the British High Commission in Lagos the Nigerian quietly admitted that the experience of Egyptian-crewed MiG-17s had been a disaster, the pilots being useless. In a confidential telex (dated 28 October 1968) back to London the British High Commission in Lagos described the two Jet Provosts already in use as being "more useful and effective in an offensive capacity than all their MiGs put together." The comment was accompanied by a recommendation that more Jet Provosts be released to Nigeria. A formal (and personal) request by letter was sent by Gowon to Prime Minister Harold Wilson on 5 November 1968 for six BAC.167 trainers. On 8 November Wilson called Enahoro and Brigadier Ogundipe (the Nigerian High Commissioner) into 10 Downing Street and formally rejected the request for BAC.167s on the basis that new-build aircraft would not be ready for eighteen months and that the RAF would have to close down units in order to release any existing aircraft. Instead Wilson suggested that the Nigerian government make an approach to Airwork Ltd who were servicing new Jet Provosts with the South Yemen and the Sudan Air Forces.[168] This of course would not have involved the British Government but whether any formal approach was made is unknown. What is known is that Soviet Air Force Antonov An-12s were once again rumbling into Kano airport.

The Nigerian Air Force therefore operated just the two Jet Provosts. They continued to operate from Kaduna, mainly in a training role for Nigerian student pilots, but were regularly detached to Makurdi for sorties against targets in Biafra. Even during early 1968 all three British pilots (Swift, Martin and Thompsett) were making regular live missions over Biafra. But, curiously, they attracted very little publicity. Then, one of them made headlines in the West German newspaper, *Frankfurter Algemeine Zertung*.

On 23 June 1969, it was reported, a "two-seat British-built training jet forced-landed in the shallow waters of a lagoon near the town of Porto Norve, Dahomey." The aircraft, fully camouflaged with Nigerian Air Force markings, was fitted with live rockets. According to the press report, "a British pilot occupied the left-hand seat". The

58: The Nigerian Air Force's two Jet Provosts were very rarely photographed. Both performed well, especially in a ground attack role, but suffered from poor maintenance. Just visible in this view of NAF701, at Benin in 1968, is the unusual serial presentation 'NAF' aft of the fuselage roundel and '701' above the fin flash. The nose cone appears to be considerably weather-beaten. The significance of what appears to be a (red?) cat figure on a white disc is unknown. In this view three of Nigeria's principal 'white mercenary' pilots pose in front of NAF701. They are (left to right) Mike Thompsett (British) and South Africans Charlie Vivier and Ares Klootwyk. The Nigerian on the far right is believed to be Captain Alfa (Ares Klootwyk Collection)

59: Air-to-air views of Nigerian Air Force MiG-17Fs are not too common. NAF608 makes a pleasing subject and displays the serial presentation style (with the roundel) adopted for the initial batch of aircraft. Also in evidence are the underwing rails for six rockets. Flying NAF608 on this occasion was Jimmy Webb, photographed by Ares Klootwyk while on a sortie from Benin. Webb and Klootwyk flew together on several occasions but the only time when Webb was flying NAF608 was on 23 November 1968 (Ares Klootwyk)

60: The profile of a MiG-17F in bomber configuration is considerably different to the standard view of it with underwing fuel tanks. Without the auxilliary fuel tanks the endurance was little more than 45 minutes. In this view, taken at Benin on 25 November 1968, MiG-17F NAF615 is fitted with two 100kg bombs ready for a night sortie against Uli strip. South African mercenary pilots Ares Klootwyk and Jimmy Webb pose for what was the first night sortie by a MiG-17F flown by a non-Egyptian pilot. Webb flew MiG-17F NAF616 the same night on an attack against Ugu (via Ares Klootwyk)

aircraft was in fact the Nigerian Air Force Jet Provost NAF701 and the pilot was indeed British; he was Mike Thompsett, one of the ex-RAF pilots hired by the Nigerian Government. His presence in Dahomey was simply an embarrassingly unfortunate result of getting lost in very low cloud over the Lagos area, and then of straying westward across an international border. Any assertions that British pilots were not flying military sorties in Nigeria had been blown.

The report in the West German press could have recorded a slightly wrong interpretation of the events. There seems little doubt that the Jet Provost NAF701 had strayed into Dahomey but instead of landing in shallow water had managed to land at an airfield where it was speedily refuelled and flown back to Lagos.[169]

Nigeria hires mercenaries

The first mercenary pilots hired by the Nigerian government arrived just after the fighting had started but were contracted specifically to fly L-29 Delfins and the impressed DC-3s. Most had, only weeks beforehand, left the Congo after the war that had raged there for some seven years had dramatically drawn to a conclusion. Among the early arrivals were David Vaughan-Games, Frenchman Pierre Berthe and two South Africans, Ivan Maritz and Bill Fortuin. All had earlier flown in the Congo civil war and several were selected for an L-29 Conversion Course in Prague but as it turned out all conversion flying was carried out by Czech instructors in Nigeria. As soon as several pilots had converted to the L-29 the Czech instructors left Nigeria. Not all of the mercenary pilots stayed either; Fortuin, who flew L-29s and DC-3s, was asked to leave Nigeria at the end of 1967, reportedly as a result of the publicity his presence had created. Vaughan-Games was later invalided out of Nigeria with a collapsed lung, caused by a blood clot after a Nigerian bomb handler had accidentally dropped an unfused 100kg bomb on his leg.[170]

Following their transfer to the military, the former Nigeria Airways DC-3s were kept at Lagos for general transport duties. A number of company pilots, especially the non-Nigerian crews, had also transferred with the aircraft, including two Poles, Roman Hrycak and Marian Kozubski. Hrycak had been the airline's Chief Pilot and had only tempted Kozubski to move down from Aden in mid-1967.[171] But Kozubski, like many Poles outside the Soviet bloc, held an intense dislike of the Russians and, when asked to ferry a group of Russian technicians up to Kano, promptly resigned his position. He travelled firstly to São Tomé in the hope of finding work with the Biafrans but eventually took up an appointment flying DC-3s with Guyana Airways. Kozubski later returned to Nigeria and remained there for much of the war but many of the mercenary pilots who took flying jobs in Nigeria simply undertook a short-term assignment for easy money. There were, of course, some exceptions and several Nigeria Airways pilots were sacked for refusing to fly for the Air Force, including two Swedish pilots, Borje Anderson and Ola Sandberg, who were expelled on 27 October 1967 after refusing to fly a government charter flight to Enugu a week beforehand.[172]

A number of the early arrivals in Nigeria were recruited by the former Congo mercenary leader, Yorkshire-born John Peters. Peters, who led the infamous Congo 5 Commando from November 1965 to February 1967, had contracted with the Nigerian government to supply pilots for the Nigerian Air Force. In January 1968 a group of pilots arrived in Lagos, consisting of some six South Africans and two Belgians. Among the South Africans was one Ares Erasmus Klootwyk, and probably one of the best combat pilots to fly with the Nigerians. The son of a senior officer in the South African Army, Klootwyk had flown with the Royal Air Force in Bahrein–serving with 152 Squadron–and eventually served several tours of duty with the Nigerian Air Force. Rated by colleagues in Nigeria as having quite exceptional flying skills, his first flight there was a thirty-minute familiarisation flight aboard one of the ex-Austrian Whirlwind Mk.2s (NAF504) on 13 January 1968; he later converted to L-29 Delfins at Benin in August 1968.[173]

The Westland Widgeon

Apart from the Whirlwinds, there was one other helicopter taken onto Nigerian Air Force stock during the civil war. This was the former Bristow Helicopters' Westland Widgeon 5N-AGA. Captured intact at the Biafran Helicopter Headquarters base at Udi, in early February 1968, the Widgeon was flown by Ares Klootwyk on 2 February from Udi to Enugu. The helicopter performed without any major snag and after an overnight stay Klootwyk and a Nigerian officer, Lt Ayuba, flew from Enugu to Oturkpo and on to Makurdi. 5N-AGA remained at Makurdi for several days before Klootwyk (accompanied by a Lt Bashim) flew the Widgeon from Makurdi to Lagos-Ikeja, via Benin.

Despite the fact that the Widgeon was still in Bristow Helicopters' livery the Nigerian Government never formally admitted to Bristows that it was one of their original helicopters. Instead 5N-AGA was repainted in an overall light grey scheme and with a large Nigerian roundel applied to the cabin sides. A newly allocated serial, NAF510, was painted along the boom. On 14 February 1968, and only twelve days after its capture from the Biafrans, Klootwyk made a brief flight from Dodan Barracks, Lagos with the Federal Nigerian leader, General Gowon, aboard.

Klootwyk made a number of flights in the Widgeon, often accompanied by other mercenary pilots or mechanics. They included the South African pilot Charlie Vivier,

61: The former Bristow Widgeon 5N-AGA looked very attractive in Nigerian Air Force markings. Complete with the serial NAF510 it stands at Lagos in between flights. Note the full serial is repeated on the nose (Ares Klootwyk)

62: Eventually, and perhaps not surprisingly. the Nigerian Air Force Widgeon was written-off in an accident. For a while it suffered from bad vibration but little, or no, investigation was made to determine the cause. In June 1968 the tail-rotor drive shaft failed as it was taking-off from Lagos airport. NAF510 was wrecked. In the background can be seen the Northern Regional Government's Heron 5N-ABH and the fin of a visiting Lufthansa Boeing 707 (Terry Peet)

63: The rear section of Widgeon NAF510 survived at Ojo Barracks, Lagos for some time afterwards. This view was taken in July 1970 at a time of a major building programme to house the thousands of Nigerian Army soldiers returning from the occupied areas of former Biafra. Quite why this section was retained remains unknown but it does illustrate the effect of a tail-rotor failure (Confidential Source)

the Frenchman Pierre Berthe and a South African mechanic, Jimmy Calderhead, who was to later gain a degree of notoriety aboard Nigeria's military DC-3s. In early June 1968 Klootwyk left Nigeria on leave having given instructions to the senior helicopter mechanic, Cliff 'Yorkie' Grimes, to establish the source of some bad vibration felt on his final flight. However, on 22 June, another British mercenary pilot, Terry Peet, who was presumably unaware of the vibration problem, decided to make a local flight. Just after getting airborne the Widgeon's tail-rotor drive shaft failed and NAF510 was wrecked in the crash that followed. Peet did not suffer any injury.

A summary of flights made by Ares Klootwyk aboard Widgeon 5N-AGA/NAF510 is as follows:

Westland Widgeon 5N-AGA/NAF510 Flights by Ares Klootwyk

Date	Flight Detail	Hours
2.2.68	Udi-Enugu (+2 passengers)	0.30
3.2.68	Enugu-Oturkpo-Makurdi (+Lt Ayuba)	2.00
7.2.68	Makurdi-Benin-Lagos (+Lt Bashim)	5.15
14.2.68	Lagos-Lagos (+ 4 passengers)	1.00
4.3.68	Lagos-Lagos (+ Jimmy Calderhead)	0.30
9.3.68	Lagos-Lagos (+ Jimmy Calderhead)	0.30
14.3.68	Lagos-Lagos (+ Pierre Berthe)	0.30
16.3.68	Lagos-Lagos (solo)	0.40
19.3.68	Lagos-Lagos (+ Charlie Vivier)	0.40
26.3.68	Flight aborted (with 3 passengers)	0.15
1.4.68	Lagos-Lagos (+ 1 passenger)	0.15
5.4.68	Lagos-Lagos (solo air-test)	0.15
8.4.68	Lagos-Lagos (solo)	0.15
17.4.68	Lagos-Keri Keri-Lagos (solo)	0.40
18.5.68	Lagos-Lagos (solo)	0.50
21.5.68	Lagos-Keri Keri-Lagos (solo)	0.30
29.5.68	Lagos-Keri Keri-Lagos (+ Terry Peet)	0.30
30.5.68	Lagos-Keri Keri-Lagos (+ Lt Okpere)	0.30
4.6.68	Lagos-Keri Keri-Lagos (solo)	0.30

Nigerian Air Force C-54 and DC-7C

At the end of 1968 the Nigerian Air Force acquired a Douglas C-54B. Lloyd International Airways had sold the aircraft, G-ARWI, to the French company Air Fret during mid-December 1968 but who immediately sold it to the Nigerian Air Force, on 14 December. The transaction was effectively between Lloyd and the Nigerian government but Air Fret acted as broker to avoid some of the restrictions in sales to Nigeria. The aircraft was ferried from Southend to Lagos, via Tripoli, by two former Air Ferry pilots, Peter 'Paddy' Roberts and Alan Breedon. Roberts stayed on in Nigeria for a while and shortly afterwards accompanied Marian Kozubski on a 45-minute acceptance flight flight out of Lagos on 17 December. Immediately afterwards the it was officially accepted by the Air Force, and allotted the serial NAF311. However, the Nigerian Air Force made little, if any, use of the C-54B due to it suffering almost continuous trouble with two of its engines.[174] NAF311 was not the only aircraft in Nigeria to have suffered with poor engines.

In propaganda terms, the acquisition by the Federal Nigerian authorities of the ex-Biafran airlift DC-7C PH-SAE proved to be one of the most valuable. The aircraft had been flown from São Tomé to Lagos on 7 June 1968 by two Americans and immediately on to Kaduna. It remained at Kaduna for several months while the Nigerians tried to make use of their new acquisition. Initially two Lagos-based mercenary pilots, Terry Peet and Henri Laurient (both being ex-Congo pilots and now hired by the Nigerians to fly DC-3s) were approached and even encouraged to operate the DC-7C for the Air Force. But both men refused on the grounds that the DC-7C's control systems were far too complex. Subsequently the two Polish pilots, Marian Kozubski and Roman Hrycak, were contracted to fly it and duly reported to Kaduna to acquaint themselves with the DC-7C.[175]

Hrycak noted that some attempt to rather crudely erase the aircraft's identity from the fuselage. The flight-deck identity showed it as being "5N-AOW" (but this was not an official allocation). After some gentle coaxing the engines were started and, at 10:40 hours on 7 September 1968, Kozubski and Hrycak took-off for a two-hour positioning flight to Lagos. Despite its rough-running and the excessive vibration the DC-7C was, a week later, impressed into Air Force service for a series of supply flights between Lagos and Port Harcourt. With hindsight, Hrycak later questioned his own sanity for attempting to fly an aircraft in such a poor state. It was effectively beyond repair and not surprisingly abandoned at Lagos several weeks afterwards.[176]

Although the flight from Kaduna to Lagos was recorded as a positioning flight, both pilots later admitted that it was more of a familiarisation flight as, despite their extensive experience, neither was officially type-rated on a DC-7. Hrycak also realised, during the flight to Lagos, that the aircraft was in a worse mechanical state than initially perceived and immediately on landing at Lagos ordered essential maintenance be carried out before its next flight.

'5N-AOW' spent almost a week undergoing correction of major snags at Lagos. Then, during the morning of 13 September it was loaded with a full cargo of 250lb and 500lb bombs. At 12:50 hours, with Hrycak in command, Kozubski in the right-hand seat and a young Nigerian, Captain Adejoh, acting as Flight Engineer, the aircraft took-off from Lagos for the first of several planned supply flights to Port Harcourt. A second flight from Lagos to Port Harcourt took place on the following day. The crew remained as before apart from Captain Adejoh being replaced by another Nigerian, Captain Ozah.

Another week of inactivity at Lagos followed before the three-man crew of Hrycak, Kozubski and Ozah were called to make another flight. At 08:00 on 19 September '5N-AOW' left Lagos for a third ammunition run to Port Harcourt. On this occasion the unloading took just under two hours before the aircraft was back in the air at 11:25 for the return leg to Lagos. It was on this flight that the aircraft suffered total loss of power from one of its engines and the landing, at 12:55 hours, was undertaken with power from only three engines.

Yet again the DC-7C was grounded at Lagos for several days. This time a locally-based Irish mechanic attended to the faulty engine. On this occasion Hrycak and Kozubski both invited the mechanic to join them as a regular Flight Engineer; he flatly refused. So with just a crew of two, the fourth arms flight to Port Harcourt took place on 23 September. The DC-7C departed Lagos at 13:15, but after flying for only about 85 miles the number two engine failed again, and without any warning. The concern on the flight-deck was now not so much the faulty engine but on not having a Flight Engineer on board.

Because the aircraft was closer to Lagos the two Poles both agreed to turn back but only when he tried to feather the engine did Hrycak realise that the problem was not just confined to a faulty engine. When he tried to engage the propeller's electrical reduction gear the effect was minimal suggesting that the entire engine's electrical system had failed. Hrycak knew that there was an alternative method of feathering the propeller by using the aircraft's hydraulic system but because the hydraulics were accentuated by electrical power this attempt also failed. Hrycak's technical knowledge of the DC-7C, albeit only fairly basic, was enough to take him to the rear of the cabin roof and to the switches that connected the engine's batteries. What he found inside the switch-box was a simple handwritten instruction that read "SWITCH OFF IN CASE OF ENGINE FAILURE", the message having presumably been left by the Irish engineer at Lagos.

With the number two engine safely shut down and the prop feathered, Hrycak and Kozubski now concentrated on an emergency three-engine landing at Lagos and with a full load of ammunition. The lack of electrical power to the engines meant that reverse-thrust could not be engaged after landing and so, as a precaution, Hrycak left the flight-deck to check that the cargo was safely secured. What he did not anticipate finding among the ammunition were five petrified Nigerian Army conscripts seated on the cabin floor. All five had somehow smuggled themselves aboard at Lagos in the hope of getting back home to Port Harcourt. Hrycak had little alternative but to add a further element of fear by explaining the likelihood of a full emergency landing back at Lagos and suggested that all five passengers find a safe corner and brace themselves for a possible overrun.

The approach to Lagos was made at marginally above the recommended stalling speed. As the mainwheels touched down Kozubski cut all power on the three remaining engines; both crew applied heavy pressure on the brakes. Gradually the aircraft slowed and managed to stop just short of the bush area at the runway's far end.

Hrycak immediately climbed down from the cockpit and discovered that not only were the aircraft's freight doors already wide open but that one of his passengers was missing. It was then that he was told by the other conscripts that the missing member was so convinced that the DC-7C was going to crash and that the entire cargo would very likely explode that he had chanced his luck by jumping out just as the aircraft was landing. Unfortunately, it seems that he seriously misjudged the speed of the aircraft and the remains of his mutilated body were later removed from Lagos' main runway.[177]

In spite of attempts to rectify its damaged engine, the DC-7C never flew again. Instead, it was pushed to the end of a disused runway and into an area of rough bush.

A summary of flights made in Nigeria by the ex-Schreiner DC-7C is as follows:

Flights In Nigeria by DC-7C PH-SAE / 5N-AOW

Date	Flight Detail	Times (Z)	Duration
7.9.68	Kaduna-Lagos	1040-1240	2.00
13.9.68	Lagos-Port Harcourt	1255-1420	1.25
	Port Harcourt-Lagos	1455-1610	1.15
14.9.68	Lagos-Port Harcourt	1050-1220	1.30
	Port Harcourt-Lagos	1610-1730	1.20
19.9.68	Lagos-Port Harcourt	0800-0920	1.20
	Port Harcourt-Lagos	1125-1255	1.30
23.9.68	Lagos-Lagos	1315-1425	1.10

Russia supplies more MiGs

In spite of the extent to which the Soviet Union assisted Nigeria at the start of the Civil War and the permanent presence of Soviet technicians at Kano's Central Hotel, there was never a continuous airlift of Soviet military hardware throughout the war period. The Soviets did also provide technicians and engineers to assist with some of the upgrading of airfields for jet equipment. Russian workers extended the runway at Kaduna airfield and, after its capture from the Biafrans, the smaller airfield at Calabar. One of the Antonov An-12s (CCCP-11416), which had formed part of the huge delivery on 18 August 1967, did return eleven days afterwards with a cargo of ammunition and spares but it was then another eight months before any more Soviet deliveries to Nigeria took place. When they did, during April 1968, it was by three Antonov An-12s of the Egyptian Air Force (SU-AOR, SU-AOS, SU-AOZ) which landed at Kano on 26 April with further MiG-17 spares. On the following day, 27 April, four Soviet Air Force/Aeroflot An-12s (CCCP-11256, CCCP-11263, CCCP-11393 and CCCP-11398)

64: *Four Egyptian mechanics at Port Harcourt are flanked by MiG-17F pilots Paul Martin (left) and the Australian, Noel Von Hoff (right). Both pilots flew several tours on Nigerian Air Force MiG-17s and on several occasions flew operational missions over Biafra as a pair (Paul Martin)*

65: *MiG-17F NAF617 was the aircraft in which Ares Klootwyk strafed the Flughjalp DC-6 TF-AAE as the latter was landing at Uli after dusk on 2 June 1969. The MiG-17F sustained minor damage by anti-aircraft fire but returned successfully to its Port Harcourt base. In this view, taken just after the raid, Klootwyk stands in the cockpit while Nigerian Air Force mechanics attend to repairs. Note the damaged starboard fuel tank; note also the apparent lack of a Nigerian fin flash on this particular MiG-17F (via Ares Klootwyk)*

66: *MiG-17F NAF616 was wrecked on 25 June 1969 when British mercenary John Pallister carried out a forced-landing on a road near Opobo, south of Port Harcourt. The emergency arose after the aircraft ran out of fuel but as the aircraft touched down the starboard wing struck a palm tree next to the road. Ares Klootwyk was flying NAF617 and returning from a separate mission at the time. Klootwyk landed and had his aircraft refuelled before taking-off to search for Pallister. After locating the wreckage Klootwyk and French mercenary Pierre Berthe flew down to the crash site in Whirlwind 2 NAF508 early the next morning. They took five passengers with them, some of whom are seen viewing the wrecked aircraft (Ares Klootwyk)*

67: *A small batch of attrition-replacement MiG-17Fs was air-freighted into Nigeria during April 1968. The four aircraft in question had their Nigerian markings applied in a non-standard fashion. NAF614 illustrates the crudely-applied serial and the 'wing' roundel on the fin. NAF614 rests at Enugu between sorties in early-1969 (Keith E. Sissons)*

68: *Although this aircraft is not armed with rockets the underwing rocket rails can be clearly seen in this view of MiG-17F NAF605 at Enugu. Unguided rocket attacks against Biafran targets were frequently made by MiG-17Fs throughout the Nigerian Civil War although strafing with cannon-fire was the more usual mode of operation (Keith E. Sissons)*

69: *An Egyptian Air Force (UARAF) MiG-17F, serial 2435, lies destroyed on the ground at Al Arish after Israeli attacks in the June 1967 war. What is clearly evident in this view is the Egyptian-designed underwing rail modification for 76mm unguided rockets. The conversion was carried out at the Egyptian Aircraft Modification Depot at Heluan, Egypt and helps to confirm the source of Nigeria's MiG-17Fs. Compare this view with pictures of NAF605 above and on page 107 (via Dr David Nicolle)*

landed. Between them the An-12s flew in four more MiG-17Fs which after assembly at Kano are believed to have been serialled NAF611-NAF614. These four aircraft effectively became attrition replacements for four similar examples lost in service. They became unique in appearance inasmuch that the presentation of serial marking was in a 'handpainted' style and with a wing-proportioned roundel on the fin. Again it is likely that some, if not all, of these aircraft originated from Egyptian stocks.[178]

Apart from the four Antonov An-12s bringing in attrition-replacement MiG-17Fs in April 1968, several further An-12 flights into Kano had brought additional spares. On 10 July 1968 Soviet Air Force An-12s CCCP-11256 and CCCP-11259 flew in, followed on 17 August by two Egyptian examples, SU-AOI and SU-AOJ, which brought in spares and armaments. But not all of the Soviet supplies were air-freighted in. On 14 June 1968 the Soviet freighter, *Nikolai Nekrasov*, docked at Lagos with a large consignment of weapons, including 100kg bombs for the Nigerian Air Force.[179]

The Federal Nigerian army advanced beyond Aba towards Umuahia and Owerri was also within artillery range. At one stage, during September 1968, Biafra's Uli strip was within a whisker of falling into Nigerian hands. But Autumn 1968 was a major turning point in the Nigerian civil war. The massive relief airlift into Biafra had been launched and French arms had started to be airlifted in to Biafra from Libreville, at a reported rate of 150 tons per week. For a while the tide of war turned in Biafra's favour. Then, over a six-week period starting on 12 October 1968, the Soviets embarked on a massive build-up of new MiGs and spares with 33 movements of Aeroflot Antonov An-12s into Kano, as follows:

Autumn 1968 Soviet Airlift of Antonov An-12 aircraft to Kano, Northern Nigeria

Date	Antonov An-12 identities
12.10.68	CCCP-11952
18.10.68	CCCP-11361, CCCP-12953, CCCP-12955
24.10.68	CCCP-12953, CCCP-12955, CCCP-12957
26.10.68	CCCP-11361
29.10.68	CCCP-12952, CCCP-12956, CCCP-12957
30.10.68	CCCP-11361, CCCP-11366
4.11.68	CCCP-11361, CCCP-12956, CCCP-12957
7.11.68	CCCP-12954, CCCP-12955
12.11.68	CCCP-11366, CCCP-12954, CCCP-12955, CCCP-12956, CCCP-12957
17.11.68	CCCP-12956, CCCP-12957
18.11.68	CCCP-12954
20.11.68	CCCP-11366, CCCP-12955
24.11.68	CCCP-11018, CCCP-11361
25.11.68	CCCP-12953, CCCP-12955
26.11.68	CCCP-12957

Those An-12s that landed between 12 October and 4 November each carried one dismantled MiG aircraft. In all some 16 new MiGs were air-freighted in. They were allocated serials NAF615 to NAF630 inclusive. The remaining An-12s that arrived during November 1968 brought in spares. A sizeable quantity of spares was also flown into Kano by a single Aeroflot Ilyushin Il-18, CCCP-75460, which made three such visits to Kano on 14, 19 and 24 November 1968.

The MiG-17F was the standard production variant with a VK-1F *Forsirovannyi* (meaning 'reheat') engine and afterburner. Standard weapon fit on this variant consisted of one 37mm N-37D and two 23mm Nudelmann-Rikhter NR-23 cannons, although sorties were often flown with just a full belt of 23mm cannon but only a half-belt of 37mm rounds. Underwing hardpoints on the MiG-17F offered a facility for up to two 250kg bombs or auxillary fuel tanks which would allow an increase in duration from 45mins to 1.15hrs at lower altitudes.

In bomber configuration the Nigerian MiG-17Fs are not known to have carried 250kg bombs but did often carry two 100kg bombs, especially after the large delivery of such bombs in June 1968. Even these could cause significant damage if targeted correctly. However, it was in a ground-attack role, using cannon or occasionally rockets, that the MiG-17F performed much better. Interestingly, the Egyptians produced a MiG-17F weapons upgrade pack at the E.A.F. Aircraft Modification Depot, Heluan. This included rails for 76mm Sakr rockets, each aircraft carrying four rockets. It is undoubtedly this upgrade which had been fitted to several of Nigeria's MiG-17Fs, again underlining the likely source of these aircraft.

Nigeria: more mercenaries

The large delivery of MiG-17Fs during the Autumn of 1968 marked a turning-point in the use of white mercenary pilots. Until then almost all MiG-17 sorties had been flown by Egyptian Air Force pilots but with markedly poor results. For over a year those Egyptian pilots attached to the Nigerian Air Force had displayed a distinct unwillingness to put themselves to any risk, especially over the war zone. (In fairness to the Egyptians, none had volunteered for duty in Nigeria and, if some reports can be believed, a number of pilots had been sent to Nigeria after performing badly in the Seven-Day War with Israel.)[180]

The L-29 Delfins were the only front-line aircraft flown by white mercenary pilots, and mainly by South Africans. But they too displayed a similar dislike to attack anything other than 'soft' targets. The prized target in Biafra was, of course, the airstrip at Uli but the fact that two damaged aircraft had sat on the strip for almost a week in August 1968 admirably demonstrated this 'unwillingness' to fly through the flak defences. The two aircraft (DC-7C '5T-TAD' and L-1049G '5T-TAH') presented an easy and attractive target for the Nigerian Air Force but on no occasion was the strip seriously attacked in daylight during the period that the aircraft were stranded there. Mechanics worked hard on both aircraft until they were declared sufficiently fit to be flown out. Both managed to fly out to São Tomé during the night of 16/17 August 1968.[181] The opportunity was lost. Whether or not Nigeria knew of the two aircraft stranded at Uli is unclear. What is clear, however, is that the Nigerian Air Force was about to quietly propose that some of those white mercenary pilots already flying DC-3s, helicopters and L-29 Delfins might be willing to convert to the MiG-17F.

The first non-Arab pilots to fly Nigeria's MiG-17Fs were two South Africans, Ares Klootwyk and Jimmy Webb, both of whom secretly converted to the type before the Russians agreed to lift their restriction. Klootwyk had been in Nigeria since January 1968. Jimmy Webb had been sent to Lagos at the beginning of November 1968 with instructions from his employer, Trans Meridian Airlines, to collect the 'stolen' DC-7C, PH-SAE. When Webb, and his First Officer, David Priest, inspected 'SAE they found that one damaged engine had effectively seized and suspected, wrongly as it turned out, that Kozubski had flown it on 100-octane fuel instead of the richer 115-octane. In view of the DC-7C's condition Webb and Priest abandoned any intention of flying it back to the UK and instead stayed on in Lagos for several days. It was during this period that Webb met Klootwyk who invited him to join the Nigerian Air Force Detachment at Benin. Two weeks later, and with several missions over Biafra completed, both men were selected to undergo a covert MiG-17F conversion course at Kano. Klootwyk and Webb flew north to Kano on Thursday 14 November 1968

70: In November 1968 Ares Klootwyk and Jimmy Webb became the first Westerners to fly a MiG 17 in action. Both were RAF-trained but conversion onto the MiG was rudimentary in the extreme. The training was carried out over a weekend when Soviet advisers were not present. Pilot's notes came in the form of an oral instruction, "you'd better make a note of this..." The set of notes on the right was used by Ares Klootwyk throughout the conflict and were written on the back of the Lagos landing chart

aboard an Air Force DC-3 ('AAM', flown by Marian Kozubski). Because of the Soviet ban on non-Arab pilots flying these aircraft and the fact that the Russians did not work over the weekends, they waited for several days. Then, on Saturday 16 November, each South African undertook twenty minutes dual instruction by Nigerian Air Force instructors; Jimmy Webb flying a MiG-15UTI (NAF601) with instructor Major Gammal, and Ares Klootwyk flying the other MiG-15UTI (NAF602) in company with Major Usman Jibrin. On the Sunday morning both of the newly-converted pilots spent an hour's solo flying MiG-17Fs, NAF614 and NAF608 respectively. Two Nigerian Air Force MiG-17Fs, NAF614 and NAF615, were then ferried from Kano to Lagos early on Monday 18 November. In order not to upset their Soviet masters the MiGs were ferried by the two Nigerian instructors, Gammal and Jibrin. At Lagos, Webb and Klootwyk then took over the aircraft and, having completed some basic range gunnery training, positioned the same two MiG-17Fs to Benin for operational sorties over Biafra. For the next few weeks NAF615 became the personal mount of Ares Klootwyk. Jimmy Webb adopted another of the new MiG-17Fs (NAF616) which he collected from Enugu on 24 November 1968 to replace the older NAF608. Both men flew their MiGs to Calabar on 27 November from where they attempted the first night interception of a gun-running aircraft on the Libreville to Uli shuttle. In this they were unsuccessful and both returned to Benin the same night. For the remaining few days of November 1968 both pilots undertook daylight missions over Biafra.[182]

The Soviets did eventually relax their restriction on who flew their aircraft and did agree to allow non-Egyptian pilots to fly the MiG-17s–but only if they were British. Under no circumstances did the Soviets allow any American pilots to be recruited to fly the MiGs. In fact, the Nigerian Government went on to employ a number of British pilots, as well as Australian, South African and even several European pilots, for MiG-17 operations. All of the recruiting was done through one agent in Switzerland. Russian officers at Kano were wary of many of these Commonwealth pilots and tried desperately to enforce the rule of allowing only Britons to fly the MiG-17s; they would frequently question a pilot's nationality but were forced to accept responses often given in what was clearly 'European-English' but which were explained as being a 'British regional accent'.[183]

By the end of November 1968 other mercenary pilots began converting to the MiG-17F. Webb returned to his job with Trans Meridian. Klootwyk also left Nigeria at the same time for a period of leave in the UK but later returned in April 1969 and stayed for the rest of the war. He eventually amassed almost 200 hours on MiG-17s, completing 189 sorties.

Two of the British pilots who ferried the Jet Provosts from Sudan to Nigeria, Paul Martin and Mike Thompsett, also converted to the MiG-17F and joined the Detachment at Port Harcourt. Thompsett, however, had the distinction of becoming the only mercenary pilot (with the Federal Nigerian Air Force) to be killed in action–on 19 July 1969. His death, or at least the officially reported version, came at the end of an evening mission to find and destroy a Biafran gunboat on the river Niger. Thompsett, it was reported, had apparently spent too much time trying to locate the gunboat and as a result his MiG-17F, NAF623, ran out of fuel while returning to Port Harcourt. The aircraft hit the ground only some 200 yards short of the runway but burst into flames on impact. The ejector seat fired on impact; Mike Thompsett's body was later found almost 100 feet away from the wreck. (There was another, and unofficial, version of events. Thompsett's death came just six weeks after the shooting-down by a MiG-17F of an International Red Cross DC-7B (on 5 June 1969). The so-called glory of shooting down an

Memorandum

From GOC

04 MAY 19**69**

To Capt Alfa

Go on the farm settlement furing your second sortie. You will go on the Ohekelem - Olakwo run. Fire the Houses. They are all in there.

Our own tps are in Okpuala. The en are now in Objs 1 to 4. They are your tgets.

Serious attacking going on now. Hurry.

COL.
GENERAL OFFICER COMMANDING,
3 MARINE COMMANDO DIVISION.

71: A fascinating document issued, on 4 May 1969, by the GOC 3 Marine Commando Division, to Capt Alfa at Port Harcourt. At the time the Division was trying to push northwards towards the recently-vacated town of Owerri and clearly required MiG-17F support along the Ohekelem-Olakwo line. Judging by the emphatic "Hurry" the Division was either under attack from Biafran troops or carrying out a determined attack itself. To meet the GOC's request Ares Klootwyk undertook a 50-minute sortie in MiG-17F NAF617 on the same date (Ares Klootwyk Papers)

enemy relief plane was not shared by all at Port Harcourt and some feelings against Nigeria's mercenary pilots ran high. So high, it is claimed, that when Thompsett was returning from a night mission (on 19 July) the Air Traffic Controller at Port Harcourt simply refused to turn on the runway lights. Thompsett was forced to circle and wait; in the end, and dangerously short of fuel, he attempted to land in darkness but the MiG-17F ran out of fuel on approach. Nobody, of course, will either confirm or deny this version of events.) But the same dissenting voice was later heard to remark, rather laconically, on the occasion of Thompsett's body being flown back to the UK; "...they arrive First Class; they leave as cargo…"[184]

While nobody would confirm or deny the precise circumstances into the crash of NAF623 and the death of Thompsett, neither would they confirm the precise details of the shoot-down of the Swedish Red Cross DC-7B. *Private Eye*, a politically satirical magazine published in London, pointed the finger at Mike Thompsett as part of an ill-informed attack against the (then) British Foreign Secretary, Michael Stewart. Other sources variously identified the pilot as "an Australian or South African mercenary pilot." Again, there was no official confirmation or denial. But Thompsett appears to have paid the price.[185]

The Biafran gunboat which Thompsett had been detailed to attack previously attracted another British pilot within the Port Harcourt MiG-17F Detachment. He was John 'Jack' Pallister, ex-RAF, and who claimed to have at one time been the personal pilot of Zambia's President Kaunda. Pallister had joined the MiG-17 squadron during June 1969 and spent almost two weeks shooting-up the gunboat but never quite succeeded in destroying it. He became known among other pilots as 'One-Wing Jack' after he forced-landed MiG-17F NAF616 on a road near Opobo, south-west of Port Harcourt, on 25 June 1969. The aircraft had simply run out of fuel during a training sortie and during the landing the starboard wing struck a palm tree beside the road. The aircraft was written-off in the ground-loop which followed.

Pallister had apparently spent his final days in RAF service flying with the Royal Aircraft Establishment at Llanbedr as had another of the Nigerian MiG-17 pilots, John Driver, who–like Pallister–also arrived in Nigeria during June 1969. Although he underwent conversion training on the MiG-15UTI and MiG-17F at Kano, most of Driver's operational sorties were with the ex-Nigeria Airways DC-3s.

The majority, if not all, of Nigeria's front-line pilots were mercenaries and whose line-of-management was directly to the most senior officer at their base. Mission orders were usually instigated by Army commanders in the field who would call upon an airfield Commanding-Officer for air support. Whichever pilots undertook the mission tended to be those who were at the airfield at the time. Very few Nigerian pilots participated in live sorties and the only recorded occasions were those when a Nigerian would act as a wingman to a mercenary leader.

MiG-17Fs often flew sorties in pairs, the first to draw anti-aircraft fire; the second to attack the target. The Biafrans never did succeed in shooting down any MiGs but their fire was often accurate. As one MiG-17F pilot later claimed, "they nearly always got the height correct but timing was poor". Nevertheless there were a number of occasions when MiG-17Fs were hit; NAF617 was hit by anti-aircraft defences around Uli strip during the early evening of 2 June 1969, on the occasion of Ares Klootwyk's infamous attack against the Flughjalp DC-6 TF-AAE. Three days later the same MiG-17F and pilot sustained further hits during a bombing sortie against Oguta. On a much later sortie over Biafra, Klootwyk attracted anti-aircraft fire while attacking Uli, on 13 September 1969. On that occasion his MiG-17F, NAF622, received damage to the underwing drop-tank.

Uli, or at best the aircraft using it, was undoubtedly the primary target for MiG-17Fs throughout 1969. Most sorties originated from Port Harcourt with two aircraft attacking, the lead aircraft circling Uli at about 1,000ft and about half-a-mile ahead of the second. This ensured that the Biafran anti-aircraft flak fire–which usually burst a few hundred yards behind the lead aircraft–had little effect against its target. A few bursts of machine-gun or cannon from the rear MiG-17F was normally sufficient to stop any firing.

Although the Nigerian Air Force had, by late-1968, been equipped with additional aircraft there is little evidence to suggest that any organisational structure, other than a very basic unit command, had been established. Headquarters of the Nigerian Air Force was at Lagos and the primary training base was at the Tactical & Training Wing at Kaduna, where all elementary flying training had been carried out on Piaggio P.149D trainers under West German guidance until the shooting war really started. No.1 Fighter-Bomber Squadron was formed at Makurdi when the MiG-17Fs arrived in Nigeria during August 1967. No.2 Fighter-Bomber Squadron was later formed at Lagos and it was from these two squadrons that Detachments were formed to operate from Benin, Enugu and Port Harcourt. The Detachments operated almost as self-contained units; one exception being an occasional deployment of MiG-17Fs to Calabar when the Nigerian Air Force tried to intercept Biafran arms flights from Libreville to Uli.[186]

'Genocide': the bomber

During the Autumn of 1968, one of the former Nigeria Airways' DC-3s, 'AAN', had been converted for a bomber role and fitted with a bomb release mechanism that was crudely simple to the extreme. It relied primarily on the muscle power of the 'bombardiers' rather than any mechanical ingenuity. A commercial-type rollermat, described as the kind found in many warehouses, was used to eject bombs up to 250lb (113kg) through the passenger entrance door which was removed before the start of any sortie.[187]

The DC-3 'bomber' was based at Benin and in October 1968 began operating a nightly sortie over Uli airstrip in an attempt to bring the Biafran relief and arms airlift to a halt. A number of mercenary pilots were seconded for these flights, the initial crew consisting of two Belgian mercenaries, Henri Laurient and an ex-Belgian Air Force DC-3 pilot, François Reip. Like many other mercenaries then flying in Nigeria, both had also served in the Congo.

Crews changed periodically within the Nigerian DC-3 'bomber' unit. Undoubtedly the best known were two South Africans, both of whom were later to enjoy local legend status. They were a 60-year old pilot, Derek 'Boozy' Bond and a Flight Engineer, Jimmy Calderhead. Bond was widely known to be a heavy drinker and, during bombing or leaflet-dropping sorties, would often be found on the flight-deck with a half-bottle of whisky in one hand. (Interestingly, when Bond arrived in Nigeria, during June 1968, he was checked-out on the DC-3 by Marian Kozubski–of whom it was said would often fly with a half-bottle of *brandy* in one hand. One is left to wonder who was checking out whom.) Calderhead, on the other hand, quickly developed a more sinister reputation. On many of the nightly missions over Uli his role was to help push the bombs out of the aircraft in the hope of hitting Uli's runway or at best destroying one of the aircraft on the ground. But, after acquiring a portable transceiver, for much of the time he would scan the frequencies used by the Biafran relief crews and interrupt their air traffic broadcasts with general taunts and threats of an imminent attack. Subsequently he coined the call-sign 'Genocide' to add a sense of self-styled macabre to his broadcasts.[188]

In spite of almost continuous attempts from the Autumn of 1968 until the end of the war in January 1970, Nigeria's efforts to put Uli strip out of action failed miserably. Part of the reason for failure can be attributed to the use of mercenary pilots flying the DC-3s within the Benin Squadron. While the war raged on and Uli continued to be used nightly, Nigeria's mercenary crews received work and pay. The accuracy of the bombing was questionable as well. Crews, flying on oxygen, would climb sometimes as high as 18,000ft over Uli before dropping bombs 'by hand'. No attempt was made to pinpoint the target or to consider wind and drift etc so that Uli often escaped unscathed. When John Driver joined the squadron in June 1969 he even discovered, among the DC-3 pilots, a degree of willingness to *avoid* hitting the target. His first seven missions over Uli were flown with the Belgian captain, François Reip; all seven flights were technically orientation flights although on none of the sorties did he see the airstrip at Uli, nor did he experience the oft-reported flak barrage from Biafran defences. Later, Driver is said to have gained a command role and conducted several sorties with a Nigerian crew but challenged other mercenary pilots over their inability to locate Uli.[189]

Nigeria receives Ilyushin Il-28s

The search for an effective bomber began at the outset of the civil war. One of the earliest attempts to develop a bombing facility was to convert a Dornier Do 27. A single aircraft, NAF151, was fitted with bomb racks and carried out live bombing tests near Makurdi during September 1967. The conversion was never fully adopted.[190]

As noted earlier the MiG-17F was used on occasions in a bomber role but its effectiveness in this guise and against jungle or bush targets was always questionable. The solution had been to introduce a dedicated bomber aircraft and in February 1968 the Nigerian Air Force received four Ilyushin Il-28 bombers. All four aircraft were manned by Egyptian Air Force crews and were operated from Calabar in the south-east, the airfield there having been upgraded by the Soviets specifically for use by the Il-28. The aircraft themselves were undoubtedly also ex-Egyptian aircraft.

At the beginning of April 1969, Nigeria received a further two Il-28s which originated, reportedly, from redundant Soviet Air Force stocks. The two new bombers arrived in a silver overall finish with no external markings at all. Both were then flown south to Lagos where they were painted in an overall camouflage scheme. In the normal numbering sequence the Il-28s would have been serialled within the NAF8xx series but no confirmed identities have been forthcoming. One is thought to have carried the serial NAF805 but the photograph from which this was deduced is too grainy to offer clear evidence.[191]

Nigeria Airways
British Midland Airways

Since the impressment of its DC-3s into the Air Force, Nigeria Airways effectively had only the four F-27 Friendships (5N-AAW, 5N-AAX, 5N-AAY and 5N-AAZ) to maintain its domestic services. Flights to the East had been suspended since April 1967 but with the re-capture of Port Harcourt the airline resumed limited services to the liberated towns of Calabar and Port Harcourt. The first of these services took place on 5 June 1968 when an F-27 made two flights into Calabar. As time passed the services did increase in frequency although they were being used more by military personnel rather than civilian passengers. Subsequently, on 22 November 1968, Nigeria Airways leased a Series 400 F-27 (JY-ADF c/n 10354) from ALIA–Royal Jordanian Airlines. The lease ran until 28 February 1969, during which time the F-27 had been registered with an out-of-sequence identity, 5N-CLN.

The Nigerian national carrier also arranged for the

72: MiG-17F NAF619 shows the standard silver finish, Nigerian fin-flash and black serial that was applied to the batch NAF618-625. In company with four Nigerian ground-handlers, ex-R.A.F pilot Paul Martin stands in front of his mount at Port Harcourt. Martin flew ten sorties in NAF619 during his second Nigerian tour. Note the effective painted camouflage applied to the concrete hard standing (Paul Martin)

73: During 1969 one of the Nigerian Air Force Ilyushin Il-28s ran off the runway at Port Harcourt. It was not seriously damaged but was effectively beyond local repair. Afterwards, local manpower was used to turn the aircraft through 180° whereupon it was simply left in situ. For some time it became a normal sight for pilots approaching Port Harcourt, as was the other unidentified wreckage to the right of the runway (Ares Klootwyk)

lease of a British Midland Airways' Viscount.[192] Initially British Midland despatched V.815 Viscount G-AVJB to Lagos on 10 November 1968, together with several flight crews, under the leadership of Captain Barry Fleming. As well as flight crews, a number of maintenance personnel were also transferred to Lagos, sufficient to support and maintain a stand-alone weekday service to Eastern Nigeria.

Routine maintenance on the Viscount was carried out over most weekends at Lagos but when 'VJB was due for a Check 1 the aircraft was flown back to the UK, on 16 May 1969, and was temporarily replaced by a BMA V.745D variant, G-AWGV. When it did return to Lagos to resume services, G-AVJB did so with a fibre-glass freight compartment fitted within the front cabin section. As a result the seating capacity had been reduced to 56 seats and from then on almost all flights were flown with full passenger and freight loads. Only one flight had to be cancelled during the entire period of operation in Nigeria.

During August 1969 Nigeria Airways took delivery of two new F-27 Friendship Srs 600s, 5N-ABA and 5N-ABB. Their entry into service brought to an end the need for the leasing arrangement with British Midland, which effectively came on 8 October 1969. The Viscount had maintained a strenuous programme during its Nigerian operation and flew three services (Lagos-Kaduna-Lagos, Lagos-Calabar-Lagos, Lagos-Port Harcourt-Lagos) each weekday and, due to the curfew in Lagos, the first flight departed at 07:00 and had to arrive back from Port Harcourt by 20:00. There were many occasions when the BMA crews were pressurised to fly urgently-required ammunition to Port Harcourt but all requests were denied. There were, however, numerous occasions when the Nigerian Army sequested the Viscount at Port Harcourt in order to repatriate wounded soldiers back to Lagos.

Pan African Airlines

While the British Midland Airways Detachment refused to yield to Nigerian Air Force pressure, one company which did frequently assist in the transferring of supplies and soldiers was the Lagos-based Pan African Airlines. Many of those who flew with Pan African Airlines (Nigeria) Ltd suspected it to be funded by America's Central Intelligence Agency; certainly it had the feel of an African equivalent of Air America. The majority of the airline's pilots were American and all funding, support and supplies came in from the USA; so much so that there seemed little doubt, especially among the crews, as to who precisely were their real paymasters.[193] Some scheduled services were flown between Lagos, Cotonou and Lomé by the company's Beech 18 and Cessna 310, but most of Pan African's operations were carried out on behalf of the Nigerian government. The company operated one DC-6A, 5N-AFT, for such freight charter work but as the war effort increased so did the demand for Pan African's services. An increasing number of DC-4/C-54s were positioned to Nigeria, all operating under American registry and in fairly non-descript colour schemes.

Once the war had started, much of Pan African's routine work was in ferrying troop reinforcements from Lagos to Port Harcourt, Calabar and Enugu. Supplies of ammunition to the same bases were also ferried aboard the DC-4s, as was a regular weekly round trip taking cash for the banks at Port Harcourt and Enugu. Frozen food and other perishable cargoes were flown from Lagos to Port Harcourt and Calabar while, towards the end of the war, DC-4s were used for ferrying raw army recruits from Calabar to Lagos for training. Other work involved the ferrying of relief material from Lagos to Calabar on behalf of the Red Cross. Surprisingly, only one aircraft was lost by Pan African during this period. It occurred during the autumn of 1968.

Late on 28 September 1968 C-54B N90427 took-off from Lagos for a routine flight to Port Harcourt. On board were fifty-five fully-armed soldiers, all reinforcements for the Nigerian Army's 3rd Marine Commando Division. By the time that the aircraft reached Port Harcourt it was after dusk and the runway landing lights were turned on. The pilot's final call was to acknowledge that he had sight of the runway but immediately after doing so the port wing-tip struck two 50ft trees, causing the DC-4 to veer into the ground, on the edge of a small village beneath the centre-line to Port Harcourt airfield. All of the soldiers were killed instantly in the fire that followed impact. John Connell, the American captain and his Swedish co-pilot, Olle Ringstrand, were also killed in the crash as was one Nigerian woman in the village.

The accident was attributed to the lack of quality approach and landing aids at Port Harcourt and as a direct result of this crash all night flights into airfields other than Lagos were stopped, although the ban was later lifted for one flight.

That flight came after the Federal Nigerian Army had made some advances in Biafra's north-west sector during April 1969. The fighting along the Enugu-Owerri front was particularly bitter and the Army suffered heavy casualties with many seriously wounded. For several days a Pan African Airlines DC-4, N11117, was positioned to Enugu to fly each day's wounded north to Kaduna for hospital treatment. The pattern of activity over this period was that the wounded soldiers would be kept at Enugu airfield until around 16:00 when between 70-80 at a time were loaded aboard and then flown north. This was the scene on 3 May 1969 when, at 17:15hrs, N11117 took-off from Enugu with eighty wounded soldiers lying on the aircraft floor, many in pain and shock and on hastily-positioned saline drips. Unfortunately a heavy thunderstorm over Kaduna that afternoon caused a widespread power failure and completely blacked-out Kaduna, including the airfield. Rather than divert to Lagos, the crew called for

74: *The International Red Cross operated on both sides of the Civil War. On the Federal Nigerian side the agency had use of a Pan African DC-4. In this view N9982H is seen unloading relief material at Calabar in February 1969. No special markings were applied to the DC-4 which still retained the basic colours of Trans Mediterranean Airlines, with whom it had operated as OD-AEA (Keith E. Sissons)*

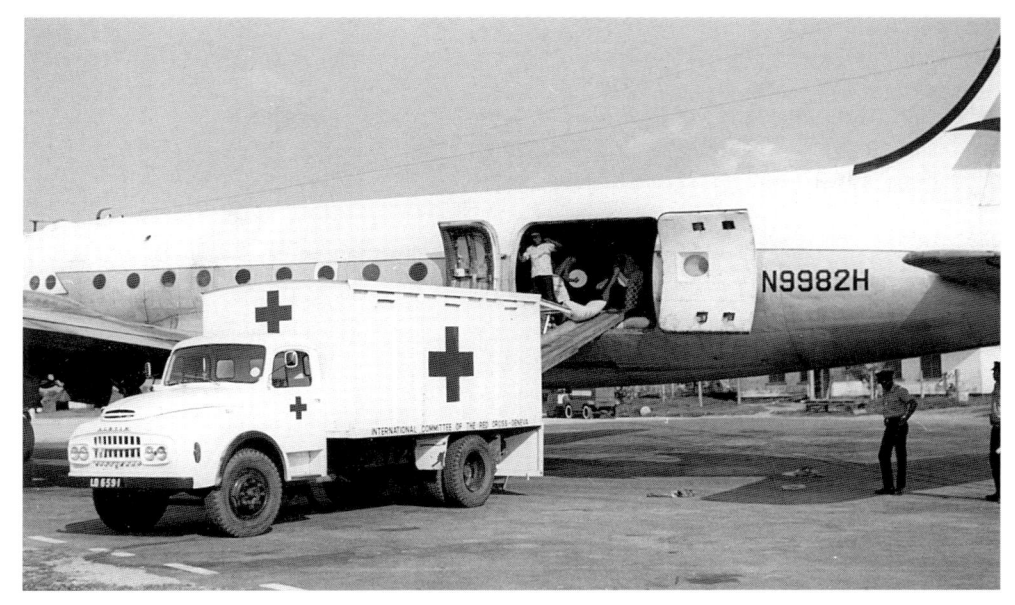

75: *On 25 April 1969 the crew of Pan African Airlines DC-4 N3934C was preparing to let-down for Enugu when the aircraft was subjected to a barrage of 'friendly' anti-aircraft fire. The crew knew that the aircraft had sustained a direct hit but were unsure of the extent of the damage. As it was still flyable the crew elected to return to Lagos where emergency facilities were markedly better than those at Enugu. N3934C landed safely. Ironically this incident was one of the very few occasions when an aircraft was actually hit! (Keith E. Sissons)*

76: *"Captain, we have a problem here!" On 22 November 1968 the Pan African DC-4 N88891 took-off empty from Lagos for a positioning flight to Port Harcourt. At the top of its climb-out from Lagos vibration caused the door hinge locking pin to fall out. The door was then torn off and wrapped itself around the leading edge of the port tailplane. Amazingly the effect on control was only minimal; the worst feeling was being able to see it from inside the aircraft. Nevertheless the aircraft was landed safely at Lagos (Keith E. Sissons)*

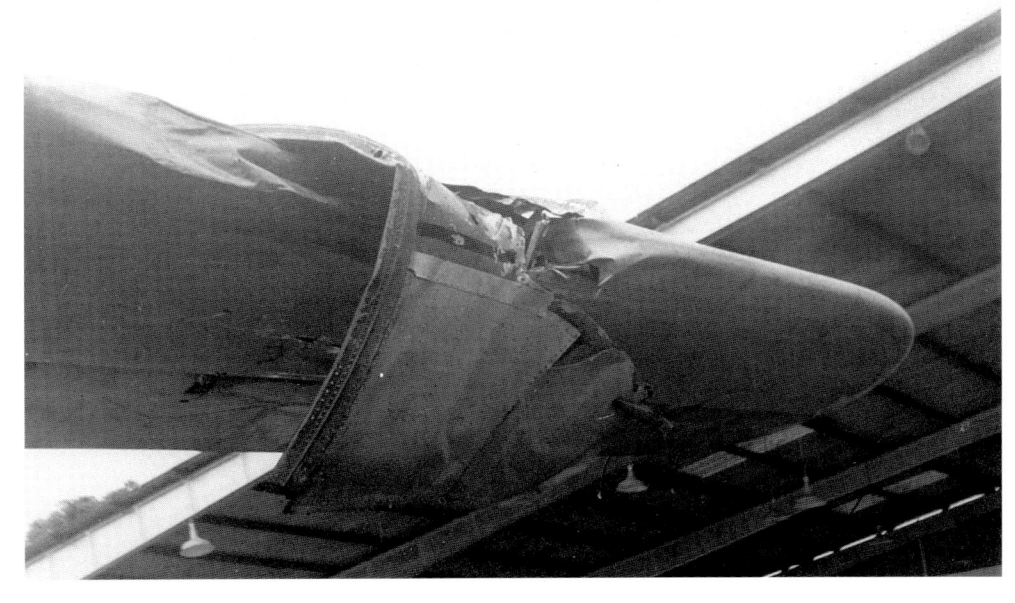

93

assistance. The Nigerian Army commander then arranged for three Land Rovers to be positioned at the end of Kaduna's runway. All three vehicles had their headlights turned on to provide a crude illumination. Crude the arrangement certainly was but it was just sufficient to allow the aircraft to land safely.

Operating within an active war zone brought a number of incidents although few were the direct result of military action. One exception occurred on 22 November 1968 when C-54B N88891 was being positioned empty from Lagos to Port Harcourt. The crew of two consisted of a British captain and a Chilean co-pilot, Ricardo Schultz. The aircraft had taken-off from Lagos at 05:50 and not long into the flight the rear cargo door blew open, became detached, and wrapped itself around the leading edge of the port elevator. The crew reduced altitude to 1,500' and despite very low cloud managed to fly the aircraft back to Lagos where it was landed safely. Fortunately the elevator spar had not been damaged and the crew clearly had a lucky escape. When the damage was later inspected at Lagos it was discovered that a locking-pin was missing from the rear door hinge bolt and that in-flight vibration had simply caused the hinge to lift off. (The forward half of the door had remained in place by the airflow.) In the event N88891, considered by many crews to have been a rogue aeroplane, was out of service for two months.

Many accidents were narrowly avoided on Pan African's Nigerian operation. On one such flight, on 2 August 1969, the same British captain was preparing to fly N88891 from Port Harcourt to Lagos with 116 wounded Nigerian soldiers on board. With so many on board and squeezed-up in the rear of the aircraft, the centre of gravity was so far to the aft that the captain found steering the nosewheel almost impossible. Despite the difficulty, however, the aircraft was successfully flown back to Lagos.

Another Pan African DC-4 did suffer damage after landing at Benin airfield, on 6 March 1969. As the aircraft, N9982H, was being taxied to the parking apron the captain took a short cut across the grass, not appreciating that the ground was soft after very heavy rain. Even with increasing engine power, the DC-4 very quickly became stuck in the soft ground. Mechanics then tried to extricate the aircraft by creating a track with wooden planks. The plan was to move the aircraft to the limit of the track, stop, move the rearward track forward again to allow taxying to the new limit and so on until reaching the runway. Unfortunately, during the first attempt, the American captain believed that momentum would carry the aircraft across the gap. He 'gunned' the engines causing the nosewheel to dig into the soft ground whereupon the aircraft became irretrievably stuck with damage to the nosewheel and engines. To all intents and purposes the aircraft was written-off by Pan African and it sat in situ for several months. Eventually, on 24 May 1969, the DC-4 became a target for the Biafran Air Force when it was rocketed by MFI-9B 'Minicons'.

Not long after the Benin incident one of Pan African's DC-4s sustained serious damage on a flight to Enugu. On 25 April 1969 N3934C had departed Lagos at 12:50; the flight had been uneventful apart from during the let-down to Enugu when the aircraft passed near Onitsha. At 6,000' the aircraft came under 88mm anti-aircraft fire and sustained a direct hit within the wing-root area. The shell blew a five-foot hole in the starboard side of the fuselage immediately aft of the wing root. The starboard flap, floor structure, aft baggage hold and fuselage skin suffered major damage, including the loss of the wing fillet.

Rather than test the meagre emergency facilities at Enugu, the crew elected to abandon the approach and immediately turned back for Lagos. Fortunately, one set of elevator cables remained undamaged thus allowing for normal flight to be achieved. At one stage, and soon after the DC-4 was hit, it was feared that the cargo doors were on the point of opening in flight so the co-pilot secured them with rope. In the meantime the company Cessna 310 had taken off from Lagos to rendezvous with the DC-4 and positioned beneath the damaged aircraft to allow the extent of the damage to be seen before a landing was attempted. To those aboard the Cessna the damage looked horrendous and for a time it seemed doubtful that a safe landing could even be attempted so, as a precaution, the crew of N3934C began dumping fuel. Hydraulic fluid had been lost, rendering the flaps useless, and when an attempt was made to lower the undercarriage fortunately the lock-up system had been rendered inoperative and the undercarriage extended by free-falling. At 16:20, after a single approach to Lagos, the aircraft touched-down safely. Nine of the soldiers on board had been injured in the attack, two of whom are believed to have died later from wounds. Repairs to the aircraft took almost two months and N3934C did not rejoin the Pan African operation until 16 July 1969. Ironically, the anti-aircraft fire that had caused the damage came, not from a Biafran unit, but from a Nigerian Army battery.

Notes

Note 146 According to John de St Jorre (*Nigerian Civil War*, published by Hodder & Stoughton 1972) one West German instructor was killed during a raid against Kaduna airfield by the Biafran B-26R and that as a result the entire team left for Europe on the following day.

Note 147 *The International Trade In Arms* by J. Stanley & M. Pearton, published for The International Institute for Strategic Studies 1972.

Note 148 *Weapons*, by Russell Warren Howe, published by Sphere Books Ltd 1981

Note 149 As related to the author by Flight Engineer Bernie Murphy.

Note 150 Details of how this loophole (for not requiring a licence to export arms from Belgium to Nigeria) was closed by a new law on 19 July 1968 are contained in The International Trade In Arms, by John Stanley & Maurice Pearton, published for the I.S.S.

Note 151 British Government Cabinet Papers 1968, PRO, Kew.

Note 152 British Government Cabinet Papers 1968, PRO, Kew.

Note 153 Foreign & Commonwealth Office Papers; PREM13/ 2257 Public Record Office, Kew.

Note 154 *Twilight of the Pistons*, by Malcolm Finnis; published privately by Malcolm Finnis 1997.

Note 155 This is the only real evidence suggesting that two of the Nord 2501D Noratlas aircraft (NAF301-302) were taken up.

Note 156 As recorded by South African pilot, Ares Klootwyk who flew the helicopter on several occasions.

Note 157 The charred remains of this helicopter are allegedly those which are currently on display at the Nigerian Civil War Museum at Umuahia. If Akahan was killed aboard a Whirlwind then it could explain why those pilots in Nigeria during 1968/69 never recorded flying NAF501, but that is purely an assumption by the author. It may also explain why most, if not all, of the Austrian Whirlwinds were grounded until progressively test-flown by mercenary pilots in 1968.

Note 158 *RAF Flying Review*, March 1968 issue

Note 159 There is confusion over the precise number of L-29 Delfins delivered to Nigeria at this time. Production records published in the monthly journal, Scramble, indicate that seven new-build examples were exported to Nigeria. Other sources show a higher number. It is possible that not all of Nigeria's L-29s were brand new aircraft.

Note 160 British Aviation Insurance Co fully investigated claims by Ghana Airways and concluded that the aircraft's fate was as described.

Note 161 *Scramble Journal*, 1997

Note 162 As observed by Kano Air Traffic Control officers and British expatriate personnel still at Kano.

Note 163 As described by Anthony Alaribe to Leif Hellström and presented in *Foreign Invaders*, by Leif Hellström & Dan Hagedon; published by MCP 1994. Reproduced by permission.

Note 164 The true source of these MiG-17s is unconfirmed. Only one Nigerian Air Force MiG-17F has apparently been identified by construction number, this being NAF609 c/n 0515317. The c/n does confirm Soviet manufacture and that it was built at Plant 153, which was at Novosibirsk in Siberia. This does not, of course, suggest that it was delivered ex-factory but the An-12s which air-freighted MiGs to Nigeria were Soviet Air Force examples and operated by a fairly "obscure squadron or unit", ie not one of the Moscow or East European-based squadrons. The implication is that the An-12s were also based in Siberia, suggesting that the MiG-17Fs did originate from the Soviet factory. Whether they were ex-Soviet Air Force examples or former Egyptian Air Force aircraft that had been returned to Siberia for refurbishment–or indeed a mix of both–may never be known. It is likely that most of the MiG-17s did in fact originate in Egypt. The overall view expressed here, however, is based on comments by Soviet military specialist, Robert J. Ruffle.

Note 165 As noted by those pilots who underwent conversion training, notably Paul Martin.

Note 166 The Sudan Air Force serials for the two Jet Provosts have not been accurately determined but it is likely that they involved the two survivors (143 and 157) of the four T.51 variants which were donated by the British Government in 1962.

Note 167 Foreign & Commonwealth Office Papers; PREM13/ 2257 Public Record Office, Kew.

Note 168 Foreign & Commonwealth Office Papers; PREM13/ 2260 Public Record Office, Kew.

Note 169 As related to the author by Ares Klootwyk who was in Nigeria at the time and was despatched on a search mission.

Note 170 *Aerojournal* 1973; article by Mike Schoeman
Note 171 As related to the author by Roman Hrycak, 18 January 1982.

Note 172 *Lagos Daily Times*, Saturday 28 October 1967.

Note 173 *Nigerian Civil War*, by John de St Jorre published by Hodder & Stoughton 1972. Plus conversations with Ares Klootwyk and Paul Martin.

Note 174 As related to the author by Keith Sissons, 16 June 1981

Note 175 As related to the author by Marian Kozubski, 1970

Note 176 As related by Roman Hrycak; times and other details confirmed by Flying Log Books of Capt Marian Kozubski.

Note 177 As related to the author by Roman Hrycak, 18 January 1982.

Note 178 Details of Kano airport movements provided by Mike Downing who was serving at Kano at the time.

Note 179 Foreign & Commonwealth Office Papers; PREM13/2258 Public Record Office, Kew.

Note 180 As outlined by Dr David Nicolle, a specialist on Egyptian military aviation.

Note 181 As observed by the author at São Tomé and by conversation with the L-1049G Flight Engineer.

Note 182 As related to the author by Jimmy Webb and Ares Kloowyk. Details confirmed by Pilots' Flying Log-books.

Note 183 As related to the author by Paul Martin.

Note 184 As related to the author by British Midland Airways engineer Alan Beardmore who watched the departure.

Note 185 It is not the author's intention to publicly identify the pilot reponsible for the shoot-down; nor to comment on the level of accuracy contained within the *Private Eye* report.

Note 186 As related to the author by Paul Martin

Note 187 *Flying Review International*, Feb 1970; article by Keith Sissons.

Note 188 As related to the author by Alan Beardmore and a number of pilots who were based in Nigeria at the time.

Note 189 As recounted by author, Mike Schoeman

Note 190 Paul Martin undertook some of the test-flying.

Note 191 All known photographs of Nigerian Air Force Ilyushin 28s do not show full Nigerian serials. Postwar views of the Il-28 at the Nigerian War Museum, Umuahia, however, show what appears to be an '05' on the nose but this could be part of a former Soviet Air Force identity.

Note 192 As related to the author by Alan Beardmore and Roy Pawson, both of British Midland Airways. Both provided details of BMA flights in Nigeria. Other details courtesy Air Britain Vickers Viscount & Vanguard, by Peter M. Davis, 1981

Note 193 Many of the incidents described here have been related to the author by Keith Sissons who was flying for Pan African Airlines at the time.

BIAFRAN RELIEF AID STARTS
Politics of relief; the war grinds on

The Nigerian naval blockade of Biafra's sea ports, which effectively denied all imports of vital Norwegian stockfish, and the fact that the Federal Army had advanced rapidly and captured important cattle-rearing areas of north-east Biafra had a fearful and far-reaching effect upon the Biafran civilian population.

As early as Autumn 1967 there was a realisation within Biafra that the suffering among the population would become a major issue. Three leading relief agencies (the World Council of Churches, CARITAS Internationalis, and the International Red Cross) began to warn that "a protein deficiency in Biafra was rapidly becoming a serious problem". The two Church organisations pressured the International Committee of the Red Cross (I.C.R.C.) to take appropriate action.[194]

Enter the Red Cross

By the very nature of its own Charter the I.C.R.C. was obliged to seek an agreement from Lagos before attempting to fly any relief aid into Biafra. In fact the International Red Cross saw a need to offer its services to both sides of the civil war and in its approach to Lagos requested specific approval to do just that. Furthermore the I.C.R.C. put forward a plan that placed overall responsibility for co-ordinating *all* relief and medical operations throughout Nigeria and Biafra firmly under Red Cross control.

That first formal request to supply aid into Biafra was made to Lagos on 13 December 1967; the request involved just one flight into Port Harcourt with a team of Red Cross doctors and a consignment of urgently-required medical supplies. Perhaps not unsurprisingly the Federal government displayed a certain degree of nervousness and stipulated that any clearance to fly into Biafra would only be given if the aircraft first landed at Lagos for a full inspection of its cargo. But, and fearing that this would lose him public credibility by accepting aid 'via the enemy', Ojukwu refused to accept any relief flights on such terms. Thus the 'cat-and-mouse' politics, that dogged and frustrated the entire International Red Cross operation in Biafra, began to emerge. It was a card that Lagos played effectively throughout the war period.[195]

By 19 December 1967 the I.C.R.C. had negotiated an agreement that allowed Lagos to lift its blockade for just two nights but only on a clear understanding that any Red Cross aircraft flown into Port Harcourt did so "at its own risk". The perceived threat ultimately manifested itself with tragic circumstances. But for the time being the International Red Cross accepted the condition.

*77 **Above:** The first aircraft leased by the International Red Cross for flights into Biafra was the Balair DC-6B HB-IBU. Red crosses superimposed onto a white block were applied beneath the fuselage and the outer wing panels. HB-IBU rests over at Santa Isabel airport, Fernando Póo island on 28 August 1968 before undertaking a night shuttle into Uli. (Michael I Draper)*

78: The first of two Biafran Air Force B-26 Invaders arrived at Enugu on 29 June 1967, after a flight from Lisbon, via Dakar, Abidjan and Port Harcourt. Registered as N12756 for the ferry flight, it had previously operated with the Armée de l'Air's Centre d'Essais en Vol (CEV) and with whom it had received a modified nose. Jean Zumbach, who stands to the extreme left of the picture, acted as a "passenger-escort" on the flight to ensure that the aircraft arrived safely in Biafra (Jean Zumbach)

79: Subsequent to its arrival in Biafra the B-26R was repainted in a camouflage scheme. It also featured a shark's teeth design on the nose and the national insignia of Biafra on the rudder. The aircraft appears never to have carried any individual identity (Jean Zumbach, via Jean Rouzé)

80: The ex-Trans World Leasing DC-7CF G-ATOB was sold to the Biafran Government very shortly after Secession was declared. It was intended to support the L-1049G 5N-07G but, because of its poor serviceability state, spent much of its life grounded. During the spring of 1968 G-ATOB spent a lengthy period at Madrid with serious engine snags, as well as a flat front tyre. Eventually the Biafrans gave the aircraft to Hank Warton in lieu of money owed but when Warton flew in to inspect it the former SS officer Otto Skorzeny and Lucien Pickett claimed to have had a shared interest in the aircraft. A Spanish court later ruled in favour of Warton (via Peter J. Marson)

97

81: During May 1968, two ex-Austrian Air Force Fouga Magisters (199 & 212) were airfreighted from Gratz to Lisbon aboard the Trans Mediterranean Airways CL-44D-4 N604SA. With the tail swung back one of the Magisters is clearly visible and about to be unloaded. In the background can be seen the Hank Warton L-1049D '5T-TAC' which was later blown up in an act of sabotage at Bissau. On board the L-1049D at the time were the Magister wings (Alex Rumley)

82: When the Federal Nigerian government announced a change in national currency at extremely short notice the Biafrans faced financial disaster. Bank vaults were emptied and cash was flown "by the planeload" to Switzerland where the Biafrans exchanged millions of Nigerian banknotes for dollars at hugely discounted rates. Two of Hank Warton's L-1049Gs were used, one of which ('5T-TAF') flew into Basle on 10 and 13 January 1968 with consignments of cash. Overnight snow and heavy icing is much in evidence as the aircraft awaits a return to Lisbo (Guido E. Buehlmann)

83: DC-7C VP-WBO was impounded at Lomé after Jack Malloch landed there on January 20 1968 with a cargo of Nigerian banknotes. Amongst other charges, the Togo authorities indicted Malloch on flying an aircraft with a false registration (ZP-WBO) although the owner suggested that he had altered the prefix letters to 'ZP' (Paraguay) because a Rhodesian-registered aircraft could have caused embarrassment to certain African countries! The aircraft eventually rotted away at Lomé (Confidential source)

84: *The initial batch of MFI-9B 'Minicons' are believed to have been later serialled BB101-BB105. Prior to their ferry flight from Gabon all had been camouflaged in the manner seen in this view. BB105 is seen here on the dump at Lagos-Ikeja having been conveyed from the former Biafran enclave as a war prize. Traces of Biafran national insignia are just visible forward of the serial (Confidential source)*

85: *The barely visible notch in the propeller of this former Biafran Air Force T-6G matches perfectly the description by José Pignatelli of how his aircraft was struck by Federal Nigerian small-arms fire. No Biafran markings were ever applied although, surprisingly, the photographer discovered a manufacturer's plate still in the cockpit which identified it as a Model T-6G-1-NH; the Manufacturer's Serial Number as 182-497 and USAF serial 51-14810. The camouflage pattern is also particularly noteworthy. When the war in Biafra ended one of Nigerian Air Force's mercenary pilots, François Reip, flew the T-6G to Lagos where it was later abandoned. It was still extant, as in this view, in May 1972 (Confidential source)*

86: *A second batch of four T-6G Texans was ready for delivery to Biafra when the war ended. After being refurbished at Cascais the former 51-14770 was repainted in what had become a standard Biafran overall camouflage scheme. Bomb racks were also fitted beneath the fuselage as seen in this view at Cascais on 18 August 1971, some 18 months after the war had ended (T. le Nobel, via D. Becker)*

87: *Braathens S.A.F.E. DC-6B LN-SUD is refuelled at São Tomé whilst C-97G N52600 awaits its turn behind. The upper surfaces of the DC-6B are painted in the 'Joint Church Aid jungle-blue' scheme although the company's red fuselage cheat-line and, unusually, roof titling remain. LN-SUD probably spent more time operating into Biafra than any other aircraft having initially operated in an all-white scheme out of Fernando Póo on the International Red Cross airlift (Phil Phillp)*

88: *After the International Red Cross decided to stand-down its airlift from Santa Isabel and Cotonou much of its stockholding of relief material was transferred to São Tomé from where Church aircraft continued to fly into Biafra. Swedish Red Cross DC-7B SE-ERF is seen visiting São Tomé on one of a number of such missions. It is a sad irony that for so long the Church airlift was denounced by the International Red Cross yet the latter was forced to hand over much of its relief material to the Churches so that it could reach starving Biafrans (Jakob Ringler)*

89: *The International Red Cross C-97Gs also joined the Cotonou-São Tomé shuttle when relief stocks were passed across to Joint Church Aid. Unfortunately neither C-97G in this August 1969 view can be identified (Jakob Ringler)*

90: The C-97G engine shop was simply an area beside the main apron. Routine on-site and outdoor maintenance was undertaken at São Tomé. The island offered no suitable hangar space and JCA's stock of replacement engines and parts stood in the open throughout the entire campaign. Reconditioned engines were occasionally flown in to São Tomé by Flying Tiger Line and other CL-44s. C-97G N52600 stands to the left (Jakob Ringler)

91: Two Joint Church Aid C-97Gs (N52600 and N52676) stand idle on São Tomé awaiting the approach of dusk before joining the nightly relief airlift into Uli. N52600 was perhaps unique in having both fish coloured blue unlike the standard blue and yellow examples, seen on N52676 (Jakob Ringler)

92 Below: One of the most evocative views to emerge from the Biafran airlift is this fine shot of C-97Gs HB-ILY and HB-ILZ formating just off the Dahomey coastline and a few miles from the CICR base at Cotonou. They were photographed from the I.C.R.C. King Air HB-GBK ostensibly just after dawn on their return from Uli (Marcel Tschudin)

101

93: Dawn breaks over Dahomey to provide a magnificent backdrop for the International Red Cross DC-6B HB-IBR as it flies just ahead of a C-97G. Both aircraft have begun letting-down for landing at Cotonou after a night of plying into Biafra's Uli strip. HB-IBR made its final sortie into Biafra during the night of 29/30 April 1969 after which it was returned to Switzerland and withdrawn from use (Marcel Tschudin)

94: Undergoing attention to its starboard inner engine at Cotonou on 6 May 1969, is the ICRC DC-6AC HB-IBT. Externally 'IBS and 'IBT were identical, both having been acquired from the defunct Air Ferry by a lease arrangement through Balair. Within 36 hours of taking this shot HB-IBT crashed in Biafra with the loss of four lives. The crash robbed the airlift of one of its most experienced pilots (Marcel Tschudin)

95: The German Government leased one of the prototype C-160D Transalls to Balair for ICRC operations as a temporary replacement for a Swedish C-130E Hercules. The Transall performed admirably and eventually joined the shuttle airlift of material from Cotonou to São Tomé after the International Red Cross operation had been forcibly shut down. The elegant blue nose of Canairelief's L-1049H CF-NAK is noteworthy in not having the KEBAC legend while the standard application of the Canadian national insignia is seen to best advantage on CF-NAL (Jakob Ringler)

96: *DC-3 'AAQ' retained its basic Nigeria Airways scheme throughout its impressed military service. It was used exclusively as a freighter and was badly shot-up by the Biafran Air Force MFI-9Bs at Escravos on 10 November 1969. Captain Marian Kozubski received serious leg and back injuries in the incident. The aircraft was sufficiently patched-up to enable a single flight from Escravos to Lagos but it is reported never to have flown again. This view, showing some of the repairs, was taken at Lagos afterwards (Confidential source)*

97: *The former Nigeria Airways 5N-AAN was one several DC-3s repainted in an overall scheme for operations with the Nigerian Air Force. In the case of 'AAN' it was an overall matt earth scheme and in this guise it was, for a while, based at Benin and used for nocturnal bombing sorties against the Biafran airstrip at Uli. This view was taken at Lagos after hostilities had ceased and the DC-3 fleet was withdrawn from use (Confidential source)*

98: *PA-23 Aztec 250C NAF001 was used as a VIP transport throughout the civil war. Many of these flights were flown by Polish-born Marian Kozubski and the aircraft regularly took Commanders to Port Harcourt, Enugu and Benin. It was also used for twin-conversion training at its Lagos base and where it was photographed outside the Delta Air Charter hangar after the war (Confidential source)*

99: There were marginal differences in the schemes applied to each of the five Canairelief L-1049H Super Constellations. CF-NAJ featured a shorter white fuselage roof band as well as a 'Peanuts' character on the starboard nose (Jakob Ringler)

100: L-1049H CF-NAK also had a short white fuselage band but had a JOINT CHURCH AID–USA title added. The Canadian fleet was a fundamental element of the nightly JCA operation throughout 1969 with relief loads up to 17 tonnes. Seen here at São Tomé preparing for a departure for Biafra, CF-NAK was later destroyed by Nigerian bombing at Uli (Jakob Ringler)

101: Apart from its nose configuration, the L-1049H CF-AEN also differed from other Canadian L-1049Hs by having the fuselage legend 'JOINT CHURCH AID' and 'OPERATED BY CANAIRELIEF' on the forward fuselage side. Note also that the 'blue-top' camouflage (a shade lighter on CF-AEN) extended much lower on the fuselage than all of the earlier Canadian Super Connies as well as being applied to the outer fins and rudders. CF-AEN is seen here on São Tomé just after its arrival there on 20 November 1969 (Jakob Ringler)

104

102: Transavia's brand-new Boeing 707 PH-TRF landed at São Tomé on 17 August 1968 with relief supplies from Amsterdam marking the first of several such charter flights from Europe by this aircraft. The 707 shares the São Tomé apron with DC-7Cs '5T-TAB' (left) and '5T-TAD' (right), each of which differed slightly in scheme and markings. Normally Hank Warton's L-1049G Super Connies occupied these apron spaces and which accounts for the widespread oil stains on the tarmac (Fr Billy Butler)

103: On a number of occasions Loftleidir CL-44 freighters operated support flights from Europe to São Tomé. Spares, including engines, were flown in as well as urgent medical supplies for immediate shipment into Biafra. Loftleidir's TF-LLJ is seen mid-way through the unloading procedure. (One wonders on the outcome of the air war had the TMA CL-44 carrying the Biafran Fouga Magisters continued to São Tomé instead of terminating at Lisbon (Jakob Ringler)

104: L-1049G F-BHBI was offered by the French Government for Biafran support operations. Its serviceability state was often in doubt and it only made a few flights to Biafra. In this view it is positioned at São Tomé outside the airport's terminal reception area (Jakob Ringler)

105

105: The initial batch of Czech-built L-29 Delfins supplied to the Nigerian Air Force was delivered during August 1967 and certainly involved seven new-build aircraft. The first two, at least, are known to have been flown to Nigeria whilst the others are believed to have airfreighted by Soviet Air Force An-12s and by sea. NAF401, the first of the batch, is seen on the Lagos runway during early 1969 and in an overall matt 'primer' scheme (Keith E. Sissons)

106: The Ilyushin Il-28 bombers supplied to Nigeria are thought to have numbered only six. Crewed by Egyptian mercenaries they never really achieved spectacular results. Unfortunately the serial number range cannot be confirmed for these aircraft as most photographs were taken with cockpit canopy covers in place. The serial appeared just beneath the cockpit side glazing. In this view of an Il-28, taken at Port Harcourt, the original green and brown camouflage appears to have been modified with a black and green scheme (Keith E. Sissons)

107: One of the Nigerian Air Force Il-28s remained unserviceable at Port Harcourt for a period during 1969 after taxying off the runway following a tyre burst on landing. The undercarriage was damaged as it ran into soft ground. In this view the green and brown camouflage pattern is clearly evident (Keith E. Sissons)

108: Although NAF618 appears in the standard format for the later batch of MiG-17Fs, it is the MiG-17F partly visible to the rear that is of interest. Signs of an earlier red fuselage band are clearly evident, a style exclusive to Egyptian Air Force MiGs and which undoubtedly confirms the origin. The MiG-17F in question is NAF605 and has underwing rails for 76mm Sakr rockets. The fitting of these was an exclusive Egyptian upgrade carried out at the Aircraft Modification Depot at Heluan, Egypt and provides further evidence of the aircraft's origin (Keith E. Sissons)

109: MiG-17F NAF625 was part of the large consignment of MiG-17Fs air-freighted in to Nigeria during the Autumn of 1968. Like others in this batch it was prepared for Nigerian service without having the national roundel applied to the fuselage serial presentation. NAF625 was photographed at Benin City during early 1969 (Keith E. Sissons)

110: Seen creating a storm of dust while running up its engine at its Enugu base during 1969, MiG-17F NAF612 of Nigerian Air Force No.1 Fighter Bomber Squadron shows clear evidence of a rear fuselage band, a marking that was peculiar to those operated by the Egyptian Air Force. NAF612 was part of a batch of four which carried a Nigerian roundel on the fin and large-style fuselage serials (Keith E. Sissons)

111: Literally at the end of the road! On the night of 28/29 June 1969 gun-running DC-4 TR-LNV prepared for take-off from Uli in full darkness. Unfortunately it was turned to face the wrong direction and attempted to take-off with only several hundred metres of runway available. TR-LNV hit trees and other obstructions before its starboard undercarriage collapsed and the aircraft slid to a halt. This view was taken the following morning–thankfully the film was removed before irate Biafran Air Force officers noticed the camera and smashed it to avoid any evidence of the crash (via Dave Goldsmith)

112: Late on 1 November 1969 DC-6A LN-FOM was destroyed at Uli by a bomb dropped by the Nigerian 'Intruder' bomber. The force of the explosion caught the DC-6A and a fire started beneath the starboard wing. The aircraft burned for some 20 minutes before the fuselage broke in two. This view was taken late on the following day (Capt. Amund Klepp)

113: By the time this shot of the wrecked DC-7C '5T-TAR' was taken mechanics had removed the engines to São Tomé island. Subsequently they were flown up to Lisbon where one was later fitted to one of the L-1049G Super Constellations. In the background can be seen the white fin, a German flag and the '7c' logo still on the rudder, evidence that this is the former D-ABAR which never acquired the late-style Südflug scheme. Compare this picture with that of the same machine on page 151 (John Trent)

114 Above left: *C-97G N52679 crash-landed onto the landing strip at Uli, Biafra during the early evening of 8 May 1969. The wreckage blocked the strip and prevented further landings that night. It also prevented several aircraft from taking-off. In the meantime, the Biafrans could only sit back and wait for the inevitable daylight attack by the Nigerian Air Force. As dawn broke, two MiG-17Fs successfully strafed the stricken aircraft. One of several stranded aircraft was the Biafran 'Grey Ghost' L-1049G '5N-07G' and whose Flight Engineer, John Trent, just happened to have a camera in his flight-bag. This view of the starboard side of the fuselage shows the fire about to consume the letters '..AID U..' of the legend 'JOINT CHURCH AID USA' (John Trent)*

115 Above right: *Another wrecked aircraft clearly visible by the side of Uli strip in June 1969 was an unidentifiable DC-3. The position of the wreckage and the location strongly suggests that this is the remains of one of the two Biafran DC-3 gunships, the former N10802 or N10803. It is possible that this picture is the result of a MiG-7F attack carried out on the 13 June 1969 (John Trent)*

116 Below: *Bristow Helicopter's Riley Dove 5N-AGF was effectively appropriated by the Biafrans when company personnel were forced to abandon it at Port Harcourt on 18 July 1967. It had previously been used by the Biafran Army when they demanded that the pilot fly a group of officers on a coastal reconnaissance sortie. It most certainly was used by the Biafran Air Force after July 1967 but when the Nigerian Air Force L-29s and Jet Provosts began aerial attacks it was repainted in a most imaginative camouflage pattern. When, following the crash of the Anson in September 1968, the author was questioned by the Biafran authorities one of those present was a BAF Officer, Godwin Ezeilo. He enquired about the likelihood of acquiring a replacement propeller for a Riley Dove especially as "Mercy Missions' Bovingdon base was close to Luton". He subsequently explained that a prop had been damaged, as well as a wing-tip, when the aircraft was ground-looped after hitting a truck on an uncompleted landing-strip. That the former 5N-AGF was later moved to the school playing-field at Uli village suggests that the location was Uli strip. The intriguing paint pattern is described as matching that of the Biafran F-27 5N-AAV. This view of the former 5N-AGF was taken in August 1970 (Tony Mabelis)*

117: Under a complex leasing arrangement two former Western Airlines L-749A Constellations joined the Biafran government fleet in Autumn 1969. Initially they operated with full US-marks and retained their former airline scheme, including the large head of a native American on the nose. The ill-fated N86525 is seen here at São Tomé awaiting departure to Biafra. Ultimately this aircraft was lost on 28.11.69 when, routeing from Faro to São Tomé, it flew into mountains 70km south of Marrakech (Jakob Ringler)

118: An attempt to remove evidence of its former owner was made to N86524 when the nose markings were removed. Both aircraft regularly flew Biafran officials in and out of Biafra as well as transporting arms and ammunition in. At São Tomé they were parked amongst the Joint Church Aid relief fleet until darkness. Subsequently FAA Inspectors visited the island and ordered the removal of US registration markings (Jakob Ringler)

119: The alteration of US-registration marks to a form of Biafran markings involved relatively minor painting. The marks N86524 became '5N86H' and which presumably satisfied the FAA Inspectors. In this view, taken at São Tomé during November 1969, the newly-amended '5N86H' takes on some essential supplies before waiting for darkness as cover for its flight to Uli (Jakob Ringler)

120: The final transformation of the former Western Airlines aircraft took place in December 1969 and involved the repainting of upper surfaces in Biafran 'blue-top' camouflage. All evidence of the former owner was removed and the aircraft was later positioned permanently to São Tomé in anticipation of a speedy escape by senior Biafran officials. When this view was taken in January 1970 the crew and groundworkers were urgently awaiting the signal from Biafra that Ojuwku was ready to flee into exile (Jakob Ringler)

121: The wide undercarriage track made it difficult for the L-1649A HP-501 to land safely at Uli and the American captain, Larry Raab, made only one trip into Biafra with this aircraft. It was used on a number of occasions on the Faro to São Tomé run and flew a number of senior Biafran officials back to Faro in the last days of Biafra's independence (Jakob Ringler)

122: L-1049H N563E arrived at São Tomé on 3 January 1970 with an Alouette II on board. For a brief period the freight doors were opened to allow cool air in—just long enough for this unique shot to be taken. Even now it is uncertain whether the aircraft was going into Biafra or had come out during the previous night. Close scrutiny of the Alouette cabin roof suggests that it is extremely dirty and looks to be "grossly unserviceable". If so then it is likely to have been air-freighted out of Biafra and is en route to Europe for repair. N563E was operating on a three-month lease to the Biafran Government at the time (Jakob Ringler)

123: *One of the factors in successfully beating the widespread starvation in Biafra was to ensure aircraft made two–or perhaps even three–shuttles per night whenever possible. In this view the Sterling Airways DC-6B OY-EAR is speedily loaded with sacks of stockfish for a second shuttle into Uli. The crew had to be airborne from São Tomé by 02:00 in order to ensure getting out of Uli by dawn (Jakob Ringler)*

124: *The lack of shadow on a bright and sunny day illustrates well the fact that São Tomé island is just a few miles north of the equator. Loading 10 tonnes of relief material by hand was therefore an exhausting task for local workers This view of Flughjalp's DC-6B TF-AAA at São Tomé shows the twin-fish insignia to best effect (Jakob Ringler)*

125: *The Nigerian Civil War is over and the former Biafran enclave has been finally overrun. On São Tomé island the Biafran relief airlift has been wound down and the operational base is being dismantled. On 23 January 1970 Biafran children from the CARITAS children's village at San Antonio on São Tomé island were flown across to Libreville for settlement into the larger Km 11 Village–so-called because of the road distance from Libreville. A group of Catholic Sisters followed on 30 January. Both flights were made with the Fred Olsen DC-6A LN-FOL which had had all of its Joint Church Aid insignia removed. In this view the Sisters are seen about to embark at São Tomé (Jakob Ringler)*

Rather than fly out of Lagos the I.C.R.C. chose to operate from the small and nearby island of Fernando Póo and it was this decision that helped to persuade Ojukwu to accept the relief flights. The island, part of Spanish Equatorial Guinea, was just less than 150 miles from Port Harcourt and offered a better opportunity for maximising the number of flights in the two-night window. A Balair DC-6B (HB-IBU), which had been chartered by the I.C.R.C., made several flights from Santa Isabel airport to Port Harcourt on 20 December 1967.[196]

Although aid had been succcessfully flown into Biafra the agreed formula for doing so was, in the eyes of the I.C.R.C., far from satisfactory and a series of negotiations for terms much more acceptable to the Red Cross Charter continued to take place on both sides. Subsequently, on 28 December the Geneva team of negotiators obtained another concession from Lagos. This time it involved a regular shuttle of flights from Fernando Póo to Port Harcourt with, it seemed, no time limit. Flights by the Balair DC-6B resumed and continued until mid-January 1968 when, without prior warning, General Gowon promptly rescinded all prior agreements. It had become clear to him that Biafran military supply flights had taken advantage of the temporary lifting of the blockade and had used the occasion as a cover for flying in and out. Gowon was, of course, quite right in his assertions; arms flights had increased and all subsequent attempts by the I.C.R.C. to tempt Lagos to change its official line met without success.

By early 1968 reports emerging from inside Biafra spoke of a disturbing situation. They noted an alarming rise in civilian deaths, solely attributable to starvation. These reports originated from representatives of several relief organisations including a number of stark messages from the International Red Cross man in Biafra, a Swiss businessman named Henrich Jaggi. Jaggi's reports highlighted a widespread protein deficiency that had already resulted in outbreaks of two associated diseases, Marasmus and Kwashiorkor. Jaggi went on to suggest to his superiors in Geneva that they launch a limited international appeal for medicine, food and clothing.[197]

Enter the Churches

A similar call for relief aid had also gone out from a group of Catholic and Protestant missionaries in Biafra. A number had been forced to abandon their missions in the face of the Federal Army advance but decided to remain with the refugees. It was those same missionaries who created a focal point at the interconfessional Queen Elizabeth Hospital at Umuahia. From that group of missionaries developed a very unique and an extremely close working relationship between the various religious groups as well as with the International Red Cross.

Initially the Umuahia group concentrated on hiring medical staff for those hospitals within Biafra and under the control of foreign medical missions. Subsequently, when the amount of aid increased dramatically, the group concentrated on organising the flow of relief aid inside Biafra. Under the leadership of three missionary doctors developed the World Council of Churches Refugee Relief Operation in Biafra and which became based upon the fusion of effort between the Christian Council of Biafra and the World Council of Churches in Geneva.[198]

Concern for the situation in Nigeria, had first been highlighted by the Catholic Church in December 1967 when two Monsignors, George Rocheau and Dominic Conway were asked by the Vatican to undertake, on its behalf, a peace mission to Lagos and Kaduna. The mission also visited the Biafran town of Onitsha but faced enormous difficulty initally in obtaining diplomatic clearance to travel on either side, especially within Biafra. The two Monsignors did visit Lagos for an audience with General Gowon who, in turn, offered freedom to travel only in areas that the government of Federal Nigeria could guarantee their safety. The authority to travel was clearly aimed at denying the Vatican's representatives access to Biafra. The Bishops of Onitsha, as well as the Biafran people, were clearly angered at what appeared to be a snub, and as a consequence they appointed Father Anthony Byrne (the Director of Catholic Social Services in Biafra) to travel to Rome and help resolve the overall situation.[199]

After several weeks in Rome, Father Byrne succeeded in convincing the Vatican to authorise a visit by the same two Monsignors to Biafra. At the end of January 1968 the two Vatican officials succeeded in reaching Biafra, travelling to Port Harcourt, via Lisbon, aboard one of Warton's L-1049G Super Constellations. When they returned to the Vatican and submitted their report to the Pope the response was immediate. Pope Paul IV commissioned Monsignor Jean Rodhain and Monsignor Carlo Bayer, respectively the President and Secretary-General of CARITAS International, to establish a relief programme for both sides of the conflict. In turn, Father Anthony Byrne was appointed as Director of the CARITAS operation in Biafra, the CARITAS operation on the Nigerian side being co-ordinated by a Lagos-based Director of Operations. The moral obligation of helping to feed hungry people had proved to be far greater than the political obligation of simply maintaining a good relationship with the Federal government. It was, with hindsight, quite a momentous decision to have taken and had a far-reaching effect on the manner in which the massive relief airlift to Biafra was operated.

CARITAS Internationalis, the Catholic agency for international aid, had been formed in 1951 expressly for the purpose of supplying humanitarian aid to areas of acute starvation. In setting up its Biafra operation, Father Byrne first flew to the Portuguese island of São Tomé to explore the possibility of establishing a relief base there. In geographical terms, the island was seen as perhaps not

126, 127: When it arrived on Fernando Póo island on 15 August 1968, the Air Mid East L-1049H Super Constellation N469C did so with the legend 'ANGEL OF MERCY' on the fuselage roof. Aboard the aircraft was Azi Riba, "leg-man" for Lucien Pickett who, allegedly with the former SS officer Otto Skorzeny, was attempting to gain access to the airlift into Uli. The cargo of stockfish had arrived from Madrid where Skorzeny had apparently arranged the customs clearance. Despite some dubious claims that the flight, and cargo, had the apparent blessing of none less than the Pope himself, the aircraft failed to gain permission to fly into Biafra. Only the aircraft's captain, the former Air America pilot, Canadian-born Axel Duch, remained involved with the relief airlift when he replaced Count von Rosen as Chief of Flight Operations at São Tomé, on 26 September 1968. The poor quality of the lower image is because it was photographed directly from a TV screen. However, it is the only known image to show the legend 'ANGEL OF MERCY' (Peter J. Marson)

the most ideal, but it was politically secure and diplomatically independent of Federal Nigeria. (In fact the Spanish island of Fernando Póo was better situated geographically but the sympathetic attitude shown by the Portuguese towards the Biafran cause outweighed the disadvantage of distance. Fernando Póo was also due to gain its independence from Spain; a political uncertainty within colonial Africa.)

After a month of preparations, CARITAS Internationalis launched its Biafra operation during March 1968. Sixty tonnes of relief material was immediately shipped from Lisbon to São Tomé, the priority being protein-rich food and medicine. The first CARITAS relief flight from São Tomé to Port Harcourt took place during the night of 26/27 March 1968.[200]

The only route from São Tomé to Biafra open to CARITAS was to make use of Hank Warton's irregular arms airlift to Port Harcourt. Fr Byrne had therefore met with Warton at the Tivoli Hotel, Lisbon and successfully negotiated a deal involving blocks of six charter flights at a cost of $3,800 per flight. Furthermore Warton agreed to undertake one free flight for every six 'paid-for' flights. The Catholic Church airlift had got under way but after Warton had completed just twenty-four flights under this arrangement, the cost factor began to cause CARITAS some considerable anxiety over the future of its relief programme.[201] There were other factors to be considered.

The impounding of L-1049G '5T-TAF' in Malta, during February 1968 had reduced Hank Warton's fleet to just one aircraft ('5T-TAG'), and although the numbers were later made up with the acquisition of two more former Lufthansa aircraft, (which became '5T-TAH' and '5T-TAK'), by mid-March 1968 CARITAS suspected, quite rightly, that the demand for arms and ammunition would always take preference over relief material. Food was, by this time, beginning to stockpile on São Tomé.

The Portuguese Governor of São Tomé, Major Antonio Jorge de Silva Sebastiao, had always turned an official 'blind eye' to Warton's gun-running activities. In any case the landing fees, sales of fuel and overnight accommodation at the island's one hotel, provided a welcome boost for the island's economy. But as the Churches began to raise the awareness of civilian starvation in Biafra so the Governer came under increasing pressure, from both W.C.C. and CARITAS to alter his standpoint. Eventually they won over his support; sufficiently enough to persuade him to issue an ultimatum to Hank Warton. Fuel supplies would, the Governor warned him, only continue to be made available for arms flights on the assurance that he undertook a proportion of relief flights into Biafra. The Governor also added a condition of his own: that in view of the flight time between São Tomé and Port Harcourt, Biafra being only 1 hour 40 minutes then each aircraft could undertake two return flights per night, each of which was capable of carrying up to $10^{1/2}$ tonnes.[202]

The Protestant World Council of Churches also used Hank Warton for relief flights into Biafra, the first of which had taken place on 22 March 1968 with a chartered L-1049G flying from Lisbon to Port Harcourt. Further flights were organised, again utilising Warton's aircraft, but (and as it did with CARITAS) the frequency became increasingly irregular; by July 1968 only six flights had been made by W.C.C. from São Tomé into Biafra. Two further flights, between Lisbon and Fernando Póo, were also funded by W.C.C., the first of which took place on 27 June 1968.[203]

Despite the Governor's support Father Byrne was still concerned at the lack of available space and at the beginning of July 1968, in one of his regular reports back to his superiors in Rome, he expressed those concerns and suggested that CARITAS organise its own separate airlift.[204] The response from CARITAS Internationalis' Secretary-General, Monsignor Carlo Bayer, was quite dramatic and, to a greater degree unexpected. Byrne was told to fly immediately to Germany and make an appeal on national television for financial aid to support the purchase and operation of their own aircraft. Within hours of the broadcast the German government had donated DM 8million, split equally between the German Catholic agency, Deutscher Caritasverband (DCV) and Das Diakonische Werk (DDW), a German Protestant relief agency.[205]

In the meantime the World Council of Churches had also been exploring alternative means of getting relief aid into Biafra and while Father Byrne was lobbying the Vatican for action, the W.C.C. was entering into a contract with an American company, Intercity Airways. On 3 July 1968 Intercity's L-1049H Super Constellation N469C (albeit with AIR MID EAST titling) flew into Geneva airport for an inspection by the W.C.C. and the application of red cross insignia *(sic)*. The contract stipulated that Intercity would undertake a minimum of 25 flights into Uli during the month of August, each flight to carry seven tonnes of relief material or 50-70 passengers.[206]

Intercity Airways was managed by an American entrepreneur, one Lucien H. Pickett, who had convinced the W.C.C. that he could break Warton's monopoly of the Uli landing-codes and procedures. This was based on the fact that one of the L-1049H's crew, a pilot named Bell, had previously flown for Warton on the arms airlift from Lisbon. Furthermore, Pickett had claimed that he could undercut Warton's charges and operate a Lisbon to Uli return shuttle for only $10,500. It was on this understanding that the W.C.C. entered into a contract with Pickett.

N469C was, at this time, being flown by a Canadian pilot, Axel Duch, who had just joined Intercity after a tour in South-East Asia with Air America. The aircraft is believed to have taken on board a cargo of relief material before its planned flight south but its movements are rather sketchy. It certainly did not fly into Biafra at this stage.

It can only be assumed that Lucien Pickett did not relate his previous assignments to the W.C.C. Like many others who turned up at that time, Lucien Pickett had a 'background'. He had first come to the fore back in July 1964 when he had operated a single L-1049G Super Constellation, N9642Z, on a series of charter flights within Europe under a company name of 'U.S. Airways'. At the end of the year the aircraft was grounded at Frankfurt for several months but re-appeared at Malta, in February 1965, with the false identity '9G-28' and being operated by 'Trans Africa Airlines'.[207] The aircraft had landed to take on fuel before planning an air-drop of weapons to rebels in the Algerian Berber mountains but delivery never took place. Lucien Pickett, who was on board the L-1049G, was arrested for violating Maltese airspace and later fined a mere $280.

Pickett was also reported to have been the owner of the infamous Canadair DC-4M2 HP-925 which, at the time of the Maltese incident, was being held by Dutch authorities at Amsterdam. It was this aircraft which much later was used by Hank Warton for the ill-fated arms flight to Eastern Nigeria in October 1966.

There is little doubt that the World Council of Churches never got value for money from Pickett, or indeed if any contract was actually signed. Pickett later had his aircraft flown to Copenhagen where he negotiated a new contract with the relief agency Danchurchaid. Under this agreement Pickett was paid $10,000 before Duch and Bell flew N469C to Madrid to uplift ten tonnes of stockfish. When the aircraft later arrived on Fernando Póo island, on 22 July 1968, the AIR MID EAST titling had been replaced with the more prophetic legend 'ANGEL OF MERCY'.

The International Red Cross takes action

Whilst the Churches were developing their own relief airlift from São Tomé, the International Red Cross faced a domestic dilemma in coming to terms with the refusal by Lagos to sanction flights into Biafra. Furthermore observers knew that until a human catastrophe occurred Lagos was unlikely to consider any change of attitude towards the I.C.R.C. Nor was there any sign of the fighting coming to an end.

Ultimately the 'fly at your own risk' policy so disliked by the I.C.R.C. forced an unusual alliance between the International Red Cross and Hank Warton, in a similar manner to that of the early Church relief operation.

On 8 April 1968 the International Committee of the Red Cross signed a contract with Biafra's primary gun-runner for five flights, each carrying exclusively relief material from Fernando Póo to Port Harcourt, the first of the flights taking place on the day of signing.[208] Inevitably Lagos immediately intervened in an attempt to stop the flights. Then, on 18 April 1968, the Nigerian Foreign Ministry issued a written authority to the I.C.R.C. giving permission for relief supply flights to be flown from Fernando Póo to Biafra–'at its own risk'.

Geographically, Fernando Póo island was ideally-suited for flights to Biafra, being approximately half the distance than from São Tomé island. Despite this benefit there were some local difficulties which frustrated the International Red Cross in their attempt to increase the frequency of relief flights. The major obstacle was that Santa Isabel airport operated only during daylight hours and the island authorities refused to extend facilities to include night opening. Biafra, of course, refused to accept any incoming flights, whether relief or arms, outside the hours of darkness and so, on the initial Red Cross flights, Warton's aircraft were positioned from São Tomé to Fernando Póo during the mid-morning. After loading of Red Cross relief material had been completed the aircraft was then flown back to São Tomé to await darkness before making the final leg into Biafra, after which the aircraft was usually then routed back to Lisbon, occasionally returning to São Tomé for refuelling.

Another factor which irritated the I.C.R.C. was that the Fernando Póo authorities were unwilling to upset its relatively large expatriate Nigerian population (as well as the influential Nigerian Embassy on the island) by openly allowing relief flights into Biafra. Customs clearance was, of course, merely a formality as Warton's aircraft always arrived empty and the outgoing cargo was carefully scrutinised, even by Nigerian embassy staff, beforehand. The Spanish continued to display their annoyance towards the I.C.R.C. in that, while all documentation correctly identified the destination as São Tomé (as well as the fact that the aircraft always headed out in a southerly direction) it was painfully obvious to all concerned precisely where the cargo was intended for.[209]

Despite the operational difficulties at Fernando Póo, Warton completed his initial contract of five Red Cross flights after which, and having made no real progress in gaining official clearance to operate its own aircraft, Geneva agreed to undertake a further five and subsequently another six flights, all of which were to take place at approximately weekly intervals. But the extra pressure for space aboard his aircraft was giving Warton considerable problems, so much so that the service he had contracted to provide was becoming increasingly difficult to maintain. Warton began to enforce delays and at times had to cancel flights altogether, due partly to a lack of available crews. Another factor was the unserviceability of his aircraft. Undoubtedly, the primary reason for cancelling some Red Cross flights was the rapidly deteriorating military situation inside Biafra, especially after the loss of Port Harcourt in May 1968 when the Biafran Army had to abandon valuable stocks of ammunition. On several occasions Warton even claimed the capture of Port Harcourt airfield by the Federal Nigerian Army as being the major reason for cancelling Red Cross relief flights.[210]

In reality the Biafran forces had already created a second airstrip by converting a stretch of the Owerri to Onitsha road, between the villages of Mgbidi and Uli, near Ihaila and which was was identified initially as 'Airstrip Annabelle' but which was later universally known as 'Uli'. A World Council of Churches flight had successfully landed at Uli during the night of 21/22 May 1968, being the first relief flight to use Uli,[211] and although they became aware that an alternative airstrip was available the International Red Cross was equally aware that Warton's masters had insisted that arms flights became the major priority.

By June 1968 Hank Warton had been forced to cancel five International Red Cross charter flights which itself led to a further crisis involving the safe storage of relief material at Santa Isabel.[212] Until the military situation had stabilised the I.C.R.C. found itself with little alternative but to wait.

Towards the end of June 1968 Warton, by now under a real threat of losing his Red Cross contract, made a serious effort to resume his relief flight schedule. At 11:00 hours on 28 June one of Warton's L-1049Gs (either '5T-TAH' or '5T-TAK'), and flown by Larry Raab, took-off from São Tomé for the short flight to Santa Isabel; it was loaded during the course of the afternoon before departing for Biafra just after dusk to operate the tenth I.C.R.C. relief flight.[213] Later the same night Raab flew the aircraft empty from Uli to Lisbon. The eleventh Red Cross flight took place on the following night (29 June) when another of Warton's pilots, August Martin, flew '5T-TAG' from São Tomé to Fernando Póo and on to Uli. After unloading its cargo Martin then flew the aircraft back to São Tomé. Warton's plan involved the allocation of August Martin and '5T-TAG' to solely operate Red Cross flights over the next few nights in order to catch up on the original I.C.R.C. schedule.

'Augie' Martin was, at the time, one of the few American black captains with a full FAA commercial rating. Since 1955, he had flown with Seaboard & Western Airlines (later re-titled Seaboard World Airlines), firstly on Super Constellations and for a while on the company's German-based C-46 Commando. At one time Martin had held the distinction of being the only black pilot with a leading American airline and when he joined Warton's outfit for flights to Biafra he was officially on leave from Seaboard World. Just four months previously he had married the niece of jazz vibraphone player Lionel Hampton and when Martin landed on Fernando Póo around midday on 30 June 1968 his wife was on board as a passenger. The other two crew members were an American co-pilot, Jesse Raymond Meade, and a South African Flight Engineer, Thomas 'Bull' Brown.[214] 'Bull' Brown was probably one of the most experienced Flight Engineers on the Biafra arms airlift; he had previously flown into Biafra with Jack Malloch's Air Trans Africa but decided to join Warton after Malloch was jailed in Togo and the Rhodesian operation was suspended.

Fully laden with $10^{1/2}$ tons of food and medicine the aircraft took-off for Uli; it arrived overhead Uli about 20:20 hours. The weather over Biafra that night was particularly bad with active tropical thunderstorms over much of the area. The runway lights were turned on, as was the standard procedure, and '5T-TAG' was lined-up for a landing. The adverse weather conditions might well have been a factor in causing the crew to mis-align the let-down because the aircraft turned onto final approach at too low an altitude. About $1^{1/2}$ miles south of the airstrip and close to the junction of the Ihiala-Oguta road, the aircraft struck rising ground. All on board were killed instantly.[215]

'Augie' Martin and his crew were the first to die on the relief airlift and in view of the wrecked aircraft lying within close proximity of Uli the local Catholic priests saw it a fitting tribute that the entire crew be buried within a new cemetary just outside the village of Uli. The graveyard was situated alongside the Uli to Ihaila road, though not easily visible therefrom. It was regularly tended by Father Joe Prendergast who also arranged for a local *Ibo* carpenter to construct four wooden headstones until marble examples could be acquired from South Africa. The crash brought home to all involved the dangers of operating a nightly relief airlift into Biafra.

For two weeks following the crash on 1 July 1968 the Red Cross airlift became the focus of much frenetic diplomatic activity The standard procedure adopted by the International Red Cross had always been to advise Lagos of the details and timings for each of its flights, primarily to avoid unwanted attention from the Federal Nigerian Navy gun-boats lying off the Nigerian coast. Lagos had openly accused the International Red Cross of allowing the aircraft to stage via São Tomé where, according to Nigerian reports, some of the relief material had been offloaded and replaced by arms. The Red Cross charter flights had, according to Lagos, been of 'mixed cargo'. The I.C.R.C. quite naturally and extremely strenuously rightly denied such accusations.

Warton, on the other hand, was not so keen that the International Red Cross passed over precise details of each flight to Lagos but did agree to make further flights as part of his contract with the I.C.R.C., in spite of the latter's request to alter the flight pattern. What the Red Cross demanded of Warton was that he delay future take-offs from Fernando Póo to dusk, or at best the last possible moment immediately prior to the closure of the airport for the night.

Hank Warton's position of being the sole non-Government operator into Uli was becoming sufficiently precarious that he had little alternative but agree to the Red Cross demands.

At the start of the Red Cross flights Hank Warton was operating three L-1049G Super Constellations, all of which were being flown with illegal Mauritanian registrations, '5T-TAG', '5T-TAH' and '5T-TAK'. There can be little doubt that the I.C.R.C. were aware that the registrations were not genuine; the Air Traffic Control officer at Santa Isabel was certainly aware but chose to ignore the fact. But the crash of '5T-TAG' brought the matter into the open and the authorities on Fernando Póo began to display their irritation to such flights. (The real source of this irritation was without doubt the strong Nigerian embassy on the island and whose staff were undoubtedly acting on instructions directly from Lagos. The relationship between the embassy and the island authorities is known to have been extremely close.)[216]

When confronted by the I.C.R.C. over the registration issue of his aircraft, Hank Warton simply promised to have them legally registered. In fact it was Warton's Operations Manager, Bertram Peterson, who undertook to legally register the aircraft. Because of Peterson's dual British/Canadian nationality he was able to register a new company, ARCO, in Bermuda and applied for registration of Warton's aircraft. The application was made immediately after the crash of '5T-TAG' and to support the application the International Red Cross Headquarters in Geneva wrote to the Director of Civil Aviation, Bermuda (on 13 July 1968) in order to expedite clearance of the necessary paperwork. But when the next I.C.R.C. charter flight flew into Santa Isabel it was made by a Super Constellation carrying the marks 'N8025'. Furthermore the crew was able to substantiate this with documentation identifying the marks as indeed being legally registered to a Super Constellation of the North American Aircraft Trading Corporation–Warton's other US-registered company. The fact that it was not an ARCO-registered aircraft, as had been expected, was, it seemed, purely "an administrative item". The Spanish authorities could do nothing but accept the declared legality of the aircraft and allowed flights to continue. Presumably they were unaware that the true N8025 had since been repainted as '5T-TAC' and also that it had crashed at Port Harcourt during February 1968, an incident which Warton had conveniently never advised the Federal Aviation Agency.[217]

Suitably repainted as 'N8025', Warton positioned the erstwhile '5T-TAH' from São Tomé to Fernando Póo on 15 July to operate the I.C.R.C.'s fourteenth relief flight.[218] The aircraft took-off almost in darkness and climbed to cruise altitude over the island before turning towards Biafra. As it did so, another aircraft turned onto the same course; it was L-1049G '5T-TAK' operating an arms flight from São Tomé. In view of the International Red Cross' insistence on advising Lagos of the flight-times and course then the crew of a crucial arms flight from São Tomé considered it to be fair game to use the Red Cross as protection for the inbound flight.

The two aircraft flew in together and, as usual, caused confusion among the Nigerian gunboat crews, so much so that they opened fire on both aircraft. For once their accuracy was fairly good and although neither aircraft was hit, both crews abandoned the flight and turned back to São Tomé.[219]

The events of 15 July 1968 had far-reaching repercussions, especially for the Biafran leaders who were furious that a desperately-needed arms flight had failed to arrive. But for the I.C.R.C. its relief programme had taken another serious blow. In a little over six months the I.C.R.C. had managed to fly just 160 tonnes of aid into Biafra. Nevertheless, because of the question of landing-codes at Uli the I.C.R.C–as were the Churches–was forced to continue using Warton's services. Faced with such a situation, and despite the slippage in flight schedules, the I.C.R.C. was virtually forced into another cash deal with Warton. This involved exclusive use of one of Warton's aircraft, but not one of the L-1049G Super Constellations.

The Italian company, Sociedad Aerea Mediterranea (SAM) was disposing of two C-46 Commando aircraft (I-SILA c/n 30271 and I-SILV c/n 392). Both were sold to a Miami-registered dealer Aaxico Sales Inc and to whom they were registered, on 17 July 1968, as N10624 and N10623 respectively. On the strength of an agreement with the I.C.R.C. Warton arranged for the purchase of N10623 (and the possible lease of N10624). As part of the terms of purchase the American Civil Aviation Bureau insisted that Warton signed documentation that, while allowing him to use them on behalf of the International Red Cross and the Churches, neither aircraft would be flown on behalf of, or chartered to, the Biafran government. Warton agreed to sign and the deal with the I.C.R.C. was confirmed. This involved Warton positioning the C-46s to Fernando Póo from where two flights per night (each carrying a minimum 5 tonnes) would be made. The I.C.R.C. even paid over to Warton SwFr300,000 (£30,000) for the first series of flights. It was this cash that enabled Warton to complete the purchase with Aaxico. He then prepared N10623 with Red Cross insignia before flying it to Geneva for inspection. Progress, it seemed, was about to be achieved.[220]

The Churches take unilateral action

The question of launching a dedicated relief airlift had first been raised at the World Council of Churches assembly in Uppsala during July 1968 when members discussed the possibility of a joint CARITAS/International Red Cross airlift from Fernando Póo to Uli. The concept was later put before the I.C.R.C. in Geneva but it met with a stern refusal, and any thoughts of co-ordinating relief flights was abandoned. Instead the Churches developed their own plan and, since large financial donations had been raised in West Germany the German Protestant (Das Diakonische Werke–DDW) and the German Catholic (Deutscher Caritasverband–DCV) Churches immediately set about purchasing five surplus Douglas DC-7C aircraft from the German carrier, Südflug.

The first of the Südflug DC-7Cs, D-ABAS, was ferried from Germany to Lisbon on Monday, 22 July 1968. It had on board a 12-tonne mixed cargo of aircraft spares and food, the latter consisting of tinned meat and dried milk. Two days later, on 24 July, a second DC-7C, D-ABAC, was ferried to Lisbon with a full cargo of stockfish.[221] Father Byrne, having concluded the purchase of the five aircraft, flew back to São Tomé on one of the early delivery flights to help organise flights into Biafra. One of the stipulations made by the Südflug was that the aircraft be re-registered before any flights into Biafra took place and that Father Byrne took on the responsibilty for ensuring that this was done. In turn, he gave this task to Hank Warton and, accordingly, the DC-7Cs were repainted with Mauritanian marks, within the same sequence that was used for the Super Constellations. The first DC-7C (D-ABAS) was given the registration '5T-TAL', following on from Warton's last L-1049G. The second DC-7C appears to have been the subject of a private joke between Warton and Byrne when it appeared as '5T-TAB', the letters being as close to a personalised identity for Father Anthony Byrne as Warton could get.[222]

Although Father Tony Byrne was effectively in charge of the São Tomé airlift, much of the groundwork was carried out by another Irish priest, Father Billy Butler. He had been the CARITAS representative at Port Harcourt until its capture by the Nigerian Army in May 1968. On São Tomé Butler was in charge of loading relief supplies onto the aircraft. Until the DC-7Cs arrived Butler would meet each of Warton's aircraft on their return from Uli and determine from the crew whether or not the aircraft would be available for relief material on the following

128: When the International Red Cross sought to establish a regular shuttle of relief aid to Biafra the Agency was forced to contract Hank Warton. As a result Warton lease-purchased two C-46 Commando freighters, N10623 and N10624. In the event no relief flights were made with the C-46s and they were used for other work. N10623 eventually passed to Warton's Swiss-based ARCO (Bermuda) Ltd fleet. N10623 is seen here at Basle on 12 October 1969 (Peter J Marson)

129: The port nosewheel door of the DC-7C to the right clearly has the letter 'C' visible; the fuselage cheat-line is solid blue and a white DC7C logo is on the top of the fin - all characteristics of the former D-ABAC and which became '5T-TAB'. The other DC-7C visible in this photograph, taken at São Tomé cNovember 1968, is another former Südflug aircraft but without the 'DC7C' fin logo and a two-tone blue fuselage cheat-line. This confirms it as being the former D-ABAD (Giorgio Torelli)

130: The false Mauritanian marks '5T-TAL' were applied to the former Südflug DC-7C D-ABAS after it had arrived at São Tomé. By the time that this shot was taken, at São Tomé cNovember 1968, the aircraft had acquired the appearance of a well-used tramp freighter in need of a good clean, evidenced by the amount of oil-stains across the flaps. To the right of '5T-TAL' is Transavia Holland DC-6 PH-TRA which operated with Nordchurchaid between 17 October 1968 and 10 February 1969. Also just in view is one of the Fred Olsen C-46R Commando freighters (Giorgio Torelli)

night. If it was then for Fr Butler the day would start at 08:00 gathering together some 10 tonnes of relief aid, some from the CARITAS store on the island and some purchased from local shops. A typical load would contain a mixture of flour, beans, salt, rice, dried fish, tins of meat, butter, sugar and milk. Non-food items would include candles, batteries, bicycles, petrol, gas-oil or kerosene. Butler would try to deliver the supplies to the airport by mid-morning; he also had full access to airport equipment and would personally move the steps to the guarded aircraft, open the freight doors, and load the aircraft. By midday Butler had usually completed his task, checked the weight distribution, ready for the crew who, if due to depart at 17:30, would start an engine check around 15:00 and refuel the aircraft. Butler's final gesture would be to hand over $1,600 in cash to the captain, Warton's fee for the short flight into Uli.[223]

The first of the new DC-7Cs to make a landing at Uli did so on the night of 26/27 July 1968, quite likely by '5T-TAB', bearing in mind the cargo it brought down from Germany. It is also likely that '5T-TAL' remained at Lisbon for some considerable time where it acted as a store for spare parts.[224]

The third of the Südflug aircraft (D-ABAR) was ferried from Germany to São Tomé, via Lisbon, on 5 August 1968, followed the next day by D-ABAD. Re-registering took place almost immediately but by now this work appeared to be done with the minimum of paintwork; D-ABAR became simply '5T-TAR', D-ABAD was repainted as '5T-TAD', but the final aircraft, D-ABAK, posed Warton a problem (as the L-1049G '5T-TAK' was still flying) and so operated for a while with just the letters '5T', but later became either '5T-TAC' or '5T-TAG'.[225]

Not long after the start of the Church airlift one of the DC-7Cs, '5T-TAD', sustained damage to its main undercarriage after landing heavily at Uli. Although the damage was relatively minor and repairable, it was sufficiently serious to enforce the aircraft to remain at Uli. '5T-TAD' was carefully taxied into one of the unloading bays (referred to as 'fingers') and then covered entirely with foliage cut down from nearby trees, as a precaution against a daylight Nigerian air attack.[226] With one aircraft lying damaged at Uli, it had not been the best start to the Church airlift but over the next few weeks a group of engineers set about repairing the DC-7C's undercarriage by airlifting spares in on subsequent relief flights. In fact '5T-TAD' spent almost ten days on the ground at Uli until the night of 16/17 August when a crew was flown into Uli aboard L-1049G '5T-TAK' and it was successfully flown out to São Tomé.[227]

While the Churches were using Warton's monopoly of the Uli landing codes to their advantage, the I.C.R.C. was still concerned over the irregularity of its own flights, especially the circumstances that had caused the cancellation of their 14th flight on 15 July. A third group, the World Council of Churches, was equally frustrated with the dependence upon Hank Warton and which had meant that its own supplies stockpiled within the ICRC Fernando Póo warehouse were not being flown in to Biafra.

In view of the Südflug aircraft being purchased jointly by Deutscher Caritasverband and Das Diakonische Werke the flight operations from São Tomé became equally divided, on a nightly basis, between the two agencies. One night the flights into Uli carried Catholic-donated cargoes, the following night a Protestant load, and so on. At the end of the month a comparison was made of the total tonnages for each agency and if, say, the Catholic tonnage was seen to be higher then the Protestant agencies then the latter was given an extra night's flight during the following month. The arrangement led to a popular report that, after landing at Uli, pilots would sometimes ask unloaders, "Who are we flying for tonight; Jesus Christ or the Pope?"

In order to allow some degree of planning flights and crew rosters from São Tomé Warton agreed to relief flights being contracted in 'packages' of six, the price for each 'packages' being $19,000 which took account of one flight within six being made free of charge. Although the arrangement seemed complicated it was designed ultimately to benefit Warton in that when the total of free flights equalled the value of the aircraft then ownership of the DC-7C's would be transferred to him. While the Churches agreed to this arrangement, they also insisted on all payments being made in cash.

Peace talks and a turning point

Not content to watch one of its leading member countries destroy itself, the elder Statesmen of Africa began moves towards getting both sides of the Nigerian Civil War to attend peace talks. Under the leadership of Ethiopia's Emperor Haile Selassie, as Head of the Six-Nation Committee on Nigeria, the Organisation of African Unity opened a conference at Niamey on 15 July 1968. General Gowon attended on the second day and, following some indecision as whether to attend, Ojukwu flew from Uli to Libreville during the night of 17/18 July for a pre-arranged breakfast meeting with President Bongo of Gabon. Ojukwu then flew north to the Niamey Conference aboard a Douglas DC-8 of Air Afrique, which President Houphouet-Boigny of the Ivory Coast had placed at his disposal.[228]

At Niamey, Ojukwu outlined his proposals for one (or even two) 'mercy corridors' either by using the river Niger to the Biafran port of Oguta or by the demilitarisation of Port Harcourt and a 10-mile wide corridor to front-line positions north of Port Harcourt from where the Biafran Red Cross would take over. To the obvious annoyance of Gowon, the O.A.U. Consultative Committee listened attentatively and indicated its assent to the Biafran case before pressing both sides to establish a land corridor and to enable food and medicines to flow into Biafra.

What appeared to have been achieved at Niamey was a formula for peace and an agreed means of supplying relief aid into Biafra. Accordingly an agenda was drawn up for what was hoped would be a much more conclusive meeting at the O.A.U. Addis Ababa conference, set to open on 29 July.

During July 1968 the I.C.R.C. increased the pace of its diplomatic process to 'legalise' its Biafra operation, the first step being the appointment, on 19 July, of Dr August Lindt, until then the Swiss Ambassador to Moscow, as the Co-Ordinator of Relief Operations. Once again the pressure on both leaders for a peaceful end to the fighting was gaining in strength, not only from the O.A.U. but also from August Lindt of the I.C.R.C. albeit those close to the situation knew only too well that no end of talking would settle the Nigeria-Biafra issue. Lindt's first aim was to meet the leaders of both sides in order to obtain a joint initiative for setting up a land corridor for bulk supplies and an immediate daytime airlift from Fernando Póo to avoid further civilian deaths from starvation. Almost ten days of intense diplomatic talks followed with almost total support from the relief organisations all of whom saw the initial step as being the one opportunity to reduce the starvation in Biafra.

Lindt achieved neither proposal but he did manage to gain one concession from the Spanish authorities on Fernando Póo; they would allow an all-night operation from Santa Isabel airport. The island's authorities also formally agreed to a limited number of direct flights from Santa Isabel to Biafra, thus finally acknowledging the real destination and removing the need for subterfuge when all flights would have to climb-out in any direction other than towards Biafra. No large-scale operation could have been mounted without those two concessions, and with Geneva anxious to get food and medical supplies moving again the only problem that dogged further progress was access to the Uli landing codes, at the time monopolised by Warton.[229]

Hank Warton had been openly denounced by Lucien Pickett as having let Ojukwu down badly when the Biafran Army needed ammunition most; Warton countered by warning Ojukwu to be wary of Pickett especially after the suspicions surrounding the sabotage incident at Bissau (when the L-1049D '5T-TAC' had been blown up). Everybody, it seemed, was prepared to publicly denounce everybody else. Ojukwu was also under enormous pressure from the relief organisations to break his enforced allegiance with Warton. Eventually he had to and the Biafran leader quietly instructed one of the delegates flying out of Uli to the Addis Ababa conference to pass a copy of the landing codes on to the I.C.R.C. delegate.

What helped Lindt in all of his discussions was a well-worn document from Nigeria's Foreign Ministry, dated 18 April 1968, and which was handed to Lindt when he took office some three months later. It was the written clearance, by Lagos, to fly into Biafra and which, according to its text, stated that the Nigerian Military Government gave I.C.R.C. permission to fly supplies from Fernando Póo into Biafra. At one of his early meetings with Gowon, after the Red Cross had stopped flights due to anti-aircraft fire, Lindt showed the Nigerian leader the document that he had inherited. Lindt added that, whatever Gowon said in refusing to allow night flights to Biafra or to stop the Nigerian Navy from shooting at Red Cross aircraft, he already had permission to fly in. Furthermore Lindt announced that he was intending to re-start flights immediately. Gowon responded by denouncing the 'official clearance note' on the grounds that it had been given at a time when the harbour of Port Harcourt was "still in the hands of the rebels–and after my troops re-conquered the town the note became invalid." Lindt countered that the note neither specified Port Harcourt, nor did it mention any time limit. Finally, Lindt used what was to become a typically-implied threat by the International Red Cross by asking Gowon how he thought world opinion would interpret the withdrawal of such permission. Gowon conceded to allow flights to resume but still on an 'at your own risk' basis and this phrase was included on a revised government note to Lindt. It also added that the Nigerian Authorities would take steps to avoid any incidents.[230]

The Red Cross starts its own flights

One of Lindt's first reactions after receiving the codes was to cable the head of Balair and request the permanent use of one aircraft; Balair responded by promising to position a DC-6B to Fernando Póo within 24 hours and on 26 July the International Red Cross signed a contract with the Swiss airline, Balair AG, for the lease of a DC-6B. On the following day DC-6B HB-IBU was flown from Geneva to Fernando Póo by Balair's chief pilot, Captain Vogel. Lindt flew back to Fernando Póo just ahead of the Balair DC-6B in order to finalise clearance with the Biafrans but on his arrival at Santa Isabel was confronted by Axel Duch, the Canadian-born pilot of L-1049H N469C, together with Intercity Airways' representative, a Mr Azi Riba, an Argentinian and who was described as Lou Pickett's "leg-man".[231] In spite of the agreement between Intercity and the Scandinavian Churches and the promises made in Copenhagen it was on Lindt's express instruction that the 'Angel of Mercy' did not fly in from Fernando Póo. There was a brief exchange in the small airport terminal at which point Lindt made it perfectly clear that Geneva did not approve of the Church's disregard for flying against the wishes of Lagos and therefore would not discuss further any suggestion of a joint I.C.R.C-Church venture with the two gentlemen.[232]

The I.C.R.C. DC-6B HB-IBU retained its basic Balair

markings but with an added red cross on a white block beneath the rear fuselage. It had also been converted to cargo configuration although some seats were retained at the rear of the fuselage. Its first flight from Santa Isabel to Uli was made during the late evening of 31 July, with 8 tonnes of powdered milk and the Red Cross Co-ordinator on board. After landing, Lindt was driven to Umuahia for a series of continued negotiations with Ojukwu; his DC-6B was flown back empty to Fernando Póo where it would stay until the call came from Biafra to go and collect him. That call came two days later whereupon the DC-6B was flown back in (on the night of 2/3 August) to pick Lindt up. In the meantime Lindt had secured the clearance for nightly supply flights into Uli.[233]

The first International Red Cross flight with a full cargo under the new agreement was flown into Uli on the night of 3/4 August, again using the DC-6B HB-IBU. On that occasion a small number of passengers were aboard, including Axel Duch, whom Lindt had granted a 'Red Cross passport' in order that he may present personally to Ojukwu his case for flying the 'Angel of Mercy', L-1049H, into Uli. Despite taking the trip into Biafra and the apparent blessing of Dr Lindt, Duch still experienced difficulty in convincing Ojukwu to allow W.C.C./Intercity flights into Biafra. Indeed it has to be doubted as to whether or not Duch actually met with the Biafran leader. In the event he decided to return to Fernando Póo but traffic chaos on Biafra's poor roads caused him to miss his return flight from Uli. Then, in what was a typical display of Red Cross arrogance, the I.C.R.C. representative in Biafra, Henrich Jaggi, later questioned the right of Axel Duch to even hold a Red Cross passport. As a result Duch was promptly arrested by the Biafran Army at Uli and held in custody until the next Red Cross flight out. Duch subsequently returned to Fernando Póo and flew N469C to São Tomé where the cargo of stockfish was finally unloaded before flying empty on to Lisbon. The L-1049H had no further involvement in the relief airlift to Biafra although Axel Duch did later return to São Tomé to become the Chief of Flight Operations for Nordchurchaid.[234]

The Red Cross airstrip

The resumption of flights to Biafra after months of seemingly frustrating inactivity, except perhaps on the diplomatic front, allowed the I.C.R.C. to publicly demonstrate its assistance to both sides of the civil war. But with only between eight and ten tonnes of relief aid bring flown into Uli each night the real effect against starvation in Biafra was still minimal. Painfully aware that the nightly shuttle was not going to meet the population's need, the Red Cross continued to pursue clearance for daylight flights but, as ever, one side or the other put up an obstacle. Then Ojukwu made a new offer by agreeing in principle to daylight flights, not to Uli, but to an alternative airstrip then under construction on the Afikpo Road, just west of the village of Obilagu.

At the time of Ojukwu's offer, the runway at Obilagu was almost completed. It lacked electrical power (necessary to provide runway lighting etc), and there was no air traffic control facility. However, for daylight operation the strip was almost useable. The I.C.R.C. agreed to make up these deficiencies at its own cost and began work on 4 August 1968 under the guidance of a Swiss architect, Mr Jean Kriller, who was also appointed as Obilagu airstrip's commandant. One of Kriller's first actions was to insist on the removal of all Biafran troops and military equipment, including some anti-aircraft guns, to outside a 5-mile radius. The neutral zone meant that, with the front line only fifteen miles from Obilagu, Biafran defences were moved precariously close to the line of fighting and only after an intervention by the Biafran leader was the area cleared. An agreement was signed on 14 August between the Biafran government and the I.C.R.C. by which the airstrip then became officially administered by the Red Cross. Work continued on a round-the-clock basis but progress was hampered by heavy rain during what is referred to as the 'small dry' season. The landing-strip was approximately 6,000ft in length and four unloading bays were constructed to one side of the runway.[235] Once the actual landing area was completed Kriller painted three large white 60-feet discs along the runway, each with a red cross superimposed, but in spite of this the Nigerian government refused to recognise the neutrality of Obilagu. And as if to prove the point, Nigerian Air Force Ilyushin IL-28s bombed the airstrip on at least three separate occasions; on 20, 24 and 31 August, although the extent of damage caused is said to have been minimal.[236]

Red Cross: the turning-point

After eight nights of flying just one return shuttle per night from Santa Isabel to Uli, the International Red Cross took the decision to double the number of flights each night. For the night of 9/10 August 1968 Red Cross schedulers planned two flights into Uli strip with the DC-6B HB-IBU. The first flight took-off from Santa Isabel at dusk and, as was now the standard routine, climbed to 18,000' by circling over the island before setting course for Uli. The DC-6B's Swiss captain, Vogel, later reported an unusually heavy, and much more accurate, flak barrage from the Federal Nigerian Navy on that night but nevertheless continued on course and landed safely at Uli. When the aircraft returned to Santa Isabel, by taking a wide detour to miss the gunboats, Vogel's description laid the foundation for reports that the Nigerians had recently taken delivery of new radar controlled-equipped gunboats. Not only was the planned second flight of the night by HB-IBU promptly cancelled but once again the entire I.C.R.C. relief effort was brought to a halt.

The Balair DC-6B had not been alone in the sky above Biafra on the night of 9/10 August. Two German Churches' DC-7Cs had 'tucked in' behind the International Red Cross flight for a safe passage. But while Vogel had con-

122

131: *When the rear section of DC-6BF OH-KDA was closed there was little, at first glance, to distinguish it from other DC-6Bs. In this view the tail hinges can just be seen as well a red tip to the top of the fin. That was the local means for instantly identifying the DC-6BF. OH-KDA rests over at Santa Isabel on 26 September 1968 (Michael I Draper)*

132, 133: *The swing-tail arrangement of Kar-Air's DC-6BF conversion OH-KDA proved to be most beneficial for carrying bulky loads. When it arrived at Fernando Póo on 28 August 1968 to join Operation 'INALWA' it brought in a number of Land Rovers. The unloading of such vehicles at Santa Isabel, even after the island's daily rain shower, proved fairly troublefree. Reversing down the narrow ramps on a blacked-out Uli strip, however, was not quite so easy and such loads were therefore normally taken in aboard the C-130E Hercules (Michael I Draper)*

tinued to Uli the Church aircraft turned back to São Tomé. The response by Warton's pilots was broadly similar to the International Red Cross pilots in that both groups refused to fly in the face of newly-positioned radar-controlled anti-aircraft guns, although the São Tomé pilots did add a slight twist. They would fly but only if their salaries were substantially increased.[237]

With the São Tomé airlift also at a standstill, Hank Warton flew south from Lisbon, not to pay over more money, but simply to tell his pilots to adopt standard 'bush-flying' tactics; they should, he told them, fly in during the final hours of daylight and at tree-top level. The reaction from the São Tomé-based aircrew was suitably scrawled across a wall outside the Pousada Geronimo hotel the following morning: "Fly With Warton; Die With Warton".

It was constantly argued that Dr Lindt's insistence on communicating precise flight details to both Lagos and the Equatorial Guinea authorities had indirectly brought the airlift to a halt. At the same time the military situation within Biafra was becoming increasingly desperate; the Biafran town of Owerri was now under serious threat and a Federal assault against Aba was widely thought to be imminent. Indeed Lagos was even now talking of a "quick kill action" to end the war. All of this was genuinely interpreted in most quarters that Biafran resistance would crumble by mid-September 1968.

Dr Lindt maintained a hectic schedule of meeting various African leaders as part of an on-going diplomatic attempt to pressure both sides of the Nigerian civil war to sue for peace and allow relief aid to be sent in to the war zone. Most leaders saw the war as an internal Nigerian problem and not as an African problem. His personal aircraft, a Mitsubishi Mu-2B (HB-LEB) had spent just three weeks in Africa but was due for a routine service in mid-August. Lindt therefore took advantage of a necessary flight from Addis Ababa, where he had met with Emperor Hailie Selassie (of Ethiopia), back to Geneva, on 11 August.[238]

The I.C.R.C. took the painful decision to wait for the collapse of Biafra's forces and then, with full clearance from Lagos, mount a massive airlift from Fernando Póo. Not unnaturally Lagos warmed to the strategy and at the same time continued to condemn efforts by the Church in flying from São Tomé, even accusing the Churches of providing food for the Biafran army. Lagos also declared that any post-war airlift of relief aid to the East would exclude any involvement from the Churches and in the belief that the collapse was imminent the International Red Cross began to arrange for the lease of a sizeable fleet of aircraft.

Other relief agencies were looking at the possibility of using their own 'dedicated' aircraft. Oxfam (together with the British Red Cross) took an option on a Pacific Western Airlines C-130 Hercules which was capable of carrying up to 20 tonnes per flight. The aircraft's Canadian owners placed a stipulation that the Hercules would only be flown under the aegis of the ICRC and only after both Gowon and Ojukwu gave a joint clearance for daylight flights into Biafra.[239] Not unsurprisingly the Nigerian leader refused to allow the aircraft to operate from Fernando Póo; Oxfam therefore let its option lapse.[240] The decision to align with the ICRC was still seen by Oxfam as the correct course of action to take and, having lost the opportunity to operate its own aircraft, immediately arranged for the purchase of a freight-configuration DC-7CF which would be handed over to the ICRC to operate on Oxfam's behalf. In anticipation of this an Oxfam official then travelled to Fernando Póo to help organise the storage and transmission of its own supplies.[241]

The real turning point: Count von Rosen arrives

Although most of the relief aid flown in from São Tomé was brought to the island by ship some consignments were flown down from Europe on charter flights. One such flight involved a Transair Sweden DC-7B, SE-ERK, which landed at São Tomé during the afternoon of 11 August 1968 with a cargo of medicines from Frankfurt. The aircraft had been chartered through a Danish priest, Pastor Mollerup, and was flown in by Transair's chief pilot, Count Gustav von Rosen.[242]

The timing of von Rosen's arrival on São Tomé could not have more prophetic. He was met on the tarmac by Father Tony Byrne who explained that all relief flights into Biafra had been suspended and urged the crew to fly the aircraft and cargo on to Uli that evening. Not unnaturally von Rosen declined the request on the grounds that, in the event of any accident, neither the aircraft nor the crew were insured for war risks. His job, he argued, had simply been to fly only to São Tomé. But continued pressure from Father Byrne, including a detailed overview of the humanitarian catastrophe then facing Biafra, made it difficult for the Swedish Count to turn his back on the situation. It was not the first time that idealistic objectives had driven von Rosen to fly humanitarian flights in theatres of war. Previous exploits had involved operations in Abyssinia, Poland, Finland and the Congo.[243]

Von Rosen's initial reaction to the pressures on São Tomé was to accompany one of Warton's DC-7C crews in an attempt to reach Uli during the night of 11/12 August. His objective was simply to assess at first-hand the chances of breaking the Federal blockade. The DC-7C was flown, firstly towards Fernando Póo, but as the aircraft approached the island it became clear that International Red Cross flights from there were still suspended, at which point the Warton crew turned back, over the island of Príncipe, to their São Tomé base.

As soon as the DC-7C landed back at São Tomé, Father Byrne called for a 'debriefing' in the small coffee-room below the airport control-tower. Undeterred by the failure of the DC-7C to reach Uli, von Rosen, together with his co-pilot and Flight Engineer, outlined a plan to fly in low over the Rivers area of Nigeria; but he needed somebody else on board who knew the area well. Father Byrne recommended Father Billy Butler, one of the Irish priests based on São Tomé and whose prime responsibility was to oversee the loading of relief cargoes. (Father Butler had previously worked at Port Harcourt and knew the region well. He was also well-known to the priests and ground-crews working at Uli and could therefore vouch for the crew.) During the course of the following day the plan was put to the island's Governor, Major Antonio Jorge de Silva Sebastiao, bearing in mind that the low-level flight, designed to break the Nigerian blockade, would be operating from his island. The Governor, a master of diplomacy, gave his blessing but in quietly displaying his fear of a reaction from Nigeria claimed that he would only be "responding to the Church's request to help save the starving children of Biafra."[244]

Later, on 12 August 1968, a coded radio message was transmitted from São Tomé to the Uli controllers warning them that a flight might well be attempted that evening. Indeed, at 16:18 hours the DC-7B SE-ERK took-off, von Rosen in command and accompanied, not just by his own crew, but also by two of Warton's pilots to act as guides for the landing procedure at Uli. Father Billy Butler and one journalist completed the crew.[245]

The early take-off time ensured that the aircraft would reach Uli just before dusk. As planned von Rosen by-passed Fernando Póo and instead flew a direct course at relatively low altitude from São Tomé. When the aircraft approached the Nigerian coastline he then took the DC-7B even lower, below sixty metres. This classic 'bush-flying' tactic–the same as suggested by Warton to his pilots several days beforehand–proved sufficiently successful to avoid detection from the Nigerian gunboats. Even more surprised was the Biafran Army when von Rosen called the Uli controller and radioed the correct coded sequence for landing. After landing von Rosen requested–and was granted–an immediate audience with the Biafran leader in his Umuahia bunker to discuss the relief airlift situation.[246] Father Butler accompanied the Swedish Count, again as a means of vouching for von Rosen's sympathies. In the meantime the DC-7B was flown back to São Tomé by von Rosen's co-pilot and was prepared for a second relief flight to Uli on the following evening. In the final hours of 13 August von Rosen rejoined his aircraft at Uli for the return sector to São Tomé, bringing out several passengers who took advantage of an available outbound flight. SE-ERK was then flown back to Malmö.[247]

In just 48 hours von Rosen had quite dramatically altered the course of relief aid to Biafra and at a time when the motivation to act was at its lowest.

When news of von Rosen's flights reached the International Red Cross on Fernando Póo the reaction was decidedly low-key; the strategy of waiting for the Nigerian 'quick-kill' remained intact, and no attempt was made to fly the Balair DC-6B HB-IBU into Biafra. But on 17 August a British-registered Avro Anson, G-AWMG, arrived at Santa Isabel, inbound from São Tomé, its crew possessing a copy of the Uli landing-codes. Furthermore the Anson crew had been given official clearance from the Biafran Government to fly in to Biafra.

Mercy Missions' Ansons

The Anson was one of two ex-RAF examples (G-AWMG and G-AWMH) acquired by Mercy Missions and which had been prepared for relief flights at a time when the relief airlift was having little or no effect in fighting the increasing starvation.

Mercy Missions had been jointly formed on 13 July 1968 by Nic Taaffe, an ex-British Eagle Airlines pilot, and John Mitchell-Smith, a commercially-rated Flying Instructor. The two pilots had met by chance at Denham airfield at a time when both were seeking new flying jobs. Subsequently, Taaffe and Mitchell-Smith had successfully inspired a pro-Biafra action group in London to help establish funding for the purchase of two Vikings at Manston, which had been declared redundant by their owner, Air Ferry. On closer inspection neither aircraft was considered suitable and the agency instead purchased two Ansons which would be used to ferry food supplies in from Fernando Póo. With hindsight the choice of the Anson seems nonsensical but it was taken at a time when the airlift to Uli was at a virtual standstill and only the occasional relief flight, chartered by the Churches or the I.C.R.C. from Hank Warton, was reaching Biafra.[248]

The two Ansons had been part of a batch of nine purchased from the Royal Air Force by C. Bilson Ltd.[249] All nine aircraft were to be cannibalised for spares but the company agreed to sell two of the aircraft to Mercy Missions, with new C of As, and to keep two others in reserve. VV958 and TX227 were both civilianised at RAF Bovingdon as G-AWMG and G-AWMH respectively while VL349 and VM351 were the two reserve aircraft, (and which were later registered G-AWSA and G-AWSB to John R. 'Jeff' Hawke on 21 October 1968 for re-sale to the USA.)[250]

The two Mercy Missions Ansons departed Bovingdon on 5 August 1968 for the first leg to Guernsey but adverse weather and low cloud over the Channel Islands forced a diversion to Jersey. Grounded initially for twenty-four hours, the weather later worsened and the Ansons, with limited blind-flying instrumentation, made no further progress for four days.[251]

The lifting of the cloudbase on 9 August 1968 enabled

134: The two Mercy Missions' Ansons were registered as G-AWMG and G-AWMH on 23 July 1968 and re-painted at RAF Bovingdon four days later. The first of the pair, the former C.19 VV958, required the minimum of painting; just the removal of Royal Air Force insignia and titling. In an effort to increase available payload most of the interior 'luxuries', including seats and an Elsan toilet, were also removed (Peter J. Bish)

135: The second of the two Mercy Missions' Ansons, the C.21 G-AWMH, was repainted in an overall white scheme to cover a camouflage pattern applied some weeks beforehand for the making of the epic film, Battle of Britain. G-AWMH is seen here shortly after its arrival at Jersey on 5 August 1968. Nic Taaffe sits in the cockpit while co-pilot John Desborough and passenger Anthony Stanscombe relax on the grass. Immediately afterwards bad weather forced both Ansons to remain grounded for several days (Jersey Evening Post)

136: During the Anson's enforced four-day stopover at Jersey the cat's face and legend "KATMANDU" was hand-painted on the nosecone of G-AWMH by a local aviation enthusiast. The Anson is seen at Port Etienne on 17 August 1968 after its enforced landing during a sand-storm. The undamaged tip of the starboard prop serves evidence of an inflight engine failure (Nic Taaffe)

137: With unnecessary items such as liferafts, documents etc removed the overall capacity of the Anson was barely over 1 tonne of relief material. The fact that the International Red Cross was averaging less than one flight per night as well as fuel shortages inside Biafra threatening distribution by road made the Anson's cargo a little more meaningful. The cargo being loaded here consists of sacks of milk-powder and Complan *(Michael I Draper)*

138: On 31 August 1968 Anson G-AWMG was loaded for a shuttle from Santa Isabel to Uli early the following morning. Small but heavy boxes of foodstuff could be easily stowed in the forward cargo compartment. John Mitchell-Smith, joint Trustee of Mercy Missions (UK) lifts cases of high-protein food into position *(Michael I Draper)*

139: The only Mercy Missions Anson to reach Biafra was G-AWMG but during the early morning of 3 September 1968 it crashed in the Methodist Leprosy Settlement at Uzuakoli. The aircraft had attempted a dawn air-drop of milk-powder to the Settlement but on the third run along the valley stray small-arms fire cut a fuel line in the starboard engine. With only one engine giving power and the aircraft still carrying a half-load the crew tried to fly out of the valley but as it neared the ridge so it struck the ground. Within hours the Nigerian Air Force was airborne and in order to avoid detection from the air the wreckage was covered with vegetation. In this view the camera-man is carefully watched by a Biafran police officer *(via Nic Taaffe)*

G-AWMG and G-AWMH to stage from Jersey to Bilbao but after landing at the northern Spanish airfield the starboard main undercarriage of 'WMH was found to have sustained damage. Closer inspection revealed that a wheel rim had fractured, possibly as a result of the landing at Jersey in poor conditions several days beforehand. Another enforced overnight stay for both aircraft allowed time to organise replacement parts to be ferried down from Bovingdon but in the meantime it was agreed that G-AWMG would ply on ahead. Nic Taaffe, and his co-pilot John Desborough, remained at Bilbao with the damaged aircraft while Mitchell-Smith (together with the author, as co-pilot, and two cameramen) staged G-AWMG on from Bilbao to Seville; on to Casablanca on 10 August and to El Aaiun (in the Spanish Sahara) on 11 August. By 15 August it had reached Abidjan (Ivory Coast), via Port Etienne (Mauritania), Bathurst (Gambia) and Robertsfield (Liberia). Precise details of the Anson's flights are as follows:

Mercy Missions Anson 19 Srs.2 G-AWMG - Flight Log

Date	Route	Flight Time	Duration	Remarks
5.8.68	Bovingdon-Jersey	1300-1440	1.40	Diversion from Guernsey due to adverse weather conditions
9.8.68	Jersey-Bilbao	1640-2010	3.30	In formation with G-AWMH
10.8.68	Bilbao-Seville	1220-1550	3.30	Delayed departure due to damage of Anson G-AWMH
	Seville-Casablanca	1735-2000	2.25	
11.8.68	Casablanca-El Aaiun	1310-1655	3.45	Throttle lever malfunction
12.8.68	El Aaiun-Port Etienne	0900-1235	3.35	
	Port Etienne-Dakar	1645-2000	3.15	Night landing
13.8.68	Dakar-Bathurst	1500-1550	0.50	Air Traffic Control delay departure
14.8.68	Bathurst-Robertsfield	1105-1625	5.20	Auxilliary fuel-tanks used
15.8.68	Robertsfield-Abidjan	1010-1330	3.20	Extra fuel tank fitted at Abidjan
16.8.68	Abidjan-São Tomé	1040-1620	5.40	Extra fuel tank used

Mercy Missions Anson 19 Srs.2 G-AWMH - Flight Log

Date	Route	Flight Time	Duration	Remarks
5.8.68	Bovingdon-Jersey	1305-1445	1.40	Diverted from Guernsey due to adverse weather conditions
9.8.68	Jersey-Bilbao	1640-2010	3.30	In formation with G-AWMG
12.8.68	Bilbao-Seville	?	3.40	
13.8.68	Seville-Agadir	?	6.10	Diversionary landing due weather
14.8.68	Agadir-Las Palmas	?	3.25	Brakes failed; repaired 15.8.68
16.8.68	Las Palmas-Port Etienne	?	4.00	Forced-landing in sandstorm

Although Mercy Missions' second Anson had suffered undercarriage snags at Bilbao, the flight by G-AWMG was similarly not without problems. During the let-down to El Aaiun the crew discovered that the port throttle lever would not travel fully through the throttle gate, making final approach and landing particularly difficult. Engineers from the Spanish Air Force Detachment there attempted repairs but the fault was not fully rectified and during the next leg to Port Etienne the throttle lever again continued to malfunction. As the Anson landed at Port Etienne the two throttle levers had to be set at considerably different positions to ensure a controlled approach. The problem also affected the port engine boost control which operated out of synchronisation with the starboard. Effectively it required four hands to land the aircraft.

At Abidjan the crew of G-AWMG considered the next leg to São Tomé, via Lomé, but were warned not to venture too close to the Togo border. Before taking-off on 16 August the crew modified the fuel system in a manner related to them by John Squire (of Aer Turas) back in Jersey. This involved the addition of a third oil-drum of fuel in pyramid fashion to the two already installed beside the flight-deck entrance. The extra fuel, together with the weight of additional cargo transferred from G-AWMH back in Bilbao, certainly put the Anson well over its recommended maximum weight. But the third fuel drum did enable 'WMG to further increase its range from a standard 600 miles to almost 900 miles—sufficient to allow the final leg to São Tomé to be flown direct, on 16 August 1968.[232]

The situation that faced Mercy Missions when the Anson landed at São Tomé was very different to the scenario that had led to the formation of the agency in the UK. By then the Churches had positioned its fleet of freight-configured (ex-Südflug) DC-7Cs to São Tomé and Count Gustav von Rosen had just re-established the relief airlift when he flew a Transair Sweden DC-7B into Uli during the late afternoon of 11 August. Flights, however, were still irregular and there was still work available for Mercy Missions.

At the time the World Council of Churches had several hundred tonnes of Norwegian stockfish stored in the I.C.R.C. warehouse on Fernando Póo but Red Cross flights from the island had been suspended since 10 August. With approval from the Biafran Government the W.C.C. appointed Mercy Missions to position to Fernando Póo and airlift the stockfish into Uli, but despite official approval the International Red Cross refused to release any of the W.C.C. supplies. In fact, apart from Mercy Missions having been given the landing codes for Uli, many of the obstacles that had prevented Axel Duch from flying the L-1049H N469C in were put forward by the Red Cross to block flights by Mercy Missions. The Norwegian stockfish remained firmly in storage. (It was a standard quip on São Tomé that "when the wind was in the right direction the smell of Red Cross stockfish could be detected back in Norway".)

Apart from the W.C.C. contract, Mercy Missions had also been briefed by Biafran envoys at São Tomé that, because of the dire shortage of suitable vehicles, there was some difficulty in moving relief material from Uli to some parts of Biafra. At the time only three airstrips were serviceable: the main roadway at Uli, a grass strip just south of Umuahia and another converted stretch of road at Obilagu, the last-mentioned having just been designated as a neutralised I.C.R.C. strip. Several other airstrips were being prepared and the leader of the Biafran delegation at São Tomé, Godwin Nsoku, put a proposal to Mercy Missions that the Ansons be used for short-hop flights inside Biafra once the additional airstrips had been completed.[253]

In the meantime and several days after the arrival of G-AWMG on Fernando Póo, a medical team from the Save The Children Fund (STCF) arrived on the island. The team had been given visas which enabled travel into Biafra aboard a Red Cross aircraft. But the I.C.R.C. aircraft was still grounded, and desperate to begin work, the team instead elected to fly in with Mercy Missions, a decision that had quite a dramatic effect. No sooner had the Red Cross learnt that the STCF were changing aircraft (by seeing the Anson being loaded with STCF equipment) then the I.C.R.C. Co-ordinator took quite an extraordinary decision. Sensing that the Anson was scheduled to fly into Biafra very early on the following morning (20 August) Lindt, without any notice given to Lagos, nor for that matter to his masters in Geneva, authorised the immediate preparation and loading of the Balair DC-6B HB-IBU for a flight to Biafra that night. A very bewildered STCF medical team was on board.[254]

The flight of the DC-6B HB-IBU into Biafra late on 19 August was made in defiance of any political considerations and even in the face of a worsening military situation in Biafra. Once again the aircraft faced the newly-acquired gunboats off the Nigerian coast and, perhaps of even greater significance, the flight was authorised specifically against Geneva's policy of waiting for the Nigerian Army's 'quick-kill'. In defiance of all that, the I.C.R.C. nightly airlift to Uli resumed on 19 August 1968 almost as abrubtly as it had stopped. Two flights a night were then achieved regularly, each flight averaging 8 tonnes. Within weeks the I.C.R.C. would expand its Fernando Póo operation, as would Nordchurchaid from São Tomé. Together they were to provide what ultimately became the largest civilian relief airlift since the Second World War.

For an effective role in the airlift to Biafra, Mercy Missions had arrived too late. At the time of its formation there was virtually no food being flown in but by the time the first aircraft had arrived at Fernando Póo events were about to overtake it. Nevertheless there were delays in starting the International Red Cross airlift, unnecessary delays which angered the World Council of Churches and who decided therefore to nominate Mercy Missions to ferry in their supplies, held by the I.C.R.C., from Fernando Póo. But the International Red Cross had flatly refused to allow any local stores to be flown in to Biafra by any agency other than itself—regardless of the fact that Mercy Missions had full clearance to fly into Biafra or that the Red Cross fleet was grounded. The only way to make supplies available to Mercy Missions was therefore to ferry stock in from São Tomé to Fernando Póo. To do this the W.C.C. hired a locally-registered DH.114 Heron CR-SAH. Unfortunately the owners of the Heron would not allow it to be flown into Biafra and so it was used solely for transferring supplies between the two islands. The cost to the W.C.C., while not immense, was an unnecessary one and did little to ease the tension between the Churches and the Red Cross.[255]

That tension emerged in an interview on Fernando Póo island, on 4 September 1968, between BBC journalist Phil Tybernham and Charles Bailiff, the World Council of Churches' Biafra Representative. The interview, part of which is quoted below, was broadcast in the UK shortly afterwards:[256]

Bailiff *"...The Red Cross were so recalcitrant—and I say the Red Cross—because they are the agency in charge of the great stockpile on this island.*

Tybernham *"Why was it, do you think, that the Red Cross refused to give them (Mercy Missions) supplies?"*

Bailiff *"Personally, I feel, it was because of the attitude of the Red Cross that they must maintain a very delicate balance or posture of neutrality with Lagos as well as Biafra. And that their Representative, Dr Lindt, was in discussion at that time with General Gowon as well as Colonel Ojukwu and that he had enunciated a position that only Red Cross personnel would be involved in any airlift operation from Santa Isabel."*

Tybernham *"What exactly is the supply situation from here (Santa Isabel) at the moment?"*

Bailiff *"Approximately that of 4,000 tonnes, at least 1,700 tonnes (have been) donated by the World Council of Churches and associated agencies; about 1,000 tonnes donated by your own OXFAM; UNICEF have donated a small amount, and other agencies, including the Red Cross, account for the other 500-600 tonnes."*

Tyernham *"So your complaint is that the Red Cross are appropriating supplies that are not theirs anyway."*

Bailiff *"Not precisely appropriating supplies but not interchanging them according to the announcement by Dr Lindt. He made a statement that these supplies would be interchangeable and I would think that a representative of one of these other agencies—regardless of which agency, but especially the World Council of Churches which represents the largest amount—requests a few tons I would think they would release a few tons, but this was refused."*

Bailiff went on to support the World Council of Churches' decision to use Mercy Missions by highlighting some of the shortcomings of the International Red Cross operation:

Bailiff *"The shortcomings to be summed up would be the incongruity of a situation where up until last night there* *were many planes sitting out at the airport—six to be exact, including a C-130 Hercules—but only one plane flying in any supplies. The rationale given is that Lagos had only approved one flight into Biafra whereas Lagos refused to allow **any** flights and said 'no flights **would** be allowed' and this one flight has been experiencing anti-aircraft flak. So we could not understand up until last night, why one aircraft could go in and for many, many days about five or six were sitting at the airport. The Red Cross, of course, are more concerned with their posture than the international view.*

Harsh criticism indeed from a major relief agency and for the first time criticism against the International Red Cross being aired in public. But it wasn't just the Churches who were becoming frustrated at the 'holier than thou' attitude of the Red Cross. Other agencies, whose supplies had been channeled through the I.C.R.C. also voiced irritation. The main complaint levelled against the Red Cross was that it was blamed for being slow off the mark in rushing supplies to the starving civilian population of Biafra; then the Red Cross faced an accusation that its pilots were too cautious to risk Federal Forces' anti-aircraft fire; for taking too much attention of orders from Lagos and for stockpiling vital supplies on Fernando Póo. The high number of Red Cross personnel on Fernando Póo also came in for much critisism, especially when no relief flights were being made–so much so that one American member of the W.C.C. team complained that *"the only effect the Red Cross has had since it arrived on Fernando Póo has been to push up the price of the local hookers."* Finally, the I.C.R.C. was charged with tying up its whole operation in miles of red tape and deliberately obstructing other mercy teams willing to fly supplies in. Geneva did, however, admit to having been slow off the mark.[257]

Ultimately the International Red Cross did release the W.C.C. supplies to Mercy Missions who had elected to attempt daylight flights into Biafra, the first of which took place during the morning of 1 September 1968. The aircraft took-off from Santa Isabel at 09:45 and flew at extremely low-level to Uli. Unfortunately, as the Anson circled Uli, the airstrip's air traffic controller did not respond to coded radio calls. The runway was crudely camouflaged yet clearly visible as was a series of obstructions which made a landing impossible. The Anson crew had no alternative but to return to Santa Isabel, where G-AWMG landed at 12:05.

On the following day a radio message from a Biafran leprosy settlement at Uzuakoli, close to the front line, reported a desperate situation and spoke of increasing deaths from starvation. The Mercy Missions team was asked to make an air-drop of milkpowder and complan. The crew agreed to fly in early on 3 September. Taking-off from Santa Isabel at 07:35 the Anson flew under strict Visual Flight Rules (VFR) and once over the Nigerian coast dropped to tree-top height all the way across Federal-held territory. Flying northwards towards Umuahia the crew, navigating by dead reckoning, found and followed the railway line to Uzuakoli. The target was then located in a valley just to the east of Uzuakoli. G-AWMG made several runs and discharged part of its cargo before the starboard engine cut on the third or fourth run along the lower part of the valley. With insufficient power to climb out the aircraft hit the rising ground and was written-off. Inspection of the wreckage later revealed that the starboard wing was holed in several places and that a fuel line had been cut. There was no doubt that the holes had been caused by small-arms fire, from below and to one side.

Mercy Missions' second Anson, G-AWMH, never reached Fernando Póo. After repairs to its undercarriage had been completed at Bilbao, Nic Taaffe and John Desborough flew on to Seville on 12 August 1968 for an overnight stop. It had been intended to fly on to Sidi Ifni on 13 August but bad weather closed in over the Sahara coast and a diversionary landing was made at Agadir instead. By the following morning the weather had cleared sufficiently to allow G-AWMH to be flown on to Las Palmas. The landing at Las Palmas was made without brakes and an enforced delay of 24hours widened the gap between the two Ansons even more. Then, on 16 August, Taaffe and Desborough flew out of Las Palmas and headed for Port Etienne. When the Anson arrived overhead Port Etienne it did so in the middle of a sandstorm and as a consequence the crew was instructed to hold off as the storm passed through. However while circling above the field the Anson's starboard engine failed. Unable to hold altitude on just one engine the aircraft then, as Nic Taaffe later described, "simply ran out of altitude and landed just short of Port Etienne's main runway." In an attempt to bring the aircraft to an abrupt halt the main undercarriage was raised and in doing so the aircraft sustained some minor structural damage. In spite of this the aircraft was not repaired immediately and took no further part in the Biafran operation.[258]

Notes

Note 194 *Nigerian Civil War* by John de St. Jorre; published by Hodder & Stoughton 1972

Note 195 For much of the time these 'cat-and-mouse' politics were acted out through the Nigerian embassy on Fernando Póo island. Many other incidents are described within Dr Lindt's book "Generale Hungern Nie", published by Zytglogge Verlag Bern 1983

Note 196 The identity HB-IBU has been quoted by the International Red Cross but has to be considered as unconfirmed.

Note 197 *The Making Of A Legend* by Frederick Forsyth, published by Penguin Books 1977

Note 198 The missionary doctors were Dr Edgar Ritchie, Dr Klein Shepherd and Dr Herman Middlekoop.

Note 199 *Airlift To Biafra*, by Tony Byrne, Columba Press 1997.

Note 200 On 26 March 1969 Father Anthony Byrne and Fr Tony Cunningham presented gifts to those pilots on São Tomé island to celebrate the anniversary of the first CARITAS flight to Biafra.

Note 201 *Ibid.,* Fr Tony Byrne.

Note 202 *Ibid.,* Fr Tony Byrne.

Note 203 According to Santa Isabel airport Tower Log-Book

Note 204 According to a report in the *London Times,* 16 July 1968, CARITAS had chartered 26 flights involving L-1049 Super Constellations. Presumably all of these were with Hank Warton.

Note 205 *Der Spiegel,* Issues 9 June 1969 & 16 June 1969.

Note 206 Situation Report, I.C.R.C. July 1968.

Note 207 *Ibid.,* Peter J. Marson.

Note 208 International Red Cross Situation Report

Note 209 As described to the author by aircrew who had operated such flights from Fernando Póo

Note 210 Conversations between the author and Warton's crews at São Tomé. Also confirmed in an interview with Rev William Aitken.

Note 211 As related to the author by Rev William Aitken.

Note 212 In addition some 500 tons of stockfish, supplied to the ICRC by the World Council of Churches, arrived at Santa Isabel docks aboard the Hossjokull on Sunday 30 June. Also en route to the island was half of a British Government's relief contribution of 62 tons (the other half having been unloaded at Lagos), 1000 tons of milkpowder from Oxfam aboard the Matropa. At the beginning of July 1968 the WCC sent 500 tons of stockfish from Norway while a further 1300 tons of stockfish, made available by the Norwegian Government, was being loaded at Bergen on 15 July. Storage was about to become a major problem and with no flights underway the situation on Fernando Póo was clearly worsening.

Note 213 Although described as an I.C.R.C. charter flight, the aircraft was also reported in the *London Times* (8 July 1968) as being chartered by the World Council of Churches.

Note 214 *Airline Management and Marketing,* January 1969 issue for background details on August Martin. Insurance sources offer evidence that the dependents of Jesse Raymond Meade attempted to sue for damages. Fr Anthony Byrne kindly added further personal details.

Note 215 *Ibid.,* Peter J Marson.

Note 216 During the course of many discussions with the author, the Santa Isabel Air Traffic Controller related, with a fair degree of open amusement, the fact that Warton's aircraft were carrying illegal identities. Other details, including dates etc, are taken from the Santa Isabel Airport Tower Log Books.

Note 217 Santa Isabel Airport Tower Log-Books.

Note 218 Santa Isabel Airport Tower Log-Books

Note 219 There is some evidence that the No.1 engine suffered some damage as the author saw it with one engine out at São Tomé several weeks later and local reports suggested that the aircraft had not flown into Biafra since the 'gunboat' incident.

Note 220 Foreign & Commonwealth Office Papers; PREM13/ 2259. Public Record Office, Kew.

Note 221 *Der Spiegel*

Note 222 *Ibid.,* Fr Tony Byrne.

Note 223 As related to the author by Rev Billy Butler

Note 224 Luis A Tavares correspondence with Peter J Marson, augmented by extracts from *Airlift To Biafra* by Fr Tony Byrne (Columba Press 1996).

Note 225 The tie-up between German and false identities remains unconfirmed but from sightings at São Tomé by the author and comparison of photographs they can be judged as correct. Each of the DC-7C aircraft had minor differences in fin markings and cheat-line styles.

Note 226 From Rev William Aitken's personal log of events at Uli.

Note 227 Much of the detail on the Uli accident was supplied by the W.C.C. Controller at Uli, Rev William Aitken. The author also spoke with the crew (and ferry crew) of 5T-TAK at São Tomé prior to take-off.

Note 228 *Ibid.,* N.U. Akpan.

Note 229 *Generale Hungern Nie,* by August R Lindt. by Zytglogge Verlag Bern 1983.

Note 230 *Ibid.,* August R Lindt.

Note 231 I.C.R.C. Situation Report, August 1968.

Note 232 Details of this exchange were related to the author by I.C.R.C. personnel on Fernando Póo.

Note 233 As related to the author by Bruce Ronaldson of OXFAM, August 1968. According to Dr Lindt he travelled to Lagos on 2 August 1968!

Note 234 Axel Duch took up a position of Flight Co-Ordinator at São Tomé on 22 August 1968 and later was appointed as the Nordchurchaid Chief of Flight Operations on São Tomé on 26 September 1968, replacing Carl Gustav von Rosen. Duch held the position until 5 March 1969.

Note 235 *Ibid.,* August R Lindt.

Note 236 *Ibid.,* Frederick Forsyth (Page 212).

Note 237 As explained to the author at São Tomé, August 1968

Note 238 *London Times,* 12 August 1968

Note 239 The aircraft involved is likely to have been the L-382B Hercules CF-PWO (c/n 382-4197) which, during this period, was described by Anglia AeroNews (June 1968) as being wet-leased by Transmeridian Air Cargo Ltd and operated throughtout Europe on a charter basis.

Note 240 *London Times,* 2 July 1968 and 6 July 1968.

Note 241 This was Bruce Ronaldson whom the author met on Fernando Póo and who provided a fair amount of background information on Oxfam and the Red Cross activity.

Note 242 The flight was the first of many chartered by religious and charity groups and which brought a host of European DC-4s, DC-6s, DC-7s and Britannias to Sao Tomé. Later the flights were co-ordinated by Nordchurchaid and Boeing 707s/DC-8Fs were used. Pastor Viggo Mollerup was the General Secretary of Danchurchaid. He later became a key figure in the Nordchurchaid operation.

Note 243 There is no doubt that von Rosen had led an exceptional life. Fighting for the underdog in foreign parts and a taste for adventure ran deep in his blood. He had flown ed Cross flights in Ethiopia at the time of the 1935-1936 Italian invasion. Later, in World War II, he aided the Dutch resistance and flew a regular courier service between Berlin and Stockholm under the nose of Hermann Göring who, by marrying von Rosen's niece, had become part of the von Rosen dynasty.

Note 244 As related to the author by Fr Tony Byrne.

Note 245 *To Faraway Places* by Fr Billy Butler, published privately.

Note 246 This meeting has become almost legendary. However Fr Tony Byrne has always questioned if indeed the meeting with Ojukwu ever did take place or whether von Rosen only met relief group officials in Umuahia.

Note 247 London Times 15 July 1968

Note 248 The pro-Biafra group included two anti-establishment stalwarts–Hanna Baneth, a German Jew who had survived Hitler's rise to power and in 1968 a member of the Save Biafra Committee, and Peter Cadogan who, in 1968, was the national secretary of the antiwar group, Committee of One Hundred.

Note 249 The nine aircraft involved were TX191/209/227/230/VL349/VM329/332/351 and VV958.

Note 250 Hawke worked fairly closely with the Mercy Missions team at Bovingdon and at one stage contemplated delivering further aircraft out to Biafra. However, these plans were dropped after the crash of G-AWMG.

Note 251 There were several occasions when the weather improved but remained bad further south towards Spain. There were also good opportunities for raising financial donations to Mercy Missions.

Note 252 Although the fuel load had been calculated to be sufficient to enable G-AWMG to reach São Tomé island midway through the flight it was realised that the upper drum was emptying twice as fast as the lower two! Some delicate activity in controlling fuel-flow by a "thumb-over-the-end-of-the-pipe" method solved the difficulty.

Note 253 The proposal was accepted by the Mercy Missions crew only as a secondary operation. However at that stage the true situation at Fernando Póo was not realised.

Note 254 Unfortunately the STCF team was evacuated out several nights later.

Note 255 While it was an irritant, it was also an attempt by the W.C.C. to force the hand of the local I.C.R.C. co-ordinator, a Swiss named Steigemann, into being less dogmatic towards relief aid to Biafra. On that the W.C.C. failed and the Heron made a number of trips between the two islands. The author took advantage of these flights and spent several stopovers at São Tomé speaking with crews on the relief and arms airlift there.

Note 256 The interview was broadcast as part of BBC TV's *24 Hours*.

Note 257 As broadcast on BBC *World At One* 4 September 1968.

Note 258 As related to the author by Nic Taaffe. The crew returned to the UK and left the Anson at Port Etienne where it was eventually repaired and Nic Taaffe returned to collect it. It eventually crashed in Liberia nine months later.

140: With an ability to fly in a cargo considerably greater than the DC-6B, the Hercules was very much a fundamental part of Operation 'INALWA'. The tail marking '71' referred to the Swedish Air Force F71 Squadron. SE-XBT is seen at Santa Isabel immediately after arriving from Stockholm on 27 August 1968 *(Michael I Draper)*

141 **Far left:** When it arrived the Swedish C-130E Hercules brought in several tonnes of milk powder and a number of Volvo ambulances *(Michael I Draper)*

142 **Left:** The natural metal finish of the C-130 was deemed unsuitable amidst fears that it looked like a military aircraft! It was therefore repainted at Santa Isabel in the standard white overall finish. Unfortunately the only ladders available on the island were the mobile steps used for the local Iberia Convair 440 or for visiting Spantax DC-7Cs. Even when a long pole was fixed to the paint brush the local mechanics could still not reach the top of the fin and rudder *(Michael I Draper)*

143: Every document produced by the Biafran Government was typed on school exercise-book paper of which there seemed to be an inexhaustible supply. When the author was given clearance to "leave Biafra on 23 September 1968" he was also given permission to pass back through Uli's Immigration Control on his return. But note how the loss of Enugu a year previously was never offiically acknowledged. Enugu continued to be used as a 'postal address' throughout the conflict (Author's Personal Papers)

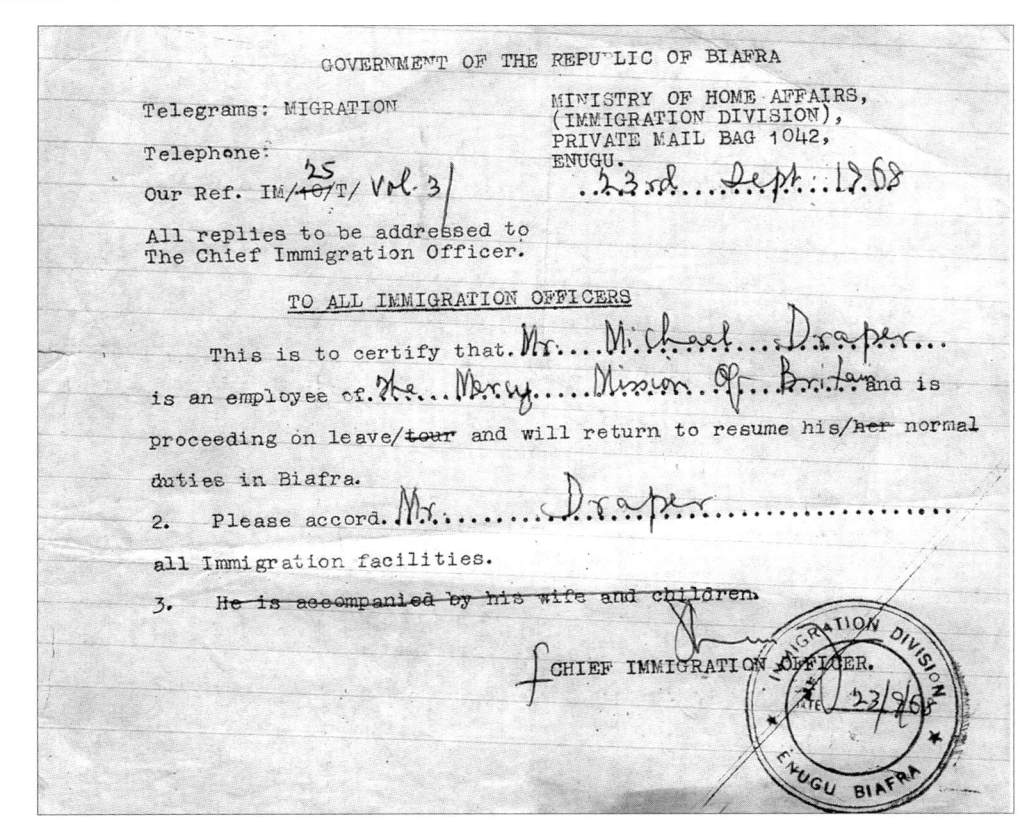

144: Mitsubishi Mu.2B HB-LEB was used exclusively by the International Red Cross co-ordinator, Dr August Lindt. It clocked up many flying hours shuttling between Fernando Póo, Lagos, Douala, Addis Ababa and other African capitals as Lindt explored supportive diplomatic means of establishing an ICRC relief airlift to Biafra (Dave Becker Collection)

145: Beech 90 King Air HB-GBK was also leased by Balair for use by Dr August Lindt. The aircraft regularly commuted between Lagos, Fernando Póo, São Tomé and Douala as Dr Lindt strove to achieve diplomatic clearance for relief flights to operate into Biafra. It is seen here at Santa Isabel, Fernando Póo, on 3 October 1968, after arriving from Lagos. On the starboard side of the fuselage the 'RED CROSS' titling was replaced by 'C.I.C.R.' (Michael I Draper)

133

ULI and UGA
The lifeline airstrips

Biafra's two main airfields were at Enugu and Port Harcourt; both had tarmac runways and a full air traffic communications facility. Three other landing-grounds existed at Calabar, Owerri and at Ogoja, all of which featured hard laterite runways but little (if any) in the way of other facilities, such as landing aids etc. The loss of Enugu, the Biafran capital, on 4 October 1967 was widely seen at the time to signal the imminent collapse of Biafran forces. Then just two weeks later Calabar, in the south-east, was lost to a successful seaborne assault by the Nigerian 3rd Marine Commando Division, on 18 October. The landing at Calabar, and a subsequent break-out to the north-east, enabled Nigerian units to effectively seal off the Biafran coastal ports as well as controlling the Biafra-Cameroons border. With road and sea communications therefore denied to them, the Biafrans were forced to transfer international communication, including valuable arms flights, to Port Harcourt despite that airfield being itself under threat from Nigerian forces at Calabar, to the east. But Port Harcourt survived for a further seven months during which period it became Biafra's main outlet to the world. Its re-capture by Nigerian forces in May 1968 came, undoubtedly, as a major blow. Huge stocks of ammunition fell into Nigerian hands when Biafrans evacuated the town. Once again it was widely anticipated that, having lost Enugu and then Port Harcourt, Biafran resistance would quickly collapse.

It was the loss of Enugu which first prompted the concept of establishing a series of secret airstrips in the Biafran bush and a team of Biafran engineers began to select possible sites. By far the easiest option in producing a traditional bush landing-strip capable of accepting an aircraft the size of a C-47 Dakota was by converting stretches of road where they ran suitably straight for a sufficient distance. Development of three sites therefore began at the end of 1967: at Uli, Uga and Awgu.[259]

It is said that that the engineer responsible for the overall layout and construction of these sites had previously been the Project Engineer for the laying of runways at Lagos and Kano airports.[260] It is also believed that Awgu was the favoured location for the first of the three strips and that work had progressed well beyond the initial stages when it was abandoned due to an increasing threat from Nigerian forces advancing from the north during the spring of 1968. At that point effort concentrated upon the second site, codenamed 'Annabelle', just to the south of the village at Uli. The decision to abandon development of Awgu proved the right one when it was eventually lost to Nigerian forces on 14 June 1968.

By far the largest of the three projected airstrips Uli became synonymous with the entire Biafran effort to survive; next to the rising sun 'national' insignia it undoubt-

146 Above: Relatively few people were in a position to photograph Uli strip during daylight but Reverend Billy Butler managed to sneak this shot as he was being driven, in a CARITAS Volkswagen car, along the side of the runway. Daylight hazards included lines of 40-gallon oil drums, positioned to prevent aircraft landing (Rev Billy Butler)

edly became the best known symbol of Biafra. The strip was converted from a stretch of the main Owerri to Ihiala road. The landing area consisted of a 6,000ft x 72ft (1,850 x 22 metres) strip of tarmac, achieved by widening the road (from its original 18 metres) to make it sufficient for operation by Douglas C-47/DC-3 aircraft. The road was relatively new and, by African standards, was well constructed having been laid by a French construction company not long beforehand. Nevertheless it was, commented one airlift pilot much later, "a nice wide road, but a damned narrow runway."

Initially, and many more were added throughout the war, some six circular bays, each with a direct link to the taxiway, were laid in the adjoining bush on the eastern side of the strip. Installed along either side of the runway was a single line of kerosene 'gooseneck' flare-pots which, when alight, marked out the extent of the landing area. Green electrical lighting had also been installed to mark out each runway threshold, and a single centre-line of red lights marked out the short-final approach at each end. To the north of Uli a single red light was affixed to the spire of Uli church and which jointly acted as an obstruction beacon and a crude navigational aid. These were the only lights installed, there being no lights along the taxi-track, nor at any of the parking-bays

By May 1968 work on a number of access and diversion roads into and around the airstrip had been completed, as had two parking areas but only two-thirds of the taxi-track (of some 16 metres in width) was finished. But in spite of Uli not being completed the Biafrans were forced to bring the strip into regular use immediately after the loss of Port Harcourt, on 21 May 1968. The first 'live' landing at Uli was made on the night of 21/22 May when a DC-7C, flown by British pilot John Phillips, arrived with a mixed cargo of military supplies and relief material.[261]

By mid-August 1968, and with the strip now in regular use, a considerable amount of additional work had measurably improved the capability of Uli to accept larger numbers of aircraft. Two-thirds of the runway 'lighting' was replaced by low-intensity electric lights and some six additional parking bays, by then referred to as 'fingers', had been laid alongside the taxi-track. The entrances to the fingers were only some 12-14 metres wide and the largest of the parking bays, measuring only 50 metres square, reflected the fact that the strip had been designed for aircraft up to DC-3 size. In total there were eight fingers all of which were referred to by number, starting at the southern (or 34) end of the runway and ending at 'Finger 8', approximately 350 metres from the northern (or 16) end.[262]

The references to the parking locations appear to have been varied; the southern end was often referred to by CARITAS personnel as 'Finger 9' while others referred to it as the 'Mgbidi end'. Others knew the southern end as simply the 'military pan' as during the early days this was the area where the arms flights were unloaded.[263] Some ground staff referred to the southern entrance as the 'Terminal Building' as there had originally been a small building which served as a government terminal, but that had been destroyed by the Nigerian Air Force very early in the airstrip's operational period. The northern end of the strip was almost always known as the 'Uli end' because of its proximity to the village of Uli. Ultimately the runway became universally known as 34/16 as a result of the required directional course settings of 344° (Runway 34) and 164° (Runway 16).

In addition to the eight fingers along the taxi-track there were, as the airlift gained momentum, other parking areas constructed at either end of the runway. At the 34 end areas had been cleared on both the east and west side, (codenamed 'Cedar 1' and 'Cedar 2'), the western pan measuring some 50 metres wide and 50 metres deep and could just contain one DC-7. The eastern pan, although considerably larger and measuring 75 metres square, was still considered suitable for only one aircraft.

At the 34 end a parking bay was cleared on the western side, again measuring approximately 50 metres square, but with considerably better access. A fourth bay, of similar dimensions, was cleared at the junction of the runway and the taxiway to 'Finger 8'.

Whilst Uli was of adequate size, and suitably equipped for the initial relief flights, it lacked many of the facilities needed for the dramatic increase in flights planned by Nordchurchaid. All of these deficiencies were listed at a meeting in Biafra, on 20 August, between the W.C.C., Nordchurchaid and the heads of the Biafran Ministry of Works and the Biafran Air Traffic Control. Afterwards, the W.C.C. representative at Uli, Reverend William ('Bill') Aitken, was invited to fly to Malmö, Sweden and to present a 'shopping-list' of items required. At the top of Bill Aitken's list was enough electric lighting to replace the remaining kerosene flares which had a tendency to be blown out every occasion an aircraft landed or took off.

Other items of equipment, vital to the needs of meeting the demands of a larger airlift included reliable replacements, or at least spare parts, for the radio Non-Directional Beacon (NDB) and the VHF Transceivers used by Uli Air Traffic Control. A new item required was a series of high-intensity fog lamps for placing at the approach to runway 34 in view of the frequent morning fog that had often forced aircraft to abandon a landing and to return to base. Additional telephone equipment to link various points on the strip to the tower and a standby generator for the landing lights were also requested by Aitken at the Malmö meeting on 26 August.

Although Bill Aitken was employed by the W.C.C. he was effectively handling every aircraft which landed at Uli and while São Tomé was despatching approximately five flights per night to Uli during late-August 1968, he was also managing arrivals by the I.C.R.C. from Fernando Póo as well as having to allow arms flights from São Tomé and Libreville.[264] Even at this early stage of the airlift there were occasions when between ten and fifteen aircraft were landing at Uli each night, all of which were unloaded by teams of Army fatigue workers under the control of one Biafran Army officer, Major Akagbogu. Operational control of Uli, however, was the responsibility of the Biafran Air Force with a Squadron Leader commanding 'Air Base Ihiala'.

The scheduling of flights by the operations staff at departure points was probably one of the most difficult of duties. Unloading generally took, during the early days of the airlift, up to an hour or more; longer if a Biafran government or arms flight was expected as these aircraft were offered priority over relief flights. This reflected the fact that in reality Uli was a military airstrip and often the unloaders were kept on the military pan–usually 'Finger 8'–to wait for a specific flight, and which in turn frequently created a shortage of unloaders for the relief flights. Flight schedules were based on ensuring the first flight of the night to Uli crossed the Nigerian coast at dusk at the earliest. If that aircraft was designated for a second flight to Uli then the latest it could leave São Tomé, for example, was 01:00 GMT in order to guarantee that it was unloaded and airborne out over the Nigerian coast before dawn broke. What did frustrate schedulers and flightcrews was that the Biafran military at Uli was not prepared to make the unloading of a relief flight a priority. Nor were those men who did the unloading willing to work at the required hectic pace, they were, after all, virtually military slave labour and (to quote Nordchurchaid) "too few in numbers, over-worked and underfed."[265]

With the installation of the improved landing-lights at Uli the next priority was a need to construct additional aircraft parking areas. During early September 1968, an urgent appeal for steel planking was sent out by Nordchurchaid. Despite several disappointments the Church Relief Service (in New York) located 13,000 square feet of aluminium planking and arranged for its purchase and shipment by air, firstly to Europe, and on to São Tomé, where it arrived on 24 September. Within four days it had been flown in to Uli and laid, principally to build a parking area known as 'Finger 1B' and along the eastern edge of the taxi-track between 'Fingers 1B' and '1A'.[266] (Not all of the aluminium planking was used at Uli; see later.)

At the same time another unloading bay was constructed by clearing the area between 'Finger 1A' and the taxi-track, some 150 metres from the area at the 34 end of the runway. This entire area inherited the name 'Finger 1A'. With the Biafran Ministry Of Works providing a good asphalt/gravel surface measuring some 60 metres square Uli was, by the end of September 1968, able to provide up to six well-surfaced parking areas. These enhanced parking areas were at 'Fingers 1A', '1B' and 'Finger 8', one bay at the end of Runway 16 and two at the end of Runway 34. All of these enlarged parking bays could adequately contain a DC-7C or an L-1049 Super Constellation.

Most of the improvements to facilities at Uli were completed by October 1968; other work had involved the construction of additional relief roads, which avoided having to cross the landing area, and the removal of some of the mounds beside the parking bays which would allow better clearance of aircraft wings when turning to park. Although all of the upgrading work had been finished there was a constant requirement for maintaining the systems and effecting repairs, the latter often necessary after night bombing by Nigerian Air Force DC-3 aircraft and daylight strafing raids by MiG-17s or, occasionally Il-28s. Night bombing of Uli, by specially-adapted Nigerian Air Force DC-3 aircraft, began during the night of 26/27 October 1968. The first casualties of the bombing occurred on the night of 5 November when a number of the Uli unloading team were killed and two crew members of a Church DC-7C were injured. After this incident, and specifically as a result of it, slit trenches were dug close to the airstrip boundary. Much later, when the bombing became more accurate, a number of protective concrete block bunkers were built alongside the unloading areas.[267]

Night bombing also brought other difficulties for the ground staff at Uli. Events leading up to the initial attack and the effect on Uli operations afterwards were graphically described by Rev 'Bill' Aitken.[268]

"On 23 October 1968 the *(Biafran)* air force telephoned the airstrip to douse all lights as an enemy plane was in the area. I was one of those who laughed. With so many planes about and no radar how could they know there was an enemy–anyhow the Nigerians had never flown at night. After an hour lights went on and we continued unloading. The same happened the next night and again on the third night–then bombs were dropped. Evidently the Biafran intelligence had been accurate. This brought in a new phase; the phase of dark silent unloading. Up till now ground power units plugged into the planes had provided light for unloading as well as background noise. Now no cars or lorries were allowed to use even sidelights while driving, torches were kept to a minimum, and all background noise and machinery was stopped so that people could listen for the distinctive noise of the bomber and of falling bombs.

"The danger moments were always while a plane was landing and immediately after it had landed, for then the bomber had had his target clearly lit up for about 30 seconds during which time he could make his bombing run. Tactics varied; at first there were large numbers of fragmentation bombs, then the policy seemed to change and six heavier bombs were used.

"The blackout led to another phase of difficulty–that of controlling the unloading. Some schoolmasters have trouble with a class of 30 boys under the ideal conditions of a classroom; but put the class into the dark and ask them to work at unloading a highly valuable cargo and even the most experienced schoolmaster would quail at the task. And the trouble was that the NCOs in charge of the Biafran air force's labour gangs were not even experienced schoolmasters. Conditions for the thief were perfect and falling bombs gave an excellent excuse for rushing off into the darkness. No wonder that some of our pilots, in a hurry to be unloaded and off the ground into the comparative safety of the air, were exasperated when the labourers seemed more interested in what they could acquire themselves than in getting the job done. But once more we had excellent co-operation from those in authority. There were senior officers whom we could trust absolutely, and though they could not be everywhere at once they made it perfectly plain to those under them that nonsense would be tolerated.

"As the relief goods became more valuable as other forms of food became scarcer, so black market prices rose and the attacks on the lorries between the airport and our central store became more determined. At first, villagers and local people would try to jump onto the back of a moving lorry, cut down the barrier tied at the back and throw something off into the roadside. Then when we put lorries into convoys, a log would be rolled across the road in front of the last one in order to cut it off from the rest. As the attacks became more subtle so we tightened our security, until finally we came in March (1969) to an armed hold up organised by the sort of black marketeers and deserters that every war produces. The air force responded with an armed escort and a week or so later there was a gun battle in which one of the attackers had his leg shattered. After that the attacks ceased."

At the same time as improvements to the parking and unloading areas were being carried out so similar improvements were being made in the Air Traffic Control and radio communications facilities. The original 'control tower' at Uli was in fact nothing more sophisticated than the rear section of a Land Rover which was usually positioned on the west side of the runway, about 1,000 metres from the northern end. At the same location was placed the electrical generator that supplied power to the runway lights together with the control switch, which allowed the Biafran air traffic controller (initially a young Biafran, Peter Areh) to verbally instruct the switcher as to when to turn on the lights. The arrangement was never ideal due often to the noise of aircraft taxiing close-by, nor was the condition of the communications equipment sufficiently good enough to be described as reliable.

After a daylight strafing attack by Nigerian Air Force L-29 Delfins during August 1968, as a result of which much of the radio equipment at Uli was destroyed, the control centre was moved to 'Air Base Ihiala', a point some 3km north of the airstrip. Unfortunately, the move did place Air Traffic Control some distance away from the runway-light controller but as night-bombing of Uli had not started at that stage the unreliable telephone link was not a major issue.

When night-bombing did start, during October 1968, runway lights were turned on for the shortest time possible. They were turned on at the incoming pilot's request and remained on for certainly no more than a minute at an absolute maximum; then extinguished immediately after touch-down, all taxiing and parking being made by using the aircraft's own lights. From this period the landing operation required a greater degree of precision by the ground staff as well as the pilots but all too often there was a slight delay in turning the lights on, thus causing an incoming aircraft to overshoot at the final moment. Unfortunately this procedure was never changed and there were many occasions when accidents were avoided by the narrowest of margins. (Indeed the landing procedure at Uli may well have been a contributive factor in the subsequent loss of C-97G N52676, during September 1969.)

By January 1969, and despite regular on-site repairs and frequent modifications, the VHF link between the Uli Controller and inbound aircraft had reached a severely dangerous state, so much so that the airlift was suspended for the night of 15/16 January to allow a meeting of controllers, relief agencies and the Biafran authorities. The primary objective of the meeting was to review air traffic procedures. Already new VHF equipment was being installed at Air Base Ihiala and a new Non-Directional Beacon (NDB) was brought into use shortly afterwards which, combined with the newly-installed high intensity fog/approach lights, greatly enhanced the bad weather approach facilities at Uli. A final improvement involved the setting-up of a Visual Approach Path Indicator (VAPI) which offered pilots greater assistance in making a correct approach to Runway 34. This equipment had been purchased, in the USA, by Flight Test Research and delivered into Uli during late-February 1969 aboard a C-97G. It was then handed over to W.C.C.'s Reverend 'Bill'Aitken who had it installed and working satisfactorily by mid-March.

It was not just the equipment which was tired and overworked. By March 1969 the Controllers at Uli had worked almost continuously for some seven months under the most testing of conditions; they were seriously overworked and certainly under-staffed. As a result the Swedish church relief agency, Lutherhjalpen, offered the services of Lars Elming, a serving officer with the Swedish Air Force from whom he was technically on leave; he arrived at São Tomé on 7 April 1969 and took up his new position at Uli several nights later. Elming introduced a number of improvements to the Air Traffic Control procedures and helped with other local improvements, including the repainting of white runway markers.

Apart from the technical difficulties associated with the equipment at Uli there were natural hazards, especially the frequent tropical thunderstorms and ground fog early

147: For a brief period in the autumn of 1968 the International Red Cross made use of an exclusively designated 'Red Cross' strip at Obilagu. Known also as Uturu the strip was converted from a stretch of the Afikpo-Okigwe road and ran approximately 08/26. In this view conscript workers sweep clear the red cross patch before touching-up the red areas. Oil drums have been placed the length of the centre-line to prevent any unscheduled landing. Note how both sides of the road have been widened at the end of the strip to allow an aircraft, up to DC-7C size, to turn through 360° for line-up and take-off (CICR/Finck; BIAF33/21)

148: When Jack Malloch's DC-4 TR-LNV crashed on take-off at Uli it overran the end of the landing-strip and came to rest further along the main road. This view shows that despite the fact that it was essentially a bush high road the tarmac did stand up relatively well to the weight of an out-of-control DC-4. It also gives an indication of the original width of the road before it was slightly widened into a landing-strip. Another view of this accident is on page 108 (Dave Goldsmith)

149: Nigerian Colonel Olusegun Obasanjo's most recorded moment came when he posed at the southern end of Uli strip within days of Biafra's surrender. It seems almost incredible that this landing strip should have been described as a "secret airstrip in the Biafran bush" when white markers and the '34' compass heading should be so prominent. At the end of the war the wrecks of seven aircraft visibly littered Uli. These remained in situ for at least fours years afterwards (Peter Obe)

in the mornings. The fog often restricted vertical visibility to 30 metres or even less. In such circumstances crews were simply forced to let down through the fog in the hope of finding the runway. Mercifully the 2,600 metre landing strip was sufficiently long enough to allow for some margin of error and often fully-laden aircraft touched-down halfway along the runway but were still able to brake in time.

For inbound flights Uli operated only between the hours of darkness, officially from 17:00 to 05:00 hours GMT. Landing was only permissible after the crew had transmitted the correct landing-code for the night. Various code styles were devised by the Biafrans and which often involved using a simple phrase, the interpretation of which was understood by both aircrew and ground controllers. The coded phrases changed regularly but as the size of the airlift increased and the time between aircraft landings reduced considerably, for pilots it became a most unpleasant task having to turn various pieces of paper in order to code and decode phrases while at the same time prepare for approach and landing manoeuvres to an airstrip in complete darkness and in a volatile airspace.

Towards the end of January 1969 the Biafran Air Force introduced a new frequency shift system for the final approach and landing phase. The new arrangement involved pilots initially contacting Biafra Area Control Centre (ACC) by using the normal code format. As soon as an inbound aircraft was established with the ACC then, and depending on traffic, weather, or enemy aircraft activity ACC would then clear the inbound aircraft to Uli whereupon pilots would then talk with Uli Tower in plain language until touchdown. Attempts at maintaining a degree of secrecy was achieved by constantly changing to pre-determined radio frequencies throughout the night. The revised system was introduced for a trial period during the night of 24/25 January 1969 but only at first for Joint Church Aid aircraft operating out of São Tomé due to the Biafrans not trusting "certain other agencies" flying into Biafra. The frequency chart for the first week of operation was as follows:

FREQUENCY CHART VALID FROM FRIDAY 24 JAN 1969 - FRIDAY 31 JAN 1969

Date	Channel A	Channel B	Channel C	Channel D	Channel E	Channel F	Channel G
24.1.69	118.4	118.7	119.5	119.9	119.1	120.7	126.2
25.1.69	130.5	128.5	122.6	129.5	128.7	119.3	118.5
26.1.69	126.6	126.8	127.2	125.1	124.3	130.8	130.3
27.1.69	119.9	119.3	128.5	118.6	119.2	124.7	118.8
28.1.69	129.1	118.3	120.1	126.0	122.8	121.7	129.0
29.1.69	118.5	122.6	128.7	118.0	126.4	118.5	118.0
30.1.69	130.4	119.9	125.1	118.6	120.8	119.3	118.9
31.1.69	120.0	126.2	118.4	123.9	119.0	128.7	125.1
Times GMT	1700-1900	1900-2000	2000-2130	2130-2300	2300-0130	0130-0230	0230-0500

The system of constant frequency changes worked well although pilots felt it unnecessary that a different set of frequencies was issued for each night. Therefore the next set of codes which were issued for the month of February 1969 showed the same frequencies being maintained for periods of four nights. There were, of course, obvious dangers to the revised system with so many aircraft inbound to the same location and all attempting landing procedures on different Air Traffic frequencies, some transmissions in code, others not.

On Tuesday 1 April 1969 a new set of landing codes was introduced and which was based on a simple three digit principle. The codes were divided into three sections, the three digits relating to each section of the code sheet. The first digit was described as a 'Constant' to indicate at a glance which section of the main code is being referred to; an 'Indicator' related to a pre-determined statement. Lastly, a 'Variant' was added and which was simply any number which did not repeat the previous two digits. At the same time, individual aircraft were also allocated three letter codes, for example DC-6 PH-TRB was coded 'RWS', DC-6B PH-TRD as 'FGH' and PH-TRZ as 'MNR'. In addition to these codes the Biafrans also used a system of 'key words' to indicate numbers; these being used when relating to flight levels and radio frequencies. Thus a crew flying DC-6B PH-TRZ and being cleared from 6,000 feet for an approach to Uli (code-named 'WW') would receive the instruction "MNR 6-4-9, Whisky-Whisky, Mozambique-Burundi", the two African States being the 'key-words' for '6' and '0'. *(A full set of landing-codes for Uli, as well as Uga, is shown on page 284)*

For many aircrew flying at night and in hostile airspace offered little room for error. Navigation over Biafra was essentially based on the 'time-and-distance' rule and which involved simply flying for a pre-determined time on a certain heading and maintaining a constant speed. The process was started by establishing the point of crossing the Nigerian coastline, either by visual contact or by gaining a radar fix. Once within approximately 50 kilometres of Uli pilots were able to navigate by homing the aircraft's Automatic Direction Finding equipment onto one of the Biafran beacons. Prior to Christmas 1968, ie before ground equipment was considerably upgraded, all inbound aircraft homed into the radio beacon 'EB', located on the western edge of Uli's runway. But with the increase in relief flight traffic (which in turn increased the risk of mid-air collision) the air traffic control pattern was altered in January 1969. A secondary reason for re-organising landing patterns was that another airstrip at Uga, and only 27 kilometres to the north-east of Uli, was brought into regular use for Biafran Government aircraft.

Uga, the second of the three sites originally selected as a bush airstrip, was hastily developed following the threatened loss of Uli during September 1968. Like Uli, the strip at Uga was converted from a stretch of the main Orlu to Awka road but instead of creating concrete hard-standings the Biafrans used a form of PSP, a pierced-steel planking system, although local reports at the time described the material as 'perforated aluminium strips'. (It is very likely that the material used for developing Uga had originally been purchased via the Church Relief Service for use at Uli - see earlier). Certainly the material was seen to be conveyed from Uli to the new site by road. By the end of 1968 the strip was declared operational, but only as a secondary strip to Uli and strictly for government and military useage only. Uga could only, in reality, be considered for emergency purposes as the actual landing strip was considerably uneven and pilots who used it complained about the undulating surface. In fact at first Uga was very rarely used, even by arms flights which continued to use Uli under the cover of relief flights. It was not until the late-Spring of 1969, after Uli had been subjected to a particularly bad spell of night-bombing, when Uga came into more regular usage. Even then, it was pressure from the Churches which brought Uga into more regular use rather than any desire to separate the two commodities of relief and arms.

The first known landing of a regular arms flight into Uga came on the night of 10/11 May 1969 when Jack Malloch flew one of his own DC-7CFs, TR-LOJ, into Uga. With him were co-pilot Clive Halse and Flight Engineer Cliff Hawthorne. None relished the idea of using Uga strip again; the landing surface was not as good as Uli with considerable amounts of loose stone and shingle. The surface proved to be a major hazard especially when putting heavily-laden DC-7CFs into reverse pitch after landing. Contrary to popular belief, very few flights were made by DC-7s or L-1049Gs into Uga.[269]

The substantial increase in the size of the airlift during the Autumn of 1968, notably from São Tomé, raised the question of creating a holding pattern and it was essentially this that emerged from the changes introduced in January 1969. The process that evolved was based upon a holding beacon 'EZ' positioned some 32 kilometres east of Uli, approximately midway between Uli and Uga. Inbound aircraft were instructed to establish their run-in on the 'EZ' beacon (244kc), make contact with the newly set-up Biafran Area Control Centre and to receive instructions for holding in a pattern around the beacon. When pilots were overhead the 'EB' Beacon (435kc) they would call to announce "overhead" to Uli, and using it as a reference to begin their landing approach pattern, flying their downwind, base-leg and short final courses on this basis. Another NDB, 'AA' Beacon (422kc) was established just to the south of Uli's 34 end. Aircraft would later report "short finals" to the tower, request "lights" and be asked to report "lights in sight". They would then be cleared to landing and given parking instructions.

Pilots flying in from São Tomé initially took a due-northerly heading to the Nigerian coastline, a distance of 238 nautical miles with an approximate flight-time of 1 hour 10 minutes, all interior and exterior lights being turned off some twenty minutes before crossing the coast. A change of heading to 025° for seventeen minutes (68 n.miles) followed by a turn to 065° for twelve minutes (48 n.miles) brought the incoming aircraft to overhead the 'EZ' Beacon where aircraft held (if necessary) at a minimum 6,000 feet and in a left-hand holding pattern.

A chart marked out in three-minute divisions allowed for a direct flight from the Nigerian coast to Uli to take exactly 24 minutes. Some pilots from São Tomé generally preferred to cross the Nigerian coast just west of Brass which was often visible by the flares from onshore oil wells.[270] A maximum airspeed of 150 knots in the holding-pattern ensured adequate separation. Or, so it was theoretically. On occasions as many as twenty aircraft were circling simultaneously, some of which were assigned the same altitude by inexperienced Biafran controllers. It was not just the Nigerian Air Force C-47 'Genocide' which offered a threat to airlift pilots–one Swedish pilot, Ulf Engelbrecht, claimed that "if all the pilots some night were to turn on rotating beacons and clearance lights, a dozen of them would die of fright at their proximity to one another!"

Most of the flights that made use of Uli were relief agency flights flying in from the three main relief bases but there is no doubt that these agencies did provide the Biafrans with a cover for arms flights and its own governmental flights. It was these last-mentioned flights which were the real target for the Federal Nigerian Air Force bombing sorties. Such, therefore, was the need for some form of anti-aircraft defence.

Light anti-aircraft guns were placed at each end of the airstrip and manned by a Biafran Army unit. There were no occasions when they managed to shoot any attacking aircraft down although as the war progressed additional gun batteries were installed. Strafing attacks by MiG-17s were frequently carried out just after dawn in the hope of catching a late departing aircraft or an aircraft forced to remain on the ground due to a temporary fault. On occasions the MiGs were lucky and at very low altitude they presented a very difficult target for Biafran anti-aircraft defences. Ultimately the Biafrans sought more imaginative means to protect Uli.

Uli survived until the very end of the civil war. There were occasions when lights broke down or Nigerian bombing damaged the runway. But amazingly it survived until the very end.

Notes

Note 259 Although Uli became synonymous with the relief airlift its planned useage was always to be as a military strip, as was Uga and Awgu. Undoubtedly there were other sites looked at also.

Note 260 It was never planned that any of the strips would be any more than a converted roadway. In this way the strip could be easily camouflaged as well as not requiring the basic foundation work. As the size of the aircraft being operated increased this sometimes did cause problems for larger and heavier aircraft.

Note 261 As recorded by Rev William Aitken in his personal diary. He did not record the identity of the aircraft but it is presumed to have been either the Biafran government's G-ATOB or the ex-Schreiner PH-SAE. The serviceability state of both of these aircraft was highly suspect and therefore in reality it is doubtful if the first landing was either of them–if indeed Rev Aitken was correct in believing it to be a DC-7C.

Note 262 As described to the author by Rev William Aitken.

Note 263 As described to the author by John Trent, a regular Flight Engineer aboard L-1049G '5N-07G' during mid-1968.

Note 264 The relief organisations worked hard at separating any handling activity of relief material to that of the arms flights. However, the gun-runners worked equally hard to integrate their movements at Uli with those of the relief flights. At no time did the relief organisations assist in unloading ammunition.

Note 265 Nordchurchaid Operations Report

Note 266 Some press reports did record several lorries taking alluminium planking northwards from Uli, leading to speculation that a second strip was being prepared. It could be, of course, that some of this material was diverted to Uga strip.

Note 267 *Ibid.*, Fr Tony Byrne

Note 268 *On The Airstrip At Uli* by Rev William Aitken, published as an article within the July/August 1969 issue of the periodical *Venture*. The text is reproduced with kind permission from Rev Aitken.

Note 269 According to Jack Malloch's aircrew who landed there.

Note 270 A number of Transavia crew used this method; it was described to the author by First Officer Phil Phillp.

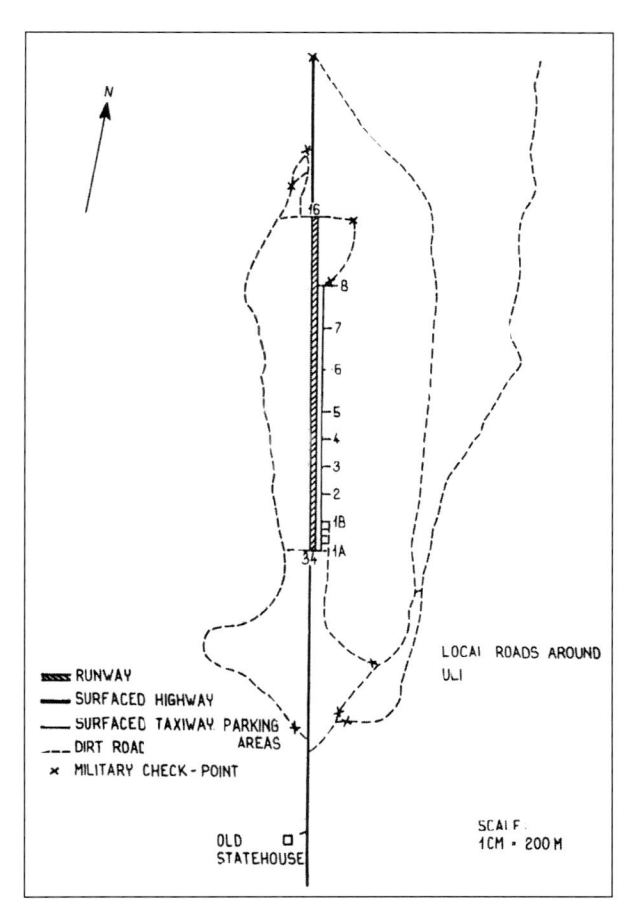

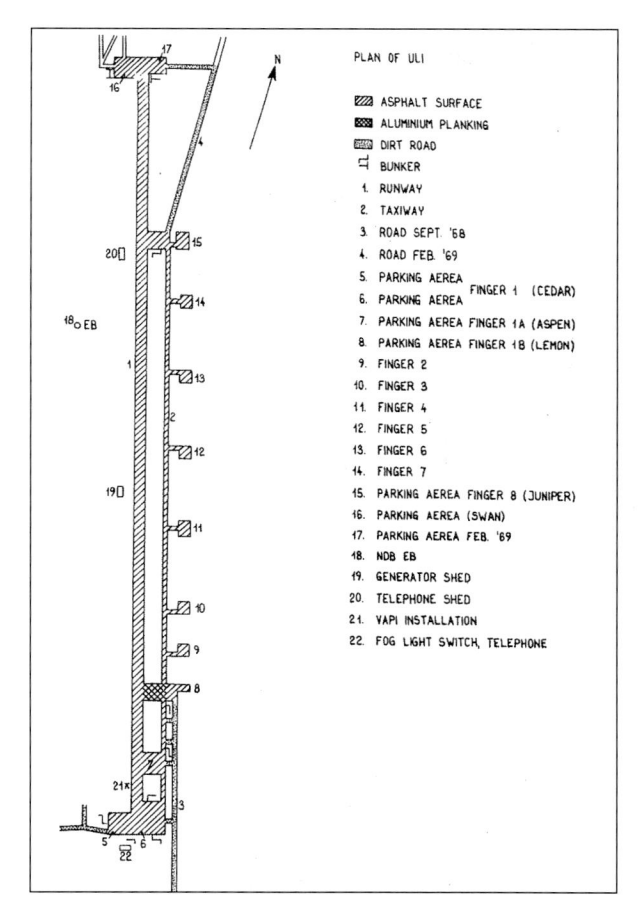

150, 151 Above: When Port Harcourt was lost to Nigerian forces in May 1968, the Biafrans were forced to open up prematurely the incomplete Uli strip for military and the occasional relief flights. The strip was merely a section of the Owerri to Ihiala road between the villages of Mbidi and Uli. Alongside the eastern side of the runway a taxiway was laid off which were eight parking bays ('Fingers'). By August 1968, when the relief operation began to gain momentum, a series of additional facilities began to be introduced. These primarily involved improved lighting and landing aids. As the airlift increased in size so the pressure on improving ground facilities increased. In September 1968 the World Council of Churches and the Biafran Ministry of Works constructed a vital link road between Finger 1A and the diversion road at the southern end of the strip. Similarly, in February 1969, another road between Finger 8 and the 16 end of the landing-strip was built. In the case of the latter terrain and drainage enforced a dog-leg pattern. This new road avoided the need to drive along the blacked-out runway when travelling, often essentially, between either end of the strip as aircraft were preparing to land or take-off. At the same time as this road was built the Biafrans constructed another parking bay (codeword 'JUNIPER') at the northern end of the strip Item 15 on the plan above). The taxiway, widened landing strip and parking-bays were constructed of a gravel and crushed rock base (obtained from river beds to the north-west of Uli) and with a locally-made bitumen top-cover. Sufficient stocks of both were maintained throughout the war for extending some bays as well as repairing bomb damage. Some 13,000sq ft of aluminium planking was obtained from the USA by Church Relief Services and air-freighted to Sao Tome in September 1968. This not only allowed for a new Finger 1B but also to widen the taxiway along the eastern edge between Fingers 1A and 1B. Ironically some of this material was also used to provide facilities at a new military strip under construction at Uga (Plans reproduced and augmented courtesy of Pastor Viggo Mollerup, Danchurchaid)

NORDCHURCHAID AIRLIFT BEGINS - JOINT CHURCH AID EMERGES
International Red Cross 'Operation INALWA' launched

Whether or not Count Gustav von Rosen ever did meet Ojukwu after his first flight into Biafra (on 12 August 1968) is almost immaterial. He certainly met with senior personnel of relief agencies in Biafra and discussed with them the outline objective of a developing plan. That plan was designed to enable the relief airlift to resume, not in the rather haphazard manner of the past, but with sufficient number of aircraft operating at a much-increased frequency. Only then, claimed von Rosen, would they be capable in helping to relieve the civilian suffering within Biafra. The Swede's plan also called for a fully co-ordinated and well-organised airlift which, as he saw it, only the Churches could effectively mount, but von Rosen also put forward two provisions; firstly that the reliance upon Hank Warton for flights to Biafra cease immediately (especially as the Churches now had the landing-codes for Uli) and, secondly, that von Rosen himself be installed as the Chief of Operations.

The suggestion that Biafra should break its alliance with Hank Warton, for both food and arms, undoubtedly found favour with Ojukwu. The Biafran army was under extreme pressure from the south and ammunition stocks were dangerously low.[271] In the knowledge that Biafran emissaries were at that time liaising with several potential new suppliers, Ojukwu acceded to von Rosen's provisions. (Arrangements for an alternative arms airlift from Lisbon were completed at a meeting on São Tomé island over the two days, 16/17 August 1968)

The day after von Rosen returned to São Tomé, on 14 August, he flew the Transair DC-7B SE-ERK back to Malmö and hurriedly arranged for a series of meetings, initially with his bosses to help draw up a charter arrangement. In the meantime, and at an I.C.R.C. press conference in Geneva, Pastor Mollerup first learned of von Rosen's recent blockade-breaking flight into Biafra. So did Axel Duch, the pilot of the 'Angel of Mercy' L-1049H, N469C, who was at the same press conference and in Geneva to help persuade the I.C.R.C. to authorise his aircraft to fly into Biafra. Immediately after the press conference closed Mollerup and Duch flew up to Malmö to meet von Rosen. The three met, on 18 August 1968, and discussed the feasibility of a new and independent airlift from São Tomé to Uli. All three agreed the basis for a further meeting with representatives of the Danish, Norwegian and Swedish church relief organisations.[272]

Enter Nordchurchaid

From the second meeting emerged the formation of an *ad hoc* air transport organisation to be known as Nordchurchaid and an agreement to charter aircraft was reached under the guidance and leadership of von Rosen.

152 Above: After experiencing continued difficulties in its Operation 'INALWA' out of Fernando Poo, the I.C.R.C opened a new base at Cotonou, Dahomey. The mainstay of the original Cotonou fleet was the C-160D Transall HB-ILN and two DC-6ACs, HB-IBS and HB-IBT (Marcel Tschudin)

Initially Nordchurchaid sought to charter aircraft for periods of fourteen days; all of the aircraft were to be drawn from Scandinavian companies in order to underline the neutrality factor of any proposed relief airlift. Von Rosen's recommendation of fleet size accounted for a total of eight aircraft (to include one spare) at São Tomé and with a frequency target of two flights per aircraft, per 24-hour period.

With seven aircraft in continual usage the burden of chartering costs under the Nordchurchaid agreement was to be divided as follows:

Folkekirkens Nodhjelp, Denmark	two-sevenths
Kirkens Nodhjelp, Norway	two-sevenths
Lutherhjalpen, Sweden	two-sevenths
Kyrkans U-landshjalp, Finland	one-seventh

By noon on 19 August 1968, just 24 hours after the new agreement had been drawn up, Nordchurchaid was in a position to publicly announce that six aircraft had already been located and that charter agreements were being signed. The six aircraft involved three DC-7Bs (SE-ERD, SE-ERI and SE-ERK) from Transair Sweden AB, a single DC-6B (OY-EAR) from Sterling Airways and two C-46R Commando aircraft (LN-FOP and LN-FOR) from Fred Olsen Air Transport.

The Transair DC-7Bs were capable of carrying a payload of 9,000kgs (9 tonnes) and under the charter agreement the company received $3,625 per São Tomé to Uli shuttle, whether or not the aircraft actually landed at Uli. Transair Sweden also received $17,500 for a return trip to Europe, necessary every fourteen days for routine maintenance work. The charter agreement between Nordchurchaid and Transair was later renewed to take effect from 3 September 1968. The renewal contract was financed slightly differently to the first and simply involved a payment (by Nordchurchaid) of $696 per aircraft flying hour plus $723 for each flight and $200 (per aircraft) for each day that the DC-7B was stationed at São Tomé.

The payload of the Sterling Airways' DC-6B was 1,000kgs (1 tonne) less than the Transair DC-7B although in time the DC-6B became the favoured workhorse of the airlift. The initial cost for chartering the Sterling Airways' aircraft (OY-EAR) was agreed at $300 per block-hour (to include handling, take-off and landing charges), plus a layover fee of $175 for each 'commenced 24-hour period'.

Finally, the agreed costs to Nordchurchaid for chartering the two Fred Olsen C-46Rs involved a rate of $388 per flying-hour providing a minimum six flying-hours were carried out each day. Nordchurchaid was obliged to pay $65 for each hour short of the 6-hour target. In fact the Norwegian owners never exercised this option on the few occasions when flights were cancelled and flying-hours fell short of target.[273]

The first of the Transair DC-7Bs to join the new Nordchurchaid fleet was SE-ERD and which departed Malmö on 22 August and routed to São Tomé, via Las Palmas and Abidjan. Aboard the first aircraft was Axel Duch, returning to São Tomé to take up a temporary appointment as Nordchurchaid's Flight Co-Ordinator until the return of von Rosen himself who, in the meantime, had began to travel extensively to enlist worldwide support for the new operation.

Von Rosen's first call was to Geneva on 19 August to meet with the International Red Cross Co-Ordinator for Biafra, Dr August Lindt, but the concept of a joint I.C.R.C./Nordchurchaid airlift–with both groups sharing operating and warehousing costs–was not acceptable to Lindt. (Lindt, in fact, believed that any joint operation could falter if one of the partners should be forced to halt flights; two independent airlifts would ensure that the flow of relief material would continue, albeit on a reduced basis. In reality Lindt still considered the Churches' operation to be technically illegal due to no prior permission being sought from Lagos. Furthermore Lindt was also mindful that sooner or later the Federal Nigerian government would achieve suitable means for grounding the Church airlift and allow the International Red Cross the sole right to humanitarian relief flights. (Events were later to prove him so wrong on all counts.)[274]

After his non-productive meeting with the I.C.R.C., von Rosen flew south to meet with his old friend, Emperor Haile Selassi of Ethiopia who, since the O.A.U. Peace Conference at Addis Ababa, had become personally involved in Nigeria's civil war. Von Rosen also travelled to New York, Washington and Toronto to persuade government and church groups to support Nordchurchaid with both financial and material aid.

When he returned to Sweden von Rosen did so to collect the third of the Transair DC-7Bs to be allocated for Biafra operations. SE-ERI departed Malmö on 3 September 1968 and was flown south to São Tomé, via Niamey. Among the handful of passengers aboard SE-ERI was Reverend 'Bill' Aitken who, while von Rosen had been drumming up support for Nordchurchaid, had managed to secure most of the equipment necessary to upgrade Uli for the expected increase in flights and tonnages.[275] There was a distinct change of attitude at São Tomé when von Rosen and Aitken landed and for Aitken it was most encouraging to see such a gathering of aircraft, all designated for relief flights.

By 5 September 1968 all six Nordchurchaid aircraft had started regular flights to Uli alongside the ex-Südflug DC-7Cs that were still being operated by the German Catholic and Protestant Churches. Later, during the same evening, 'Bill' Aitken boarded one of the German Church DC-7Cs for the final leg of his flight to Uli. (Aitken recorded in his diary that not only has he "been encouraged at the sight of so many aircraft at São Tomé" but that when he later landed at Uli he was "left speechless upon learning that the strip was now accepting up to fourteen flights per night."[276]

The increase in relief flights to Uli was not just due to the start of the Nordchurchaid operation from São Tomé. There had been some quite dramatic developments at the International Red Cross base on Fernando Póo.

Operation 'INALWA': the Red Cross fleet grows

I.C.R.C. Directors in Geneva continued to lobby for daylight flights into Biafra. The flights were seen as necessary until the much-favoured neutral land corridor could be established, and in preparation for the likely sanctioning of those daylight flights, the International Red Cross had begun to request additional aircraft through Governments and/or national Red Cross agencies. Sweden promised a C-130E Hercules while Denmark, Finland and Norway also promised one aircraft each.

The first aircraft to arrive at the International Red Cross base on Fernando Póo island was a Swedish Air Force C-130E Hercules (84001), chartered by the Swedish Red Cross, and temporarily civilianised with the marks SE-XBT. It landed at Santa Isabel on 27 August, having routed from Stockholm via Casablanca and Robertsfield, Liberia. The Hercules was followed, on 28 August, by two DC-6B aircraft on a direct charter to I.C.R.C., LN-SUD from Braathens S.A.F.E., and OH-KDA from the Finnish charter company, Kar Air. The latter aircraft was unusual in being a 'swing-tail' DC-6BF conversion and which allowed the carriage of bulky loads through a rear entry door. A third new arrival involved a Sterling Airways DC-6B OY-BAS, which arrived on 30 August, and to complete the fleet of six was the Martinair DC-7C PH-DSL, chartered by the Dutch Red Cross, and which arrived at Santa Isabel from Amsterdam via Palermo, on 6 September 1968.

Unlike the Church aircraft, most of the new arrivals assigned to the International Red Cross had been repainted in Europe with a highly-visibile white overall scheme and with standard red cross insignia. There were two exceptions. Firstly, of course, was the Balair DC-6B HB-IBU, which was still in its basic airline scheme but with red cross insignia beneath the wings only. The other exception was the Swedish Air Force C-130E which had retained its standard natural metal finish but with red cross insignia. All Air Force insignia and markings had been erased although they were still visible to a casual eye, a fact that did not go unnoticed by staff from the Nigerian embassy on the island. Shortly after its arrival SE-XBT was repainted at Santa Isabel in a white overall finish but nowhere on the island was there a ladder tall enough to reach the upper part of the fin. The white overall scheme therefore excluded these parts.

With most of its fleet positioned on Fernando Póo island within the prescribed timescale, the I.C.R.C. finalised plans for what was described as Operation 'INALWA': **In**ternational **A**ir**L**ift, **W**est **A**frica, provisionally timed to commence on 3 September. Victor Hug was appointed the commander of INALWA, his deputy being a Swede, Sven Lampell, who some years previously had commanded the fighter aircraft element of UN operations in the Congo. Another change of personnel involved the captain of the Balair DC-6B HB-IBU, which was now being flown by Guy Steiner. Prior to the launch of INALWA, the International Red Cross had completed some 47 flights into Biafra and which had ferried 398 tons, 219 tons of which had been flown in during the month of August 1968 on board the Balair DC-6B HB-IBU.

Just prior to the start of Operation 'INALWA' Lindt gathered a meeting of flight captains to finalise the flying aspects. All of the pilots agreed that the best option was to continue night flights into Biafra and to fly above the Nigerian flak. (In fact the only pilot willing to fly to Biafra in daylight was the Finn.) During the first night of Operation INALWA (3/4 September) the four I.C.R.C DC-6Bs each made one flight into Biafra with a combined load totalling 30 tonnes. On the following night only the three Scandinavian DC-6Bs flew in, the Kar-Air aircraft achieving two round trips. A week later, during the night of 11/12 September, the Martinair DC-7C PH-DSL joined the nightly airlift. And so it continued...

All of these flights were made from Fernando Póo to Uli, the Red Cross strip at Obilagu still not being ready to receive incoming flights.

Obilagu: the Red Cross strip

There still remains some considerable doubt as to precisely when the exclusive Red Cross strip at Obilagu was first used. Geneva announced, on 4 September 1968, that two Red Cross aircraft, one Swiss and one Scandanavian, had landed at Obilagu for the first time during the previous night. But one of the problems at Obilagu was the lack of any runway lighting. That fact alone precluded its use and in a display of clear irritation at not being allowed to use Obilagu, Lindt came up with an intriguing solution. He ordered all available personnel on Fernando Póo to find and collect as many empty wine bottles as they could find; by the end of the day the Balair DC-6B HB-IBU was loaded with empty beer, wine and champagne bottles, sufficient in number to establish two lines of gooseneck flares along the landing strip at Obilagu. Lindt also sent the INALWA boss, Sven Lampell, into Biafra on the same flight to ensure that the bottles reached Obilagu.[277]

On 6 September the Swedish Hercules flew into Biafra for the first time; it is also likely that this marked the first occasion that the International Red Cross used its own exclusive airstrip. The exclusivity did not, however, last for very long.

The increase in relief aid being flown in by the Churches and the International Red Cross was the result of several months of worldwide publicity for the plight of Biafra's civilian population. Of greatest concern were Biafra's children who had come to symbolise the need for such a massive relief effort. The flow of food into Biafra had started in real earnest. But for Biafra independence was far from being secure.

The advance by the Nigerian Army's 16 & 17 Brigades (3 Marine Commando Division) towards Owerri progressed slowly. Federal troops found it hard-going, especially as the advance was along a wide front line which, while stretching Nigerian resources, also caused a massive strain on Biafran efforts to defend Owerri yet still hold on to the equally-important town of Aba. When the Nigerian assault against Aba began on 24 August the Biafrans fought hard to defend the town but their stocks of ammunition had run desperately low. So low were the stocks that the Biafrans were forced to abandon Aba on 4 September. To the west the Nigerian Army's 15 Brigade made a very decisive dash towards the town of Oguta on 10 September 1968. The Biafrans could do nothing but panic; again the defenders' ammunition was virtually exhausted partly due to a lack of incoming arms flights. The speed of the Nigerian advance around Oguta brought Nigerian guns dangerously close to Uli airstrip and such was the sheer panic within the Biafran camp that the airstrip was abandoned. For four nights (12-15 September) the relief organisation's ground personnel at the strip were ordered away from the area and during the same period no flights landed at Uli.

With Uli abandoned and feared to have been lost the International Red Cross routed all of its flights into Obilagu. On the night of 13/14 September four Red Cross aircraft (DC-6BF OH-KDA, DC-6 OY-BAS, DC-7C PH-DSL and C-130E SE-XBT) landed with, between them, 33.7 tonnes of milkpowder, lentils and medical equipment. The Hercules flew in three Volvo ambulances. All four aircraft made just one return flight into Biafra that night, but the jubilation on Fernando Póo at having been able to fly into Biafra, despite the reported loss of Uli, was later tempered by the realisation that the Biafran leadership, desperate for shipments of arms from Libreville, had instructed several military flights to land at Obilagu as well. The implications of Red Cross personnel constructing an exclusive airstrip which was then shared by gun-runners were all too horrifying to imagine, but the Red Cross managed to avoid embarrassment.

Although the Nigerians had successfully advanced as far as Oguta, and therefore to within just a few miles of Uli, the most forward units had effectively outstretched their line of communication, so much so that within several days the same units were forced to withdraw from Oguta (on 15 September) to avoid becoming encircled by the Biafran Army. Biafra's relief in re-establishing their hold on Oguta allowed the strip at Uli to reopen but within twenty-four hours the Biafrans were forced to admit the loss of Owerri. With the reopening of Uli on the night of 15/16 September incoming flights began to use both Uli and Obilagu strips, although it was primarily I.C.R.C. aircraft which used the latter. The number of inbound flights, despite two strips being available, were below previously achieved levels and on the night of 16/17 September only seven flights landed at the two strips. One of the I.C.R.C. flights on that night took Dr Lindt into Biafra for a showdown meeting with Ojukwu over the use of Obilagu for arms flights and other non-Red Cross aircraft. His meeting with the Biafran leader was brief and non-productive. Lindt returned to the island base with little other than a very terse warning that both of the Biafran airstrips were now under Biafran Air Force control. Lindt had little alternative but to advise his pilots that once in Biafran airspace to land at whichever strip was available to them. The matter did not end there. When the C-130E SE-XBT landed at Obilagu on 19 September the pilot was met on the ground by a "heavily-bearded officer" (who may well have been Ojukwu himself although Ojukwu was not the only Biafran to sport a beard!). The officer instructed the pilot of the Hercules that the Biafran Government now wanted exclusive use of Obilagu and that all future Red Cross flights should use Uli which, it was also announced, had since re-opened.[278]

While Uli had been under threat from the Nigerian Army around Oguta and Owerri, the Nigerian 1st Division had launched an assault against the Obilagu airstrip, as part of a drive towards Umuahia. The Red Cross airstrip fell into Nigerian hands on 23 September 1968, as well as the Red Cross relief distribution centre at Okigwe. Obilagu had been the first neutral airfield in the history of International Red Cross operations–it had lasted just thirty days. Ironically it had only been used exclusively by the Red Cross on seven of those days.

Operation 'INALWA' rolls on: changes in the air fleet

For the first month of Operation 'INALWA', ie the period covering the nights of 3/4 September until 29/30 September, the I.C.R.C. completed 141 flights from Fernando Póo to Biafra. This brought the total number of Red Cross flights to 190 with a combined total of relief aid amounting to 1,680 tonnes. During a similar period (from the night of 1/2 September to 27/28 September) the German DC-7Cs and Transair DC-7Bs flew 189 trips from São Tomé to Biafra, to take the Church airlift's total to 283 flights and an accumulative 2,830 tonnes. Almost a year after the first concerns had been raised by a group of clergy in Biafra the relief airlift to Biafra was at last very much underway.

153: During daylight hours the I.C.R.C.'s 'INALWA' fleet was parked on an overspill apron near the Santa Isabel control tower. The International Red Cross was never satisfied with its operations based on the island for a number of reasons, including the pending political independence of Spanish Equatorial Guinea. Only the fact that Santa Isabel airport continued to be administered from Madrid ensured the relative safety of the I.C.R.C. In this view of the 'INALWA' fleet (two DC-6Bs, one DC-7C and C-130E SE-XBT) are seen in the overspill area on 26 September 1968. In the distance the Swiss DC-6B HB-IBU can just be seen on the main ramp area (Michael I Draper)

154: DC-7C PH-DSL was chartered from Martinair by the Dutch Red Cross for participation on the I.C.R.C. airlift to Biafra. It staged south via Palermo, to Santa Isabel on 6 September 1968 in the customary overall white scheme and red crosses on the fin, above and below the fuselage. It made its first flight into Uli on the night of 11/12 September 1968. By the end of the year it returned to Amsterdam, and on to Stansted for scrapping. PH-DSL was photographed on Fernando Póo island on 26 September 1968 (Michael I Draper)

155: Apart from the traditional fin markings, the Balair DC-6B HB-IBR was also painted in an overall white scheme for Biafra operations. Red crosses were applied to the rear fuselage underside and beneath the outer wing sections. On 30 April 1969 HB-IBR returned from Cotonou to Basle where it was withdrawn from use and subsequently scrapped (Mike J. Hooks)

Changes within the I.C.R.C. 'INALWA' fleet of aircraft were made frequently during the Autumn of 1968 as each short-term charter contract was completed and a new one started. Maintenance requirements also took aircraft back to Europe as no facilities existed on Fernando Póo island. The first of the original fleet to leave Santa Isabel was the Kar-Air DC-6BF OH-KDA which departed for Helsinki on 23 September, followed by the Balair DC-6B HB-IBU to Geneva, on 25 September. Shortly afterwards the Sterling Airways DC-6B OY-BAS returned to Copenhagen on 28 September after completing forty flights into Biafra while the Swedish Red Cross C-130E SE-XBT returned to Stockholm, via Frankfurt on 25 October, for essential maintenance. The Hercules was scheduled to return to Fernando Póo on 15 November for a second Swedish Red Cross charter of just one month until 15 December. While it was back in Stockholm the Swedish Red Cross chartered the ex-Internord DC-7, SE-CNE, for the period 30 October until 15 November.

The Martinair DC-7C PH-DSL, chartered by the Dutch Red Cross, returned from Santa Isabel to Amsterdam on 26 October and was replaced by DC-6A PH-MAM which arrived at Santa Isabel on 11 November 1968, also on a short-term charter to the Dutch Red Cross. Another of the original 'INALWA' fleet, the Braathens DC-6B LN-SUD returned to Oslo on 8 November 1968 after completing 130 flights from Fernando Póo.

Because of its ability to carry up to 18 tonnes of cargo per flight, the return of the Swedish Red Cross Hercules caused a serious shortfall in capacity on the I.C.R.C. airlift. Although it had been replaced by the DC-7 SE-CNE the use of an aircraft such as the C-130E clearly had benefits other than capacity. The I.C.R.C. successfully persuaded the Canadian Red Cross to charter a C-130E Hercules from the Canadian Armed Forces. The I.C.R.C. schedule called for the Canadian Hercules to start flights into Uli on 28 October 1968. In fact two Canadian aircraft were involved; firstly C-130E 10314, which departed Canada on 12 October for operations on the Federal Nigerian side, and 10322 which positioned to Santa Isabel for flights into Biafra.

C-130E 10314 staged Ottawa to Recife on 12 October 1968 for an overnight stay. On 13 October it was flown from Recife to Ascension Island for a second stopover before flying the final leg to Lagos on 14 October. The crew was captained by 'Les' Hussey, one of Canada's most experienced transport pilots. The relief operation in Federal Nigeria, however, was continuously frustrated by unreasonable demands by the Federal Government which could have involved the aircraft and crew ferrying military supplies to front-line areas. The Canadians had selected Enugu and Calabar airfields as those ideally placed for relief operations but the Federal Government reacted by advising the Hercule crew of the unsuitability of those airfields for such operations. Eventually the aircraft was withdrawn from Nigeria without completing a single flight. Sadly, 10314's captain, Les Hussey had developed an illness caused by a parasite caught at Lagos. It was to dog his flying role for the rest of his life.

Operations were no less difficult for the crew of C-130E 10322 based on Fernando Póo. For a while the Canadian Air Force crew refused to accept commands from the INALWA chiefs, but after some communication with Ottawa, flights by the Canadian C-130 eventually started. When night bombing of Uli commenced on 26/27 October Canadian Armed Forces chiefs began to be aware of just how vulnerable their aircraft was to such attacks. 10322 was promptly recalled to Ottawa. It had operated from Santa Isabel for less than a week and had completed just twelve flights into Uli, airlifting 220 tonnes of relief aid.

The removal of the Canadian Hercules from the nightly Biafra roster most certainly had an impact. The German Red Cross managed to solve the situation by chartering one of the C-160D Transall prototypes from the German Government but there was still a slight shortfall in capacity as the C-130E averaged 18 tonnes per flight while the Transall was scheduled for carrying four tonnes less. Although it was civilian registered as D-ABYG the Transall was re-registered to Balair, as HB-ILN, and presumably to avoid causing embarrassment between the Germans and Lagos.

The Transall did not arrive at Santa Isabel until 5 November, due primarily to Balair not able to locate a pilot suitably-rated on the C-160D. The Transall was scheduled to remain part of the Santa Isabel 'INALWA' fleet until the end of the year but almost came to grief after just four nights. While on the ground at Uli, the Transall sustained twenty hits during an attack by a Nigerian MiG-17F. The damage was relatively minor and not sufficient to stop a return flight to Fernando Póo but the incident brought INALWA to a halt again. Pilots refused to fly into Biafra until Lindt received a personal assurance from Lagos that the Nigerian Air Force would stop attacking International Red Cross at Uli. No assurances were ever received and the incident also did little to enhance the already-strained relationship between Biafra and the International Red Cross. In fact that relationship worsened to such an extent that Ojukwu openly accused Lindt of "showing the enemy the way to Uli"! Gradually pilots were re-assured and flights from Fernando Póo were restarted.

Almost a permanent feature of 'INALWA' was the Swiss Red Cross DC-6B HB-IBU, which returned to Santa Isabel after a brief period of maintenance. The Balair DC-6B operated into Biafra throughout the October and November period. The only change took place at the beginning of November when the International Red Cross took over the role of charterer, a change that also involved a repaint, at Basle, into the customary all-white colour scheme.

Apart from those aircraft carrying relief cargoes into Uli each night one other aircraft became almost a permanent feature in the area. That was the Mitsubishi Mu-2B HB-LEB which was leased by the International Red Cross for the personal use of Dr Lindt. The Mu-2B had first been leased when Lindt was appointed to the role of I.C.R.C. Co-Ordinator back in July 1968. After a period of overhaul in Switzerland it returned to Santa Isabel on 7 September and shuttled almost daily between Fernando Póo and Douala. Less frequent were trips from the island to Lagos. On one of the flights to Lagos smoke was seen coming out of the instrument panel. Fortunately it had occurred just after landing but it signalled the need to replace the aircraft. The replacement was a Beech King Air and which arrived at Lagos on 1 October 1968 in order to take Lindt back to the island base at Fernando Póo.

Details of the ferry flight from Basle to Lagos, which involved night-stops at Las Palmas and Robertsfield International, was as follows:

King Air HB-GBK - International Red Cross Charter

Date	Route	Flight Times	Hours
29.9.68	Basle-Malaga	0700-1125	4.25
	Malaga-Las Palmas	1205-1600	3.55
30.9.68	Las Palmas-Port Etienne	0600-0830	2.30
	Port Etienne-Dakar	0930-1200	2.30
	Dakar-Robertsfield	1330-1700	3.30
1.10.68	Robertsfield-Lagos	0600-1030	4.30

The French Red Cross

While the International Red Cross acted as an 'umbrella' operation from Fernando Póo and with aircraft operated under a sub-contract basis with its European agencies, the French Red Cross operated independently from Libreville, in Gabon. By design, the French Red Cross never did attract the degree of publicity gained by the I.C.R.C., something which later had enormous benefits in June 1969 when a Swedish Red Cross DC-7B was shot down en route to Uli. Indeed the French Red Cross continued to operate from Libreville until the very end of the civil war.

The early relief flights organised by the French Red Cross had involved a Transunion DC-6B F-BOEX during the Summer of 1968. The DC-6B, flown by a Captain Bourdens, subsequently sustained slight damage at Uli. The aircraft was later flown out safely to Libreville but Bourdens appears to have by then given up operations in to Biafra.

It was during this period that another Frenchman, Roger Morançay, arrived at Libreville with an Air Fret Bristol 170, thought to be F-BCDR, one of three operated by Air Fret. There is no doubt that a number of flights were undertaken by the Bristol 170 but the needs of Biafra required aircraft of greater capacity.[279]

At the same time elements within the French Government began to urge Air France to release aircrew with current L-1049G ratings for secondment to Libreville. Air France eventually gave in to pressure and at the end of August 1968 one full crew, identified as Mnrs Chauve, Gréard and Diou, was released to fly Air Fret's newly-registered L-1049G Super Constellation F-BRAD to Gabon. On 7 September 1968 the aircraft departed Orly and staged via Luqa (Malta) and Douala (Cameroons) to Libreville where, for at least a month, the aircraft became based.

Officially the L-1049G, F-BRAD, was undertaking 'training flights' and at the same time evaluating suitable routes from Libreville to Biafra, often via Douala where the aircraft refuelled. Interestingly the only fuel available at Douala was 95/115 grade but the L-1049G required 115/145 Octane. The lower grade was kept for DC-4 aircraft but could be used by the L-1049G as long as the crew operated engines in an 'auto-rich' position. The result of this was a 4-metre long flame out of each exhaust at particular power settings and which was frequently visible when overflying the island of Fernando Póo. Not only was the aircraft very visible but the French crew rarely maintained radio silence and on some occasions even reported departure times or estimated arrival times to and from Biafra. Over a number of successive nights, the Santa Isabel Control Tower Log recorded the French crew reporting their position as follows:

"At 13,500' abeam Fernando Póo 2225; en route Biafra to Libreville"
"Departed Douala en route to Biafra; abeam Fernando Póo at 1910"
"Departed Douala en route to Biafra; abeam Fernando Póo at 1856"
"Abeam Fernando Póo 0047 ex-Biafra; ETA Libreville 0140"

The aircraft made similar calls nightly until at least 1 October as it flew food in to Biafra. Often, on return flights from Uli to Libreville, the L-1049G was used for bringing starving children out and the only difficulty which threatened the operation was the concern by the Cameroons government in losing its good relationship with neighbouring states if it openly supported flights into Biafra.

The L-1049G was taken off the nightly roster during October 1968. The Bristol 170 was also retired and in their place came two C-54A/DC-4s, newly-registered as F-BRHC and F-BRHE. Both of the new arrivals retained their previous operator's basic scheme, both of which had been acquired from Air Algerie. The two DC-4s operated nightly from Libreville to Uli until the beginning of 1969 when they were both replaced. The new arrivals were two former Tunis Air examples, again operating in

156: The control tower at Abidjan provides the backdrop on 26.12.68 for French Red Cross DC-4 F-BRHC. This was one of several C-54s acquired by Air Fret from Air Algerie and positioned to Libreville for flights into Uli (Roger Caratini)

157: Air Fret's L-1049G F-BRAD operated out of Libreville for periods throughout the conflict, some flights being on behalf of the French Government. It is thought to have been involved in air-freighting the first batch of MFI-9Bs to Libreville. Towards the latter stages of the war F-BRAD acquired the Biafran 'blue-top' colour scheme as seen here when it visited Abidjan on 23 November 1969 (Roger Caratini)

very basic schemes. F-BRHQ, the first of the new pair, had been acquired by Air Fret on 2 January 1969 and the other, F-OCNU, followed almost two months later, on 27 February 1969.

Changes by the Churches: Transavia replaces Transair

Changes had also taken place among the Church relief airlift at São Tomé. During the second week of September 1968 Transair Sweden replaced their DC-7B SE-ERD with another DC-7B, SE-ERE[280] but on 16 October 1968 the Nordchurchaid-Transair contract expired and was not renewed. In six weeks of operating the airlift the Transair DC-7Bs had performed a total of 63 shuttle-flights from São Tomé to Uli, carrying a total of 567 tonnes.

In the same six weeks of Transair operating the airlift the situation had changed measurably. The German Churches' DC-7Cs had continued to operate as had the two Fred Olsen C-46R Commandoes. But such was the increase in flights that the São Tomé stocks of relief aid had, on several occasions, dwindled to extremely low levels. To remedy the situation, Axel Duch had ordered the two Fred Olsen C-46R Commandoes (LN-FOP & 'FOR) to transfer some of the World Council of Churches' stockfish held in the I.C.R.C. warehouse on Fernando Póo. For two days (14 & 15 September 1968) the two C-46Rs operated a shuttle between Fernando Póo and São Tomé and transferred a total of 43½ tonnes of stockfish.

The Transair DC-7Bs were succeeded on the Nordchurchaid airlift by a mixed DC-6/DC-6B fleet from the Dutch charter company, Transavia. The contract with Transavia differed considerably from that agreed with Transair in that it involved a complex tri-partite lease agreement, signed on 9 October 1968, between Transavia (Limburg) NV, Loftleidir AG (of Iceland) and Nordchurchaid. The contract also specified a longer (six-week) period with Nordchurchaid holding an option to extend the leasing arrangement for three weeks at a time. Each extension involved a guaranteed number of flying-hours based on an average utilisation of five hours per aircraft per day. Three aircraft were allocated initially, the first being DC-6, PH-TRA, which arrived on the island on 16 October, followed by two DC-6Bs; PH-TRD on 19 October and PH-TRL six days later. Before leaving their Schiphol base, all three aircraft had been re-configured to cargo format enabling them to carry slightly more than a standard DC-6/DC-6B, as well as each having had the cargo compartments fitted with a protective material as a precaution against possible corrosion from shipments of salt. The cost of this modification was borne by Nordchurchaid in addition to the agreed charter costs of $315 per block-hour, for the DC-6, and $355 for each of the DC-6Bs.[281]

On the strength of the Nordchurchaid charter contract, Transavia began recruiting additional aircrew, all experienced on DC-6/DC-6B. Three complete crews were positioned to São Tomé involving the company's chief pilot, New Zealander Captain Holmes, the Icelander Captain Thorstein 'Tony' Jonsson, Canadian Captain Don Merriam and a Jugoslav, Capt Kamensec. Two British First Officers joined the initial group, Phil Phillp and Mike Waddington, the latter being a grandson of the Governor of the Bank of England. Three Flight Engineers, Eric Littlewood, 'Jock' Chisholm and Bernie Murphy, completed the initial crews. Each of the newly-appointed captains was asked to sign a Temporary Service Employment Agreement. The terms involved a standard rate of $1500 per month, plus $30 per hour over 75 hours per month. While living on São Tomé captains were paid an additional $30 per day and finally a Fulfilment Bonus of $20 per day was paid at the end of each three-month period.

Accidents and incidents

Mounting an airlift on the scale planned by Nordchurchaid brought, not unnaturally, enormous logistical difficulties. One of the major problems facing the planners was maintaining an adequate supply of aviation fuel on São Tomé. Local stocks of fuel had never been designed to support a high level of movements and at the start of relief operations all of the fuel required was shipped across from Luanda in drums and then trucked to the airport's tanks. The tanks at São Tomé were sufficient to support only one night's flying. As the size of the airlift increased so Shell built a new fuel storage depot at a site between the airport and the town; this store was dedicated solely for use by relief aircraft. Even so there were still occasions when the task of supporting the São Tomé airlift with a regular supply of fuel in sufficient quantity was met with difficulty. The worst moment occurred much later, on 27 April 1969, when the Shell depot on the airport road exploded and 1.6million litres of aviation fuel were lost as well as all local stocks of methanol, oil and hydraulic fluid which had burned in the fire which followed. The incident, which claimed the lives of four local workers, is known to have been an act of sabotage by a group of Nigerian infiltrators. It threatened to shut down the entire Church airlift but within hours the São Tomé Governer granted permission for Norchurchaid to draw from military reserves on the island. No flights were cancelled as a result of the fuel store fire although until adequate stocks of Methmix, necessary as a power booster, could be flown in from Europe, aircraft either used water injection or flew 'dry'. This meant having to reduce cargoes by 10% owing to the reduced engine power.[282]

The growth in the size of the relief airlift also created increased pressure on space at Biafra's Uli airstrip, not just in parking and unloading arrangements but purely due to the number of aircraft moving around the strip in almost total darkness at any one time. Uli had never been designed for such a high number of movements and the congestion on the ground not unnaturally raised the odds of an incident. It did not take long to occur.

During the night of 3/4 October 1968, and just after it had been unloaded, one of the German Church's DC-7Cs, '5T-TAR', was being taxied from the 'Swan' receipt pan to the runway holding point at the 32 end when it suffered a brake seizure in its port main undercarriage. Its position obviously created a dangerous obstruction and the Uli Air Traffic Controller broadcast an urgent appeal to incoming pilots, approaching Runway 16 that they should land as short as possible. Unfortunately a French pilot (flying a French Red Cross DC-6B, F-BOEX) and inbound from Libreville was unaware of the ATC instruction and landed normally, his aircraft's wing-tip striking the port side of the stranded DC-7C's cockpit.

'5T-TAR' sustained damage to the cockpit steering controls as well as to the aircraft's hydraulic system, creating further difficulty in moving the stranded aircraft off the runway. Uli was not a modern strip with adequate emergency vehicles and equipment but it was staffed by ground-based personnel who were always prepared to improvise. A blocked runway necessitated such action to avoid bringing the airlift to a standstill. With a length of rope looped through the nosewheel assembly the DC-7C was eventually towed by two lorries to a position just off the main landing strip, an operation that took a number of hours to complete but was achieved before dawn broke. '5T-TAR' was immediately covered by loose foliage as a camouflage protection against likely air strikes while an urgent request was passed to São Tomé for a proper towbar to be flown in during the following night. Several nights later a Belgian flight-engineer, named Malmquist, was flown in to Uli and who succeeded in starting the DC-7C's engines. Again, with assistance from several lorries, a team of willing hands managed to manoeuvre the aircraft along the taxiway and into one of the 'finger' bays. The brakes on the aircraft's port undercarriage were still in a seized state and the whole operation was carried out with the port wheels being dragged along the dirt surface just off the edge of the taxiway. Safely camouflaged with palm leaves, '5T-TAR' was almost immediately assessed by Malmquist as useful for spares recovery only. From then onwards mechanics periodically flew in from São Tomé to rob it of parts necessary to keep the other DC-7Cs serviceable. Eventually, and inadvertantly, the Biafrans relaxed their control in changing the camouflage cover to such an extent that it had become clearly visible to marauding Nigerian MiG-17Fs. It was ultimately destroyed during a series of daylight attacks.[283]

The French DC-6B (F-BOEX) which had collided with the DC-7C on 3 October had also sustained damage but only to the port wing-tip. It too had been forced to remain at Uli overnight, and for several days afterwards. In fact the presence of F-BOEX at Uli was a potential embarrassment to the French authorities who were keen to maintain a very low profile over its involvement in Biafra. It was heavily camouflaged by foliage to allow mechanics to work safely. Even before the aircraft had been temporarily repaired with a replacement wing-tip the operators had flown a non-French crew (Irishman, 'Bluey' Gardiner and an American Flight Engineer, Tom Archer) into Uli to bring the aircraft out to Libreville.[284]

On São Tomé some concern was expressed during October 1968 as to the legality of Warton's fleet of DC-7Cs. The concern was raised by the organisers of the relief airlift who knew that the Mauritanian identities were purely a figment of someone's imagination. Only one of the aircraft, the DC-7CF (the former G-ATOB), was legally registered, as VR-BCT. Warton's manager at São Tomé, Bertram Peterson, was therefore forced to arrange for the remaining aircraft to be similarly registered in Bermuda. By the end of the month '5T-TAB', '5T-TAG', '5T-TAD' and '5T-TAL' had been registered as VR-BCW, VR-BCX, VR-BCY and VR-BCZ respectively. Not that being legally registered implied they were all fully serviceable. Each had received only rudimentary servicing since being purchased from Sudflug in July 1968 and, under normal circumstances, all would have been grounded. At the end of October 1968 only one, for example, had any radar equipment still in working order; all of them had permanently lengthy snag lists. Not surprisingly, crew members were asked before each flight to Biafra to sign a form claiming they were flying 'at their own risk'.

Night-bombing of Uli strip by Nigerian Air Force C-47s began after dusk on 26 October 1968. Although it was fairly indiscriminate and not too accurate the bombing did have the effect of halting International Red Cross flights for a night. The bombing almost claimed its first casualty during the night of 5/6 November 1968. A Church DC-7C, almost certainly VR-BCZ, landed at Uli shortly after midnight between two attacks by the Nigerian 'Intruder' bomber. While the 10 tonne cargo of stockfish was being unloaded two of the crew, Captain Kjell Erik Bäckström, from Sweden, and his Norwegian First Officer, 'Ollie' Olsen, were standing on the strip, with Father Desmond McGlade. What occurred next still remains uncertain. Either the 'Intruder' dropped a small number of anti-personnel bombs or a small stockpile of ammunition left beside an adjacent parking-bay exploded. All three men were caught in the blast, Bäckström receiving fragment injuries to his back and legs while one of Olsen's lower legs was badly shattered. Olsen and Bäckström were both fortunate; elsewhere, twelve Biafran conscript unloaders had been killed. Nevertheless Olsen's injuries required urgent surgery. It was therefore decided that he should be flown, aboard an International Red Cross aircraft, to Fernando Póo for immediate hospital attention.[285]

In the darkness of Uli, it was difficult to estimate the number of hits received by VR-BCZ but the aircraft was certainly holed or dented in over one hundred places. Two of the engines developed oil leaks, caused by flying debris, and a punctured outer main tyre had to be hacked off to

158: During October 1968 the stranded and badly-damaged DC-7C '5T-TAR' was finally spotted at Uli by the Nigerian Air Force. MiG-17Fs and L-29s made repeated attacks which eventually resulted in at least one direct hit. A tiny fraction of the fuselage cheat-line confirms the identity. Even at this stage of destruction Biafran mechanics were still able (and willing) to remove the engines and unbent propellors to act as spares for Faro-based Government L-1049Gs! See also picture 113 on page 108 (John Trent)

the bare rim. In spite of his injuries Bäckström, and his German Flight Engineer, Nubler, took the decision to attempt a flight back to São Tomé.

Shortly after take-off from Uli the oil pressure on Number Four tank fell dramatically. Flight Engineer Nubler shut the engine down and feathered the prop. Worse still, Bäckström began to lose consciousness due to the intense pain from injuries to his thigh. The Flight Engineer radioed São Tomé to explain the predicament whereupon another DC-7C was immediately ordered to take-off and head north and attempt a rendezvous with the inbound damaged aircraft. The second DC-7C was flown by a Scot, Captain John McOmie, who turned on all navigation and landing lights in the hope that Bäckström would have a high-visibility illuminated target to aim for. The plan worked. Bäckström saw McOmie's aircraft ahead of him and was guided safely back to São Tomé.[286]

Immediately the DC-7C landed the crew were taken to the island's hospital; Kjell Erik Bäckström had three pieces of metal removed from his body and recovered from his injuries. In fact, just three weeks after the incident, he was back on the nightly flight-roster. Olsen also recovered but his badly injured leg had to be amputated. He never flew again. As for the aircraft, it was declared unserviceable and sat at São Tomé for a while. Somebody, at Bäckström's request, counted the holes in it; there were 122 in total.[287]

The losses mount

It was said that John McOmie was a qualified doctor and the son of a Royal Navy Admiral. He was certainly a highly-respected pilot among the São Tomé group. Tragically, and shortly after the Bäckström incident, he lost his life in the first fatal accident of the Church relief operation. The crash occurred on the night of 7/8 December 1968 and involved the DC-7C, '5T-TAD'/VR-BCY.[288] The circumstances surrounding the incident again highlighted the communications difficulties at Uli, as the first suggestion of a crash had been given by a Transavia DC-6B crew as they climbed down to meet the Uli groundstaff. The Transavia pilot reported, to 'Bill' Aitken, seeing an "intense flare which lasted for less than a minute, just to the south of Uli". The flare was not immediately associated with the crash of an incoming aircraft and it was not until much later that Aitken questioned the offloaded cargo figures against the night's planned despatch schedule. The figures simply suggested that one aircraft had "not been unloaded". A telephone call to Uli Air Traffic Control offered a recommendation that Aitken speak with the airfield commander but again no admission of a crash. Immediately dawn broke Aitken drove, with Father Aengus Finucane, south of the airstrip towards where the Transavia crew had reported seeing the intense flare. They eventually arrived at the scene of the crash. The DC-7C had been destroyed by fire and Aitken's first move was to help remove the badly mutilated bodies of the crew and try to make an attempt at identification. A badly burnt briefcase marked 'Capt. John McOmie' had somehow survived the fire; at least the pilot was identified. Aitken then returned to Uli to relay the information back to the W.C.C. centre at Umuahia. He was amazed to learn afterwards that crews from São Tomé had carried out a comprehensive search of the sea area between the island and the Nigerian coast in the firm belief that the DC-7C had gone down in the sea.[289]

All four occupants of '5T-TAD'/VR-BCY died instantly. The bodies were taken to the small hospital at Ihiala for formal identification and burial. By chance Fr Billy Butler, a São Tomé-based CARITAS Priest, was in Biafra at the time having spent several days escorting the President of CARITAS Italy around a number of feeding centres. Although the President had left Biafra Rev Butler had stayed on in Biafra to accompany an Irish Redharc television crew around the enclave. It was while at Amaimo, during the mid-morning of 8 December, that Butler received a visit from one of the Uli priests asking that, as he personally knew all the pilots at São Tomé, he return to the strip and help to identify four dead aircrew. Apart from John McOmie the crew had consisted of a German First Officer, Heinz Raab, Flight Engineer Richard Holzman as well as an American, Arthur 'Tommy' Thompson.

Late in the afternoon of 8 December 1968, all four crew members were buried in the small graveyard at Uli Church, next to the four graves of the L-1049G Super Constellation '5T-TAG' (which had crashed on approach to Uli almost six months previously). The DC-7C crew were buried with full military honours; three Irish priests offered Mass and the choir of Ihiala Seminary sang. The Last Post was sounded and a number of Biafran Army soldiers fired a volley of shots. As the shots were fired and the names of the dead crew were called out, so the sound of the first of that night's arrivals could be heard approaching the strip.[290]

Like all aircraft crashes there was another sad irony attached to the loss of '5T-TAD'. 'Tommy' Thompson's official capacity on the flight had been as a passenger as it was his night off the duty roster. He had a current C-46 Commando rating (having been flying one of the Fred Olsen C-46s on the airlift) and on the night in question was unofficially acting as a "trainee DC-7 First Officer". In fact he was due to be rostered for the first time aboard the DC-7C on the following night as a replacement for John McOmie who was due to return to Scotland on the following day for a spell of Christmas leave. McOmie was simply performing a final 'checking-out' role for Thompson.[291]

Various theories were put forward in determining the cause of the crash, including pilot error when it was revealed that the aircraft's wing-tip had struck tree-tops as it had turned onto final approach to Uli. On the other hand, other pilots who had flown '5T-TAD'/VR-BCY had –on several occasions–queried the accuracy of some of the aircraft's instruments, especially the artificial horizon and the altimeter. They claimed that these items had provided misleading data. However, it seems that these reports had been checked out and the aircraft had been declared serviceable only the day before its fatal flight.

The conclusion arrived at by investigators was that the aircraft had crashed after hitting trees, its low altitude probably resulting from a decision by the crew to fly below some low cloud. Other crews reported that the cloud was extremely low on the night. Not surprisingly the cause was put down to human error.

Nordchurchaid employed flight crews from across the globe, mostly from Europe and the USA. Some joined simply to build up hours; others took their holiday leave from major airlines purely to 'enjoy' the chance of flying DC-6s and DC-7s. A number joined purely for the financial rewards; there were few other legal opportunities for earning such high wages. Some flight crews, on the other hand, flew solely for religious reasons but then soon found that landing on a small strip at night and sometimes under the threat of bombing proved too frightening and required greater skills than they could muster; most of those left shortly afterwards.

Problems for the the Red Cross

Many of the crews flying with the International Red Cross came, as it were, with the aircraft. But in establishing a huge nightly airlift into Biafra, with all the complexities of approach and landing at Uli in the most testing of circumstances, the I.C.R.C. experienced many of the problems that had also faced the Churches. Regular and torrential rain together with low visibility over Biafra frequently made landing at Uli even more hazardous. Bad weather often reduced the I.C.R.C. shuttle-rate to only two flights per night during the final months of 1968. But the International Red Cross faced other problems some of which were never encountered by the Churches on São Tomé island. For example, unlike the relationship between Nordchurchaid and the São Tomé authorities, that which existed between the I.C.R.C. and the authorities on Fernando Póo was never an amicable one.

Operation 'INALWA' had only been underway for two weeks when the I.C.R.C. faced its first 'political' crisis. It involved a shortage of aviation fuel on the island. In reality there was no shortage as a fully-laden tanker had been waiting to be unloaded in Santa Isabel docks for several weeks. But the Spanish Equatorial Guinea authorities unnecessarily checked, double-checked, and checked again all of the required import documentation. It was all performed at a painfully slow rate. Ultimately the I.C.R.C. became impatient and queried the length of time that it took to check a piece of paper. It was at that point

the same authorities then embarked upon another delaying factor; they decided that the only pipeline between the docks and the airport ought to be carefully inspected to ensure that it had not been contaminated by any liquid other than aviation fuel. As fuel stocks at Santa Isabel airport fell dangerously low, Red Cross aircraft returning from Uli were instructed (by Geneva) to divert and refuel at Douala, in the Cameroons.[292]

The hallmarks of collusion between Lagos and Equatorial Guinea were always just below the political surface on Fernando Póo; the fuel fiasco was a prime example. The real source of the interference was always suspected to be the island's Federal Nigerian embassy. It was undoubtedly a decisive factor in delaying the replenishment of fuel tanks at the airport. But there were other and more serious factors for the I.C.R.C. to consider.

On 12 October 1968 Spanish Equatorial Guinea gained independence from Spain to become the Republic of Equatorial Guinea. Independence brought a new President, Francisco Macias Ngueme, who was not slow in displaying dictatorial tendencies. There was one area, however, outside his immediate control; under the terms of independence Spain would continue to control the airport at Santa Isabel for the forseeable future. Nevertheless, it was well known among International Red Cross personnel on the island that Nigerian Foreign Minister Ankpo had met with the new President in order to persuade him to make life increasingly difficult for the Red Cross. More incidents of petty interference followed until, towards the end of December 1968, a major crisis on the island brought relief flights to a halt.

Dr August Lindt had taken advantage of the need for scheduled servicing of his King Air HB-GBK by taking a ride back to Geneva. Lindt's short and temporary absence from Fernando Póo allowed the authorities there to raise mischief by levelling some serious accusations against the Red Cross' operation. The first that Lindt became aware of the latest governmental interference was when he received an en route message while returning to the island aboard his newly-overhauled King Air.

When Lindt landed at Santa Isabel, on 21 December 1968, the situation that faced him was almost too farcical to be true. Soldiers at the airport had, the previous evening, made an unannounced inspection of cargo aboard Red Cross aircraft and found drums of diesel oil. The same soldiers declared these items to be "war material". As a result Lindt's deputy, Sven Lampell, had been immediately arrested and thrown into the island's jail for the night. The real reason for stopping flights into Biafra at that time is thought to have been more associated with a two-day visit to Equatorial Guinea by a Federal Nigerian government mission which, coincidentally, arrived on 21 December.

President Macias lifted the embargo on 23 December

and allowed flights to resume on the following night, 24 December, in what he described to Lindt as "a Christmas present". But pressure from the island's authorities resumed immediately after Christmas 1968. Within a few days an announcement banned the ferrying from Fernando Póo to Biafra of diesel oil and oxygen bottles. The accusation levelled against the I.C.R.C. implied that the diesel oil was being used, not for Red Cross distribution vehicles within Biafra or to power theatres at Biafran Red Cross hospitals, but for the generators which provided power for Uli's electric runway lighting. The accusation was, of course, quite ludicrous, but the true reason for this latest ban was later put forward by Lindt. It seemed one of the Red Cross pilots spoke his mind when the Guinean Internal Minister turned up at Santa Isabel airport, with the Nigerian Consul in tow, both drunk and creating a disturbance. The ban was simply the official response.[293]

The constant interference and extremist antics of the new Equatorial Guinea government were seen by the I.C.R.C. to be an on-going, if not permanent, feature of the airlift out of Fernando Póo. But the airport at Santa Isabel offered adequate facilities for the size of the Red Cross fleet at the time and had a major benefit in being relatively close to Biafra in flying time, but any recurring stoppage in flights was always likely to upset the battle against civilian starvation. Ultimately, there was no alternative for the I.C.R.C. but to re-locate and establish an alternative relief base before scaling down any activity from Fernando Póo.

Operation 'BULLDOG'

Finding a new relief base did not prove an easy option. The ideal choice would have been a move to Douala, in neighbouring Cameroons. Facilities at Douala were good; indeed 'INALWA' aircraft had used Douala for refuelling on a number of occasions when stocks on Fernando Póo were low. Douala was also reasonably close in flying time; indeed sympathy towards Biafra had been demonstrated by the Cameroons leader when a guarantee of safe passage had been offered for a Twin Otter into a landing-strip close to the Cameroons/Biafra border had the Biafran leader wanted to evacuate in an emergency. Nevertheless the same leadership refused to consider Douala as an operational base for Operation 'INALWA'.

Libreville, in Gabon, was also a very serious contender and had first been mooted as a Red Cross base as early as 25 July 1968 but was never adopted and instead the International Red Cross continued its operations from Fernando Póo. But so serious was the search for an alternative base that the I.C.R.C. gave the codename 'Operation Bulldog' for the likely transfer to Libreville.[294] It fell to some of those governments supporting the I.C.R.C. to first envisage problems in operating out of Libreville. The obvious difficulty was that Libreville had become a primary staging-post for Biafran arms and, despite the fact that the French Red Cross was already operating from there, the military association with Libreville proved sufficient reasoning to abandon any notion of moving to Gabon.

Negotiations took place with a number of other governments, including those of Ghana, Togo and Dahomey. In Federal Nigeria's eyes, both Togo and Ghana were thought to be non-runners when they made over-stringent demands on the International Red Cross; Dahomey, on the other hand, was seen as going either way. In an effort to discourage the President of Dahomey from entering into any agreement with the International Red Cross, the Nigerian government therefore took an unexpected step. They quietly sent the volatile Commandant of Lagos-Ikeja airport, Major Paul Dixon, on a quick quasi-official visit to Cotonou, on 22 January 1969. Aboard a Nigeria Airways PA-27 Aztec 250 (5N-AAR) he was flown from Lagos to Cotonou by a British captain, Rod Price. Accompanying the two men were some hastily-prepared gifts of fish, meat and other food items. After just a 45min flight, the aircraft landed at Cotonou at 11:55. Throughout the course of the afternoon Dixon met with Dahomey's President and put forward Nigeria's case. At the end of the day the Aztec took-off from Cotonou (at 18:15 hrs) and flew Dixon back to Lagos.[295]

Major Paul Dixon's effort to dissuade the International Red Cross and the Dahomey President from forging an understanding proved fruitless. On 28 January 1969 both parties agreed terms for the use of Cotonou airport as an alternative I.C.R.C. relief base. Preparations began immediately and within days the new base was brought into use.

The Order of Malta

Another humanitarian airlift, albeit on a much smaller scale, had been successfully operating out of Libreville for some time. It involved two C-47As operated by the French relief agency, *Oeuvres Hospitalières Françaises de l'Ordre de Malte*. Two French Air Force C-47s had been released from the Armée de l'Air storage unit (EAA.601) at Chateaudun and registered as F-BRAM and F-BRAN on 6 September 1968. The first of these aircraft, C-47A F-BRAM, was flown to Libreville by a former Air France pilot with the intention of starting up a Libreville-Uli airlift. However, the start of the operation was frustrated by various administrative difficulties and by mid-November 1968 no flights had taken place.[296]

A replacement pilot, Jean-Renaud Guillemot, was recruited by Oeuvres Hospitalières Françaises de l'Ordre de Malte during November 1968. A serving French Air Force pilot with 15 years of service, Guillemot in turn recruited several additional French crew members who included co-pilot Edouard Bacci, Flight Engineer René Dousot and Navigator Aimé Portet.

159: The French agency, Oeuvres Hospitalières Françaises de l'Ordre de Malte, ran a little-publicised operation out of Libreville. Two ex-French Air Force C-47s were allocated, the first of which (F-BRAM) is seen at Abidjan on 23 November 1968 on its first outbound flight from its Libreville base. Its first visit to Uli occurred on 9 January 1969 and throughout its operation flew with civilian markings on its port wing only. Although the roundel was crudely erased, the French Air Force serial '48994' was retained on the fin (Roger Caratini)

160: Libreville, January 1969. A group of Biafran children await their turn to climb aboard DC-3 F-BRAM for the flight from Libreville to Abidjan and on to Bouaké, Ivory Coast. These children had already spent between 15-30 days at Libreville undergoing medical care before being flown to Bouaké for recuperation. Eventually they would be returned to Biafra. They were the fortunate ones who benefited from a small campaign that never hit the media headlines (Jean-Renaud Guillemot)

161: The regular four-man crew of the Oeuvres Hospitalières Françaises de l'Ordre de Malte DC-3 F-BRAM are seen among this group. They are, from left to right: Jean-Renaud Guillemot (captain), René Dousot (flight engineer), Édouard Bacci (co-pilot) and Aimé Portet (radio operator/navigator). Next to the captain are two nurses while to the centre is Colonelle Werth, the Israeli director of the children's centre at Bouaké, Ivory Coast (Jean-Renaud Guillemot)

The DC-3, F-BRAM, was test-flown by Guillemot at Libreville on 22 November 1968 and on the following day flew to Abidjan where it remained overnight. During the course of 24 November Guillemot returned to Libreville via São Tomé. Operations were, at long last, underway although F-BRAM did not operate its first sortie into Biafra until 9 January 1969 when it operated a return shuttle from Libreville to Uli.

Over a period of several months a number of sick children were brought of Biafra to Gabon for care and convalescence at a Libreville centre run by volunteer doctors. Most had been brought out aboard French Red Cross DC-4s, although after the 9 January trip the DC-3 was used on occasions for airlifting more children out. After some 2-4 weeks of tratment in Gabon these children were then flown in groups aboard the DC-3 to Bouké, in the northern Ivory Coast. The long flight from Libreville to Abidjan was invariably made under cover of darkness to avoid any possible interception from the Nigerian Air Force and only the final leg to Bouaké was made in daylight.

The recuperation centre at Bouaké was run on behalf of the French agency by an Israeli commandant nurse, under whose care many sick and starving Biafran children were nursed back to full health. In time, the operation came under the auspices of Joint Church Aid. By April 1969 the flying operation was scaled down and taken over by other aircraft normally used on the Libreville relief airlift, notably the DC-6Bs chartered by Africa Concern. The two DC-3s, F-BRAM and F-BRAN, were then returned to Armée de l'Air charge, although there is some doubt as to whether or not the latter was actually used at all.

Notes

Note 271 Warton's fleet of L-1049G Super Constellations had dwindled to only two and of those '5T-TAH' had been declared a "technical" write-off at São Tomé.

Note 272 Nordchurchaid Operations Report

Note 273 Nordchurchaid Operations Report

Note 274 Events took a dramatic turn with the shoot-down of a Swedish Red Cross DC-7; see Chapter 9 for details.

Note 275 Interview between Rev 'Bill' Aitken and the author

Note 276 Interview between Rev 'Bill' Aitken and the author

Note 277 *Ibid.,* August R Lindt

Note 278 *Ibid.,* August R Lindt

Note 279 *Le Laboureur de Nuages,* by Suzanne Morancay (1970)

Note 280 Nordchurchaid Operations Report

Note 281 Nordchurchaid Operations Report

Note 282 Nordchurchaid Operations Report

Note 283 Interview between Rev 'Bill' Aitken and the author

Note 284 Tom Archer became prominent in the sale of several former Luftwaffe C-47 aircraft which were subsequently operated by the Biafran Air Force. The Irishman, "Bluey" Gardiner - Capt W.H. Gardiner – had for many years flown alongside Larry Raab at Lufthansa on the L-1049Gs purchased by Hank Warton. He later became involved in crew-training Jack Malloch's crews on the former Aer Turas DC-7CFs.

Note 285 *Ibid.,* Fr Tony Byrne

Note 286 Details of the incident were related to the author by Flight Engineer Bernie Murphy. Bäckström later returned to São Tomé and held the position of Deputy Chief of Flight Operations from 7 January 1970 until 1 February 1970 when the Nordchurchaid base was wound up.

Note 287 As related to the author by Fr Tony Byrne.

Note 288 Nordchurchaid insisted that Hank Warton legally register his DC-7C. All were registered in Bermuda to ARCO (Bermuda) Ltd

Note 289 Interview between Rev 'Bill' Aitken and the author

Note 290 As described to the author by Fr Billy Butler

Note 291 As related to the author by Father Aengus Finucane of Africa Concern. Father Finucane was based at Uli strip during this period. As well as knowing the crew, he also knew full details of the incident.

Note 292 International Red Cross daily Situation Report.

Note 293 *Ibid.,* Frederick Forsyth; Penguin Books 1977

Note 294 *Ibid.,* August R Lindt

Note 295 As related to the author by Rod Price, former Nigeria Airways pilot; times etc extracted from Pilot's Flying Log-Book.

Note 296 *Le Trait d'Union,* Issue 152. Also, as related to the author by Jean-Renaud Guillemot.

"FLY NOW – PRAY LATER"

The Church airlift is consolidated; Joint Church Aid is launched; International Red Cross opens new base at Cotonou

Joint Church Aid and the USA

It was at a two-day meeting in Rome, on 8-9 November 1968, that the term 'Joint Church Aid' was first used. That Rome meeting, at which a number of groups had been invited, including Nordchurchaid and the German Churches, had been arranged by Caritas Internationalis to find ways of increasing the capacity of the relief airlift. Those attending the meeting agreed that a C-130 Hercules was probably the ideal selection of aircraft type for any massive airlift but that the chartering costs were greater than any one agency could finance. It was therefore put forward that a jointly-financed plan to charter a C-130 be put into action. A name was needed to represent the various agencies now involved in this project and so the title Joint Church Aid emerged.

The Hercules never materialised but the name 'Joint Church Aid' did remain as an umbrella for referring to the joint effort by the various churches and denominations who were airlifting supplies into Biafra. In fact it became the common terminology for the São Tomé-based airlift.

162 Above: The introduction of former USAF C-97G Stratofreighters marked a significant increase in airlift capabilities. Loading and unloading was made easier by the rear doors clearly visible here. Some cynics referred to Joint Church Aid as "Jesus Christ Airlines". (Jakob Ringler)

The name became especially associated with a number of C-97G Stratofreighters which were later supplied by the USA and which operated under the title 'Joint Church Aid-USA'. Along with these American C-97Gs came a small number of pilots, some of whom had joined solely for religious motives. It was with these pilots in mind that the initials 'JCA' became known, among some cynics, as 'Jesus Christ Airlines'.[297]

Like much of the western world the conscience of America began to wake up to the situation in Biafra during the Summer of 1968. Initially, the State Department had urged Biafra to support a neutralised land corridor, a stance that was announced by Joseph Palmer, the Assistant Secretary for African Affairs.[298] But for many Americans this position did not go far enough and as far as the situation in Biafra was concerned the Johnson Administration was being accused of inaction and passivity. Senator Eugene McCarthy even called upon the President to request UNICEF to establish a mandatory airlift to Biafra.

McCarthy's rival for the Democratic nomination, Vice-President Hubert Humphrey was more emphatic and called for the I.C.R.C. to "take prompt and risk-taking initiatives". Within three months Richard Nixon had taken power in the White House and by the end of November

1968 Under Secretary of State, Nicholas de B. Katzenbach, had been charged with setting up an emergency task force on Biafra.

Material aid from the USA was made available, largely due to Senator Edward Kennedy's efforts, and on 28 December 1968 it was announced that eight Boeing C-97G Stratofreighters would be divided equally between the I.C.R.C. and Joint Church Aid. All of the C-97Gs were seconded from Air National Guard squadrons and leased to Flight Test Research Inc. of Long Beach, California, who also hired the crews. The four Joint Church Aid aircraft were delivered first and were ferried across the Atlantic in pairs, N52915 and N52679 arriving at São Tomé, via Abidjan, on 25 January 1969, followed by N52631 and N52676 on 9 February. All four C-97Gs, later to become known locally as 'Kennedy Babies', were in a standard bare metal overall finish with all Air National Guard insignia and markings removed. Each aircraft carried a 'JOINT CHURCH AID-USA' fuselage legend and a 'double-fish' insignia on the fin and forward fuselage.[299]

CANAIRELIEF and Africa Concern

Jointly formed in November 1968 by the Canadian Presbyterian Church and OXFAM Canada, another constituent member of the Joint Church Aid group was CANAIRELIEF. At the same time a company, CanRelief Air Ltd was registered specifically for the purchase and operation of suitable aircraft.

The Canadian charter company, Nordair, had placed two of its L-1049H Super Constellations, CF-NAJ and CF-NAM, in storage at Dorval and it was the first of these, CF-NAJ, which was purchased on 13 December 1968 at a cost of $C108,000. The crews were hired almost exclusively from Nordair but the job of organising spares and clearing all of the necessary administrative procedures delayed the departure of CF-NAJ until 17 January 1969 when it finally left Toronto for São Tomé. The initial shuttle into Uli took place during the night of 24/25 January.

Detached from the São Tomé relief base and operating independently was the Irish agency, Africa Concern, working out of Libreville, in Gabon. Africa Concern had been formed in Dublin during March 1968 out of an appeal for help by several Irish priests. The agency had despatched one charter flight from Dublin; by 18 February 1969, when the mv *Archon* sailed from Ireland, Africa Concern had despatched four shiploads of relief supplies to São Tomé and Libreville. Such was the co-operation now apparent between the various relief agencies that the *Archon* called at Genoa to load 1,000 tons of rice from Interchurchaid of Switzerland and which was later unloaded at the two relief bases. From Libreville, part of the cargo was airlifted to Uli aboard a Belgian-registered DC-6A OO-GER, chartered from Belgian International Air Services jointly by Africa Concern Ltd and Dr Gypens of the German agency, Forderungsgesellschaft Fur Afrika.[300]

Further shipments by Africa Concern involved the dispatch of mv *Edward Schupp* from Birkenhead with 1,440 tonnes of relief material, 890 tonnes of which was unloaded at São Tomé on 21 May 1969, the remainder being delivered to Libreville

Back on São Tomé, the arrival of the last of the four Joint Church Aid C-97Gs and the first of the Canairelief L-1049Hs enabled the German Churches to take a decision regarding the future of the DC-7Cs which Hank Warton had operated on their behalf for over six months. The DC-7Cs were by now so badly in need of attention; indeed one of them, VR-BCZ (the former '5T-TAL'), had collected so many holes that it was referred to as 'The Whistling Giant' and even had the name 'The Whistler' painted on the nosewheel door on account of the sound created by the airflow across so many bullet and shrapnel holes. Two of Warton's DC-7Cs, VR-BCW (ex-'5T-TAB') and VR-BCZ (ex-'5T-TAL') were flown from São Tomé to Basle, via Lisbon, on 9 February 1969; these were followed two months later by VR-BCX (ex-'5T-TAC'), on 3 April 1969. Their departure marked the end of Hank Warton's association with Biafra.

New pilots

The arrival of new aircraft onto the airlift brought new pilots and aircrew. The turnover of crews remained at a high level as many lasted only a short period. Some remained a little longer, others lasted the entire course. A number, tragically, were killed during operations.

Typical of the new breed of pilots joining the São Tomé airlift at the end of 1968 and turn of 1969 was British-born Alex Nicoll, latterly a regular captain flying Hawker Siddeley Tridents with Kuwait Airways. Nicoll was a highly-experienced pilot with almost 18,000 flying hours logged and, like a number of other pilots on the airlift, was a former wartime Royal Air Force pilot. After completing several tours with 15 Squadron on Stirlings and Lancasters, Alex Nicoll entered postwar civilian aviation through the independent sector. He came into contact with the Polish entrepreneur, Marian Kozubski, and together they formed several independent British airlines, including the ill-fated Falcon Airways in 1959. It was a telephone call from an old Australian friend, Verdun Polley, that took Alex Nicoll to Schiphol over the 1968 Christmas holiday for a Boxing Day checking-out flight on a Transavia DC-6B. A return flight to Paris as Verdun Polley's First Officer, on the regular Transavia flower run, was sufficient to judge Nicoll as an acceptable pilot for the Biafran operation.

At 16:00 hours on 1 January 1969, Alex Nicoll, accompanying a Canadian captain, Don Merriam, took-off from

163: *Another quietly successful relief campaign was operated by the Irish agency, Africa Concern. Operating out of Libreville the DC-6B OO-GER, leased from Belgian International Air Services, occasionally visited São Tomé, as seen in this view (Jakob Ringler)*

164: *Belgian International Air Services acquired the DC-6B OO-HEX from Trans Union in January 1969. Soon afterwards it replaced OO-GER on the relief airlift and became one of the most colourful on the relief airlift. It operated out of Libreville for most of the time on charter to Africa Concern and CARITAS Ireland. Towards the end of the airlift it operated on alternate nights from São Tomé (Dave Becker Collection)*

165: *The Canadian relief agency, Canairelief, joined the São Tomé relief airlift in January 1969 with just one L-1049H Super Constellation, CF-NAJ, and sufficient funding for a 3-month operation. The aircraft operated in its former Nordair scheme but with the CANAIRELIEF legend and Jointchurchaid 'twin-fish' insignia on the fins. Tragically, the aircraft was lost on 3 August 1969 when it crashed short of Biafra's Uli strip, killing all on board. It is seen here, prior to delivery, at Montreal on 29 December 1968 (Y. Franklin)*

Schiphol aboard another of Transavia's DC-6Bs (PH-TRZ) for a positioning flight to São Tomé, routeing via Luxembourg, Tripoli and Accra. The aircraft, replacement for PH-TRL, landed at São Tomé at 12:40 hours on the following day, ending just over 17 hours of flight-time and with only an hour's break at each refuelling stop. After a 36-hour rest period Nicoll was rostered with another British Transavia captain, Eddie Roocroft, for the first of two São Tomé to Uli shuttles that night. On the following night, 4/5 January, he again completed two shuttles, on that occasion back alongside the Canadian, Don Merriam. A final 'route & process checking-out' took place during the night of 5/6 January when two return flights to Uli were made in company with the Icelander, Tony Jonsson. After a successful return to São Tomé at 05:15 hours on 6 January, Nordchurchaid put Nicoll onto the 'captain's roster' and from that moment he appeared on the duty roster almost every night. In fact Alex Nicoll went on to accrue an amazing number of flights from São Tomé, as did Don Merriam. Tragically, both men were to later lose their lives while flying into Biafra, albeit in separate incidents.

More incidents...

Night bombing of Uli by the Federal Nigerian Air Force 'Intruder' DC-3 continued throughout the early part of 1969, and on a number of occasions managed to cause some interruption to the relief airlift. Occasionally the Nigerian bomber successfully hit or caused damage to aircraft, one such incident involving Transavia DC-6B PH-TRD on the night of 9/10 February 1969.

The DC-6B had turned onto final approach for Uli when the crew called the customary coded sequence that demanded the runway lights to be turned on for the briefest of periods. Almost immediately afterwards the Nigerian 'Intruder' released a cluster of small bombs, and for once his aim was accurate. One of the bombs hit the runway directly ahead of the landing DC-6B but the crew managed to brake sufficiently hard to stop just in time. The aircraft had missed being hit by the main explosion but flying debris had caused some structural damage to the fuselage. PH-TRD was taxied into one of the 'fingers' for unloading while the World Council of Churches' Controller at Uli, Reverend 'Bill' Aitken dashed onto the runway to inspect it for damage. Despite the bombs being relatively small, one had caused a sizeable crater towards the 34 end, ie the southern end of the runway. As Aitken stood in darkness considering what effect the damage might have for other landing aircraft, he heard the unmistakable roar of a Super Constellation being summoned on full-power for its take-off run. Immediately Aitken ran forward, frantically flashing a torch at the approaching aircraft as it gathered speed towards him. Mercifully, the flight-deck crew saw Aitken's torch-light albeit only at the last moment, and cut all four engines and applying maximum brake pressure at the same time. The aircraft was Canairelief's L-1049H CF-NAJ and it managed to stop literally a few feet short of the runway damage. Not surprisingly, one of its tyres burst as it had skidded to a halt. Aitken was allowed to clamber aboard the Super Constellation and, from a standing position in the cockpit, guided the Canadian captain safely around the damaged runway and to a new holding-point just to the north of the crater. It meant a shorter take-off run, and despite a burst tyre, the Super Connie successfully got airborne for the return flight to São Tomé. For the rest of the night 'Bill' Aitken's car was parked just ahead of the bomb damage, the owner using headlights in sequence with the runway's landing-lights to warn other aircraft on final approach. At the same time conscripted Biafran soldiers hurriedly filled in the hole; by daylight only a top-cover of tarmac was required. By the following evening aircraft were again able to use the entire length of Uli's one runway.[301]

Although Reverend Aitken's action had certainly averted a major incident, daylight on São Tomé revealed that Canairelief's only L-1049H Super Constellation had sustained some damage. Although only superficial, and probably caused by the initial explosion at Uli, the damage was beyond the ability of local São Tomé-based mechanics. CF-NAJ was therefore flown to Europe for repairs, arriving in the UK at Luton on 12 February. But, as the aircraft was associated with the Biafran airlift, local companies were quietly warned against working on the aircraft. Undeterred, the crew flew the aircraft on to Paris where a more liberal view was taken towards involvement with Biafra. Air France carried out the repairs but it had been a ludicrously expensive exercise. The final cost, including the ferry flights to the UK and on to Paris, eventually amounted to some $25,000–all to repair several shrapnel holes. The Canairelief L-1049H was repaired and declared fully serviceable within two weeks, returning to São Tomé on 27 February 1969.[302]

Up to the incident at Uli, CF-NAJ had completed 28 return flights to Uli and during March 1969 made sixty flights into Biafra without further incident. Canairelief's chief pilot, Captain J. Patterson achieved a personal milestone on 9 March 1969 when he completed his 100th trip to Uli. (Not all of these trips were, of course, with Canairelief.)

...and even more incidents

More incidents followed. During the night of 21/22 February 1969 an English pilot, John Knox, was being 'check-examined' by the Icelander, Tony Jonsson, aboard the DC-6B PH-TRL. The circumstances were curiously similar to those that had taken place a fortnight beforehand. On the night in question the Nigerian 'Intruder' DC-3 dropped an unusually accurate load just as the Transavia DC-6B touched-down from the 16 end. As always the ground-crews took cover but clearly saw the silhouette of the landing aircraft against the flash of the exploding bombs. The main impact had just missed the runway on that occasion and the DC-6B slowed to a taxi-pace and parked at Uli's most southern 'finger' for off-loading. In the darkness the crew examined the aircraft for structural damage and found no obvious signs of having been hit. It was only when Jonsson and Knox prepared for the return leg to São Tomé did they discover that many of the DC-6B's systems were not responding. A second, and closer, examination revealed that a small piece of shrapnel had entered the top of the cockpit and caused extensive damage to the electrical systems, and magnetoes etc. The crew had no alternative but to abandon any immediate plans for take-off and prepared for an overnight stay at Uli. A group of Biafran conscripts were mustered together and helped tow the aircraft towards the extreme edge of the unloading bay, the undercarriage nosewheel being 'kick-steered' into the required direction.

Later, after the last of the night's aircraft had taken-off, a Biafran Ministry of Works' lorry was used to tow the DC-6B out of the loading-bay, along Uli's runway, and into a 'finger' with better protection of nearby trees and undergrowth. Again, steering the aircraft into the parking-area was achieved by having soldiers kick the nose-wheel into the desired direction. At the same time other soldiers began to hack down trees to allow the aircraft's wings to pass. The DC-6B was then covered completely with palm-leaves and branches to camouflage it from above, and from any marauding Nigerian MiG-17 that usually strafed the airstrip at dawn and throughout the day.

To avoid any concern back at the São Tomé base, Bill Aitken radioed a sufficiently obscure message that simply announced that "Tony and friends spending another day in Biafra". The message indicated trouble with the aircraft but that the crew members were safe. Another message, sent by Aitken later during the day, requested a replacement switch panel and wiring, and which was flown into Uli aboard the first shuttle of the following night.

Accompanying the replacement parts was a young Dutch radio mechanic who wasted little time in setting about repairing the damaged DC-6B. The cockpit windows were totally blacked-out to allow the mechanic to work in as much light as possible but the full extent of the damage was worse than originally thought; it meant that simply replacing the switch panel was insufficient. Aitken, overlooking the repair work, later described what followed as "a little ingenuity with a soldering-iron", as everybody else left the Dutchman to work alone. At around 02:00 hours the young mechanic emerged from the cockpit and asked if a crew could start the engines and prepare for a return flight to São Tomé. Not even the Biafrans–who were masters at improvising–had been prepared for such a rapid repair and had to admit to not having a single vehicle available to help tow the DC-6B clear of those trees which had not been cut down. Tony Jonsson successfully started the engines and very carefully taxied the aircraft (in a 'zig-zag' manner) out of the pan while his co-pilot, John Knox, led on foot with two torches. Finally, at just before 05:00 hours Jonsson and Knox lined up on Uli's runway and successfully took-off.

For the Uli controllers the departure of PH-TRL was an immense relief. But relief turned to utter amazement when, during the following night, among the aircraft inbound from São Tomé was the DC-6B PH-TRL, and with a full load. The aircraft had been passed sufficiently fit on São Tomé but was later grounded on 24 February following a report that the DC-6B was losing oil. Mechanics discovered that the aircraft had indeed lost oil and that an oil pipe had been completely severed–presumably by a piece of shrapnel from the same bomb that had caused its grounding at Uli three nights previously.[303]

The International Red Cross begins operations from Cotonou

1969 opened with the International Red Cross deep in crisis. Its fleet was still grounded at Santa Isabel, the result of another ban imposed by the Equatorial Guinea government. Although flights were subsequently allowed to resume Geneva still remained unconvinced that any resumption would not again be interrupted again by further unsubstantiated accusations.

The setting-up of a second base in Dahomey, Nigeria's immediate western neighbour, had never been a serious option but was only decided upon in the light of political developments on Fernando Póo. To attempt an increase in operations out of Fernando Póo was also not an option for consideration. Indeed Balair had completed, in early January 1969, a leasing agreement for two DC-6AC aircraft specifically for Red Cross work and that these had been flown to Basle but held back for several weeks pending the completion of an operational base at Cotonou airport.

Both of the Balair DC-6ACs had, since new, operated with a number of companies within the British Air Holdings group, latterly with Air Ferry. The Group had elected to close down Air Ferry and as a result both aircraft (G-APNO & G-APNP) were ferried to Lydd, Kent on 9 October 1968 and placed into short-term storage. Balair's requirement for additional aircraft to meet its increasing commitment to the International Red Cross Biafran operations subsequently led to a lease/purchase agreement with Air Ferry. The agreement involved the hiring of both aircraft for a 3-month period at US$22,000 each per month.[304] As well as hiring the two aircraft Balair also hired a team of ground engineers from Air Ferry, again on a three-month contract.[305] Under the terms of the leasing agreement the aircraft were ferried to Wymeswold for a Check 1 Inspection, after which they were positioned to Southend for acceptance. By now re-registered as HB-IBS and HB-IBT they were flown from Southend to Basle on 11 and 12 January 1969 respectively where they were

The arrival of the Joint Church Aid C-97Gs allowed the surviving German Churches' DC-7Cs to be retired. Under the terms of the contract with Hank Warton the aircraft had amassed sufficient 'free' flights for ownership to be transferred to Biafra's former gun-runner.

166 Left: *DC-7CF VR-BCT, formerly owned by the Biafran government under the identity of G-ATOB, was ferried from São Tomé to Basle on 3 April 1969 in company with the standard DC-7C VR-BCX. The lack of cabin windows identifies VR-BCT as the freighter version*

167 Left: *Marginal differences to the fuselage cheatline and nose-cones were other features that further differentiated these two 'white-tailed' aircraft. VR-CBX, left, operated on the relief airlift with initially just '5T' as an identity but later it operated as either '5T-TAC' or '5T-TAG'*

168: *The dark-blue fin and two-tone blue cheat-line was always characteristic of DC-7C VR-BCZ which for a while operated the relief airlift with Warton's spurious identity '5T-TAL'. It was also known as 'The Whistler' on account of the number of bullet holes along its lower fuselage. After its ferry flight from São Tomé to Basle on 9 February 1969, it was never flown again and was eventually broken up at Basle (All by Mike J. Hooks)*

repainted in an all-white scheme with large red crosses on the fin, lower rear fuselage and lower wing-tips. 'INTERNATIONAL RED CROSS' titling was applied to the fuselage.

The agreement between the I.C.R.C. and the President of Dahomey was based on a number of assurances from both parties. For its part the International Red Cross agreed that it would support its operation at Cotonou by using local transport companies and people as far as possible. Essential supplies would also be purchased within Dahomey. There were, for this small African country, other commercial benefits. The Dahomey government successfully negotiated standard-rate landing fees for each aircraft movement as well as a 10% transfer tax for all relief aid flown into Cotonou. Supplying the starving population in Biafra did not come cheaply and, based on normal useage, the I.C.R.C. faced paying fees of approximately £1,600 per aircraft, per month. For the Red Cross there were some other costs to consider. Unlike Santa Isabel, which featured secondary parking areas and a lengthy runway, the facilities at Cotonou needed to be upgraded and the International Red Cross spent approximately £20,000 on constructing a new tarmac parking area at Cotonou airport, purely for its own aircraft. Shell Petroleum also invested the same amount for additional refuelling facilities designed to allow more than one aircraft to be refuelled at any one time. It is reported that the Dahomey exchequer benefitted by some 800,000 Marks from the International Red Cross airlift.[306]

One of the real penalties in flying from Cotonou was the greater distance from Biafra and therefore the additional flight-time required in flying into Uli. Three shuttles per night from Santa Isabel had been achieved on several occasions and there were nights when four or even five flights had been made by individual aircraft from Santa Isabel. Schedulers considered that three return flights from Cotonou would be the absolute maximum but Geneva considered this to be rightly justified if the new airlift was able to operate without any political interruption.

To offset the slight reduction in nightly tonnages as a result of transferring to Cotonou, the I.C.R.C. elected to continue operating out of Santa Isabel. As a further precaution against possible political interference the aircraft fleet was carefully divided. Cotonou would become the base for solely Swiss-registered aircraft, all of which were leased from Balair AG; operations from Fernando Póo became the sole domain of the Swedish Red Cross. The Swedish DC-7, SE-CNE, therefore remained at Santa Isabel and where it was joined by two Swedish DC-7Bs, SE-EDU and SE-ERO. The Martinair DC-6A PH-MAM, which had been based at Santa Isabel since mid-November 1968, had already been ferried back to Schiphol/Amsterdam on 23 December. Flight crews were also appointed on a basis of nationality, they being drawn from countries that had declared no allegiance to either side in the Nigerian civil war.

The Balair DC-6B HB-IBR and the C-160D Transall HB-ILN were transferred from Santa Isabel to Cotonou during late-January 1969. The two ex-Air Ferry DC-6Acs, HB-IBS and HB-IBT, which had been held back at Basle were also ferried down to Cotonou. First of all they repositioned to Geneva from where they departed together for Cotonou late on 29 January. The ferry flight involved two stops, firstly at Marseilles to collect a ground power unit and later a refuelling stop at Niamey. HB-IBS and HB-IBT both arrived at Cotonou during the afternoon of 30 January 1969 and were immediately loaded for a flight into Uli that evening.

The start of Red Cross operations out of Cotonou did not pass without incident. On the first night the Transall, HB-ILN, was refused permission to land at Uli on its first attempt. The crew returned to Cotonou with a full load. An incensed Dr Lindt decided that he, himself, would accompany the second attempt to land at Uli and so joined the French captain and Swiss co-pilot (the veteran Balair captain, Guy Steiner). When the Transall entered the Holding Pattern over Biafra landing permission was again denied by Uli's controllers. While the aircraft circled the night sky above Uli Lindt tried desperately, but in vain, to contact Ojukwu direct. Eventually, the crew advised Uli that they were returning to Cotonou for a second time. As the crew prepared to head for home landing permission was unexpectedly given whereupon the aircraft landed. Once on the ground Lindt sought out the reasons for the unnecessary delay. It then emerged that the Commander of Uli (no less than Major Godwin Ezeilo, the Commander of the Biafran Air Force) had taken a personal decision not to allow the I.C.R.C. aircraft to land on its first attempt. No rational explanation was given, nor was the question of an apology even contemplated. It was not just the Transall which was held up; one of the DC-6ACs had also spent a considerable time in the Uli holding pattern and was not called forward by the Uli Air Traffic Controller. It too had returned to Cotonou with a full load but not flown in to Uli until the following night.[307]

Even the second night was not without incident. When a Red Cross DC-6AC landed at Uli one of the mainwheel tyres burst. Under normal operating conditions the aircraft would have been grounded but in view of the dawn threat of attack by MiG-17s, the crew elected to fly back to Cotonou with one damaged tyre. Back at the Red Cross base the British engineers were appalled to learn that the Swiss captain had taken off with a blown tyre. The mainwheels of a DC-6, when retracted, are very close to fuel lines inside the wing nacelle; had the tyre began to burn during its take-off from Uli, the engineers argued, the chances of an in-flight fire were very real. But the crew simply shrugged their shoulders. Such was the routine on the Biafran airlift and was a situation that the Churches had actively faced on several occasions.[308]

If the British ground staff was shocked at the manner in which the Balair DC-6AC was flown back to Cotonou,

163

then the procedure adopted for replacing the damaged tyre was almost beyond their comprehension. Balair had had the foresight to include a spare mainwheel tyre in the spares stockholding at Cotonou but the only available wing-jack was on the island of Fernando Póo. There was no time the get the jack transferred to Cotonou in time for a second shuttle that night. Red Cross officials irrationally demanded that mechanics construct a makeshift jack from a number of orange boxes stacked close-by. At the same time the I.C.R.C. Cotonou Manager, in a burst of uncontrollable rage, arrogantly asked the engineers what their wives would think if they were to read in the next day's press that "the population of Biafra had nothing to eat because four Britons would not change a wheel!"

The faulty tyre was changed during the following morning, 1 February, but the manner in doing so was typically unorthodox. A French engineer, employed locally by Air Afrique, produced a railway sleeper, chamfered at one end, and which was placed directly in front of the good wheel. The aircraft's engines were then started and with a sudden hefty burst of power the good wheel ran forward, up the chamfered edge and onto the flat portion of the sleeper whereupon the brakes were sharply applied. The braking action caused the DC-6AC to yaw violently to a halt but the manoeuvre had positioned the undercarriage in such a fashion that the faulty tyre was clear of the ground. Without any further trouble the tyre was then successfully replaced.[309]

In spite of the various operational difficulties, and the fact that only 14 tonnes of relief aid had been flown in on the first night, at least the I.C.R.C. had established its secondary air-bridge from Cotonou.

Fernando Póo: a reprieve

It was vitally important that the Cotonou base succeeded. The situation on Fernando Póo never improved, if anything it worsened. One factor alone that irritated the newly-independent government of Equatorial Guinea was that the Spanish authorities continued to manage Santa Isabel airport. That meant that landing fees etc were paid directly to Madrid; the local government gained nothing, another reason for interference.

On 11 February 1969 Dr Lindt received an official letter from the Foreign Minister of Equatorial Guinea. In it the Minister demanded that the International Red Cross remove all of its foodstocks from the island within 30 days. At the same time the Minister was cautious by insisting that there would be no restriction, however, on flights in the meantime. Once again Lindt found himself embroiled in West African politics. Not only was President Macias still causing trouble, but Lindt was also the subject of a complaint by Nigeria to President Zinzou of Dahomey over the new Red Cross base at Cotonou. Within a fortnight Nigeria closed its border with Dahomey.[310]

Against mounting pressure from its Nigerian neighbour, the Dahomey government agreed to a Red Cross request to increase the number of aircraft based at Cotonou, from four to seven. I.C.R.C. was expecting delivery of a fleet of Boeing C-97Gs and this paved the way, if necessary, for a run-down of its operations at Santa Isabel.

There was an interesting turn of events on Fernando Póo at the end of February 1969. Angered by the dictatorial manner in which he ran the colony, the civilian population on the island began a series of local riots. The focus of the riots was Macias himself and on the last days of the month Macias and his ministers fled the island to Bata, on the African mainland. Lindt waited several days for the tension to die down. Then, and as the C-97Gs began to arrive in Cotonou, he flew to Bata in his King Air (HB-GBK) for a showdown with Macias. According to his testimony, Lindt agreed to pay landing fees directly to the Equatorial Guinea government. He also agreed to ferry rice and powdered milk from Fernando Póo to Bata for school meals. But in return he made a number of demands; Macias agreed, on 17 March 1969, to allow the Red Cross to position a fourth aircraft to the island and to lift the forthcoming ban on flights to Biafra. Later that same evening three Swedish Red Cross aircraft (DC-7Bs SE-EDU & SE-ERO and DC-7 SE-CNE) flew supplies from Santa Isabel to Uli to re-open the island base.

The Red Cross receives C-97Gs

Delivery of four Boeing C-97G freighters, leased from Flight Test Research Inc to the International Red Cross, began during February 1969. All were initially flown from the USA to Basle in an overall silver finish, ie standard USAF scheme but with all Air National Guard titles removed. Each of the four aircraft were flown across the North Atlantic under Swiss registry. The first to arrive at Basle was HB-ILW which was ferried from Santa Maria on 16 February 1969, followed shortly afterwards by HB-ILZ on 22 February and later by HB-ILX on 15 March, and by HB-ILY on 30 March.[311]

Unlike the Joint Church Aid C-97Gs, those operated by the I.C.R.C. were repainted at Basle in an overall white 'high-visibility' finish, the first of which, HB-ILW, was rolled out by 22 February 1969. It also had an 'INTERNATIONAL RED CROSS' legend on the fuselage with red crosses marked on the fin and on the fuselage underside. The same aircraft was the first to arrive at the Cotonou base from where it joined the airlift to Biafra, during the late evening of 31 March 1969. HB-ILZ made its first appearance in Biafra on the night of 3/4 April, and HB-ILY followed five nights later, on 8 April. The last-mentioned differed slightly in its markings, having the fuselage legend 'COM. INTERNATIONAL RED CROSS'. It is possible that the last of the quartet, HB-ILX, was initially considered ill-equipped to commence operations immediately as it was subsequently ferried from Basle to

169: The first two of an initial four Boeing C-97G Stratofreighters for Joint Church Aid arrived at São Tomé on 25 January 1969. N52679 and N52915 routed from Miami via Abidjan where the former was photographed during a brief refuelling stopover. All previous USAF Air National Guard markings were removed prior to the ferry flight and each had the 'twin-fish' logo liberally applied to the fuselage and fin (Roger Caratini)

170: C-97G HB-ILY was ferried through Shannon on 30 March 1969. All Air National Guard markings had been erased in the USA but strangely the USAF serial 52-2626 was retained on the fin. The next stage was to repaint the aircraft in an all-white scheme with red cross insignia before it was positioned from Basle to Cotonou on 7 April 1969 (Malcolm Nason)

171: The I.C.R.C established a second base at Cotonou at the end of January 1969. The airport was almost literally on the beach. In this view three DC-6s and two C-97Gs are visible, one of the latter still in silver overall finish as well as two Dahomey Air Force C-47s. Evidence of expanding the parking area is supported by new earthworks, part of the agreement between the I.C.R.C. and the Dahomey Government (Marcel Tschudin)

Tel Aviv on 22 April 1969 for attention by Israeli Industries. It later flew to Gatwick on 14 May to uplift a cargo of brand-new Land Rover vehicles for use in Biafra. HB-ILX eventually joined the airlift to Uli on the night of 17/18 May.

The air-freighting of vehicles into Uli represented only a small perentage of cargoes airlifted in. All were delivered for Red Cross teams operating inside Biafra. The bulk of the relief material flown in consisted of Norwegian stockfish and milkpowder. Corn meal mixture was a frequent priority as was salt, but items tended to differ slightly and depended largely on specific requirements by the Red Cross teams inside Biafra. The supply of food was based upon a balanced and mixed diet aimed specially at reducing the spread of disease caused by starvation.

There were, of course, occasions when the make-up of relief material created more of a difficulty than helping to solve the overall problem. At one stage tinned food, for example baked beans or condensed milk, were flown in but which created enormous problems at food-distribution centres due to a complete lack of tin-openers in the Biafran bush. Some shipments simply did not make sense and on one occasion the Swiss Red Cross is reported to have flown in a large consignment of quality Swiss cheese, something that the Biafrans had to be shown how to use–or even eat–as it had never been seen in Africa before. Flour was another commodity flown in occasionally during the early days of the airlift but because there was no yeast in Biafra the relief workers were forced to mix it with palm oil.

Red Cross: rosters and routes

Flight scheduling from Cotonou by the I.C.R.C. planners accounted for a minimum of two return shuttles to Uli during the hours of darkness but also allowed for a third shuttle by several of the aircraft if time and circumstances allowed.

I.C.R.C. crews were advised of the duty roster and flight schedule only after the Chief of Flight Operations had been advised of the daily aircraft availability. The schedule was then announced as late as mid-morning for that night's operation. Examples of typical schedules, those for the nights of 2/3 and 4/5 April 1969, illustrate a mixed DC-6/C-160 roster and another with C-97Gs as well:

II.C.R.C./ C.I.C.R. FLIGHT-SCHEDULE FOR OPERATION 2/3 April 1969

Flight No:	Type:	Aircraft:	STD Cotonou	STA Uli	STD Uli	STA Cotonou
01	DC-6A/B	HB-IBS	1700	1840	1910	2030
02	DC-6A/B	HB-IBT	1715	1855	1925	2045
03	DC-6B	HB-IBR	1730	1910	1940	2100
04	C-160	HB-ILN	1830	2010	2050	2210
05	DC-6A/B	HB-IBS	2110	2250	2320	0040
06	DC-6A/B	HB-IBT	2125	2305	2335	0055
07	DC-6B	HB-IBR	2140	2320	2350	0110
08	C-160	HB-ILN	2310	0050	0130	0250
09	DC-6A/B	HB-IBS	0120	0300	0330	0450
10	DC-6A/B	HB-IBT	0135	0315	0345	0505
11	DC-6B	HB-IBR	0150	0330	0400	0520

DEADLINES: 1700 GMT and 0215 GMT. ALL TIMES ARE GMT

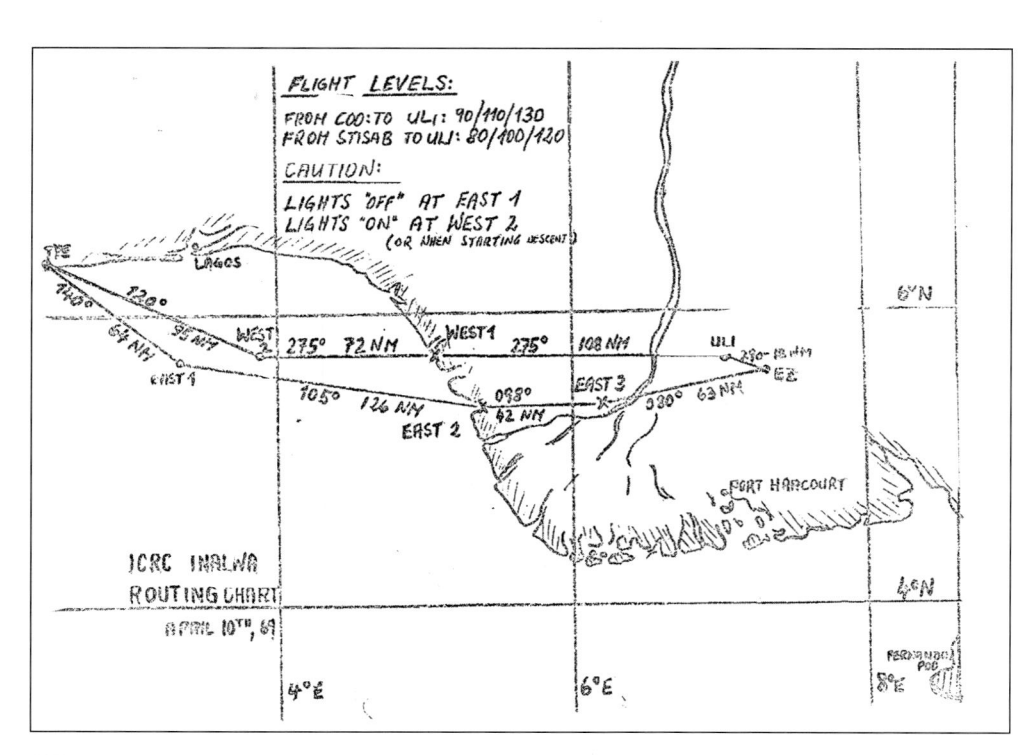

172: The route given to International Red Cross aircrew changed slightly each night although the changes were marginal. This example, for the night of 10/11 April 1969, shows that aircraft covered 313 miles from Cotonou to Uli and only 275 miles on a more direct route homebound. This chart also illustrates the closer proximity of Fernando Póo (less than half the distance) but the political situation was considerably more volatile there than at Cotonou (Marcel Tshudin)

I.C.R.C./ C.I.C.R. FLIGHT-SCHEDULE FOR OPERATION 4/5 April 1969

Flight No:	Type:	Aircraft:	STD Cotonou	STA Uli	STD Uli	STA Cotonou
01	DC-6B	HB-IBR	1700	1840	1910	2030
02	DC-6A/B	HB-IBT	1710	1850	1920	2040
03	C-97G	HB-ILZ	1730	1930	2010	2130
04	C-160	HB-ILN	1740	1920	2000	2120
05	DC-6A/B	HB-IBS	1800	1940	2020	2140
06	C-97G	HB-ILW	1900	2100	2140	2300
07	DC-6B	HB-IBR	2110	2250	2320	0040
08	DC-6A/B	HB-IBT	2125	2305	2335	0055
09	C-160	HB-ILN	2240	0020	0100	0220
10	DC-6A/B	HB-IBS	2250	0030	0110	0230
11	C-97G	HB-ILZ	2300	0100	0140	0300
12	C-97G	HB-ILW	0100	0300	0340	0500
13	DC-6B	HB-IBR	0130	0310	0350	0510
14	DC-6A/B	HB-IBT	0150	0330	0410	0530

DEADLINES: 1700 GMT and 0215 GMT.
ALL TIMES ARE GMT

I.C.R.C./ C.I.C.R. FLIGHT-SCHEDULE FOR OPERATION 4/5 May 1969

Flight No:	Type:	Aircraft:	STD Cotonou	STA Uli	STD Uli	STA Cotonou
01	C-97G	HB-ILZ	1630	1830	1900	2020
02	DC-6A/B	HB-IBS	1640	1820	1850	2010
03	DC-6A/B	HB-IBT	1655	1835	1905	2025
04	C-97G	HB-ILY	1715	1915	1945	2105
05	DC-6B	TF-FRA	1900	2040	2110	2230
06	DC-6A/B	HB-IBS	2050	2230	2300	0020
07	DC-6A/B	HB-IBT	2105	2245	2315	0035
08	C-97G	HB-ILZ	2120	2320	2350	0110
09	C-97G	HB-ILY	2205	0005	0035	0155
10	DC-6B	TF-FRA	2315	0055	0125	0245
11	DC-6A/B	HB-IBS	0100	0240	0310	0430
12	DC-6A/B	HB-IBT	0115	0255	0325	0445
13	C-97G	HB-ILZ	0210	0410	0440	0600
14	C-97G	HB-ILY	0255	0455	0525	0645

DEADLINES: first take-off at 1630Z Latest arrival Cotonou at 0200Z for 3rd flight
ALL TIMES ARE GMT

The second schedule illustrates well the complexity facing the schedulers when including a mix of three basic aircraft types. The scheduled flight-time from Cotonou to Uli varied between 1hr 40mins for the DC-6B and C-160 Transall and two hours for the slower and heavier C-97G. Often a DC-6B, or the C-160 Transall, was scheduled to depart Cotonou after a C-97G but would then be slotted in to land at Uli. All of the times shown on the Flight-Schedules were, of course, dependent on there being no difficulties in landing at Uli. Factors such as adverse weather conditions over Biafra or the presence of the Nigerian DC-3 'Intruder' frequently had an effect on the night's operations.

As the I.C.R.C. Boeing C-97Gs became increasingly available for joining the shuttle to Uli so the schedulers at Cotonou had to take fullest advantage of the difference in air speeds between them and the DC-6B. Thus the first departure of the night was almost always made by a C-97G, as was the final return flight. Taking a longer time to reach Uli meant that the first departure from Cotonou could be made before the normal deadline of 17:00.

By May 1969 the slightly earlier fall of dusk allowed earlier departures. Rosters also included the first time the Icelandic-registered DC-6B TF-FRA operated by an Icelandic agency, Fragtflug. It had been purchased by Fragtflug on 1 May 1969 from the American dealer, Boreas Corporation, having previously operated with Japan Air Lines and whose markings it partially retained.

The flight schedule issued for the night of 4/5 May 1969 was as follows:

The routeing of flights from Cotonou to Biafra followed a series of standard patterns which, apart from the final let-down procedure into Uli, changed slightly each night. Typical of a route pattern from Cotonou was that announced to rostered flight crews for the night of 10/11 April 1969. (See opposite)

Immediately after taking-off from Cotonou aircraft set a south-east course (140°) and out over the Atlantic to 'Checkpoint East 1', a distance of some 64 nautical miles and where the standard instruction to turn all lights out came into effect. At the same time a course change to 105° brought the aircraft to the point where the Nigerian coast was overflown, a point referred to as 'East 2'. A second course change to 098° (for 42 n.mile) and a further change to 080° (for 63 n.miles) was sufficient to take aircraft overhead Uli's 'EZ' Holding Beacon. From the Holding Area, aircraft were slotted into the final let-down and approach to Uli, at which stage flights from Cotonou were phased into a landing pattern which included aircraft inbound from São Tomé, Santa Isabel and Libreville. It was also at this stage that crews faced the most frenetic part of the operation, especially if the Nigerian Air Force was active in the area. To avoid the risk of collision over Biafra, especially when approaching the Holding Area, aircraft from Cotonou to Uli were instructed to maintain flight-levels of 9,000, 11,000 or 13,000 feet while those aircraft inbound from Santa Isabel were ordered to keep at 8,000, 10,000 or 12,000 feet.

The return flight from Uli to Cotonou was considerably simpler and involved setting an immediate course of almost due west (275°) until a final course-change at a point just 95 n.miles from base.

The arrival of the C-97Gs at Cotonou added significantly to the capacity of the I.C.R.C. airlift and allowed the C-160D Transall HB-ILN to be returned to Germany for essential maintenance. Given the general operational conditions the C-160D had performed extremely well; in fact when the Transall joined the Cotonou airlift a spares holding of some 12,600 units was transferred with it but only twenty-seven of those items had apparently been used.[312] From 1 April 1969, however, HB-ILN began to suffer from technical snags and shuttles were forcibly cancelled. It was again grounded by snags on the night of 9/10 April when the decision to return to Europe was taken. The Transall returned to Germany for a major overhaul at VFW's Bremen factory as well as a renewal of its airworthiness certificate. To the irritation of the I.R.C. the Bonn government refused to lease a replacement aircraft and the Transall never did return to the airlift.

The introduction of the C-97Gs also allowed the well-utilised DC-6AC HB-IBS to be temporarily taken off the nightly roster, on 7 April, for an overhaul as well as allowing the Balair DC-6B HB-IBR to be returned off-lease on 30 April. From the beginning of May 1969 the nightly I.C.R.C. Cotonou schedule became based on two C-97Gs and two DC-6ACs.

Operational conditions began to improve during April 1969. On the night of 28/29 April the I.C.R.C. recorded its most successful night since the relief airlift began when the Cotonou and Santa Isabel bases each launched twelve flights to Uli. It brought the Red Cross total flights to Biafra up to 1,597 and the total tonnage up to 15,922. On the following night I.C.R.C. broke its record again with 26 flights landing at Uli, an achievement that was never bettered. Paradoxically the high nightly achievements coincided with Dr August Lindt's arrival in Biafra to discuss the question of daylight flights.

Flughjalp is formed

It was not just the International Red Cross who were achieving an astonishing rise in flights. The Joint Church Aid airlift from São Tomé had also dramatically increased. But 1969 had not started without difficulties.

Arriving with the J.C.A. C-97Gs in February 1969 was a group of twenty-seven new American aircrew, the result of a successful recruitment campaign in the USA. But after several flights into Biafra, many pilots among the new group described the risks to be far greater than presupposed. Part of the risk was reportedly attributed to several aircraft having witnessed patrolling MiG-17Fs flying alongside them as they approached the Nigerian coast. The new pilots demanded an extra $50 per trip 'danger money' but Joint Church Aid, in not wishing to discriminate against those pilots flying for other agencies, refused to meet the demands. For a while the same crews refused to fly and nightly tonnages dropped from an average 140 tonnes to 70 tonnes per night.[313]

By April 1969, by which time many of the troublesome pilots had been replaced, nightly averages had not only resumed to earlier proportions but were beginning to exceed them. On the night of 4/5 April 1969 the São Tomé airlift recorded its 2,000th successful relief flight into Biafra. By the end of that month Joint Church Aid had completed 2,279 flights from São Tomé; the 2,500th flight was recorded on the night of 27/28 May 1969. But while tonnages had dramatically increased so had the costs, and the Scandinavian members of J.C.A. were beginning to seek ways of saving money–even as much as a 25% saving on the rising transportation costs. There were other problems facing the airlift schedulers and another human one. Transavia, from whom half the aircraft were chartered, was applying pressure over the working arrangements for pilots and aircrew. The problem was associated with the number of hours crews could legally work for; the demands of operating into Biafra meant that legal limits were constantly being broken. Ultimately it meant that under Dutch civil aviation regulations, Transavia could no longer continue its charter agreement with Nordchurchaid in using Dutch-registered aircraft.

The solution to both problems was found by establishing a new and non-profit making company specifically for humanitarian relief work. The company was named Flughjalp H.F., the English translation being, Aid By Air. Formed on 18 April 1969 and registered in Reykjavik, Iceland, Flughjalp was essentially owned by three partners - Nordchurchaid with a 45% share, the protestant Evangelical Lutheran Church of Iceland (35%), and the Icelandic airline, Loftleidir (20%). Most of the Dutch-registered DC-6 and DC-6B aircraft that were being used on the Nordchurchaid Biafra relief airlift were in fact owned by Loftleidir but operating under a lease agreement with Transavia. The only visible change to the aircraft on the airlift was a simple change in registration letters. Subsequently aircraft were repainted in a standard colour scheme with the characteristic 'double-fish' badge and the new company name.[314]

Flughjalp H.F. formally acquired ownership of its first two aircraft on 8 May 1969 with the purchase of two DC-6Bs, TF-LLC and TF-LLE, both of which were, at the time, on lease to Transavia as PH-TRZ and PH-TRL respectively. In fact both had already been operating on the airlift for some time. The two aircraft in question were both at São Tomé at the time of the change and where their new Icelandic registrations TF-AAA and TF-AAB were applied. Flughjalp H.F. also purchased the two DC-6s PH-TRA and PH-TRB and a DC-6B, PH-TRC all of which, unlike the earlier DC-6Bs, were actually owned by Transavia. The purchase of these three aircraft was formally completed on 12 May 1969 on which date they were re-registered in Iceland as TF-AAD, TF-AAE and TF-AAF respectively. (PH-TRB was already at São Tomé at the time and was repainted as TF-AAE on the island.)

A sixth aircraft was also acquired by Flughjalp but was

173: Inside a Flughjalp DC-6B during the unloading process at Uli strip, on 25 April 1969. Already one Biafran conscript worker is on board the aircraft and with a customary polythene bag tucked into his belt. At an opportune moment he will secretly slit open a sack of food and speedily fill the bag, ready for sale on Biafra's black market. If caught, however, the young man faced severe punishment–a military firing-squad (Phil Phillp)

done so in a rather complicated arrangement. It involved another DC-6B, PH-TRD, an aircraft owned by Loftleidir but at the time leased to Transavia. Like several of the other aircraft acquired by Flughjalp PH-TRD was already positioned at and operating from São Tomé. But rather than purchase it outright, Flughjalp agreed to a charter agreement with the aircraft's owner, Loftleidir, after the aircraft had completed routine servicing back at Schiphol. In order to satisfy the Dutch authorities, the DC-6B PH-TRD was restored to the Icelandic register as TF-LLA so that it could be ferried from São Tomé to Amsterdam, via Tripoli on 26 May. After reaching Schiphol in the early hours of 27 May 1969, the charter arrangement between Loftleidir and Flughjalp became effective and at that point TF-LLA was immediately re-registered to Flughjalp as TF-AAG.

The formation of Flughjalp did have a desired effect on Nordchurchaid's operational costs. The cost of chartering a DC-6B from Transavia had been $355 per blockhour; the new rate for leasing a DC-6B from Loftleidir was reduced to $262 per blockhour. Of those aircraft purchased by Flughjalp, the company had to pay for all aspects of their operating costs, including fuel, insurance, maintenance and spares - apart from the cost of buying the aircraft in the first instance.

The difficulty over maximum flying hours was also overcome. Under international rules aircrew were limited to a legal maximum 120 flying hours within any 28-day period without taking a mandatory rest period. Some pilots were achieving more than 120 hours by having themselves rostered under false names, sometimes with the name of a captain who had long left the airlift. As all of the aircraft were now operating under Icelandic registry the ex-Transavia captains were issued with Icelandic Commercial Licences, under which flying restrictions were considerably more relaxed. From then on it became quite normal for pilots to average 180 hours per month and sometimes in excess of 200 hours.[315]

One of the major frustrations felt by the Joint Church Aid group was that its operation was always viewed in a vastly different manner to, say, that of the International Red Cross. J.C.A. organisers very much wanted its operations from São Tomé to be openly recognised as being, as indeed they were, legitimate, valid and as politically independent as the Cotonou and Santa Isabel-based I.C.R.C. airlifts. The trouble was that São Tomé had traditionally become associated with Hank Warton's ragged fleet of tramp aircraft operating Biafran arms flights. Even though Warton had long departed the island, the perception of a well-organised Joint Church Aid relief airlift was never readily obvious to the outside world. The one visible example of this was the mixture of chartered aircraft all in their owner's standard colour schemes. An attempt to remedy this misconception was made by standardising on the appearance of aircraft used on the Joint Church Aid airlift.[316]

In fact the Joint Church Aid fleet became standardised in three different formats. The Icelandic and Scandanavian DC-6/DC-6Bs were repainted in an overall dull blue scheme with the characteristic double 'mirrored-fish' insignia on the fin. The C-97Gs retained their natural metal finish and the Canairelief L-1049Hs retained their overall blue scheme.

The Flughjalp fleet was the first to appear in the new colour scheme when they were repainted at Schiphol during maintenance periods, although not all of the aircraft were repainted in an identical fashion. TF-AAA, TF-AAE and TF-AAG did appear the same with 'JOINT CHURCH AID' titling on both sides of the fuselage. TF-AAB emerged with the 'JOINT CHURCH AID' legend on the port fuselage side and 'FLUGHJALP' on the starboard side while TF-AAF flew with the 'FLUGHJALP' legend on both sides of its fuselage. Other minor differences involved the colour shading of the fish insignia on the fin.

174: With the return of Transavia DC-6B PH-TRL to Amsterdam for an overhaul, Transavia despatched a replacement, PH-TRZ, to São Tomé. This had been leased by Transavia from Loftleidir, specially for the Nordchurchaid airlift to Biafra. It was photographed at Amsterdam-Schiphol on 1 January 1969 immediately before Captains Don Merriam and Alex Nicoll took off for the flight south. Routeing via Luxembourg, Tripoli and Accra PH-TRZ landed at São Tomé at 12:40 on 2 January. Note the unorthodox combination of markings: Loftleidir colour scheme and titling, Dutch registration and Joint Church Aid 'twin-fish' emblem beside the main door. This aircraft spent a year operating the airlift, less brief periods in Europe for routine servicing but was re-registered as TF-AAA midway through this period (via Peter J. Marson)

175: With the formation of Flughjalp during April 1969 DC-6B PH-TRZ was re-registered as TF-AAA. It is seen here at Amsterdam in May 1969 still wearing its original scheme. Just visible on the nosewheel door is the legend 'THE MOULES MAN' and which was applied during its first Biafran tour (via Peter J. Marson)

176: Transavia DC-6 PH-TRB operated out of São Tomé in standard scheme and later acquired the 'twin-fish' insignia. With the formation of Flughjalp in April 1969 PH-TRB was re-registered TF-AAE and carried those marks by the time it returned to Amsterdam for servicing in May 1969 (Unknown)

177: Although a poor quality photograph, it does show Flughjalp DC-6 TF-AAE at São Tomé after being flown out from Uli following an attack by Nigerian MiG-17Fs. Already the DC-6 has "lost" an engine, having been deemed suitable only for spares use. Note that TF-AAE operated with a white-top scheme (Jakob Ringler)

178: During May 1969 the DC-6B TF-AAA was repainted at Schiphol into the classic Joint Church Aid 'blue-top' camouflage scheme and 'twin-fish' emblem on the fin. Initially the lower fish was coloured. Most of the Icelandic registered aircraft carried the 'FLUGHJALP' legend on the fuselage and 'AID BY AIR' on the nose. TF-AAA is seen arriving at Prestwick on 16 January 1970 for storage, its Biafran role over. Note the name 'The Moules Man' on the nose (Unknown)

179: DC-6B TF-AAB was repainted in full Flughjalp markings at Schiphol during June/July 1969. On 15 July 1969 it was scheduled to leave Amsterdam for ferrying to São Tomé but developed a serious water-methanol leak just before take-off. There was then doubt as to whether the captain was DC-6B-rated; departure was therefore postponed until the following morning to allow a full daylight sector between Amsterdam and Tripoli. At 0805, on 17 July, TF-AAB's Icelandic and British crew took-off from Tripoli for Cotonou where it refuelled for the final leg to São Tomé. It eventually arrived on station at 2115. It is seen at Prestwick at the end of the airlift (Unknown)

A period of accidents

"Always–unspoken in the background–Death lurks carrying his scythe and lantern."

Approaching and landing at night onto what was essentially no more than a converted roadway was dangerous enough. To dramatically raise the number of aircraft landing and taking-off under such conditions each night considerably increased the accident stakes. Varying skills and experience of aircrew, the tension from the threat of bombing, the mix of relief and arms flights using the same stretch of roadway to land on and the relative crudeness of landing aids and systems were all factors designed to make accidents a certainty. Some pilots, they say, even developed a so-called death wish. Yet, given those circumstances, most of the incidents were treated as fairly minor. The International Red Cross would often report back to Geneva a "technical snag", such as one occasion when, at Uli, a Biafran Army lorry accidentally reversed into the wing of a Balair DC-6AC and damaged the inside edge of an elevator hinge. The damage was decided insufficient to keep the aircraft grounded and the crew therefore flew it back to Cotonou safely. It was, said the report next day, a "technical snag". Other incidents occurred and were put down to the mental strain of operating under such conditions. On another occasion a newly-recruited American Flight Engineer forgot to switch on water methanol when one of the Balair DC-6ACs took-off from Uli on full-power, a lapse that could have caused a serious loss of power at a very critical moment. Similarly, on another departure from Uli, a Flight Engineer retracted the undercarriage too early on take-off and nearly caused a serious accident.

Given such conditions it is almost unbelievable that the first serious accident of 1969 did not occur until the night of 6/7 May 1969. Furthermore in the nine months since Operation 'INALWA' began it was the first accident to involve a Red Cross aircraft. It involved the Balair DC-6AC HB-IBT.

The International Red Cross Flight Operations manager at Cotonou had planned to despatch five aircraft on the night in question, each scheduled to complete three return trips to Uli. HB-IBT began its first shuttle when it took-off from Cotonou at 16:35 hours and later landed at Uli at 18:13. Unloading took an amazingly short period of fourteen minutes before the aircraft was airborne again at 18:35 for the return flight to Cotonou, where it landed at 19:42 hours.

After being refuelled and speedily re-loaded with a full cargo of dried fish, 'IBT took-off from Cotonou at 20:31; its sister aircraft, HB-IBS, followed five minutes behind. The two aircraft then selected and maintained separate flight levels in accordance with the Red Cross arrangements, 'IBT at 9,000 feet, 'IBS at 7,000 feet. Both aircraft were operating on the same radio frequency and as 'IBS overflew the river Niger, its captain heard Uli Air Traffic Control clear the lead aircraft (HB-IBT) down to 6,000 feet. Then the crew was instructed to change to the Uli Tower frequency before gaining clearance for a direct approach on a right base leg to runway 16. The same controllers requested the crew of HB-IBS to overfly Uli at 4,000 feet and then to land on runway 16 immediately afterwards but from a left base leg.

At 21:52 the crew aboard HB-IBS heard what became the last radio call from its sister aircraft: "Could I have the runway lights please, I think I am very close to the field, may be on short final." A few seconds later the crew of 'IBS saw the runway and approach lights switched on, but then some thirty seconds afterwards they witnessed a very large explosion to the north of runway 16 and with an immediate huge fire.

DC-6AC HB-IBT crashed some distance to the north of Uli and during the following night two accident specialists (Mnsrs Hier and Heimoz) were flown from the Red Cross base at Cotonou into Biafra in order to carry out a full investigation of the crash. They found the wreckage of HB-IBT to be strewn along a definite path which acknowledged the correct final approach pattern to runway 16. It was also clear that the aircraft had been on a course heading of 220 degrees, suggesting that it was almost lined up for the approach to land. The aircraft's main undercarriage was fully extended, but it had collided with palm trees that rose up to 20 metres about 10km north of Uli's runway. Contact with the palm trees had first caused the outer wings and starboard elevator to be ripped away and which clearly ruptured the aircraft's main fuel tanks. With fuel pouring from the wing tanks there had been no way of avoiding a fire breaking out once impact had occurred. The aircraft hit the ground some 200 metres beyond the first bent palm trees and evidence pointed to the fact that the port undercarriage and engines took the main impact before the primary explosion.

The conclusion that both investigators came to as to the reason for the crash was to some extent rather vague. There was no obvious mechanical defect that would have caused the crash. (HB-IBT had undergone a routine Check 3 at Cotonou only the day before the accident and its condition had been found to be good.) The reported visibility at Uli at the time of the accident was up to 16km and, apart from some scattered cirrus cloud, was a clear sky with virtually no wind. The crew, all of whom were Swedes, was suitably-qualified for the Biafran operation and the pilot, Captain Carl Baltze, was considered to be the most experienced captain on the I.C.R.C. airlift. The ultimate conclusion arrived at by the investigators was that the crash had occurred due to "the very difficult conditions for a direct approach to an unlit runway, and that in doing so the aircraft had come into contact with the ground prematurely".[317]

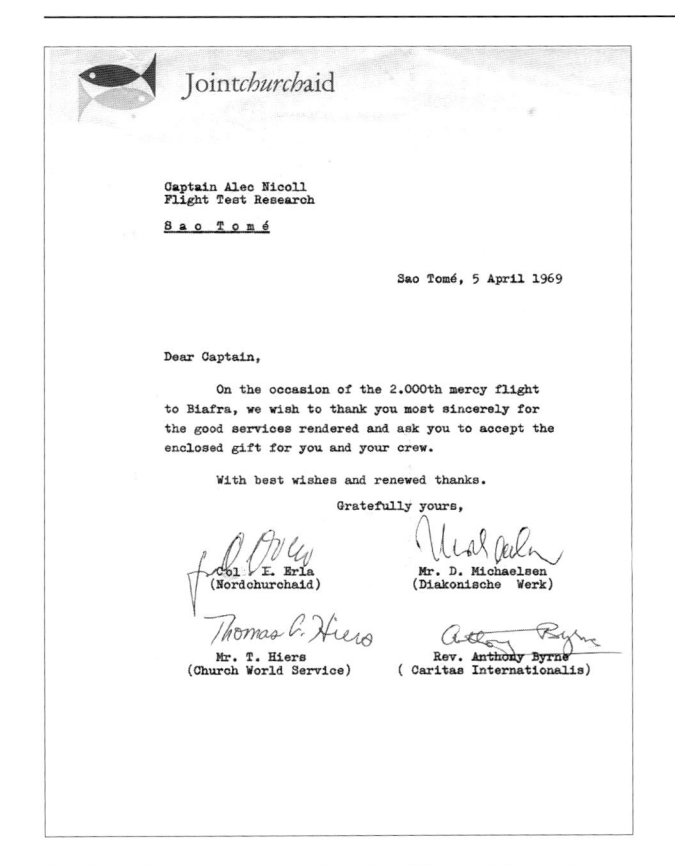

180 Above: During the night of 4/5 April 1969 the Joint Church Aid relief airlift from São Tomé achieved its 2,000th flight into Biafra. To show their gratitude the representatives of the four primary JCA agencies gave a token gift to all captains at São Tomé (Via David Nicoll)

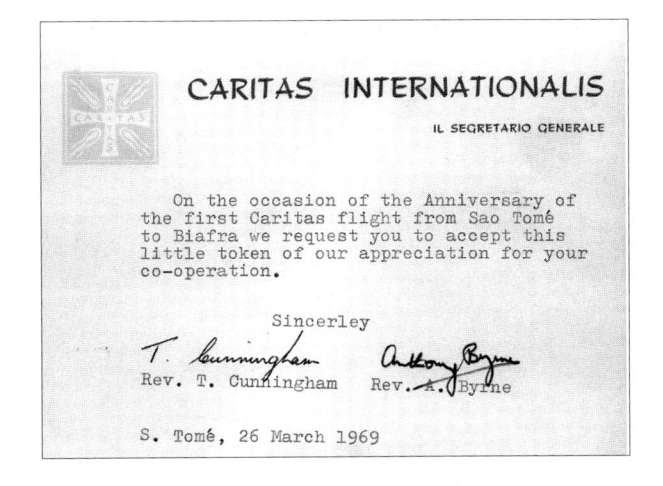

181 Above: 26 March 1969 marked the first anniversary of the start of CARITAS relief flights from São Tomé to Biafra. From very small beginnings, and by chartering space aboard Hank Warton's L-1049G Super Constellations, the airlift had reached massive proportions. Instrumental in the growth of the airlift were two Irish Catholic Priests, Father Anthony Byrne and Father Tom Cunningham. In spite of the enormous workload and administrative difficulties that the airlift created, all pilots at São Tomé received a simple but meaningful token. The message is clearly self-explanatory (Via E. Roocroft)

Joint Church Aid: two lucky escapes

Within a month of the I.C.R.C. DC-6AC crash the Joint Church Aid airlift suffered the loss of two aircraft, although neither involved any loss of life. The first occurred on the night after the crash of HB-IBT, when one of the American-crewed C-97Gs, N52679, crash-landed onto the runway at Uli during the early evening of 8 May 1969. In fact, the C-97G had been slotted in as the night's third arrival, immediately after the Biafran Government's L-1049G '5N-07G'; the first arrival had been an International Red Cross DC-7B (SE-ERP). The DC-7B landed safely as did the L-1049G, but the C-97G literally crash-landed onto Uli's landing strip. With the runway blocked the Uli controllers had no alternative but to shut down operations for the night and all other aircraft attempting to land that night were ordered to return to base. The cause of the crash-landing was initially blamed on the collapse of the aircraft's nose-wheel but a subsequent announcement by Joint Church Aid attributed the accident to pilot error. Word on São Tomé spoke of the crew simply forgetting to lower the undercarriage. There was even one–perhaps tongue-in-cheek–suggestion that, because of the noise level inside a C-97G and the height of the flightdeck off the ground, none of the crew realised that the aircraft had made a wheels-up landing until the captain tried to turn off the runway.[318]

Fortunately the accident had occurred towards the beginning of the night's operations and therefore only two other aircraft were stranded on the strip. Even so the activity on the strip descended to sheer pandemonium. The C-97G had not caught fire but was sitting in the centre of Uli's runway. Workers began to unload the cargo while others began the task of trying to move the stranded wreck. The first attempt involved trying to raise the nose section and to drag the aircraft clear, which did not work.

The answer, or so it seemed, was to reduce the striken C-97G to manageable pieces before attempting to move it clear. For once the Biafrans were almost thankful for dawn and the anticipated arrival of the Nigerian Air Force. The MiG-17Fs strafed and bombed the American freighter setting it alight almost immediately. The other two aircraft on the strip, the Grey Ghost L-1049G and the Swedish Red Cross DC-7B, had been well camouflaged and were not attacked. By midday on 9 May 1969 the C-97G had almost completely burnt out; it had also broken up in the fire and had become reduced to moveable size. By late afternoon the runway had been cleared and swept; by dusk Uli was ready for another night's operations. The first movements of the night involved the departures of '5N-07G' and SE-ERP to São Tomé and Fernando Póo respectively.

The second of the losses involving an aircraft of Joint Church Aid was a much more serious affair and occurred during the night of 2/3 June 1969 when one of Flughjalp's

DC-6s landed at Uli with a full load of stockfish. The aircraft, TF-AAE, was being flown by the Australian captain, Verdun Polley, with his co-pilot, Harold Snelholm and flight engineer Hordur Eiriksson. Polley made his first approach to Uli and, as per the usual routine, called for the runway lights to be turned on at the last moment. As the lights came on he found himself, on this occasion, too low and considerably off the centre line; he immediately took the decision, and not for the first time since joining the relief airlift eight months earlier, to overshoot and try again. But this occasion Verdun Polley made an unforgiveable error. Instead of climbing up to re-establish with Uli's beacon he decided to make a 360° turn to port and make a second approach. Polley counted the four turns until knowing that he was back on final approach. Again, he called for the runway lights to be turned on and again he was off the centreline but this time a long way out and only at 200feet. Polley switched on the DC-6's landing lights and corrected his line of approach. Leaving the lights on was a second mistake.[319]

Two Nigerian Air Force MiG-17Fs were patrolling the area that night and hoping to pick out a suitable target at Uli. Verdun Polley's DC-6, with landing lights blazing as it approached to land, was a perfect target for a head-on attack. The DC-6 was in a slightly nose-down attitude and as the two MiGs also attacked in a diving profile the two pilots (actually a South African and a Briton) could aim for the landing lights without being blinded.[320]

One of the MiGs fired at least two rockets; the other strafed with cannon-fire. As TF-AAE touched-down so the cannon fire hit the runway and exploded upwards, either side of the cockpit. The attack had clearly been from a directly head-on position. The DC-6 landed and the engines put into immediate reverse pitch. In darkness the aircraft slewed off the strip and came to a halt in a shrub area.

Following immediately behind Verdun Polley's aircraft was a second Flughjalp aircraft, the DC-6B TF-AAD, flown by two Britons, Eddie Roocroft and Phil Phillp, and a Belgian Flight Engineer, Jos de Pau. The crew just caught sight of the exploding cannon shells and rockets. At the same time the Uli Controller announced that the strip was closed while enemy fighters were in the vicinity. Roocroft continued his approach and landed, without lights, further along the strip.

Despite TF-AAE sustaining direct hits there were no injuries among the crew and Verdun Polley eventually managed to taxi the DC-6 clear of the landing area and into a parking bay. A carefully-worded signal, requesting engineers to be flown in aboard the second-wave of flights, was then relayed back to São Tomé. Verdun Polley and his crew decided to remain at Uli in order to examine and assess the full extent of damage in daylight. In the meantime the Biafrans covered TF-AAE with the standard foliage camouflage to reduce the threat of it being caught again by any marauding Nigerian MiG-17F after daybreak.

In fact the damage sustained by TF-AAE was initially assessed as being sufficiently repairable to allow the aircraft to be flown out of Uli. The main fuel tanks had been ruptured but the auxilliary tanks (in the outer wing sections) were undamaged and contained enough fuel to make São Tomé. The major problems involved broken hydraulic cables and two flat mainwheel tyres. There was also some cannon damage to the fin but thankfully the rudder hinges were untouched. Two spare wheels and a wing-jack were brought in on the second shuttle of the night but at every attempt to jack up the wing the thin bitumin surface of Uli's tarmac collapsed. It was therefore decided that, as there was one shattered tyre on each side, it was easier simply to remove the torn tyres and leave bare rims. As regards the hydraulics, some of the repairs were effected by using pipes and fencing wire. With the threat of further MiG-17 attacks there was no room for repairs 'by the book'.

Just past midnight, in the early hours of 4 June, Polley took the decision to fly TF-AAE back to base. The plan was to fly at low altitude to the coast and then climb. The approach to land at São Tomé was made with hydraulic pressures reading zero, no brakes and very little fuel. Verdun Polley landed at just above stalling speed and then allowed the aircraft to gently ground-loop to a halt.

Daylight on São Tomé allowed a closer and more detailed inspection of the aircraft. This revealed that TF-AAE had, in fact, suffered extensive structural damage, so much so that it was considered too serious for repair. The aircraft was effectively stripped of its engines and all useable components, including the complete nosewheel assembly.[321]

Without doubt the crew of TF-AAE had had a very narrow escape. Several nights later, however, luck ran out for a Swedish Red Cross DC-7B crew.

The ultimate shoot-down

The attack by two MiG-17Fs against the Flughjalp DC-6 had signalled what appeared to be a significant change of tactics by the Nigerian Air Force. The change was undoubtedly in retaliation for renewed air attacks by the Biafran Air Force, which had just received a small force of MFI-9B aircraft. On 22 May 1969, the MFI-9Bs had begun a series of air-raids against Nigerian airfields. Ironically the MFI-9B force was led by the former Biafran relief pilot, Gustav von Rosen.

The introduction of new tactics by the Nigerian MiG-17Fs was also driven by changes within the Nigerian Army field of command.

During May 1969 Major Atto was replaced as Com-

1969 FLIGHT LOG

Date Day/Month/Year	Aircraft Type	Markings	Pilot's Function on board	Place and Time for Departures & Arrivals From	To	Flight times Pilot in Command	Co-Pilot	Dual
April 21	DC 6 B	TRE	P1	Ams - Orly - Ams		3.20		
" 26	"	TRE	"	2 Prof Checks		2.35		
May 15	"	AAA	"	2 shuttles to ULI		8.00		
" 16	"	"	"	2 shuttles " "		7.35		
" 17	"	AAB	"	3 " " "		11.46		
" 19	"	"	"	2 " " "		7.35		
" 20	"	AAA	"	2 " " "		8.45		
" 22	"	"	"	3 " " "		10.40		
" 24	"	AAD	"	3 " " "		10.41		
" 26	"	"	"	2 " " "		7.41		
" 27	"	AAE	"	3 " " "		11.07		
" 29	"	AAD	"	2 " " "		8.09		
" 30	"	AAE	"	3 " " "		10.35		
June 1	"	AAE	"	3 " " "		10.30		
" 2	"	AAE	"	½ " " "		2.00		
" 3	"	"	"	½ " " "		1.45		
" 6	"	AAB	"	1 " " "		4.06		
" 7	"	AAD	"	2 " " "		7.05		
" 9	"	AAA	"	2 " " "		7.16		
" 10	"	AAA	"	2 " " "		7.15		

PAGE TOTALS: 148.25
Totals brought forward: 20117.15 | 648.35 | 67.45
TOTALS TO DATE: 20265.40

TOTAL FLIGHT TIME: 20,982 Hrs. — Mins.

PORT HARCOURT

Year 1969 Month	Date	Aircraft Type and Mark	No.	Captain or 1st Pilot	Co-pilot 2nd Pilot Pupil or Crew	DUTY (Including number of day or night landings as 1st Pilot or Dual)	Day Flying 1st Pilot	2nd Pilot	Dual	Night Flying 1st Pilot	2nd Pilot	Dual	Total Cols. 1-6
						Totals brought forward	3820/20	94/45	315/40	157/30	40/05	31/55	4447/05
JUNE	2	MIG 17	623	SELF	SOLO	LAGOS - PORT HARCOURT (C-46) (HIT BY A/C HIT A/C)	1.00						1.00
	2	MIG 17	617	SELF	SOLO	STRAFING A/C ON ULI STRIP				1.15			1.15
	3	MIG 17	617	SELF	SOLO	P.H. to ENUGU, STRAFING AT UGA STRIP (A/A)	1.00						1.00
	3	MIG 17	617	SELF	SOLO	ENUGU to P.H. STRAFING VEHICLES ON ROADS OWERRI AREA	1.00						1.00
	3	MIG 17	617	SELF	SOLO	Recce IHIALA STRIP (A/A)				1.20			1.20
	3	MIG 17	617	SELF	SOLO	Recce IHIALA STRIP (A/A)				1.15			1.15
	4	MIG 17	617	SELF	SOLO	STRAFING OGUTA (A/A)	1.15	4.15					1.15
	4	JETPROVOST	701	SELF	THOMPSETT	RECCE IHIALA STRIP	(1.30)		1.30			*	1.30
	4	MIG 17	617	SELF	SOLO	Bombing OGUTA (2 ROCKETS)	.45						.45
	5	MIG 17	617	SELF	SOLO	Bombing OGUTA (HIT BY A/A)	.45						.45
	5	MIG 17	617	SELF	SOLO	BIAFRAN A/C INTERCEPTION, NONE SEEN	1			1.10			1.10
	6	S/55	508	SELF	BERTHE	TO SCENE OF CRASHED DC6 (PILOTS DEAD) (SE-ERP) SWEDISH RED CROSS	3.10	9.00				H	3.10
	7	S/55	508	SELF	THOMPSETT	TO SCENE OF CRASHED DC6	2.30					H	2.30
	11	JETPROVOST	701	SELF	THOMPSETT	LAGOS - PORT HARCOURT	1.15					*	1.15
	12	MIG 17	617	SELF	SOLO	STRAFING NORTH OF ABA	.45						.45
	12	MIG 17	617	SELF	SOLO	Recce IHIALA (A/A)				1.05	7.35		1.05
	13	MIG 17	617	SELF	SOLO	P.HARCOURT - ENUGU (A/A) STRAFING IHIALA, HIT 2 DC3s ON GROUND	1.00						1.00
	13	MIG 17	617	SELF	SOLO	ENUGU - P.HARCOURT (A/A) Recce UDIARH AREA FOR REBEL AUSTER D FIRED ON A/C (A/A)	1.10	15.40					1.10
	13	MIG 17	617	SELF	SOLO	STRAFING ULI STRIP				1.30	9.05		1.30
	13	MIG 17	617	SELF	SOLO	STRAFING N. OF OWERRI + N. OF ABA	.45	16.25					.45
	14	MIG 17	617	SELF	SOLO	Recce ULI STRIP, also UGA				1.30			1.30
	17	MIG 17	622	SELF	SOLO	Recce ULI and UGA strips (A/A)				1.20	11.55		1.20
	18	MIG 17	617	SELF	SOLO	Strafing at ULI and UGA (A/A)	1.15	17.40					1.15
						Totals carried forward	5.15 / 3838/00			169/			5.15 / 25

182 Top: Verdun Polley recorded "half a return shuttle to Uli" on 2 June 1969. In fact his DC-6 TF-AAE was attacked by a Nigerian Air Force MiG-17F just as it touched down on Uli's landing-strip. It was undoubtedly one of the luckiest escapes of the airlift. Amazingly, Polley flew the DC-6 out to Sao Tome the following night to complete the remaining "half shuttle"

183 Above: South African mercenary Ares Klootwyk, flying Nigerian Air Force MiG-17F NAF617, recorded hitting an aircraft on Uli strip during a night mission. Although he mistakenly records a C-46, the aircraft was in fact the DC-6 TF-AAE. Note the entry for 5 June 1969 describes the night of the shoot-down of the Swedish Red Cross DC-7 SE-ERP

184: The Swedish Red Cross acquired a sizeable fleet of DC-7B aircraft during 1969 for operations out of Fernando Póo under the International Red Cross umbrella. SE-ERO appears in standard white overall scheme with red crosses liberally applied in the standard ICRC positions, ie. Above and below the wings and fuselage, on the nose and finally on the fin (Unknown, via P.J. Marson)

185, 186: The shooting-down of Swedish Red Cross DC-7B SE-ERP on 5 June 1969 was undoubtedly the most outrageous act of the Nigerian Civil War. The aircraft had crossed the Nigerian coastline in full evening daylight and presented itself as an easy target for a pair of mercenary-crewed Nigerian Air Force MiG-17Fs patrolling out of Port Harcourt. The DC-7B came down close to the village of Eket where, shortly afterwards, Federal soldiers are seen man-handling a section of wreckage. Such was the impact that all four crew were killed instantly but only two bodies were ever found (Peter Obe)

mander of the MiG-17 Port Harcourt Detachment by a Nigerian Air Force Captain, Gbadamosi King who, on 28 May, was summoned by General Olusegun Obasanjo, the newly-appointed CO of the Army's 3 Marine Commando Division. In spite of facing operational difficulties in not having any efficient navigational aids, nor an effective ground-to-air communications system, Obasanjo demanded better and immediate results from the MiG-17F pilots. King, under no illusion of the task being demanded of him, managed to request replacement equipment from Lagos within days.[322] The attack against TF-AAE was the first of the immediate results. Within days another attack by the Port Harcourt-based MiG-17Fs brought devastating results when an inbound Swedish Red Cross DC-7B, SE-ERP, was shot down.

By the turn of June 1969 the International Red Cross had flown almost 2,000 shuttle flights into Uli, from both Santa Isabel and Cotonou. Since the opening of the Cotonou base, the I.C.R.C. had reduced its fleet on the island to just four Swedish Red Cross DC-7Bs, but each of the aircraft there had sometimes managed four return flights to Uli on nights when flights were allowable. Only the local riots and the attempted coup against President Macias during February/March 1969 had interrupted flights from the island for any given length of time.[323]

Precise details surrounding the events of the night of 5/6 June 1969 will always, undoubtedly, contain a degree of uncertainty. Even the passing of time has not offered a full explanation and various published sources have offered theories, all of which differ in some minor detail. What has not been disputed is that SE-ERP had, since its arrival at Santa Isabel on 26 April 1969, completed almost 100 shuttles into Uli; that on the night in question was undertaking the first of three planned flights, and that its cargo consisted almost totally of rice.

One of the most graphic accounts suggested that the Air Force Detachment at Port Harcourt received a tip-off from Lagos as to the departure time of the DC-7B SE-ERP from Santa Isabel, together with its estimated speed and bearing. A MiG-17F was scrambled from Port Harcourt and flown on an east-south-easterly heading in order to rendezvous with the DC-7B after it had crossed the Nigerian coastline. The information relayed from Lagos stated that the aircraft would cross midway between Port Harcourt and Calabar but the MiG pilot initially experienced some difficulty in finding the I.C.R.C. aircraft. Eventually, and risking the danger of running out of fuel, a final search across the evening sky revealed the all-white DC-7B. The American captain of the DC-7B, Captain David Brown, was apparently then ordered to land at Port Harcourt or at Calabar but the demand was ignored. The call was repeated but the pilot remained unyielding at which stage the Mig-17F pilot re-positioned his aircraft to the rear of the DC-7B and fired several short cannon bursts. The DC-7B sustained numerous hits and came down in bush near Eket.[324]

Frederick Forsyth provides some finer detail on the incident:

"At 17:38 hours on that Thursday evening Captain Brown took off from Fernando Póo with his cargo...... If he made any mistake it was in leaving too early for Biafra. The sky was a brilliant blue, without a cloud, and the sun was still well above the horizon. It was habitual for planes leaving São Tomé to depart at this hour, for with the longer journey they only came over the Biafran coast after 19:00, that is after dark. Dusk is very short in Africa. The light starts fading in June around 18:30 and by 19:00 it is dark. But with the much shorter journey (only 60 miles) from Fernando Póo to the coast, he came over the coast about 18:00 in brilliant daylight. At 18:03 his voice was heard on the Fernando Póo control tower, and by other Red Cross pilots on the same run. He gave no call-sign, and the voice was high-pitched with alarm. He said: 'I'm being attacked... I'm being attacked.' His switch went dead, there was a moment's silence, then a babble on the ether, with Fernando Póo asking for the identification of the caller. Thirty seconds later the voice came back on the air. 'My engine's on fire... I'm going down...' Then there was silence."[325]

Within a fortnight the identity of the pilot responsible for the shooting-down of DC-7B was known among the crews at São Tomé. They believed him to be one of the few remaining South African pilots still contracted to fly MiG-17Fs. Inside Nigeria, and among the group of mercenary aircrews who lived in relative luxury at the Ikeja Arms hotel in Lagos, word also had it that he was a South African pilot and who even spoke of aiming cannon-fire at the DC-7Bs port wing-tip, striking the outer engine. Over drinks in the hotel bar, he had allegedly claimed that, after firing his first shots, the nose of the Red Cross DC-7B rose sharply before entering a stall, after which at least two of the crew members opened the freight doors and started to throw some of the cargo out before the aircraft went down, not in a sudden dive, but in a gradual and controlled descent.[326]

Other mercenary pilots in Nigeria claim that two MiG-17Fs had in fact been scrambled from Port Harcourt on the night of 5/6 June, flown by Ares Klootwyk and Mike Thompsett. (Thompsett was later killed flying a MiG-17F when it ran out of fuel while returning to base.) The justification among the pilots at Port Harcourt, and the primary reasoning for shooting at the I.C.R.C. aircraft was a widely-felt frustration that the "personal financial greed of mercenary pilots on Fernando Póo had encouraged departures to be made earlier and earlier." It was known that, on top of their regular salary, International Red Cross pilots, who consisted primarily of Swiss, Swedes and Americans, received a nightly bonus of an extra $50 for the first return shuttle to Uli, and an extra $100 for the second and subsequent shuttles. The increase for the second and third shuttles was specifically designed to encourage pilots to make more than just a single shuttle per night. They were, claimed some MiG pilots, "pushing their luck a bit too much, and needed to be brought down to size".[327]

Precisely which of the two MiG-17Fs fired the fateful shots is hard to establish and however hard those responsible tried later to justify their actions, one fact remained; the incident caused the loss of four lives. Apart from the American captain, David Brown, those who died were two Swedes, co-pilot Stig Carlson and Loadmaster Harry Axelson and a Norwegian Flight Engineer, Kiell Pettersen All were killed instantly as the aircraft hit the ground. Sadly only two bodies were ever recovered from the wreckage. But there was a final irony. The American pilot, Captain David Brown, had originally flown into Biafra with Hank Warton. That was an angle missed by the Nigerians.

A second DC-7B, SE-ERO, had been following the unfortunate 'ERP while four aircraft (C-97Gs HB-ILX and HB-ILY), DC-6AC HB-IBS and DC-6B TF-FRA) were already en route from Cotonou. Immediately that news of the action was relayed from Santa Isabel to Cotonou all aircraft were recalled and all other flights of the night were cancelled. For the International Red Cross the shooting-down of the DC-7B effectively brought the airlift to a halt and, not for the first time, the question of flying relief aid into Biafra became dominated by a period of intense political bargaining between Lagos and Geneva.

Shoot-down: the aftermath

Dr August Lindt flew to Moscow early on 10 June 1969 primarily to collect his personal effects. Before he left, he issued instructions with the Cotonou Operations Chief, Nils Wachtmeister, that a series of 'proving flights' should be made from Cotonou to Uli. The one provision of the planned four flights was that all should take place strictly during the hours of darkness. Should the proving flights be successful and without any harassment from the Nigerian Air Force then Lindt intended to resume regular flights, initially to begin with and steadily increase their frequency until they reached the pre-5 June level.[328]

Not unnaturally the shooting-down of the DC-7B SE-ERP had an equally dramatic effect on the airlift out of São Tomé. The Joint Church Aid fleet had all returned to their base on the night in question while the full impact of the incident was carefully considered. More than anything else the feeling among the São Tomé crews was one of intense annoyance that their opposite numbers on the Nigerian side were now aiming for the man and not the aircraft. One Nordchurchaid captain, Eddie Roocroft, put forward a plan that all available aircraft should make a daylight flight from São Tomé and in line abreast formation approach the Nigerian coastline. One of their number would then call on Port Harcourt's frequency and "dare the MiG-17 mercenary pilots" to make another attack. The notion, albeit a popular one among aircrews, was not accepted by the Nordchurchaid planners.[329] At least one C-97G, N52676, flown by British pilot Alex Nicoll, flew in to Uli on the night after the shoot-down, as did several Icelandic DC-6s, all without incident. Flights did continue at a drastically reduced rate of only two or three flights per night. These flights accounted for, at the most, only about one-tenth of the end-May flow of relief material which had amounted to some 300 tonnes per night.

At Cotonou, on 10 June 1969, the Icelandic DC-6B TF-FRA was fuelled up for what the International Red Cross described as the first of two 'proving flights' into Uli that night. Both flights were made by the Icelander, Lofto Johanssen and the aircraft returned safely on both occasions. Two more proving flights were scheduled for the night of 12/13 June 1969, again to be flown by Johanssen in the DC-6B TF-FRA. But only hours before Johanssen was due to take-off from Cotonou an official at the US Embassy in Geneva telephoned the International Red Cross headquarters with a warning of "unspecified dangers" and urged them not to fly that night. The same caller issued an identical warning to the Joint Church Aid chiefs who were, at the time, attending a Plenary session at Lucerne. News of the warning was immediately passed on to São Tomé by which time seven aircraft were already in the air. One, in fact, had landed at Uli, two others were in the Uli holding pattern (and therefore allowed to land) but the remaining four were recalled to São Tomé. The second shuttle of the night by all seven J.C.A. aircraft is reported to have been cancelled.[330]

Investigations into the true source of the telephone call, as well as the extent of the 'unspecified dangers", began on the following morning. The nature of the threat turned out to be a report that the Nigerian Air Force had recently received a small number of Sukhoi night-fighter jets; the source of the report emerged to be the American Embassy in Lagos. Furthermore it later transpired that the reasoning behind the original warning had been due to "political problems at Cotonou". At that point the J.C.A. Operations Director promptly dismissed the whole episode as being nothing more than a domestic Red Cross problem and immediately ordered a resumption of flights from São Tomé for the following night, 13/14 June, albeit still at a carefully considered reduced rate.

What was fast proving to be a well-orchestrated conspiracy directed against the International Red Cross brought further difficulties when Lindt, having returned from Moscow, then flew to Lagos. Aboard his personal King Air (HB-GBK) Lindt landed at Lagos on 14 June in a final attempt to resolve the relief flight situation. But Lindt never managed to meet the Federal leaders; instead he and the crew were promptly arrested (by the Airport Commandant, the volatile Nigerian officer, Captain Dixon, for landing his aircraft without, allegedly, any proper authorisation. If there *was* a Federal conspiracy against the I.C.R.C. then it had now begun to manifest itself–even more so several hours later when, and after being held for several hours, Lindt was expelled from Lagos and declared *persona non grata*. For the International Red Cross and for Lindt personally it had to be the final humiliation.

Dr Lindt was forced to leave Lagos aboard a scheduled airline flight to Douala. On 19 June 1969, he formally resigned his post.

Eager to resume its operations the I.C.R.C. lodged a request with the Nigerians, on Friday 20 June 1969, for permission to operate one daylight flight from Lagos to Uli. For a long while the request went unanswered. Then, on 30 June, the Federal Nigerian government issued its sternest warning yet to any relief agency attempting to fly into Biafra without official clearance. The threat was delivered personally by Nigeria's Information Commissioner, Chief Anthony Enahoro who, and in the strongest terms possible, insisted that all supplies "by air, sea, river or land" must be cleared by the Nigerian armed forces and police "after thorough inspection in Lagos or other approved points in Federal areas". "Only supplies which had been inspected by Federal authorities would be allowed through the blockade", Chief Enahoro continued, before adding that the Federal Government would have to be satisfied that relief supplies which go through "do not prove a cover for the transportation of arms and other war materials, such as spare parts for radio, vehicles, aircraft and fuel, as well as non-relief personnel." Enaharo concluded by implying that the Nigerian Air Force would again shoot down any aircraft which attempted to break that blockade.

Ultimately the International Red Cross did accede to Nigerian demands and agreed to undertake a number of flights to Biafra on the night of 4/5 August 1969, all of which routed via Lagos for a full inspection by Federal authorities. The I.C.R.C. had planned three flights for the night involving two C-97Gs, HB-ILY and HB-ILZ, together with the DC-6B TF-FRA. To ensure the maximum load possible, all three aircraft were stripped of all non-essential equipment but in the event only two aircraft flew in, the DC-6B and the C-97G HB-ILZ. Both landed at Lagos before flying east to Uli, where they landed shortly after 02:00 hours to unload 27 tonnes of medicine and a small quantity of food for Red Cross teams based in Biafra. The I.C.R.C. aircraft remained at Uli for some period of time before taking-off for the return leg to Lagos where a further inspection took place prior to their return to Cotonou.[331]

In spite of having successfully negotiated for a temporary lifting of the ban on its flights to Biafra, the International Red Cross did not, in fact, resume its airlift to Biafra and no further flights took place. Aircraft of the Swedish Red Cross detachment on Fernando Póo, which had undergone minor fleet changes to meet maintainence requirements, including the arrival of DC-7B SE-ERR on 9 May to replace SE-EDU, were ferried to Cotonou where they joined the rest of the grounded I.C.R.C. fleet.

The Churches carry on

Joint Church Aid did carry on relief flights from São Tomé. In spite of the events surrounding the loss of the Red Cross DC-7B and facing continued threats from the Federal Nigerian government, Joint Church Aid elected to resume a full nightly flying programme. The decision to resume flights was taken by the São Tomé Director of Operations, Colonel T Wichmann, who had visited Uli shortly beforehand and had found that harassment from the Nigerian Air Force was considerably less than they had been led to believe. By the end of July 1969 Joint Church Aid nightly tonnage achievements had returned to the level regularly achieved prior to 5 June.

The Irish agency, Africa Concern, which had also continued flights in the wake of the shooting down of the Red Cross DC-7B, also increased the frequency of its flights out of Libreville. By 30 June 1969 Africa Concern had completed 61 flights from Libreville with a total of 638 tonnes of food, medicines and agricultural supplies. The agency's DC-6B, OO-HEX, was also utilised by other agencies, one of which involved ferrying 20 tonnes of seed rice from Abidjan to Uli. The Philadelphia-based Biafra Relief Fund Inc also used the Africa Concern DC-6B for flying salt from Abidjan to Uli. After its own aircraft had been returned to French Air Force charge l'Oeuvres Hospitalières Françaises de l'Ordre de Malte used OO-HEX for flying 150 Biafran children from Uli to Abidjan for care and recuperation.[332]

The Joint Church Aid fleet had also undergone some minor changes and at the end of July 1969 included the original C-97Gs N52631 and N52676, plus an attrition-replacement, N52600, which had arrived from Miami on 16 June. A fourth C-97G, N52915, had been ferried to Tel Aviv on 20 July for an overhaul by Israeli Aircraft Industries. Four Flughjalp aircraft were on strength at São Tomé involving the DC-6 TF-AAD and three DC-6Bs TF-AAA, TF-AAB and TF-AAF. The third element of the Joint Church Aid fleet involved the Canairelief L-1049H Super Constellations which by now accounted for four aircraft: CF-NAJ, CF-NAK, CF-NAL and CF-NAM.

Canairelief's finances at the start of its Biafra operation in January 1969 had been just sufficient to support a three-month period with one L-1049H Super Constellation, CF-NAJ. A highly-vigorous campaign by the Canadian press to highlight the extent of Biafra's plight had reaped enormous financial benefits for the Canadian agency. So much so that on 24 April 1969 Canairelief announced the purchase of Nordair's three remaining Super Constellations, the first of which, CF-NAK, was flown from Montreal to São Tomé on 2 May 1969. CF-NAM followed on 2 June, while the last of the four, CF-NAL, landed at São Tomé on 30 July 1969.

187 Above: Apart from Transavia, Martinair was the only other company willing to allow large jets to use the relatively short runway at São Tomé. DC-8 Freighter PH-MAS was a regular visitor to the island operating variously from Amsterdam or Frankfurt on behalf of the religious groups that later formed JCA. Relief material, passengers, replacement aircrew and general support equipment was brought down. Larger and bulkier loads were often brought in aboard Trans Meridian Air Cargo CL-44s, one of which, G-AXAA, is seen taxying to the main apron in this view, taken on 22 December 1969 (Jakob Ringler)

188 Centre left: The reason for the TMAC CL-44 staging into São Tomé was to bring in direct from Tucson, Arizona, a newly-overhauled Pratt & Whitney R-4360 engine for the JCA. C-97G fleet. Quite why it requires five men to drive a fork-lift truck is not clear...(Jakob Ringler)

189 Left: ...but if many hands make light work of unloading a fully-laden DC-8F then seven men and one open lorry must be the order of the day. In fact it did take much of the day to unload a DC-8F. Support services and equipment on São Tomé island were typical of early colonial Africa. Despite bristling with radio aerials, the control tower and buildings in the background clearly belong to a different generation to the aircraft in view (Jakob Ringler)

190, 191: When the Fred Olsen Air Transport DC-6A LN-FOL arrived on São Tomé in November 1969 as a replacement for LN-FOM, it brought in a full load of Norwegian stockfish. The cargo was unloaded for short-term storage as all cargoes being flown in to Biafra were varied and depended on precise requirements from the feeding stations. the island is situated virtually on the equator and loading at the height of the day was not made any easier by the shortage of fork-lift trucks etc. All loading and unloading was carried out by hand although there was much local labour available on the island. LN-FOM was the last of the Church airlift aircraft to leave São Tomé (Jakob Ringler)

192: The Sterling Airways DC-6B OY-EAR operated the Biafra airlift from São Tomé on two separate periods; for a month in 1968 and for two months at the end of the war. For its second period it was fully painted in 'JOINT CHURCH AID' markings, ie a 'blue-top' camouflage and 'twin-fish' insignia. The Sterling aircraft were also unusual in operating with the last two letters on the nosewheel door (Unknown via P. J. Marson)

193 Left, 194 Below right: Routine servicing was carried out 'al fresco' style but as the island sits virtually on the equator, undertaking engine maintenance beneath the São Tomé sun was not too much of a chore. In any case the hinged engine covers of the L-1049H offered some protection. Note in the top view the Canairelief jeep and the engineless Flughjalp DC-6 TF-AAE in the background. The lower right picture offers a good view of the L-1049's engine access panels *(Jakob Ringler)*

195 Far left: The view from the flight-deck of a C-97G was quite extraordinary. In this view of N52876, which was unusual in having the 'last-three' repeated on the nose, the positioning of the Jointchurchaid twin-fish insignia is seen to best advantage *(Jakob Ringler)*

196 Left: The nose of an International Red Cross C-97G is just visible on the main ramp area at São Tomé. It has just landed from Cotonou with sundry spares and relief aid from the Red Cross store there. A typically-marked Joint Church Aid C-97G, N52915, sits in the background and dwarfs an AERANGOL DH. 104 Dove, CR-LKE, which made visits to the island from time to time in lieu of the usual DC-3 service from Luanda *(Jakob Ringler)*

182

More accidents

Averaging payloads of 15 tonnes per flight the Canairelief Super Constellations played a vital role in the Joint Church Aid airlift. By the end of July 1969 the agency had successfully completed almost 250 flights into Uli with a total delivered cargo of 3,800 tonnes. But, sadly, Canairelief too suffered from tragic losses. The first occurred on the night of 3/4 August 1969 and involved the original aircraft, CF-NAJ.

The aircraft, with an exceptionally full CARITAS load of 5 tonnes of medicine and almost 12 tonnes of salt and rice, was being flown by one of the airlift's most experienced of pilots, Captain Donald Merriam, although he had only recently transferred across from the Flughjalp DC-6B fleet. His co-pilot was another Canadian, Ray Levesque, while the Flight Engineer was 37-year old Vince Wakeling. 27-year-old Loadmaster Garry Libbus, from Montreal, completed the crew and who was standing-in for a sick colleague in spite of his wife and children having just flown from Canada to Amsterdam to meet him there.

CF-NAJ took-off from São Tomé at almost exactly 22:00 and joined the Uli Holding Pattern in the normal manner, letting down for landing at about 23:40 hours. As was the standard practice, Merriam called, at 23:45, for Uli's landing lights to be turned on. A minute later the message was repeated but on that occasion, according to other pilots sharing the same frequency, Merriam spoke in a more urgent manner and simply demanded, "Lights on, Uli". It is unclear whether or not the runway lights were in fact ever turned on. The controller was known to have been particularly nervous on that night due to the presence of the Nigerian 'Intruder' bomber overhead. Whether or not he did was rather immaterial.

It later transpired that when Merriam had transmitted his final and urgent request the aircraft was some 15 miles to the north of Uli, near to the village of Uga. The aircraft was making a slow and very wide turn to the left, suggesting that the initial landing approach had been abandoned. At the time of impact Merriam had completed three-quarters of a full (360°) turn for a second approach to Uli's Runway 16, ie from the north. Between the aircraft and the strip was a hilly area and CF-NAJ was very close to a ridge. Then, at 23:50, the Super Connie hit trees on the crest of the ridge. The aircraft then skidded down the northern slope and exploded.

By the time that Biafran rescuers reached the scene of the crash the aircraft had completly burnt out, the crew having died instantly. At noon on the following day a Catholic missionary priest held a service locally and later in the day the remains of all four men were buried in the small Anglican churchyard close to Uli airstrip.

Within two months of the loss of CF-NAJ a crash involving a Joint Church Aid C-97G during the night of 26/27 September 1969 robbed the airlift of another of its most experienced pilots.

Captain Alex Nicoll had joined Transavia at the beginning of the year but after completing one tour he resigned and returned to the U.K. When a group of American C-97G pilots had found the airlift too dangerous and left to return to the USA Joint Church Aid was left desperately short of suitable crews. Alex Nicoll was called and tempted to return to São Tomé. He did so on 1 March 1969 and immediately began flying in on the C-97Gs. Eventually he became the C-97G Chief Pilot–in spite of the fact that until March 1969 he had never previously flown one.

On the night of the accident Nicoll had been rostered to oversee a flight by a newly-recruited US Air National Guard pilot, John Wilson. On their first flight of the night the aircraft, N52676, made what was later described as a normal approach to Uli but, it seems, because the Nigerian 'Intruder' bomber was in the area the Uli controller turned off the runway lights. The C-97G abandoned its approach and made a full circuit before making another attempt to land, but as it made its second line-up for Uli it had apparently lost altitude in the long 360° turn and began its second approach at too low an altitude. After hitting the tops of several tall trees, N52676 immediately plunged into the ground and exploded. That was the reasoning offered by Flight Test Research, operators of the C-97G. Other reports simply attributed the cause to "a combination of unfortunate circumstances"[333] and clearly did not rule out human error. An on-site investigation did later establish a theory. It seems that N52676 suffered an engine malfunction on its first approach to land which was the reason for carrying out a full circuit and try again. This, it is believed, allowed time to close-down and feather the dead engine. Unfortunately, some reports allege, the crew feathered the wrong engine. With a full load, and a loss of power from two engines and on a final approach in total darkness, a crash was virtually inevitable. All five crew died instantly.[334]

The Nigerian Air Force 'Intruder' was known to be in the Uli area at the time of the C-97G crash and indeed there was some suspicion that the Nigerian aircraft had interfered with the C-97G's approach. This was subsequently disproved. On the night in question the 'Intruder' DC-3 was being flown by an Englishman who, immediately after seeing the crash, had a brief conversation with relief pilots on the Uli frequency. Icelander Tony Jonsson who, at the time, was attempting to land a DC-6B immediately behind the C-97G interrupted the 'Intruder'. For once taunting threats were not being broadcast and instead a conversation that underlined a peculiar degree of mutual respect emerged. That conversation was later recounted by Father Joe Prendergast who, at the time of the accident, had been at Uli and also listening in on the approach frequency:[335]

Intruder: "There's a huge fire just south of the airstrip. I'm afraid one of your planes has crashed."
Uli Tower: "Who is this speaking?"
Jonsson (*interrupting*).... "I see the fire also. It is probably the C-97. Did you shoot it down?"
Intruder: "No, I haven't dropped anything yet."
Jonsson: "Will you bugger off for a while and give us a chance to see what has happened?"
Intruder: "Very well. I'll do nothing for 30 minutes... and believe me, I'm very, very sorry."

Notes

Note 297 The phrase was originally coined by some of the American pilots

Note 298 *West Africa* magazine, 3 August 1968 issue.

Note 299 As related by John Trent, Flight Engineer aboard L-1049G '5N-07G'

Note 300 Africa Concern document, 'Recent Developments'

Note 301 As related to the author by Rev William Aitken

Note 302 Canairelief Operations by Brian Harris (unpublished manuscript)

Note 303 As recounted by Rev William Aitken

Note 304 'One Remarkable Six' by Robert M Stitt, *Air Enthusiast* Issue 67

Note 305 The team of British mechanics consisted of Radio Engineers Phil Townsend and Ron Blake, as well as Electricians Fred Greap, Frank Strainge and Eddie Edgar. All were based at Cotonou for three months.

Note 306 *Der Spiegel* magaine

Note 307 *Ibid.*, August R Lindt

Note 308 As related to the author by British mechanic Phil Townsend

Note 309 As related by Phil Townsend

Note 310 *Ibid.*, August R Lindt

Note 311 *Aviation Letter*

Note 312 *Jetstream*, August 1969 issue

Note 313 It was reported by other airlift crews that the American crews who arrived with the C-97Gs were fundamentally "weekend military fliers - high on self-esteem, but low in confidence." There were occasions when C-97Gs would return to São Tomé without landing due to being unable to make contact with Uli's weak ND Beacon. There were even reports that some Americans left after discovering that were working for black masters!" To be fair, some American ANG crews did last the course and played a tremendous role in the airlift.

Note 314 Many of these schemes were slightly different; some of the dimensions of the fish were also very slightly different.

Note 315 One of the pilots who regularly achieved 180+ hours was Eddie Roocroft who joined the Nordchurchaid airlift on 17 December 1968 and remained at São Tomé until 19 June 1969.

Note 316 It is unfair to describe the Church airlift in such unflattering terms but visually the apron at São Tomé sometimes did represent a "secondary apron full of tramp freighters at any South American airfield".

Note 317 Extracts from the official crash enquiry into Balair DC-6AC HB-IBT.

Note 318 As described by John Trent who was on the strip that night and spoke with the crew immediately afterwards.

Note 319 As described to the author by Verdun Polley and quoted in his as yet unpublished autobiography

Note 320 As described to the author by Ares Klootwyk

Note 321 As described to the author by Jakob Ringler

Note 322 *Ibid.*, General Olusegun Obasanjo

Note 323 *Ibid.*, Frederick Forsyth

Note 324 *Ibid.*, General Olusegun Obasanjo

Note 325 *Ibid.*, Frederick Forsyth

Note 326 As recounted to the author by Alan Beardmore.

Note 327 As related by MiG-17F pilot Paul Martin.

Note 328 *Ibid.*, August R Lindt

Note 329 The architect of this plan was Eddie Roocroft and who later related details to the author

Note 330 *Ibid.*, Fr Tony Byrne

Note 331 *Ibid.*, August R Lindt

Note 332 Details quoted from *Africa Concern–Recent Developments*, dated 4 July 1969.

Note 333 Church World Service press release

Note 334 As related to the author by Phil Phillip

Note 335 Quoted from personal correspondence between Fr Joe Prendergast and Mrs Emily Nicoll, reproduced by kind permission.

197: Late in the evening of 26 September 1969, the Joint Church Aid C-97G N52676 crashed just short of Uli strip. Five crew were killed including Joint Church Aid's Chief Pilot, Alex Nicoll. Reverend Billy Butler was in Biafra at the time and raced to the scene just after dawn on 27 September. By then only the fin and starboard outer wing section were recognisable (Rev Billy Butler)

BIAFRA
Old Faces; Old Aircraft; New Faces; New Aircraft

Many of Biafra's emissaries had spent the initial months of independence urging western powers and other African states to recognise the breakaway regime. Independence was over a year old before the world at large took note of the desperate struggle within Biafra.

Four African states did offically recognise Biafra. The first, Tanzania, did so on 13 April 1968 when President Nyerere explained that the unity of a country "can only be based on the general consent of the people involved" and that he was "convinced that unity cannot be maintained by force". Nyerere's declaration was certainly not with the consent of the British Government, nor was recognition of Biafra by Zambia, on 20 May 1968.[336]

Of greater concern to Britain, but more significant for Biafra, was the recognition by two French colonies, by the Ivory Coast on 4 May and by Gabon four days later, on 8 May 1968. Unlike the two British colonies, the decision by Ivory Coast and Gabon had the very hallmarks of having official support from Paris. Indeed, several months later

198 Above: Jack Malloch's L-1049G VP-WAW operated the arms airlift into Biafra almost throughout the entire Nigerian Civil War. For much of that period it retained the scheme of its former owner, the Brazilian national airline, VARIG. When Malloch was held in a Togo jail the L-1049G was at Woensdrecht, Holland undergoing an overhaul by the Dutch company, AVIOLANDA. It is seen stored outside their hangar in September 1968 just prior to being ferried south to Gabon. It then joined the arms airlift out of Libreville and Abidjan (John Wegg Collection)

on 31 July 1968, President de Gaulle ventured as close to official recognition by France as one could possibly get. The motivation for de Gaulle's action was possibly twofold; to underline continued French support in the expectation of favourable oil concessions resulting from a Biafran military victory, or more simply a verbal attack against Britain at a time when Anglo-French relations were at an extremely low ebb.

It was, of course, a huge disappointment for Ojukwu that France–and for that matter, Portugal also–never formally recognised Biafra as an independent state. The Portuguese strategy in assisting Biafra through its African colonies was both vital and visible. Key staging-posts at Sal, Bissau, Luanda and São Tomé allowed unrestricted movements of arms to Biafra. Biafran government aircraft also operated without interference by officials encouraged to turn a distinctly blind eye. Even the military side of Lisbon's international airport had openly become virtually a Biafran base. (Later, operations were transferred to Faro, on Portugal's southern coast.)

French support, on the other hand, was much less visible yet was probably greater. Staging-posts at Abidjan and Libreville, and to a lesser degree at Dakar, were as equally vital to Biafra as were the Portuguese colonial staging-posts. Furthermore the governments of Ivory Coast and Gabon later supplied huge stocks of arms and ammunition, all of which were immediately replenished by France. It was a very thin disguise by the originator.

The rise and fall of Henry Warton

Until January 1968 Biafra had two gun-running operations supporting its fight against the Federal Nigeria Army. They were run respectively by Hank Warton and Jack Malloch. Then, on 20 January 1968, Malloch, and others, was arrested at Lomé and spent the next five months in a Togo prison. Warton took over the entire gun-running operation and even took on the reponsibility for operating the Biafran government's 'Grey Ghost' L-1049G Super Constellation '5N-07G'. In effect Warton acquired a monopoly of Biafra's military option and that was undoubtedly the determinant factor that ultimately led to his downfall.

Biafra's military position changed dramatically during 1968. There were serious military losses as well as some dramatic victories but the gains were short-lived and the losses irreversible. In almost every case the cause of the loss was a dire shortage in Biafran firepower. Port Harcourt had undoubtedly been Biafra's greatest loss in May 1968. It allowed the Federal Nigerian Army to strengthen its southern line ahead of a major assault northwards against the Biafran towns of Owerri, Aba and Umuahia. By August 1968 the Biafran Army was defending against a well-equipped Federal Army on three fronts. Unfortunately Warton was unable to provide sufficient flights to meet Biafra's demand for arms and ammunition.

Throughout 1968 Hank Warton's monopoly had meant that only he could extend space to the relief organisations. To meet increased demands he had acquired two additional L-1049G Super Constellations ('5T-TAH', '5T-TAK') and a single L-1049D variant ('5T-TAC'). But Warton lost four of his aircraft during the year: in crashes at Port Harcourt and another near Uli, an act of sabotage at Bissau and one seized by authorities at Malta. As at August 1968 he had just two remaining L-1049Gs, one of which ('5T-TAH') was stranded at Uli for a week in a "grossly unserviceable" state (until flown out to São Tomé during the night of 16/17 August). The final aircraft ('5T-TAK') was similarly in need of attention but still on the flight roster. It had become unrealistic to expect Warton to be in a position to meet Biafra's dire needs with one aircraft. And the battle for Aba was about to start.

Hank Warton bows out–ungracefully

During September 1968 Hank Warton was finally sacked as Biafra's principal provider of arms flights. He was ordered to remove the two remaining L-1049Gs from São Tomé island as they were taking up valuable apron space. The first to depart was '5T-TAK' which was flown out empty, and on three engines, on 20 September 1968. Three days later it arrived at Lisbon and where, because of its overall state and condition, it was simply abandoned.

Sister aircraft '5T-TAH' was in a worse state and failed to make it back to Lisbon. In fact it too flew out of São Tomé on three engines–the Number 2 prop was feathered –on 28 September 1968. The crew headed firstly for Abidjan where the aircraft landed safely. However they refused to fly any further and abandoned the Super Connie there and then.

Hank Warton was said to have suffered a bad heart attack; it was not life-threatening but he had been forced to move to Switzerland for recuperation. That was the official line for ending Hank's monopoly of arms supplies. But he did not completely sever his link with the Biafran airlift; he still had his contract with the German Churches and continued to operate the four surviving DC-7Cs on the relief airlift to Uli. Warton had also acquired an additional DC-7C from the Biafran government in lieu of money owed to him which he claimed, at one stage, to have been almost $450,000. The new aircraft was the DC-7CF G-ATOB, the infamously unserviceable aircraft which had stood at Madrid for several months.[337]

When Warton travelled to Madrid to inspect the aircraft he did so accompanied by his 'front-man' Bertram Petersen and his lawyer. He knew that he would find the aircraft in an unserviceable state but other things he had not expected. Shortly after his arrival in Madrid, Warton was confronted by Lucien Pickett's 'leg-man', the little Argentinian, Azi Riba. Riba claimed that the Biafrans had had no right to give the aircraft away as "it was not theirs to give". It was jointly owned, Riba told Warton, by Lucien Pickett and Otto Skorzeny, the former SS Officer. Warton, together with his lawyer, took his case to a Madrid court who later accepted Hank's claim as being rightful and duly released the DC-7CF to him. In the meantime his Canadian associate, Bertram Petersen, made use of his good connections with the Bermuda Department of Civil Aviation and arranged for the aircraft to be re-registered in Bermuda as VR-BCT, on 25 July 1968, to a new company, ARCO (Bermuda) Ltd. It received some servicing and some fairly rudimentary paintwork before joining the other DC-7Cs on the relief airlift to Biafra.[338]

The fall and rise of Jack Malloch

Hank Warton's main rival, the Rhodesian gun-runner Jack Malloch, had been released from jail in Togo on 5 June 1968. He had been put on a plane to Europe from where he made his way back to Rhodesia to assess the damage sustained by his company as a result of his five-month absence.

A number of Jack Malloch's crews had transferred across to Hank Warton's operation. Others had joined legitimate companies operating in southern Africa. Malloch's two aircraft, the DC-4 VP-YTY and the L-1049G VP-WAW, were both at Woensdrecht, Holland where AVIOLANDA had impounded them in lieu of money owed for overhaul and other maintenance work carried out. But Malloch still had influential friends in high places. There can be few doubts that some of those friends were close to the upper reaches of the Quay d'Orsai in Paris.

When de Gaulle made his astonishing announcement of Biafran support on 31 July 1968 it had clearly not been an overnight decision. There had been some ominous signs of preparation for some time, since in fact the recognition of Biafra by Gabon and the Ivory Coast. According to the German mercenary Rolf Steiner, who had enlisted

with the Biafran Army and had a habit of waiting at Uli to meet the inbound ammunition flights, the first arms cargo from Libreville was flown in to Uli during the night of 13/14 July 1968.[339]

Reports passed on from the German Ambassador in Libreville, at the beginning of August 1968, indicated that arms for Biafra were being flown in each night by a "French DC-3". The same report (which did not identify the aircraft) claimed that it was housed by the Gabonese Air Force and loaded inside one of the Air Force's hangars. It also mentioned that a DC-4 was expected to join the operation "shortly". Again, no identity was given. The very fact that German diplomatic staff in Libreville seemed aware that a DC-4 was about to arrive may well have been associated with the recent–yet mysterious–sale of a German-registered DC-4. The aircraft, D-ADAR (c/n 18378) and part of the Transportflug fleet, had been sold to a Frenchman, named as Gilbert Bourgeard, on 6 August 1968.[340] (The DC-4 has never been reported since its sale and certainly does not appear to have re-registered. Photographs taken at Salisbury at the end of the Nigerian Civil War show a DC-4 being scrapped alongside Jack Malloch's L-1049G CS-TLF. The DC-4 had apparently been given to Malloch by the French Government but was found to be seriously corroded and scrapped shortly afterwards. Details of any usage in Biafra remain unclear.)

Managing the increase in French material aid for Biafra was almost personally the responsibility of Jacques Foccart, de Gaulle's *Secrétaire-Général aux Affaires Africaines et Malgaches auprès de la Présidence*. Foccart's link man with Biafra was reported to be Jean Mauricheau-Beaupré, a former Resistance member and an experienced conspirator. 'Monsieur Jean', as he was sometimes referred to, was an adviser in the President's Office in Abidjan. He also controlled the purse strings and appears to have been the driving force behind reinstating Jack Malloch onto the Biafra arms run.[341]

Jack Malloch's outstanding and overdue account with the Dutch company, AVIOLANDA, was settled in full and the impoundment on his two aircraft lifted. The first to leave Woensdrecht was the DC-4 VP-YTY, now fully overhauled and repainted in a revised two-tone blue scheme—not dissimilar to that carried by the DC-7C VP-WBO when it was impounded in Togo. Clive Halse, one of Jack Malloch's most loyal of pilots, travelled to Woensdrecht in September 1968 to ferry the DC-4 south to Libreville. By now under South African registry, as ZS-FLO, the DC-4 was flown by Halse (with co-pilot Craxford and Flight Engineer Bill Townsend) to Las Palmas on 16 September and on to Abidjan the following day. At Abidjan, on 18 September, the registration was changed to newly-allocated Gabonese marks TR-LNV and as such the DC-4 was positioned to Libreville for Biafra flights. Its first arms shuttle into Uli was made by the same crew during the night of 20/21 September.[342]

199 Above: *In a key speech on 31 July 1968, President de Gaulle announced official French support for the Biafran cause but stopped just short of declaring formal recognition. Reaction in London caused, as it was probably designed to do, immediate concern within the corridors of Whitehall. The rate of telex exchanges between British Embassies in Africa and the Foreign & Commonwealth Office increased dramatically as London tried to determine the impact of de Gaulle's actions in French-speaking Africa as well as trying to establish the likely level of any French military aid to Biafra. Then, amongst this frenzy of cypher activity, came Telex 169. Sent to Yaoundé, Cameroons, it passed on intelligence details gleaned from the German Ambassador in Libreville who, in turn, had gathered details from the French Ambassador.*
The 'additional DC-4' remains something of a mystery but could relate to any of a series of Air Fret DC-4s that operated the Biafra run from September 1968. Alternatively, it could well have referred to a former Transportflug aircraft, D-ADAR (c/n 18378), which was sold to a Gilbert Bourgeard on 6 August 1968 and which simply disappeared immediately afterwards. The extent to which this aircraft was used in Biafra, if at all, is unknown but its fate at the end of the war is certainly a little clearer when it was given to Jack Malloch as a replacement for his ill-fated TR-LNV (Reproduced by kind permission of the Public Record Office)

Jack Malloch personally brought the L-1049G Super Constellation out of Woensdrecht, although Clive Halse was with him in the right-hand seat. Like the DC-4 a week beforehand the Rhodesian marks were changed to South African for the ferry flight. As ZS-FAA, the L-1049G departed Woensdrecht on 24 September 1968 and was flown to Las Palmas for an overnight stay.[343] On the following day it staged on to Abidjan where the aircraft also took on a newly-allocated Gabonese identity. Then, and as TR-LNY, Malloch, Halse and Hodges positioned the Super Connie to Libreville but it was not until the night of 2/3 October that it was first flown into Uli. For a week the L-1049G operated almost nightly on an Abidjan-Uli-São Tomé-Abidjan arms run, the visits to São Tomé necessary for refuelling with high-octane fuel. Jack Malloch was back in business.

Malloch: more aircraft

At the end of 1968 Malloch's operation out of Libreville was stretched. The DC-4 (TR-LNV) and the L-1049G (TR-LNY) were both being worked almost every night and left little opportunity to maintain Biafran requirements when routine servicing was due. Once again, assistance from the French was sought. It came with the transfer of a second DC-4.

The DC-4 was due to be ferried to Malloch by a French crew but the Rhodesian asked one of his Flight Engineers, Cliff Hawthorne, to fly to Paris and meet with the French mercenary Bob Denard. Denard, banned from re-entry to Africa since the Congo fiasco, was now working for the French Government and had arranged for an additional aircraft and crew to be made available to Malloch's gun-running operation. Hawthorne's job was simply to ensure that the transaction went smoothly.

The aircraft involved was F-BBDD, one of the former Air France fleet of DC-4s which had been operating on the French Domestic Postal System (Centre d'Exploitation Postale Metropolitan) since June 1967. The postal fleet was being replaced with new F-27 Friendships and the DC-4s had been declared redundant. Bob Denard had also arranged for a two-man crew, including a South African captain named Koller who, it was said, had been the pilot of a DC-3 hijacked in the Congo by a group of escaping mercenaries led by Bob Denard.[344]

Cliff Hawthorne joined the crew at Paris/Le Bourget but the delivery flight was not as smooth as had been expected. Departure from Le Bourget took place on 17 January 1969 but after just ninety minutes flight engine trouble forced a diversion into Poitiers. It took almost a week to deliver and install a replacement engine and it was not until 22 January that F-BBDD resumed its ferry flight with a Poitiers-Las Palmas sector. Then, via a refuelling stop at Abidjan, F-BBDD arrived at Libreville on 24 January and shortly afterwards began operating into Biafra. Koller, in fact, remained at Libreville for a brief period and undertook at least one flight into Uli with Malloch's DC-4, TR-LNV, on the night of 27/28 January.

Apart from periods of necessary routine maintenance, and a six-monthly C of A renewal on 29 May 1969, F-BBDD remained on the Libreville arms airlift throughout much of 1969. At the end of November 1969 it was officially issued with a *Certificat de Na igabilité* (temporary C of A) that was restricted to just one flight. This enabled it to be ferried to Toulouse (probably on 2 December 1969) for a major overhaul.[345]

Malloch: enter the DC-7Cs

The first of several redundant DC-7C aircraft was acquired by Malloch, in February 1969. It was one of the original K.L.M. aircraft, PH-DSC, but which had latterly operated with Martin's Air Charter. M.A.C. sold it to the London-based Autair Ltd on 6 February 1969 who immediately re-sold to a French aircraft broker based at Le Havre, Pollet & Fils. In fact, the sale was handled by the new Managing Director of Aer Turas, John Squire (the same John Squire who almost a year previously had ferried the fuselages of two former Austrian Air Force Fouga Magisters from Lisbon to São Tomé). The M.A.C. DC-7C was then ferried to Lisbon and on to Salisbury. Shortly afterwards it was re-registered in Gabon as TR-LOK, although whether it actually carried those marks externally all the time is doubtful. (An "unidentified" DC-7C made frequent visits to São Tomé during mid-1969 for refuelling purposes. It was known by relief crews on the island as being part of the gun-running fleet at Libreville but it was not totally unidentifiable. The name 'Yellow Sea' was still visible on the nose–the original K.L.M. name given to PH-DSC.)

By the Spring of 1969 Malloch's active fleet at Libreville consisted of the two DC-4s and a single DC-7C. The arrival of the DC-7C enabled Malloch to despatch the L-1049G TR-LNY back to Salisbury on 17 February 1969 for servicing. It returned to Libreville on 3 March and (under the command of Clive Halse) worked throughout much of the month before returning to Salisbury on 20 March for further routine servicing. Then, on 30 March 1969, it was back on the roster (this time with a Captain Alexander) for what was to become its final Biafran tour. The tour started with a positioning flight to Waterkloof to collect a 10-tonne cargo of arms before heading north to Luanda and Libreville. From Libreville, the next night, TR-LNY staged into Uli, unloaded and returned to Libreville via a refuelling stop at São Tomé. The same pattern followed for the next week although some nights landing in Biafra was abandoned due to either bad weather or enemy aircraft activity over Uli. On 9 April, TR-LNY had taken off from Libreville for another routine arms supply flight when it suffered a hydraulic failure and a failure of No.4 engine. Under Alexander's control, the aircraft

200: During the course of the Nigeria-Biafran war a number of aircraft just seemed to 'disappear'. One was DC-4 D-ADAR which, on 6 August 1968, was sold by Transportflug to Frenchman, Gilbert Bourgeard. At the end of the Biafran war it was broken up at Salisbury, Rhodesia alongside Jack Malloch's L-1049G CS-TLF. Could this have been the "anticipated French Government DC-4" mentioned in confidential British Embassy telex signals (Henry Kinnear)

limped into São Tomé and then back to Libreville and then three days later made a three-engine ferry flight south to Luanda. After a night stopover 'LNY took-off on three engines but just fifteen minutes after climbing out the Number 3 engine failed and the aircraft returned to land at Luanda on just two engines.[346]

The Super Connie remained grounded at Luanda for almost seven months throughout 1969. Its life as a gun-running aircraft into Biafra had ended although it was eventually repaired and was finally flown out on 6 November 1969 by Clive Halse and Colin Miller. The aircraft was ferried from Luanda to Salisbury where it underwent a complete overhaul and eventual restoration to VP-WAW

The final month of TR-LNY's operation on the arms airlift can be summarised as follows.

Flight-Log: L-1049G TR-LNY March-November 1969

Date (or Night of)	Route	Hours Day	Hours Night
30/31.3.69	Waterkloof-Luanda		5.55
31.3.69	Luanda-Libreville	2.55	
	Libreville-Uli		2.20
	Uli-São Tomé		1.45
1.4.69	São Tomé-Libreville		1.00
1/2.4.69	Libreville-Uli		2.10
	Uli-São Tomé		1.40
	São Tomé-Libreville		0.55
2/3.4.69	Libreville-Uli		2.20
	Uli-São Tomé		1.55
	São Tomé-Libreville		0.55
3/4.4.69	Libreville-São Tomé		3.40
Abandoned landing at Uli due to bad weather over strip			
	São Tomé-Libreville		4.50
	Libreville-São Tomé		0.50
	São Tomé-Libreville		4.40
4.4.69	Libreville-São Tomé	0.40	
4/5.4.69	São Tomé-Uli-Libreville		4.45
5.4.69	Libreville-São Tomé	0.45	
5/6.4.69	São Tomé-Uli-Libreville		4.30
6/7.4.69	Libreville-São Tomé-Libreville		4.40

Abandoned landing at Uli due to strafing of runway

7.4.69	Libreville-São Tomé	1.40	
7/8.4.69	São Tomé-Uli-Libreville		2.40
9/10.4.69	Libreville-São Tomé-Libreville		1.45
12.4.69	Libreville-Luanda	3.15	
13.4.69	Luanda-Luanda	0.20	

The enforced grounding of L-1049G TR-LNY posed a problem for Malloch. Biafra's need for military aid had not lessened and Malloch urgently needed replacement aircraft.

The Irish company, Aer Turas, had bought four freight-configured DC-7CFs from K.L.M. during February 1969. The first pair were retained for the company's use (as EI-ATT & EI-ATU) but the other two were available for resale and a deal was agreed between John Squire and "Bluey" Gardiner (both of Aer Turas) and Jack Malloch The two aircraft involved in the sale were EI-ATW (ex PH-DSG) and EI-ATV (ex PH-DSI). Again, the deal was brokered by Pollet & Fils after which both aircraft were ferried to Paris/Le Bourget, on 26 April and 27 May 1969 respectively. Both were subsequently flown on to Lisbon before being ferried south to Salisbury. Part of the original purchase deal between K.L.M. and Aer Turas was that the Dutch airline would repaint the four aircraft into Aer Turas' scheme. They therefore arrived in the new green and yellow Aer Turas scheme–hardly the appropriate pattern for a nightly arms airlift into Biafran bush airstrips. The white roof area on both aircraft was overpainted in what was becoming a standard 'Biafra blue-top' scheme. This was carried out at Salisbury before entering service. They were also re-registered as TR-LNZ (ex EI-ATV) and TR-LOJ (ex EI-ATW) to Jack Malloch's company, *Cie. Gabonaise d'Affrétements Aériens*, more widely known by the shorter title of Affretair.

By 7 May 1969 the first of the two new DC-7CFs (TR-LOJ) was ready to join the Biafran arms airlift out of Libreville and was ferried from Salisbury by Jack Malloch on 8 May. Then, during the late afternoon of 10 May,

'Uncle' Jack positioned 'LOJ from Libreville to São Tomé before flying into Biafra that night.

In fact Malloch took TR-LOJ not into Uli but into the dedicated arms strip at Uga. It was not the gun-runners' favoured strip, due to the loose soil and undulating landing surface, but pressure from the Churches had successfully persuaded arms flights to be routed into Uga instead of Uli whenever possible. After departing from Uga, the DC-7CF returned to São Tomé to refuel and then back to Libreville just before daybreak.

Like Hank Warton (his American former counterpart) the Rhodesian gun-runner Jack Malloch virtually managed the company single-handedly. But unlike Warton, Malloch did much of the flying himself; he preferred to fly many of the arms flights into Uli personally. For the remainder of May 1969 Jack Malloch made a further five flights into Biafra aboard DC-7CF TR-LOJ before flying north to collect a second DC-7CF. Details of Malloch's flights for that period are as follows (all flights are aboard DC-7CF TR-LOJ):

Flight-Log of Jack Malloch aboard DC-7CF TR-LOJ for the period 10-20 May 1969 inclusive

Date (or Night of)	Route	Hours Day	Hours Night
10.5.69	Libreville-São Tomé	1.00	
10/11.5.69	São Tomé-Uga-São Tomé-Libreville		4.35
11/12.5.69	Libreville-Uli-São Tomé-Libreville		4.30
12/13.5.69	Libreville-Uli-São Tomé-Libreville		4.50
13/14.5.69	Libreville-Uli-Abidjan		4.50
14.5.69	Abidjan-Lisbon	8.45	
16.5.69	Lisbon-Abidjan	6.10	3.40
17/18.5.69	Abidjan-Uli-São Tomé-Libreville	1.40	4.30
19/20.5.69	Libreville-Uli-Abidjan		5.00
20.5.69	Abidjan-Lisbon	8.35	

201, 202: Jack Malloch acquired two DC-7CFs from Aer Turas during 1969 for use on the nightly arms run from Libreville to Biafra. The second of the pair to be delivered was TR-LNZ which was ferried south, via Paris, on 27 May 1969. The DC-7CFs were heavily worked on the Libreville arms run yet, given the circumstances, performed admirably. Routine servicing was carried out at Malloch's base at Salisbury but whenever these aircraft returned to Rhodesia the registration letters were immediately masked over to avoid them being identified. The subterfuge was not always successful, as evidenced in these views of TR-LNZ taken at Salisbury just after the collapse of Biafra (via Dave Becker)

During the late spring of 1969 Malloch's original DC-4, TR-LNV, (the former VP-YTY) sustained some minor damage at Libreville when a fork-lift truck struck the port aileron. The damage was minor but beyond the capability of local mechanics. The aircraft was due for a service anyway, so it was flown back to Salisbury. Instead of repairing the aileron, the entire wing (and engines) was replaced with that from another DC-4, VP-YTU, which Air Trans Africa was then scrapping at Salisbury. In fact, the wing was almost brand new, having been fitted when VP-YTU's original wing attachments were discovered to have badly corroded. TR-LNV emerged from its overhaul almost a new aeroplane but almost immediately afterwards it was lost in Biafra in a most unfortunate manner.

Events began to unfold early on 24 June 1969 when TR-LNV was ferried, by Affretair's Captain John Gibson, from Salisbury to Libreville. Two nights later, on 26 June, John Gibson (plus co-pilot Bill Wragg and Flight Engineer Dave Goldsmith) attempted to fly from Libreville to Uli with a full cargo of ammunition. As the aircraft crossed the Nigerian coastline, however, the crew became increasingly nervous of the bright moonlight and clear skies. A Swedish Red Cross DC-7B had been shot down only three weeks previously and John Gibson took the precautionary decision to turn back over Port Harcourt and return to Libreville. On the following night the same crew flew TR-LNV, still with the same cargo of arms, on a second attempt at getting into Uli. On this occasion Biafran Air Traffic Control began warning of dangerous thunderstorms across Biafra. The crew tried to skirt some of the bad weather but it was not the weather for landing on a bush strip in the dead of night and with a heavy and highly explosive cargo. Added to that the crew began to experience some flak, then realised they were lost, and turned south when it was feared that they were close to Lagos. For a second night, the DC-4 returned to Libreville without landing in Biafra.[347]

A third attempt to fly to Uli was made during the evening of 28 June 1969. For that night Jack Wight was in the captain's position; the other crew members were the same as the previous two nights: co-pilot Bill Wragg and Flight Engineer Dave Goldsmith. The plan for the night of 28/29 June was slightly different in that two DC-4 flights to Uli would be attempted–but not by the same aircraft. (To complete two shuttles with the same aircraft was out of the question as it took too long to reload with heavy cases of ammunition at Libreville and then unload it all at Uli before daybreak. The crew were therefore rostered to make one shuttle in TR-LNV and then immediately after returning to Libreville make a second shuttle aboard F-BBDD which had already been loaded.)

TR-LNV took-off from Libreville at 18:45. On this occasion there were no difficulties in crossing the strip of Nigerian-held territory and landing at Uli from the southern approach. The difficulty came when taking-off.

As was customary only the outer engines were shut down for the process of unloading which, on that night, was achieved in quick time. The crew was anxious to return to Libreville because the other DC-4, F-BBDD, was known to be waiting fully loaded with arms. As TR-LNV began the process of departing Uli, Flight Engineer Dave Goldsmith felt the aircraft being steered to the right onto the runway and assumed the pilots had either back-tracked while he was concentrating elsewhere or that they were going for a short take-off run. There was also confusion as to whether or not the Uli controller had in fact given clearance for take-off. Nevertheless, full power was requested and the throttles were set to maximum. The DC-4 was just reaching the stage of lifting the nose-wheel when the landing-lights picked out bushes and trees directly ahead. Instinctively, all power was cut and brakes were applied but the aircraft could not be stopped in time. The starboard main undercarriage struck an embankment laid across the runway and was immediately torn away. The aircraft then sank onto its belly and proceeded to slide along the strip.[348]

Even before the aircraft came to a halt the crew of three were out of their seats and running towards the rear of the empty fuselage. As the undercarriage had collapsed the jump was not very high and all three men managed to get out and run clear before fire broke out. So hasty had been the evacuation that the engines were still turning as the crew ran into the bush. None suffered any injuries.

It was only then that the full impact of the confusion became apparent. TR-LNV had turned onto the strip–but facing the wrong direction. There simply was no runway available.

Ironically Jack Malloch was also on Uli strip that night having flown in a second arms cargo aboard the DC-7CF TR-LOJ. It was not long before Malloch realised that an aircraft had crashed in an attempt to take-off. He had immediately sensed that it was his DC-4 which was involved and sent two of his own crew, Paul Rex and Henry Kinnear, down to the end of the strip to investigate. At the final parking bay the crew of a Flughjalp DC-6B expressed concern, having watched helplessly as the DC-4 ploughed off the end and into the trees. Then they discovered the crew to be safe and already arranging to hitch a flight out. Jack Malloch was relieved to learn that he did not have to break the news of three dead men to their wives but then his relief turned to anger. He had lost his treasured DC-4, the personal gift from the former Congo leader, Moise Tshombé.

As so often was the case in the Biafran War there was a final twist of irony that night. When Jack Malloch flew back to Libreville for breakfast and a rest, news was just beginning to break that Moise Tshombé (who had been held in Algiers since his aircraft was hijacked on 1 August 1967) had mysteriously died that night in an Algiers jail. Somebody went over and told Malloch the news. Malloch just shrugged and quietly remarked *"his aircraft just died with him…"*[349]

The Zambian Dakotas

When Zambia accorded Biafra diplomatic recognition on 20 May 1968, it was followed very shortly afterwards by the offer of two C-47/DC-3 aircraft, one reportedly given free and the other sold. Interestingly, given the fact that he openly announced support for Biafra, it seems that Zambia's President Kaunda took steps not to publicise the deal and was particularly anxious that the Federal Nigerian government did not learn of the transaction. The aircraft were provided by the Zambian Government and without doubt originated from Zambian Air Force stocks. They were allocated civilian registrations 9J-RIF and 9J-RIG and flown to Libreville, Gabon during August 1968.

One of the two DC-3s was noted by the British Ambassador to Cameroons when he passed through Libreville on 19 August. This is thought to have been 9J-RIF, as 9J-RIG was known to be still at Lusaka on 31 August 1968 and about to be delivered to Libreville. It is doubtful that, once handed over to the Biafrans, either aircraft ever returned to Zambia. This could be further supported by the fact that the Zambian Department of Civil Aviation cancelled the two registrations approximately ten days after their delivery to Biafra; 9J-RIF was cancelled on 29 August 1968, followed by 9J-RIG on 11 September.[350]

US sources later reported to the British Embassy in Lagos that the two aircraft were re-serialled after their arrival at Libreville: 9J-RIF became '439B' and 9J-RIG became '704B'. (The explanation for these serials is unknown but they do resemble a style adopted by the French Aéronavale for use on its C-47s whereupon, for example, C-47 43-49824 became simply '424'; 43-49468 became '468' and 44-77101 was serialled '701' etc.)[351]

It is understood that both of the Zambian aircraft were provided by Kaunda in the belief that they were to be used for ferrying relief aid into Biafra but evidence suggests that they were very quickly put to use in carrying military supplies. Both aircraft were crewed by Biafran Air Force personnel and both sustained damage in a number of incidents.

One of the Biafran pilots complained to one of Jack Malloch's Flight Engineers about the rough-running of the aircraft and had become quite scornful of the Zambian donation. When Cliff Hawthorne, the engineer in question, took a closer inspection of the engines he discovered that the propeller tips were badly scuffed and bent. It was the result, he believed, of either an over-rotated take-off or a very poor landing at Uli. Hawthorne also suggested to the Biafran Officer that somebody should check out the engine's reduction gear casing which was more likely to have cracked and which was probably the true cause of the vibration. So much for pre-flight checks![352]

One of the two former Zambian C-47s crashed at Uli on 16 March 1969. (It is likely that this crash involved 9J-RIG, if only on the basis that a C-47 abandoned at Libreville at the end of the war appeared to have carried the marks, 9J-RIF.)

The crash was remembered by other Biafrans as having occurred on the night of St Patrick's Day 1969. The C-47 had landed at Uli with a cargo of ammunition. It was unloaded and then took-off empty from Uli for the return flight to Libreville. Immediately after getting airborne the Biafran Air Force pilot, Captain Emane Ngwu, radioed Uli tower to explain that he was experiencing difficulties with the aircraft and that he was being forced to make an immediate emergency landing back at the strip. Ngwu also reported that he did not have sufficient time to complete a full circuit of Uli and instead decided to make a tight 180° turn so as to land from Uli's 16 end. The runway landing lights had been turned off, due more than anything else, to the fact that the Nigerian 'Intruder' bomber was circling overhead. Ngwu, it semed, had no alternative but to attempt a landing in the dark and was obviously unable to see the runway properly. Not surprisingly, the C-47 touched-down off centre; in fact the mainwheels touched to the right of the main landing strip. To those who, in the darkness, could just make out the approaching aircraft, it was seen to land extremely heavily, bounced badly, then veered to the right, but managed to remain airborne until the starboard wing hit trees along the side of the airstrip. It then cavorted uncontrollably into the bush. All aboard: Captain Emane Ngwu, co-pilot Ernest Ike and Supernumery David Inyang, were killed instantly. All were later buried with full military honours in the Uli graveyard.[353]

The German Dakotas

The purchase of three former West German Air Force C-47s was part of a plan which, like so many others, was just simply bizarre. On the other hand, had it worked then the idea would have been considered brilliant.

In a manner similar to a number of attempted purchases for the Biafran government the 'German C-47' episode began with a germ of an idea. It was part of a concept to deal with regular strafing attacks of Uli by Nigerian Air Force MiG-17Fs. Von Rosen had claimed that the best way to deal with the MiGs was to attack them at their bases; he also claimed that the aircraft best-suited for such an operation would be small and single-engined, such as the Provost, the T-6G Texan or the MFI-9B. Other groups favoured a concept based on the experience of USAF AC-47 "Gunships" in Vietnam. The one difference being that instead of shooting downwards at the ground the Biafran gunships were designed to fire upwards.

1.

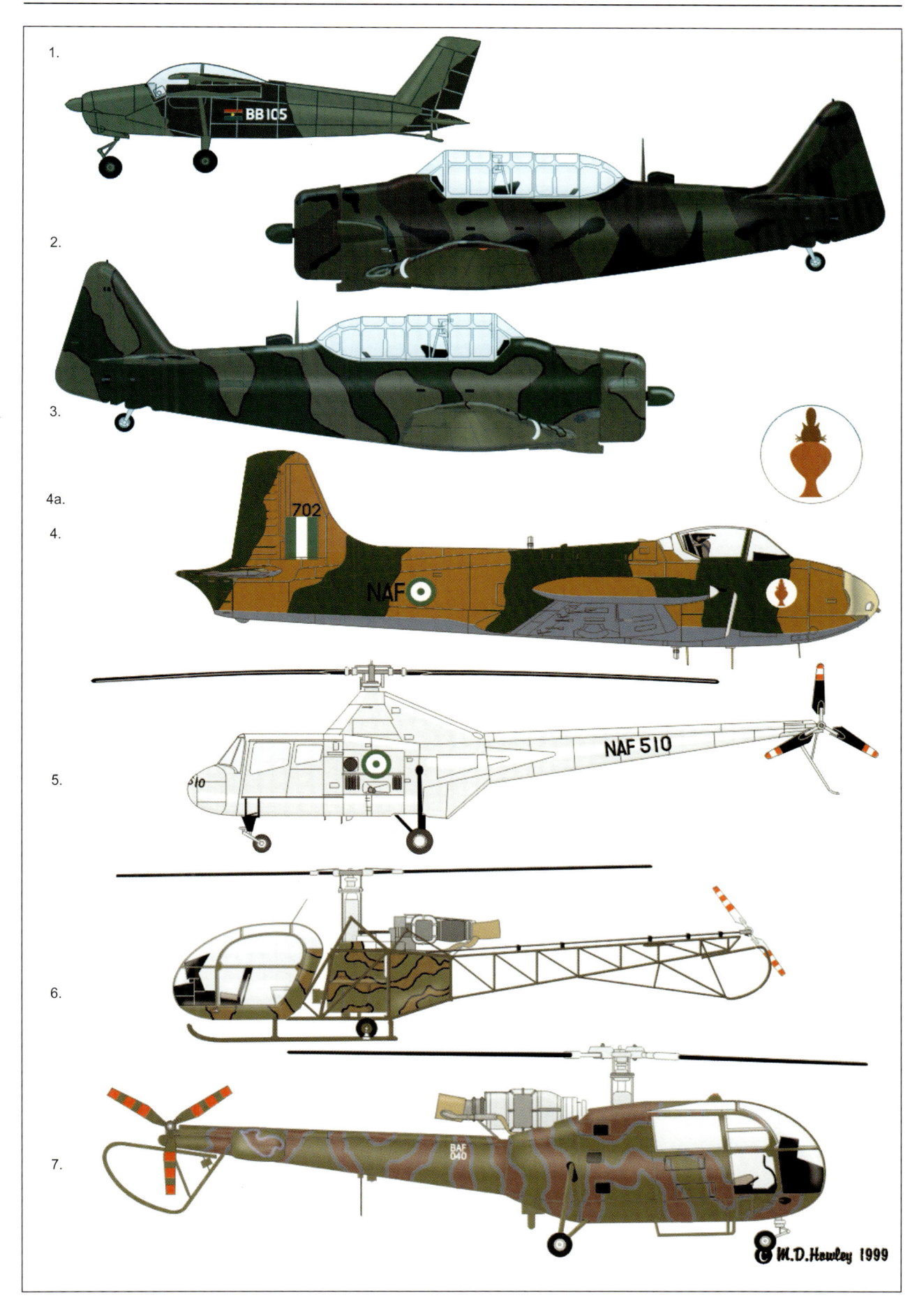

2.

3.

4a.
4.

5.

6.

7.

193

194

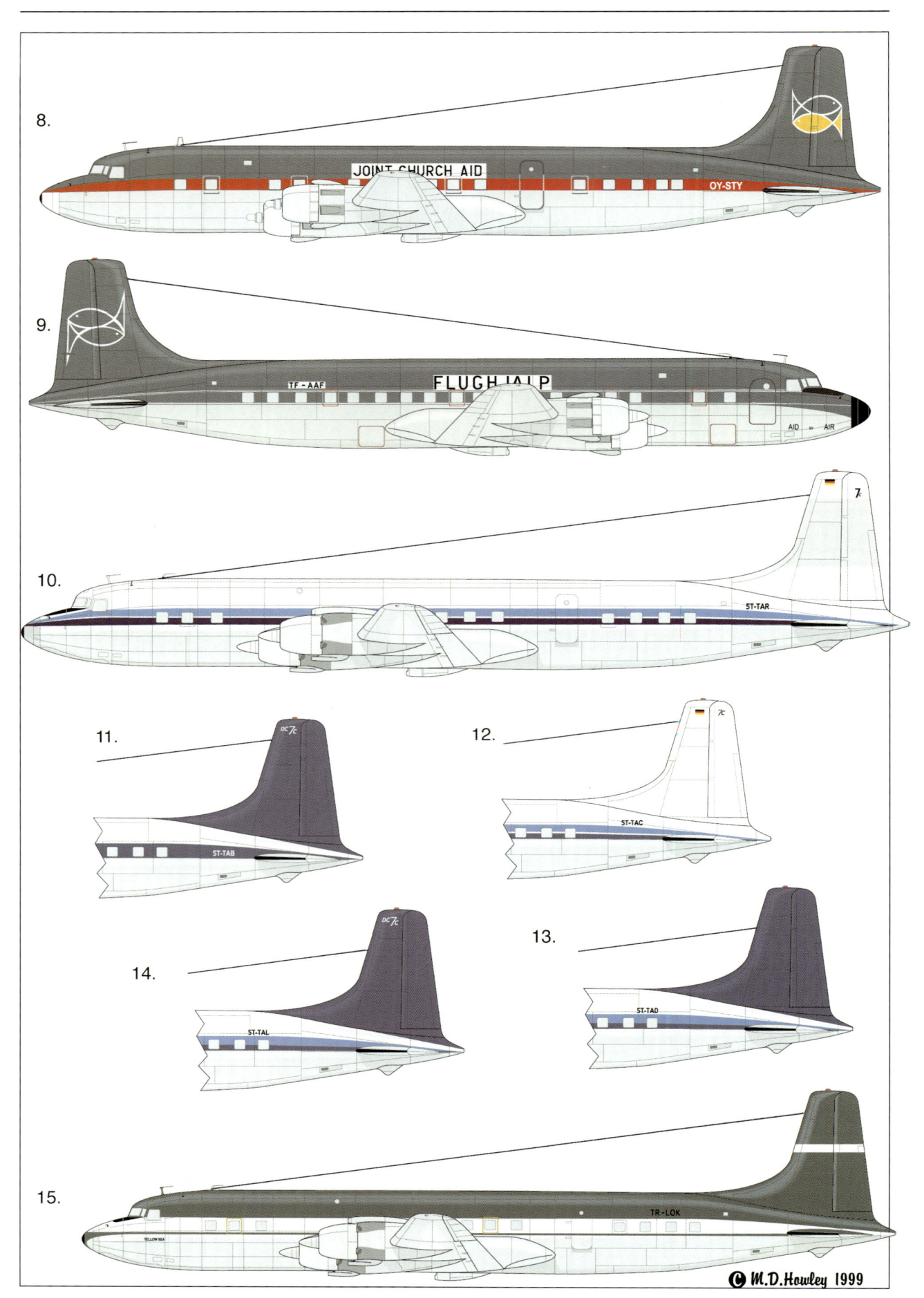

16. HB-IBU

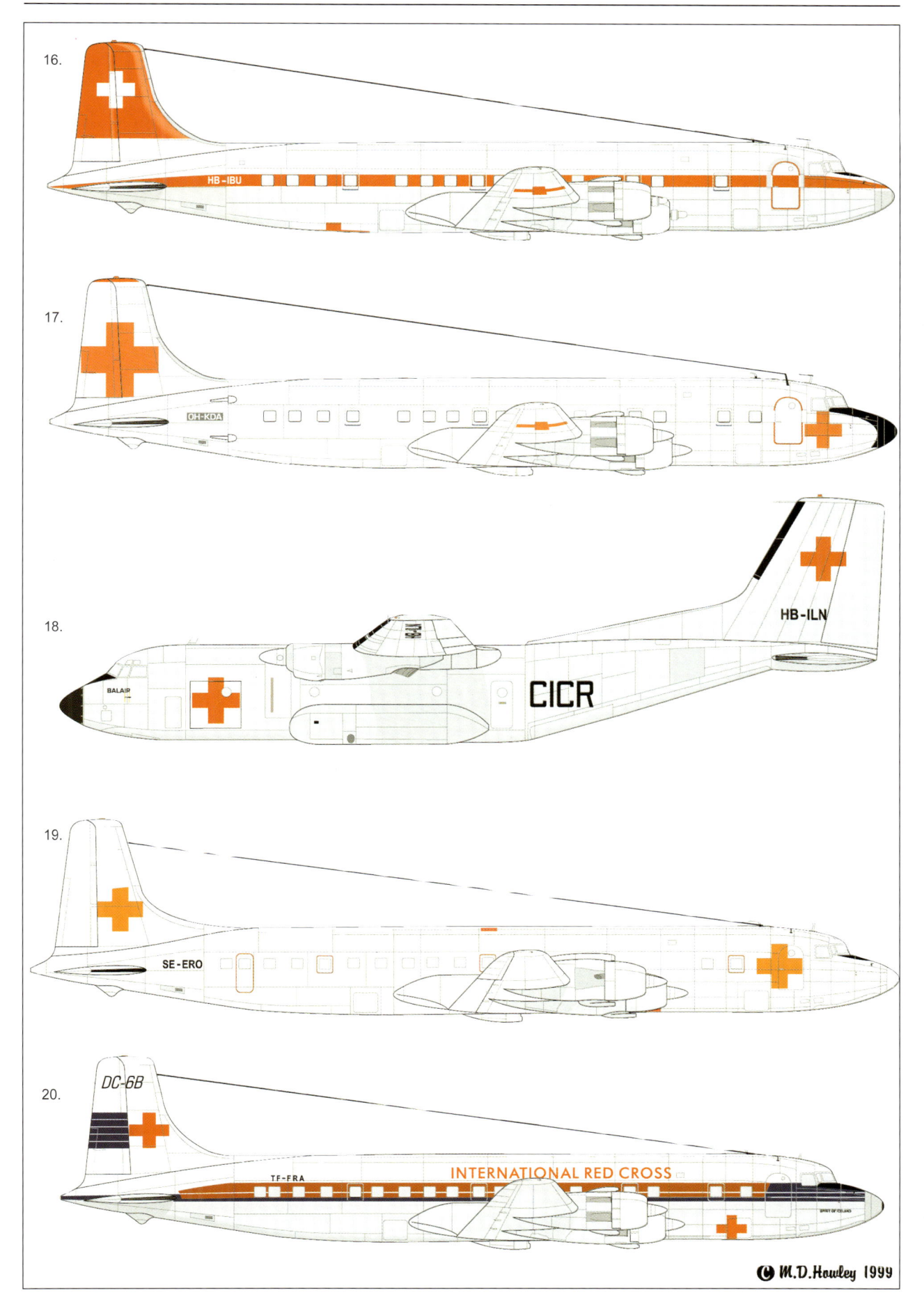

17. OH-KDA

18. BALAIR — CICR — HB-ILN

19. SE-ERO

20. DC-6B — TF-FRA — INTERNATIONAL RED CROSS

M.D.Howley 1999

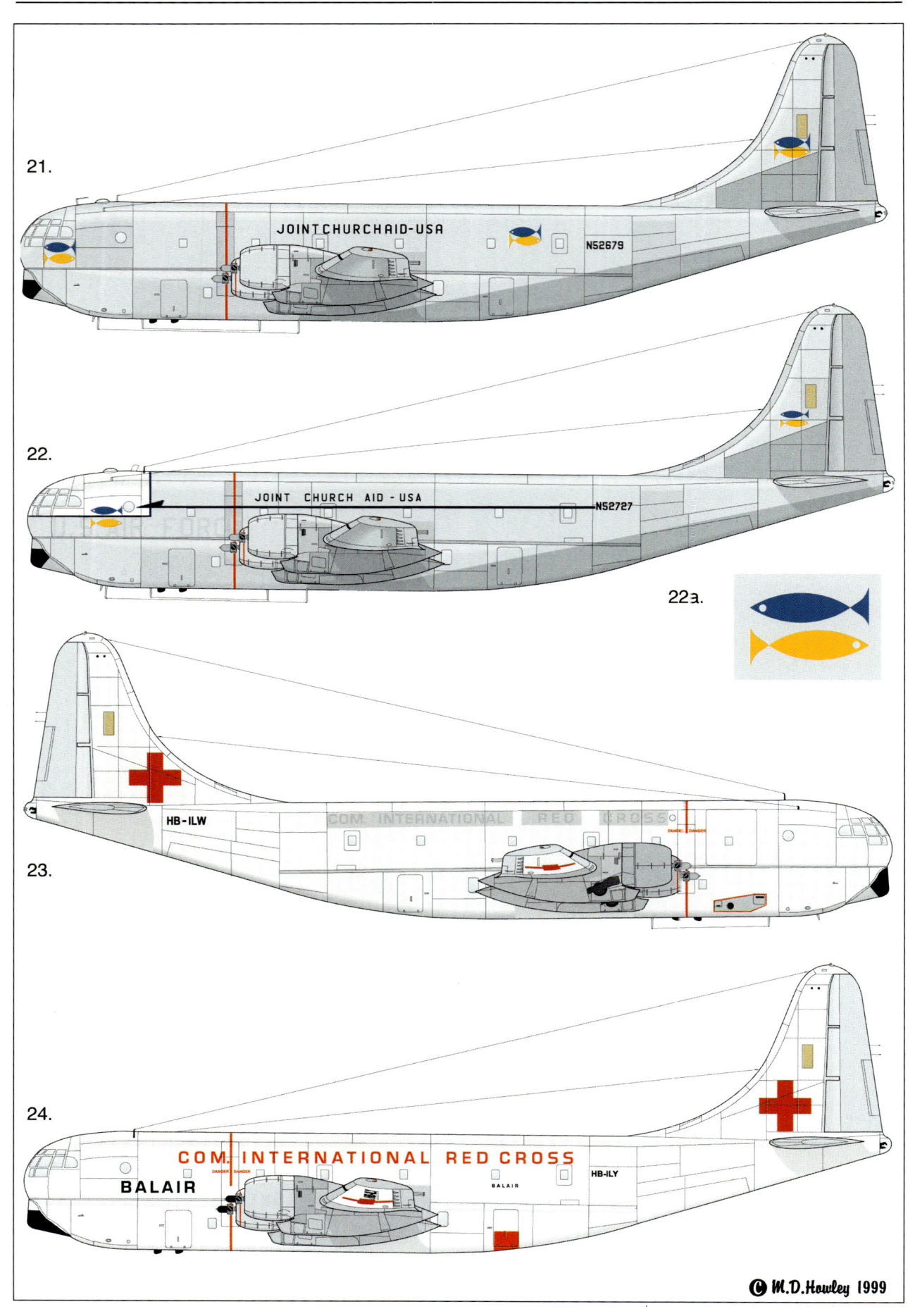

21.

JOINTCHURCHAID-USA N52679

22.

JOINT CHURCH AID - USA N52727

22a.

23.

HB-ILW COM. INTERNATIONAL RED CROSS

24.

COM. INTERNATIONAL RED CROSS
BALAIR BALAIR HB-ILY

© M.D.Howley 1999

25.

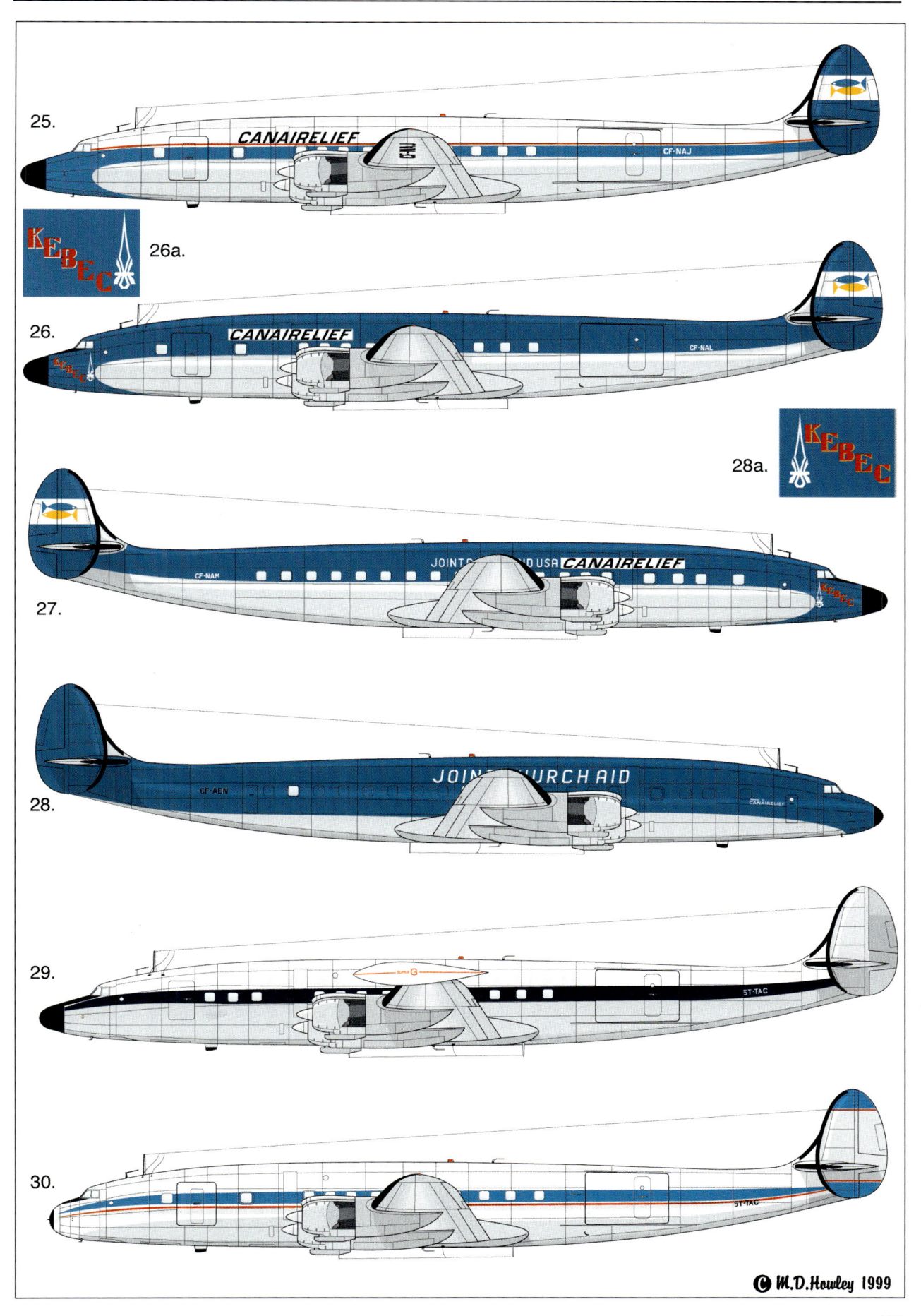

26a.

26.

28a.

27.

28.

29.

30.

© M.D.Howley 1999

197

31.

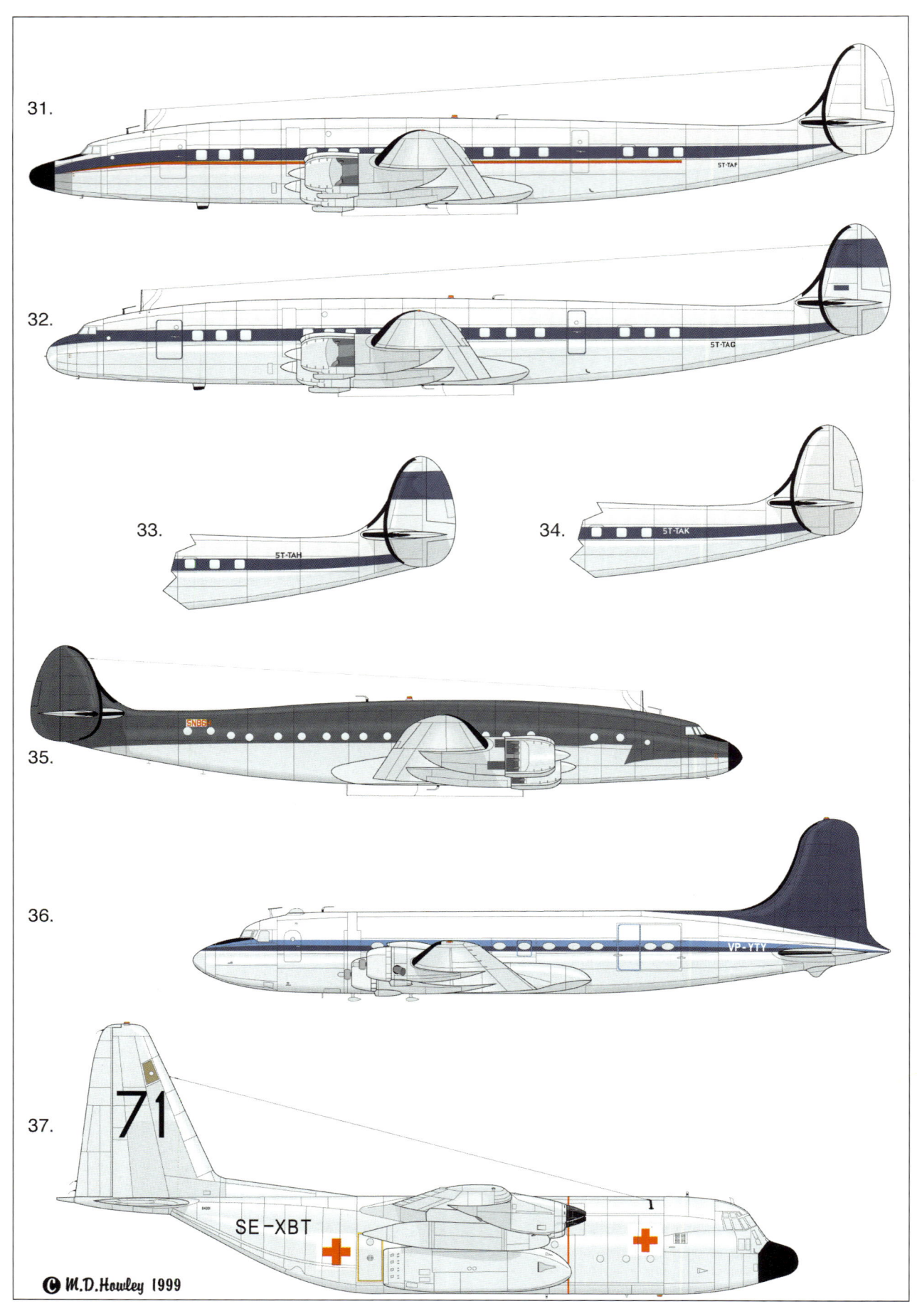

32.

33.

34.

35.

36.

37.

© M.D.Howley 1999

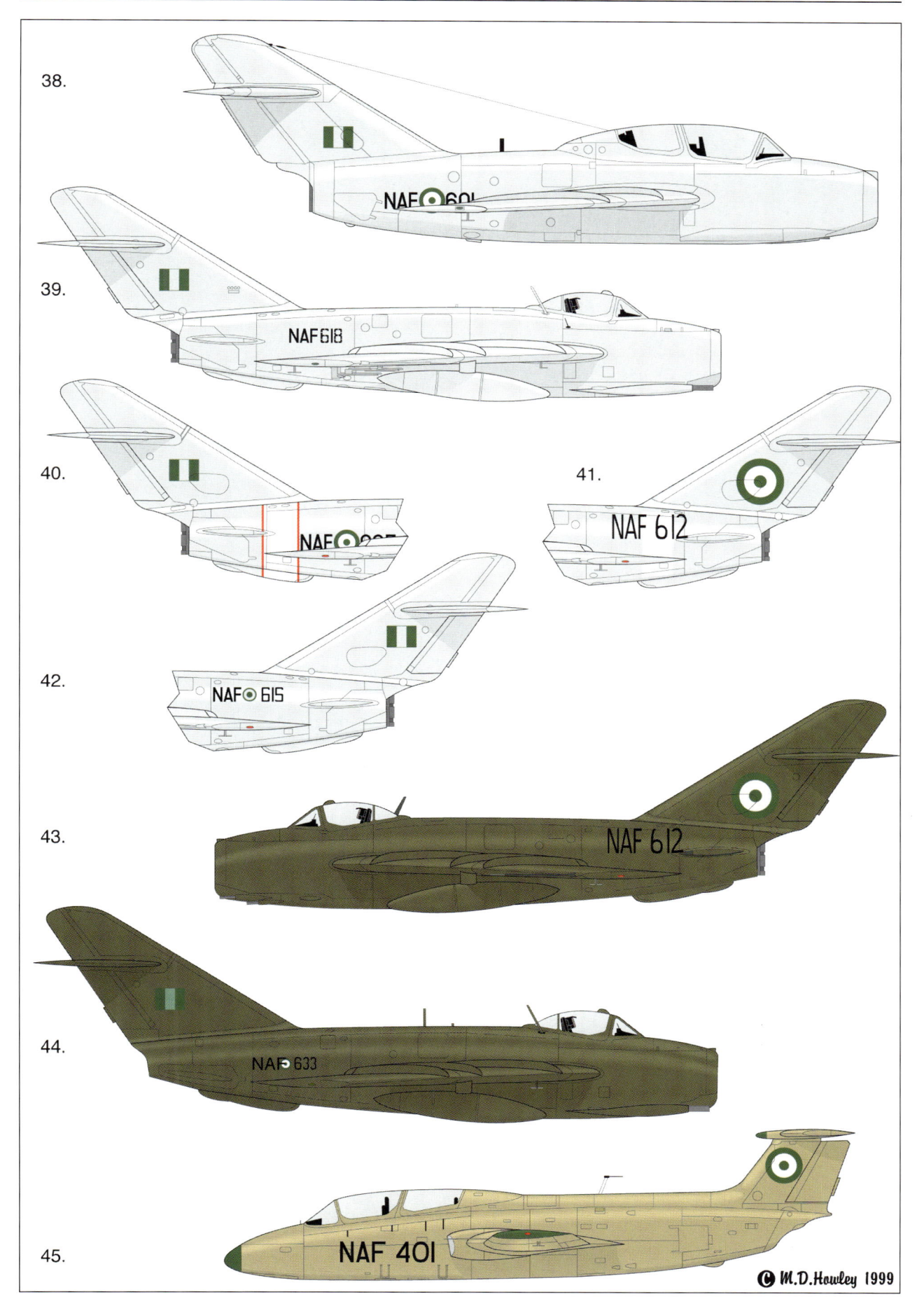

38.

39.

40.

41. NAF 612

42. NAF 615

43. NAF 612

44. NAF 633

45. NAF 401

© M.D.Howley 1999

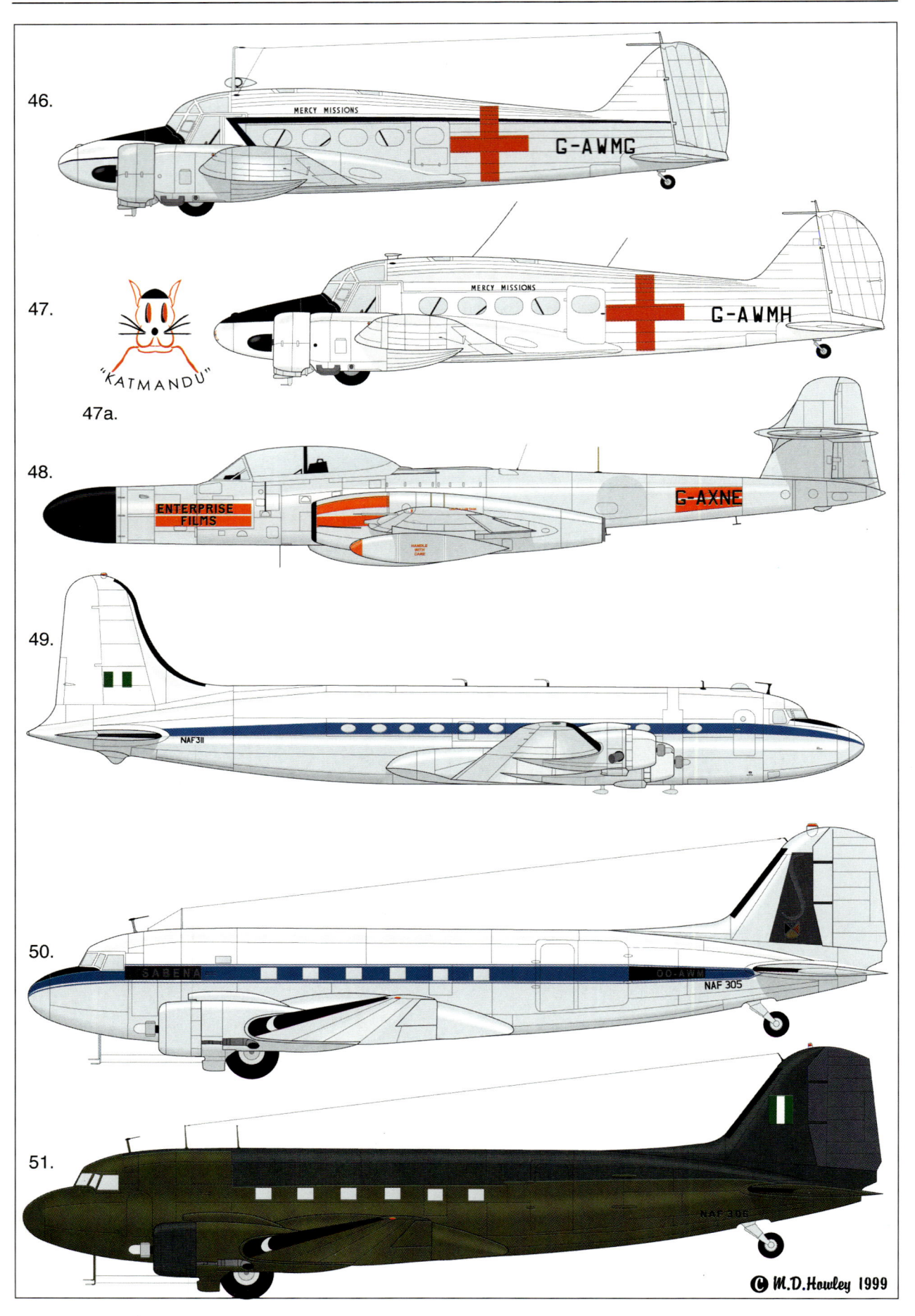

46.

47.

"KATMANDU"

47a.

48. ENTERPRISE FILMS G-AXNE

49. NAF 311

50. SABENA OO-AWM NAF 305

51. NAF 306

© M.D. Howley 1999

200

53.

54.

55.

56.

57.

© M.D.Howley 1999

203: As a direct result of air attacks by Biafran Air Force T-6Gs the Nigerian Air Force began repainting all war-zone MiG-17s in an overall dark green scheme. A general view of the apron at Lagos-Ikeja immediately after the end of the war shows a variety of aircraft. Behind MiG-17F NAF612 is an L-29 Delfin, a Dornier 27, and a Dornier 28. To the right of the MiG-17 can be seen the former Biafran Air Force T-6G Texan (Keith E. Sissons)

204: To facilitate conversion training onto the MiG-17F, the Nigerian Air Force received several two-seat MiG-15UTI 'Mongol' variants. These were based at Kano in Northern Nigeria where NAF601 is seen landing after a training circuit during 1969 (Keith E. Sissons)

205: Two Meteor NF.14s are visible in this view of Faro on 13 September 1969. To the left, and in a turquoise scheme, is G-ASLW whilst G-AXNE is seen in the foreground. After fitment of cannon barrels both jets departed Faro for Biafra. Also visible is the C-47D N10801, still in its former Luftwaffe white and day-glo scheme. Like the Meteors, the C-47 was purchased for operations in Biafra but also never arrived. It remained at Faro for a further eight years (Paul Baxter)

206: Fully-loaded and awaiting departure from São Tomé is L-1049H N7776C. The armed guard standing beneath the wing ensured the security of aircraft and cargo (and suggested the nature of the cargo!) Members of the Church airlift were advised not to fraternise with Biafra's gun-runners but that did not stop Father Byrne's assistant, Jakob Ringler, from taking this view, nor, surprisingly, did the guard intervene either (Jakob Ringler)

207: Abandoned at Libreville at the end of the war was one of the arms airlift C-47s. It appears to carry a Zambian prefix and which could suggest 9J-RIF or 9J-RIG. Careful scrutiny also offers the identity 'AF-...' which signifies a former Zambian Air Force serial. If indeed this is one of the two Biafran C-47s then the authors' guess is that it is 9J-RIF only on the basis that 'RIG was reported as having been camouflaged. However there is no sign of the recorded Biafran Air Force serial '439B' (P.Boy)

208: Jack Malloch acquired three DC-7Cs during 1969, two of which had been converted to DC-7CF configuration. The exception was TR-LOK, the former Martin's Air Charter PH-DSC. Owing to high-octane fuel being unavailable at Libreville, these gun-running aircraft refuelled at São Tomé most nights Note that the original KLM name 'Yellow Sea' appears on the aircraft's nose (Jakob Ringler)

203

209: *The characteristic 'blue-top' camouflage applied to Canairelief's L-1049H Super Constellations is well-portrayed in this view of CF-NAM, at São Tomé during 1969. The 'KEBEC' legend is in red, outlined in white while the 'dagger' motif is in plain white. Note that the 'JOINT-CHURCHAID USA' legend has been added aft of the CANAIRELIEF fuselage title. Note also how the 'blue-top' is extended stylishly across the nosewheel door (Phil Phillp)*

210: *When, after the end of the relief airlift, the Joint Church Aid C-97Gs flew out of São Tomé to Basle they were immediately scrubbed clean of any JCA insignia. For a brief period N52631 was re-registered to Balair as HB-ILK but eventually returned to Davis-Monthan AFB for storage and scrapping (Guido E. Buehlmann)*

211: *C-97G HB-ILZ first arrived at Basle on 22.2.69 after being ferried across the Atlantic via Brussels. It arrived in silver overall finish and devoid of any markings except its Swiss registration and the former USAF serial O.20857. Its appearance belied the fact that it was a redundant 15-year old military freighter. It was later repainted in Red Cross insignia and flown south to Cotonou on 28.3.69 (Guido E. Buehlmann)*

212: The small hamlet of San Antonio on São Tomé island became the location for a temporary children's home. The simplistic design of the two main living units made assembly easy. These children had been flown out of Biafra where they were fed and tended by CARITAS nurses. Ultimately they were returned to Biafra when fully restored to good health (Jakob Ringler)

213: The Governor of São Tomé island played a delicate and diplomatic role in the fortunes of Biafra. He allowed Biafra airlift aircraft to refuel on the island regardless of the nature of their cargo. It all helped the island's economy as well as the innocent children of Biafra. He certainly supported the San Antonio Childrens Village where he is seen giving out Christmas presents at the end of 1969 (Jakob Ringler)

214: CARITAS Austria donated a complete warehouse to the relief effort based on São Tomé island. It was delivered by ship and reassembled close to the airport by local workers. The bulk of the relief aid arrived on the island by ship, briefly stored, and then trucked across to the aircraft. By the end of 1969 the Church relief operation had reached massive proportions and saved many thousands of Biafran lives (Jakob Ringler)

206

Airstrips in Biafra 1968 - 1970

- UDI May 67 - February 68
- UGA March 69 - January 70
- OZUBULU June 69 - January 70
- ULI May 68 - January 70
- OBILAGU September 68
- URUALLA June 69 - January 70
- MBAWSI November - December 69
- PORT HARCOURT May 67 - May 68
- Construction abandoned

Locations: Onitsha, Enugu, Udi, Awka, Awgu, Afikpo, Nnewi, Okigwe, Uzuakoli, Ihiala, Orlu, Mbidi, Uli, Owerri, Umuahia, Ikot-Ekpene, Uyo, Aba, Port Harcourt, Calabar

Legend: Airfield or airstrip in existence before the war / Airstrips using roads

Africa

Name changes
- Salisbury is now Harare
- El Aaiún is now Laayoune
- Bathurst is now Serekunda
- Fernando Poó is now Malabo
- Port Etienne is now Nouâdhibou

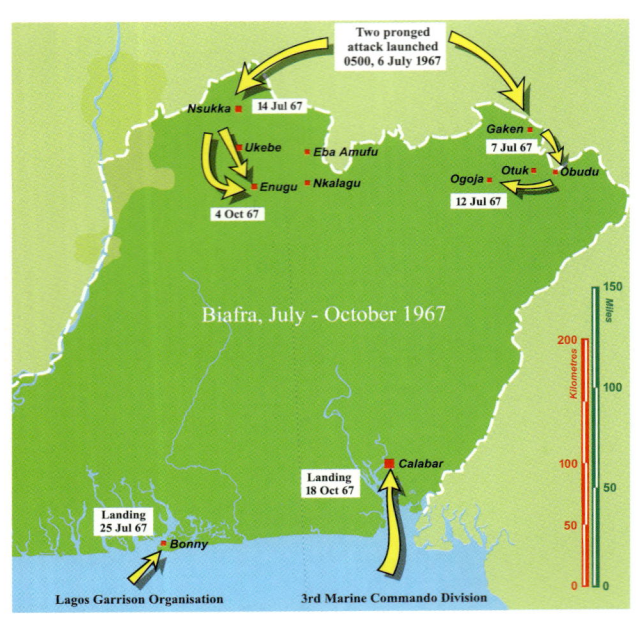

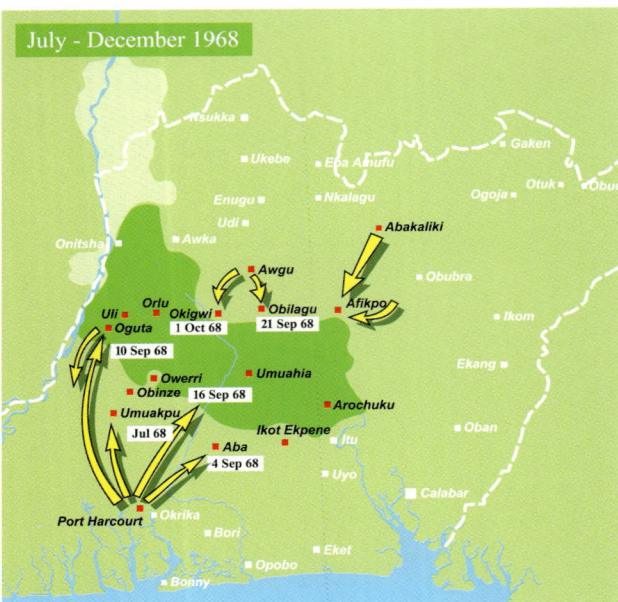

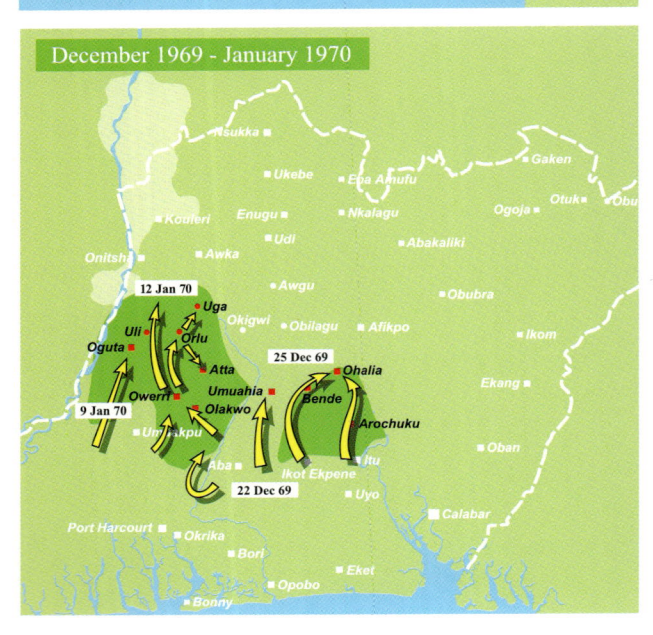

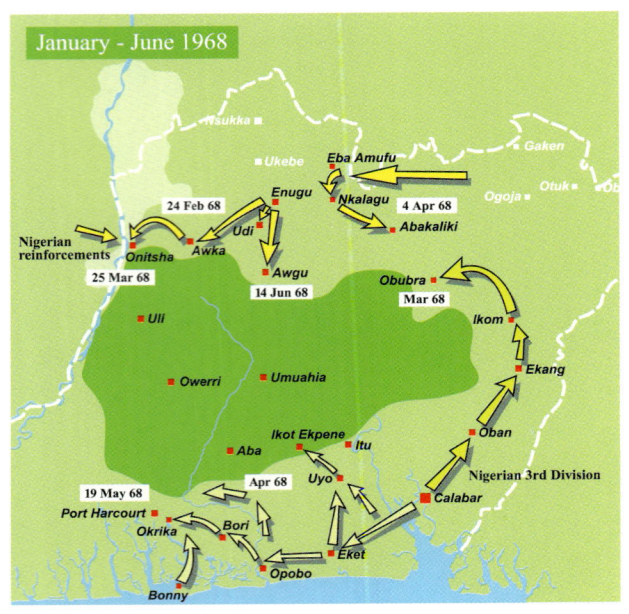

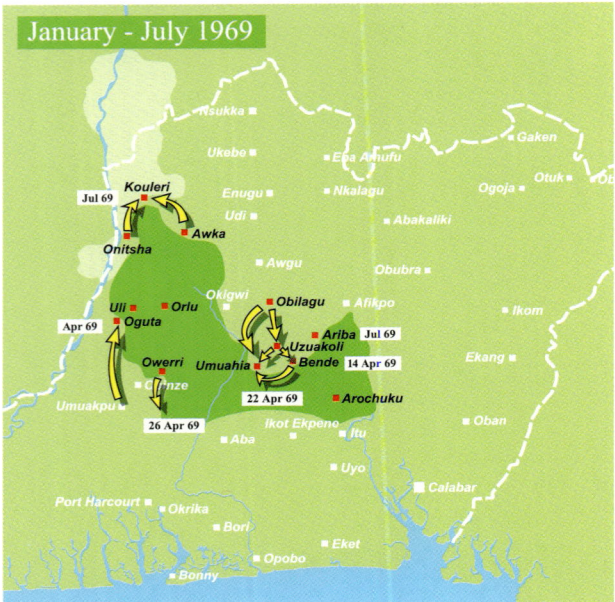

The land war started with a two-pronged Nigerian assault along Biafra's northern border. Then, on 9 August 1967, Biafran forces attacked and secured the entire Mid-West Region. The action slowed the Nigerian advances but by 6 October Nigerian forces (in the West) had pushed the Biafrans back across the Niger. As the final stage of withdrawal took place, the Nigerians attacked Enugu. A landing at Calabar swiftly followed. Nigeria's 1st Division advanced southwards from Enugu but progress was slow and the Division was held back by strong resistance for almost the entire war. In the south, the 3rd Marine Commando Division broke out from Calabar in January 1968 and eventually captured Port Harcourt in May 1968, thus completely land-locking Biafra. By the end of 1968 the Nigerian Army had captured Aba, Owerri and briefly held Oguta from where Uli strip came into range. The Biafrans later recaptured Owerri in April 1969 and held it until the final phase. 1969 saw gains and losses on both sides but the frontline remained fairly constant. The Nigerians captured Umuahia in April but later lost it.

The final stages of the war began in December 1969 when Nigerian forces successfully broke through from the south and cut Biafra in two. The easterly portion was cleared before the final thrust took the Nigerians towards Uli and Uga. A field surrender was signed at Amichi, just south-east of Nnewi, on 13 January 1970

Three Luftwaffe C-47s had originally been sold through the West German Government's Frankfurt-based surplus disposal agency, VEBEG. They were sold for to Luxembourg Aero Service, the owner of which was Tom Fuller, a former Seaboard World Flight Engineer with dual American-Luxembourg nationality. They were later registered in the USA as N10801, N10802 and N10803 in the name of Thomas M. Fuller (of 1 Rue Bender, Luxembourg City). None of the C-47s were flown to Luxembourg and instead Fuller kept them at the border airfield of Trier. The first of the trio, N10801, was then flown on to Lisbon on 12 September 1968 before positioning to the Portuguese coastal airfield of Faro.

It is believed that by the time of the flight by N10801 to Faro all three had been purchased by the German-American dealer, Ernest Koenig. (In fact, all three were later re-registered to E. Koenig, of PO Box 25082, Oklahoma City, USA–the official address of the Federal Aviation Agency.)

There was, if reports are accurate, considerable money to be made in redundant C-47s; VEBEG had sold them for $5,000 each; Koenig paid $11,000 for each of the aircraft while the Biafrans are said to have agreed $45,000 on receipt of the aircraft in Biafra.[354]

It was not until March 1969 that N10802 and N10803 were flown from Trier to Faro where both were fitted with a crude bomb release system similar to that thought to have been used in the Federal Nigerian 'Intruder' bomber aircraft. Only two of the C-47s were destined for delivery to Biafra, the remaining aircraft, N10801, would stay at Faro in reserve. The two nominated for delivery were then fitted with additional fuel tanks inside the fuselage although this was primarily associated with their delivery flight more than anything else. Other preparations for the delivery flight to Biafra involved blocking out part of the registration letters so that they read simply '802' and '803'. Both aircraft still retained their Luftwaffe camouflage and looked every bit a pair of military aircraft, especially '803' which still had an extended nose section, previously fitted by the Luftwaffe for NASARR trials.

'802' was the first of the two C-47s to depart Faro, with a 65-year old American pilot, formerly with Hank Warton, in command (thought to be George 'Robbie' Robertson), and a co-pilot believed to be named Grimwood. The aircraft staged around West Africa, arriving at Abidjan on 2 April 1969, before making the final sector into Uli.

'803' took-off from Faro exactly a week afterwards but was immediately forced to return when the Automatic Direction Finding (ADF) system failed to work on the first leg. After two days of undergoing repairs at Faro, '803' again set out for Biafra with an Australian pilot, 'Bunny' Sommerville, in command and John Mitchell-Smith, formerly with Mercy Missions (UK), as co-pilot/navigator. Engineer Bryan Mather was also aboard this aircraft. The first stage of '803''s flight, from Faro to Porto Santo, was uneventful but at the end of the second stage, when the aircraft reached Bissau, Sommerville promptly quit. It was no surprise to the others; he had continually complained throughout the flight of the appalling condition and general serviceability state of the aircraft. His place was taken by a Briton, thought to have been named Archer, and under whose command '803' continued from Bissau to Abidjan on 11 April and on to São Tomé before flying into Uli.[355]

Neither aircraft carried any cargo when they flew in to Uli; nor had they been converted to their projected gunship role. One of the C-47s, '802', was, within days of arriving in Biafra, flown across to Uga strip where it was pushed back into the bush and camouflaged with leaves and branches. '803' remained at Uli. It too was pushed into a clearing and camouflaged from the air. In the meantime mechanics were waiting for a delivery of components in sufficient number that the C-47s could be converted into gun-ships, fitted with a number of fast-firing 9mm guns at the rear and along the inside of the fuselage.

The gun arrangment was originally conceived in such a way that they fired rearwards through an opening in the rear fuselage cone; another gun would also be fitted on a platform that extended just out of the side fuselage door. Their primary target was the Nigerian MiG-17Fs that regularly attacked Uli at dawn. The attack profile of the MiGs was almost always the same. The first pass was at a relatively high altitude before reducing height quickly to make a low run across the airstrip from the north. The objective of the armed C-47s was to be airborne at dawn and to fly towards Uli at very low altitude, one aircraft from the north and one from the south, each C-47 flying to the right of a centre-line so as to not be on a collision course. The crew would be advised by radio from a ground controller of the point at which the MiG-17 began his run in. Then, on a signal from the ground controller, all of the guns aboard the C-47s would be fired upwards in such a manner that would involve the MiG-17 literally flying through a shower of bullets.[356]

Due to a dire shortage of aviation fuel in Biafra, neither of the C-47s was flown for some time after their arrival. Both aircraft are also reported to have suffered trouble with radio equipment, a key factor in the success of their role. (For these two reasons alone, a very disillusioned Bryan Mather decided to leave the group; he took a flight out to São Tomé and eventually back to the UK.)[357]

One of the C-47s, '803', is known to have been flown (by Mitchell-Smith) to Libreville during the night of 4/5 May 1969 where, on the following day, work started on fitting brackets for 9mm guns beside the fuselage doorway. Several nights later it was flown back into Uga, then across to Uli, and stored.

215: There may well have been an attempt to have the former Luftwaffe C-47D readied for ferrying to Biafra towards the final stages of the war. It arrived at Faro in a standard Luftwaffe 'white-top' scheme but after the aircraft had stood for over a year it was repainted with what had become the Biafran 'blue-top' scheme. In the event it was never ferried to Biafra and it stood at Faro until 1978 when it was eventually ferried back to the USA, via the UK (Unknown)

216: Towards the end of 1968 three surplus ex-West German Air Force C-47s were purchased by the Biafran Government. Two reached Biafra during April 1969, the first of which was N10802 although its registration was crudely shortened to '802' during its stopover at Faro. It was photographed at Abidjan on 2 April 1969 during the final leg into Uli. The bizarre role for this aircraft, and its sister aircraft '803', was an attempt by the Biafrans to create a small squadron of aerial gunships in an effort to strike back at the Nigerian MiG-17s (Roger Caratini)

217: The second of the two former Luftwaffe C-47s to reach Biafra involved N10802 which flew simply as '803'. The nose extension identifies the aircraft as one of several modified for research and development purposes with the Luftwaffe Fernmelde-Lehr und Versuchsregiment 61 (FVSt) at Lechfeld. '803' was delivered to Biafra a week after '802' and is seen here at Abidjan on 9 April 1969 (Roger Caratini)

Almost immediately Nigerian Air Force MiG-17Fs began making dawn attacks against Uga as well as continuing raids against Uli. It was, the Biafrans felt, almost as if the Nigerians "had been tipped off that the gunship C-47 was at Uga". Although the aircraft was not hit the suspicions remained. Eventually the Biafrans vented their distrust of all British crew and arrested John Mitchell-Smith. He was expelled from Biafra and flown back to Faro on 24 May 1969. He played no further part in the Nigerian war, nor did a number of British mechanics at Faro. The suspicions were, of course, totally groundless.

The precise fates of the two ex-Luftwaffe C-47s are unclear but neither was reported after May 1969. At least one Biafran C-47 was later used for flying in fuel for the MFI-9B 'Minicon' squadron but this could have been the survivor of the two former Zambian C-47s. Another C-47 is reported to have flown into Mount Cameroon one night while flying from Libreville to Uli but no confirmation of this is to hand. There is, in the meantime, no evidence to suggest that either aircraft ever actually performed their designated aerial gunship role.

It might be, of course, that the two former German C-47s were destroyed in Biafra; caught by the Nigerian Air Force in one of the many strafing, rocket or bombing raids they enacted against the Biafran airstrips. There is, in fact, a rather cryptic entry which appears in the Flying Log-Book of MiG-17F pilot Ares Klootwyk. It appears against 13 June 1969. Klootwyk took-off from Port Harcourt in MiG-17F NAF617 for a strafing mission against Uli and then planned to land at Enugu. During the raid he attracted, as usual, Biafran anti-aircraft fire from near Uli but records that he hit two DC-3s on the ground. He did later question whether there were one or two DC-3s on the strip; certainly he recollected one DC-3 in a "light-coloured, perhaps unpainted" finish. This may well suggest the unpainted '802'. In the heat of the moment, of course, he may have been mistaken but Klootwyk was certainly not one for making false claims. Nor was Paul Martin who claims to have strafed a damaged C-47 at Uli much later in the war, during December 1969.

'Biafra Airways': a change of strategy

When Jack Malloch was arrested in Togo and Hank Warton adopted the role of sole arms supplier he took on one other responsibility as well.

Since August 1967 the Biafrans had operated its own L-1049G, the so-called 'Grey Ghost' Super Constellation, "5N-07G". The Biafrans continued to own the aircraft and control to where it flew and what it carried but, from January 1968, Warton took on the role of supplying crews and organising the maintenance etc. This, as Warton saw it, was part of the monopoly deal negotiated with the Biafrans.

Warton, of course, was paid a fee for managing the 'Grey Ghost' but not as much as when operating his own aircraft. For that reason alone '5N-07G' did not undertake a tremendous number of flights during 1968; it spent much of the time at Lisbon where Hank's mechanics would occasionally rob it of some vital item to keep their own fleet of L-1049Gs serviceable. Then came the wind of change during the summer of 1968.[358]

The French government raised its level of assistance for Biafra at the end of July 1968. Within two months the question of supplying arms and ammunition would be solved with the appointment of Jack Malloch as a replacement for Hank Warton. But Malloch was not taking over the responsibility for operating the 'Grey Ghost'. That responsibility was being kept by the Biafrans themselves. The question of who would supply additional aircraft or crews was discussed at a meeting between Biafran emissaries and several leading characters at the Pousada Geronimo on São Tomé island, on 16 August 1968.[359]

What emerged was a new arrangement of short- and long-term leases. The new set-up was to be managed from Lisbon by a Biafran, H. Onobugu. The Chief Engineer was an American, Jack Crosson; two other Americans, John Fluney and Ed Short, were also hired as senior mechanics. Ironically, all three Americans had until then worked for Hank Warton.

In the meantime various groups began to organise aircraft for leasing agreements. Within three weeks of the São Tomé meeting an export license had been lodged with the British Board of Trade for two redundant Canadair C-4s (DC-4Ms).

A British connection

The gathering of dealers at the Pousada Geronimo, São Tomé, on 16 August 1968, was hugely significant. Senior Biafran government negotiators had, despite the most senior Minister suffering acute malaria, openly invited tenders to operate on behalf of the Biafran government. Most of the tenders involved leases by a number of American operators. At least one offer, and probably the first to be received, came from a British operator as part of an overall bid to launch a Biafran national airline once the fighting had stopped.

The plan involved a pair of British Midland Airways Canadair C-4s, G-ALHS and G-ALHY. Retired by B.M.A., both aircraft were officially sold, on 19 October 1968, to a hitherto unknown British operator, Chartwell Aviation. In fact, Chartwell had no connection with aviation at all; it was simply a Kent-based car retailer who agreed to put up a guaranteed sum of money to cover the purchase price of the two C-4s. The responsibility for operating the two aircraft rested with the broker, Templewood Aviation Ltd, whose Operations Manager had,

211

on 6 September, already applied to the Board of Trade for an export licence covering the two aircraft.

On the strength of an agreed lease/charter arrangement with the Biafrans, Templewood hired four ground engineers (Ashcroft, Russell, Moore and Lameroa) and two complete flight-crews. The latter included Captains Bailey and Norman, plus two First Officers, Don Bullock (who had just left the bankrupt Air Ferry) and the Dutchman, Peiter Dezeeuw who had joined Templewood as part of a frustrated deal to supply the Biafrans with a number of Swedish Hunter jets. Since the Hunter deal had collapsed Dezeeuw had enrolled with the Bedfordshire Air Centre at Cranfield during August 1968 to gain an American CPL rating. The cost of the course was born by Templewood Aviation, although in the event Dezeeuw failed to complete the course.[360]

The agreement between Templewood and the Biafrans involved two separate operations. Firstly, a return Lisbon-Bissau-São Tomé-Uli flight for which the Biafrans would be charged $13,000 for each round trip, conditional on a minimum of ten trips. The other option involved the aircraft being permanently positioned to São Tomé from where they would complete two shuttles into Uli each night at a charge of $5,800 per trip providing that they completed a minimum of twenty shuttles to Uli.

The first of the C-4 Argonauts to depart the UK should have been G-ALHS, on Sunday 21 October 1968. Its flight plan simply showed a positioning flight to Zurich but its ultimate destination was widely believed to be Lisbon. There was also a suspicion that the plan was to fly to Lisbon via either Prague or Vienna where the aircraft would uplift an undisclosed cargo.

British Midland had officially withdrawn G-ALHS on 16 October 1968 and G-ALHY on 6 November, but in the event neither aircraft ever left East Midlands airport. As the first of the two Argonauts was preparing to depart for the first stage to Zurich, officers of HM Customs, having received an earlier tip-off in Switzerland as to the precise intention of the group involved, successfully convinced the captain to return to the ramp area. The aircraft was detained and the crew questioned. In fact, no charges were brought against either the crew or indeed against Templewood. All that the Customs wanted was a signed declaration that neither of the two aircraft were destined to operate the airlift into Biafra. Templewood was not prepared to give such an undertaking in writing and abandoned any further attempt to fly the aircraft out of the UK. Eventually, both aircraft were scrapped at East Midlands airport during 1970.

A French connection?

The whole Lisbon operation (which later moved to Faro) was shrouded in mystery. It eventually became referred to as the 'Phoenix' operation; even the Biafrans themselves used the name 'Phoenix', referring to 'Phoenix Airlines' or 'Phoenix Air Transport' but nobody quite knew the exact name of the company operating out of Portugal. Nor, for that matter, did anybody know who was financing it.[361]

By the Autumn of 1968 the state of the Biafran economy had seriously deteriorated. When secession was announced in May 1967, Biafra had been able to finance the purchase of armaments and supplies from private arms dealers to fight what was probably seen then as a brief war of independence. But the decision by Lagos to introduce new currency at short notice in January 1968 had rendered valueless millions of old Nigerian pounds still in Biafran hands. It is believed that Biafra's foreign-exchange reserves were exhausted by April 1968 and that by September 1968 the country was bankrupt. So, who did financially support the new operation?

What is known is that France used its secret service fund to supply something over £2million worth of arms and related military assistance over the September-December 1968 period. France perhaps saw a unified Nigeria as a threat to French-speaking West Africa. The real prize, however, was the likely gains by French oil interests and the substantial concessions that until then had been enjoyed by British oil companies. These concessions would have become bargainable with a Biafran victory. Therefore, the true funding of the new Portuguese-based operation was probably French, and not, as it appeared to be, American funding. Alternatively, it might well have been both. One observer remarked shortly afterwards; "Maybe the French financed the whole operation but hired Americans. In that way it would look like a secretly-funded American set-up–a CIA set-up. Of course, the CIA would deny any involvement–heck, the CIA was still denying any involvement in Vietnam. That would convince everybody it really *was* a CIA set-up. So, it probably was funded by the French!"

An American connection

Towards the end of September 1968 the first of several L-1049G Super Constellations arrived in Portugal to join the Biafran government operation. Reports told of 'N480C' landing at Lisbon on the 25th September. The identity has never been officially proved and its lack of other markings (apart from a red fuselage cheat-line) ensured that whatever secrets the aircraft had, they remained well-hidden. A second L-1049G was first reported at Lisbon on 1 October and seen to carry a Panamanian registration, HP-475. Officially this aircraft was still registered to the South American company, *Cia. Interamericana Export-Import*.

The third new arrival was first noted at Lisbon on 7 November 1968 and may well have been the same aircraft that was earlier reported as 'N480C'. On this occasion it was correctly identified as N8338, an L-1049G legally registered (on 21 November) to Jack A. Crosson but with a Miami address. (Crosson, of course became the front man for the Biafran operation at Faro.) Shortly after its arrival at Lisbon the L-1049G N8338 was re-painted with the illegal Biafran marks '5N-83H', a change that required the minimum of painting.

During the Spring of 1969 the original 'Grey Ghost' L-1049G Super Constellation '5N-07G', which had operated continuously for almost two years, was finally grounded. Sorely in need of a major overhaul it was instead abandoned at Lisbon. An American pilot, Al Carstens, claimed to have made the final flight from São Tomé to Lisbon.

Not long after the grounding of '5N-07G' the Biafran government secured the lease of an American-registered L-1049H Super Constellation. It was registered as N7776C (legally!) and officially owned by Leasing Consultants Inc. and flew regularly from Lisbon (and later from Faro) to Biafra from July 1969 until the end of the war.

The summer of 1969 also saw two L-749A Constellations join the Biafran government airlift. Both had previously been operated by Western Airlines whose livery included a large native American head on the aircraft's nose. They arrived at Faro with their American registrations, N86525 and N86524 (in late-July and late-August 1969 respectively) and initially operated on the Biafra run as such and, indeed, retained their rather dramatic airline livery. All that had to change after a visit to São Tomé (during late-Autumn 1969) by two FAA inspectors. They raised some questions about the legality of US-registered aircraft running guns and associated military equipment into Biafra. As a consequence the two L-749As were applied with Biafran identities, '5N85H' (ex-N86525) and '5N86H' (ex-N86524). (Note that the new identities were not hyphenated.) They were also repainted, on the upper fuselages, in a blue-grey camouflage scheme, a pattern that was extended to other aircraft employed on the airlift. Curiously, the need for 'Biafran' camouflage and identities was not seen as necessary for the L-1049H aircraft.

The allocation of the registration '5N-83H' bears an uncanny similarity to Biafra's 'Grey Ghost' Super Constellation, which operated for several years with the equally spurious marks '5N-07G'. The similarity has even caused observers to offer evidence of an official Biafran Aircraft Register with various theories as to how the sequence was managed. An inescapable suggestion is that '5N-07G' was, in fact, the **seventh** *fixed-wing aircraft to have been acquired by the Biafrans during 1967; therefore the later Super Constellation could possibly have been the* **83rd** *entry onto this reported register. Two Constellations secured later were allocated '5N85H' and '5N86H' and which offered further 'evidence' of this sequential theory.*

The meaning of the suffix letters 'G' and 'H' have also been surmised to have referred to the year of registration, 'G' being 1967 and 'H' indicating 1968, the series reflecting that 1961 had been the first year of independence in Nigeria. But this theory can be discounted by the fact that the later Constellations were 're-registered' during 1969.

The so-called Biafran registrations appear to have been crude corruptions of the existing American marks, but those responsible for applying the illegal letters did not just alter the existing ones. In fact a cardboard template was made and the letters sprayed on as if the change was carried out legitimately by professional engineers.[362]

The author has found no real evidence that these identities bear any relationship to a sequential register although alternatively they offer no rational reason for the marks '5N-07G' but does concede that the aircraft was indeed the seventh aircraft acquired. Furthermore the author suggests that as all published references to other Biafran 'registrations' have not been supported by photographic evidence, then these reports are completely spurious.

218: The first evidence that the missing Biafran Government L-749A Constellation '5N85H' had crashed came from an AP Press Telex dated 11 July 1970. Amnesty International had investigated the disappearance of the aircraft on behalf of concerned relatives of one of the passengers. This ended widespread speculation that the aircraft had been hijacked, with its crew and passengers being held at some unknown location (Hank Warton Personal Papers)

```
MARRAKECH, MOROCCO, JULY 11 (AP) MOROCCAN AUTHORITIES
HAVE FOUND A QUANTITY OF ARMS AND THE REMARKABLY PRESERVED
BODIES OF EIGHT EUROPEANS IN THE WRECK OF AN AIRCRAFT BELIEVED
TO BE ONE ## OF BIAFRASXX GREY GHOSTS...THE GUNRUNNERS THAT
KEPT SECESSIONIST STATE ALIVE DURING ITS WAR WITH NIGERIA.
THE WRECK OF THE PLANE, WHICH VILLAGERS SAID CRASHED LAST
NOVEMBER, WAS REVEALED WITH MELTING SNOWS SOME 70 KILOMETERS
SOUTH OF HERE IN THE OUKAIMEDEN MOUNTAIN RANGE AT AN ALTITDE
OF 3000 METERS.
THE BODIES WERE BURIED LOCALLY. IT WAS SPECULATED THAT
THE SIX PASSENGERS IN ADDITION TO THE PILOT AND COPILOT
WERE MERCENARIES. BUT MOROCCAN AUTHORITIES WOULD NOT SAY
 IF THEY HAD DETERMINED THEIR IDENTITY AND DECLINED TO
  PROVIDE ADDITIONAL DETAILS. (END)
                                  JULY 11
```

219: The former RAPSA L-1049G HP-475 arrived at Lisbon in September 1968 and was one of the first aircraft to operate for the Biafrans after Hank Warton was fired. It continued to operate the Faro to Biafra run until the end of the war in January 1970 and is seen here, on São Tomé, during late-1969 just before the final leg into Uli (Jakob Ringler)

220: One of the first aircraft to be used by Biafra's 'Phoenix' operation was the L-1049G Super Constellation '5N-83H'. By the time that this view was taken, outside the 'Phoenix' hangar at Faro on 13 November 1969, it had been withdrawn from use and its engines removed (Ian P. Burnett)

221: The name 'ENDEAVOUR' was stylishly applied to the nose of L-1049G Super Constellation '5N-83H' during its time on the Biafra run. From an earlier decade the manufacturer's original 'Super G' logo still looked as fresh as when it was applied, in 1955, when she was built for the Portuguese national airline, T.A.P. (Unknown)

214

222: *The prototype L-1049H Super Constellation was originally built in 1956 for QANTAS as VH-EAM. It was retired by the end of 1962, after which it was owned and operated by a number of dealers and minor airlines until June 1969 when acquired by Leasing Consultants Inc. During August 1969 it first appeared at Lisbon on lease to the Biafran Government, operating with minimal markings and carrying arms from Faro to Uli, often via São Tomé. In this view N7776C is seen during a stopover at Faro on 13 November 1969 (Ian P. Burnett)*

223: *L-1049G F-BHBI was donated by the French Government for use by the Biafran Government. Its use, however, was severely restricted due to the poor state of the engines. After only one, or possibly even two, trips to Biafra 'HBI suffered a multiple engine failure while routeing back to Faro. Being close to the Canary Islands at the time the crew elected to make an emergency landing at Lanzarote. No attempt was made to repair the aircraft and it was simply abandoned there. This view, taken during October 1972, shows it still retaining its former Air France livery but without the classic seahorse insignia on the nose (via Peter J. Marson)*

224: *The DC-6B TR-LOX was registered to Jean-Claude Bergey in October 1969 and joined the arms airlift out of Libreville late in the war. It was repainted in the traditional Biafran 'blue-top' camouflage and had the name 'APOLLO' applied to the nose. In this view TR-LOX is seen at Douala, Cameroons (Unknown)*

Notes

Note 336 John de St Jorre (*The Nigerian Civil War*) quoted an experienced observer of African affairs as believing Tanzania's recognition of Biafra was a case of President Julius Nyerere doing "the wrong thing for the right reasons." The same source quotes President Kenneth Kaunda of Zambia being strongly influenced by Nyerere. The security of Biafra, both men believed, would be strengthened at the negotiating table by political recognition. The actions of the French colonial countries was, of course, for completely different reasons.

Note 337 G-ATOB was (according to *Piston Engine Airliner Production List* by A.B. Eastwood & J. Roach) bought on 25 July 1968 but temporarily re-registered as TI-1065P on 8 October 1968. This was possibly for post-overhaul test-flight purposes but further details are unknown.

Note 338 According to Hank Warton the aircraft did work some flights on the relief airlift from São Tomé but Nordchurchaid records do not offer any evidence to support this.

Note 339 *The Last Adventurer; From Biafra to the Sudan* by Rolf Steiner; published by Weidenfeld & Nicolson 1978

Note 340 Ibid,. A.B. Eastwood & J. Roach.

Note 341 Ibid,. John de St Jorre

Note 342 According to entries shown in the Flying Log-book of Clive Halse. The marks ZS-FLO were officially not taken up.

Note 343 The marks ZS-FAA were officially allocated for operation by Protea Airways and are quoted from the Flying Log-book of Clive Halse.

Note 344 As related to the author by Cliff Hawthorne

Note 345 According to the records of French specialist Jean Delmas

Note 346 It was fairly normal to ferry the L-1049G on three engines as a means of saving fuel and wear. On this occasion the use of three engines was by necessity.

Note 347 According to those crew members mentioned within the text.

Note 348 As related separately to the author by Jack Wight and Dave Goldsmith.

Note 349 As related by Flight Engineer Henry Kinnear who was present at the time.

Note 350 The official entries for these two aircraft within the Zambian Directorate of Civil Aviation records are shown in hand-writing. All other entries are typed suggesting that the process was extremely hurried. Unfortunately no other details are given. The sighting at Lusaka was recorded in *Blackbushe Movements* (October 1968 issue), published by B.A.R.G.

Note 351 The explanation, although plausible, may be wrong as no aircraft without a known fate can be attributed to any with such a serial.

Note 352 As reported to the author by Cliff Hawthorne

Note 353 As related to the author by Willy Murray-Bruce.

Note 354 *Sunday Times*, 27 July 1969.

Note 355 According to Bryan Mather and John Mitchell-Smith

Note 356 As described to the author by John Mitchell-Smith

Note 357 As related to the author by Bryan Mather 4 December 1972

Note 358 As related by Hank Warton and John Trent

Note 359 By accident the author was present at the hotel at the time and believed it to be quite normal that the hotel bar and lounge should be so full of guests. The Biafrans later explained why so many American citizens were present.

Note 360 Much of the following text is taken from private documents held by Alex Rumley

Note 361 The name 'Phoenix' was in fact first used by a group of Britons attempting to export Meteors from the UK. It served as a cover to foil HM Customs investigators, but the Biafrans at Faro adopted it.

Note 362 Air Britain Soviet aircraft specialist, Bob Ruffle, discovered the template stuffed behind a seat on the aircraft several years later. He then handed it over to Peter J Marson as a souvenir. The template can be seen to have acted for both 5N85H and 5N86H.

225: After the end of the Biafran operation Jack Malloch repainted his DC-7CFs in an equally anonymous scheme. This postwar view was taken on 29 December 1971 after it crash-landed on Libreville's Runway 16 at the end of a routine flight (AG244) from Salisbury. As the undercarriage was lowered the aircraft lost all hydraulic pressure, forcing the crew to use reverse thrust and air brakes (which caused three tyres to burst on touchdown). Unfortunately the reverse thrust failed on No.4 engine causing the aircraft to swerve to the left and run onto soft sand beside the runway. (Peter J Cooper)

BIAFRAN AIR FORCE OPERATIONS
Establishing Biafra's 'Second' Air Force

The T-6 Texans

Attempts by Biafra to acquire single-engine fighter-attack aircraft had begun very shortly after secession was declared. Initially a batch of twelve North American T-6G Texans was involved. All had originally been supplied to the French Air Force under a US Government Mutual Defence Aid Pact and were part of a large number in storage at Châteaudun and which had been placed for disposal by the French during 1965. They were disposed of to a number of buyers, notably a Belgian-French sugar-beet farmer at Allé sur la Lys, who bought one batch while others had been sold to various dealers, including twelve to the dealer, *Établissements Godet* (or Gaudet).[363]

It was the batch bought by Godet that became the subject of a long and frustrating acquisition by the Biafran government. Details of those twelve are in the accompanying table:

226 Above: The original batch of five MFI-9B 'Minicons' at 'Camp I' in Libreville, where they act as a backdrop for a group photograph of the three Swedish and two Biafran pilots selected for the delivery flight to Biafra. From left to right: Martin Lang, Willy Murray-Bruce, Count Gustav von Rosen, Augustus Okpe, and Gunnar Haglund. It is worth noting the various paint finishes on the aircraft, in particular the high-contrast finish on the machine just behind the pilots, and the complete absence of any markings. The precise location of 'Camp 1' has never been made known but it is suspected to be the small airfield at Lambaréné, south-east of Libreville. The airfield provided an opportunity for pilots to simulate bush-flying techniques and to practice low-level attack procedures, but conditions in the Biafran bush proved to be considerably different (Pierre Mens)

Serial	C/n	Total Hours	Fuselage marking
50-1306	168-570	4819	1306; code L
51-14770	182-457	7077	114770; code 24
51-14794	182-481	5221	14794; code KH
51-14798	182-485	5285	114798; code KY
51-14800	182-487	8209	14800; code 21
51-14810	182-497	7983	14810; code J
51-14873	182-560	4427	114873; not coded.
51-14959	182-646	5855	14959; code KK
51-14991	182-678	6683	14991; code KG
51-15046	182-733	5814	15046; code KC
51-15051	182-738	5890	115051; code KC
51-15083	182-770	5640	115083; code KI

The first recorded evidence of any Biafran involvement with T-6Gs is contained within a contract agreed between Texsel Sales & Services (a Swiss-based associate company of Templewood Aviation Ltd) and Biafra's London-based agent, Austin Okwesa. It is possible, of course, that Texsel simply acted as a broker for a sale between Godet and Biafra.

The Texsel contract involved twelve T-6Gs bought by the Biafrans for an agreed US$12,000 each. The cost included delivery to Biafra in four separate batches, each of three aircraft, with flights into Biafra being made at a maximum interval of seven days commencing Sunday 3 December 1967. The price also included VOR and 12-

Channel radio equipment fitted to each aircraft, as well as four .50 machine-guns and external underwing bomb racks. The contract was signed by Anthony Paris (on behalf of Texsel Sales & Service) and Austin Okwesa, on 25 November 1967. The only provision contained within the contract was that the Biafrans deposit a Letter of Credit for US$ 144,000 at Texsel's Swiss bank by 29 November.[364]

Although the contract had been signed during November 1967 none of the T-6Gs physically moved immediately and the agreed delivery date proved to be unrealistically optimistic. In fact all twelve aircraft remained stored in a warehouse within the Rochefort-La Rochelle area. It was not until March 1968 that they were finally shipped out of France and south to Lisbon.

Even the arrival of the twelve T-6Gs at Lisbon did little to enhance Biafra's chances of operating a squadron of ground-attack aircraft. The condition of the aircraft was poor; they required a fair amount of attention and maintenance and the engines needed an overhaul. All of this work had to be carried out in Portugal, or at least outside Biafra. The naval blockade of Biafran ports and the general war situation precluded any delivery to Biafra other than by air and even then under their own power.

In fact none of the aircraft were moved away from the Lisbon dock area for several months. Eventually they were moved by road to Cascais airfield in Portugal where they remained for almost eighteen months.

The Provost T.1s

Frustration at the non-delivery of the T-6Gs was widely felt among officers of the Biafran Air Force officers and an attempt to procure alternative aircraft began in Umuahia during the early Autumn of 1968. Initial discussions explored the possibility of acquiring a batch of ex-RAF Hunting P.56 Provost T.1s which were known to be in storage and probably available for sale. But this attempt met with even less success than the twelve T-6G Texans.

Ironically the concept of acquiring Provosts was first mooted, in September 1968, during a chance discussion at the Queen Elizabeth Hospital, Umuahia, Biafra between Count Gustav von Rosen and two members of the British Mercy Missions team. Von Rosen outlined Biafra's basic requirement as needing to meet two fundamental objectives; firstly, and most importantly, as an armed counter-insurgency aircraft, as was the role envisaged for the T-6G Texans. The secondary role for the Provosts was as a fast and versatile means of moving urgent drugs by air within Biafra. The latter role was at one stage being offered to the Mercy Missions' Ansons but in reality the aircraft were most unsuitable.[365]

The six Provosts in question were among the last of the type to be operated by the RAF and latterly had flown with the Central Air Traffic Control School (CATCS), at Shawbury. All had been placed in storage at 27 Maintenance Unit at Shawbury where they were later put up for disposal by the Ministry of Defence. All six were purchased by Target Towing Aircraft Co Ltd, a company formed on 18 October 1967 by Tony Osborne with his wife, Lesley Ann Osborne.[366]

Once the purchase was confirmed the Provosts were allocated civil registrations on 8 November 1968, as G-AWTB - G-AWTG, in order that they could be flown from Shawbury to Blackbushe. In spite of this all were actually ferried in military markings although several had their fin-flashes crudely erased. WV421/(G-AWTF) was the first to be ferried to Blackbushe, on 13 November 1968; the remainder made the flight on the following day. All except one aircraft were then picketed out on the main terminal apron. The exception was WV540/(G-AWTG) which Tony Osborne used as a personal daily 'air-taxi' between Blackbushe and Stapleford Tawney. But Blackbushe was an extremely visible airfield and its owner, Air Vice Marshall Don Bennett, was instantly wary of the group's intentions. The six aircraft were therefore flown from Blackbushe to Fairoaks Airfield, Surrey, on 20 November 1968, as follows:

Provost Flight Detail: Blackbushe-Fairoaks 20 November 1968

Identity	ATA Fairoaks	Ferry Pilot
XF691/(G-AWTE)	1600	Tony Osborne
XF554/(G-AWTD)	1615	Richard Kingsmill
XF838/(G-AWTB)	1615	.... Wright
XF693/(G-AWTC)	1715	.... Wright
WV421/(G-AWTF)	1715	Tony Osborne
WV540/(G-AWTG)	1715	Richard Kingsmill

Osborne began to openly float the notion that he had acquired the Provosts for export and that they were destined specifically for the Zambia Flying Doctor Service; H.M. Customs & Excise Office suspected, quite rightly, that they were destined elsewhere, especially after Count Gustav von Rosen had publicly recommended that Biafra be "provided with an air strike capability". Customs officers reacted by visiting Fairoaks to forcibly remove the engine starter motor from each aircraft, and thus rendering them immobile.[367]

The activities of Tony Osborne, and especially those of Target Towing Aircraft Ltd, were by that time the subject of an official government investigation and, apart from the unwanted attention over the Provosts, Osborne was also facing bankruptcy charges. To avoid any further difficulty with the Provosts, Osborne arranged for the registered ownership of all six aircraft to be transferred to a young aircraft engineer from Coventry, Bryan Mather. The C.A.A. was notified of the 'sale' on 9 December 1968,

227: The original contract for the supply of twelve ex-French Air Force T-6G Texan aircraft to Biafra was signed on 25 November 1967 between Biafrais London-based arms buyer, Austin Okwesa and Tony Paris of Texsel Sales & Service. It was almost two years before the aircraft involved began to arrive in Biafra. By that time the war was reaching its dramatic climax and their effectiveness became severely reduced by a lack of fuel and increasingly low morale (Alex Rumley Personal Papers)

```
                            CONTRACT.

DATED THE 23rd NOVEMBER, 1967.

This contract is made between Texsel Sales and Services, c/o Union Banque
Suisse, 8 Rue de Rhone, Geneva and the State of Biafra, represented by
Mr. A. Okwesa, c/o Schweizer Volksbank, Zurich.

The seller sells and the buyer buys twelve (12) T6 Harvard piston engine
light attack aircraft for the sum of U.S. $12,000. per aircraft delivered
by flight to............................

The buyer contracts to open an irrovocable, confirmed, divisable and
transferable Letter of Credit for the full amount in favour of Account Number
308/797.00V. at the Union Bank of Switzerland, Head Office, Geneva, Switzerland
to be paid against the presentation of the relevant invoice and a certificate
from Air Traffic Control.......................that the aircraft have
landed there.

It is further agreed that the aircraft will be delivered in four (4) seperate
flights at a maximum of seven (7) day intervals, commencing Sunday 26th 3rd
December, 1967. provided that the Letter of Credit is in our Bank by
Wednesday the 29th November, 1967.

It is also agreed that the aircraft will be delivered three (3) at a time,
and that part delivery will be accepted in each stage, unless prior
agreement is received from the buyer to deliver in larger groups.

It is also agreed that a Letter of Credit will be at our Bank on
Wednesday the 29th November, 1967. for the sum of U.S. $144,000. that
being the total amount in full, stating that part delivery is acceptable.

It is also agreed that the above prices include the following equipment:-

                    a.)     VOR RADIO.
                    b.)     12 CHANNEL MARCO.
                    c.)     4-.50 MACHINE GUNS.
                    d.)     EXTERNAL BOMB RACKS.

It is also agreed that if the first delivery is not made on the above
stated date, this contract and Letter of Credit are deemed cancelled.

This contract is subject to the aproval of the Quartermaster General.


SIGNED ON BEHALF OF THE BUYER.          SIGNED ON BEHALF OF THE SELLER.


A. OKWESA.                              A. PARIS.
```

228: Through intermediaries, the Biafran Air Force purchased twelve T-6G Texans from French sources at the end of 1967. By March 1968 they had been shipped from France to Lisbon and stored beside a wharf in Lisbon's dock area. This view was taken shortly afterwards and shows the twelve dismantled aircraft. In the foreground is 114873 which was one of the few to later be delivered to Biafra (Luis A. Tavares)

229: During the winter of 1968 a Blackbushe-based group attempted to sell six ex-RAF Provost T.1 aircraft to Biafra. The aircraft were initially registered to Target Towing Aircraft Ltd, the same company which later attempted to deliver several Meteors to Biafra. HM Customs & Excise became concerned about the group's intentions and physically removed the starter motors from each of the aircraft. Subsequently the Provosts, which had been moved from Blackbushe to Fairoaks, were dismantled and re-sold, eventually finding their way to the Rhodesian Air Force after Biafra had collapsed. None of the aircraft ever carried their UK registrations and only on WV540, seen here at Fairoaks, was there any attempt made to cover the British military markings (David Pope)

230: The Biafran Air Force was reformed during mid-1969 with the acquisition of five MFI-9Bs from Swedish sources. All were purchased on the premise of being bought for a Flying School in Tanzania. Three of them (SE-EUE, SE-EUN and SE-EWF) were in fact acquired from the manufacturer and are seen here in Gabon awaiting re-assembly. Note the beer bottles on the rear fuselage of the nearest machine (Pierre Mens)

and on 3 January 1969 the aircraft were re-registered to their new owner. Mather, a former engineer with ACE Freighters, had been invited to join the group to help re-assemble the aircraft overseas but it is likely that he signed Board of Trade documents indicating a change of ownership without realising the full implications. Whatever the case, it helped to cover the fact that Osborne's 'Target Towing Aircraft' team was meeting with Gunter Meisner, President of the so-called International Association for The Promotion of Arts and Sciences, based in Berlin. Meisner later admitted that he was purchasing the Provosts on behalf of the Biafrans, but unfortunately he was never quite sure as to who legally owned the aircraft and, worse still, exactly who was representing the owner. Nor did he realise that H.M. Customs & Excise had already shown more than a passing interest in their movements. In the event the aircraft were allegedly sold for cash twice, the respective deals being agreed at exactly the same time but to different buyers and at different venues. Even so Meisner reportedly paid between £3,500-£4,000 for the Provosts but because of actions taken by British Customs he was unable to move them out of the country.

The administrative side of the deal was allowed to be completed when the C.A.A. cancelled all six registrations, on 24 March 1969, on their 'sale to Germany'. At the same time most of the team involved in the Provost deal flew out to Portugal in March 1969 having been contracted to ferry a pair of ex-Luftwaffe C-47s from Faro to Biafra.

Had everything gone smoothly and to plan none of the Provosts were ever likely to have reached Germany. It had been intended to ferry all six aircraft from Fairoaks to Cherbourg from where, after being dismantled, they were to be shipped to Lisbon and then flown to Faro for the fitment of weapons. Armament was to consist of a machine-gun pack fitted to each of the aircraft's fixed-undercarriage legs.

Ultimately Gunter Meisner was forced to sell the six Provosts for scrap and all passed to a West London aircraft dealer, reportedly for a total sum of £210. They were subsequently dismantled at Fairoaks, crated, and placed into storage at a warehouse in Kilburn, west London. Meisner proved to be the loser as, of course, so did the Biafrans. The real winner in the Provost deal was the Rhodesian Air Force which eventually received the six aircraft in 1973 via a complex and circuitous shipping route, designed to avoid export sanctions which were in force at the time.[368]

The MFI-9B 'Minicons'

Count Gustav von Rosen always considered that a small two-seat training aircraft built by Malmö Flyg Industri (MFI), a subsidiary of SAAB, under the designation MFI-9B, would ideally meet a Counter-Insurgency (COIN) role in the Biafran bush. In fact the MFI-9B, which had been dubbed 'Mili-trainer' by the manufacturer, was essentially a version of the standard MFI-9 but with a strengthened wing-structure to permit the insertion of two hardpoints for military stores. Apart from an evaluation batch of ten for the Swedish *Flyg apen* (under the service designation Sk.80) the military market had failed to be attracted to the SAAB MFI-9B. Nevertheless the structural features were incorporated into the standard MFI-9B of which over forty had been sold to civilian customers. The evaluation batch had since been returned to the manufacturer and stored; availability of suitable aircraft was therefore not an issue. Furthermore, as the MFI-9B was considered to be a civil aeroplane, there appeared to be little threat of contravening Sweden's export licensing laws.

The first approach to Malmö Flyg Industrie was made, not by von Rosen, but by the Tanzanian embassy in Stockholm. Embassy officials enquired about the suitability of the MFI-9B as a training aeroplane for what was apparently planned as a Government-sponsored flying school in Tanzania. The ambassador also let it be known that the proposed flying-club was seeking suitably-experienced flying instructors. (There was, of course, no reason to link the purchase of aircraft that had initially been designed as a military aircraft with the fact that Tanzania was one of the few African countries to have formally recognised Biafra.)

Another report suggested that a former Swedish pilot, and doctor in Rome, Dr Solve Webster, was planning to establish an Italian-based company known as Aircraft Lease Company for the hiring of aircraft for use in ore-prospecting.[369] The same report states that a deal, involving five MFI-9B aircraft and spares, amounting to a total cost of $60,000 (£21,000), was finalised in a Zurich bank between Rudolph Abelen, the head of MFI, and an unnamed Tanzanian. (The total cost of refitting, plus the salaries of the Swedish pilots and technicians apparently cost Biafra a further $140,000).[370]

Five MFI-9B trainers were flown from Sweden to the French airfield of Toussus-le-Noble; they staged through Rotterdam on 26 and 27 April 1969 and all carried Swedish civilian registrations: SE-EUE, SE-EUL, SE-EUN, SE-EWE and SE-EWF. The ferry pilots were all Swedish nationals and whose job simply involved flying the aircraft to Toussus; only one of the Swedes, an engineer named Per Hazelius, remained with the aircraft in France. Hazelius had been retained by the group to re-assemble the aircraft '"in Tanzania" but when one of the MFI-9Bs was flown to a French military base near the Atlantic coast for 'testing' his suspicions were apparently aroused. Nevertheless he elected to remain with the group.

The MFI-9B selected for 'testing' was reportedly measured by French Air Force technicians for underwing rocket fittings and for the aircraft's electrical system to be changed from 12-volt to 24-volt. In the event no armament was actually fitted and the MFI-9B was returned to Toussus-le-Noble where it, and the other four, were dismantled, crated, and then air-freighted from Le Bourget to Libreville, Gabon aboard two Air Fret L-1049G Super Constellations.[371]

Together with two Swedish technicians, Bengt Weithz and Sigvard Torsten Nilsson, a second group of Swedish pilots left Sweden on 10 May 1969 and had flown ahead to Libreville direct. This group consisted of the project leader, Count Gustav von Rosen, Martin Valdemar Lang and Gunnar Haglund. When the MFI-9Bs arrived in Gabon they were immediately taken to a bush strip just south-east of Libreville (a strip referred to by the Group as 'Camp I') where each aircraft was re-assembled and fitted with two underwing French-made rocket pods, each pod capable of carrying six 68mm Matra rockets. The aircraft were also repainted in an overall two-tone green camouflage scheme, fitted with an auxilary fuel-tank in the cockpit's right-hand seat, and test-flown.

It was at this point that the Swedish engineer Per Hazelius realised that there never had been any intention to form a flying school in Tanzania, (even though von Rosen had allegedly advised Hazelius that the proposed 'flying school' had temporarily moved to Gabon). He promptly left the group and returned to Sweden. But joining the group in the Gabon bush were two Biafran pilots, Augustus Okpe and Willy Murray-Bruce, both of whom were experienced pilots with the Biafran Air Force. Both had originally been with the Biafran Helicopter Squadron at Udi and until their arrival at 'Camp I' were employed on the Biafran Government airlift from Faro to Uli.[372]

The flight to Biafra

Within a month of leaving Sweden the five civilian-registered MFI-9Bs were armed, repainted in an overall camouflage finish and made ready for delivery into Biafra. On 20 May 1969 the Swedes were officially accepted by the Biafran Air Force. Von Rosen was given the rank of Wing Commander, Martin Lang became a Captain while Gunnar Haglund became a Flight Lieutenant.

As part of the final preparation the three Swedish pilots were flown into Biafra to spend a day inspecting several secret airstrips already selected and prepared for operations. They then flew immediately back to Libreville. The final leg, from Gabon to Biafra, took place in daylight on Thursday 22 May 1969.

Before departing from Gabon each MFI-9B was given a final test-flight and then allocated (on a semi-permanent basis) to the five pilots. Mechanics made a final check of each aircraft. Rocket pods were checked and the firing systems checked again. Each pilot was issued with a pack of biscuits and a large bottle containing drinking water. The air temperature at ground level was 35°C. The aircraft were heavy with additional fuel and full weapon load.

All five MFI-9Bs flew a line-astern formation with von Rosen in the lead aircraft. Martin Lang took the number two position, followed by Gunnar Haglund and the two Biafrans. Willy Bruce brought up the rear slot. The strategy was to maintain a flight-level of 500ft until reaching the Nigerian coastline from where they would then fly even lower. Occasionally, von Rosen gave short and concise instructions in Swedish; Gunnar Haglund relayed the message in English to Okpe and Bruce. Apart from several very short instructions the five pilots maintained radio silence throughout. But as the Nigerian coastline approached Willy Bruce broke silence and began to broadcast a concern that his aircraft was slowing up. The others ignored his concerns. Okpe tried to stop Bruce, who was by now clearly displaying frayed nerves, from transmitting and possibly giving up the element of surprise. Then, just to the south of Port Harcourt, the lead aircraft began to enter a small but intensive rainstorm. The forward formation closed up and von Rosen radioed back to advise the two Biafran pilots on how wide the rain belt was.

By the time that the three lead aircraft crossed the Nigerian coast they were again flying in clear sunlight. The beaches were deserted and peaceful. They flew northwards towards Port Harcourt and then turned due east to attack the town's airfield. The five aircraft had by now effectively become two groups, some 5-10 minutes apart. The lead group began to attack the airfield at 14:05, just over three hours after taking-off from Gabon.

The MFI-9Bs spent about ten minutes attacking Port Harcourt. The first run was in line astern; then von Rosen radioed an instruction to attack the control tower. Rockets were fired from two MFI-9Bs at the tower and towards the hangar immediately behind the tower. Gunnar Haglund and Martin Lang then reformed as a pair, joined with von Rosen, and all three turned north towards Biafra. South of Owerri, and safely over Biafran territory, von Rosen radioed the two Biafran pilots. Okpe replied that he was following behind and that he too had successfully rocketed Port Harcourt airfield. There was no call from Willy Bruce.

In fact, when Bruce flew through the low belt of raincloud he had inadvertently made a gradual turn and emerged to an open sky. He had lost sight of the others. Still extremely nervous and feeling increasingly agitated, his primary concern began to turn towards his fuel supply. The planned time-over-target had always been a critical factor and quite simply he was now scared of running-out of fuel. Therefore, instead of attacking Port Harcourt, Bruce flew on to locate Uli where, despite having become temporarily lost, he was the first of the group to land.

The main force of four MFI-9Bs landed, as planned, at the Biafran Air Force's new base at 'Camp II', adjacent to Biafra's secondary airstrip at Uga. It was much later in the day that the Swedes learnt of Willy Bruce's disorientation but that he was safe and well.[373]

231: At 60-years old, the Swedish adventurer, Count Gustav von Rosen, displayed no sign of taking life easier. His involvement in Biafra's fortunes was purely idealistic. He even claims to have managed the acquisition of the MFI-9Bs personally. Von Rosen also helped to train two of the Biafran pilots selected to fly with the MFI-9B Squadron. Their conversion was carried out at 'Camp 1' where von Rosen is seen in this view (Pierre Mens)

232: Shortly after their arrival and re-assembly in Gabon, all five MFI-9Bs were repainted by hand in an overall gloss camouflage scheme using locally purchased Valspar paints. Martin Lang, one of the Swedish pilots, adds the second colour to an unidentified MFI-9B at the secret base south-east of Libreville. The base became known within the group as 'Camp I' (Gunnar Haglund, via Freddy Stenbom.)

233: During their working-up period at 'Camp I' the MFI-9Bs were fitted with two underwing rocket pods, each of which contained six 68mm SNEB rockets. No special work was required as the MFI-9B was designed with built-in hard-points. Note how even the propellor has been crudely camouflaged. No national markings or visible external serial identites were applied at this early stage although immediately prior to departure for Biafra each pilot personally marked his aircraft with a minute identity (Pierre Mens)

234: When the Biafran MFI-9Bs targeted Enugu airport late on 26 May 1969 four aircraft attacked in two pairs. Martin Lang's aircraft sustained damage from Nigerian defensive small-arms fire as well as striking trees during his first run across the target. The aircraft returned to base safely. Damage to the rear fuselage is clearly evident in this view, as is a Biafran roundel, presumably coloured red, black and green. How many MFI-9Bs were given roundels is not known. At least one source claims the camouflage pattern matches that applied to MFI-9B SE-EUL, c/n 53 (Gunnar Haglund, via Freddy Stenbom.)

223

The flight from Gabon to Uli, including the hit-and-run rocket attack against Port Harcourt airfield, had taken almost $3^{1}/_{2}$ hours. The attack had not only taken the Nigerians by complete surprise but several aircraft on the ground had been damaged. The attackers claimed damage to two MiG-17Fs and two Ilyushin 28s, although subsequent reports from the Federal Nigerian Air Force suggested that all apart from one MiG-17F were later repaired - if indeed they were hit at all. One MiG-17F was certainly damaged beyond repair by the MFI-9Bs; this was NAF620 which had been collected from Kano just two days previously.

The Nigerian MiG-17F Detachment at Port Harcourt reacted immediately after the Biafran attack. At least one MiG-17F, NAF617 flown by Ares Klootwyk, was scrambled for a reconnaissance sortie to cover the areas of Owerri and Aba in the belief that secret Biafran bush strips were located somewhere along that line. But Klootwyk failed to find any sign of the Biafran airstrips. In fact it was to take a week before the Nigerian Air Force discovered the location of any of the Biafran Air Force MFI-9B bases.

Biafran Babies fight back

News of the attack against Port Harcourt was immediately flashed around the world. The squadron of MFI-9Bs became dubbed by the world's press as the 'Biafran Babies'; they were also termed as 'Minicons', the origin of which has never been fully explained but is thought to have been a corruption of the *intended* 'Mini-Coin', a phrase implying '**mini**ature **co**unter-**in**surgency aircraft'.

Two days after their arrival in Biafra, on Saturday 24 May 1969, four Biafran MFI-9Bs carried out a second attack. This time the target was the airfield at Benin, base airfield for MiG-17Fs and the infamous 'Intruder' bomber. The aircraft were flown by von Rosen, Lang, Haglund and Augustus Okpe; Willy Bruce was not included.

Take-off from their Biafran base was in pre-dawn darkness, so timed as to surprise the Nigerians at first light. The four attackers divided into two pairs for the attack. Lang and Haglund attacked from the west while the other two attacked from the east. Von Rosen's 'Minicon' suffered a malfunction in its firing mechanism, probably a temporary electrical snag, which prevented him firing any rockets. Martin Lang attacked an anti-aircraft position on the airfield's western boundary as well as the control tower, before the group turned for home.

The return flight from Benin almost ended in disaster. Several of the aircraft were low on fuel when they crossed back into Biafra. An added problem was that the base strip proved to be so well camouflaged that at least two of the pilots had trouble in locating it. Von Rosen's electrical fault extended to the radio and virtually prohibited the group leader from guiding his men back to base. Then,

and after circling for some time trying to locate the strip, one of the pilots saw a strip and landed. The others saw him landing and followed. The strip had been found more by luck than judgement, and all four landed safely. In fact it is believed that the strip at which the attackers landed was not the same as that from which they had taken off from earlier; this was a strip which became 'Camp III'.

A Nigerian Air Force MiG-17F was said to have been destroyed on the ground at Benin as was a DC-4. The latter was the Pan African Airlines DC-4, N9982H, which had been unserviceable since 6 March 1969 with a damaged nosewheel and engines, and had been declared a write-off since the Biafran Air Force had earlier attacked Port Harcourt on 22 May. Pan African did later admit the loss of N9982H.) Reports from Lagos added that six people were killed in the raid and eight more had been injured. Some superficial damage was sustained by airport buildings.[374]

There was no grand plan for systematic air attacks by the 'Minicons' and each target was selected individually. With Port Harcourt and Benin successfully attacked, the next obvious target was Enugu. The former Biafran capital, Enugu was now one of the Nigerian Air Force's 1st Bomber Squadron's three bases. The decision to attack Enugu airfield was taken the day after the Benin raid. The attack was calculated to coincide with dusk on Monday 26 May.

Willy Bruce was still showing signs of 'battle stress' and so the Enugu raid was again carried out by just four 'Minicons'.[375] The plan to attack Enugu airfield involved two groups of two aircraft. Each pair would attack the airfield from opposite directions–as had been the case at Benin. All four would, however, initially approach from the west, ie out of the sun. Von Rosen and Okpe would attack the eastern side and then turn north while Haglund and Lang would hit the western side of the airfield and then turn south. In their escape both groups were to take advantage of hilly areas surrounding Enugu. That was the plan but the raid did not go fully to plan.

All four 'Minicons' took off from their Biafran base at 16:00 hours. They flew due west across the Niger, then turned due north until reaching the same parallel as Enugu. A ninty-degree turn to the right brought them directly in line for an approach to Enugu from the west. The final approach was at extremely low-level. As he crossed the airfield boundary Gunnar Haglund believes that he saw a MiG-17F preparing for take-off. He fired almost all of his rockets at the MiG. Most of the rockets struck the ground close to the Nigerian jet but he doubted that any actually hit it. It was certainly hidden in the smoke from exploding rockets and possibly damaged by debris. Haglund admits that he concentrated for too long on the state of the MiG-17F, a mistake that caused his starboard wing to hit a small bush. The 'Minicon' received a major jolt but sustained little damage.

Haglund fired off his remaining rockets at the Terminal building and then set course for base. Martin Lang's aircraft, hit by defensive small-arms fire at the end of his first attacking run, had also suffered damage after it had struck trees, causing leaves to partially block the engine air intake. He took a direct course back to base. Okpe and von Rosen flew back to base (at 'Camp II') together following the same route as taken on the inbound run while Haglund flew a wider arc to the north. He met up with his two comrades on the approach to base but then lost them in the darkness. With his fuel gauge reading empty, Haglund broke radio silence and called for lights at Uga strip to be briefly turned on. This allowed him to take a bearing to 'Camp II' where he landed safely.

In reality, the Enugu raid had been a fiasco and almost ended in disaster. Although the element of surprise was successfully achieved and another Ilyushin Il-28 was claimed as destroyed, the Biafrans failed to hit anything other than the hulk of a former Biafran Air Force B-26R Invader and the DH.114 Heron VP-WAM which had also been previously wrecked and discarded. Two 'Minicons' had sustained minor damage in the raid and again the landing back at Base had caused enormous difficulties. For several days the Biafran Air Force rested while improved lighting and landing procedures were worked out. Sundry repairs to two MFI-9Bs were also required.

Since the Biafran attack against Port Harcourt on 22 May 1969, the Nigerian Air force had spent each day searching for the Biafran Air Force MFI-9B base. Suspected areas had been photographed from the air but it was not until 29 May 1969 that Nigerian MiG-17Fs found and successfully strafed one of the Biafran bases.[376] One MiG-17F sortie confirmed that the target was, in fact, a 'Minicon' base; a second sortie 20 minutes later saw another MiG-17F attack the same strip. In the attack the squadron's chauffeur was killed and nine others were injured.

The strip attacked by the MiG-17Fs contained just two 'Minicons'; the other three were at Camp II. Neither aircraft was damaged despite the MiG-17Fs strafing with 37mm cannon fire and dropping 100kg 'splinter' bombs. As if to underline this, the Biafran Air Force carried out a daring dusk attack against the power station at Ughelli, in the Mid-West Region, later on the same date.

The Ughelli raid called for four 'Minicons' to attack; three from Camp II flown by von Rosen, Lang and Haglund and a fourth, flown by Okpe, which would operate from the other strip, the strip earlier attacked by Nigerian MiG-17Fs. The group intended to rendezvous over a village en route but not until the main group of three were circling and waiting for Okpe did von Rosen learn that due to technical difficulties Okpe had not taken off. Thus only three 'Minicons' took part in the Ughelli attack.

The attacking group arrived over their target at 18:45. It had been intended that two groups of two would attack from opposite directions in the same manner as had been performed previously. As they approached the power station it looked different to how they had expected and a change of attack profile saw all three aircraft make a very low-level line astern attack. Each pilot released a salvo of rockets immediately after the aircraft in front had fired and turned away. Von Rosen and Lang attacked as planned and Haglund followed. Unsure how many rockets he had fired, Haglund then claims to have made a second approach and fired two more rockets into the complex. It later transpired that the power station did sustain damage and was unable to operate for two/three weeks although some reports suggest that it was up to six months before power was fully restored.

A new type of target

Until the Ughelli attack the Biafran Air Force 'Minicons' squadron had specifically targeted the Nigerian Air Force. Ughelli was a considered a legitimate target as it was the primary source of power that served Benin airport, the base from which the DC-3 'Intruder' bomber operated. However, 30 May 1969 was Biafran National Day and it signalled a major change in target selection.

For some time Biafran soldiers had surrounded a Nigerian force in Owerri. The Nigerians were well dug in and could not be dislodged. The 'Minicons' were therefore brought in to support Biafran ground troops. The pilots were specifically briefed by Biafran Army officers who outlined the importance of securing the objective. The plan was again very simplistic. Four aircraft would fly in two pairs towards Owerri but fly westwards to Obigwe; then south before turning through 180° and attacking the Nigerian force from the south. The two pairs would then fly separately over different roads out of the area and shoot-up any opportunity target that may be seen. Each pilot was briefed to divide the number of rockets equally the known enemy position and opportunity targets. The Biafran Army would then make their main ground thrust. That was the plan...

The four 'Minicons' took-off in order to reach their target by 17:00 hours. Everything went to plan until they reached the target. Von Rosen and Martin Lang were flying ahead of Augustus Okpe and Gunnar Haglund; all four at extremely low-level. The lead pair had difficulty finding the enemy position and so both climbed to approximately 300ft and began circling. At the same time Von Rosen and Lang constantly radioed each other, one asking the other if either could see the target. Okpe and Haglund also circled but at tree-top level. None of the pilots saw any sign of Nigerian positions, nor were there any opportunity targets, and so the group returned home without firing a rocket. Biafra's National Day celebrations were a little sombre.

235: One of the ex-Swedish MFI-9B 'Minicons' is positioned within its dispersal bay at Uga strip during the final month of the war. The starboard MATRA rocket-launcher pod is clearly visible beneath the wing. The simplistic overall two-tone camouflage scheme suited well the operational conditions of Biafran bush strips. Biafran Air Force Officer, Johnny Chuco, stands beside his aircraft as minor attention to the cockpit is carried out (A. Alves Pereira)

236: A Biafran Air Force MFI-9B 'Minicon' in its bush clearing beside Uga strip. This view shows well the positioning of the underwing rocket pods (A. Alves Pereira)

237: When this picture of a battle-weary MFI-9B was first published it was believed to be carrying the serial BB-903. However, closer examination suggests that it could be BB-103 and that part of the serial is hidden where the fuselage panelling has been forced apart. The damage was caused by two MiG-17Fs in a strafing attack against the Biafran strip at Ozubulu on 29 November 1969 (Karl Bruno Ljungberg, via Freddy Stenbom)

During the course of the following day the Biafran Army visited Biafran Air Force HQ to de-brief the pilots. The Army officers reported that all the time the four 'Minicons' had been circling the Nigerian ground forces were firing constantly and using a variety of weapons. It was, everybody agreed, amazing good fortune that any of the four aircraft returned to base in one piece.

The night after the Owerri raid, the three Swedish pilots left Biafra to return to Sweden. Two Swedish support technicians, Sigvard Nilsson and Bengt Weithz also returned. Ironically, it was while travelling back that news broke of the shooting-down of a Swedish Red Cross DC-7B. At the time it was reported by Lagos that the incident was in direct retaliation for the Biafran 'Minicon' raids.

One other Swede was hired for Biafran Air Force 'Minicon' operations. A former Swedish Air Force pilot, Rune Norgren arrived as his Swedish compatriots were returning home. He flew some missions but did not appear to stay in Biafra for too long.[377]

During July 1969 Rune Norgren is credited with carrying out 21 attacks, mostly against front-line positions in support of the Biafran Army. Ground attacks were divided between the northern front (ie north of Onitsha) and the southern front, to the south of Owerri. Norgren was also something of a loner; many of these sorties were solo efforts although Biafra's only other competent 'Minicon' pilot at that time, Augustus Okpe, flew occasionally as Norgren's wing-man. In fact Norgren's first mission in Biafra was alongside Okpe. Two 'Minicons' took off from Base, headed for Orlu and then headed south towards Owerri and on to Obigwe. The Biafran Army had laid out ground locater markers to indicate the target, an enemy concentration and a large house thought to be used as an ammunition store. Okpe attacked from the west; Norgren from the east. But as the two aircraft turned for home they experienced anti-aircraft fire from positions believed to be under Biafran control. In fact what Norgren had flown through was so-called 'friendly-fire'. It subsequently transpired that the Biafran Army had not been advised by the Biafran Air Force that the raid was imminent. A signal had been sent but the message had not reached the front.

Both pilots returned to the same target the next day. This time they were successful in rocketing the Nigerian ammunition store on their second run over the target. The explosion was considerable and nearly caught Norgren's aircraft. As a result of the confusion caused by the second 'Minicon' sortie the Biafran Army was able to take advantage of the situation and capture the village.

More MFI-9B 'Minicons' arrive

During August 1969 the Biafran MFI-9B force was supplemented by four more examples. Three of the four (SE-EUB, SE-EUP and SE-EWB) had gathered at Copenhagen, from where they departed on 21 July while the fourth (SE-EFU) flew from Skovlunde on 22 July; all four later staged through Rotterdam on 23 July, en route to France from where, like their five predecessors, they would be air-freighted to Libreville.

According to contemporary press reports the four additional aircraft had been purchased, on behalf of the Abidjan Flying Club, by an unnamed African. One of those who had sold an MFI-9B was a Dr Arne Nyholm who negotiated the sale of SE-EWB (c/n 47) on behalf of the Karlskoga Flying Club. Nyholm is reported to have been paid 60,000 Swedish kroners (£4,888) for the aircraft, some 7,000kroners (£566) more than the Flying Club had paid out for it just several months beforehand.[378]

After the second batch of MFI-9Bs had been acquired from Swedish sources all further attempts to secure MFI-9Bs were blocked by the Swedish authorities even though, in Sweden at least, von Rosen had become a figure of almost folklore-reputation. The Swedish press described the Biafran War as 'Von Rosen's Holiday War' in view of his taking summer leave from his airline job to participate. But the entire MFI-9B episode had gained worldwide publicity and had become an embarrassment to the traditionally neutral Swedish government.

Whether or not all four of the second batch were flown into Biafra remains unrecorded. Several were kept in Gabon for basic and refresher training purposes. What is clear is that the Biafran Air Force allotted serial numbers to the MFI-9Bs but not in a straightforward fashion. From contemporary photographs two batches of serials appear to have been allocated. One series ran consecutively from BB101 to BB105; the other was in the BB90x range. Of the latter, BB903, BB905 and BB909 can be confirmed. If the 'missing' serial is logically BB907 then that may explain why some contemporary reports spoke of fourteen Minicons, ie five plus nine, operating in Biafra.

The Biafran identities were applied to the fuselage side just aft of the cockpit canopy and adjacent to a Biafran national insignia. It is likely that each aircraft also had the serial repeated on the underside of the wing–one of them certainly did. The precise meaning of the serial prefix 'BB' is likely to have been a reference to the 'Biafran Babies' by which these MFI-9Bs had become affectionately known.

Biafran MFI-9B operations continued throughout August and September 1969, principally from their original 'Camp II' base but also from a second base some two miles south of Uga, close to the junction village of Urualla. On the same road as Uga, this second base became known as 'Camp III'. Two other Forward Strips were later constructed, using strips adjacent to roads; one on the same road as Biafra's main Uli strip, but lying to the north between Okija and Ozubulu, the other situated in the east of Biafra at Mbawsi, just south of Umuahia.[379]

The Gabon Training School

The is little doubt that while von Rosen and his Swedish team had re-established a capable Air Force element the Biafran High Command, rather than rely upon Europeans, preferred to have its own pilots operating live missions. There were a number of *Ibo* pilots available, all loyal to the Biafran cause and, most of whom, had previously been with Nigeria Airways or the Nigerian Air Force. Few however held a command status and none were trained fighter pilots. The need for basic and continuation training was of paramount importance if von Rosen's 'Minicon' operation was to succeed.

With the departure of Martin Lang, Gunnar Haglund, Rune Norgren and the support personnel the Biafran Air Force was effectively left with just one pilot, Augustus Okpe. Von Rosen returned to Biafra in August 1969 to supervise pilot selection and training. A Training School was set up in Gabon, at the original 'Camp I' with MFI-9Bs from the second batch of four aircraft. Two Swedish instructors, Kristian Kristensen and Nils Holmer, also arrived at 'Camp I' in August 1969 to establish the first pilot course. One other Swede, Karl-Bruno Ljungberg–a former Swedish Air Force pilot and a SAAB Design Office executive–arrived at 'Camp I' in August 1969. Ljungberg's role was effectively Biafra's Chief Technical Officer but he did undertake some operational instruction flying live sorties in Biafra, as did Nils Holmer for a brief period.

The initial group of pilots to be trained by Kristian Kristensen consisted of four Biafrans and included two of the original pilots, Augustus Okpe and Willy Bruce. A third, identified only as Goody, was deemed to be one of Biafra's most competent pilots but a fourth failed to reach an acceptable standard.

Two more groups of Biafran pilots were trained during late-August and September 1969. Some had been receiving flying-training elsewhere in Europe pending delivery of various other aircraft, the majority of which never materialised. If there was a preference it was to have aircraft flown by half-trained pilots rather than fully-trained pilots but no aircraft.

Initial training in Gabon involved an MFI-9B conversion course, basic daylight tactical flying skills and rocket-firing practice. With this part of the programme completed pilots were then flown into Biafra for operational flight training and which involved live sorties. A second course in Gabon took pilots on through basic Instrument Flying and Night Flying skills. Only after that course were pilots then declared fully fit for active combat in Biafra.

By the end of September the Biafran Air Force could boast ten fully-trained pilots, nine of whom were Biafrans. The exception was the German, Friedrich Herz, who had returned to operational flying in Biafra after a break of almost two years, since the loss of the Biafran B-25s in December 1967.

'Minicon' attacks continue

During October 1969 Biafran 'Minicon' activity was significantly stepped up. The operation was by now divided into two separate units, 45 Squadron and 47 Squadron. Neither unit could be described as being of standard squadron strength and at best could only offer two or perhaps three serviceable aircraft at any one time.

The Biafran Air Force Command described a sortie against Benin airfield, on 10 October 1969, as one of its most effective yet. The claim was undoubtedly erroneous but there is no doubt that a raid on Benin did take place. It involved four MFI-9Bs, flown by Friedrich Herz and three Biafrans, Ibi, Alex and Benny. The Biafrans attacked initially from the north and all four aircraft made several passes before turning for home. Biafran claims included the destruction of a DC-4, at least one MiG-17F, an arms dump, a navigation beacon, sundry vehicles and the deaths of 28 men including the Chief of Nigeria's Air Force. The DC-4 was undoubtedly the hulk of N9982H which had been the subject of a Biafran 'Minicon' attack nearly five months previously.

Whatever the true facts of the Benin raid were, some injuries did undoubtedly take place. While the Biafran Air Force was attacking the airfield a Nigeria Airways F-27, 5N-AAY, flying the late-running scheduled service WT120 from Lagos, was about 10-15 minutes out. The crew called Benin Tower for landing clearance but received no answer. Having already flown over a Non-Directional Beacon which was not working the F-27 crew simply presumed an electrical failure had hit the area and that that was also the reason for Benin Tower not responding to their calls. (For that period, it was a normal situation in West Africa.) Flying the F-27 on that day was a Dutchman, Captain Fred Gacobs and a British First Officer, Jim Leahy. Neither had any reason to be concerned and so continued the approach for landing. Then, a frantic late call was transmitted from Benin's Air Traffic Controller; he simply ordered the Nigerian F-27 to "get out, get out, get out!" Thankfully, the crew had already switched on the water-methanol mix as per a company instruction when operating to the former Eastern Region. The additional power that it gave to the two engines was astonishing. The F-27 climbed steeply, was immediately turned around and flown directly back to Lagos. Neither pilot knew it at the time but the reason for the Tower not responding to their initial calls was because the Air Traffic Controller was lying on the floor of the Tower with both ankles badly injured. He had heard the F-27 crew report their position but, not unnaturally, had experienced considerable difficulty in reaching for the transmitter. In fact, the MFI-9Bs were still shooting up Benin as

238, 239: *Just before Count Gustav von Rosen brought his SAAB MFI-9B force into Biafra he flew in to inspect several possible airstrip bases on 13/14 May 1969. The first of these was located just to the north of Uga strip and consisted of a length of asphalt road. After being selected it became known in Biafra as 'Camp II'. In these two views the strip is seen as first inspected by von Rosen and Lang in company with the prospective Base Commander and two Biafran officers. The long (early morning) shadows suggest that this view is facing north-west which 'Camp II' and Uga certainly did. (In fact this strip may even be Uga!) The attempt at camouflaging the landing-area with palm fronds is fairly rudimentary and was not too successful. The second view purports to illustrate the same strip after the camouflage was improved. In fact in the lower view there are at least two men walking along the strip, neither of whom are clearly visible (Gunnar Haglund, via Freddy Stenbom)*

240: *A second batch of MFI-9Bs was acquired by the Biafran Air Force during July 1969; like their predecessors all originated from Swedish sources, via France. The additional four aircraft allowed the formation of a second squadron and it was possibly these aircraft which received Biafran serials within the BB-9xx sequence. In this view a badly-damaged BB-905 is seen on the Lagos dump at the end of the war after it was conveyed back from former Biafra by road. Just barely visible is a 'painted-out' Biafran flag forward of the serial (Confidential Source)*

the F-27 was preparing to join 'long finals'. For the F-27 it was a lucky escape.[380]

Nigeria's oil installation became the focus of several Biafran attacks. On 14 October 1969 four 'Minicons' attacked the Mobil installation at Sapele and set alight one of the petroleum storage tanks. The same aircraft also attacked the dock area and hit the mv *Freetown* which was waiting to sail to Hull and on to Hamburg. On the evening of 30 October three aircraft raided the Shell-BP storage facility at Forcados. On that occasion the Biafrans were specifically targeting a new offshore oil export terminal but they failed to locate it on the first run. A Dutch-registered tanker, *Niso* was rocketed and holed in several places above the waterline. A second tanker was slightly damaged as were some service barges moored offshore at the new Terminal. One of the barges was sunk and several men suffered slight injuries but no serious damage was inflicted.

One hazard that faced Biafran pilots was an attempt by the Nigerians to interfere with (or even jam) Biafran radio frequencies. On several occasions 'Minicon' raids were frustrated by the inability to call base. The source of the interference was a transmitter set up by the Nigerians at Mbiama, north-west of Port Harcourt. Two 'Minicons' were detailed to attack the radio station on 25 October. The attack, led by Friedrich Herz, proved successful; the transmitter was located and destroyed. Sorties after that date were rarely interrupted by enemy radio interference.

Notes

Note 363 According to Simon Hare, in an interview with the author on 13 August 1973, Établissements Gaudet (or Godet) purchased 24 T-6Gs from this batch but that only twelve were involved in the Biafran deal. It is also reported that a number of T-6Gs were stored at Rochfort La Rochelle at the time and this may have related to the same aircraft.

Note 364 Private papers of Alex Rumley

Note 365 The author was involved in such plans in São Tomé in August 1968

Note 366 Osborne had previously purchased an ex-RAF Anson 19 (TX166) and had it registered to his wife, Lesley A. Osborne, on 25 July 1968 as G-AWML, and in an effort to gain a full Certificate of Airworthiness had freely offered his services (as well as the Anson) to Mercy Missions in return for the funding of a C of A. Despite Osborne applying a charitable legend along the fuselage 'Biafra–Save The Children' the Mercy Missions team turned down his offer in the knowledge that Osborne had no real intention ever to fly the aircraft to Biafra.

Note 367 Von Rosen made the announcement at the International Biafran Aid Conference in New York during December 1968.

Note 368 These details first appeared in *Roundel*, bi-monthly historical journal published by the British Aviation Research Group.

Note 369 *Sunday Times*, 1 June 1969.

Note 370 *The New Mercenaries* by Anthony Mockler; published by Sidgwick & Jackson 1985.

Note 371 One of the aircraft was F-BRAD; the other is thought to have been F-BRNH.

Note 372 Interview between Willy Murray-Bruce and the author

Note 373 Interview between Willy Murray-Bruce and the author

Note 374 Interview between Keith Sissons and the author

Note 375 Interview between Willy Murray-Bruce and the author

Note 376 As related to the author by MiG-17F pilots based at Port Harcourt at the time.

Note 377 This and many other facts relating to MFI-9B operations in Biafra first appeared in *Gerillapilot I Biafra* by Gunnar Haglund, published in Sweden by Allt om Hobby 1988.

Note 378 *Sunday Times*, 27 July 1969.

Note 379 It is possible that the Mbawi strip was already in existence as a landing-strip was known to be in the Umuahia area when the town was Ojukwu's headquarters in autumn 1968.

Note 380: As related to the author by Jim Leahy; other details from Flying Log-books

241: There is no doubt that the two Meteor TT.20s SE-DCF and SE-DCH were en route to Faro when they landed at Charleroi, Belgium. Their owner, Herbert Berg, had signed both aircraft over to Target Towing Aircraft Ltd, the same company that had been involved in despatching two Meteor NF.14s from Britain to Portugal. After Interpol had alerted European forces, both of the Swedish Meteors were grounded and they eventually were abandoned in Belgium (Unknown)

THE METEOR JOB

Britain, as far as the Nigerian civil war was concerned, faced a dichotomy. From a political viewpoint, the British government under Labour Prime Minister, Harold Wilson, was unquestionably aligned with the Federal Nigerian government in Lagos. The British public, on the other hand, felt increasingly compelled to encourage and support action that helped to stem the starvation raging within Biafra. Nevertheless, no official assistance for the Biafrans was offered and relief aid was channelled mainly through Oxfam and Save The Children Fund.

Material aid from Britain did involve a number of unofficial attempts to supply the Biafran government with a range of aircraft; some attempts successful, others not so. One of the most active companies supporting Biafra with material assistance operated from within almost a stone's throw of Windsor Castle.[381]

Through Templewood's Swiss associate company, Texsel Sales & Service, the company later negotiated the sale of a batch of twelve former French Armee de l'Air T-6G Texans. Shortly after that deal the Windsor-based company had attempted to broker a deal involving four Hunter F.50 jets but that deal fell through when the Swiss

242 Above: The former R.A.E. Bedford Meteor NF.14, G-AXNE, took-off from Blackbushe late on 6 September 1969 for a positioning flight to Exeter where it was refuelled and customs-cleared on a temporary XS29A permit on the following day. In this view, taken on departure at Blackbushe, Graham Spencer Taylor is flying from the front-seat and Templewood Aviation's director, Alex Rumley, occupies the rear seat (David Pope)

financier died suddenly. Two Fouga Magisters were successfully exported from Austria and would have arrived in Biafra had the wings not been blown up in an act of suspected sabotage at Bissau. Ultimately, in mid-1969, came Templewood's most ambitious project yet. It involved up to three Meteor jets being exported from the UK–in fact, in total, some five Meteors were involved in the attempt to provide the Biafran Air Force with teeth.[382]

In the final event none of the Meteors ever reached Biafra and those involved in the affair later faced a series of charges resulting in a rather unconvincing showdown trial at Berkshire Assizes.

The Swedish-German connection

The 'Meteor-job' effectively began during the Spring of 1969 and involved two TT.20 variants, SE-DCF (c/n 5562) and SE-DCH (c/n 5549). The two Meteors had been part of a fleet of target-towing aircraft operated by the Swedish quasi-military organisation, Svensk Flygtjanst AB. This company operated military aircraft on behalf of the Swedish Air Force. Both of the Meteors had been in storage at Malmö from March 1965 until mid-1968 when they were completely refurbished by Swedish Airworks Ltd.

On 14 (or 15) March 1969 SE-DCF and SE-DCH were ferried from Malmö to Billund, in Denmark, having been sold to Kjeld Motensen; by 21 March they had been flown on to Cologne, in West Germany. All available evidensuggests that the two Meteors had been re-sold to a German company for target-towing duties on behalf of the German Luftwaffe.

In fact the buyer was a German aircraft dealer, Herbert Berg, who traded from Karlsruhe as Flugzeughandelsgesellschaft Karlsruhe (FHGK). Berg was also a business associate of Target Towing Aircraft Ltd's Tony Osborne who had previously been associated with the attempted export of six former RAF Provost T.1s. Osborne and Berg jointly operated the International Jet School at Karlsruhe. (The school was later described as being part of Lorraine Aviation Ltd, a company jointly owned by Osborne's wife and his father-in-law - neither of whom were deeply involved in aviation. Lorraine Aviation Ltd was also linked with another Osborne company, International Aviation Services. It was a complicated web of semi-active companies of which little was known. However, Osborne's more general activities were fairly well-known to the British authorities.)[383]

Herbert Berg was also well known to the German authorities and who were quietly watching his activities. Berg operated another aircraft which became closely associated with the Biafran support base at Faro. This was the Dornier Do 28A, D-IBIF, originally owned by Rosenthal Porzellan AG, but which had been in storage at the manufacturer's airfield at Oberpfaffenhofen between October 1968 and March 1969. Herbert Berg acquired the Dornier and made several ferry flights to Faro. For a short while it was based at Faro where it acted as a commuter facility for Biafrans travelling between there and Lisbon. It was also used for flying across to Cascais (where a number of Biafran T-6G Texans were stored) but towards the end of April 1969 it sustained damage to the undercarriage when it was ground-looped while landing at Cascais –reportedly by the former Biafran B-25 pilot, Friedrich Herz.[384]

Faro had probably been the intended destination of the two Swedish Meteors. The original flight-plan had been declared as routeing from Billund – Bremen – Karlsruhe – Bordeaux. In fact both jets remained at Cologne for a brief period until 11 May 1969 when they were ferried to Gosselies/Charleroi, in Belgium. They remained at Gosselies for several months due to "technical difficulties".

The British Meteors

Within several weeks of abandoning the Provost deal Tony Osborne was facing financial ruin; at an insolvency hearing he disclosed debts of £8,364 and assets of only £195, He was declared bankrupt in May 1969. But within two months he was at the centre of an extraordinary deal involving the attempted export of three Meteors from Britain.

Rolls-Royce, during the 1960s, operated several jet aircraft, mainly company 'hack' aircraft including the Meteor NF.14 G-ASLW. For most of the time it was used by a number of company pilots for "continuation flying" purposes. In July 1969 it was due for its annual C. of A. inspection and overhaul. At the same time the company considered the value in keeping the aircraft. Company pilots were now able to maintain their "jet hours" on a Hawker Siddeley 125 (G-AWYE) which Rolls Royce had just begun leasing from the Swiss company Transair through the Windsor broker, Templewood Aviation. Templewood was therefore asked as to the market value and sales potential. Not only could Templewood supply an estimated value for the Meteor they could even offer Rolls-Royce a potential purchaser.

On 4 July 1969 Templewood's Tony Griffin took Tony Osborne to the Rolls-Royce facility where he was introduced as the owner and Curator of the British Historic Aircraft Museum at Southend. By the end of the day a purchase price of £5,500 for the Meteor had been agreed and, despite his apparent adverse financial position, Osborne handed over a cheque. (In turn, Rolls-Royce then paid Templewood a 10% handling commission.)

At 10:54Z (11:54 local) on Saturday 5 July 1969, a PA-30 Twin Comanche, G-AVHW, landed at Hucknall airfield, inbound from Gatwick via Sleap. There was one passenger on board the hired aircraft–the new owner of Meteor NF.14 G-ASLW. Osborne's intention had been to fly to Sleap to collect a pilot whom Osborne had contracted to ferry the Meteor from Hucknall to Hurn. The pilot had not shown up at Sleap; nor was he at Hucknall but there was, it seemed, an easy and immediate solution. Osborne then asked Rolls-Royce if they could deliver the Meteor to Bordeaux (for a cash fee of £50!). Rolls-Royce refused but did agree to have a company pilot fly the Meteor to Hurn on the following day. Osborne accepted the offer and then flew back to Elstree, departing Hucknall at 13:18Z (14:18).

At 09:31Z (10:31), on the following morning, Osborne returned to Hucknall aboard the Twin Comanche G-AVHW. On this occasion he was accompanied by a Peter Wheatley, a pilot friend of Templewood's Alex Rumley and who had been contacted at very short notice as a result of Osborne's original pilot not showing up. Wheatley had agreed to fly the Meteor on from Hurn but asked to accompany the Rolls-Royce pilot on the Hucknall-Hurn leg so as to re-familiarise himself with the Meteor.

The Twin Comanche was the first to leave Hucknall, at 09:15Z (10:15), with Tony Osborne aboard. At 09:30Z (10:30) Meteor NF.14 G-ASLW took-off with Rolls-Royce pilot James Patrick at the controls and Peter Wheatley in the rear seat. Finally, the company's 125, G-AWYE, flew from Hucknall to Hurn, ostensibly on a test flight, but acting as a crew ferry to take James Patrick back to Hucknall.

The Meteor was the last of the trio to land at Hurn after Patrick and Wheatley had circled for some time to burn up excess fuel. When the aircraft landed, at 10:30Z (11:30), the two wing tanks and the ventral fuel tank were all empty. Within minutes the aircraft was officially handed over to Osborne and the Rolls-Royce pilot left to return to Hucknall aboard the 125.

Immediately after handing over the aircraft Tony Osborne instructed refuellers to replenish the tanks. There was some difficulty at first with the fuel couplings but, in the mistaken belief that he was working on an aircraft owned by Rolls-Royce, an employee of Shell very quickly assembled a new coupling and filled the two droptanks and the two fuselage tanks. In total the Meteor took on some 390 gallons of kerosene–all invoiced to Rolls-Royce at Hucknall.

James Staples, a Customs Preventive Officer at Hurn airport was approached by two men at 12:45 with a request to complete customs clearance for the Meteor. The two men produced typed copies of an XS.29A (30-day temporary export permit) and an XS.155 (General Customs declaration, showing Bordeaux as the destination) both duly signed by pilot Peter Wheatley on behalf of Target Towing Aircraft Co Ltd. Staples validated the XS.29A and allowed the pilot to proceed.

It had taken just 48 hours since Tony Osborne had first inspected the Meteor. Nobody had chosen to question how a recently declared bankrupt had managed to purchase a military jet fighter (albeit unarmed) with a company cheque and allowed to take delivery and knowingly for immediate export–possibly before the cheque had even been cleared. But the plan worked, and it was to work again.

With Peter Wheatley in command of the Meteor NF.14 G-ASLW when she left Hurn, the rear seat (the navigator's seat) was now occupied by Templewood Aviation partner, Alex 'Sandy' Rumley. Rumley was no stranger to fast jets; before becoming a partner in 1968, he had just concluded a tour in Aden, on Hunter FGA.9s. (He had come to Templewood in response to an advertisement for four pilots required for the Swedish Hunter F.50 deal. That episode was never finalised but Alex Rumley stayed to help out with the Fouga Magister deal. Subsequently, when one of Templewood Aviation's partners resigned on 20 September 1968, Rumley was invited to join the company board.)

G-ASLW landed at Bordeaux after a direct flight from Hurn as planned. It was again refuelled and positioned for a night stopover. Then, early on the following morning, Monday 7 July 1969, the part of the plan that was never previously discussed openly was put into action. The aircraft took off from Bordeaux and immediately climbed to its maximum altitude of 41,000 feet before setting course for crossing the length of Spain and down to the Portuguese coastal airfield at Faro. No flight-plan had been lodged and, as far as Rumley can recall, neither he nor Wheatley contacted any Spanish air-traffic control zones en route.

Meteor G-ASLW: the spares

Within a few days of the Meteor's arrival in Portugal, Tony Osborne hired a Piper PA-24 Comanche, G-ARIE, from the Surrey & Kent Flying Club at Biggin Hill and flew down to Faro. The flight detail, which almost replicated that of the outbound Meteor, was as follows:

PA-24 Comanche G-ARIE Flight Routeing

Date	Flight Routeing	Flight Time
11.7.69	Biggin Hill - Blackbushe	0.30 hrs
	Blackbushe - Hurn	0.30 hrs
	Hurn - Bordeaux	2.15 hrs
	Bordeaux - Faro	4.00 hrs
12.7.69	Faro - Rennes	6.00 hrs
	Rennes - Gatwick	2.00 hrs
14.7.69	Gatwick - Elstree	0.30 hrs
	Elstree - Biggin Hill	0.30 hrs

Osborne never gave a reason for flying south to Faro but it served to suggest he was chasing the Meteors. Unfortunately, it later provided evidence of Osborne's involvement in knowingly exporting the aircraft to Biafra.

Included within Rolls-Royce's original sale price was a small stockholding of spares and ground-handling equipment. Other spares were made available and sold separately, the cost of which would be agreed at a later date. Nevertheless some of these spares were collected by Tony Osborne, on 16 July, and conveyed by road back to Blackbushe. It was on this occasion that Osborne first spoke of the aircraft going to Africa, It was, he claimed, being fitted with cameras for aerial survey work although he failed to mention which country.

On the following day Tony Osborne returned to Hucknall aboard a Blackbushe-based Cessna 180, G-ASYI, flown by Richard Kingsmill. They uplifted the remaining spares and flew them back to Blackbushe.

The Cessna 180 was not unloaded at Blackbushe. Instead, and on the following morning, Dick Kingsmill flew the aircraft on to Hurn where he requested customs clearance for an outbound flight to Bordeaux. Typically, no prior notice for customs clerarance had been given. But on this occasion the Customs Officer demanded an export licence for the spares as well as an explanation. Kingsmill argued that the spares were urgently required for the Meteor, G-ASLW, which was in France on a 30-day export permit but had broken down at Bordeaux with brake trouble. It could not, it seemed, be flown back until the spares had been fitted. There was, of course, little reason to deny export clearance even if the spares included tyres, brake pads, alternator, cockpit windows, hydraulic pump, and boxes of sundry pipes, nuts and bolts. Kingsmill also argued that these items were not technically being exported as they would be "returning" to the UK albeit fitted to the Meteor. Hurn customs suspected otherwise but allowed the spares to be flown out on an XS29A temporary export licence.

In fact, the Cessna 180 did not fly to Bordeaux; instead it routed from Hurn directly to Biarritz (on 18 July 1969) and then on to Seville before heading further south to Faro. Two days after leaving Hurn the spares were at Faro.

A second Meteor flies out

By mid-August 1969 a number of factors should have alerted the British authorities. The Meteor NF.14 G-ASLW (sold to, but never re-registered to Target Towing Aircraft Co Ltd) had exceeded the 30-day limit of its temporary export permit. A simple telephone call to Bordeaux would have established the fact that it had flown on to Biafra's Portuguese base at Faro. Osborne had publicly displayed sympathies towards Biafra by parading his Anson, G-AWML, around the UK with 'Save Biafra Campaign' titles on its roof. It was also widely known within aviation circles that Osborne had been declared bankrupt and that a number of questions were being asked about the precise status of his aircraft museum at Southend. Finally, almost everybody involved in the frustrated sale of the Provosts (also registered to Target Towing Aircraft Co Ltd), and which HM Customs forcibly immobilised at Fairoaks, had all fled the country–to Faro, and on to Biafra.

Why then did nobody raise an alarm bell when, on 20 August 1969, Tony Osborne arrived at RAE Bedford with the intention of buying a second Meteor NF.14?

This second Meteor was an ex-RAF example, WS804, which had latterly been operating with the Royal Aircraft Establishment at Bedford. It had been declared redundant and put up for disposal by the Ministry of Technology. Ironically, Tony Osborne was on the M.O.D. Harrogate mailing-list for tender applications of retired service aircraft. But although Osborne presumably knew that WS804 was available for sale it was not he who made the initial move. That came from an acquaintance of Osborne (and for that matter, of Templewood Aviation); one Tony Paris of P.B. Export Sales (Cavendish Square) Ltd. Claiming to be acting as an agent of a film company, Paris telephoned the Ministry of Defence at Harrogate on 19 August 1969 and enquired as to whether the M.O.D. had any Meteor jets for sale. Harrogate confirmed that WS804 was available for purchase and invited Paris to inspect the aircraft at RAE Bedford and, if suitable, to make an offer through Harrogate.

Tony Paris visited Bedford on 20 August and, not having a deep knowledge of aviation, made only a perfunctory inspection of the Meteor. Officers at Bedford even suggested that he returned with an engineer. Nevertheless Tony Paris did telephone Harrogate on the following day and verbally offered £4,000, an offer which was immediately accepted. Two provisions, however, were put forward by the M.O.D. Firstly, that the aircraft should not be flown without the issue of a Certificate of Airworthiness and, secondly, that the aircraft not be exported without the express approval of the Board of Trade. The first point effectively stopped the Meteor from being flown out of Bedford so, on 25 August, Paris made a request to the M.O.D. that, for a fee, they arrange delivery to Blackbushe as part of the purchase conditions. The M.O.D. accepted this request but charged Paris £100 for doing so.

Anthony Paris paid over £4,100 to the M.O.D. Cashier in London on 27 August and immediately called Harrogate to release the aircraft. But Harrogate knew Paris only

243: The very thought of going to war with an aircraft displaying liberal patches of RAF 'day-glo' may have been part of the ruse in diverting attention from HM Customs & Excise. Certainly part of the plan was the legend 'ENTERPRISE FILMS' and which was applied in black engine lacquer. G-AXNE was ferried to Blackbushe on 5 September 1969 (as WS804) but departure was delayed due to flat batteries. The Meteor finally departed the UK and flown to Faro where it joined sister-aircraft G-ASLW (Paul Baxter)

244: Immediately the Meteor NF.14 G-AXNE arrived at Faro work began on re-fitting cannon barrels. The work was carried out in the Biafran 'Phoenix' hangar and was completed in several days. By the time this view was taken the Meteor was armed and ready to go (Paul Baxter)

as an agent and needed the identity of his client, to which Paris gave the name, Target Towing Aircraft Co Ltd. An alarm bell immediately rang. Harrogate refused to allow the sale to this company but not for all the obvious reasons. It seemed that Tony Osborne had not settled an outstanding account of £300 for twelve parachutes when he had purchased the six Provosts in November 1968. Harrogate therefore asked Paris to give an undertaking, in writing, that the Meteor was not re-sold to Target Towing Aircraft Co Ltd. Paris agreed to this condition but then later visited Harrogate personally, on 3 September, and paid Osborne's outstanding debt in cash.

In the meantime Osborne had travelled to Bedford on 26 August to personally inspect the Meteor. Two days later, on 28 August, the Board of Trade accepted Osborne's registration application and allocated the Meteor the civil marks G-AXNE in the name of Target Towing Aircraft Co Ltd.

The embarrassing hitch involving Target Towing's outstanding unpaid account caused a 48-hour delay. That meant that Peter Wheatley, who had again been hired to deliver the Meteor, could not perform that task due to a previously arranged flying commitment. A pilot from RAE Bedord, Flt/Lt Ian G. Conradi was nominated to fly the Meteor from Bedford to Blackbushe which he did on 5 September 1969.

Immediately after landing at Blackbushe the military marks were erased and replaced by the new civilian letters, G-AXNE. The legend 'ENTERPRISE FILMS' was also painted on the nose–in engine lacquer, owing to no black paint being available–as part of a ruse to convince the British authorities that the Meteor was, like its sister aircraft G-ASLW, to participate in a forthcoming film about the Korean war.

To replace Peter Wheatley the group succeeded in hiring another civilian pilot, Graham Spencer Taylor. The Cessna 180 G-ASYI was despatched to RAF Shawbury to collect him but when, on the morning of 6 September, Taylor arrived at Blackbushe he learnt from Templewood's partner, Alex Rumley, that the Meteor's main batteries had lost their charge overnight but that a local garage in Yateley had organised a booster-charge. Again, the departure was delayed. It was late in the day when the batteries were re-installed but the crew still had difficulty in starting the engines and it was only then that the full extent of the problem was realised; Alex Rumley had flown Vampires and Hunters while Graham Spencer Taylor's only previous jet experience had been on Vampires.

While the crew had been trying to get the Meteor engines started Tony Paris was trying to convince the airport authorities at Exeter to remain open long enough to accept the arrival of G-AXNE. Eventually the correct starting procedure was determined and G-AXNE was ready for take-off from Blackbushe at 17:00 hours. Exeter finally agreed to remain open and the Meteor was flown down to the west country for a night stopover.

Early the next morning, as 'XNE was topped up with 379 gallons of fuel, the crew arranged for a customs clearance–again without the usual 24 hours notice. The destination given by Taylor and Rumley was Bordeaux and therefore, like its sister aircraft, 'XNE was allowed to leave the country on a temporary XS29A export permit. The aircraft took-off from Exeter around 13:00 hours.

Taylor and Rumley in fact flew south to Bordeaux on Sunday 7 September where the aircraft was temporarily grounded for some minor repairs to the ignition system. The delay meant that Taylor had to return to the UK to meet previously arranged flying commitments; his schedule had not considered possible delays. During the morning of Tuesday 9 September a replacement pilot, Richard Spurrell, arrived at Bordeaux by scheduled flight. Almost immediately he climbed into the Meteor to undertake the final leg to Faro; Rumley again occupied the rear navigator's seat. In the same manner as the first Meteor (G-ASLW), the flight to Faro was made at maximum altitude and once again without any contact with Spanish air traffic control. By late afternoon on 9 September both of the Meteors, G-ASLW and G-AXNE, were together and safely on the ground at Faro.

Biafra: a third Meteor?

Having successfully flown two Meteors out of the UK, the group then turned towards acquiring a third Meteor. This was G-ARCX, a hybrid NF.11/14 variant, which for several years had been operated by Ferranti Ltd.

On 18 September 1969, Tony Paris contacted Ferranti Ltd to discuss a purchase price. Ferranti was offering the aircraft to Paris for £3,500, plus £1,500 for various modifications that Ferranti had fitted previously. There was also a sizeable spares holding, available for £3,000. Paris agreed to buy the aircraft but, as usual, the sale was conditional on gaining M.O.D. approval for the purchase as well as any subsequent re-sale that Paris might have had in mind. By now, the Ministry of Defence was becoming, quite naturally, concerned at the number of errant Meteors that were in breach of temporary export permits. The sale to Paris was, not surprisingly, refused.

Arming and delivering the Meteors

As part of the standard conditions of sale by the Ministry of Defence both of the Meteors had had their weapon fit blanked-off or removed. In the case of G-ASLW, it had already been removed anyway. The next priority for the two Biafran Air Force Meteors was to restore the cannon installation although live ammunition was not going to be fitted on Portuguese soil. The agreed fit involved four 20mm cannons mounted in two pairs outboard of the engines and underwing bomb racks, each to hold four 500lb bombs.

The origin of the armaments is unclear. Surviving documents suggest that they were obtained from Europe through two arms dealers, Harry Briggs and Ernest Koenig. British customs officers believed that they had been collected by Kingsmill "from a field in Belgium" but later accepted that they had come from the group's store at Slinfold, Sussex. In fact, Richard Kingsmill was subsequently charged and tried for "illegally exporting four 20mm cannon barrels, out of Biggin Hill on 18 September 1969 aboard the Cessna 180 G-ASYI."

If, indeed, Kingsmill had collected the cannon barrels from Slinfold then that lends credence to an amusing aside involving Osborne and his museum. Among the exhibits was a SAAB J-29F, 29640, which had been donated by the Royal Swedish Air Force apparently in the mistaken belief that the museum was an official British institution. The J-29F was conveniently fitted with four 20mm Hispano Suiza cannons which are thought to have been the cannons involved. Osborne claimed that he "could not be accused of stealing from his own aeroplane" and, in any case, nobody else would know; he had already removed a number of items from the cockpit. When the barrels were removed the effect was to considerably alter, even more so, the aircraft's centre-of-gravity. By the following morning, the reduction in forward weight had caused it to slowly tilt backwards, and very visibly, onto its tail.[385]

By 20 September 1969 both of the Meteors at Faro had weapon packs fitted and both were ready for onward delivery to Biafra. Early on the following morning both Meteors took off within a short time of each other. G-ASLW, still in its turquoise and white scheme, was flown by Templewood's Peiter Dezeeuw while G-AXNE was being flown by either Richard Spurrell or Graham Taylor.

G-AXNE, still carrying its 'ENTERPRISE FILMS' legend headed for Funchal, in Portuguese Madeira and within several days had been successfully flown on to Dakar and Bissau, Portuguese Guinea. At Bissau, 'XNE had shown signs of trouble with one of its engines and was temporarily grounded.[386]

The other Meteor, G-ASLW, had also set out for Madeira on its first leg but was then grounded with several minor snags; a sudden change in the weather also caused a delay in departing. Dezeeuw eventually flew 'SLW out of the island on 28 September, and to avoid any interference from 'unfriendly' countries stuck to his planned course of keeping well offshore. But in a desperate attempt to make up for lost time Dezeeuw attempted to make for Bissau in one hop. Inevitably, the aircraft ran short of fuel.

Some miles short of his target airfield Dezeeuw had no alternative but to eject from the Meteor and allow the aircraft to ditch in the Atlantic. Some reports, later denied as rather fanciful, related how Dezeeuw had drifted for several days in a liferaft-dinghy before being picked up by a ship. In fact he had ejected fairly close to a ship which picked him up and later landed him, ironically, back at Cape Verde. He later made his way back to Lisbon aboard a scheduled T.A.P. flight.

The full weight of diplomatic effort by the British Foreign Office ensured that the Meteor G-AXNE never departed Bissau. By most accounts the Biafran Meteor saga ended at Bissau. But the group, and especially Tony Osborne, continued in their attempt to provide Biafra with Meteor jets.

Tony Osborne revisited his German business associate, Herbert Berg, to discuss means of getting the two Swedish-registered TT.20s (SE-DCF and SE-DCH) down to Portugal. Both aircraft had been effectively abandoned at Gosseilles/Charleroi some four months previously although in the meantime the Belgian company, SIAI, did apparently undertake some servicing work on the aircraft.

Berg signed the two aircraft to Target Towing Aircraft Ltd on 29 September 1969 (in exchange for Osborne's AT-16 Harvard, G-AXCR, which the Swiss Air Force had donated to Osborne's museum). This then allowed Osborne to apply for UK civil registration but the Civil Aviation Authority turned down his application–on the basis that his cheque had been dated *31* September 1969. (Why on earth Osborne would wish to apply for British registration when two other Meteors with which he was associated had overstayed temporary export permits is almost beyond credibility.)

A month later, Herbert Berg applied for registration in Germany, and the Meteors were allocated the marks D-CAKU and D-CAKY, on 29 October 1969. However, when the German authorities learnt that the aircraft were probably intended for Biafra and that both the British C.A.A. and, apparently, the American F.A.A. had both already turned down requests for registration, the Germans too refused to register them. The marks were promptly cancelled a week later, on 7 November 1969. With that the story did come to an end–apart from the obvious repercussions.[387]

The investigation

The war in Biafra was still being waged when HM Customs began enquiries and taking interviews from those involved. The alarm was raised when, on 14 October 1969, Customs officers at London-Heathrow stopped Tony Paris as he passed through to catch an outbound flight. They found that he had a considerable amount of cash on him. (Exchange Controls were in force at the time and which restricted the amount of cash any one individual could take out of the country.) Together with the cash, Paris had been given written instructions to contact Harry Briggs (an arms dealer based in Paris) and procure Meteor spares–quantity and not quality–and forward them to a group of known Biafrans at Faro. These instructions were wrapped around the wad of banknotes. Tony Paris then, it seems, chose to tell the entire story and over the next month or so two Senior Investigation Officers, interviewed all of those involved in the 'Meteor job'.

Much of the prosecution case against the accused was quite straightforward. Two Meteors had been flown out of the UK on temporary XS29A export permits and had not been returned. The individuals concerned were known to have all been arranging deals which involved supplying aircraft to Biafra. It was the armament aspects that caused some considerable concern, especially in the export of 20mm cannon barrels etc.

Richard Kingsmill was the subject of interrogation by Sydney Hoy (an H.M. Customs Senior Investigation Officer) at Gatwick on 18 November 1969:

Hoy: *"Have you ever been to Belgium?"*

Kingsmill: *"No."*

Hoy: *"Dezeeuw, who was flying G-ASLW when it went down in the sea off the West African coast, said that in Faro he had paid an Englishman £600 for bringing down to Faro 4 x 20mm Hispano Suiza cannons. The cannons were ferried in a Cessna from a field in Belgium. Did you make this trip?"*

Kingsmill: *"Christ no. I've never been to a field in Belgium. I only went down to Faro once with a few spares."*

Hoy: *"I thought you did more than one trip to Faro."*

Kingsmill: *"No—wait, I did another one with Richard Miller. About three months ago."*

At that stage Dick Kingsmill began to get confused over how many flights to Faro he had actually made. It convinced the customs investigators that Kingsmill was as involved as the others.

Sydney Hoy later travelled to Germany where he (and another Customs Officer, a Mr Rosser,) met and questioned Tony Osborne on two occasions. From the first interview:

Hoy: *"Have you any knowledge of the movements of the Meteors between July and October 1969?"*

Osborne: *"Yes. The Board of Trade told me they had left Faro."*

Hoy: *"Did you know of their movements before you saw the Board of Trade?"*

Osborne: *"No, not until then"*

Hoy: *"In what way? Didn't you ask a British pilot if he would pick up some Hispano Suiza cannons in Belgium and take them to Faro?"*

Osborne: *"No. I don't know anything about armaments."*

Later in the interview:

Hoy: *"Did you know before we had told you that G-ASLW went straight on to Faro?"*

Osborne: *"No, I didn't. I sent the Cessna G-ASYI about a week later with the spares to Bordeaux. Dick Kingsmill found the aircraft was not there; he went to the tower and checked, was told that it went to Faro so he took the spares on because he knew the company was based in Faro."*

237

Rosser: *"Did you specifically request Kingsmill to make this trip for you?"*
Osborne: *"Yes, I did."*

Hoy: *"We've seen Kingsmill. He never went to Bordeaux, he went to Biarritz."*

Osborne: *"Here we go again. He was told to go to Bordeaux."*

Later in the interview........

Hoy: *"Let's leave these doubtful matters and refer to your trip to Faro in the Comanche, G-ARIE."*

Osborne: *"I wanted to see Phoenix and also to get some flying hours in so I jumped into the Comanche and went down to Faro."*

Hoy: *"How did you know Lima Whiskey had not remained at Bordeaux?"*

Osborne: *"Because Kingsmill told me, he phoned me from Faro."*

Hoy: *"My memory is that Comanche G-ARIE went out on 11 July but Kingsmill in G-ASYI did not go out until 18 July."*

Rosser: *"So you wouldn't have sent Kingsmill to Bordeaux would you, Mr Osborne?"*

(Long pause) No reply

Hoy: *"Your recollection is wrong, Mr Osborne."*

The charges and the verdicts

Osborne's recollections were wrong on a number of points, as were those of Richard Kingsmill. Kingsmill was later arrested by police as he was leaving the country through Dover docks, on 27 April 1970. On the same date Tony Osborne, Tony Paris, Alex Rumley and Tony Griffin were all arrested by Berkshire police. All were charged with various offences relating to the Meteors. Kingsmill, a court later decided (on 26/27 May 1970), *had* illegally exported the four 20mm cannon barrels, taken from the group's Slinfield store and flown out of Biggin Hill on 18 September 1969 aboard the Cessna 180 G-ASYI. He was fined £100.

Osborne had maintained that he had been utterly duped into "leasing the Meteors to an American film company, whose intentions were, with hindsight, rather questionable". In the eventual outcome, the court expressed its opinion of Osborne's claim of innocence by fining him £700 for illegally exporting military aircraft.

The others were also fined what can only be described as rather contemptuous amounts and then freed.

There was a final, and perhaps fitting irony to the Meteor episode. Neither of the two Meteors which reached Faro had fired guns for many years and there was considerable doubt, even by their suppliers, that the guns fitted would actually have worked satisfactorily. There were no facilities in Portugal to test-fire the guns, nor was there en route. The first test-firing would have taken place in Biafra. As one of those involved later reflected, "with so many MiG-17s based around the Biafran borders I would not have liked to have flown a mission in one of those Meteors just to test a set of time-expired guns!"

Notes

Note 381 The company was Templewood Aviation Ltd. The address later proved extremely beneficial in that some clients believed that being so close to Windsor Castle that it was a quasi-governmental organisation. The owners of the company of course did not seek this impression deliberately.

Note 382 Details are contained within the personal papers of Alex Rumley. Much of the detail contained within this chapter and relating to the activities of Tony Osborne, Tony Paris and Richard Kingsmill have been based on original prosecution documents, kindly made available by Alex Rumley.

Note 383 Great concern had been shown over the nature and activities of the "British Historical Aircraft Museum" at Southend. Osborne's activities concerning the Provosts G-AWTB-WTG were also well known.

Note 384 It has been reported that the Dornier 28 suffered undercarriage damage as a result of Frederick Herz attempting to land it with a broken leg while his co-pilot operated the rudder controls. Unfortunately nobody can corroborate the story and some doubt must be expressed considering Berg reportedly broke his leg in December 1967 and the Dornier crashed during April 1969.

Note 385 It is ironic that Osborne believed the SAAB J-29F to be his property. The Royal Swedish Air Force donated the aircraft on a "permanent loan" basis in the belief that it was going to a national aviation museum. The aircraft was even presented at RAF Cranwell before flying on to Southend on 13 June 1967. An added irony was that the Swedish Government had declared an arms embargo to both sides of the Nigerian civil war yet the cannon barrels for the Meteor had been removed from an aircraft still technically owned by the Swedish Air Force. It should be pointed out, however, that according to Swedish Air Force records the cannon barrels were removed prior to delivery to the UK.,

Note 386 G-AXNE was abandoned at Bissau. A photograph of the Meteor at Bissau, taken by Al J Venter, appeared in *Air Enthusiast* February 1972 issue

Note 387 *Aviation Letter*

THE NIGERIANS CLOSE IN
Biafra's Final Hour

Biafra: the T-6G reappears

Despite losing their two Meteor NF.14 jets, the Biafrans did manage to receive some additional aircraft towards the end of 1969. These were several T-6G Texans from the batch of former French Air Force examples that had being lying dormant in Portugal for almost a year-and-a-half.

The first sign of any movement occurred during the early Summer, probably during June 1969, when the Cascais-based company, SEAMA (*Sociedade de Exploração de Aerodromos e Manutenção de Aerona es SARL*) began the task of restoring them to flying condition.[388]

By September 1969 overhauls of four T-6Gs had been completed and each had been successfully test-flown at Tires. All four had been repainted an overall matt drab olive-green on all surfaces, with irregular patches ('splinters') of matt dark green outlined in extra-dark green superimposed–basically a three-tone matt green scheme with the top 'splinter' green applied in a manner not unlike that applied to the Biafran F-27 Friendship some two years previously. The pattern differed slightly on all four. None carried any national markings, nor did they carry any external identification. The only clue to their origin was the original manufacturer's plates showing the c/n etc (which surprisingly were left intact). By September 1969 overhauls of the first batch of four aircraft was complete and a start on the second batch of four had just begun. Aircraft included within the first two batches were as follows:

T-6G Overhauls by SEAMA First Batch

C/n	USAF Serial	French Serial/Code
182-485	51-14798	114798/KY
182-497	51-14810	14810/J
182-560	51-14873	114873/-
182-738	51-15051	115051/KC

T-6G Overhauls by SEAMA Second Batch

C/n	USAF Serial	French Serial/Code
182-457	51-14770	114770/24
182-481	51-14794	14794/KH
182-487	51-14800	14800/21
182-678	51-14991	14991/KG

As it turned out only the first batch of four overhauled T-6Gs left for delivery to Biafra. These were dismantled

245 Above: *Canairelief L-1049H Super Constellation CF-NAK operated on the nightly Nordchurchaid airlift for just over seven months. During the night of 17/18 December 1969 it sustained a direct hit at Uli by a bomb dropped by the Nigerian Air Force C-47 'Intruder' aircraft. After fire had consumed the aircraft, only the tail section remained recognisable. This entire section was later towed to one side of the strip and crudely hidden with palm fronds (via Peter J. Marson)*

at Tires and prepared for shipment from Lisbon to Bissau, Portuguese Guinea. They arrived at Bissau docks during mid-October 1969 after which each was immediately conveyed to Bissau airfield where pilots, who had already flown down from Faro aboard one of the Biafran Government flights, were waiting.[389]

The group of pilots and engineers hired by the Biafran government to fly the four T-6Gs marked quite a departure from previous groups. Since the civil war in Nigeria had started Portuguese support for Biafra had amounted to allowing the use of its airfields and colonial bases for transit staging-points. True, there had been the occasional Portuguese pilot or engineer working for Biafra but the T-6G operation involved a team consisting entirely of Portuguese nationals. Four Portuguese Air Force Reserve pilots had been contracted, in July 1969, to ferry the T-6Gs south to Biafra and then operating them as part of the Biafran Air Force.

The four were Artur Alves Pereira, José Eduardo Peralta, Armando Cró Brás and Gil Pinto de Sousa, the last named having previously worked under contract to the Biafran Air Force when he briefly flew one of the B-25 Mitchells, in 1967. To support the T-6Gs inside Biafra were two Portuguese engineers, Faustino Borralho and Jorge Cãncio, both of whom had been contracted at the same time. The pilots were offered contracts involving a 'retainer' of US$1,000 per month whenever outside Biafra which rose to US$3,000 when operating inside Biafra. Each pilot was also paid a further $1,000 to deliver the aircraft and bonus allowances were payable for special missions, eg attacking oil tanks, enemy military columns and, of course, the MiG-17 bases.[390]

Not everything went smoothly and even before the group had left Bissau several incidents had flared into disagreements. One of the pilots, Armando Cró Brás, decided to break his contract at Bissau and return to Portugal. At the same time there appears to have been an attempt to stop further progress when the locally-based Portuguese Air Force Commander argued that the group, albeit technically Portuguese civilians, should not become involved in Biafra's war. The group insisted that they were nothing other than delivery pilots and although it was an unsubstantiated claim it proved nevertheless a convincing one. The Commander allowed the aircraft to leave Bissau.

Since one of the pilots had left the group it was decided to ferry the T-6Gs to Abidjan in one group of three, with the remaining aircraft following on later. The three aircraft took off from Bissau and headed out to sea in order to follow the coastline offshore. However, shortly after take-off, one T-6G suffered engine trouble and a second began to experience problems with its radio. Both aircraft were returned to Bissau leaving just one, piloted by Gil Pinto de Sousa, to fly on alone. De Sousa later crossed the Ivory Coast border and landed at the coastal airfield of Sassandra with fuel tanks virtually exhausted. After taking on fuel the T-6G was flown the final short stage to Abidjan where Gil Pinto de Sousa left the aircraft and returned to Bissau. His plan was to join Pereira and Peralta in ferrying the remaining three T-6Gs but in order to conserve fuel this second ferry flight took a more direct and overland course to the Ivory Coast. Yet again the group used Sassandra for refuelling before staging on to Abidjan.

All four Biafran T-6Gs remained at Abidjan for several days while the three pilots (and support personnel) considered the military situation inside Biafra. Pereira and de Sousa decided to hitch a ride aboard a Biafran Government Constellation flight to Uli, where they could gain a first-hand assessment of precisely what the operational conditions were inside Biafra. Peralta remained at Abidjan and reportedly spent his time trying to convince the Biafrans there that a training school should be established at Abidjan. The concept of such a school at Abidjan was rejected. The Biafrans clearly needed every available pilot and aircraft to help fight an increasingly weakening military situation. Thus it was at that point that Peralta became the second pilot to leave the group and returned to Lisbon; his T-6G remained at Abidjan and in fact was never flown into Biafra.

Peralta's place was taken by a newly-recruited Portuguese pilot, José da Cunha Pignatelli, and when de Sousa and Pereira returned from Biafra the three pilots agreed to undertake the final leg to Uli during the evening of 30 October 1969. Although the three T-6Gs were flown from Abidjan to Uli direct, all three pilots set slightly different courses. The two Portuguese engineers flew on ahead aboard a Biafran Government flight to await their colleague's arrival but only two of the T-6Gs successfully managed to land at Uli.

Alves Pereira had followed a pre-determined route that took him directly over Takoradi (in Ghana), then out over the sea past Togo, and Dahomey to continue almost due eastwards towards Escravos and the river Niger where he had planned to arrive just after sunset. The final leg to Uli was to be flown in Visual Flight conditions (VFR) but the weather had become overcast with a low-lying belt of stratus cloud. Initially undeterred, Pereira changed course to almost direct north but in cloud he had allowed his aircraft to drift to the west and found himself being shot at. Taking a definite easterly direction Pereira descended to 2,000ft and tuned into the Uli Beacon. Although the Uli controller responded to Pereira's calls for the landing-lights to be switched on, the presence of the Nigerian 'Intruder' bomber necessitated the lights being temporarily turned off as Pereira made his final approach. After an abortive initial approach the T-6G landed at Uli on its second attempt. Shortly afterwards, José Pignatelli landed at Uli and both aircraft were pushed into a makeshift shelter for the night.

Of the three T-6Gs which had set out from Abidjan, it

246: Gil Pinto de Sousa was contracted by the Biafran Government, during 1969, to fly Biafran Air Force T-6G Texan aircraft. On the final stage of the delivery flight from Abidjan to Uli, the aircraft's ADF malfunctioned and he bailed out over the Benue Plateau area of Nigeria. Captured shortly afterwards, de Sousa spent some four years in a Nigerian jail without trial, or even charges being brought. He is seen in this specially posed view beside the wreckage of his T-6G which is surrounded by Nigerian police and army officers (Africa Press)

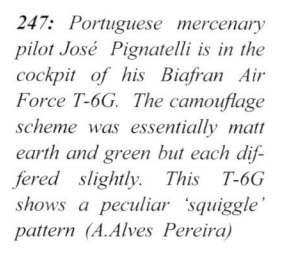

247: Portuguese mercenary pilot José Pignatelli is in the cockpit of his Biafran Air Force T-6G. The camouflage scheme was essentially matt earth and green but each differed slightly. This T-6G shows a peculiar 'squiggle' pattern (A.Alves Pereira)

was the last to leave, the one flown by Gil Pinto de Sousa, that encountered difficulties and never made it to Uli The aircraft's Automatic Direction Finder (ADF) had failed during the flight, forcing de Sousa to continue navigating by dead reckoning. Inevitably, as darkness fell over unfamiliar terrain and with few notable landmarks, de Sousa became lost. He transmitted several MayDay calls in the hope of being heard by relief airlift pilots and perhaps being guided in. But the chances were slim, as were the chances of locating the Biafran strip at Uli. Ultimately the aircraft ran short of fuel and de Sousa decided to abandon the flight and bail out by parachute. The T-6G crashed approximately 125 miles south of Keffi, in the Benue Plateau. (Gil Pinto de Sousa was arrested on the following day and taken to Lagos where he was fully interrogated and placed in detention. Never brought to trial in spite of his obvious 'mercenary' status, he was held at Lagos for almost five years.)

During the early daylight hours of 31 October the two T-6Gs that had managed to arrive in Biafra safely were flown from Uli, by Pereira and Pignatelli, to their permanent base at the nearby Uga strip. As if to underline their achievement in successfully arriving in Biafra the pilots, Pereira and Pignatelli, made a low pass of the Biafran Air Force HQ en route, followed by a loop and a slow roll undoubtedly to the delight of the Biafran Air Force commander, General Godwin Ezeilo. In spite of having only two aircraft the newly-arrived T-6Gs were accorded independent status as the Biafran Air Force's 42nd Squadron. The squadron was immediately declared operational and under the command of Captain Artur Alves Pereira.

In the meantime the Biafran Air Force MFI-9Bs had been divided into two operational units and accorded squadron status as the 45th Squadron and the 47th Squadron.

Nigeria: more MiG-17s

The principal front-line element of the Federal Nigerian Air Force was the MiG-17F but by Autumn 1969 a number had become unreliable and in serious need of major servicing and repair. Some spares had been supplied during April 1969 but even these could not keep all of the MiGs flying. The Federal Nigerian Government continued to request, from the British Government, assistance in the shape of fighter aircraft - even citing the fact that Biafra was attempting to procure jet aircraft from British agents. Always the answer was negative.

Eventually the Nigerian Air Force did receive replacement aircraft when, on 13 October 1969, five Soviet Air Force An-12s (CCCP-11365, CCCP-12952, CCCP-12953, CCCP-12955, and CCCP-12956) landed at Kano. Each An-12 carried one MiG-17. Four days later CCCP-11365 and CCP-12956 returned with a cargo of MiG-17 spares while, on 18 October, the other three Antonov An-12s (CCCP-12952, CCCP-12953 and CCCP-12955) flew back into Kano with, between them, three more MiG-17s. Even that was not the end of this mini-airlift; two more loads of MiG-17 spares and sundry other armaments were flown in on 21 October (CCCP-12956 & CCCP-12957) with a final two consignments (CCCP-12953 & CCCP-12955) arriving on 22 October 1969. (It is likely that some of these loads included the 122mm artillery guns that were later described by some reports as a key factor in bringing the war to a conclusion. Other reports suggest that the guns arrived but were never used in the final offensive.)

The eight MiG-17s airfreighted in during October 1969 were non-afterburner variants (basic MiG-17, known by NATO as 'Fresco-A' variants). All had fomerly operated with the East German Air Force where they were designated MiG-17*blatt* (*blatt* simply meaning *nothing*, ie no sub-type). They were, to all intents and purposes, very basic (and probably early production) examples of the standard MiG-17. By late-November 1969 the first five MiG-17*blatten* (NAF631 to NAF635) had been ferried from Kano to No.2 Fighter Bomber Squadron's main MiG-17 bases at Enugu, Port Harcourt and Lagos. The remaining three (NAF636 to NAF638) were ferried, like the earlier examples, to forward bases by British mercenary pilots during December 1969.

Biafra: the T-6G is operational

The first operational sortie by the Biafra T-6Gs has been especially difficult to date, particularly as Nigerian reports from front line areas rarely identified the aircraft type. One raid against Port Harcourt airfield, early on 10 November 1969, involved both of the T-6Gs. Operating out of Uga, Port Harcourt represented only six or seven minutes flight-time to target. That allowed ample time for a direct attack from the north and then make an anti-clockwise 270-degree turn to port, and carry out a second run across the airfield. Both aircraft then escaped to the west before turning northwards and back to base. On the first run the T-6Gs attacked a group of MiG-17s parked on an unprotected and open ramp area. The attacking pilots claimed the destruction of three, or possibly four, MiG-17s destroyed but local sources deny this. They did admit to the loss of a Pan African Airlines DC-4, N480G, which was hit on the second run across the airfield. This was one of the few occasions that the DC-4 was not undertaking a military flight; it had a cargo of food for several Port Harcourt hotels. It was also an occasion when for once the crew had not remained with the aircraft. American captain 'Pop' Garrett and British First Officer Tony Dorman

248: A Biafran ground-handler places branches over the engine of a Biafran Air Force T-6G at Uga to protect it from attack by the Nigerian Air Force. Just visible is a notch on the aircraft's propeller, undoubtedly identifying the aircraft as that flown by José Pignatelli and which was hit by Nigerian small-arms fire on several missions. It is also quite likely it is this aircraft which was flown back to Lagos after the end of the war (A. Alves Pereira)

249 Above: When the war ended the second batch of T-6Gs was ready for delivery, but all four remained in Portugal where they were later scrapped. Here the former 51-14770 looks pristine and fresh from overhaul in spite of this shot being taken on 18.8.71, eighteen months after Biafra's collapse. Note the underwing bomb-racks still fitted (via Dave Becker)

250 Right: When the Portuguese ferry pilot, Peralta, landed at Abidjan while delivering a T-6G to Biafra he heard reports of intense Nigerian anti-aircraft fire. He elected not to venture any further. His T-6G remained at Abidjan (Roger Caratini)

had fortunately wandered off just before the Biafran attack and therefore escaped injury. Less fortunate, however, were some twenty Nigerians unloading the aircraft and who were all killed in the attack.

The Port Harcourt raid was described by one of the British mercenary pilots (with the MiG-17 Detachment there) as "not one of the usual flying-club type of raids by von Rosen's crowd, but a highly professional attack and using highly-accurate rockets". According to the same pilot this raid destroyed one of the resident MiG-17Fs (NAF615) as well as one Ilyushin Il-28 which was passing through at the time. Two MiG-17Fs (NAF621 & NAF622) were scrambled immediately after the Biafran raid but their respective pilots, Paul Martin and Ares Klootwyk, were both unable to track the Biafran attackers back to their base. (The loss of MiG-17F NAF615 was immediately made good by transferring NAF612 from Enugu.)

On the same day as the Port Harcourt raid by the T-6Gs, three Biafran MFI-9Bs and one T-6G attacked the oil companies' air-strip at Escravos. The attackers hit their target around lunchtime and released rockets against a small hangar and several aircraft, including a Nigerian Air Force Dornier 27 parked beside the strip. The Biafran aircraft struck just as a Nigerian Air Force DC-3, 'AAQ' had landed on a supply flight from Lagos.

The DC-3 was taxying off the landing strip and sustained fourteen direct hits; its pilot, Marian Kozubski, received serious leg injuries that almost put an end to his flying career.[391]

Nigeria reacts; MiGs turn green

Three days after the attack against Port Harcourt, on 13

November, a Nigeria Airways F-27 Friendship, 5N-AAX, inbound from Lagos, landed at 13:50. The F-27 was operating a Government Charter flight (Flight GC025) with ammunition and soldiers. The crew, Captain Rufus Orimoloye and a British co-pilot, Rod Price, approached Port Harcourt cautiously, having learnt of the destruction caused in the raid several days beforehand. But when they landed the crew found no sign of any damage. Everything had been cleared and it was as if the attack had never taken place. The only change was the speed at which the F-27 was unloaded, but there was a specific reason for this. A revised procedure for visiting aircraft now called for a MiG-17F to rendezvous with the F-27 as it crossed the river Niger and then make a wide 'defensive circuit' of the airfield while the cargo was being unloaded. Only after 5N-AAX had taken-off (at 14:05) and passed over the Niger, on its return to Lagos, did the MiG-17F break off to land back at Port Harcourt.[392]

The impact of the Biafran Air Force attack had been quite serious. Precautions were at last being taken. Speed had become an important factor; the duration of the MiG-17, without underwing fuel tanks, was barely more than 45 minutes.

The Biafran air raid against Port Harcourt also had quite a dramatic effect on some of the mercenaries based there. One of the British MiG-17F pilots reacted by writing a paper on airfield defence systems and which recommended the construction of parking-bays in jungle clearings as well as the painting of parking areas and taxi-tracks in green paint. Various other systems and procedures were recommended, including the introduction of an airfield standby procedure with a daylight watch and an air-raid warning bell. The Commanding Officer of the Port Harcourt MiG-17 Detachment, Captain Bayo Lawal, dutifully accepted the report with an air of some indifference. Nevertheless, he promptly signed it, and sent it on to NAF HQ at Lagos–only then to find himself promoted immediately to the rank of Major. Rather ironically another of the report's recommendations was that front-line MiG-17s should be repainted in overall two-tone green camouflage and that one of Lawal's first orders (as a Major) was to instruct the same British pilot responsible for compiling the report to ferry one of the based MiG-17Fs (NAF612) to Lagos for repainting. When the pilot flew in to Lagos on 24 November 1969, he was quite surprised to find a MiG-17, one of the former East German Air Force non-reheat examples (NAF633), already camouflaged and awaiting his collection. NAF612 therefore became the *second* Nigerian MiG-17 to be repainted in what was actually an overall single-shade dark-green scheme. *(Several more MiG-17s were repainted and were in evidence in the October 1970 Independence Day flypast, but the programme is thought not to have involved more than a handful of aircraft.)*

More Biafran attacks

Four days after the Port Harcourt raid the Norwegian ship mv *Titania* was attacked, just after midday on 14 November, by two Biafran aircraft, both identified as MFI-9Bs, as it was unloading at the John Holt & Co wharves, at Warri docks. In what had become a standard attack profile, the Biafran aircraft made two runs across Warri docks. On the second run the attackers also caught an American steamer, *African Crescent*. The latter sustained six direct hits causing damage to its superstructure. The ship's bridge was also damaged in the attack and one passenger cabin was gutted by a resultant fire. The steamer was temporarily repaired at Warri and two days later, on 16 November, the *African Crescent* sailed for Lagos. As for the *Titania,* it had been holed in three places and a small fire had broken out on board but, apart from a minor injury sustained by the Second Mate, there were no serious injuries as a result of the raid.[393]

Towards the end of November 1969 one of the two Biafran T-6Gs was temporarily deployed to the forward

251: The shorter exhaust identifies this as one of eight non-afterburning MiG-17 blatt variants delivered in November 1969. All were former East German Air Force examples. After re-assembly at Kano NAF633, the third of the batch, was delivered to Lagos by Paul Martin on 15 November 1969 where it was repainted in an overall dark green scheme. NAF633 was then collected by another British mercenary pilot on 25 November 1969 and ferried to Port Harcourt where this view was taken shortly afterwards (Ares Klootwyk)

strip at Mbawsi, just south of Umuahia. Biafran Army Intelligence reports had indicated that Nigerian units were gathering along the Aba-Umuahia road. The T-6G, fully armed with 68mm rockets and machine-guns, attacked the column and caused a large number of casualties. The Nigerian Air Force MiG-17 detachment at Port Harcourt was immediately alerted and ordered to catch the Biafran T-6G as it landed at Mbawsi but by the time that the MiG-17 managed to get airborne the T-6G had escaped unscathed. MiG-17s did subsequently locate the Biafran strip at Mbawsi and several retaliatory attacks were carried out against the strip on 26 November and 1 December in the hope of either hitting the aircraft on the ground or rendering the strip sufficiently deniable for use. But the T-6G had already transferred back to its Uga base.

In the meantime the 'Minicons' were brought into an action which took several days against a Nigerian ground force massing for an attack from the west and south-west of Owerri. The first sign of the build-up came on 20 November when two Biafran MFI-9Bs, flown by Willy Bruce and Friedrich Herz, attacked artillery guns near Kwale, on the west bank of the river Niger. It was reported by Intelligence Units at the time, albeit unconfirmed, that the artillery consisted of newly-delivered Soviet 122mm long-range guns. Other reports told of Divisional HQ using a schoolhouse on the eastern bank at Omoku. Several 'Minicon' sorties were flown against the new target at Omoku on 25 November but Biafran Intelligence later admitted that the HQ was not at Omoku but at Obrikon, several miles to the north. One MFI-9B reconnaissance sortie was flown to Obrikon late on 26 November and attracted heavy anti-aircraft fire. Nigerian soldiers were seen to be massing artillery for a concentrated assault.

The Biafran Air Force planned a decisive attack against Obrikon for 28 November with three MFI-9Bs. Friedrich Herz was to lead the attack with two Biafrans, Sammy and Alex, in support. The three aircraft, operating from Ozubulu strip, flew direct to Obrikon but as they turned to start their attack all came under heavy anti-aircraft fire. The attack was immediately abandoned and Herz called his two wingmen to see if either aircraft had been hit. Alex did not respond to Herz' radio calls and was seen to make a wide turn as if to head back to base. The remaining two aircraft then resumed the attack and fired rockets against their designated target. Biafran Air Force HQ, listening in to enemy frequencies, heard the Nigerian commander in Obrikon calling Port Harcourt for air support from MiG-17s. It confirmed the importance of the target but it seemed that the Nigerian Air Force was not ready to respond to the calls. Back at their base Sammy's aircraft was found to have taken five direct hits; Freddy's aircraft was undamaged. Of Alex, however, there was no sign.

Shortly after daybreak on 29 November, at 06:40, Friedrich Herz and Sammy carried out a search mission in an attempt to find Alex's aircraft but there was no sign of it. Later in the day the same two pilots made yet another rocket attack against the Nigerian units massing at Obrikon. Biafran Air Force HQ again heard the call for MiG-17 support. This time Port Harcourt was ready; the Army Commander received a brief acknowledgement "MiGs in 3 minutes". Unfortunately Biafran HQ was not in direct radio contact with the 'Minicon' and was unable to warn the pilots until too late.

The Nigerian Air Force launched two MiG-17Fs in a bid to catch the Biafran MFI-9Bs. The South African mercenary Ares Klootwyk was quickly airborne in MiG-17F NAF621 while British pilot, Paul Martin, followed immediately aboard NAF624. The Biafrans returned to Ozubulu unaware of the danger facing them. Then came the codeword "Yankee, Yankee!" to indicate enemy aircraft in the vicinity. Herz managed to land safely and taxied quickly to the edge of Ozubulu strip and beneath some trees. As soon as Sammy had landed he brought his MFI-9B to a halt, jumped out of the cockpit, and ran for cover. Klootwyk could see the Biafran aircraft sitting on the strip and brought his MiG in for a successful strafing run. The aircraft exploded. The two MiG-17Fs then made another run and caught and damaged Herz' MFI-9B, believed to be BB-103, with 37mm cannon fire. (The wing and fuselage of the MFI-9B were badly damaged.) Paul Martin then flew over the Ozubulu base for a final run to photograph the damage. Both MiG-17Fs then returned safely to Port Harcourt.[394]

For the Biafran Air Force, November 1969 had ended badly but the worst news came in early on 30 November. The wreck of Alex Agbafuna's 'Minicon' had been found in shallow water, close to the front line but on the Biafran side. Alex's body was still in the cockpit. Three of the other pilots drove to the crash site to bring the body back home and it was then they realised that Alex had been shot in the neck by small-arms fire. One of the rockets had fired on impact and caused a fire although crashing in a small river had prevented the fire from totally destroying the aircraft. Whether Alex had died from the bullet wound or whether he drowned afterwards was not clear but it did explain why he did not respond to Herz' radio calls over the target area.

In spite of receiving reinforcement pilots from the Training School in Gabon the morale within the Biafran Air Force was, by early December 1969, exceedingly low. Aircrew had been particularly upset at the loss of Alex Agbafuna.

But it was not just 'Minicon' pilots whose morale had dropped. One of the two Portuguese pilots who arrived with the T-6Gs, José Pignatelli, appeared to have suffered a deep psychological trauma after only two weeks in Biafra; he had also taken to drinking a locally-brewed alcohol. Pignatelli returned to Abidjan one night ostensibly to collect a third T-6G, the aircraft left at Abidjan by

José Peralta after he had decided to quit the operation. Pignatelli flew to Abidjan after hitching a ride out of Uli aboard a returning arms flight. But he never did collect the T-6G; in fact he was never seen in Biafra again. Nor was the Portuguese engineer, Borralho, after he was sent back to Europe during December 1969 with a considerable sum of money to buy urgently-needed T-6G spares, although to his credit the war was over before he had a chance to return.

The German pilot, Friedrich Herz was, for a while, the only European flying MFI-9Bs of Biafra's 47th Squadron. Of his final sorties in Biafra, two almost ended in disaster. Late on 13 December 1969 Herz carried out a night raid against an enemy front-line target but on the return flight to base the aircraft's radio failed. His only alternative was to fly north along the River Niger until he reached the town of Onitsha. At that point he knew from experience that to fly on a heading of 120° for 11 minutes would bring him directly over one of the 'Minicons' former bush strips. In the darkness, Herz found enormous difficulty in recognising landmarks as he circled over what he believed to have been the strip. He then saw a green light and then three hand-held torches appeared. With fuel running dangerously low Herz had no alternative but to land towards the lights. Amazingly he landed safely only to find that his guides had been a group of Biafran soldiers who recognised the sound of an MFI-9B.

The second incident occurred two nights later, on 15 December 1969. Two 'Minicons', flown by Friedrich Herz and Augustus Okpe, were detailed to attack Ughelli. Take-off was timed for 18:15hrs to allow the attackers to reach their target just after dusk. Moonlight was just sufficient to allow the two aircraft to maintain visual contact. Okpe took the lead with Herz just behind and slightly above but as they were approaching their target Okpe appears to have made a serious error. He flashed the aircraft's landing light, an error that was seen by enemy soldiers on the ground. The enemy opened fire but it was Herz' aircraft that took the hit. He reduced altitude instantly and saw Okpe's aircraft begin to weave to avoid getting hit. Augustus Okpe avoided the enemy fire and apparently managed to make the target and fire off a number of rockets. Herz' aircraft began to vibrate erratically and the engine lost 25% power. He lowered the flaps slightly and immediately set course back to Biafra. The engine also began losing oil pressure, which eventually dropped to zero, and the engine began to sound as if about to seize. Then, as Herz approached Biafran territory he decided to abandon any attempt to land at base and instead land at the main Uli strip. He radioed Uli and managed to convince the Controller to temporarily halt the relief flights. At almost exactly 22:30 Herz lined up for final approach to Uli but his landing was not quite to plan. As the 'Minicon' touched-down it swung violently to port. Herz instantly increased power and landed again, this time just with the starboard wheel. Then with the nosewheel down he sharply applied the brakes. The aircraft came to a halt on the strip and Herz climbed out quickly. Unloaders and other helpers ran onto the strip and physically lifted the damaged aircraft clear of the landing area.

Herz managed to get a lift back to his base by road. Then, once dawn had broken and the threat of a MiG-17 attack had gone, mechanics set about repairing the 'Minicon'. It seemed that a magneto had been damaged by small-arms. The fuselage had eight bullet-holes in it but of greater significance was the fact that the port mainwheel was missing.

The situation inside Biafra by mid-December 1969 was becoming almost intolerable. The Biafrans were suffering heavy civilian casualties through artillery fire and Nigerian Air Force attacks. On 17 December a meeting was held at Biafran Air Force Headquarters. Several Army officers attended, as did three MFI-9B pilots, Tommy, Benny and Friedrich Herz. The Army, it seemed, desparately wanted the Air Force to start attacking specifically-civilian targets in Nigeria as a means of retaliation. The pilots openly disagreed claiming that civilian targets in Nigeria bore no military significance to the Biafran war effort and in any case would undoubtedly increase the enemy's morale and resolve to further attacks.

A week after the Strategy meeting Friedrich Herz returned to Europe for a three-week Christmas break. This left only Biafran pilots with the squadron. In the meantime General Godwin Ezeilo, the Biafran Air Force Commanding Officer, had made an attempt to find additional pilots, not only to replace Friedrich Herz but also to replace the Portuguese T-6G pilot, Pignatelli. Word went out to the various agencies still supporting the Biafran cause. Two Europeans did arrive in Biafra early in December 1969. One was Pieter Dezeeuw, the Dutchman who just weeks beforehand had ditched the Meteor NF.14 G-ASLW into the Atlantic Ocean while undertaking the delivery flight from Faro to Biafra. He had made his way safely back to Portugal and then back to London; his Windsor-based employer then answered a call from Biafra for an experienced C-47/DC-3 by offering Dezeeuw the job in Biafra. The other European pilot who arrived in Biafra turned out not to be a pilot at all, only an Engineer.[395]

Nigeria: the first 'Final Push'

Signs of a 'final push' by the Nigerian Army became evident during November 1969 with the arrival of large numbers of reinforcement troops to all three Federal Divisions; the new recruits were sufficient for several new Battalions to be formed. The arms shipments from the Soviet Union had also resumed during the previous month and which included a number of long-range 122mm heavy artillery guns. These were seen particularly as having the sufficient power and range to become a key and decisive factor in any breakthrough against Biafran resistance. But despite the fact that no Nigerian Army gunners had received any formal training, and thus denying front-line units the immediate use of these weapons, the final offensive was launched.[396]

If there were signs of a final Nigerian push, there were few signs, at the end of November 1969, that Biafran resistance was close to a dramatic and swift collapse. The enclave had retracted steadily and considerably during the course of the year but Owerri and Orlu, the only towns of any significant size remaining under Biafran control, were still considered, by the Biafrans, to be safe. Even the Nigerian Air Force 'Intruder', which continued to bomb Uli at night had had little effect on reducing the nightly arms and relief airlift. Indeed, during the final two months of the war, Nordchurchaid managed to airlift some of the highest nightly tonnages of the entire war. But, sadly, not without sustaining further losses.

Relief airlift: two more losses

Just two weeks after the loss of Alex Nicoll and four other crew members aboard the Joint Church Aid C-97G, Canairelief suffered damage to one of its L-1049H Super Constellations. CF-NAM sustained damage from bomb fragments while it was being unloaded at Uli during the night of 7/8 October. At first, the damage (which seemed to be confined to the wings) appeared to be largely superficial and as all systems were still functioning satisfactorily the crew managed to take-off from Uli and fly safely back to São Tomé. But, as so often happened in the past, daybreak allowed engineers to take a closer look at the L-1049H and discover damage of a much more substantial nature. The aircraft was not declared irrepairable but the damage was sufficient to warrant a flight back to Europe for repairs.

In the light of the difficulties experienced back in February 1969 when Canairelief had tried to arrange for repairs to CF-NAJ, the agency decided to take a much simpler option. CF-NAM was removed from the São Tomé roster and instead nominated as a valuable source for spares.

In the light of the withdrawal of CF-NAM, as well as the earlier loss of CF-NAJ in a crash near Uli during August 1969, Canairelief faced a future with just two serviceable aircraft (CF-NAK & CF-NAL). The agency's Montreal headquarters did agree to fund a replacement aircraft, and organised the immediate purchase of an ex-Capitol International Airways L-1049H (N1927H) which, since March 1968, had been in storage at Wilmington, Delaware. The aircraft was flown to Montreal for a routine inspection and at the same time was repainted in the standard (albeit slightly lighter) 'blue top jungle camouflage" scheme with white titling. The titling was different to the previous aircraft in that it read 'JOINT CHURCHAID' and 'OPERATED BY CANAIRELIEF'. By now re-registered as CF-AEN, the replacement L-1049H departed Dorval, Canada on 9 November 1969 and flew to London-Heathrow, before flying on to Amsterdam on 15 November. It eventually arrived at São Tomé on 20 November, but immediately became the subject of a major difficulty. Nobody at Canairelief, it seems, had advised the island's authority of its pending arrival. Therefore none of the Operations personnel had requested a permit to position the aircraft to São Tomé. As the Governor himself had to sign the permits there was considerable anxiety among the airlift planners as to the reaction from the island's Governor. In the meantime Canairelief was refused clearance to operate from São Tomé and CF-AEN was re-positioned to Libreville on 26 November. Only then could Canairelief request the necessary clearances which, in spite of the Governor's anger, were approved. CF-AEN remained at Libreville overnight and returned to the island on the following day and joined the shuttle to Uli during the night of 28/29 November.

Night bombing of Uli by the Nigerian Air Force 'Intruder' had stopped during October 1969 but then suddenly resumed on the night of 1/2 November. A Fred Olsen DC-6A, LN-FOM, and being flown by Amund Klepp, had just landed, around 18:45 hours on the first of its two scheduled flights for the night when the 'Intruder' released several bombs. The DC-6A was being taxied into one of the "fingers" when the bomb struck the runway, about 80 yards from the aircraft. The force of the explosion caught the aircraft and shrapnel hit one of the starboard engines. The aircraft still had some 8,000ltrs of fuel on board which immediately ignited. Very quickly the fire engulfed the starboard wing; another fire broke out towards the rear of the fuselage.[397]

As soon as the fire started Flight Engineer Bill Hough forced open the cockpit door and climbed over a full load of stockfish to reach the two passengers, Father Dick Kissane and Brother Walter Maccagno. Bill Hough then managed to open the rear cargo door and tied a rope to a stanchion to allow all three to swing out from the aircraft away from the flames and safely negotiate the drop of 15 feet to the ground. The three men crawled across the melting tar of the tarmac, all sustaining burns as they did so. While this was happening, so the two remaining crew members, Captain Amund Klepp and First Officer Bill Markant had successfully made hasty exits through the cockpit windows.

All five men were taken to the nearby Ihaila Hospital and kept there overnight, three being treated for minor burns. The three-man crew returned to São Tomé during the following night but, as for the DC-6A LN-FOM, it had continued to burn for some twenty minutes before the fuselage broke into two. Unfortunately the entire cargo of stockfish was also lost. (It was said that the smell of burning stockfish could be detected across the entire Biafran territory for much of the night and the next day)[398]

252: No worse for wear is the impression given by the three crew members of the Fred Olsen DC-6A LN-FOM burnt out at Uli during the night of 1/2 November 1969. Captain Amund Klepp, Flight Engineer Bill Hough and First Officer Bill Markant escaped injury but spent a night in a Biafran hospital before being airlifted back to São Tomé on the following night. In this view the crew pose outside the hospital before leaving for Uli strip (Amund Klepp)

Joint Church Aid: changes

Towards the end of October 1969 the relief effort out of São Tomé underwent some minor operational changes. The Joint Church Aid schedule was still managed by the source of the relief material, ie agreed concept of 'one night Protestant (W.C.C.) cargo, next night Catholic (CARITAS) cargo'. The concept, introduced in August 1968, continued to work well and there was no real need for changing. In Libreville, however, where Africa Concern (and CARITAS Ireland) operated a separate relief airlift, food and medical stocks had been exhausted. The Belgian International Air Services DC-6B OO-HEX, used almost exclusively on the Africa Concern airlift, flew into São Tomé on 30 October 1969 and operated from the island on alternate, CARITAS, nights. This proved to be a more effective way of managing relief material and co-ordinating flights than simply replenishing the empty warehouse at Libreville.[399]

There was also a change in the management of the Joint Church Aid C-97G fleet. Until October 1969 those aircraft on São Tomé had been operated by the San Francisco-based company, Flight Test Research Inc. Operations were, of course, on behalf of Joint Church Aid but administrative support, spares support and base to line communications (and vice versa) were distant and sometimes difficult. From 22 October, Balair took over the responsibility for the operation of the C-97Gs. One effect of the change was the transfer of support equipment and some spares from the International Red Cross base at Cotonou. Ironically, much of this was ferried over to São Tomé aboard the Balair C-160D Transall HB-ILN.

Not everything ran smoothly to plan. Flying ever-increasing quantities of relief material into Uli at night was fine but only if the re-distribution system inside Biafra during the following day could effectively deliver to the network of feeding stations. It naturally placed a huge strain on vehicles in a country ravaged by war and where petrol/diesel supplies were controlled and reserved for the Biafran Army. Breakdowns frequently occurred and the need for replacement vehicles became desperate. New lorries arrived by ship at São Tomé docks, but then came a blow; on 12 November the US Government banned the use of the C-97Gs for transporting the new lorries into Biafra. Unfortunately the C-97Gs were the only aircraft available that could take the vehicles which could be viewed as military equipment. The lorries were never flown in.

Another sensitive issue was the question of flying in diesel fuel for existing re-distribution vehicles. The American pilots had been refusing to fly in fuel since late-September 1969 and the fuel shortage in Biafra had reached crisis level. (In fact, the fuel was flown in from Libreville aboard the B.I.A.S. DC-6B and several Biafran Government-owned aircraft.) But Joint Church Aid planners continued to urge aircrew to carry in diesel fuel. Eventually a solution was agreed upon and which was finally introduced on the night of 5/6 December. One of the J.C.A. C-97Gs had one of its tanks disconnected from the aircraft's integral fuel system so that it could be used for transporting fuel for the lorries inside Biafra. The solution seemed more dangerous than carrying loose drums. On those nights that diesel fuel was ferried in to Biafra, fuel from the C-97G's wing-tank was drained into barrels on the strip at Uli while other workers unloaded relief material from the aircraft's main hold.

Relief airlift breaks all records

One of the war's greatest ironies remains the simple fact that a hitherto unlikely alliance of religious groups (Joint Church Aid) had dared to continue where traditional (Red Cross) agencies became fearful to tread. Since the International Red Cross stood its airlift down in June 1969, following the loss of the DC-7B, holding the constant threat of starvation at bay became virtually the sole responsibility of the São Tomé relief airlift. It meant that some changes had to take place.

During August 1969 CARITAS Germany donated a large warehouse to allow for the greater quantities of relief material to be stored on São Tomé. Measuring 165metres by 30metres, the warehouse was assembled on the edge of the island's airfield. 15,000 tonnes of food could now be stored adjacent to the aircraft ferrying it nightly in to Biafra. Within days of it being re-assembled, I.C.R.C. C-97Gs began ferrying the Red Cross stocks of food and medical equipment stored at Cotonou across to São Tomé. Stocks of salt as well as Red Cross support vehicles were flown in from Fernando Póo, all of which was ferried into Biafra by Joint Church Aid aircraft. Not only food and medicine was brought in by the I.C.R.C. One C-97G arrived from Geneva with a group of *Ibos* who had been receiving medical treatment in Swiss hospitals. In fact J.C.A. initially tried to refuse access to these people and for a short while their future was in question; ultimately they were flown in to Biafra.

With the increased level of activity at São Tomé it was not surprising that records were beginning to be broken. During the night of 18/19 September 1969 the island's airlift managed to get 20 flights into Uli, carrying a total of 255 tonnes. The nightly average for that month was between 16-18 flights; a significant increase over an average 12 flights per night for August 1969. The September high lasted for just over two months.

By December 1969 the number of relief flights out of São Tomé were reaching its peak. The Canairelief L-1049Hs, for example, were exceeding all of their best previous achievements. In fact they managed during that December, for the only occasion of the entire airlift, to exceed 100 landings at Uli in a month. That this figure was achieved is quite staggering in the light of continued night bombing and a deterioration of Uli's landing surface. One close encounter involved the L-1049H CF-NAL which escaped with minor damage at Uli on the night of 13/14 November when a bomb landed just to the rear of the aircraft. One unloader and five others were injured.

A milestone was achieved on the night of 25/26 November 1969 with the 4,500th Church relief flight into Biafra, the actual flight being by one of the Norwegian DC-6s (DC-6A LN-FOL or DC-6B LN-SUD). Then, on the night of 29/30 November 1969 the São Tomé-based fleet managed to get 22 flights safely into Uli; between them they airlifted some 277 tonnes. In fact December 1969, the last complete calendar month of operations, produced the greatest number of flights by Joint Church Aid within any previous period. The highest number of flights made during any one single night of the entire J.C.A. airlift was achieved on 7/8 December 1969 when 27 flights were successfully landed at Uli, carrying in a record 364 tonnes of relief aid. J.C.A.'s total for the month of December amounted to a staggering 545 flights into Uli.

Eleven aircraft had been available for flights on the night of 7/8 December; one C-97G (N52727) was declared unfit and taken off the flight roster. Of the other regular J.C.A. airlift participants two of the Icelandic DC-6s (TF-AAD and TF-AAF) were undergoing overhaul at Prestwick and one of the Joint Church Aid C-97Gs (N52631) was midway through an overhaul in Tel Aviv. A breakdown of each aircraft's cargo despatched on the night of 7/8 December illustrates well the make-up of the Joint Church Aid airlift, and the following table shows the order in which aircraft were loaded and flown from São Tomé to Uli:

Aircraft	Type	Trip No.	Cargo (Weight in kgs)	Weight (kgs)
LN-FOL	DC-6A	1	474 sacks rice	10,896
CF-NAK	L-1049H	1	253 sacks oatmeal	12,827
			127 cartons tinned milk	2,667
TF-AAB	DC-6B	1	156 sacks oatmeal	7,909
			176 sacks nutricia	2,992
TF-AAH	DC-6B	1	138 sacks oatmeal	6,996
			177 sacks nutricia	3,009
TF-AAA	DC-6B	1	144 sacks oatmeal	7,300
			20 cartons plastic sacks	500
			157 cartons meat	2,041
			16 boxes food	463
LN-SUD	DC-6B	1	138 sacks oatmeal	6,996
			177 cartons nutricia	3,009
N52876	C-97G	1	97 sacks rice	2,250
			540 sacks Formula 2	12,744
CF-AEN	L-1049H	1	212 sacks oatmeal	10,748
			338 cartons medicine	5,746
N52915	C-97G	1	97 sacks rice 540	2,250
			sacks Formula 2	12,744
CF-NAL	L-1049H	1	233 sacks oatmeal 351	11,813
			cartons medicine	4,183
N52600	C-97G	1	97 sacks rice	2,250
			540 sacks Formula 2	12,744
TF-AAH	DC-6B	2	193 boxes meat	2,509
			20 sacks egg powder	1,000
			280 sacks rice	6,496
N52876	C-97G	2	97 sacks rice	2,250
			540 sacks Formula 2	12,744
CF-NAK	L-1049H	2	65 drums diesel oil	11,700
			10 drums motor oil	2,000
			30 bales stockfish	1,350
			19 sacks egg powder	950
LN-SUD	DC-6B	2	474 sacks rice	10,997
CF-AEN	L-1049H	2	711 sacks rice	16,495
N52600	C-97G	2	97 sacks rice	2,250
			540 sacks Formula 2	12,744
TF-AAA	DC-6B	2	119 boxes dry milk	2,499
			20 sacks egg powder	1,000
			293 sacks rice	6,496

Aircraft	Type	Trip No.	Cargo (Weight in kgs)	Weight (kgs)
LN-SUD	DC-6B	2	244 boxes Bouillon	1,000
			400 sacks milk powder	10,000
N52600	C-97G	3	97 sacks rice	2,250
			540 sacks Formula 2	12,744
N52876	C-97G	3	97 sacks rice	2,250
			540 sacks Formula 2	12,744
CF-AEN	L-1049H	3	20 sacks noodles	1,000
			20 sacks egg powder	1,000
			193 boxes meat	2,509
			517 sacks rice	11,994
N52915	C-97G	2	97 sacks rice	2,250
			540 sacks Formula 2	12,744
CF-NAK	L-1049H	3	20 sacks noodles	1,000
			20 sacks egg powder	1,000
			193 boxes meat	2,509
			474 sacks rice	10,996
TF-AAB	DC-6B	2	193 boxes meat	2,509
			20 sacks egg powder	1,000
			319 sacks rice	7,400
N52915	C-97G	3	97 sacks rice	2,250
			540 sacks Formula 2	12,744
LN-FOL	DC-6A	2	474 sacks rice	10,996
Total		**27**		**363,546 kgs**

Two nights later, on 9/10 December the same fleet achieved 22 flights with 286 tonnes. The ability to achieve such a high number of flights on these nights can be attributed to a brief lull in the fighting which accompanied the arrival at Uli of the Conservative Party's opposition Leader of the House of Lords, Lord Carrington. He had been sent to look at both sides of the war.

Uli - Biafra: "There but for the grace…"

The brief respite in Nigerian attacks against Uli during the visit to Nigeria of Lord Carrington did have some unexpected benefits. The reduction in the level of attacks lasted for almost a week afterwards and had an added benefit for two of Biafra's gun-running aircraft which, under normal circumstances, would have been easy targets for the MiG-17s. On the night of 16/17 December unloaders at Uli had just finished offloading ammunition from a DC-7CF, TR-LOK. Captain Clive Halse called for engine start-up but then discovered that the aircraft's batteries had run flat. Fearing that the DC-7CF might be stranded (and unable to get away before daylight) one of the crew noted that another gun-runner from Libreville, the DC-6B TR-LOX, was being unloaded in an adjacent bay. One of the crew ran across the strip to seek assistance. Both crews agreed on a plan of action; the captain of the DC-6B agreed to the Flight Engineer removing his aircraft's batteries and then re-connecting them to the DC-7CF, an operation that became increasingly tense as dawn drew nearer. Eventually the crippled DC-7CF's engines were started. The batteries were then again disconnected and returned to the DC-6B. Out of courtesy Halse then waited for the DC-6B to depart before taking his turn for take-off. By now, dawn had fully broken and, in broad daylight, the DC-7CF crew nervously edged the aircraft off from Uli and across the strip of Federal-held territory before climbing to cruise altitude and setting normal course for Libreville. The MiG-17s had missed an opportunity.[400]

The threat of being caught on the ground at Uli after daybreak was a major worry for any aircrew irregardless of what their cargo was. When Clive Halse returned to Uli on the night of 18/19 December with the next ammunition flight he ordered that the Number 3 engine be kept running all the time that the aircraft was on the ground. Tragically the local unloaders were unused to being so close to an aircraft with the engines running; in the chaotic darkness of Uli at night one of the Biafran labourers ran into the propeller. He was killed outright. The Flight Engineer later made the rather laconic entry "returned with red props" in his log-book. (The entry was a stark contrast to the usual "returned with green props" on occasions of hitting the tops of trees on final approach to Uli!)[401]

The lull in the fighting was only shortlived and nightly bombing raids against Uli resumed with the Nigerian 'Intruder' aircraft introducing a new bombing technique. This involved the dropping of magnesium flares before any bombs were released. Such an attack took place on the evening of 17 December when a flare was released at approximately 19:30 and which lit up the entire airstrip. The 'Intruder' then lined up to drop two bombs, neither of which caused any serious damage. Another full circuit brought the 'Intruder' over the strip when a third bomb was released; again no serious damage. On the fourth circuit the "Intruder"'s aim was still off target but on the next circuit the bombardier scored a hit.

The Canairelief Super Constellation CF-NAK had positioned to Uli's 'Finger No.2' and was almost unloaded when the magnesium flare was dropped, at which point all of the Biafran unloaders took to the safety of nearby bunkers. The aircraft's pilot, Captain Bill Fox, and the crew followed while the 'Intruder' released his series of bombs. Fox watched as the fifth bomb struck the ground no more than five feet in front of the Number 3 engine. The aircraft was immediately engulfed in flames and within several minutes the trucks that were still parked beside the front and rear cargo doors were also alight. As the aircraft burned out of control so the 'Intruder' began machine-gunning the immediate area denying the Biafrans a chance of conducting any fire fighting action. The fire continued unabated and eventually CF-NAK was completely destroyed, leaving only the distinctive triple-fin tail section which had broken away at the peak of the fire.

Mercifully, there were no injuries sustained during the bombing of CF-NAK but flights were seriously disrupted

253: Canairelief L-1049H Super Constellation CF-NAK operated on the nightly Nordchurchaid airlift for just over seven months. During the night of 17/18 December 1969 it sustained a direct hit at Uli by a bomb dropped by the Nigerian Air Force DC-3 'Intruder' aircraft. After fire had consumed the aircraft, only the tail section remained recognisable. This whole section was later pushed to one side of the strip. In this view, taken immediately after the Biafran surrender, a group of Nigerian soldiers pose victoriously on the tailplane section (Topix)

for the remainder of the night. Bill Fox and his crew managed to secure a return ride to São Tomé aboard a Joint Church Aid C-97G.[402]

The loss of CF-NAK had a dramatic effect on Canairelief"s operation. The agency had begun operations with just one L-1049H but since the airlift had began four more had been acquired. Two had since been involved in accidents and a third was grounded at São Tomé for spares recovery. Only CF-AEN and CF-NAL were, by now, declared flyable. A decision was therefore taken to restore CF-NAM to an airworthy state and to achieve this parts were ordered from Montreal. Work at São Tomé proceeded with some pace and eventually it was test-flown, on 17 January 1970. By then it was too late to return to the airlift.

A fuel crisis

The number of record flights being chalked-up by the relief airlift crews despite the bombing of a Canairelief L-1049H at Uli brought a real sense of drama to the struggle of maintaining the massive relief airlift. But in reality the drama was only just beginning to unfold.

By mid-December 1969 the increase in the number of flights was having a dramatic effect on São Tomé's ability to keep up with the demand in fuel. At the same time the Churches began to suspect that the oil companies were enforcing what was effectively a boycott of aviation fuel.

Eventually, on 22 December, a tanker arrived at São Tomé. Not only did it arrive late after having steamed from Angola at only 7 knots but it was later discovered that the fuel was contaminated. The effect on the airlift was immediate. Flight rosters were re-arranged so that only one flight per aircraft per night was planned. Ironically, two nights later, on Christmas Eve 1969, the Church airlift passed another milestone with its 5,000th flight into Uli.

During the course of 30 December fuel tankers began to arrive at the island. They had been diverted to São Tomé from other destinations and the airport's fuel tanks could be suitably replenished. The flight programme resumed its normal schedule.[403]

The final 'Final Push'

The attack began on 22 December 1969 by two Brigades (12 & 17) of the Nigerian Army's 3rd Division. The strategy was clearly to break through the Biafran line of defence north of Aba and in such strength to allow a further push to enable the southern front-line to link up with the 1st Division at Umuahia. The objective was simply to cut the remaining area of Biafra into two halves, and by Christmas Day the Nigerians had successfully done so.

For Biafra, the military situation was virtually hopeless as its dispirited army desperately fought against overwhelming enemy firepower and numbers. The will to defend had weakened measurably; the morale within the Biafran Air Force dropped even further as a dire shortage of aviation fuel effectively grounded the remaining MFI-9Bs and T-6Gs. Even with sufficient fuel reserves for just a handful of sorties against Nigerian positions, the Biafran Air Force continued to sustain some serious losses.

At the turn of the new year the Biafran Air Force 47th Squadron had consisted of five pilots including the newly-

254: Towards the end of the Nigerian Civil War the Biafran Air Force could claim just one surviving Alouette II, seen here at Uga strip. In this view the Alouette is being covered with branches to act as temporarily camouflage against air attacks by the Nigerian Air Force. Shortly afterwards this Alouette became unserviceable and is thought to have been the same helicopter as that seen aboard the L-1049H N563E (A. Alves Pereira)

255: When L-1049H N563E staged through São Tomé on 3 January 1970 an Alouette II was seen to be inside. It is possibly the same Alouette as seen above (and which was known to be unserviceable). But by this time officials inside Biafra knew the war was almost over. Would they therefore have sent an Alouette out for repair or did they acquire a replacement? If it was on the way out, then where did it go to? Did Ojukwu plan to use an Alouette for a quick escape to Uli? After 30 years there are still questions unanswered! (Jakob Ringler)

appointed Squadron Leader, Alves Pereira. Within a few days tragedy would strike one of the MFI-9B's squadron.

On 4 January 1970, one of the Air Force's most popular and accomplished pilots, Ibi Brown, was killed. Operating out of Ozubulu strip, Brown had been part of a small group detailed to attack an enemy concentration several miles to the north, within the Awka sector. The attack was carried out under enemy fire but the precise position of the front-line was extremely fluid. Some details of the incident still remain vague but it is thought that Brown flew directly over an enemy concentration and hit by small-arms fire. Other reports from an another pilot on this sortie believes that Ibi Brown was making a very tight turn, became disorientated, stalled and hit trees and exploded. Other reports described the aircraft as simply exploding in mid-air, possibly caused by a rocket detonating as Brown began his attack run. Whatever the true facts were the result was nevertheless inevitable. The 'Minicon' hit the ground in 'no-man's land' and was left to burn out. Nigerian soldiers reached the wreckage during an advance on the following day. Flt/Lt Ibi Brown's death was yet one more serious blow to Biafran Air Force morale and taken very badly by other members of the squadron. At that point the will to fight on then simply evaporated.

The 'final of the final' Nigerian offensives started in earnest early on 7 January 1970, again led by Nigeria's 3rd Marine Commando Division in a drive from the southeast. Three Nigerian Brigades (12, 14 & 17) advanced rapidly along the west bank of the river Imo as villages were simply abandoned by dispirited and out-manoeuvred Biafran soldiers. Okpuala fell by nightfall on 7 January and the Olakwo bridge was captured on the following day bringing the key Biafran town of Owerri within

256: As the Nigerian Army's final offensive got under way so the clandestine arms airlift from Libreville to Biafra continued its nightly momentum. Surrounded by cases of ammunition CIA Vietnam veteran Ed Davis brings a sense of humour to Jack Malloch's nightly operation. Taken on 23.12.69 the nose of DC-6B TR-LOX is just visible to the right, DC-7CF TR-LOK to the left. In the background is a C-47, thought to be the same example that was abandoned at Libreville with Zambian marks visible (Henry Kinnear)

artillery range. By nightfall on 9 January, when 17 Brigade had managed to advance as far as the Njaba river at Awomama, Uli strip was under serious threat of Nigerian artillery fire.[404]

It has been said that after the loss of Ibi Brown and his aircraft, Biafra's MFI-9B force consisted of just one remaining airworthy example; similarly of the two T-6Gs only one was fully airworthy. As a result operations were virtually suspended and the surviving pilots began to make plans for their own safety. Of considerable concern was the number of white advisers still in the enclave and who were by now facing a very real danger of being caught by the speed of the Nigerian advance.

General Godwin Ezeilo, Biafra's Head of the Air Force, visited the squadron late in the afternoon of 8 January and quietly announced the imminent departure of the Biafran leader. It was, according to Ezeilo, perhaps the right time for Pereira to leave Biafra as well. Passage aboard one of the last Biafran Government flights out of Uli could be arranged that night. After that the situation was seen as becoming very uncertain. The other four pilots in the squadron were Biafrans and it was they who urged Pereira to leave Biafra before the final collapse. In fact Pereira did try to make the journey south to Uli later that evening but the roads were so overcrowded with countless confused and panic-stricken refugees that the journey was hopeless. Pereira returned to his base where the squadron's only remaining serviceable T-6G had been kept. It then became, amidst the panic on the ground, the subject of quite a remarkable escape flight out of Biafra.

The decision to use it for an escape flight was taken early on 9 January. There was still sufficient fuel available for a flight to Gabon.

Most of the squadron's pilots were willing to remain inside Biafra and take a chance on being captured by Federal forces. There was, however, one exception; Flt/Lt Larry Obiechi was a Biafran but not an Ibo and for that reason he felt unsafe waiting for the Nigerian Army to overrun his position. There was also a suspicion that he had somehow been involved in the hijacking of the Nigeria Airways F-27 Friendship (5N-AAV) before the war. He was therefore allowed to join Pereira and occupy the rear seat of the T-6G. The aircraft took-off from Uga and flew at low-level initially before climbing above a cloud layer which covered the entire southern area of Biafra that day. Keeping the African shoreline always in sight, the Biafran T-6G passed abeam Fernando Póo island and the Cameroons. Later, and still keeping out to sea, the aircraft passed Equatorial Guinea and eventually arrived at Libreville where it was landed safely. The T-6G was handed over to Sr Henrique Madail, a Portuguese pilot with the Gabon Presidential Guard and into whose fleet it was incorporated.[405]

Biafra: Ojuwku flees to exile

Although its advance into the remaining Biafran-held territory had been swift the Nigerian Army almost stopped in its tracks, on 9 January 1970. In fact the Divisional Commander turned his attention to mopping up resistance in the "other half" of Biafra, the area around Arochukwu. For the main Biafran enclave it was a brief respite but just sufficiently long enough to allow the Biafran High Command to take some very decisive measures, including the confused departure of Colonel Ojukwu from the airstrip at Uli.

The events leading up to the final and dramatic departure of Colonel Ojukwu were subsequently and later very graphically described by Biafra's Chief Secretary, Mr N.U. Akpan.[406]

"The Governor *(Ojukwu)* had arrived at Owerri on the evening of Thursday 8 January, in a hurried flight from Madonna, forty miles away, his permanent residence since the fall of Umuahia. It had been a confused and panic-ridden ride for everybody. The Federal troops had crossed the Imo River at more than two points. And Imo River had always been regarded as the most effective barrier against the enemy. Shells were falling in Madonna. Early in the morning (of 8 January) we had been told that the Federal troops were 29 miles from Owerri along the Aba-Owerri road, By noon they were less than 15 miles away. I phoned the Commanding Officer, Brigadier Kalu, who told me that the situation was now hopeless and advised that any contingency plans made should be put into immediate effect."

Akpan's reference to a "hurried *flight* from Madonna" is intriguing and one that does not necessarily indicate a flight by an aircraft. Nevertheless one interesting arrival at São Tomé on 3 January 1970 had been an L-1049H Super Constellation, N563E, reportedly flown in by Larry Raab, an old-hand on the arms airlift. N563E was operating under a four-month lease arrangement between Carolina Aircraft Leasing Corporation and the Biafran Government since November 1969. Positioned just beside the aircraft's cargo doors and clearly visible from outside was an SE.3130 Alouette II helicopter but with no obvious signs of any markings. The precise reason for it being there was not made evident at São Tomé, but after dusk the L-1049H took off, presumably for Uli with the Alouette still aboard. Curiously there was no sign of any rotor blades aboard the L-1049H; nor was there any obvious supply of Jet-A1 fuel, necessary to power the Alouette's Astazou engine. (It is possible, of course, that there was still an adequate stock of paraffin—even home-made paraffin—in Biafra which, in the short term, the Alouette could have used without suffering irrepairable damage to its engine.) Equally curious was Raab's comment that the Alouette was being flown into Biafra to be positioned close to "a very senior Biafran official's residence should he be in need of moving out to Uli in haste." This was possibly the first real indication that the Biafran leadership was preparing to give up its struggle for independence.

By Friday 9 January 1970, Biafra's primary airstrip at Uli was now just as important for evacuating relief workers and refugees as it was in receiving the last deliveries of relief material. In all, some seventeen flights landed at Uli during the night of 9/10 January and this was in spite of no runway lighting until 22:00 due to a rocket having earlier damaged the power supply. Among those that managed to land was Africa Concern's DC-6B OO-HEX which evacuated twenty refugees to Libreville on what turned out to be the agency's final Biafra flight. Among other refugees flown out of Uli on the night of 9/10 January were the wives of Christopher Mojewku, Philip Effiong, Chukwudima (together with all of their children) and Mrs Akpan. Also aboard the flight was the Governor's wife and children who were offloaded at São Tomé in order to board another aircraft to Lisbon while all of the remaining passengers continued on to Abidjan.

Frank Dolha, Canairelief's Operations Manager at São Tomé, maintained a diary during his time on the airlift and which vividly records some of the events during the confused final week before Biafra's military collapse. For Saturday, 10 January 1970 he recorded:[407]

"We *(a Canadian L-1049H)* were scheduled out *(of São Tomé)* as Number 3 at 17:10Z with a C-97G ahead of us. When we arrived at the airport we were advised that Major Hanssen of JCA and Captain Tony Jonsson of Aid By Air had sent a message to São Tomé requesting that all aircraft depart 30 minutes before scheduled time. We became suspicious of this request and did not attempt to leave early, so as not to arrive over Nigeria during daylight.

257: The L-749A Constellation '5N86H' made one of the final Biafran Government flights out of Uli strip when, in the early hours of 12 January 1970, it took Colonel Ojukwu and senior ministers into exile at Abidjan. The registration marks, applied in red lettering, are clearly a corruption of the previous US identity, N86524. Later on 12 January '5N86H' flew on to Faro where it was subsequently abandoned (Roger Caratini)

"The first C-97 went mechanical *(unser iceable)* and the second one took-off at 17:10Z. *(Canairelief L-1049H)* CF-NAL with Captain Peter Knox took-off immediately after him. Juan Da Silva went on the flight to help offload since we did not want to take chances in case no offloaders would be available at Uli. As the first aircraft reached Uli they were told *(by radio)* that Uli was closed and that they were not cleared to land. Captain Knox insisted that he must land and for an excuse said that he was short of fuel. Then *(Major)* Hanssen and Captain Jonsson, who were on the ground at Uli, came on the radio *(whereupon)* Jonsson explained to Knox precisely where the runway had been damaged and advised him of the best procedure for landing. The lights along one side of the runway were out as they had had difficulties in repairing them in time for the arrival of our *(Canairelief)* aircraft.

"Just prior to darkness the *(Uli)* area was bombed and strafed, but Captain Knox landed safely. None of the regular offloaders were in sight, so the cargo was offloaded by the crew and passengers waiting to board. 80 people, mostly relief workers but some Biafrans, boarded the aircraft before the aircraft took-off for São Tomé. The crew reported ground-fire to the east *(of Uli)* with some fires and roads jammed with cars. After CF-NAL had landed most of the other aircraft returned to São Tomé as Uli Control was not clearing them to land.

One Joint Church Aid C-97G did manage to gain permission to land. The cargo was unloaded and the aircraft took-off with nine nuns aboard. Captain Jonsson *(who had just recently been in Biafra to evaluate the conditions at Uga strip)* returned to São Tomé aboard CF-NAL. Later that same night Jonsson took an empty DC-6 from São Tomé to Biafra. He managed to land at Uli and brought back 21 passengers *(most of whom were Red Cross staff)*."

On Saturday 10 January the southern half of Biafra, including the largest remaining town of Owerri, fell to the rapidly-advancing Nigerian Army. The control tower at Uli was abandoned on 10 January apart from a single priest who remained at the radio to warn incoming flights that all of the Biafran staff had fled into the bush and that the landing strip had been damaged by Nigerian shelling. In spite of this Joint Church Aid still planned an attempt to fly in and managed to get one DC-6B into Uli and on which 56 relief workers succeeded in getting out.

Akpan describes the events leading up to Ojukwu's departure from Biafra, during the night of 10/11 January 1970:

"...We started moving around midnight, but instead of turning towards Ihaila and Uli we went towards Akokwa and Uga. I did not understand for I had not then learnt that someone had telephoned from Uli to say that the airstrip had been put out of action by Federal planes, which had bombed the runway. For that reason all flights, including the one that was to take us, had been diverted to Uga. We stopped several times on the road to Uga for unexplained reasons. A few miles from Uga we stopped for thirty minutes, with vehicles pulled into the roadside, and lights out.

"Again no explanation was given, but those of us following immediately behind could see a vehicle driven forward and so deduced, rightly or wrongly, that someone had been sent to check conditions at the airstrip. After some time the car returned. Then there was a sudden movement back in the direction from which we had come. We turned round and followed without knowing or asking why.

"We finally reached the (Uli) airstrip. The huge cargo plane was waiting in the pitch darkness. Several people, apart from those who had travelled in the Governor's entourage, were already at the strip, ready to leave. The news of the number of people who had left the previous night from the Governor's own town Nnewi had gone round, and people who could make it had travelled to the airstrip to leave or at least send out their families, if they could.

"The Governor announced that only those in the 'delegation' were to travel in the waiting plane, while others should go to another side of the airstrip and board a French Red Cross plane. A senior government official who had come to the airstrip with his family, intending to leave as well, was assigned the duty of separating the sheep from the goats - those in the delegation and those who were not. In the end everyone from Nnewi and a few favoured others boarded the plane with us, while all the rest, including the family of Colonel Achuzia, were to travel in the Red Cross plane. We learnt on reaching Abidjan the following day that, as a result of a disagreement between Colonel Achuzia and the pilot, the Red Cross plane took off leaving almost all the prospective passengers behind."

The question that most people on the island were asking by now was of when Uli would finally be put out of action. Since the night of 8/9 January some 500 metres of Uli's runway had been unusable due to the number of bomb craters. But the strip could still be used and late on 10 January the L-749A '5N86H', which had been stationed at São Tomé for several days, was flown into Uli for its final mission to Biafra. The crew had been specially selected. In the left-hand seat was the aircraft's regular captain, an American named Hank Coates; his co-pilot for the flight was a Biafran named Osakwe while the Flight Engineer was a Briton. All three were probably the most experienced crewmen still flying on Biafra's 'Phoenix' run.

At a little after midnight on the morning of Sunday 11 January 1970, Ojukwu, together with a number of key Biafran government officials, made their dramatic flight to exile aboard the L-749A.[408] Another source puts the departure time at about 02:00hrs. They were flown out of Uli to Abidjan.

255

258: The only L-1649A Starliner Constellation to participate in Biafran operations was the Panamanian-registered HP-501. Former Warton pilot Larry Raab flew the aircraft on several arms supply flights to Portugal and later admitted that the aircraft had flown into Uli, from São Tomé, on just one occasion on 9/10 January 1970. It made its last Biafran flight from São Tomé to Faro on 11 January 1970 (with a number of senior Biafran officials onboard), after which it was flown to Douala and abandoned (Unknown)

Two other aircraft had also managed to land at Uli on the night of 10/11 January, both from Libreville. The French Red cross aircraft described by Akpan was an Affretair DC-7CF, TR-LOK, usually employed for arms and ammunition flights and was flown in by a Rhodesian crew (Captain Ed Davis, co-pilot Colin Miller and Flight Engineer Bill Rheeder. (The same crew had flown TR-LOK on a Libreville-Uli-São Tomé-Libreville shuttle the previous night to evacuate a number of French and South African 'advisers'. There was also talk that this would act as a reserve for Ojukwu should the L-749A be unable to perform the flight.) TR-LOK landed at Uli a little after 22:00 hours and unloaded some fuel and ammunition but its primary objective was to evacuate a number of French doctors and Biafran children. Conditions on the airstrip that night were, however, wholly chaotic. Some time after the DC-7CF landed, two trucks arrived on the strip with a group of sick Biafran children. Then two Mercedes cars drove onto the strip and, in the darkness, pulled up behind the L-749A '5N86H' which was parked opposite the Affretair DC-7CF. Apart from carrying the wives of several Biafran Government officials, the cars were clearly overloaded with luggage. Thankfully the cars parked behind the L-749A; in front of it and they would have blocked the exit of the DC-7CF. From the flightdeck Ed Davis could see soldiers running everywhere, all close on uncontrollable panic. Davis had kept one of the DC-7CF's engines running–a standard procedure to cover the event of a battery failure–and ordered his crew to restart the other three. Outside the aircraft the situation turned to sheer mayhem; a group of Biafran soldiers could be seen running in the darkness towards TR-LOK. With guns at the ready, they immediately prevented any of the children from boarding the aircraft. Then, and undoubtedly aware that Ojukwu himself was about to fly out of Uli within a very short while, the same soldiers tried to get the crew to allow another group of influential Biafrans, their families and baggage to climb aboard the DC-7CF. But when several of these soldiers began firing guns to calm the panic Ed Davis ordered his Flight Engineer, Bill Rheeder, to kick away the ladder at the back of the aircraft. At the same time, and on his captain's instruction, Colin Miller applied increased power. TR-LOK moved forward; Ed Davis turned the aircraft to the right and onto the runway, immediately applying full power for take-off. The crew had noticed a new and fairly large hole in the runway on landing but with an empty aircraft on full power Davis managed to lift the nosewheel in time to miss the hole on the take-off run. The mainwheels passed either side of it just as Davis urged the aircraft off the ground in what was an extremely short take-off. After setting course for Libreville a Biafran stowaway appeared at the cockpit door. He had hidden in the toilet while all the shooting was going on. Quite who he was nobody knew but he was handed over to Gabonese officials after TR-LOK landed at Libreville during the early hours of 11 January 1970.[409]

During the course of the following day representatives from all of the J.C.A. relief companies on São Tomé island met to discuss the deterorating situation in Biafra. The steady steam of high-ranking Biafrans had been able to pass on some details of the situation inside Biafra before some 80 or so departed the island for a direct flight to Faro aboard the L-1649A HP-501.

It was now widely known on São Tomé that Ojukwu had fled Biafra during the early hours. It was also known that Uli was virtually unuseable; only some of the runway lights were working, the Navaids were out of order and at least one-third of the runway was beyond repair. Nevertheless Joint Church Aid agreed on an attempt to get six aircraft into Biafra that night (11/12 January), in two waves of three. Frank Dolha recorded the following:

"The six aircraft nominated to fly in to Uli consisted of an initial three with the other three aircraft taking-off after a report had been received from the first group. We thought that we might have to use the airstrip at Uga - 16 miles north-east of Uli.

"Captain Jonsson took-off from São Tomé first, in a DC-6B, followed by a C-97 and then a second DC-6B. Canairelief had one aircraft in the second group.

"Captain Jonsson got into Uli and brought back five passengers; the C-97 landed, delivered his load but returned empty as there was no-one else at the airstrip. Again Uli Airport Control reported ground-fire and advised the second DC-6B that Uli was closed. *(The second DC-6B) returned to São Tomé without landing."*

In spite of getting two aircraft into Uli, Joint Church Aid acknowledged only the delivery of ten tonnes of relief aid during the night of 11/12 January. More than anything else the São Tomé-based crews believed that Uli was damaged beyond repair and that they had undoubtedly made the last relief flights into Biafra. There was another meeting of relief agencies at São Tomé's Geronimo Hotel on 12 January where concern was raised over the plight of possibly as many as thirty relief workers still trapped inside Biafra and who, it was now believed, may have been waiting at Uga instead of Uli. Throughout the day attempts to make some form of radio contact with Biafra were unsuccessful. The assumption that relief workers had been waiting at Uga became more logical and offered sound reasoning to send one aircraft in an attempt to land there. In any case it was suspected that Uli had probably fallen to Nigerian soldiers during the day but it was agreed that a second relief aircraft would fly towards Uli in the hope that a surviving VHF communications link might establish the true military position at both airstrips - even if either aircraft is unable to land.

Frank Dolha again recorded in his diary:

"Captain Jonsson again went in first as he had inspected the strip at Uga and knew the surrounding area. We (Canairelief) volunteered to go second and try Uli after Jonsson had landed and taken-off from Uga. A third aircraft would get airborne in order to relay messages to São Tomé. All went to plan and Jonsson established contact with Uga. All beacons were reported to be operating satisfactorily. However Uli was reported to be out, presumably captured by the Nigerians. Captain Jonsson landed at Uga and kept two engines running while the aircraft was unloaded. Once this had been completed a group of Biafrans and a few whites began to board the aircraft in disorder, all pushing and shoving. 45 passengers had boarded when gunfire was heard and a speedy take-off was initiated. Bullets hit the co-pilot's windshield, cracking it. Bullets also hit the side of the aircraft's fuselage. The DC-6 was able to take-off and returned safely to São Tomé. After take-off the Uga Controller advised the crew that the gunfire was believed to have come from Biafrans who wanted to board the aircraft.

"All the time that the DC-6 was on the ground at Uga, Canairelief L-1049H CF-AEN (piloted by Captain Engineer) was circling above the airstrip. They reported gunfire in the area and because of Captain Jonsson's experience did not land at Uga, instead returning to São Tomé. Captain Jonsson reported that no other white people or relief workers were at Uga and that most of the 45 passengers that he evacuated were Biafrans."

Father Anthony Byrne also recalled the flight to Uga by Jonsson:

"Later (on 12 January) Father Tom Cunningham flew with Captain Jonsson and an Icelandic crew in a spirited attempt to use the airstrip at Uga to get in further medical supplies. The facilities were poor and they had just unloaded their cargo when the Nigerian soldiers began to overrun the airstrip. In the ensuing panic, soldiers and civilians scrambled on board the JCA aircraft." As the aircraft had been hit several times by machine-gun fire, Jonsson was forced to take off in a hurry, so much so that the door may still have been open. Fr Cunningham did manage to close the door. They were lucky to get back to São Tomé at all.[410]

Indeed the crew (apart from Captain Jonsson, consisting of First Officer Einar Gudlaugsson and Flight Engineer Runolfur Sigurdsson) was extremely fortunate to not only have landed at Uga but then to have made a safe return to São Tomé as only hours before landing in Biafra, Major-General Philip Effiong (Ojukwu's Chief of General Staff, and who remained in Biafra after Ojukwu's departure) had announced what amounted to an unconditional surrender by Biafran Armed Forces. The announcement was broadcast at 16:40 hours on 12 January 1970 and signalled the end of the Nigerian Civil War. The flight, which was made by DC-6B TF-AAH, had technically been made after the surrender. Biafran forces had capitulated amid scenes of panic and chaos. Certainly advancing Nigerian forces had made a dash for Uli but whether the shooting at Uga had come from Nigerian or Biafran troops will probably never be clear.

Inevitably there was confusion at the end. Fr Tom Cunningham, who had personally offloaded about two tonnes of Stockfish from the rear door, later reflected on what was the final effort to aid Biafra. His main priority in getting Jonsson to fly into Uga was to evacuate a number of relief workers and priests. Some of the priests had previously been captured by Federal forces earlier in the war but had been deported, only to return to Biafra later. His concern was that Lagos would take a much different viewpoint if they caught them back in the country. There were still a number of missionaries and relief workers in the Biafran enclave; indeed they had made their way to the airstrip in the hope of being evacuated out. But they had all gone to Uli and not Uga.

When TF-AAH landed at Uga and taxied to a parking bay Fr Cunningham could see that people on the ground appeared agitated and so, as if to calm them when the doors opened, he quickly put on his long white soutane. In the half-light, people would see and trust the emergence of a priest. He began to unload the stockfish; it was a relatively easy cargo to move and throw down to the ground but then machine-gun fire began to be heard above the noise of the two inner engines which had been kept running. People began to clamber aboard and Cunningham called to Jonsson to take-off immediately. There was no sign of the priests that the aircraft had flown in to collect. In fact they had begun to make the 15-mile journey from Uli to Uga but in the chaos of the Biafran collapse there was no likelihood of them arriving in time.

Even before the DC-6B took off from Uga it had sustained a number of direct small-arms hits. Jonsson started the other two engines but a red light indicated that the rear door was still open. Co-pilot Einar Gudlaughsson went to the rear of the aircraft to close the door whereupon flight engineer Sigurdsson took the right hand seat. The aircraft was quickly taxied back onto the strip for takeoff. Gudlaughsson managed to return to his seat just as Jonsson applied full power for takeoff. TF-AAH became airborne under fire from the ground. It had been hit in about twenty places including around the cockpit windows. Some of the passengers who had managed to scramble aboard had also taken bullet wounds. Among those who managed to get on board were several Biafran soldiers, still carrying their weapons although these were freely surrendered once in the air. Fr Cunningham addressed the injured as best he could although he had no medical equipment to offer. He could offer a brief respite to those injured during the take-off by tearing off the lower half of his soutane and from it made a number of tourniquets to help stem the flow of blood from the more serious wounds.

Even now, thirty years on, the sequence of events is confused. Fr Byrne is still sure that the door was not closed, co-pilot Gudlaughsson believes that he closed it before racing forward to the flight deck; Fr Cunningham states that he had tremendous difficulty in closing the door but that he managed it just after the aircraft got airborne. The door, he says, simply swung round and slammed shut but it was not locked. Whatever the true facts were, Cunningham much later reflected, it was a very sad and chaotic end to an equally sad and chaotic war.

Jonsson climbed to to nearly 10,000 feet and then handed control to Gudlaughsson who completed the rest of the homeward flight. With the landing at São Tomé during the early hours of 13 January 1970, so ended the massive relief airlift into Biafra. The two principal relief agencies, Joint Church Aid and the International Red Cross, although the latter had not flown in to Biafra since August 1969, had completed 7,350 flights into Biafra with a total of 81,300 tonnes of food and medical supplies. Almost 5,500 of these flights had been made by the Churches from São Tomé. The achievement was significant in reducing starvation and saving Biafran lives, but it had not, unfortunately, been achieved without some cost. During the sixteen months between September 1968 and January 1970 some fifteen aircraft had been destroyed, either on the ground, or on approach to Uli with the sad loss of some 25 crew lives.[411]

Notes

Note 388 As watched and recorded by Luis A. Tavares

Note 389 The second batch of four T-6Gs were retained at Cascais but because of the military situation in Biafra none ever left Portugal.

Note 390 'Texans In Biafra', by João Vidal, *Air Enthusiast* Issue 65. Much of the following text is based on this article.

Note 391 Details of the incident have been taken from the Personal Flying Log-Books of Marian Kozubski. Kozubski was invalided back to the U.K. for a long spell of medical care at Odstock Hospital, Salisbury. Although he continued to suffer frequent pain, he did return to Nigeria during April 1970 and began flying F-27 Friendships with Nigeria Airways.

Note 392 As related to the author by Rod Price, a First Officer with Nigeria Airways. Other details from Flying Log-Books.

Note 393 Lloyd's List Marine Casualties

Note 394 As related to the author by Ares Klootwyk. Also based on details within *Gerillapilot I Biafra* by Gunnar Haglund.

Note 395 'Texans In Biafra', by João Vidal, *Air Enthusiast* Issue 65.

Note 396 Many press reports attribute the Nigerian Army's success to the newly-delivered 122mm artillery weapons. Post-war reports suggest that only four of these arrived at the front and while some test-firings were carried out the main supply of ammunition did not arrive until the final week of the war, and even then only reached one Federal Division.

Note 397 As related to the author by Amund Klepp

Note 398 As related to the author by Jakob Ringler, assistant to Fr Tony Byrne on São Tomé island. Aside from the unfortunate loss of vital food, the incident did become one of the most widely-told stories of the airlift.

Note 399 The plan was worked out by Jakob Ringler who related the details to the author.

Note 400 As told to the author by Flight Engineer Cliff Hawthorne who was aboard the DC-7CF.

Note 401 As described to the author by two of the crew.

Note 402 According to Brian Harris (of Nordair) five Biafran unloaders were killed in this incident at Uli.

Note 403 As related to the author by Jakob Ringler

Note 404 *Ibid.,* Olusegun Obasanjo

Note 405 *Ibid.,* João Vidal (*Air Enthusiast* Issue 65)

Note 406 *The Struggle For Secession 1966-1971* by N.U. Akpan; published by Frank Cass 1972.

Note 407 Extracted from Frank Dolha's diary by Brian Harris; reproduced by kind permission.

Note 408 Among Biafran government officials who flew into exile with Ojukwu were Dr M.I. Okpara (Ojukwu's political adviser), N.U. Akpan (Chief Secretary, Government of Biafra), Major-General Madiebo (G.O.C. Biafran Army). The time of 02:00 hours is given by John de St Jorre in *The Nigerian Civil* War.

Note 409 As related to the author by Colin Miller.

Note 410 Fr Tony Byrne describes how the door was ripped-off during the flight back but Fr Cunningham since admitted to the author that this part of the story " might just have been a trifle exaggerated!" It was nevertheless one of the most amazing flights of the entire airlift.

Note 411 Details of the 25 crew members killed are given within the Appendixes. Different figures have been quoted in other publications and certainly more were killed in flying into Biafra. However this figure relates in this instance just to those flying relief aid.

POSTSCRIPT

The speed of Biafra's final collapse came as a complete surprise to many, even to those in the respective front lines. But for the darkness, the scenes at Uli and Uga strips as Biafra's leaders, other senior officials and a number of white advisers desparately tried to escape being caught, proved as visually chaotic as the final rooftop moments that closed the Vietnam war. For Nigerian forces the end was something of an anti-climax and despite fears in Biafra of widespread retribution by Federal forces, the war ended in an encouraging posture of reconciliation. One of the Nigerian MiG-17 pilots based at Port Harcourt described the end there as "one day made to feel important and needed; the next feeling rather like a pork pie in a synogogue!". [412]

Just after the capitulation of Biafran forces, Lord Hunt visited Uli strip and was driven at speed three times along what had undoubtedly become the most famous landmark of the war. Hunt later reported that the runway was still in relatively good condition, with just two or three craters a third of the distance from the south (34) end. The wrecks of seven aircraft and the 35 (sic) graves of their crews (together with the graves of 122 Biafran groundcrew) added a certain poignancy to the scene.

259 Above: At the end of the Biafran war, all of the International Red Cross C-97Gs were flown back to Basle prior to being ferried back to the USA. In this view, taken on 28 February 1970 from the Basle control tower, the forward pair are believed to be HB-ILW and HB-ILX while the rear two are HB-ILY and a former Joint Church Aid example HB-ILF. Note the two Hank Warton/ARCO DC-7Cs on the adjoining apron. (Richard Braun)

Hunt considered the postwar rehabilitation of the former Biafran state to be honourable and orderly although once the situation returned to normal some actions by the so-called 'victors' were less than honourable. Shortly after Lord Hunt's visit the Federal Nigerian Army bulldozed the Uli graveyard in an attempt to remove the memory of Biafra. It was one of the few unnecessarily callous acts of victory.[413]

Most of the non-Biafran advisers, including pilots and technicians, did indeed manage to escape on the last flights out of Biafra. One European pilot, Peiter Dezeeuw, is thought not to have made it and believed to have been killed as Nigerian forces overran the last remaining areas of Biafra. Certainly, he has not been heard of since the day before the capitulation of Biafran forces. With the exception of Larry Ubechie, who managed to fly out as passenger aboard the last airworthy T-6G, most of the Biafran MFI-9B pilots took their chances and remained in Biafra. Most were questioned by Nigerian forces but none faced formal charges or arrested for any offence relating to their flying activities. Most resumed a normal life in Nigeria. At least one former MFI-9B pilot, Willy Murray-Bruce, was "roughed-up" a little bit but, after a brief spell of living in London, took up a command role with Nigeria Airways, as did his contemorary Augustus Okpe.

With the war over the Joint Church Aid airlift on São Tomé was grounded although in the weeks immediately following the end of the war several crews attempted to ferry in supplies. On each occasion the aircraft remained in international airspace south of Port Harcourt and attempted to make radio contact with the Nigerian Army for permission to land at Uli but received no response. On one occasion the crew of a Fred Olsen DC-6A succeeded in contacting the Nigerian Air Traffic Controller at Kano but the offer of assistance was politely but curtly denied by a request that the captain put his intentions in writing to the authorities in Lagos.[414]

Of the relief aircraft, many remained in position for several weeks in the hope that Lagos would allow the stockpiles of relief material to be flown in to the former Biafran strips. As at 20 January there were still twelve aircraft parked at São Tomé, including C-97Gs N52600, N52631, N52915; L-1049H Super Constellations CF-AEN, CF-NAL and the recently restored CF-NAM); the sole DC-6A LN-FOL, and DC-6Bs OY-STY, TF-AAB, TF-AAF, and TF-AAH). One other DC-6B, TF-AAG, was also present at São Tomé but this had never actually operated into Biafra.

Canairelief personnel departed São Tomé en masse, aboard the L-1049H CF-AEN. The aircraft, flown by Canadian Captain Olliver landed at Downsview, Toronto on 29 January 1970. Canairelief had flown 674 shuttles into Uli, carrying a total of 10,650 tonnes. Something amounting to $C2,500,500 had been raised to maintain the operation.

Canairelief attempted to sell its fleet of three L-1049H Super Constellations; one, CF-AEN, was almost sold to a Greek charter company but the sale fell through and it was instead ferried back to Canada where it was later withdrawn from use and in times broken up. Jack Malloch, the Rhodesian operater of Air Trans Africa and Affretair, made an offer for seven of the engines as spares and replacements for his DC-7CFs but the offer was rejected on the basis of preferring to sell the complete aircraft apart frpm not wishing the break the UN sanctions against Rhodesia! No other potential buyers could be found and the two remaining L-1049Hs, CF-NAL and CF-NAM, were simply abandoned at São Tomé. To this day they still remain in one corner of the airfield.

The aircraft fleets were also finally disposed of; those Icelandic-registered DC-6Bs that were owned by Flughjalp, were flown to Prestwick for essential maintenance and storage. All but one were later donated to the Government of Peru to assist with post-earthquake operations there, the exception being TF-AAD which was subsequently broken up at Prestwick. (In fact it is believed that the aircraft were sold to Peru for $1 each.)

Technically, the C-97G fleet remained the property of Flight Test Research Inc and all of the surviving I.C.R.C. and Joint Church Aid aircraft were returned to the USA, the Red Cross examples reverting to US-registry before flying across the Atlantic.

In spite of not having flown into Biafra since August 1969, the Red Cross fleet at Cotonou still stood at some nine aircraft (C-97Gs HB-ILW, HB-ILX, HB-ILY, HB-ILZ and DC-7Bs SE-EDU, SE-ERF, SE-ERO, SE-ERR and SE-ERS).

The Swedish Red Cross sold almost all of its DC-7Bs to the French charter operator, Compagnie Air Fret. In the meantime Lagos did allow the International Red Cross to make some flights into the former Biafran enclave, the first of which was simply a test-flight to evaluate the route in daylight. This took place on 24 January 1970 when the C-160D Transall HB-ILN flew from Cotonou to Lagos before flying medical supplies on to Enugu. It departed Enugu with a full load of wounded soldiers who were flown north to Kaduna. Later in the day the C-160D returned to Cotonou to re-load with more supplies before flying east to Calabar. On 25 January HB-ILN flew Cotonou-Lagos-Enugu again and then, on 28 January, it flew Cotonou-Lagos-Port Harcourt. All International Red Cross flights stopped on 9 February. No more were ever made.

260: DC-6B TF-AAH was the last aircraft out of Biafra but used Uga instead of Uli in the dying minutes of Biafran independence. Icelander Tony Jonsson, who was probably the most experienced of airlift captains, took TF-AAH into Uga to bring out a number of missionaries and priests. They missed the flight but some civilians did manage to clamber aboard under gunfire. The aircraft, seen here at Prestwick in February 1970 in full JOINT CHURCH AID livery, was later "sold" to the Peruvian Government for $1. (Peter J Bish)

The British & US Aid Airlift to Nigeria

Within hours of the collapse of Biafra and the end of the Nigerian Civil War, a Royal Air Force Hercules C.1, XV217, was loaded with medicines at Lyneham on 12 January 1970. For two days the aircraft remained at Lyneham awaiting clearance to land at Lagos, but the Nigerians, in wanting to demonstrate its insistence "to avoid any government meddling in our internal affairs" refused to give landing permission. The Hercules never left the UK and, on 14 January, it was unloaded and stood down.

President Nixon announced, on 12 January, an emergency relief aid fund of $10million with USAF support. C-141A aircraft, drawn from 436, 437 and 438 Military Airlift Wings, were immediately allotted for Operation 'Gallant Lift', an airlift from Charleston to Lagos, via Ascension Island. But again the Nigerian government refused to accept any military aircraft. The Operation was stood down but eventually, on 24 January, the Nigerians agreed to six demilitarised C-141As operating into Lagos. The aircraft carried only the legend 'UNITED STATES OF AMERICA', the US flag and their serial number. Missions commenced with the departure of two aircraft from Charleston on 27 January (although the second, 67953, later aborted.) Arrivals at Lagos began on the morning of 28 January and 21 landings were made in Nigeria before the airlift stopped on 9 February 1970. In all, the USAF airlifted in 10,000 blankets, Ford and Dodge lorries and a fully-equipped field hospital.[415]

British Crown Agents also responded to a Nigerian request for an assortment of drugs to be flown in aboard civil aircraft. To meet the Nigerian criteria the British Government chartered a number of civilian-registered L-382 Hercules aircraft (N921NA, N7951S, N9227R, N9232R, N9263R and CF-PWN) and for several weeks an airlift of lorries, equipment and other aid was ferried from Manston to Lagos.

Wrapping It All Up

Apart from the aircraft on São Tomé island there were a number of other factors to attend to and for that purpose a skeleton staff remained in place for several months after the Biafran war ended. There was the question of the Biafran children's village and hospital which had been established by CARITAS on the island at San Antonio. All of those at São Tomé were flown to Libreville for settlement into the larger village at 'Kilometre Eleven'– 11kms out of Libreville. The children were flown to Libreville on a series of shuttles made by the Fred Olsen DC-6A LN-FOL which had been retained at São Tomé long after the others had been returned to their owners. For this series of flights all of the JOINTCHURCHAID markings and insignia were removed.

There was also the question of the massive stocks of relief aid held at São Tomé. Warehouse stocks on the island, as at 10 February 1970, accounted for 6,474 tonnes of relief aid. The Nigerians refused to take any and the Churches distributed it throughout other central African centres, notably in Angola and Gabon. Most of it was transferred by ship but several aircraft from the São Tomé airlift were retained for airfreighting out some supplies.

Three flights by the Fred Olsen DC-6A took 26.5 tonnes to the Church World Service in the Central African Republic. Some forty flights by both LN-FOL and a Sterling DC-6B transferred 490 tonnes to Libreville for the Biafran children's hospital in Gabon. One flight by LN-FOL took 10 tonnes to the children's hospital at Abidjan. The remaining stocks were transferred by ship: 2,516 tonnes to Cotonou, 1,531 tonnes to Angola, and 186 tonnes to Gabon. 1,158 tonnes were donated locally in São Tomé while 258 tonnes of salt were re-sold locally on the island. Only 298 tonnes of aid was lost,destroyed by a tornado which hit the island, on 15 April 1970.

As at 10 February there was still some 4,000 tonnes of supplies at Cotonou. A cargo ship, Pluto, was expected to sail from Cotonou on 11 February to collect 1,000 tonnes of relief material held at Libreville. All of these supplies were donated to countries outside Nigeria.[416]

When the Executive Working Group of Joint Church Aid met, in Geneva, for the last time on 16 April 1970 it heard delegates' report on the dismantling of the São Tomé base and the re-distribution of relief material held on the island. With that completed it was possible to dissolve Joint Church Aid. It had operated the largest civilian food airlift in history. To the Executive Working Group it had simply "fulfilled the purpose for which it was created".[417]

The final departures from São Tomé island were Father Tony Byrne and his Austrian deputy, Jakob Ringler. Together they, and hundreds of others, had helped to manage and operate probably the largest civilian relief airlift ever mounted in the western world. It never saved Ojukwu's dream of an independent state of Biafra—it was never intended to—but it certainly did save several million civilian lives caught up in a vicious African civil war. Sadly, but perhaps inevitably, it had cost some lives.

But the memory of it all still lives on.

Notes

Note 412 All of Nigeria's white mercenary pilots had their contracts terminated immediately.

Note 413 This was part of an effort by Nigeria to "wipe out the memory of Uli and the vital lifeline" as reported in the *Daily Telegraph* 22. 1.70.

Note 414 *Ibid.*, Gunnar Haglund.

Note 415 USAF HQ AFRHA Files Alabama, Reference K3203.

Note 416 CARITAS Summary Documents, January 1970.

Note 417 Nordchurchaid Operations Report.

261 Above: "...all flights took place under conditions of war. At night aircraft were compelled to fly at short-spaced intervals and without the aid of navigation or anti-collision lights; without air traffic control en route; approaches and landings had to be made in completely darkened terrain without obstacle lighting; taxi-ing and taking-off with no lighting whatsoever. All these circumstances were aggrevated by the latent danger of the aircraft being shot down by Nigerian Air Force fighter aircraft or Biafran ack-ack; the oppressive heat in the cockpit and the penetrating odour of the stockfish cargo, the extremely hot humid nights at Uli airstrip, located in the middle of the Biafran bush. A further fact to be taken into consideration is the necessity of flying exclusively at night, leaving the pilots only the possibility to rest during the daytime which, in view of the climatic conditions, was possible only to a limited extent. All these factors inevitably led to an extremely physical drain on the crew and this must certainly have had an effect on their reflexes. Nigerian air-raids on Uli airstrip during the approaches of the aircraft were frequent up to four weeks before the accident. The whole area was often illuminated by flares (sic) and the airfield bombarded. The Biafran anti-aircraft guns, for their part, shot at all aircraft without any discrimination." Little wonder that losses occurred. The above is quoted from the official investigation into the fatal crash of DC-6AC HB-IBT six miles north of Uli which was carried out by the Swiss Federal Department of Transport, Communications & Power. The wreckage shows clearly the extent of the damage caused by fire after it hit ground north of Uli strip late on 6 May 1969. This was the scene which faced ICRC investigators on the following morning. Note that the heat of the fire has revealed the former UK registration marks, G-APNP *(Don Dornan)*

262 Left: When Captain Augie Martin, his wife, and his two crew members were killed on 30 June 1968, local priests laid out a new cemetery close to Biafra's Uli strip. Sadly there were other deaths over the next 18 months. The graves of 'Bull' Brown, August Martin and his wife, Richard Holzman, Hans Raab, Emane Ngwu and Vince Williams (sic) are being tended to in this view *(Lasse Jensen)*

APPENDIXES

TABLE 1:
AIRCRAFT ACQUIRED/OPERATED BY BIAFRAN GOVERNMENT FORCES (in chronological sequence of acquisition)

Identity	Type	C/n	Previous History & Fate
F-OCJS	SA318C Alouette II	1980	New-build helicopter. C of A issued 20.2.67. Delivery to Eastern Nigeria government unconfirmed but highly likely. Presumed lost at Udi.
F-OCJT	SA318C Alouette II	1982	New-build helicopter. C of A issued 20.2.67. Delivery to Eastern Nigeria government unconfirmed but highly likely. Presumed lost at Udi.
F-OCJP	SE3160 Alouette III	1389	New-build helicopter. C of A issued 17.2.67. Delivery to Eastern Nigeria government unconfirmed but highly likely. Presumed lost at Udi.
F-OCJQ	SE3160 Alouette III	1394	New-build helicopter. C of A issued 15.2.67. Delivery to Eastern Nigeria government unconfirmed but highly likely. Presumed lost at Udi.

One of the above Alouette III helicopters was re-serialled BAF040 and captured as such by Federal Nigerian forces at Udi in February 1968. This example, and other Biafran Alouettes, may have been damaged during a NAF Jet Provost attack on 9.10.67.

Identity	Type	C/n	Previous History & Fate
5N-AAK	Douglas DC-3	13921/25366	ex USAAF C-47A-30-DK 43-48105, A65-58, VH-TAL, VR-NCK Nigeria Airways. Impounded at Enugu 5.4.67 and impressed. Believed destroyed by NAF Jet Provost at Enugu 10.9.67.
5N-AAV	F-27 Friendship 200	10216	ex PH-FEF & Nigeria Airways. Hijacked by Eastern State soldiers 23.4.67. Written-off after mid-air explosion over Lagos on 7.10.67.
9G-AAD	Douglas DC-3	12199	ex C-47A-5-DK 42-92402, FZ641, G-AGJW & Ghana Airways. Seized by Biafran forces 15.6.67. Abandoned at Port Harcourt after reportedly destroyed in a NAF L-29 attack August 1967.
5N-AER	Hawker Siddeley 125/1B	25099	ex HB-VAU. Delivered to Paris/Le Bourget 24.6.67 and based there for European duties. Damaged at Port Harcourt but ferried to Sao Tome February 1968. Postwar to the Nigeria Aircraft Trades School, Zaria.
N12756	B-26R Invader	7245	ex USAAF A-26B-40-DL 41-39531, N64Y, FrAF 4139531. Arrived at Port Harcourt 29.6.67. Damaged by NAF Jet Provosts at Enugu September 1967 and later abandoned there October 1967.
5N-AIA	SE.3130 Alouette II	1866	ex F-BLOJ & Aero Contractors (Nigeria) Ltd. Appropriated 13.7.67. Last reported at Cascais/Tires, Portugal March 1970.
5N-AIB	SE.3130 Alouette II	1209	ex F-WIEK, H-5, F-BOEG & Aero Contractors (Nigeria) Ltd. Appropriated 13.7.67. Believed crashed between Owerri and Onitsha, date unknown.
5N-ABV	Westland Widgeon	WA/H/1	ex G-AKTW, G-APPR & Bristow Helicopters Ltd. Appropriated 15.7.67. Suffered "on-ground" damage at Port Harcourt shortly after being seized.
5N-AGA	Westland Widgeon	WA/H/3	ex G-ALIK, G-APPS & Bristow Helicopters Ltd. Appropriated 15.7.67. Captured intact by Nigerian forces at Udi February 1968. Impressed into Nigerian Air Force as NAF510.
5N-AGL	Westland Widgeon	WA/H/140	ex G-AOZD & Bristow Helicopters Ltd. Appropriated 15.7.67. Seriously damaged in heavy landing near Uli, date unknown. Rotor blades still extant January 1970.
5N-AGF	Riley Dove 400	04246	ex SAAF105, G-ASUV & Bristow Helicopters Ltd. Appropriated 18.7.67. Believed seriously damaged after hitting a vehicle while taking-off from an uncompleted Uli strip. Still extant at Uli village school January 1970.
"5N-07G"	L-1049G Super Constellation	4514	ex F-BGNE. Ferried Paris – Lisbon 10.8.67. Abandoned at Lisbon mid-1969 and used for spares. Eventually scrapped.
G-ATOB	Douglas DC-7CF	44875	ex N733PA, N7334. UK marks cancelled 2.10.67. Used by Biafran Government until abandoned at Madrid April 1968. Transferred to ARCO (Bermuda) Ltd and reg'd VR-BCT 25.7.68. Reported as briefly registered TI-1065P 8.10.68 but later restored to VR-BCT.
-	RB-26P Invader	27591	ex USAAF A-26B-50-DL 44-34312, FrAF 4434312, F-BMJR. Ferried Lisbon to Port Harcourt mid-August 1967. Damaged while landing at Port Harcourt 3.12.67; not repaired.
-	TB-25N Mitchell	108-33194	ex USAAF B-25J-25-NC 44-29919, N9868C. Ferried to Port Harcourt October 1967. Crashed on landing at Port Harcourt 3.12.67.
-	TB25J Mitchell	108-37566	ex-USAAF B-25J-30-NC 44-31491, RCAF 5245, N8013. Ferried to Port Harcourt October 1967. Abandoned at Port Harcourt May 1968, later destroyed there.

Fates of the B-25 Mitchells are unconfirmed but believed to be correct. The details are based on the assumption that the aircraft which crashed at Port Harcourt on 3.12.67 had a glazed upper nose section; N8013 is known to have had a solid nose section when disposed of by the RCAF.

Identity	Type	C/n	Previous History & Fate
5N-ABY	Hiller UH-12E	2233	ex Bristow Helicopters Ltd. Not used; recaptured by Nigerian forces at Ughelli December 1967.
5N-AGE	Hiller UH-12E	2129	ex Bristow Helicopters Ltd. Not used; recaptured by Nigerian forces at Ughelli December 1967.
PH-SAE	Douglas DC-7C	45469	ex JA6302, PH-SAE & Trans World Leasing. Ferried Cambridge – Lisbon 6.3.68 for lease to the Biafran Government. "Unauthorised flight" from São Tomé to Lagos 7.6.68 and impressed into Nigerian Air Force, possibly as '5N-AOW'.
-	T-6G-NT Texan	168-570	ex USAF 50-1306, FrAF 50-1306. Scrapped at Cascais/Tires, Portugal
-	T-6G-1-NH Texan	182-457	ex USAF 51-14770, FrAF 51-14770. Scrapped at Cascais/Tires, Portugal
-	T-6G-1-NH Texan	182-481	ex USAF 51-14794, FrAF 51-14794. Scrapped at Cascais/Tires, Portugal
-	T-6G-1-NH Texan	182-485	ex USAF 51-14798, FrAF 51-14798. Fate not known
-	T-6G-1-NH Texan	182-487	ex USAF 51-14800, FrAF 51-14800. Not delivered; sold to E.J.V. Gomes 1970 and scrapped.
-	T-6G-1-NH Texan	182-497	ex USAF 51-14810, FrAF 51-14810. Abandoned Biafra January 1970, flown to Lagos and scrapped.
-	T-6G-1-NH Texan	182-560	ex USAF 51-14873, FrAF 51-14873. Fate not known
-	T-6G-1-NH Texan	182-646	ex USAF 51-14959, FrAF 51-14959. Scrapped at Cascais/Tires, Portugal
-	T-6G-1-NH Texan	182-678	ex USAF 51-14991, FrAF 51-14991. Scrapped at Cascais/Tires, Portugal
-	T-6G-1-NH Texan	182-733	ex USAF 51-15046, FrAF 51-15046. Scrapped at Cascais/Tires, Portugal
-	T-6G-1-NH Texan	182-738	ex USAF 51-15051, FrAF 51-15051. Fate not known
-	T-6G-1-NH Texan	182-770	ex USAF 51-15083, FrAF 51-15083. Scrapped at Cascais/Tires, Portugal

Identity	Type	C/n	Previous History & Fate
'439B'	Douglas C-47B	?	ex 9J-RIF Zambian Government & Air Force. (Zambian registration cancelled 29.8.68.) Believed abandoned at Libreville January 1970.
'704B'	Douglas C-47B	?	ex 9J-RIG Zambian Government & Air Force. (Zambian registration cancelled 11.9.68.) Possibly the aircraft which crashed at Uli 16.3.69.
'801'	Douglas C-47D	16490/33238	ex USAAF C-47B-35-DK 44-76906, KN597, WGAF 4476906. Bought by T.M. Fuller/Luxembourg Aero Service 3.7.68; flown to Faro as N10801. Not flown to Biafra and abandoned there. Eventually ferried to the USA 6-19.2.78.
'802'	Douglas C-47D	15991/32739	ex USAAF C-47B-25-DK 44-76407, KN368, WGAF 4476407. Bought by T.M. Fuller/Luxembourg Aero Service 27.8.67; flown to Faro as N10802. Delivered to Biafra 4/69. Believed lost in Biafra.
'803'	Douglas C-47B/NASARR	15977/32725	ex USAAF C-47B-25-DK 44-76393, KN360, WGAF 4476393. Bought by T.M. Fuller/Luxembourg Aero Service 14.6.68; flown to Faro as N10803. Delivered to Biafra 4/69. Believed lost in Biafra; possibly destroyed at Uli 13.6.69 by MiG-17F NAF617.
BB-	MFI-9B	44	ex 801-44, SE-EUN (Registered to AB MFI.) Ferried Malmo/Bulltofla to Toussus-le-Nobel 26.4.69. Cancelled 30.5.69. Fate not known.
BB-	MFI-9B	51	ex 801-50, SE-EWE (Registered to AB MFI.) Ferried Malmo/Bulltofla to Toussus-le-Nobel 27.4.69. Cancelled 30.5.69. Fate not known.
BB-	MFI-9B	52	ex 801-51, SE-EWF (Registered to AB MFI.) Ferried Malmo/Bulltofla to Toussus-le-Nobel 27.4.69. Cancelled 30.5.69. Fate not known.
BB-	MFI-9B	53	ex SE-EUL (Registered to AB MFI.) Ferried Malmo/Bulltofla to Toussus-le-Nobel 27.4.69. Cancelled 30.5.69. Fate not known.
BB-	MFI-9B	59	ex SE-EUE (Registered to AB MFI.) Ferried Malmo/Bulltofla to Toussus-le-Nobel 27.4.69. Cancelled 30.5.69. Fate not known.
BB-	MFI-9B	32	ex SE-EFU (Registered to L-E Fredlund, Malmo) Ferried Copenhagen/Skovlunde- Antwerp-Toussus le Nobel 22.7.69. Cancelled 10.9.69. Fate not known.
BB-	MFI-9B	46	ex 801-46, SE-EUP (Registered to M. Danielsson) Ferried Copenhagen/Skovlunde- Antwerp-Toussus le Nobel 22.7.69. Cancelled 8.8.69. Fate not known.
BB-	MFI-9B	47	ex 801-47, SE-EWB (Registered to Karlskoga Fk) Ferried Copenhagen/Skovlunde- Antwerp-Toussus e Nobel 21.7.69. Cancelled 7.8.69. Fate not known.
BB-	MFI-9B	56	ex SE-EUB (Registered to Ljungbyheds Fk) Ferried Copenhagen/Skovlunde- Antwerp-Toussus le Nobel 21.7.69. Cancelled 8.8.69. Fate not known.

Note that the first batch of five MFI-9B 'Minicons' were reported as serialled BB101-BB105. The second batch is believed to have been serialled BB903, BB905, BB907 & BB909 but this remains unconfirmed. Tie-ups with Swedish identities are unknown. BB103 is known to have been badly damaged at Ozubulu strip, Biafra 29.11.69 when the strip was attacked by MiG-17F NAF621. One MFI-9B stalled on take-off from Ozubulu (date unknown) and was later conveyed to Orlu for static display. Two others are known to have been destroyed in flying accidents in Biafra on 28.11.69 and 4.1.70.

BB105 and BB905 were conveyed to Lagos after the war but later returned to the Civil War Museum, Umuahia. It is believed that at least one of the MFI-9Bs was returned to Gabon for repair, or possibly held back in Gabon for training purposes. After the Nigerian Civil War it was impressed into the Gabon Presidential Guard as TR-KGA.

Of the three T-6Gs whose individual fates are not known, one crashed in Nigeria on delivery (in October 1969) while attempting to locate and land at Uli. Another was abandoned at Abidjan during the same delivery phase while a third was successfully flown out of Biafra to Libreville several days before the Biafran surrender.

Conventional wisdom suggests that the B-25 N8013 was ex-USAF 44-31481 and therefore allotted the c/n 108-37556. However this aircraft was one of five former Royal Canadian Air Force examples (N8010 thru N8014) which were sold to Bellomy Aviation Inc, Miami in October 1963. In the correspondence supporting the block sale the Canadian D.O.T incorrectly gave the former USAF identity for RCAF5245 as 44-31481, instead of 44-31491. The FAA was unaware that any error had been made and therefore the true identity has never officially been correctly recorded. There is also a great deal of conflicting published data concerning North American B-25 manufacturer's serial numbers (c/ns). Two sources were examined: a listing of civil B-25s in AMCAR35/Sept 1987 (based on 'US Military Aircraft Designations & Serials') and a similar listing published in the American Aviation Historical Society Journal, Spring 1978. It has now become accepted that the AAHS listing (assembled by William T Larkins) is the correct version. The above data is therefore based on that listing.

The identities of the former Zambian Douglas C-47B/DC-3 aircraft are unknown, having not been recorded by the Zambian DCA. However their 'Biafran' identities appear to be based upon a similar system adopted by the French Navy for a number of their C-47s. If that is the case then the identity '439' could be a corruption of 43-48039, 43-48139 or 43-48239 et seq. Similarly, '704' could be derived from 44-76204, 44-76304, 44-76404 et seq. However no C-47s contained within these sequences have fates unaccounted for.

263: *The Biafran Air Force MFI 9Bs operated from bush strips with considerable impunity and the Nigerian pilots found that despite knowing their locations the terrain and tree cover made them difficult targets from the air. Biafran pilot Johnny Chuco is seen in the cockpit of an unidentified MFI-9B during December 1969 (A. Alves Pereira)*

TABLE 2:
OTHER AIRCRAFT PURCHASED BY/FOR BIAFRAN GOVERNMENT BUT NOT DELIVERED

Identity	Type	C/n	Previous History & Fate
199	Fouga CM.170 Magister	199	ex Austrian Air Force 4D-YF. Abandoned at São Tomé
212	Fouga CM.170 Magister	212	ex Austrian Air Force 4D-YI. Abandoned at São Tomé
G-ALHS	Canadair C-4 Argonaut	164	Acquired by Chartwell Aviation for operation by Templewood Aviation on airlift. Delivery frustrated by HM Customs & Excise. Scrapped at East Midlands Airport.
G-ALHY	Canadair C-4 Argonaut	170	Acquired by Chartwell Aviation for operation by Templewood Aviation on airlift. Delivery frustrated by HM Customs & Excise. Scrapped at East Midlands Airport.
G-AWTB	P.56 Provost T.1	PAC/F/342	ex XF838. Acquired by G. Meisner for onward ferry to Cherbourg & Lisbon. Not delivered and dismantled at Fairoaks 1970. Sold to Trans Global Supply Ltd. Delivered to Rhodesian Air Force as R6317 in 1971.
G-AWTC	P.56 Provost T.1	PAC/F/338	ex XF693. Acquired by G. Meisner for onward ferry to Cherbourg & Lisbon. Not delivered and dismantled at Fairoaks 1970. Sold to Trans Global Supply Ltd. Delivered to Rhodesian Air Force as R3616 in 1971.
G-AWTD	P.56 Provost T.1	PAC/F/285	ex XF554. Acquired by G. Meisner for onward ferry to Cherbourg & Lisbon. Not delivered and dismantled at Fairoaks 1970. Sold to Trans Global Supply Ltd. Delivered to Rhodesian Air Force as R3614 in 1972.
G-AWTE	P.56 Provost T.1	PAC/F/336	ex XF691. Acquired by G. Meisner for onward ferry to Cherbourg & Lisbon. Not delivered and dismantled at Fairoaks 1970. Sold to Trans Global Supply Ltd. Delivered to Rhodesian Air Force as R3165 in 1972.
G-AWTG	P.56 Provost T.1	PAC/F/086	ex WV540. Acquired by G. Meisner for onward ferry to Cherbourg & Lisbon. Not delivered and dismantled at Fairoaks 1970. Sold to Trans Global Supply Ltd. Delivered to Rhodesian Air Force as R63071971.
SE-DCF	A-Whitworth Meteor TT.20	AW.5562	Not used; abandoned at Charleroi, Belgium
SE-DCH	A-Whitworth Meteor TT.20	AW.5549	Not used; abandoned at Charleroi, Belgium
G-ASLW	A-Whitworth Meteor NF.14	AW.5814	ex WS829/Rolls-Royce Ltd/Target Towing Aircraft Ltd. Ferried Hucknall-Bournemouth-Bordeaux 6.7.69; arrived Faro 7.7.69. Crashed into Atlantic Ocean 28.9.69.
G-AXNE	A-Whitworth Meteor NF.14	AW.5803	ex WS804/RAE Bedford/Target Towing Aircraft Ltd. Ferried Bedford-Blackbushe 5.9.69; arrived Faro 9.9.69. Abandoned at Bissau c21.9.69 while on delivery.

TABLE 3:
AIRCRAFT OPERATED BY HANK WARTON ON BEHALF OF BIAFRAN GOVERNMENT AND THE GERMAN CHURCHES.

Identity	Type	C/n	Previous History & Fate
'I-ACOA'	Canadair DC-4M2	137	ex CF-TFM, 'HP-925', 'BR-HBP'. Crashed near Garoua, North Cameroons 11.10.66 during a pre-Biafran arms flight.
'5T-TAB'	Douglas DC-7C	45187	See Table 5
'5T-TAC' (1)	L-1049G Super Constellation	4645	ex EC-AQN, N8025. Acquired by Warton c29.6.67; registered to North American Aircraft Trading Corp. 8.8.67. Repainted as '5T-TAC' early-October 1967. Crashed at Port Harcourt February 1968.
'5T-TAC' (2)	L-1049D Super Constellation	4166	ex LV-ILW. (possibly converted to L-1049H/03 standard.) Purchased May 1968; ferried Miami-Lisbon 22.5.68. Blown up at Bissau 4.6.68.
'5T-TAC' (3) or '5T-TAG' (2)	Douglas DC-7C	45310	See Table 5
'5T-TAF'	L-1049G Super Constellation	4618	ex CS-TLC. Acquired 10/67; officially bought by North American Aircraft Trading Corp 8.11.67. (Portuguese marks cancelled 23.11.67). Impounded at Luqa 16.2.68.
'5T-TAG' (1)	L-1049G Super Constellation	4642	ex D-ALOF. Bought by North American Aircraft Trading Corp 8.12.67 and ferried Hamburg-Lisbon same date. (German marks cancelled 13.12.67) Crashed on approach to Uli 1.7.68.
'5T-TAH'	L-1049G Super Constellation	4647	ex D-ALID. Bought by North American Aircraft Trading Corp 23.2.68. (German marks cancelled 29.2.68) Abandoned at Abidjan 28.9.68. Reported still extant 1978.
'5T-TAK'	L-1049G Super Constellation	4640	ex D-ALEC. Bought by North American Aircraft Trading Corp 8.3.68. (German marks cancelled 9.3.68) Ferried São Tomé-Lisbon 20-23.9.68 and abandoned. Subsequently broken up at Lisbon 1981.
'5T-TAL'	Douglas DC-7C	45548	See Table 5
'5T-TAR'	Douglas DC-7C	45308	See Table 5
N10623	C-46A Commando	392	ex I-SILV. Acquired ex-Aaxico Sales Inc July 1968 for ICRC operations. Returned to the USA, routeing Lydd-Prestwick-Keflavik 27.8.70.
N10624	C-46A Commando	30271	ex I-SILA. Acquired ex-Aaxico Sales Inc July 1968 but possibly not purchased outright and therefore not used. Returned to the USA, routeing via Prestwick 10.12.68.

TABLE 4:
AIRCRAFT OPERATED BY THE 'PHOENIX GROUP' ON BEHALF OF THE BIAFRAN GOVERNMENT

Identity	Type	C/n	Previous History & Fate
HP-475	L-1049G Super Constellation	4551	Ferried Miami-Lisbon 9/68. Named 'ANGEL OF PEACE' on airlift. Landed at Abidjan at end of war and abandoned. Impounded 3/70 and broken up 1/71.
N8338/ '5N-83H'	L-1049G Super Constellation	4616	Purchased by J.A. Crosson 21.11.68 but ferried Miami-Lisbon 7.11.68. named 'ENDEAVOUR' and re-registered '5N-83H'. Withdrawn from use at Faro Autumn 1969.

Identity	Type	C/n	Previous History & Fate
N7776C	L-1049H Super Constellation	4801	Owned by Leasing Consultants Inc, Miami. Ferried Miami-Lisbon August 1969. Later stored at Faro 1/70-3/70 when flown back to Fort Lauderdale, FL. Broken up 1973.
N86524/ } '5N-86H' }	L-749A Constellation	2660	Lease-purchased by Robert W. Cobaugh 31.10.69 from Concare Aircraft Leasing Corp and used on airlift from 9/69. Re-registered '5N86H'. Abandoned at Faro 1/70 and broken up 1979.
N86525'/ } '5N85H' }	L-749A Constellation	2662	Lease-purchased by unknown agent (from Carolina Aircraft Corp) for use on Faro airlift. Re-registered '5N85H'. Crashed in the Oukaimeden mountain range, 70km south of Marrakech 28.11.69 reportedly as a result of 3-engine failure.
N563E	L-1049H Super Constellation	4833	Leased by Robert W Cobaugh (from Carolina Aircraft Corp) for four months from November 1969 (probably to replace '5N-83H'). Returned to Fort Lauderdale, Florida, at end of war. Broken up 1975.

TABLE 5:
AIRCRAFT USED ON NORDCHURCHAID/JOINT CHURCH AID RELIEF AIRLIFT

Identity	Type	C/n	Operator	Previous History & Fate
CF-AEN	L-1049H Super Constellation	4821	Canairelief.	Arrived São Tomé 20.11.69 (from Montreal) Dep 25.1.70 to Toronto, arriving 29.1.70.
CF-NAJ	L-1049H Super Constellation	4828	Canairelief.	Arrived São Tomé 17.1.69 (from Montreal). Dep'd 10.2.69 to Paris for servicing; returned São Tomé 27.2.69. Crashed near Uli 3.8.69.
CF-NAK	L-1049H Super Constellation	4829	Canairelief.	Arrived São Tomé 2.5.69 (from Montreal). Destroyed by bombing at Uli 17.12.69.
CF-NAL	L-1049H Super Constellation	4831	Canairelief.	Arrived São Tomé 30.7.69 (from Montreal). Abandoned at São Tomé. Still extant August 1999.
CF-NAM	L-1049H Super Constellation	4832	Canairelief.	Arrived São Tomé 2.6.69 (from Montreal). Sustained damage at Uli 7.10.69; flown back to São Tomé for spares recovery. Later restored and test-flown 17.1.70 but abandoned at São Tomé. Still extant August 1999.
LN-FOL	Douglas DC-6A	44907	Fred Olsen A/Transport.	Arrived São Tomé 12.11.69 (from Oslo) to replace LN-FOM. Ferried São Tome-Stavanger 4-7.3.70
LN-FOM	Douglas DC-6A	45375	Fred Olsen A/Transport.	Arrived São Tomé 13.9.69 (from Oslo). Destroyed by bombing at Uli 1.11.69.
LN-FOP	C-46R Commando	27049	Fred Olsen A/Transport.	Arrived São Tomé 1.9.68 (from Oslo); departed 21.3.69 to Oslo.
LN-FOR	C-46R Commando	30252	Fred Olsen A/Transport.	Arrived São Tomé 23.8.68 (from Oslo); departed 23.9.68 to Oslo.
LN-SUD	Douglas DC-6B	44060	Fred Olsen A/Transport.	Arrived São Tomé 2.12.68 (from Stavanger); departed 10.2.69 to Stavanger for servicing. Returned to São Tomé 20.2.69 (from Copenhagen). To Stavanger 22.3.69 for servicing. Returned to São Tomé 24.4.69 (from Stavanger). To Stavanger 25.7.69 for servicing; returned to São Tomé 13.8.69. To Stavanger 19.10.69 for servicing; repainted and returned São Tomé 8.11.69. To Stavanger 30.12.69. Withdrawn from use and scrapped at Stavanger.
N52600	Boeing C-97G	16625	Flight Test Research Inc	(ex USAF C-97G 52-931). Arrived São Tomé 16.6.69 (from Miami). To Tel Aviv 13.12.69 for servicing; returned São Tomé 3.1.70. To Cotonou 23.1.70; to Basle 27.2.70 and re-registered HB-ILL. Returned to USA 12.5.70 as N52600. To Davis-Montham AFB. Fate probably as N52727
N52631	Boeing C-97G	16662	Flight Test Research Inc	(ex USAF C-97G 52-2631). Arrived São Tomé 9.2.69 (from Miami). Named 'PRETTY PENN' To Cotonou 23.1.70; to Basle 28.2.70 and re-reg'd HB-ILK. Returned to USA and stored at Davis-Montham AFB. Fate probably as N52727
N52676	Boeing C-97G	16707	Flight Test Research Inc	(ex USAF C-97G 52-2676). Arrived São Tomé 9.2.69 (from Miami). Crashed near Uli 26.9.69.
N52679	Boeing C-97G	16710	Flight Test Research Inc	(ex USAF C-97G 52-2679). Arrived São Tomé 25.1.69 (from Miami). Crash-landed at Uli 8.5.69; destroyed during a Nigerian AF MiG-17F raid on 9.5.69.
N52727	Boeing C-97G	16758	Flight Test Research Inc	(ex USAF C-97G 52-2727). Arrived São Tomé 30.10.69. To Tel Aviv 5.1.70 for overhaul. To Basle 24.2.70 and re-registered HB-ILG. Returned to USA as N52727 25.2.70. To Davis-Montham AFB and scrapped by Southwestern Alloys, Tucson AZ.
N52876	Boeing C-97G	16570	Flight Test Research Inc	(ex USAF C-97G 52-876). Arrived São Tomé 20.10.69 (from Miami). To Cotonou 19.1.70; to Basle 28.2.70 and re-registered HB-ILH. Returned to USA as N52876. To Davis-Montham AFB. Fate as N52727.
N52915	Boeing C-97G	16609	Flight Test Research Inc	(ex USAF C-97G 52-915). Arrived São Tomé 25.1.69 (from Miami). To Tel Aviv 20.7.69 for overhaul; returned São Tomé 31.8.69. To Basle 22/23.1.70 and re-registered HB-ILF (repainted 30.1.70). Returned to USA as N52915 11.3.70. To Davis-Montham AFB. Fate as N52727.
OY-BAS	Douglas DC-6B	43837	Sterling Airways.	Arrived São Tomé 3.10.68 (from Copenhagen). To Copenhagen 2.11.68.
OY-EAR	Douglas DC-6B	43836	Sterling Airways.	Arrived São Tomé 26.8.68 (from Copenhagen). To Copenhagen 28.9.68. To São Tomé 22.9.69 (from Copenhagen). Returned to Copenhagen 30.11-1.12.69.
OY-STY	Douglas DC-6A/B	44175	Sterling Airways.	Arrived São Tomé 12.12.69 (from Copenhagen). To Copenhagen 30.1.70.
PH-TRA	Douglas DC-6	43124	Transavia.	Ferried Amsterdam-São Tomé 16/17.10.68. To Amsterdam 10.2.69. Re-registered TF-AAD qv.
PH-TRB	Douglas DC-6	43130	Transavia.	Arrived São Tomé 19.11.68 (from Amsterdam). To Amsterdam 12/68 for servicing; ferried to São Tomé 10/11.1.69. To Amsterdam 2.2.69; returned São Tomé 7.3.69. Re-registered TF-AAE at São Tomé qv.
PH-TRC	Douglas DC-6B	43560	Transavia.	Arrived São Tomé 15.2.69 (from Amsterdam). Ferried to Amsterdam 17-

Identity	Type	C/n	Operator	Previous History & Fate
PH-TRD	Douglas DC-6B	44120	Transavia.	22.3.69. Re-registered TF-AAF qv Arrived São Tomé 19.10.68 (from Amsterdam). To Amsterdam 14.12.68 for servicing; returned São Tomé 21.12.68. To Amsterdam 2.3.69; ferried Amsterdam-São Tomé 17-18.3.69. Ferried São Tomé-Amsterdam 26-27.5.69 as TF-LLA. Re-registered TF-AAG qv.
PH-TRE	Douglas DC-6B	44118	Transavia.	Ferried Amsterdam-São Tomé 9-15.3.69. Returned to Amsterdam for repairs. Ferried Amsterdam-Tripoli-São Tomé 19-20.3.69. Ferried São Tomé-Nice-Amsterdam 27-28.3.69. Re-registered TF-AAH qv.
PH-TRL	Douglas DC-6B	44425	Transavia.	Arrived São Tomé 25.10.68 (from Amsterdam). Returned to Amsterdam 30.12.68. To São Tomé 9.1.69; returned to Amsterdam 18.3.69. To São Tomé 4.4.69. Re-registered TF-AAB qv
PH-TRZ	Douglas DC-6B	44121	Transavia.	Ferried Amsterdam-São Tomé 1-2.1.69; returned Amsterdam 17.2.69. Ferried Venice-São Tomé 1-3.3.69 (after overhaul by Aero Navalle). Re-registered TF-AAA (by 15.5.69) and ferried to Amsterdam 26.5.69.
SE-ERD	Douglas DC-7B	45089	Transair Sweden.	Ferried Malmo-Las Palmas-Abidjan-São Tomé 22-23.8.68. To Malmo 7.9.68.
SE-ERE	Douglas DC-7B	45331	Transair Sweden.	Arrived São Tomé 11.9.68 (from Malmo). To Malmo 26.9.68.
SE-ERI	Douglas DC-7B	45339	Transair Sweden.	Arrived São Tomé 3.9.68 (from Malmo). To Malmo for servicing 19.9.68; returned São Tomé 24.9.68. To Malmo 10.10.68.
SE-ERK	Douglas DC-7B	45451	Transair Sweden.	Ferried Malmo-São Tomé 9-11.8.68. Returned Malmo 13.8.68; ferried Malmo-São Tomé 15-16.8.68. Damaged 20.8.68 (on 9th Biafra flight). To Malmo 12.9.68; returned São Tomé 17.9.68. Flown to Malmo 18.10.68 and withdrawn from use.
TF-AAA	Douglas DC-6B (ex PH-TRZ)	44121	Flughjalp/Aid by Air.	Repainted at Amsterdam 26.5.69. Arrived São Tomé 8.6.69 (from Amsterdam). To Prestwick 17.9.69 for servicing; to Amsterdam 17.10.69; to São Tomé 23.10.69. Ferried Amsterdam-Prestwick 16.1.70 for storage. Departed Prestwick 30.7.70 to Reykjavik, en route to Peru. Later serialled FAP380. (Registration marks cancelled 7.8.70.)
TF-AAB	Douglas DC-6B (ex PH-TRL)	44425	Flughjalp/Aid by Air.	Repainted at Amsterdam 20.6.69. Ferried Amsterdam-Tripoli-Cotonou-São Tomé 16-17.7.69. (Reported at Schiphol 24.8.69 & 13.9.69.) Ferried Amsterdam-Prestwick 28.9.69 for servicing. Ferried Prestwick-Amsterdam-São Tomé 5-7.11.69. Named 'YOGI BEAR'. Ferried São Tomé-Las Palmas-Prestwick 28-29.1.70 for storage. Departed Prestwick 8.7.70 to Keflavik, en route to Peru. Reserialled FAP381. (Registration marks cancelled 16.7.70.)
TF-AAD	Douglas DC-6 (ex PH-TRA)	43124	Flughjalp/Aid by Air.	Bought by Flughjalp 21.5.69 on arrival at São Tomé (from Amsterdam). To Amsterdam 22.8.69 for servicing. Ferried Amsterdam-São Tomé 15-16.9.69. Reportedly sustained nosewheel damage at Uli. Ferried São Tomé-Las Palmas-Prestwick 25.11.69. Registration cancelled 10.12.69 and used at Prestwick for BAA Fire Service.
TF-AAE	Douglas DC-6 (ex PH-TRB)	43130	Flughjalp/Aid by Air.	Bought by Flughjalp 12.5.69. ferried Amsterdam-São Tomé (via Copenhagen) 23-24.5.69. Damaged at Uli 2.6.69 during dusk attack by MiG-17F NAF617. Temporarily repaired and ferried Uli-São Tomé 3.6.69. Not flown again and used for spares recovery. Registration cancelled 4.6.69. Remains dumped in sea off São Tomé 1970.
TF-AAF	Douglas DC-6B (ex PH-TRC)	43560	Flughjalp/Aid by Air.	Repainted Amsterdam 12.6.69. Arrived São Tomé 19.6.69 (from Amsterdam). Ferried Amsterdam-Prestwick 30.10.69 for servicing. Ferried Prestwick-Amsterdam 12.12.69 and on to São Tomé. Ferried São Tomé-Las Palmas-Prestwick 29-30.1.70 for storage. Departed Prestwick 10.7.70 to Keflavik, en route to Peru. (Registration cancelled 10.8.70.)
TF-AAG	Douglas DC-6B	44120	Flughjalp/Aid by Air.	Repainted at Amsterdam 25.12.69. Arrived São Tomé 14.1.70 (from Amsterdam). Ferried São Tomé-Las Palmas-Prestwick 1.2.70. Later to Peru (departure details unknown). Registration marks cancelled 2.7.70. (Never actually flown into Biafra.)
TF-AAH	Douglas DC-6B (ex PH-TRE)	44118	Flughjalp/Aid by Air.	Believed arrived São Tomé 5.10.69 (from Amsterdam). To Prestwick 8.11.69 for servicing; ferried to Amsterdam 27.11.69. To São Tomé 28.11.69. ferried São Tomé-Las Palmas-Prestwick 29-30.1.70. Departed Prestwick 1.7.70 to Keflavik, en route to Peru. Reserialled FAP379. (Registration cancelled 6.7.70.)
'5T-TAB'	Douglas DC-7C	45187	German Churches.	Arrived Lisbon 24.7.68 (as D-ABAC). (German registration cancelled same date.) Re-registered VR-BCW to ARCO (Bermuda) Ltd 28.10.68. Ferried to Basle 9.2.69; re-registered N9498 9.10.70. Impounded Basle 5.3.71 due to bankrupty. To Geneva 9/74 for use by airport fire authority as 'HB-SSA'.
'5T-TAC'	Douglas DC-7C	45310	German Churches.	Arrived Lisbon 13.8.68 (as D-ABAK). (German registration cancelled 14.8.68.) Re-registered VR-BCX to ARCO (Bermuda) Ltd 28.10.68. Ferried to Basle 3.4.69; re-registered N9499 9.10.70. Impounded Basle 5.3.71 due to bankruptcy and broken up there 1980.
'5T-TAD'	Douglas DC-7C	45545	German Churches.	Arrived Lisbon 6.8.68 (as D-ABAD). (German registration cancelled 7.8.68.) Re-registered VR-BCY to ARCO (Bermuda) Ltd 28.10.68. Crashed on approach to Uli, Biafra 7.12.68. Registration cancelled 9.12.68.
'5T-TAL'	Douglas DC-7C	45548	German Churches.	Arrived Lisbon 22.7.68 (as D-ABAS). (German registration cancelled 24.7.68.) Re-registered VR-BCZ to ARCO (Bermuda) Ltd 28.10.68. Ferried to Basle 9.2.69. Not flown again and stored. Broken up at Basle, December 1970.
'5T-TAR'	Douglas DC-7C	45308	German Churches.	Arrived Lisbon 5.8.68 (as D-ABAR). (German registration cancelled 6.8.68.) Sustained damage at Uli 3.10.68. Later destroyed by Nigerian Air Force bombing.
OO-GER	Douglas DC-6A/B	43826	Africa Concern.	Chartered from Belgian International Air Services. Returned to Belgium (by April 1969) and sold to SIDMA.

Identity	Type	C/n	Operator	Previous History & Fate
OO-HEX	Douglas DC-6B	45478	Africa Concern.	Chartered from Belgian International Air Services (probably soon after acquisition from Trans Union 23.1.69).
SE-EKZ	Beech 95-55 Baron		Nordchurchaid.	Chartered from United Aviation. Departed Malmo 27.8.68 to São Tomé for communications/ferry duties. Returned to Malmo at end of Transair contract.

264: Braathens S.A.F.E. DC-6B LN-SUD at São Tomé with C-97G N52600 behind. The upper surfaces of the DC-6B are painted in the Joint Church Aid 'jungle blue' scheme although the company's red fuselage cheat-line remains. LN-SUD probably spent more time operating into Biafra than any other aircraft, having initially operated in an all-white scheme out of Fernando Póo on the International Red Cross airlift (Phil Phillp)

TABLE 6:
AIRCRAFT USED IN BIAFRA BY THE INTERNATIONAL RED CROSS & ASSOCIATED AGENCIES

Identity	Type	C/n	Operator	Remarks
HB-IBR	Douglas DC-6B	44165	Balair	Arrival date unknown. Ferried Cotonou-Basle 30.4.69 and withdrawn from use.
HB-IBS	Douglas DC-6AC	45531	Balair	Acquired by Balair 11.1.69. ferried Geneva-Marseilles-Niamey-Cotonou 29-30.1.69. Ferried Cotonou-Basle-Geneva 19.5.69. To Basle 14.6.69 off contract.
HB-IBT	Douglas DC-6AC	45532	Balair	Acquired by Balair 11.1.69. ferried Geneva-Marseilles-Niamey-Cotonou 29-30.1.69 Crashed north of Uli 6.5.69.
HB-IBU	Douglas DC-6B	44088	Balair	Arrived Fernando Póo c26.7.68. Remained on-station until year-end; returned to Basle off-contract.
HB-ILN	C-160D Transall	A-03	Balair	Leased from German Government 26.10.68. Apart from servicing periods, remained on-station until end of ICRC 'INALWA' operation. Briefly operated out of Lagos at end of civil war.
HB-ILW	Boeing C-97G	16765	Balair	(ex USAF C-97G 52-2734). Ferried Santa Maria-Basle 16.2.69; to Cotonou 3/69. Returned to Basle 23.2.70 off-contract. To USA; stored at Davis-Montham AFB. Scrapped by Southwestern Alloys, Tucson AZ.
HB-ILX	Boeing C-97G	16619	Balair	(ex USAF C-97G 52-925). Ferried Santa Maria-Basle 15.3.69. To Tel Aviv 22.4.69. Ferried Geneva-Cotonou c16.5.69. Returned to Basle 4.4.70 off-contract. To USA 29.4.70. Stored at Davis-Montham AFB. Fate unknown (but presumably same as HB-ILW).
HB-ILY	Boeing C-97G	16656	Balair	(ex USAF C-97G 52-2626). Ferried USA-Basle (via Shannon) 30.3.69; ferried Basle-Cotonou 7.4.69. Returned to Basle 23.2.70 off-contract. To San Antonio/USA 17.3.70. Stored at Davis-Montham AFB. Later donated to Pima Air Museum, Tucson AZ.
HB-ILZ	Boeing C-97G	16551	Balair	(ex USAF C-97G 52-857). Ferried USA-Basle (via Brussels) 22.2.69. Ferried Geneva-Palma-Cotonou 28.3.69. Ferried Cotonou-Tel Aviv 19.5.69 for overhaul. Returned to Cotonou. To Basle 23.2.70 off-contract. To USA and stored at Davis-Montham AFB. Fate as HB-ILW.
LN-SUD	Douglas DC-6B	44060	Braathens S.A.F.E	Arrived Fernando Póo 28.11.68. Returned to Oslo 8.11.68.
OH-KDA	Douglas DC-6BF	45202	Kar-Air O/Y	Arrived Fernando Póo 28.8.68 (from Helsinki). Ferried to Basle 23.9.68 and returned to Kar-Air off-contract.
OY-BAS	Douglas DC-6B	43837	Sterling Airways	Arrived Fernando Póo 30.8.68. Returned to Copenhagen 28.9.68 and immediately chartered to Nordchurchaid (see Table 5).
PH-DSL	Douglas DC-7C	45180	Martinair	Arrived Fernando Póo 6.9.68. Returned to Amsterdam c26.10.68; sold to Trans Meridian Air Cargo 19.12.68 and ferried to Stansted (same date) for scrapping.
PH-MAM	Douglas DC-6A	44257	Martinair	Arrived Fernando Póo 10/68. Returned to Amsterdam 23.12.63.
SE-CNE	Douglas DC-7	44143	Swedish Red Cross	Purchased by Swedish Red Cross 11/68 and leased to ICRC 27.11.68. Withdrawn from use at Cotonou 4/69 and broken up.
SE-EDU	Douglas DC-7B	45399	Swedish Red Cross	Ferried Geneva-Fernando Póo c13.2.69. Returned to Europe 13.5.69. Sold to Air Fret 5/70 but withdrawn from use at Nimes and eventually broken up there.
SE-ERF	Douglas DC-7BF	45232	Swedish Red Cross	Purchased 5/69 but believed not used on Biafra airlift. Sold to ARCO International 8/70 as VR-BDP. Immediately re-registered VR-BDQ 26.8.70.
SE-ERO	Douglas DC-7B	45202	Swedish Red Cross	On-station at Fernando Póo 3/69. Ferried Fernando Póo-Luqa-Basle 13.5.69. On-station at Fernando Póo late-5/69. Sold to Air Fret as F-OCPZ 14.8.70.

Identity	Type	C/n	Operator	Remarks
SE-ERP	Douglas DC-7B	45401	Swedish Red Cross	On-station at Fernando Póo 4/69. Shot down over Eket, Nigeria 5.6.69 by Nigerian Air Force MiG-17F.
SE-ERR	Douglas DC-7B	45404	Swedish Red Cross	On-station at Fernando Póo 4/69. Sold to Air Fret 5/70 and cannibalised at Nimes for spares recovery.
SE-ERS	Douglas DC-7B	45238	Swedish Red Cross	Acquired by Swedish Red Cross 6/69 but used on airlift to Biafra. Sold to Air Fret as F-OCOQ 6.3.70.
SE-XBT	C-130E Hercules	4039	Royal Swedish Air Force	Arrived Fernando Póo 27.8.68. Returned to Stockholm 29.10.68 off-contract.
TF-FRA	Douglas DC-6B	45060	Fragtflug	Purchased by Fragtflug 1.5.69 and ferried to Basle same day. To Cotonou 3.5.69. To Basle by 23.10.69. Re-registered TF-OAA 12/69 for lease to UNICEF
10322	C-130E Hercules	4192	Canadian Armed Forces	Completed 12 flights to Biafra from Fernando Póo 10/68 before recalled to Canada
HB-GBK	Beech King Air	LJ-45		Used by Dr August Lindt from 8/68 as a successor to Mu-2B HB-LEB.
HB-LEB	Mitsubishi Mu-2B	009	Pilatus AG	Used by Dr August Lindt 7-8/68. Returned to Geneva (from Addis Ababa) 11.8.68.
SE-EDT	Dornier Do.28D-1	4012	Swedish Red Cross	Arrived Cotonou 8.4.69 for brief use by ICRC.

265: When the Swedish Red Cross C-130E Hercules SE-XBT was returned to Sweden it was replaced by the C-160D Transall HB-ILN, which performed admirably on the I.C.R.C. airlift out of Cotonou. For the relief operation it was leased and operated by Balair under Swiss registry. This view by an unidentified photographer shows it at Basle in April 1969 during one of its periods back in Europe for routine servicing

TABLE 7:
AIRCRAFT OPERATED BY FRENCH AGENCIES

Identity	Type	C/n	Remarks
F-	Bristol 170 Freighter Mk.31		One of three aircraft owned by Air Fret and used on occasions for support duties. F-BBGF (c/n 13141), F-BCDR (c/n 13140) or F-BFOT (c/n 13162).

Of the three Bristol 170 Freighters F-BBGF was active until at least mid-1968 despite its last C of A being issued 27.11.67 but restricted until 27.1.68. F-BCDR had its C of A renewed on 7.8.68 but restricted until 8.11.68; on 20.11.68 it was officially suspended at Nimes. F-BFOT had its C of A suspended on 28.6.66 but was not withdrawn from use until April 1969. It was reported to be derelict at Port Gentil in December 1974 but this remains unconfirmed. On the above evidence it would seem that the aircraft used in Biafra was probably F-BCDR.

Identity	Type	C/n	Remarks
F-BHBI	L-1049G Super Constellation	4634	Operated by Air Fret until C of A expired 31.3.69; stored at Nimes until August 1969 when donated to Biafra by French Government. Abandoned at Lanzarote after emergency landing late-1969.
F-BOEX	Douglas DC-6B	45478	Owned by Trans Union; used by Air Fret for French Red Cross flights. Damaged at Uli October 1968; flown out to Libreville. French marks cancelled 12/68; sold to B.I.A.S. 23.1.69 and re-registered OO-HEX.
F-BRAD	L-1049G Super Constellation	4519	Air Fret. Ferried Orly-Luqa-Douala-Libreville 7.9.68. Operated by Air Fret until 11/69.
F-BRAM	Douglas C-47A	9644	ex USAAF 42-23782, FrAF '43.48994'. C of A (3-month) issued 3.9.68; registered 6.9.68 for operation by Oeuvres Hospitalières Français de l'Ordre de Malte. C of A later extended to 3.12.68 and later to 11.10.69. returned to EAA.601/FrAF charge 8.4.69 and later sold to the Chad Air Force 14.8.69 as 48994/"TZ-341". Registration cancelled late-1970.
F-BRAN	Douglas C-47B	33401	ex USAAF 44-77069, FrAF 44.77069. C of A (3-month) issued 3.9.68. Registered 6.9.68 for operation by Oeuvres Hospitalières Français de l'Ordre de Malte. C of A expired 3.12.68; not renewed and believed not used. Transferred to Niger Air Force as 5U-MAD on 24.4.69.
F-BRAP	Douglas DC-4 (C-54E)	7460	Acquired by Air Fret 8.10.68 (ex 7T-VAT) and leased to Air Afriqur from 25.10.68; returned to Air Fret 6.6.69 for use in Biafra. C of A renewed at Libreville 8.10.69. Subsequently withdrawn from use at Nimes 3.2.70 but restored 27.4.70 for transfer to Air Comores.
F-BRHC	Douglas DC-4 (C-54A)	10372	Acquired by Air Fret 22.10.68 (ex 7T-VAD). Operated by the French Red Cross from October 1968. C of A expired November 1968 but still active December 1968. Withdrawn from use at Nimes August 1969, registration cancelled 28.1.70. Scrapped at Nimes.
F-BRHE	Douglas DC-4 (C-54A)	10413	Acquired by Air Fret 6.11.68 (ex 7T-VAS). Operated by the French Red Cross (possibly from October 1968); returned to Air Fret at end of civil war.

Identity	Type	C/n	Remarks
F-BRHQ	Douglas DC-4 (C-54A)	3096	Acquired by Air Fret 2.1.69 (ex TS-APM). Underwent a serviceability check at Douala 7.7.69. C of A renewed at Nimes 21.1.70; ferried Nimes-Libreville (via Luqa 5.2.70) and eventually re-registered TT-DAA October 1970.
F-OCNU	Douglas DC-4 (C-54A)	3073	Acquired by Air Fret 27.2.69 (ex TS-BLH). Operated by the French Red Cross. C of A expired August 1969 and not renewed indicating almost certainly that this could have been the aircraft reported as destroyed in an incident at Uli shortly beforehand. The registration was cancelled 28.1.70.

See Table 8 for details of DC-4 F-BBDD. It is also possible that DC-4/C-54B D-ADAR (c/n 18378), which is known to have been sold by Transportflug of Germany to a Mnsr Gilbert Bourgeard on 6.8.68, was also involved in the French arms airlift out of Libreville. It is known to have passed to Jack Malloch towards the end of the civil war.

266: *DC-4 F-BRHQ joined the Libreville-based French Red Cross airlift in the autumn of 1969. The French airlift almost exclusively used DC-4s, all of which were leased from Air Fret. F-BRHQ clearly shows its former Tunis Air livery during a stopover at Abidjan (Roger Caratini via Jennifer M. Gradidge)*

TABLE 8:
AIRCRAFT OPERATED INTO BIAFRA BY JACK MALLOCH

Identity	Type	C/n	Remarks
VP-YTY	Douglas DC-4 (C-54A)	10397	Operated by Air Trans Africa. Ferried to Woensdrecht for overhaul (date unknown). Ferried Woensdrecht-Las Palmas-Abidjan 16-17.9.68 as ZS-FLO. Re-registered to Affretair 18.9.68 as TR-LNV; ferried as such Abidjan-Libreville same date (see below).
VP-WAM	DH.114 Heron 1b	14008	Operated by Air Trans Africa. Chartered by the Biafran Government September 1967 but captured intact by Federal Nigerian forces at Enugu c4.10.67. Later destroyed after a series of air attacks by the Biafran Air Force.
VP-WAW	L-1049G Super Constellation	4685	Operated by Air Trans Africa September 1967 until 17.1.68 when ferried Lisbon-Woensdrecht for overhaul. Impounded but later released and ferried Woensdrecht-Las Palmas-Abidjan 24.9.68 as ZS-FAA. Re-registered TR-LNY and repainted at Abidjan 26.9.68 (see below).
VP-WBO	Douglas DC-7CF	45463	Sold by Südflug to Meliso Anstalt, Vaduz/Liechtenstein 8.11.67. German marks D-ABAN cancelled 20.11.67 after handover at Amsterdam same date. Operated by Air Trans Africa. Impounded at Lomé, Togo 20.1.68 after flying Lisbon-Lome as 'ZP-WBO'. Abandoned at Lomé.
TR-LNV	Douglas DC-4 (C-54A)	10397	ex VP-YTY, ZS-FLO. Repainted as TR-LNV Abidjan 18.9.68 and ferried Abidjan-Libreville same date. Written-off at Uli 28.6.69 after crew attempted to take-off in the wrong direction.
TR-LNY	L-1049G Super Constellation	4685	ex VP-WAW, ZS-FAA. Repainted at Abidjan 26.9.68 and ferried Abidjan-Libreville same date. Suffered severe engine trouble at Luanda 13.4.69 and grounded; abortive ferry flight out 1.5.69. Grounded until 6.11.69 when ferried Luanda-Salisbury for major overhaul. No further Biafran involvement.
TR-LNZ	Douglas DC-7CF	45188	Acquired by Cie Gabonaise d'Affrétements Aériens (Jack Malloch) 26.5.69 (ex EI-ATV of Aer Turas). Delivered Shannon-Paris/Le Bourget 27.5.69. (Irish marks cancelled 22.8.69.)
TR-LOJ	Douglas DC-7CF	45186	Acquired by Cie Gabonaise d'Affrétements Aériens (Jack Malloch) 25.4.69 (ex EI-ATW of Aer Turas). Delivered Shannon-Paris/Le Bourget 26.4.69. (Irish marks cancelled 30.4.69.) Ferried Salisbury-Libreville 8.5.69 for Biafran arms operation.
TR-LOK	Douglas DC-7C	45182	Acquired by Cie Gabonaise d'Affrétements Aériens (Jack Malloch) 6.2.69 (ex PH-DSC of Martin's Air Charter). Reportedly re-registered in Gabon as TR-LQP July 1972.
F-BBDD	Douglas DC-4-1009	42936	Owned by Air France but "lent by French Government" to Jack Malloch; ferried Paris-Libreville 17-24.1.69. Operated throughout 1969. 6-month C of A renewal at Libreville 29.5.69. On 27.11.69 the C of A was restricted to "one single ferry flight" to enable ferry Libreville-Toulouse for long-term overhaul 2.12.69-19.3.70. Subsequently used by Air France in Antilles until sold to Tchad Air Force February 1973 as TT-NAA.

TABLE 9:
MISCELLANEOUS AIRCRAFT OPERATED IN SUPPORT OF BIAFRA

Identity	Type	C/n	Remarks
G-AWMG	Avro Anson C.19		Ex-VV958. Operated by Mercy Missions UK. Written-off in forced-landing at Uzuakoli, Biafra 3.9.68 following a small-arms strike in starboard engine.
G-AWMH	Avro Anson C.21		Ex-TX227. Operated by Mercy Missions UK. Damaged during forced-landing at Port Etienne 16.8.68; repaired but later written-off in a crash at River Cess, Liberia 20.6.69. Not flown into Biafra.
N469C	L-1049H Super Constellation	4847	Operated by Air Mid East July-August 1968. Arrived Fernando Póo 22.7.68 for Biafra flights. Not given clearance for flights. Returned to Europe and on to USA.
TR-LOX	Douglas DC-6B	44695	Registered to Jean-Claude Bergey 23.10.69; named 'APOLLO'. Impounded at Brussels 1970; later re-registered TR-LQE December 1970.
'ZP-TBV'	L-1049G Super Constellation	4581	Reported as being used in support of the Biafran Government during March 1968.
HP-501	L-1649A Starliner	1036	Owned by Nittler (& others); flown by Larry Raab October 1969 thru January 1970. Abandoned at Douala and broken up there 1980/81.

267: On 12 July 1969 an anonymous DC-4 was inside Jack Malloch's hangar at Salisbury, Rhodesia, displaying marks that prove beyond any doubt that this aircraft is the former D-ADAR. Its involvement in Biafra still remains a mystery. Less mysterious is the L-1049G CS-TLF in the background but note that the Commer van still carries the title 'Rhodesian Air Services', two years after the title was dropped (Jerry Boyd)

TABLE 10:
FEDERAL NIGERIAN AIR FORCE AIRCRAFT INVENTORY 1960-1970

Apart from maintenance records, it has not been possible to source official military data in Nigeria. Much of the following has therefore been based on external sources and pilots' flying log-books.

Type	Serial Range	C/n	Remarks
PA-27 Aztec 250C	NAF001	27-3703	ex N6419Y. Acquired May 1967 and used as a Nigerian Air Force VIP aircraft throughout the conflict.
Dornier Do-27A-4	NAF101-NAF110	522/523/484/493/ 494/497/485/495/ 490/501	ex Luftwaffe. Handed-over and delivered to Nigerian Air Force 1963/64.
Dornier Do-27A-4	NAF151-NAF160	469/476/478/525/ 482/486/487/498/ 503/511	2nd Batch; delivered to Nigerian Air Force 1965
Dornier Do-28B-1	NAF170-NAF174	3093/3094/3095/ 3096/3099	New-build aircraft; ex D-IBUT, D-IBUU, D-IBUV, D-IBUW, D-IBUZ respectively. NAF170 reported as written-off 12.1.70
Piaggio P.149D & Focke-Wulf P.149D*	NAF201-NAF214	273/284/285/287/ 289/302/187/263/ 265/277/291/292/ 293/297	Supplied to Nigeria 1964/65 in two consecutive blocks of 6 & 8 respectively. NAF207 c/n 187 is a Focke-Wulf built example. All others built by Piaggio.
VFW N.2501D Noratlas	NAF301-NAF310	090-093,165-170	New-build aircraft. Only NAF301 & 302 consigned but later returned to Germany. All others diverted off-contract to the Israeli Air Force.

Type	Serial Range	C/n	Remarks
Douglas DC-3 (C-47A/B)	AAL	13919/25364	ex 5N-AAL (Cancelled 16.8.67) Reported damaged at Lagos 17.1.68. No further details
	AAM	6071	ex 5N-AAM (Cancelled 28.8.67)
	AAN	13606	ex 5N-AAN (Cancelled 4.8.67)
	AAP	13304	ex 5N-AAP (cancelled 4.8.67)
	AAQ	9874	ex 5N-AAQ (Cancelled 4.8.67). Damaged at Escravos 10.11.69 by Biafran MFI-9B raid. Temporarily repaired for one flight to Lagos and immediately abandoned there.
	NAF303	13847/25292	ex OO-AWZ (Cancelled 24.6.69); initially test-flown at Lagos 26.6.69.
	NAF304	20776	ex OO-CBW (Cancelled 13.6.69); initially test-flown at Lagos 26.7.69.
	NAF305	12318	ex OO-AWM (Cancelled 6.6.69). Grounded after only 18hrs in NAF service; used for spares recovery at Lagos 1969.
	NAF306	9865	ex OO-AWK
	NAF307	12767	ex OO-AWN (Cancelled 29.10.69). After arrival in Nigeria discovered to be suffering from excessive corrosion. Not flown after delivery flight and abandoned at Kaduna.

The former Nigeria Airways DC-3s operated throughout the civil war period. By 1972 all (except AAM) were derelict at Lagos; AAM later joined the open store.

Type	Serial Range	C/n	Remarks
Douglas DC-4 (C-54B)	NAF311	18349	ex G-ARWI. Arrived Lagos 14.12.68 but not used operationally. Stored at Lagos until finally broken up there April 1977.
LET L-29 Delfin	NAF401-NAF410	792508-792512/ 792527-792528/ 993329/993330/ 993421	NAF401, 403, 405 & 410 are reported to have been sold to Ghana 1989; NAF404 & 409 were all reported active postwar. It is possible therefore that NAF402, 406, 407 & 408 may have been lost in accidents during the civil war period.

Although LET records show 10 new-build aircraft supplied ex-Czechoslovakia, it is generally accepted that the c/n sequence indicates 7 built in 1967 and 3 in 1969. However, two mercenary pilots (Jimmy Webb and Ares Klootwyk) recorded making numerous flights in NAF408 during October & November 1968. This offers evidence that NAF401 & NAF402 (the only two L-29s to be flown to Nigeria; the others arrived by sea/air-freight) may have originated from Soviet stocks and that the 10 new-build examples were NAF403-NAF412.

Type	Serial Range	C/n	Remarks
WS.55 Whirlwind Srs 3	NAF502	WA241	ex G-APDY Bristow Helicopters Ltd (UK registration cancelled 27.9.67.)
WS.55 Whirlwind Srs.2	NAF501 NAF503-NAF509		Eight examples from the range WA244-WA249 & WA300-WA302. All former Austrian Air Force. NAF508 is known to have been c/n WA300; all other link-ups unconfirmed.

One theory suggests that the first of 8 Whirlwind Srs.2s was test-flown as NAF501 but crashed shortly afterwards on 9.8.67 killing a Nigerian Chief of Staff. As a result, and due to non-availability of suitable pilots, the remaining Whirlwinds were stored indefinitely. Then, when qualified mercenary pilots arrived they were made airworthy. One mercenary pilot is known to have test-flown the Whirlwinds at Lagos as follows: NAF503(15.1.68), NAF504 (13.1.68), NAF505 (17.1.68), NAF506 (4.3.68), NAF507 (25.3.68) and NAF508 (20.4.68). Any further details for NAF509 remain unknown.

Type	Serial Range	C/n	Remarks
WS.51 Widgeon Srs.2	NAF510	WA/H/3	ex 5N-AGA & Biafran Air Force. Captured at Udi, Biafra February 1968 and impressed into Nigerian Air Force service. Crashed at Lagos 22.6.68 after a failure of the tail-rotor drive shaft. Wreckage stored at Oji Military Camp, Lagos until broken-up in June 1970.
MiG-15UTI ('Mongol')	NAF601-NAF602		Probably ex-Egyptian Air Force stocks. Air-freighted to Kano 18.8.67.
MiG-17F ('Fresco-C')	NAF603-NAF630	NAF609 is reported to have c/n 0515317.	NAF605 ferried Kano-Lagos 29.6.69; to Port Harcourt 1.7.69; Port Harcourt-Enugu-Kano 23-24.11.69. NAF609 ferried Kano-Kaduna 12.7.69. NAF612 ferried Enugu-Port Harcourt 11.11.69; to Lagos 24.11.69. NAF614 transferred Lagos-Enugu 8.12.69. NAF615 destroyed by Biafran Air Force T-6G at Port Harcourt 10.11.69. NAF616 ferried Enugu-Benin 24.11.68. Crashed near Opobo 25.6.69. NAF617 ferried Port Harcourt-Lagos-Kano 9-11.7.69. Ferried Enugu-Kano 4.12.69. NAF619 ferried Port Harcourt-Enugu 9.12.69; to Kano 14-15.12.69. NAF620 ferried Kano-Lagos-Port Harcourt 20-21.5.69. Damaged beyond repair by Biafran Air Force MFI-9Bs at Port Harcourt 22.5.69. NAF622 ferried Kano-Port Harcourt 25.7.69; ferried Kano-Enugu 15.12.69. NAF623 ferried Lagos-Port Harcourt 2.6.69; Port Harcourt-Lagos-Kano 28-29.6.69. Ferried Kaduna-Port Harcourt 12-14.7.69. Crashed near Port Harcourt 19.7.69. NAF625 ferried Port Harcourt-Lagos 30.5.69.

Most, if not all, Nigerian MiG-17Fs are reported to have originated from Egyptian Air Force stocks, possibly via the Soviet Union. Egypt is known to have received a quantity of Polish-built MiG-17Fs under the designation LiM-5P. Some of the Nigerian aircraft may well have been such examples. NAF603, 604, 606, 607 and 610 are believed to have been written-off in Nigerian service prior to November 1968. No visual or photographic evidence is to hand to suggest that NAF627, 628, 629 and 630 ever entered active service during the civil war.

Type	Serial Range	C/n	Remarks
MiG-17Blatt ('Fresco-A')	NAF631-NAF638		NAF631 written-off in crash landing at Makurdi 19.12.69 NAF632 ferried Enugu-Port Harcourt 23.11.69 to replace MiG-17F NAF605. NAF633 delivered Kano-Kaduna-Lagos 15.11.69; ferried Lagos-Port Harcourt 25.11.69. NAF635 delivered Kano-Kaduna-Enugu 24.11.69 NAF636 delivered Kano-Kaduna-Enugu 3.12.69; ferried Enugu-Port Harcourt 9.12.69 NAF637 delivered Kano-Kaduna-Enugu 4.12.69 NAF638 delivered Kano-Kaduna-Lagos 7-8.12.69.

All eight MiG-17Blatt variants originated from East German Air Force stocks and were airfreighted to Nigeria in two batches; NAF631-635 on 13.10.69 and NAF636-638 on 18.10.69. It is likely that no further deliveries of MiG-17 aircraft took place.

Type	Serial Range	C/n	Remarks
Jet Provost T.51	NAF701-NAF702		NAF701 forced-landed at Porto Norve, Dahomey 23.6.69 and it is unconfirmed if it was returned to Nigeria. NAF702 remained active throughout the civil war period.

Both Jet Provost T.51s originated from Sudan Air Force stocks and were flown Al Khurtum (Khartoum) -Kano August 1967 by British pilots. They were undoubtedly the former Sudanese Air Force 143 and 157 but their precise correlation to NAF701 & 702 remains unknown.

Type	Serial Range	C/n	Remarks
Ilyushin Il-28	NAF801-NAF806		4 aircraft delivered by air February 1968 and probably from Egyptian Air Force stocks; 2 further examples acquired from Soviet sources in April 1969. One example, quoted as NAF805, has been seen at the Civil War Museum, Umuahia with the serial '05' on the nose but in a manner that suggests it to be a former Soviet code. It is not known if any Nigerian Il-28 ever carried full serials as shown above.

268: During 1969 the Nigerian Air Force acquired five ex-SABENA Douglas DC-3s to supplement those previously 'impressed' from Nigeria Airways. NAF305 flew less than 20 hours in Nigeria before being grounded for spares recovery. It ended its days at one side of Lagos airport. Former SABENA insignia and Belgian marks, OO-AWM, were soon very clearly visible (Confidential Source)

TABLE 11:
PAN AFRICAN AIRLINES (NIGERIA) LTD – FLEET LIST 1967-1970

Pan African Airlines (Nigeria) Ltd was formed in August 1961 as the largest subsidiary of Africair Inc, Miami US, which also had extensive financial interests in Nigeria. Based at Lagos, Pan African Airlines has been described as partially owned by the CIA but not as an outright proprietary. At one time some 80% of Pan African's revenues came from a single US government contract for an air service to remote outposts in West Africa. (Africair Inc also had very close relationship with the American CIA.) By 1972 the airline was a subsidiary of Miami-based Dispatch Services Inc which also controls Tropical Aircraft Sales (Nigeria) Ltd.

Carolina Aircraft Corporation is a Miami-based company specialising in cargo aircraft for charter, leasing, sales and maintenance. Owned by the Boy brothers (James and Carl Boy), subsidiary companies are Concare Aircraft Leasing Corporation (of Tulsa, Oklahoma) and Florida Aircraft Leasing Corporation (of Fort Lauderdale, Florida).

Identity	Type	C/n	Remarks
N480G	Douglas DC-4	42920	Bought by Carolina Aircraft Corp April 1968; leased to Pan African April 1968. Destroyed 10.11.69 at Port Harcourt during a Biafran Air Force T-6G attack.
N529D	Douglas DC-4	10748	Bought by Carolina Aircraft Corp December 1969. Transferred to Florida Aircraft Leasing 1.10.70.
N3934C	Douglas DC-4 (C-54B)	27243	Bought by Florida Aircraft leasing Corp October 1968; leased to Pan African October 1968. Damaged at Lagos 12.10.68 and repaired. Damaged in flight over Onitsha 25.4.69 but repaired. Transferred to Air Facilities Inc January 1970.
N9982H	Douglas DC-4	10513	Bought by Carolina Aircraft Corp 5.2.68; leased to Pan African early 1969. Damaged 6 or 8.3.69 at Benin. Not repaired. Destroyed 24.5.69 during a Biafran Air Force MFI-9B attack against Benin.
N11117	Douglas DC-4 (C-54A)	3077	Bought by Aviation facilities Inc 2.11.68. Stored at Lagos May 1970. Sold to East Coast Aviation Corp 10.11.72 and transferred to south-east Asia.
N88891	Douglas DC-4 (C-54B)	10505	Bought by Carolina Aircraft Corp 6.9.67; transferred to Florida Aircraft Leasing 1.9.68 and leased to Pan African October 1968. Damaged in flight between Lagos-Port Harcourt 22.11.68 but repaired. Sold to Aviation Facilities Inc 1.4.69. Stored at Lagos May 1970. Sold to East Coast Aviation Corporation 10.11.72 and transferred to south-east Asia.
N90427	Douglas DC-4 (C-54B)	10445	Bought by Florida Aircraft Leasing October 1967; leased to Pan African from May 1968. Crashed 28.9.68 on approach to Port Harcourt. 2 crew and 55 Nigerian soldiers were killed.
N73675	Douglas DC-7CF	44878	Bought by Florida Aircraft Leasing 24.3.69. In service by October 1969 and used for flying supplies Miami-Nigeria throughout 1969.
5N-AFT	Douglas DC-6A	44069	Bought from Japan Air Lines December 1965. Damaged 20.4.68 but repaired. Sold to Air America April 1969 and re-registered N1535.

269: *Anonymous in the extreme! Apart from their registration letters Pan African's fleet of DC-4s typified the low key aspects of their Nigerian operation, much of which was described by crews as "boring and routine". On occasion crews would sometimes undertake "diversionary formation flying" as in this view of N88891 during a flight from Port Harcourt to Lagos. A white top, silver undersides and a solid blue cheat-line could almost describe a Hank Wharton DC-7C (Keith F. Sissons)*

270: *Even more nondescript is N480G, again photographed from a sister aircraft en route from Port Harcourt to Lagos during May 1969. This DC-4 was later caught on the ground at Port Harcourt on 10 November 1969 and destroyed by a Biafran Air Force T-6G (Keith F. Sissons)*

271: *It was not always the carrying of military supplies and soldiers that provided work for Pan African's fleet of DC-4s. Occasionally they ferried food for hotels in Port Harcourt and Enugu or, as in this view of N11117 at Makurdi, undertook a regular money-run to replenish bank stocks. N11117 operated unscathed until the end of the Nigeria war. Subsequently it operated on similar para-military duties in southeast Asia (Keith F. Sissons)*

TABLE 12:
FATAL ACCIDENTS INVOLVING AIRCRAFT DURING BIAFRAN OPERATIONS

Date	Aircraft/Registration	Operator	Personnel killed	Nationality
7.10.67	F-27 5N-AAV	Government of Biafra	Andre Cessou (Captain)	French
			Jacques Languillaume (Co-pilot)	French
			Bernard Bret (Flight Engineer)	French
			Christian von Oppenheim (Passenger)	Belgian
			'Simone' (Female passenger)	Tunisian
			Oyii Emmanuel (Biafran Air Force/passenger)	Biafran
			Charles Nweke (Biafran Air Force/passenger)	Biafran
			1 unidentified B.A.F. male passenger	Biafran

Crashed c00:30hrs after exploding in mid-air over Lagos while undertaking an attempted bombing-raid at the time.

| 3.12.67 | B-25 | Biafran Air Force | Sam Ezunor (Navigator) | Biafran |

Crashed on landing at Port Harcourt at the end of a bombing sortie during the night of 2/3.12.67. All other crew survived.

1.7.68	L-1049G '5T-TAG'	Hank Warton	August Martin (Captain)	American
			Jesse 'Bill' Raymond Meade (Co-pilot)	American
			Thomas "Bull" Brown (Flight Engineer)	South African
			Mrs Martin (Passenger)	American

Crashed 1½ miles miles south of Uli strip while on final approach to land night of 30.6/1.7.68.

7.12.68	Douglas DC-7C/VR-BCY	ARCO Bermuda (Warton)	John McOmie (Captain)	British
			Heinrich 'Heinz' Raab (First Officer)	German
			Richard Holzman (Flight Engineer)	German-American
			Arthur 'Tommy' Thompson (Trainee F/O)	American

Crashed approximately 3 miles south of Uli strip, Biafra while on final approach to land, night of 7/8.12.68.

16.3.69	Douglas DC-3/'704B'?	Government of Biafra	Emane Ngwu (Captain)	Biafran
			Ernest Ike (Co-pilot)	Biafran
			David Inyang (Supernumery)	Biafran

Crashed at Uli strip, Biafra while attempting to make an emergency landing shortly after taking-off on a flight to Libreville.

6.5.69	Douglas DC-6AC/HB-IBT	International Red Cross	Carl Eric Baltze (Captain)	Swedish
			Hellmut Scharck (First Officer)	West German
			Carl Gösta Sternhag (Flight Engineer)	Swedish
			Bo Valentin Almgren (Loadmaster)	Swedish

Crashed at 21:52hrs, 6 miles north of Uli, Biafra while turning towards final approach to land, after a flight from Cotonou, Dahomey.

5.6.69	Douglas DC-7B/SE-ERP	Swedish Red Cross	David Brown (Captain)	American
			Stig Carlson (First Officer)	Swedish
			Kjell Pettersen (Flight Engineer)	Norwegian
			Harry Axelsson (Loadmaster)	Swedish

Shot down at c18:03hrs by a Nigerian Air Force MiG-17F over Eket, Nigeria while undertaking relief flight to Uli

3.8.69	L-1049H/CF-NAJ	Canairelief	Donald Merriam (Captain)	Canadian
			Raymond Levesque (First Officer)	Canadian
			Vincent Wakeling (Flight Engineer)	Canadian
			Garry Libbus (Loadmaster)	Canadian

Crashed at 23:46hrs near Uga, Biafra and some 15 miles north of Uli while turning onto final approach for landing at Uli although at least one report suggests that the crew mistakenly tuned into Uga Beacon and were therefore inadvertently on approach to Uga strip

26.9.69	C-97G/N52676	Joint Church Aid	Alex Nicoll (Captain/Instructor)	British
			John Wilson (Trainee Captain)	American
			Robert Maynard (First Officer)	American
			Charles Kelly (Flight Engineer)	American
			Charles J. Cox (Loadmaster)	American

Crashed into rising ground approximately 1½ miles south of Uli strip, Biafra while on final approach to land at Uli.

28.11.69	L-749A/'5N85H'	Government of Biafra	Unidentified Captain	?
			Unidentified First Officer	?
			A.Nubler (Flight Engineer)	German-American
			Plus 5 passengers	?

Crashed into the Oukaimeden mountain range, 70km south of Marrakech, Morocco while routeing Faro-São Tomé.

| 28.11.69 | MFI-9B/BB-? | Biafran Air Force | Alex Agbafuna (pilot) | Biafran |

Hit by small-arms fire near Obrikon and crashed into a nearby river.

| 4.1.70 | MFI-9B/BB-? | Biafran Air Force | Ibi Brown (pilot) | Biafran |

Hit trees and exploded during a rocket attack against Nigerian targets south of Awka.

The twenty aircrew killed in the crashes on 1.7.68, 7.12.68, 16.3.69, 3.8.69 and 26.9.69 were all interred at the graveyard beside Uli Church, Biafra.

TABLE 13:
KNOWN FATAL ACCIDENTS INVOLVING AIRCRAFT DURING NIGERIAN OPERATIONS

Date	Aircraft/Registration	Operator	Personnel killed	Nationality
9.8.67	Whirlwind Srs.2 (?)	Nigerian Air Force	Col. Joe Akahan	Nigerian
	Crashed near Makurdi, Nigeria. Further details not known.			
28.9.68	Douglas DC-4 N90427	Pan African Airlines	John Connell (Captain)	American
			Olle Ringstrand (Co-pilot)	Swedish
	Crashed on approach to Port Harcourt, after a flight from Lagos. 55 Nigerian soldiers also killed aboard the aircraft.			
19.7.69	MiG-17F NAF623	Nigerian Air Force	Mike Thompsett (pilot)	British
	Ran out of fuel while approaching Port Harcourt airfield. Pilot ejected but at too low an altitude to survive.			
15.10.69	L-29 Delfin NAF4xx	Nigerian Air Force	Col. Shittu Alao (pilot/NAF Commander)	Nigerian
	Crashed while attempting to force-land, lost and out of fuel at Uzebba, 45 miles (72km) north of Benin.			

TABLE 14:
UNSUBSTANTIATED AIRCRAFT CLAIMS BY FEDERAL NIGERIAN GOVERNMENT

Date	Type	Details of Claim
21.3.69	Douglas C-47	Reported to have crashed at Uli while under attack by Nigerian MiG-17Fs (This could refer to a known crash of a C-47 at Uli on 6.3.69; see Table 12.)
22.3.69	?	Unidentified aircraft shot down while on approach to Uli
23.3.69	?	Unidentified aircraft bombed while landing at Uli and set alight.
23.3.69	?	Unidentified aircraft destroyed on ground at Uli.
24.4.69	?	Two aircraft destroyed on ground at Uli during an early morning air-to-ground attack. (This might involve the Biafran Air Force C-47s '802' or '803'.)
11.7.69	Douglas DC-4	Two DC-4s were reported as destroyed on the ground at Uli as a result of night bombing. On 23.7.69 the Biafrans denied Federal Nigerian reports of two DC-3s and one DC-4 destroyed "during the past few days". (It is possible that these reports involved the DC-4 TR-LNV which crashed at Uli 28.6.69 and might also explain the disappearance of DC-4 F-OCNU.)
23.7.69	?	Unidentified aircraft destroyed on the ground at Uli strip by night-bombing.
7.9.69 ?		Biafran gun-running aircraft claimed as destroyed at Uli strip by night-bombing.
16.12.69	Douglas C-47	Claimed to have been destroyed at Uli strip by night-bombing.

TABLE 15:
SUMMARY OF INTERNATIONAL RED CROSS FLIGHTS TO BIAFRA

Period of Operations & Base	Period	Flights	Tonnage (tonnes)
Santa Isabel to Biafra (pre-INALWA)	April 1968 to 2 September 1968	47	398
Operation INALWA			
Santa Isabel to Biafra	3 September 1968 to 6 June 1969	1,114	10,943
Operationa INALWA			
Cotonou to Biafra	1 February 1969 to 11 June 1969	867	9,659
Total		2,028	21,000

TABLE 16:
SUMMARY OF JOINT CHURCH AID FLIGHTS TO BIAFRA (BY MONTH)

Month	Monthly Total	Accumulative Total	Average Flights per night	Remarks
Pre-September 1968	94	94	-	Mostly by Warton DC-7Cs and Transair Sweden DC-7Bs
September 1968	207	301	6.7	Independent airlift gains momentum
October 1968	244	545	7.6	Transavia replaced Transair Sweden
November 1968	218	763	7.3	
December 1968	221	984	7.1	Warton takes full ownership of Church DC-7Cs
January 1969	309	1293	10.0	Canairelief L-1049H and JCA C-97Gs introduced.
February 1969	211	1504	7.5	Crew shortages affect number of flights
March 1969	453	1957	14.6	
April 1969	322	2279	10.7	
May 1969	347	2626	11.2	
June 1969	122	2748	4.0	Shoot-down of Swedish Red Cross DC-7B
July 1969	321	3069	10.4	
August 1969	337	3406	10.9	
September 1969	404	3810	13.5	
October 1969	365	4175	11.8	
November 1969	423	4598	14.1	
December 1969	545	5143	17.6	Record number of flights and tonnages.
January 1970	171	5314	14.3	Biafra finally collapsed 12 January 1970

TABLE 17:
SUMMARY OF NORDCHURCHAID/JOINT CHURCH AID MONTHLY FLIGHTS TO BIAFRA BY COMPANY

Month	Church DC-7C	ARCO DC-7C	Transair DC-7B	Sterling DC-6B	F.Olsen C-46 DC-6/A	Transavia DC-6/B	Braathens DC-6B	Canairelief L-1049H	JCA C-97G	Aid by Air DC-6B
Pre Sept 68	62		28		2	2				
Sept 68	77		86	10	34					
Oct 68	100		22	40	38	44				
Nov 68	87			2	46	83				
Dec 68		41			32	110	38			
Jan 69		55			28	166	41	13	6	
Feb 69		10			20	97	26	15	43	
Mar 69					27	179	38	56	153	
Apr 69						181	7	29	105	
May 69						48	57	57	99	86
Jun 69							6	37	33	46
Jul 69							39	41	119	122
Aug 69							33	31	125	148
Sept 69				14	35		55	76	115	109
Oct 69				56	55		20	85	62	87
Nov 69				44	27		39	90	122	101
Dec 69				32	49		59	113	156	136
Jan 70				18	16			34	49	54
Totals	326	106	136	218	409	908	458	677	1187	889

TABLE 18:
AIRLIFT STATISTICS (NOVEMBER 1969) FOR JOINT CHURCH AID

Company	Aircraft Type	No. of Aircraft	Flights Completed	Flights Aborted	Total Cargo Delivered (lbs)	Average Payload (lbs)
Joint Church Aid	C-97G	4 (1 standby)	122	18	3,994,558	32,742
Braathens	DC-6A	1	39	8	878,677	22,530
Canairelief	L-1049H	3 (1 u/s)	90	15	3,097,655	34,419
Flughjalp	DC-6/DC-6B	4 (1 standby)	101	16	2,333,496	23,104
Fred Olsen	DC-6A	1	27	6	652,651	24,172
Sterling	DC-6B	1	44	6	919,736	20,903
Total			423	69	11,876,813	

TABLE 19:
AIRLIFT STATISTICS (DECEMBER 1969) FOR JOINT CHURCH AID

Company	Aircraft Type	No. of Aircraft	Flights Completed	Flights Aborted	Total Cargo Delivered (lbs)	Average Payload (lbs)
Joint Church Aid	C-97G	4 (1 st'by)	156	13	5,287,821	33,896
Braathens	DC-6A	1	59	1	1,362,213	23,088
Canairelief	L-1049H	4 (1 u/s)	113	10	4,007,353	35,463
Flughjalp	DC-6/DC-6B	4 (1 st'by)	136	20	3,132,254	23,031
Fred Olsen	DC-6A	1	49	7	1,186,132	24,207
Sterling	DC-6B	1	32	1	704,840	22,026
Total			545	52	15,680,613	

TABLE 20:
JOINT CHURCH AID FLIGHT SCHEDULE FOR FRIDAY 7 MARCH 1969

Operator	Identity	Type	Captain	STD São Tomé	STA Uli NDB	ETD São Tomé	ETA Uli NDB
Canairelief	CF-NAJ	L-1049H	Patterson	1615	1800	2100	2245
Transavia	PH-TRC	DC-6B	Widmark	1625	1805	2115	2255
Braathens	LN-SUD	DC-6B	Hokbrant	1635	1810	2125	2315
Joint Church Aid	N52679	C-97G	Nicoll	1645	1835	2145	2325
Transavia	PH-TRZ	DC-6B	Evensen	1710	1850	2215	2355
Joint Church Aid	N52676	C-97G	Cutler	1720	1900	2240	0020
Fred Olsen	LN-FOP	C-46	Klepp	1730	1930	2345	0145
Transavia	PH-TRL	DC-6B	Merriam	1745	1925	2315	0055

TABLE 21:
JOINT CHURCH AID FLIGHT SCHEDULE FOR THURSDAY 25 DECEMBER 1969

Operator	Reg'n	Type	Captain	STD São Tomé	STA Uli	ATD São Tomé	ATA São Tomé
Canairelief	CF-AEN	L-1049H	Fox	1650	1840	1655	2035
Joint Church Aid	N52876	C-97G	?	1700	1850	1825	2155
Joint Church Aid	N52727	C-97G	?	1710	1900	1725	2145
Sterling	OY-STY	DC-6B	Ostergaard	1720	1910	1710	2045
Aid by Air	TF-AAH	DC-6B	Ledant	1730	1920	1745	2130
Aid by Air	TF-AAB	DC-6B	Gislasson	1740	1930	1755	2200
Braathens	LN-SUD	DC-6B	Steen	1750	1940	1800	2145
Canairelief	CF-NAL	L-1049H	Engineer	1800	1950	1805	2210
Braathens	LN-FOL	DC-6A	Flatval	1810	2000	1835	2255
Canairelief	CF-AEN	L-1049H	Fox			2120	0105
Joint Church Aid	N52876	C-97G	?			2310	0231

Operator	Reg'n	Type	Captain	STD São Tomé	STA Uli	ATD São Tomé	ATA Uli
Joint Church Aid	N52727	C-97G	?			2300	0326
Sterling*	OY-STY	DC-6B	Ostergaard			2125	0225
Aid by Air	TF-AAH	DC-6B	Ledant			2220	0201
Aid by Air	TF-AAB	DC-6B	Gislasson			2321	0322
Braathens	LN-SUD	DC-6B	Steen			2240	0224
Braathens**	LN-FOL	DC-6A	Flatval			–	–

* Although "actual" times are shown, "real actual" times for DC-6B OY-STY are: departed São Tomé 1704; arrived Uli 1846. Took-off Uli 1904; landed São Tomé 2034. Took-off São Tomé for second shuttle 2122, landed Uli 2308. Took-off Uli 2338, landed Libreville 0112; took-off Libreville 0143, landed São Tomé 0226. Total flying time for the night, 7hr 15min.

** Fred Olsen DC-6A LN-FOL returned to São Tomé with No.4 engine out. Its second shuttle was cancelled.

TABLE 22:
EXAMPLE OF NIGHTLY FLIGHTS BY INDIVIDUAL AIRCRAFT ON I.C.R.C. AIRLIFT

Space does not permit a full listing of each flight by individual aircraft for each night of the relief airlift. The following tables serve to illustrate an example of nightly operations for the period 24 April to 22 May 1969. Details have been extracted from daily Situation Reports sent by telex to Geneva from the respective Operation 'INALWA' bases at Santa Isabel (Fernando Póo) and Cotonou (Dahomey). (Apart from the note regarding SE-EDU, all comments are taken exactly as reported at the time.)

Nightly flights from Santa Isabel (Fernando Póo) to Biafra:

Night						Total	Remarks
24.4.69	SE-EDU(4)	SE-ERO(4)			SE-ERR(3)	11	SE-ERR returned to base with a full load on its 4th shuttle due to engine trouble
25.4.69	SE-EDU(4)	SE-ERO(4)				8	
26.4.69	SE-EDU(2)	SE-ERO(3)	SE-ERP(2)			7	All other flights were cancelled due to bad weather at Uli, Biafra.
27.4.69	SE-EDU(3)	SE-ERO(3)	SE-ERP(3)			9	
28.4.69	SE-EDU(4)	SE-ERO(4)	SE-ERP(4)			12	
29.4.69	SE-EDU(4)	SE-ERO(4)	SE-ERP(4)			12	
30.4.69	SE-EDU(1)	SE-ERO(1)				2	
1.5.69		SE-ERO(2)	SE-ERP(1)			3	The low number of flights is due to momentary lack of fuel at Santa Isabel airfield.
2.5.69	SE-EDU(2)		SE-ERP(2)			4	
3.5.69	SE-EDU(2)	SE-ERO(2)	SE-ERP(2)			6	All other flights cancelled due to lack of fuel at Santa Isabel airfield.
4.5.69	SE-EDU(4)	SE-ERO(4)	SE-ERP(4)			12	
5.5.69	SE-EDU(2)	SE-ERO(2)	SE-ERP(2)			6	
6.5.69	SE-EDU(2)	SE-ERO(2)	SE-ERP(2)			6	
7.5.69		SE-ERO(1)				1	SE-ERP grounded due to technical difficulty; SE-ERR grounded due to lack of fuel at Santa Isabel. (The night of 6/7.5.69 marked the final Biafra flights of SE-EDU.)
8.5.69			SE-ERP(1)		SE-ERR(-)	1	SE-ERR returned to base with a full load due to engine trouble.
9.5.69					SE-ERR(1)	1	
10-15.5.69							no flights due to DC-7Bs SE-ERP & SE-ERR engaged in charter flights between Europe and Africa.
16.5.69				SE-ERP(3)		3	
17.5.69				SE-ERP(1)		1	
18.5.69							no flights made from Santa Isabel
19.5.69				SE-ERP(3)		3	
20.5.69				SE-ERP(2)		2	
21.5.69							no flights made from Santa Isabel
22.5.69		SE-ERO(3)	SE-ERP(3)			6	

Nightly flights from Cotonou (Dahomey) to Biafra

24.4.69		HB-IBR(3)	HB-IBS(2)	HB-IBT(2)		HB-ILY(2)		9
25.4.69		HB-IBR(2)	HB-IBS(3)	HB-IBT(3)	HB-ILW(2)	HB-ILY(3)		13
26.4.69		HB-IBR(2)	HB-IBS(1)	HB-IBT(1)				4
27.4.69		HB-IBR(2)	HB-IBS(2)	HB-IBT(2)	HB-ILW(1)	HB-ILY(2)		9
28.4.69		HB-IBR(3)	HB-IBS(3)	HB-IBT(3)		HB-ILY(3)		12
29.4.69		HB-IBR(2)	HB-IBS(3)	HB-IBT(3)		HB-ILY(3)	HB-ILZ(3)	14
30.4.69			HB-IBS(3)	HB-IBT(3)		HB-ILY(3)	HB-ILZ(2)	11
1.5.69			HB-IBS(2)	HB-IBT(1)		HB-ILY(2)	HB-ILZ(3)	8

All other scheduled flights for the night cancelled due to technical trouble and lack of time.

2.5.69			HB-IBS(3)	HB-IBT(3)		HB-ILY(3)	HB-ILZ(3)	12
3.5.69			HB-IBS(3)	HB-IBT(3)		HB-ILY(1)	HB-ILZ(2)	9
4.5.69	TF-FRA(1)		HB-IBS(3)	HB-IBT(3)		HB-ILY(3)	HB-ILZ(3)	13

Nightly flights from Cotonou (Dahomey) to Biafra

5.5.69	TF-FRA(3)		HB-IBS(3)	HB-IBT(3)		HB-ILY(3)	HB-ILZ(3)	15

During the night of 5/6 May eleven refugees flown from Biafra to Cotonou.

6.5.69	TF-FRA(3)		HB-IBS(3)	HB-IBT(1)		HB-ILY(3)	HB-ILZ(1)	11

Later during the night of 6/7 May the Red Cross sent to Biafra two accident specialists from its Cotonou base, Mr Hier and Mr Heimoz to investigate the crash of DC-6B HB-IBT. The coffins containing bodies of the four crew members were flown from Uli to Cotonou aboard HB-ILZ.

7.5.69	TF-FRA(3)			HB-ILY(2)	HB-ILZ(3)	8
8.5.69						

On request of the CICR delegation in Biafra, no further flights were made to Uli, due to airstrip being congested following the crash of a Jointchurchaid C-97.

9.5.69	TF-FRA(3)	HB-IBS(3)	HB-ILW(2)			8

All other flights cancelled due to technical trouble.

10.5.69	TF-FRA(1)	HB-IBS(3)		HB-ILY(3)		9
11.5.69	TF-FRA(3)	HB-IBS(3)	HB-ILW(1)			7
12.5.69	TF-FRA(3)	HB-IBS(3)				6

During the night of 12/13 May three refugees flown to Cotonou

13.5.69	TF-FRA(3)	HB-IBS(3)	6
14.5.69	TF-FRA(3)	HB-IBS(3)	6

HB-ILY grounded due to lack of crew

15.5.69	TF-FRA(3)	HB-IBS(3)		6
16.5.69	TF-FRA(3)	HB-IBS(3)	HB-ILY(3)	9

During the night of 16/17 May five refugees flown to Cotonou

17.5.69	TF-FRA(2)		HB-ILX(2)	HB-ILY(2)	6

All other flights cancelled due to technical trouble and lack of time

18.5.69	TF-FRA(3)		HB-ILX(3)	HB-ILY(2)	8
19.5.69	TF-FRA(2)		HB-ILX(2)		4

All other flights cancelled due to technical trouble and lack of time

20.5.69	TF-FRA(2)		HB-ILX(2)		4
21.5.69	TF-FRA(2)			HB-ILY(2)	4
22.5.69	TF-FRA(3)		HB-ILX(2)	HB-ILY(3)	8

Author's note: On the night of 29/30.4.69, the International Red Cross achieved 26 shuttles into Uli strip, the highest nightly number of flights. The total involved five aircraft from Cotonou and three from Santa Isabel.

272: The former Japan Air Lines markings were always evident on DC-6B TF-FRA. It was purchased by Fragtflug on 1 May 1969 for operations on the Cotonou I.C.R.C. airlift and made its first flight into Uli during the night of 4/5 May that year. It went on to complete 82 shuttles into Biafra, including one special flight into Uli on the night of 4/5 August, several months after the Red Cross airlift had effectively stopped Note that a larger red cross was later applied to the fuselage side towards the end of the Biafran operation (Dave Becker Collection)

TABLE 23:
EXAMPLE OF NIGHTLY CARGOES AIRLIFTED TO BIAFRA ON I.C.R.C. AIRLIFT

The following tables serve to illustrate an example of nightly relief cargoes for the period 24 April to 9 May 1969. Details have again been extracted from daily Situation Reports sent by telex to Geneva from the respective Operation 'INALWA' bases at Santa Isabel (Fernando Póo) and Cotonou (Dahomey).

NIGHTLY CARGOES FROM SANTA ISABEL (FERNANDO PÓO) TO BIAFRA:

Night	Milk Powder	Rice	Dried Beans	Stockfish	Mixed Tin Food	Salt	Miscellaneous	Total
24.4.69	52.0			44.5			Baby milk powder 10.0 Miscellaneous items 7.5	114.0
25.4.69	21.0	10.5		10.0			Baby milk powder 43.5	85.0
26.4.69	17.0			41.5			Baby milk powder 15.0	73.5
27.4.69	41.5	10.5		31.0		10.5		93.5
28.4.69	93.5						Baby milk powder 32.5	126.5
29.4.69	73.0			31.0			Baby milk powder 10.5 Luncheon meat 10.5	125.0
30.4.69					21.0			21.0
1.5.69	10.0				10.5		Luncheon meat 10.5	31.0
2.5.69	20.5				21.0			41.5
3.5.69				31.0	31.0			62.0
4.5.69	31.0	31.0		31.5		31.0		124.5
5.5.69	1.5				49.5	11.0		62.0
6.5.69		19.0		10.5		21.0	Corn 1.0 Luncheon meat 10.5	62.0
7.5.69				10.0				10.0
8.5.69				10.0				10.0
9.5.69				2.5			Irish stewing steak 7.0 Food for teams 1.0	10.5
10.5.69	no flights to Biafra							
11.5.69	no flights to Biafra							
12.5.69	no flights to Biafra							
13.5.69	no flights to Biafra							
14.5.69	no flights to Biafra							
15.5.69	no flights to Biafra							
16.5.69				10.0			Irish stewing steak 21.0	31.0
17.5.69				10.0				10.0
18.5.69	no flights							
19.5.69		10.0		21.0				31.0
20.5.69			10.5			9.5		20.0
21.5.69	no flights							
22.5.69		10.5				19.5	Irish stewing steak 20.0 Cornmeal 10.5	60.5

NIGHTLY CARGOES (IN TONNES) FROM COTONOU (DAHOMEY) TO BIAFRA:

Night	Milkpowder	Rice	Dried Beans	Corn Meal Mixture	Stockfish	Miscellaneous	Total
24.4.69	13.5			8.0	56.5	Household soap 13.5 Spare Parts 1.0 Technical materials 0.5	93.0
25.4.69	13.5			62.0	58.0	Soap 13.5	147.0
26.4.69					25.0	Various 9.0 Food for Teams 3.0	37.0
27.4.69	13.4			27.0	56.0	Soap 2.0 Refridgerators 0.1	98.5
28.4.69	13.5			56.5	54.0	Miscellaneous 4.0	128.0
29.4.69	67.0			13.5	75.0	Miscellaneous 4.0 Car 1.0	160.5
30.4.69	13.5			54.5	52.0	Miscellaneous 8.0 Food for Teams 3.0	131.0
1.5.69	13.5			54.5	23.5	Miscellaneous 8.0	99.5
2.5.69	13.5			68.0	55.5	Medicine 7.5	144.5
3.5.69	13.5			27.5	55.0	Miscellaneous 8.0	104.0
4.5.69	13.5	12.0		81.0	37.0	DDT-treated Rice seed 10.0 Miscellaneous 3.0	156.5
5.5.69	13.5	29.0		78.5	52.0	Medical supplies 7.0 Butane Gas 0.5	180.5
6.5.69	13.5	25.5	24.0	27.5	30.0	Miscellaneous 12.0	132.5
7.5.69 nil	13.5	25.5	24.0	41.0			104.0

Night	Milkpowder	Rice	Dried Beans	Corn Meal Mixture	Stockfish	Miscellaneous	Total
9.5.69	13.5	12.0	22.5	13.5	23.0	Food for Teams 5.0; Misc 5.0	94.5
10.5.69		12.0	25.0	41.0	26.0	Miscellaneous 5.0	109.0
11.5.69	13.5	12.5	25.0	13.5	20.5	Medical supplies 1.0	72.5
12.5.69		12.5	25.0		29.5	Miscellaneous 2.0	69.0
13.5.69		12.5	25.0		29.5	Miscellaneous 2.0	69.0
14.5.69		12.5	12.5	12.5	25.5	Miscellaneous 6.0	69.0
15.5.69		12.5	12.5	12.5	25.5	Miscellaneous 6.0	69.0
16.5.69		12.5	25.0	27.0	18.0	Medicine 24.5 Miscellaneous 2.5 Butane Gas 0.5	110.0
17.5.69	26.0		9.5	27.0		Medicine 10.5 Cars/Food for teams 3.0	76.0
18.5.69	24.0	13.5	25.0	37.5		Rations 3.5 Food for teams 2.0	105.5
19.5.69	9.5	13.5	12.5	13.5		Food for teams 3.0	52.0
20.5.69	23.0	13.5	12.5			Miscellaneous 3.0	52.0
21.5.69			12.5	26.5		Food for teams 4.5 Salt 5.0; various 3.0 Disinfectant 0.5	52.0
22.5.69	20.0	3.5	25.0	37.0		Various 6.0 Cotton prints 10.0	101.5

273: DC-7 SE-CNE made its first flight into Uli from Fernando Póo during the night of 1-2 December 1968. Its last shuttle occurred on the night of 31 March-1 April 1969, after which it was flown to Cotonou where it was grounded for use as a spares source. By the time this view was taken, on 28 December 1970, the DC-7 been pushed to beyond the far end of Cotonou's single runway and had lost all engines, most of its windows and the majority of instruments. All Red Cross insignia, as well as the Swedish registration marks had been deleted (Confidential Source)

274: When not flying on the nightly airlift and snatching a few hours sleep, life on tropical São Tomé was divided between the hotel balcony, the bar and the palm-fringed sandy beaches. Relaxing in this view are (left to right, clockwise) ... Shultz, Captain Anderson, Fin Almten, Emil Erla (Chief of Flight Operations 13/3/69-10/5/69), Verdun Polley (Chief Pilot, Flughjalp), ... Andreason and Phil Phillp (Phil Phillp)

275: When the crew of heavily-loaded Aer Turas DC-7CF EI-ATT landed at São Tomé they used the entire length of the runway and then announced that the aircraft was desperately short of fuel. Not only that, but the cargo inside was "hot and delicate". After taking on fuel EI-ATT completed its journey to Libreville where it unloaded ammunition for the arms airlift into Biafra (Jakob Ringler)

276: The Lagos scrapyard was a treasure trove at the end of the Nigerian civil war. A door from a wrecked Whirlwind shows clearly the Nigerian Air Force roundel as well as the former Austrian Air Force insigne (Confidential Source)

277: Attacks by Biafran T-6G Texans caused widespread paranoia amongst senior Nigerian military personnel. So much so that when Nigeria Airways' VC-10 5N-ABD was reported missing on 20 November 1969 the Port Harcourt MiG-17 Detachment was immediately ordered to reconnoitre Uli and Uga for evidence of a hijack. In fact the VC-10 had crashed on approach to Lagos. The ensuing fire was said to have destroyed evidence of a Biafran shoot-down or sabotage but in the event all such reports were dismissed (via Peter J Cooper)

283

```
C O D E D   C A L L   S I G N    PH-TRZ = MNR   PH-TRB = RWS   PH-TRD = FGH

MONDAY   TUESDAY   WEDNESDAY   THURSDAY   FRIDAY   SATURDAY   SUNDAY
  O T      W W        V V          I I       H H      M C       V V      IHIALA
  M M      B B        T T          L L       E E      V V       O O      BRIDE CONTROL
  K K      J J        P P          G G       S S      A A       Z Z      UGA

Sao Tome = ZF   ABIDJAN = SC   LIBRAVILLE = WO   SANTA = EY   LISBON = GJ
```

SEC B — CODES — MEANINGS

Code		Meaning
AC 418 at 35 Morocco-Egypt-Burundi		1. MY ESTIMATE IS 35, FL 120
ACC 426 Morocco-Egypt-Burundi		2. CLEARED TO EZ HOLDING PATTERN FL (120)
ACC 437		3. NO DELAY EXPECTED
ACC 442 at (40)		4. E A C AT (40)
AC 453		5. REQUEST EZ BCN FREQ FOR THE DAY
ACC 461 Egypt-Sudan-Burundi		6. EZ BCN FREQ FOR THE DAY IS (250) K/CS
ACC 475		7. CONFIRM RECEIVING TH BCN
AC 489		8. NOT RECEIVING
ACC 490		9. STANDBY WILL CHECK BCN
ACC 404		10. BCN CHECKED OK PLEASE CHECK YOUR TUNING

SEC C

Code		Meaning
AC 613		1. RECEIVING THE BCN
AC 627		2. ENTERING THE HOLDING PATTERN
ACC 632 KAMPALA BURUNDI		3. DESCEND/CLIMB TO FL (90)
ACC 649 (WW) MOZAMBIQUE BURUNDI ..		4. CLEARED FOR AN APP TO (WW) FROM FL (60)
ACC 650 (WW) CH. A.		5. QSY (WW) TOWER ON ..M/CS REPORT CONTACT
AC 664 (WW)		6. CONTACT WITH (WW) TWR COMMENCING APP
AC 671		7. UNABLE TO CONTACT TWR THIS FREQ
ACC 685		8. CONTINUE APPROACH AIRPORT SAFE
ACC 696		9. GND RADIO FAILURE STDBY THIS FREQ FOR FURTHER CLEARANCE
ACC 608 Sudan - Burundi		10. DISCONTINUE APPROACH RETURN EZ FL (50)

SEC D

Code		Meaning
AC 810 (WW)		1. REQUEST (WW) BCN FREQUENCY
ACC 826 (WW) Canary-Sudan-Egypt .		2. (WW) BCN FREQUENCY IS (452) K/CS
ACC 837 (WW)		3. EN A/C ACTIVITIES AT (WW) WOULD YOU LIKE TO ATTEMPT APPROACH FOR LANDING
ACC 841		4. REQUEST YOUR PRESENT LEVEL
ACC/TWR 853		5. WE HAVE LANDLINE PROBLEMS ESTABLISH RADIO CONTACT WITH TWR/ACC AND REPORT BACK
ACC 864		6. THE RUNWAY IS DAMAGED
ACC 872 Egypt		7. LANDINGS NOT POSSIBLE IN THE NEXT (2) HOURS
AC 885		8. UNABLE TO HOLD ANY FURTHER REQUEST ROUTE CLEARANCE TO LEAVE YOUR AREA
ACC 898		9. YOU HAVE NO CLEARANCE TO PROCEED ANY FURTHER RETURN TO YOUR AERODROME OF DEPARTURE
AC 809		10. LEAVING YOUR AREA

SEC F   CONSTANTS - INDICATORS - VARIANTS FROM 1st - 15th APRIL

DATES	1st	2nd	3rd	4th	5th	6th	7th	8th	9th	10th	11th	12th	13th	14th	15th
SEC B	4	1	2	4	3	5	1	7	4	3	9	2	3	8	9
CONSTANT SEC C	6	3	9	2	7	2	4	2	8	6	2	8	4	4	0
SEC D	8	5	1	6	8	3	6	4	1	2	4	6	7	0	6

NUMERAL CODES - FOR FREQUENCIES AND LEVELS ONLY.

MOROCCO 1   SUDAN 5   KAMPALA 9
EGYPT 2   MOZAMBIQUE .. 6   BURUNDI 0
BULAWAYO 3   ZANZIBAR 7   VIA .... • (DECIMAL)
CANARY 4   GALILEA 8

278 and 279 Above right: *All radio transmissions between aircrew and Biafran Air Traffic Control were in code. Each aircraft cleared for flight into Biafra was issued with a three-letter coded call-sign which was revised every fortnight when a new set was flown from Lisbon to the relief bases at Libreville and São Tomé. This set was introduced in April 1969*

280 Right: *After a period of changing frequencies every night, Biafran Air Traffic Control relented to relief agency pressure and agreed to keep landing frequencies the same for four successive nights. The procedure was still complex, but the risk of confusion was slightly lessened. See page 139 (via E. Roocroft)*

GUIDE TO UNDERSTANDING THE NEW CODE

1. The whole Code is now divided into Sections A - G.
2. Sections B, C, D constitute main body of the code.
3. Section E is self explanatory.
4. Section F contains the table for changing codes nightly valid for 2 week for a start.
5. Whole system is based on the principle of three figures. THE CONSTANT THE INDICATOR, THE VARIANT.

First figure is called the "Constant", and it indicates at a glance which section of the main body of the code is being reffered to, eg. on the 1st of April the "Constant" for section B is 4 Section C is 6 Section D is 8.
On the 8th of April, it is 7, 2, 4 respectively.

Second figure is self explanatory. It indicates which actual transmission is being referred to in section B, C, D according to the numbering separating Codes and Meaninga.
Third figure is any digit at all to complete the first two; provided it is not repeated as a variant in same section.

EXAMPLES

The example shown on the code is the actual shape of the code applicable for Tuesday April 1st 1969.
Other examples are:-
        13th April: 357 means "Requestin EZ bcn frequency" (Sec. B)
                     472 means "Unable to contact Tower" (Sec. C)
                     769 means "Runway is damaged" (Sec. D.

INDICATOR   Numerical Sequence as shown in relevant Sections
VARIANT   Any number to complete 3 digits proviede it is not repeated as a variant in same section.

SEC G Tx. with Tower continues in plain language expept for requesting of frequencies
     TX. must be reduced to minimum especially during approach for landing

---

Roocroft

FEB FREQUENCY CHART
VALID FROM 1st - 28th FEB 1969.

TOP SECRET

DATES	CHANNEL A 1700-1900	CHANNEL B 1900-2000	CHANNEL C 2000-2130	CHANNEL D 2130-2300	CHANNEL E 2300-0130	CHANNEL F 0130-0230	CHANNEL G 0230-0500
1st-4th (Inclusive)	118.4	130.5	126.6	119.9	129.1	118.0	130.4
5th - 8th "	118.7	128.5	126.8	119.3	118.3	122.6	119.9
9th - 12th "	119.5	122.6	127.2	128.5	120.1	128.7	125.1
13th- 16th "	119.9	129.5	125.1	118.6	126.0	129.0	118.6
17th- 20th "	115.1	128.7	124.3	119.2	122.8	126.4	120.7
21st- 24th "	120.7	119.3	130.8	124.7	121.7	118.5	119.3
25th- 28th "	126.2	118.5	130.3	120.6	129.0	118.2	123.9

- For clarity please note, our operational day starts from 1700 hrs GMT - 0500 hrs GMT next morning.

  Please note, from 1700 hrs GMT on 4th Feb 1969, ACC frequency changes to 118.9 m/cs

- For Uli Tower, Mother frequency remains = 120.5 m/cs.

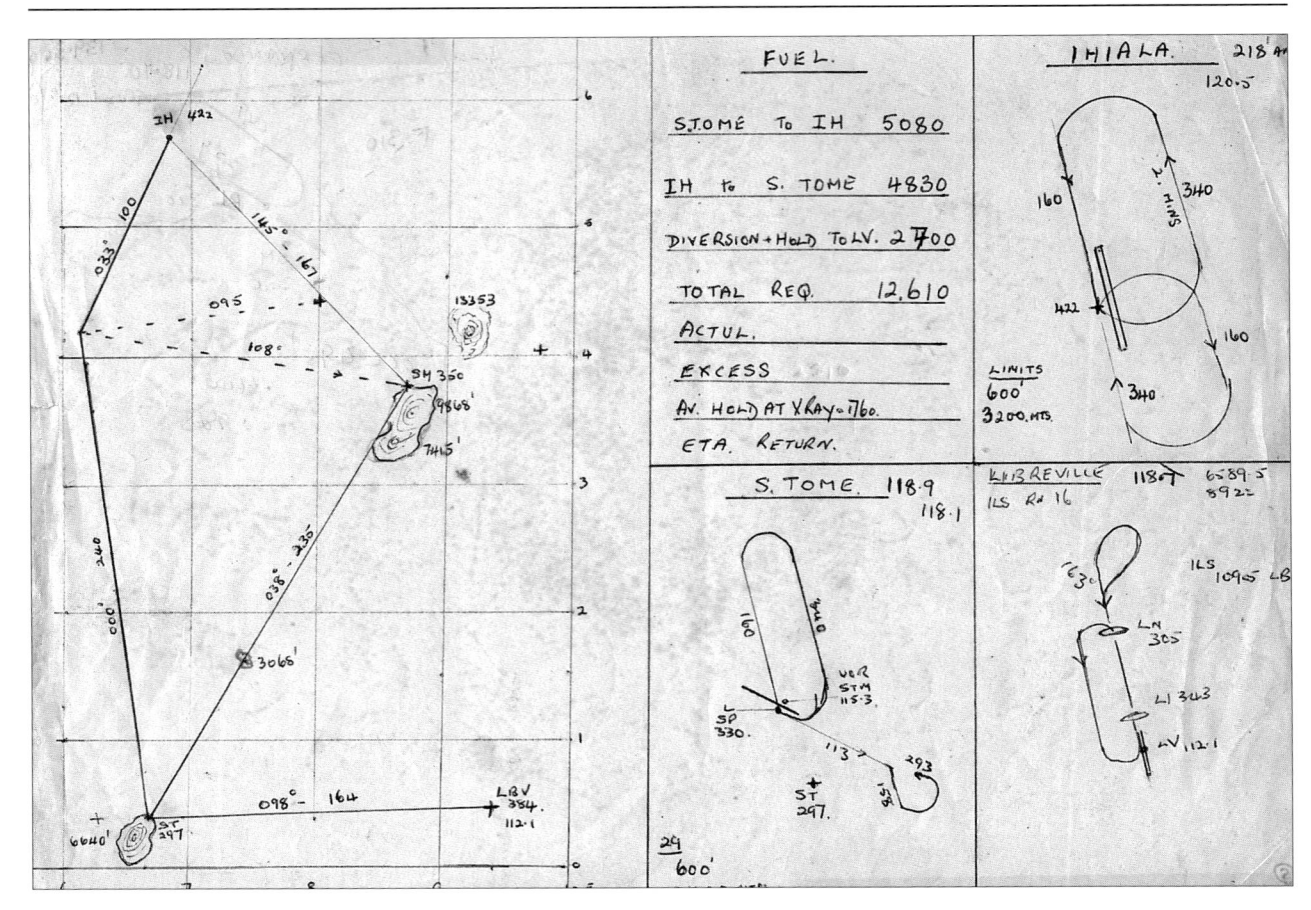

281 Above: Flight crews adopted many varying measures to ensure a safe shuttle into and out of Biafra. During the early days of the relief airlift from São Tomé there were few official charts for the area and some pilots were forced to create their own. This chart was used by Transavia First Officer Phil Phillp throughout the Autumn of 1968. The left-hand route chart shows the preferred route from São Tomé and north to Ihiala (Uli) by using a "due north and slight dog-leg" approach to the Ihiala (IH) beacon. The island of Fernando Póo is also shown with Mount Cameroon just to the north of it. Note also the guide for fuel requirements registered for a DC-6B and which also contains a reserve for holding or diversion to Libreville (Reproduced courtesy of Phil Phillp)

282 Below: When the Nigerian Civil War ended in January 1970 the relief agencies operating out of São Tomé had a huge stockpile of relief material on the island. A fair amount was transferred across to Libreville to help feed the many Biafran children brought out earlier from the war zone. Much was also shipped across to Angola to support feeding-programmes there. In this view Father Tony Byrne, the primary driving-force behind the São Tomé airlift, is seen (in sunglasses and carrying a briefcase) just after arriving at Luanda aboard the PA-30 Twin Comanche CR-LGL. His mission to Angola was simply to determine the most suitable method for re-distributing surplus food to feeding-centres in the Angolan bush. Mission completed, Tony Byrne returned to his native Ireland for a considerably quieter life (Jakob Ringler)

CAPTIONS TO ARTWORK

PAGE 193:

1: Biafran Air Force MFI-9B BB105, captured at Ozubulu January 1970. The first batch of MFI-9Bs were painted in a gloss brown and green scheme. Serial BB105 in white and small Biafran flag forward of serial.

2: T-6G (ex 51-14810) Biafran Air Force, Lagos January 1970. Three-tone green overall finish except for natural metal canopy framework.

3: A different scheme on what purports to be Biafra's "other" T-6G consisted of a two-tone green with one shade outlined in 'squiggle' pattern, probably in black. The pattern was similar to the Alouette II and may have been added in Biafra.

4: NAF701, Jet Provost T.51 1968. Both Jet Provosts were repainted before delivery. From pilot's memory the colours were a standard matt green/earth brown camouflage. Note the split serial, NAF being aft of the roundel and 701 above the fin flash.

4a: The precise meaning of the side emblem on Jet Provost NAF701 is obscure. It appears to be a pot or vase or possibly the rear view of a cat and (based on pilots' recollection) is thought to have been dull red.

5: NAF510, Westland Widgeon, Lagos May 1968. Light grey overall with black serial on boom and repeated on nose cone.

6: Unmarked Alouette II, January 1970. The base colour appears to be French Army matt green with earth brown edged in matt black. The tail-rotor and nose camouflage pattern is assumed.

7: BAF040, Alouette III, Lagos January 1970. Base colour appears to be French Army green with random 'mauve-brown' camouflage. It is possible that the camouflage was originally edged in matt black. Serial BAF040 is in white and stencilled. The tail rotor colours are assumed.

PAGE 194:

8: OY-STY DC-6B Sterling Airways typifies the final Joint Church Aid scheme. Standard company colours but with Biafran 'blue-top' camouflage and twin-fish insignia as shown

9: TF-AAF DC-6B Flughjalp. 'Blue-top' camouflage and outlined 'twin-fish' insignia. Later in the airlift the legend and insignia was replaced to match OY-STY above. Note that TF-AAF was the only Flughjalp DC-6/B with the black weather-radar nose.

10-14: At the time of joining the airlift the Südflug fleet was midway through a livery change (from white fin to blue fin). '5T-TAC' and '5T-TAR' retained the old scheme and differed in the size of the '7C' rudder logo. '5T-TAD' and '5T-TAL' featured the revised Südflug livery and only differed in the former not having a 'DC7C' logo on the fin. '5T-TAB' was quite distinctive in having a solid-blue fuselage cheat-line.

15: TR-LOK, DC-7C, São Tomé 1969. The 'blue-top' camouflage of Jack Malloch's DC-7C had a greener shade than the relief aircraft based on São Tomé. Note the original KLM name 'YELLOW SEA' on the nose.

PAGE 195:

16: HB-IBU, DC-6B, Fernando Póo September 1968. Standard Balair scheme with Swiss white cross on fin. Red Cross insignia (on white block) applied beneath the rear fuselage and outer wings.

17: OH-KDA, DC-6BF, Fernando Póo September 1968. Overall matt white scheme with Red Cross insignia on nose, fin and outer wing undersides. Note the red tip to the upper fin/rudder.

18: HB-ILN, C-160D, Transall Cotonou March 1969. Natural metal overall finish with characteristic Red Cross blocks on nose and fin. It is believed that underwing insignia appeared beneath the starboard wing only.

19: SE-ERO, DC-7B, Fernando Póo April 1969. The Swedish Red Cross fleet operated in a matt white overall finish with Red Cross insignia in a more florescent orange-red shade. Note the application on the fuselage roof.

20: TF-FRA, DC-6B, Fragtflug, Cotonou May 1969. White upper fuselage and fin; natural metal lower surfaces. Former Japan Air Lines rudder and fuselage cheat-line markings still extant. 'SPIRIT OF ICELAND' legend on nose. A much larger Red Cross insignia was later applied to the fuselage side (see page 280).

PAGE 196:

21-22a: The Joint Church Aid C-97Gs operated in natural metal overall finish will all USAF markings erased. N52727 retained a white section on the flight-deck roof surround and a black arrowhead cheat-line. All had the 'twin-fish' insignia in blue and yellow. Note how the JOINT CHURCH AID legend is one word on N52679.

23-24: The International Red Cross C-97Gs operated in a uniform matt white overall finish with Red Cross insignia in standard positions. Note the BALAIR legend on nose and mid-fuselage. HB-ILW is shown with titling removed as noted at Basle, Switzerland, in January 1970.

PAGE 197:

25: Canairelief L-1049H CF-NAJ in standard NORDAIR blue and white scheme with blue fuselage cheat-line edged uppermost in red.

26: Canairelief L-1049H Super Constellation CF-NAL in Biafran 'blue-top' camouflage with the 'twin-fish' insignia

26a: The symbolism of the white dagger or fleur-de-lys and 'KEBEC' legend carried by CF-NAL is unknown. Presumably it has French-Canadian connotations, 'Kebec' being an archaic form of 'Quebec'.

27: Canairelief L-1049H Super Constellation CF-NAM. The CANAIRELIEF legend has been augmented by JOINT CHURCH AID USA.

28: Canairelief L-1049H Super Constellation CF-AEN with much enlarged JOINT CHURCH AID legend and a reduced 'Operated by Canairelief' legend on the forward fuselage. The Biafran 'blue-top' camouflage extended much lower on the fuselage than all other L-1049Hs.

28a: CF-NAM carried a similar 'dagger' emblem and logo to CF-NAL but with yellow outlines to the letters.

29: Former Iberia L-1049G Super Constellation '5T-TAC' (c/n 4645). The red fuselage cheat-line has been repainted in dark blue. The 'SUPER G' logo was retained on the wingtip fuel tanks

30: This L-1049D was the second '5T-TAC' (c/n 4166). White upper fuselage, fin and rudder, remainder of fuselage and wings natural metal. Sky blue fuselage cheat line and upper and lower fin tips with very fine additional red cheat lines. This aircraft did not have the weather radar nose extension, but had a small black nose cone.

PAGE 198:

31: '5T-TAF' L-1049G Lisbon 1968. All former TAP markings were removed although the blue cheat-line was added and a false identity added to the rear fuselage.

32-34: The three former Lufthansa L-1049G Super Constellations operated by Hank Warton retained their basic Lufthansa scheme of white fuselage roof, natural metal lower areas and dark-blue cheat-line. The German flag and Lufthansa insignia on the fin was overpainted in blue on '5T-TAG'and '5T-TAH' whilst the LUFTHANSA titling was overpainted in white. '5T-TAK' had all markings overpainted in white, the false registration also being in white.

35: '5N86H' L-749A, Faro 1970. The final scheme applied to the former Western Airlines L-749A featured the Biafran 'blue-top' camouflage. Note the identity in red but with the H on the blue.

36: VP-YTY, DC-4, Abidjan 1968. The Air Trans Africa DC-4 was repainted during 1968 in a two-tone blue scheme virtually identical to the revised Südflug scheme. White fuselage roof and natural metal undersides provided an unusual appearance for one of the Libreville gun-running fleet.

37: SE-XBT, C-130E Hercules, Fernando Póo September 1968. The Swedish Red Cross Hercules arrived on station in natural metal overall and with most Swedish Air Force markings removed. The squadron identity 71 was still on the fin and the serial 84001 was still on the rear fuselage.

PAGE 199:

38: NAF601, MiG-15UTI, Kano 1968. Natural metal overall scheme. Nigerian green/natural fin flash while a standard-sized roundel divides the serial.

39-43: Nigerian MiG-17Fs operated in several schemes; NAF618 represents the final batch delivered and features the serial without a roundel. Earlier aircraft from this batch, NAF615-617 featured a roundel with a non-standard width outer band, the 'white' part being natural metal; NAF612 illustrates a crude hand-painted application and a large 'wing' roundel on the fin. NAF612 was later repainted in December 1969 in overall dark-green but the serial presentation was unchanged. At least one MiG-17F, NAF605, displayed the white fuselage band that was

287

exclusively applied to Egyptian Air Force examples. It is believed that on those occasions where the 'white' section of the fin flash was edged in green, the white was, in reality, natural metal.
44: MiG-17blatt NAF633, Port Harcourt December 1969. One of a very few repainted in overall dark green. Note the standard-sized roundel within the serial. The fin flash seems to have lacked the white component.
45: Most L-29 Delfins operated in overall unpainted finish but two examples (NAF401 & 402) are believed to have operated in an overall primer gold-yellow. All featured green nose cone, fin-fillet and wing-tips.

PAGE 200:
46-47: Anson G-AWMG retained its basic Royal Air Force Transport Command scheme but G-AWMH was repainted overall matt white to cover a previously-applied 'film company' camouflage scheme. The cat insignia and inscription (47a) was applied on the nose cone, the relevance of which has been lost with time.
48: Meteor NF.14 G-AXNE, Blackbushe, September 1969. Only the RAF fin flash, roundel and serial were deleted prior to UK departure. Registration and legend were applied in black engine lacquer.
49: DC-4 NAF311 retained its basic Air Ferry scheme; natural metal overall, white fuselage top and blue cheat-line.
50-51: Nigerian Air Force DC-3 NAF305 had its former SABENA insignia and registration OO-AWM crudely overpainted before service entry. NAF306 (51) at Lagos January 1970 was repainted overall dark green (to match MiG-17F NAF612 etc) but operated with a rudder in dark-blue.

PAGE 201:
52-54: The Ilyushin 28s operated in several schemes. One example at Port Harcourt was very crudely overpainted in what appeared to be matt black. Another example was delivered in a 'desert' style scheme but was later repainted locally. The standard Nigerian finish featured a grass-green slightly lighter than the national insignia green and very dark green.
55-56: The two Biafran B-26 Invaders appear to have been painted in a similar camouflage style. Upper surfaces were green and brown camouflage, the brown crudely edged in black (or black-green). It is believed that the undersides were pale blue. Whether the RB-26P (56) carried any 'national' insignia is unknown.

283, 284: When Jakob Ringler learnt that two of the Canairelief L-1049H Super Constellations had sat motionless on São Tomé for the past 30 years he elected to make a special trip back to the island in July 1999. Now serving as homes for countless tropical insects and snakes, many of which were decidedly unfriendly, both aircraft are fundamentally complete although they have suffered from the tropical weather conditions. Both the JOINT CHURCH AID and CANAIRELIEF markings remain visible. Years of hardship and material shortages have tempted villagers to systematically remove internal panels and windows in order to repair their buildings and homes, although strangely the island inhabitants have found no use for the two spare Wright Turbo compound engines which were stored inside each aircraft and which still remain there, untouched, to this day (Jakob Ringler)